# PORN ARCHIVES

# PORN ARCHIVES

Tim Dean, Steven Ruszczycky,

and David Squires, editors

DUKE UNIVERSITY PRESS

Durham and London 2014

Printed in the United States of America on acid-free paper ♾
Designed by Amy Ruth Buchanan
Typeset in Quadraat and Quadraat Sans by Tseng Information Systems, Inc.

Library of Congress Cataloging-in-Publication Data
Porn archives / Tim Dean, Steven Ruszczycky, and David Squires, editors.
pages cm
Includes bibliographical references and index.
ISBN 978-0-8223-5671-4 (cloth : alk. paper)
ISBN 978-0-8223-5680-6 (pbk. : alk. paper)
1. Pornography—History. 2. Pornography in popular culture. 3. Pornography—Social aspects.
I. Dean, Tim, 1964– II. Ruszczycky, Steven, 1981– III. Squires, David D., 1984–
HQ471.P57 2014
363.4′7—dc23 2014019387

ISBN 978-0-8223-7662-0 (e-book)

Duke University Press gratefully acknowledges the support of the University at Buffalo (SUNY),
which provided funds toward the production of this book.

Cover art: Untitled "paste-up" by Jess Collins, circa 1950s. © The Jess Collins Trust; used by permission.
Image courtesy of the Poetry Collection of the University Libraries, University at Buffalo, the State
University of New York.

# CONTENTS

# ACKNOWLEDGMENTS

Porn Archives began life during the spring of 2010 as an international conference, "At the Limit: Pornography and the Humanities," which was held at the University at Buffalo in conjunction with the graduate seminar The History and Theory of Pornography. We are grateful to the many students, faculty, and administrators at Buffalo who helped make the conference and the seminar so successful. For financial support, we thank the departments of anthropology, comparative literature, English, history, and visual studies; the Baldy Center for Law and Social Policy; the Center for the Study of Psychoanalysis and Culture; the Digital Humanities Initiative at Buffalo; the Gender Institute; Rodolphe Gasché; Steve McCaffery; and Ewa Plonowska Ziarek. We wish to acknowledge especially Buffalo's Humanities Institute (including its Cultural Studies Research Workshop and its Queer Theory Research Workshop), which provided most of the funding for the conference and the primary intellectual context for Porn Archives, as well as a subvention that helped to defray publication expenses. We thank the dean of the College of Arts and Sciences, Bruce D. McCombe, whose vision for revitalizing the humanities at Buffalo made such a difference. Others at Buffalo—María Almanza, Wendy Belz, Leah Benedict, Mary Carr, Sara Eddleman, Mary Foltz, James Godley, Lydia Kerr, James Maynard, Steven Miller, Nick Mugavero, Dustin Parrott, Matt Pieknik, Jana Schmidt, Bill Solomon, and Divya Victor—significantly contributed to this project. We express gratitude to Frances Ferguson for visiting Buffalo to discuss her work on pornography and to Zabet Patterson for speaking at the conference. Finally, we thank our wonderful contributors for their patience and good humor, as well as their readiness to think beyond the conventional academic frameworks for understanding pornography.

Our editor at Duke University Press, Courtney Berger, has been a model of tact and professionalism in shepherding Porn Archives through the review process. We are grateful for her editorial guidance and for securing three anonymous reader reports that helped us substantially improve this volume. Loren Glass's chapter, "Up from Underground," was originally published in *Counterculture Colophon: Grove Press, the Evergreen Review, and the Incorporation of the Avant-Garde* (2013). We gratefully acknowledge Stanford University Press for permission to reprint it here.

# INTRODUCTION

## Pornography, Technology, Archive

Tim Dean

The volume's title, *Porn Archives*, conjoins terms with opposing connotations: pornography evokes an ostensibly private experience, while the archive conjures publicly accessible records; porn tends to be semisecret, unofficial, and stigmatized, while archives signify officialdom and state approbation; porn's appeal lies partly in its lack of respectability, whereas archives are nothing if not respectable—so much so, in fact, that putting pornography into the archive is widely regarded as a good way of killing its appeal. If porn is juicy, then the archive is dry as dust. Archives offer sites of preservation and permanence, whereas porn is commonly considered to be ephemeral and amenable to destruction, no less so by its fans than by the police. Given these opposing meanings, in what sense can we speak of "porn archives"?

This volume is built on the premise that pornography as a category emerges in tandem with the archive, through historically specific procedures of sequestration. Rather than being opposed, pornography and the archive come into being together as functions of modernity. Although historians and critics (such as Lynn Hunt, Walter Kendrick, and Frances Ferguson) have recognized pornography as a central feature of modernity, insufficient attention has been paid to the role of archiving practices in pornography's historical development. We suggest that it is impossible to understand the contemporary proliferation of porn without appreciating the history of its archivization. The chapters assembled here respond to that gap in historical understanding by thinking through the complex interrelationship between various pornographies and the archives that condition them.

This project has become both possible and necessary as a result of rapid advances in digital technology that, over the past decade or so, have dramatically increased not only access to porn but also awareness of the significance of archival techniques. Whether or not we consult porn online, we're all constantly accessing archives electronically in ways that prompt reflection on the status of the archive. In this context, it has become evident that critical discussion of digital porn would benefit from a much broader historical consideration of predigital archiving practices, all of which depend on different media technologies. Hunt, for example, argues that "it was only when print culture opened the possibility of the masses gaining access to writing and pictures that pornography began to emerge as a separate genre of representation."[1] It is the conjoining of a new technology with widespread access to it that makes pornography possible. Focusing on the technologies of print culture, Hunt pushes the date for "the invention of pornography" as far back as the sixteenth century, toward the dawn of modernity.

However, others locate that date later, not least because the word *pornography* was coined in English only in the mid-nineteenth century (its French cognates appeared slightly earlier). Sexually explicit images seem always to have existed, but pornography as a category of aesthetic, moral, and juridical classification is a modern invention. The story of the discovery of Pompeii, rehearsed by Walter Kendrick in *The Secret Museum*, helps to account for this invention by showing how the category of pornography was created at the same time as an archive to house the erotic objects being unearthed.[2] Although it took most of the eighteenth century and much of the nineteenth to dig out those Roman cities that had been buried by the eruption of Vesuvius in 79 AD, very early in the process sexually explicit frescoes and artifacts came to light. Many of these discoveries featured the god Priapus, who, as Kendrick observes, "can be identified by his gigantic erect phallus, often out of all human scale."[3] Priapus is the original avatar of the well hung. One might say that the story of the discovery of Pompeii is a tale of archaeologists encountering way more dick than they could possibly handle.

Yet the archaeological process in southern Italy represents something more, since it set in motion a shift in the archaeology of knowledge. Too valuable to be destroyed, the Pompeian artifacts were considered too provocative to be displayed alongside other ancient discoveries; hence, they prompted a new classification, that of pornography, which enabled their preservation via sequestration. In other words, what the sexually explicit images and objects provoked was not simply outrage or lust but a special kind of archive. Here the term *archive* refers to both a physical space for holding the sexually explicit and a conceptual system for grasping it (an archive in the Foucauldian sense). The physical space was a locked chamber at the Museo Borbonico, an institution that—significantly for the link between archives and nationhood— became the National Archaeological Museum of Naples. The conceptual system likewise entailed an apparatus for segregating sexually potent material and strictly regulating access to it. By 1866 the locked room at Museo Borbonico, stuffed with erotic artifacts from Pompeii, was known as the Pornographic Collection (Raccolta Pornografica).[4]

Modern information science distinguishes between a collection and an archive; technically they are not the same thing. And Kendrick, in his account of the discovery of Pompeii, does not describe the sequestration of explicit material as archiving. But using the term *archive* more capaciously—as researchers increasingly have been doing across a range of disciplines—enables us to appreciate how the gesture of separation that creates "pornography" in the mid-nineteenth century creates along with it an archive, a new system of classification and preservation. The crucial difference between ancient and modern approaches to explicit material is that at Pompeii it was not hidden but integrated with other aspects of civic and domestic life. In contrast, the nineteenth century invented pornography by insisting on its segregation from public view. As Michel Foucault argues with respect to madness and confinement, it is the fundamental gesture of segregating certain kinds of people from the rest of society that brings the new category—in this case, madness as a specifically clinical diagnosis—into existence.[5] Just as the seventeenth century's locking up of heterogeneous social elements in former leprosariums enabled the creation of a new kind of illness, so the nineteenth century's locking up of sexually explicit artifacts enabled the creation of a new genre. And just as there can be no mental illness without the institution of the hospital, so there is no pornography without the institution of the archive.

## The Archival Turn

This volume draws on, and contributes to, the "archival turn" that has magnetized attention across a range of disciplines over the past few decades, from history, philosophy, and anthropology to cultural studies, information science, and law. Interest in the archive responds to a widespread concern with questions of cultural memory and the ways in which societies choose to preserve the past or permit its disappearance. Broadly speaking, the significance of archives lies in their role as institutions, furnished with an array of technologies, for preserving or erasing the past. The artifacts discovered at Pompeii could have been destroyed, as most erotically explicit material has been destroyed throughout the centuries; but instead they were preserved, via the paradoxical method of concealment, because they offered a particular kind of historical evidence. Even as they preserve traces of the past, however, archives are distinguished by differing degrees of publicness: the more sensitive their holdings, the harder they are to access. As Jennifer Burns Bright and Ronan Crowley explain in their contribution to the volume, modern libraries that hold material regarded as obscene frequently leave those holdings uncataloged or archive them via a separate, less transparent cataloging system. Archives preserve, but, in so doing, they always regulate access to what they preserve, thus helping to shape what is remembered and what forgotten. Much of the recent interest in archives stems from this basic recognition that archival practices, far from innocent, are politically loaded.[6]

"Secret files were and are perceived to be the opposite of democracy," observes the legal theorist Cornelia Vismann in her fascinating study of archival technologies.[7] Just as archives include certain things by excluding others, so they also routinely exclude particular classes of witness to what they include. This is no less the case for the often unofficial porn archives that interest us than for the official state archives discussed by Vismann. In both cases, relations of power mediate the criteria of inclusion and exclusion in ways that merit investigation. Archival research entails not just grubbing around to see what the archive contains but also analysis at the metalevel, in an effort to make visible the constraints determining otherwise imperceptible principles of inclusion, classification, and access. It is this metalevel of analysis that Foucault is referring to when, in *The Archaeology of Knowledge*, he differentiates archives from statements, discourses, and institutions.[8] The significance of these distinctions for our purposes lies in their implication that researching porn archives involves focus less on the sexually explicit image or text per se than on the archival systems that condition their intelligibility as pornographic to begin with. The chapters collected here demonstrate how archival work is thus highly theoretical and abstract at the same time as it is ineluctably empirical, particular, and rather dirty.

Archival dirt may take the form of dust from disintegrating documents and artifacts; it may take the form of smut associated with illicit sexual representations; or it may take the form of political dirt generated by the friction of ceaseless microstruggles for power.[9] The claim that archives, far from serving as neutral repositories, are closely tied to political power has been developed by Foucault, Jacques Derrida, and many others. Derrida, for example, traces the etymological links between archive and authority in order to suggest that "there is no political power without control of the archive"; indeed, he contends that "effective democratization can always be measured by this essential criterion: the participation in and the access to the archive, its constitution, and its interpretation."[10] What is particularly relevant to the study of pornography in Derrida's critique is his insistence that archives confer authority, including disciplinary authority. Every academic discipline has its archives, broadly understood, and without archival authorization any discipline founders. As Linda Williams argues, the scholarly study of pornography requires archives for its disciplinary legitimacy.[11] Yet, since obscenity always threatens to undermine authority (whether of an individual or an institution), pornography's presence in the archive represents a double-edged sword. Pornography in the archive is at once legitimated and potentially corrosive: what kind of a library (or museum) are you running if it's chock full of porn? Porn archives, ostensibly authorizing the legitimacy of the study of pornography, may simultaneously undermine the authority of the archive. The contributors to this volume negotiate that tension in differing ways, as have many archivists and pornographers before them.

In *Archive Fever*, Derrida pursues a related tension that seems to inhere in the archive. By describing archivization in terms of Freud's concept of the death drive, Derrida shows how archival power consists in the capacity to destroy as well as to preserve. It is not merely that institutions such as libraries are often compelled to deaccess or destroy some of their holdings in order to make room for new ones but, more fundamentally, that the urge to archive necessitates destruction. This argument is especially pertinent to the place of pornography in the archive because porn is routinely deemed more worthy of destruction than of preservation. Only rarely is porn valued as a form of knowledge in its own right or as making a contribution to understanding the history of sexuality. What kind of archaeology of human sexuality would be possible without porn archives? Another way of framing this question would be to ask why we need the distance of centuries to grasp that sexually explicit representations (such as those unearthed at Pompeii) are historically valuable and merit preservation. As the outlandish dimensions of Priapus suggest, pornography does not need to adhere to the criteria of documentary realism in order to furnish vital evidence about human sexuality.

The evidence furnished by pornography may be historical, sexological, erotic, or forensic. Everyone instinctively knows that pornographic evidence displays distinct values in different contexts. And it is precisely because archives, insofar as they record the past, offer potentially forensic evidence that porn archives are so frequently destroyed rather than preserved. In recent years, we have become increasingly aware of how pornography—which now is more readily produced and disseminated than ever before—can be incriminating. Your porn archives may be used not only by you but against you. The capacity of archivization to destroy as well as to preserve is nowhere more apparent than in the juridical realm (not to mention the court of public opinion). Just ask Anthony Weiner, the New York congressman whose inadvertent circulation, via Twitter, of a picture of his penis shattered his hitherto successful political career.

Although by priapic standards Weiner appeared quite impressive, the photographic evidence of his hungness could not have been more damaging. When, early in the summer of 2011, his secret archive of risqué self-portraits emerged into the glare of mainstream media attention, the destructive power of archivization became fully evident. To observe that Weiner was sufficiently well hung to fuck himself is to say that his porn archive caught up with him once its forensic potential was unleashed. Of the many lessons to be drawn from this morality tale, not the least significant involves the capacity of new technologies to exceed—and thus, in a sense, to outsmart—even their most experienced users.[12] Weiner was done in as much by the archival properties of digital technology as by sexual explicitness. In this respect his case, far from exceptional, is exemplary. Key features of digital technology exceed the intentions of *any* user, with far-reaching implications for porn and its archivization.

## Pornography in the Age of Its Digital Reproducibility

Weinergate, as the affair became known, was mediated as a scandal not of pornography per se but, more specifically, of sexting. As new technologies give rise to new possibilities for pornographic representation, we require new terminology, new legislation, and new social norms to accommodate it. The neologism *sexting*—derived from the relatively recent use of *text* as a verb to describe using a mobile-phone keypad to create and send typed messages—primarily refers to the use of a smart phone, with its built-in camera, to make and transmit sexually explicit messages and images. While we were not really paying attention, our phones morphed into porn-production devices. And not just our phones. Originating with mobile-phone practices, the term *sexting* has been extended to cover the production of explicit images through personal computers, web cameras (camming), and video-game systems as well. Hunt's observation—that pornography emerges with the conjunction of a new technology and widespread access to it—has never been more relevant. Yet what distinguishes the new image technologies from their predecessors is the ease of reproducibility, which lends every mobile-phone photo unprecedented potential for viral circulation. Now anyone with a phone and Internet access may become a pornographer.

This circumstance has elicited widespread concern, in part because teenagers, legally defined as children, are among the most active practitioners of sexting. When, as happens with increasing frequency, a teenage girl uses her cell phone to send her boyfriend a nude photograph of herself, she unwittingly renders them both vulnerable to indictment under child-pornography statutes. Paradoxically, she is both the producer of the pornographic image and, if she is under eighteen, its legally defined victim.[13] Since, in the United States, it is illegal even to possess material defined as child pornography, her boyfriend likewise becomes vulnerable to felony charges. In 2009, for example, a fourteen-year-old girl from New Jersey faced child-pornography charges and sex-offender registration requirements after she posted on her MySpace page nearly thirty photographs of herself naked.[14] As a Harvard Law

School report on this new phenomenon makes clear, the problem lies in how "once it is out of the hands of the minors involved, a sexted image is indistinguishable from any other sexually explicit image of a minor."[15] Needless to say, a sexted image is distinguished precisely by the alacrity with which it escapes the intention and control of its author.

Social hysteria around kiddie porn, discussed by Steven Ruszczycky in his contribution to the volume, distracts our attention from the broader issues entailed by digital technology's transformation of pornography. Weinergate made spectacularly evident that it is not just teenagers who barely know what they're doing when they use their phones to take naked pictures of themselves. To focus on youngsters sexting or to engage in hand-wringing over Weiner's antics is to treat as exceptional and, hence, as avoidable something that actually now implicates everyone. Much of the furor around Weinergate involved scapegoating a prominent figure for our own libidinal investment in, and promiscuous use of, the technologies that tripped up his career. Statistics suggest that sexting has become a routine part of young people's erotic lives and, indeed, that digital technology has made potential pornographers of us all.[16] The archival properties of this ubiquitous technology escape any individual's control, not merely that of an impulsive teenager or a reckless congressman. Far from merely contingent or anecdotal, the ungovernability of the digital image represents an essential part of its structure.

Here I'm referring to the manner in which digital images automatically encode metadata that serve an archival function. Sexting furnishes a basis for legal intervention because the technology it employs generates pornography and its archive simultaneously. The fact that every digital image, no matter how amateur, is accompanied by a comparatively sophisticated archive of information bears more than forensic significance. It means, too, that every digital image has virtually unlimited audience potential built into its structure, and consequently any digital image can be displaced from its original context with startling ease. In a marvelous discussion of the Abu Ghraib archive, W. J. T. Mitchell explains this transformation in the conditions of photography:

> The digital camera is a radically different technical apparatus from the analog camera: it is not just lightweight and easily concealed, but linked in unprecedented ways to a vast infrastructure of reproduction and circulation. . . . We have to think of the digital camera, not only as an extension of the eyes and memory of an individual, but as linked very intimately to a global network of collective perception, memory, and imagining via e-mail and postings on the Internet. . . . It is as if digital images are directly connected to the filing cabinets where they are stored and the retrieval system that

makes their circulation possible, carrying their own archiving system with them as part of their automatism.[17]

As a result of this transformation in the production and circulation of images, we start to see how the ease with which digital porn is created is matched only by the difficulty of fathoming its implications. It is not just particular images that have gone viral but imagery itself—with the metaphor of viral replication becoming a recurrent trope for attempting to grasp these changes.[18] The study of pornography, far from suffering a dearth of archives (as Williams laments), thus confronts a surfeit of them. We have more porn archives than we know what to do with. Now the problem lies in how the proliferation of image data outpaces any capacity to measure, analyze, or comprehend it. If, as suggested apropos Pompeii, pornography comes into existence with the archive, then that claim is more than substantiated in our current digital era—although what is meant by the term *archive* has shifted. And while the nineteenth-century archives that preserved sexually explicit material did so by rigorously restricting access, one of the distinguishing features of contemporary digital archives is their extraordinary accessibility. What once was preserved only by virtue of secrecy now manifests, thanks to the properties of digital technology, secrecy as its least likely characteristic. Today anyone with access to Wikipedia can view an image of *Pan and the Goat*, probably the most provocative statue found at Pompeii.

Further, everyone can just as easily upload to the Internet pictures and videos of themselves naked or having sex. Despite the exponential growth of the porn industry in recent years, most explicit digital imagery falls under the rubric of amateur productions. Ordinary people use their phones and personal computers to produce porn for the purpose of seduction, rather than for commercial purposes (though who or what is being seduced may not be readily discernible). The young man who masturbates upon waking is unremarkable, even archetypal; but the legion of young—and not-so-young—men who use their laptops' built-in cameras to record this morning ritual, in order to post it online, are engaged in a form of sexual activity that has yet to be accurately named or understood. Likewise, using a phone to take a picture of one's genitals and then posting it online needs to be recognized as a new sexual act, perhaps a novel kind of foreplay. To characterize such behavior as simple exhibitionism or to invoke it as evidence of a "culture of voyeurism" is to diagnose without understanding it.

Whether or not we categorize such practices as sexting, it would be easy to describe them, following Foucault, as so many confessions of the flesh, wherein the deployment of sexuality takes advantage of new technological opportunities for inciting sex to speak.[19] From this perspective, what's involved in the amateur production of explicit digital imagery is less any individual agency or desire than the agency of a transindividual force that acts through us in order to regulate our sexuality. We may think we've mastered the technology, but we do not control its broader implications, any more than we control the fate of images posted online. Indeed, from a certain perspective, the new digital technologies master us.

## Archives of Affect, Counterarchives

If there is no pornography without an accompanying archive, then we need to consider more specifically what porn captures and preserves. The discussion of digital imagery makes clear that pornography archives information of at least two kinds. First, each image encodes precise metadata that enables both unlimited reproduction of the image and forensic tracking of its provenance. However, the production of such images serves a broader tracking function by intensifying surveillance of our bodies and sexualities. To participate in sexting or online porn, in any shape or form, is to be constantly disclosing information about one's desire and thus to be working within the regulatory deployment of sexuality. This point—which may come as unwelcome news to those who imagine their online activities as politically resistant or necessarily transgressive—emphasizes the degree to which digital technologies capture and preserve information without their users' consent. When I see a sign at the entrance to the gym's locker room stating that the use of cellular phones is forbidden, I'm being alerted to a similar point. Almost everyone now has the technology to capture surreptitiously images of others and information about them—a fact that exponentially multiplies potential sites of porn production. Our bodies are subject to surveillance more than ever before.

This Foucauldian take on digital sex, while far from unwarranted, might be understood as one of many manifestations of a paranoid approach to pornography. It's another way of expressing the widespread fear that pornography is intrinsically harmful. A less paranoid approach would acknowledge that, in addition to archiving information, *pornography archives pleasure*. The elementary recognition at the heart of this volume is that porn is itself an archive—of sex, of fantasy, of desire, of bodies and their actions, and of pleasure. Pornography, at least in its photographic forms, preserves evidence of something that is otherwise transient and ephemeral. It enables intimacy to enter the archive, and it is valuable for that reason alone. Indeed, pornography offers evidence about a whole gamut of social issues and desires by showing us things that otherwise tend to remain imperceptible. Much of the confusion about pornography's value stems from the objection that its representations are not realistic ("my body doesn't look like that"). But as the case of Priapus suggests, pornography need not be realistic to furnish valuable evidence; realism is just one of several valid criteria in archival research.

The nineteenth-century archaeologists and curators tasked with handling priapic artifacts intuited something that contemporary scholars have begun to emphasize—namely, that archives contain not just information but also affect. What stirred the Victorians' apprehension was their sense of the artifacts' capacity to arouse uncontrollable feelings of lust in the viewer. Recent scholarship on archives, especially that inspired by feminist, queer, and postcolonialist methodologies, has stressed the affective dimension of the archive—though without considering feelings specifically of pleasure or lust.[20] Perhaps because this scholarship has tended to focus primarily on so-called negative affects, it has been reluctant to acknowledge that pornography constitutes a massive archive of heterogeneous feelings and affects. In order to grasp how sexuality works in modern culture, we need to appreciate that porn, too, is an archive of feeling. Certainly this is a major source of pornography's significance for those whose desires depart from social norms—as many of the chapters collected here attest. By preserving traces of nonnormative pleasures, porn facilitates not only the tracking but also the reactivation of these pleasures; and it may do so without requiring imaginary identification to experience them. Porn archives are important not least because sexual minorities use them as a form of cultural memory.[21]

This understanding of pornography's archival capacity stems partly from a queer perspective on porn and partly from scholarship that has enlarged our sense of what constitutes an archive. Taking stock of how pornography archives affect in addition to information entails recognizing that the notion of the archive bears more than one meaning. "The term 'archive' has become a kind of loose signifier for a disparate set of concepts," observes one surveyor of the field.[22] It is not simply a question of how the archives of virtual data held in digital images complicate traditional conceptions of the archive as a repository of documents. More fundamentally, the issue of the archive concerns the dramatic expansion of the term to cover unofficial, idiosyncratic, and personal collections of material, in addition to those that historically have served the nation-state. According to this perspective, an individual scholar's assemblage of various sources, just as much as an amateur's stash of comics or porn, may be regarded as an archive. The term now encompasses private as well as public collections and, indeed, spans cultural dimensions, ranging from the most modest, disordered groupings of material to the macro level of discursive systems (à la Foucault).

Work on the archive has been motivated as much by the desire to legitimate new fields of inquiry (no discipline without its archive) as by the conviction that unofficial archives may be turned against their official counterparts.

The official story—of a nation, a people, an ethnicity, or a sexuality—can be contested by the hitherto unsanctioned stories contained within marginal archives. Here what the archive holds is political resistance. This insight, developed from Walter Benjamin's rethinking of historiography via Foucault's account of subjugated knowledges, has led to research on what are variously known as counterarchives, migrant archives, and queer archives: a multi-pronged, cross-disciplinary project of identifying, collecting, and preserving the traces of that which otherwise remains obscure, ephemeral, itinerant, and precarious.[23] *Porn Archives* contributes to this cross-disciplinary project in manifold ways, even as the counterarchival status of pornography remains equivocal. On the one hand, what Rodrigo Lazo says of migrant archives—that they "reside in obscurity and are always at the edge of annihilation"—applies equally to porn archives.[24] This becomes evident when one considers, for example, the archive of early twentieth-century stag films preserved by the Kinsey Institute archive in Bloomington, Indiana. As Williams explains: "An archive of stag films is not like any film archive. It was not acquired to preserve film history but as a record of sexual practices; all of its films were illicitly made and distributed and no one properly 'owns' their copyright. It is something of a miracle—and a tribute to Alfred Kinsey's voracious, nonjudgmental interest in everything having to do with sex—that this archive exists at all."[25] Since porn is regarded as ephemera, the conditions that facilitate its archivization remain so contingent, often depending on the zeal of a particular individual, as to make its preservation seem miraculous. On the other hand, however, porn is routinely archived for mundane commercial reasons. The recent digitization of *Playboy*'s entire fifty-seven-year magazine run, featuring "every pictorial, interview, centerfold, investigative reporting piece, story, cartoon, advertisement and image that ever appeared in the magazine," represents a valuable resource for scholars of pornography and postwar U.S. culture.[26] As a record of mainstream erotic tastes made available for profit, iPlayboy.com hardly constitutes a counterarchive. Yet to the extent that non-target audiences, such as queer and feminist scholars, may use it against the grain, this new online resource nevertheless harbors significant counterarchival potential.

The *Playboy* example helps clarify how the term *counterarchive* refers less to a determinate place or archival content than to a strategic practice or a particular style of constituting the archive's legibility. Less an entity than a relation, the counterarchive works to unsettle those orders of knowledge established in and through official archives.[27] By exposing the libidinal investments that a given regime prefers to keep out of sight, porn archives may disrupt the dominant narrative, even as they also may consolidate the deployment of sexuality by tracking and molding their subjects' desires. In the end, pornography remains too heterogeneous to consistently qualify as counterarchival. Its heterogeneity as a category also explains why it makes little sense to take a position either "for" or "against" it. The antiporn-anticensorship battles of previous generations relied on essentialized notions of what pornography is and does. However, when one considers the full range of existing porn archives, as well as the role of archivization in shaping porn's meanings, then both pro and anti positions ultimately become untenable.

## Passions of the Collector

Antiporn critiques, whether feminist or otherwise, tend to take representations in which men dominate women as defining pornography. By thus assuming a heterosexual paradigm, criticism on pornography, both popular and academic, has a harder time grasping either porn's heterogeneity or the variety of functions it may fulfill. *Porn Archives* attempts to redress that imbalance by queering the critical perspective on pornography in various ways. More than considering simply nonheterosexual content, the contributors investigate the counterheteronormative uses to which porn—whether mainstream or marginal—may be put. Examining porn in terms of its archivization involves analyzing explicitness as something whose meaning and effects, far from self-evident, are context dependent. Such a perspective entails taking some distance from the feminist debates that brought the study of pornography into academia in the first place.[28] Or, rather, the perspective entails reframing those debates in queer terms by acknowledging that gender is only one factor, not necessarily the most important one, when considering sexuality and its manifestations. As the chapters collected here demonstrate, categories of racial difference, ethnic difference, national difference, able-bodiedness, and generational difference need to supplement—indeed, to displace—sexual difference as the principal axis structuring erotic intelligibility. Otherwise, lacking a broadly conceived queer perspective, critics of porn unwittingly reinscribe the heteronormative framework that organizes so much of social and cultural life, including mainstream pornography.

A queer perspective on pornography makes visible the artificiality of the normative division of desire into straight and gay. This is another way of saying that the notion of sexual identity is itself an artifact of heteronormativity. The closer one looks at various pornographies, the more clearly one sees how little porn respects sexual-identity categories. This point became evident in what is now regarded as a classic work of porn archiving, Samuel Delany's *Times Square Red, Times Square Blue*, a book that collated the author's reminiscences of life in the porn theaters of New York's Times Square over several decades, until the theaters' destruction under the Rudy Giuliani administration during the late 1990s.[29] Working as an informal, idiosyncratic, yet nonetheless passionate archivist, Delany undertook a labor of preservation through storytelling, in the face of a concerted, long-term program of annihilation. His book documents how the Times Square porn theaters fostered beneficent relationships, often interracial and cross class, among their legion of patrons; in turn, those relationships, social as well as sexual, conditioned the meaning of the images screened. Dramatizing how the films' heterosexual content did nothing to deter erotic activity among the almost exclusively male audience, Delany underscores the irrelevance of sexual-identity categories to the experience of pleasure in these institutions. Porn enables ostensibly straight men to come together in ways that don't always reinforce heteronormativity.

As with many of the chapters collected here, Delany's work makes plain that researching and archiving pornography is rarely characterized by scholarly objectivity. Instead, it partakes of what one of the editors of Benjamin's archive calls "the passions of the collector."[30] Benjamin, himself a major archivist, took the figure of the collector (as well as that of the ragpicker) to embody his ethics of historical salvage, where value is found in what has been discarded as outmoded or worthless. Any archive constituted in this manner, but especially a porn archive saved from obliteration thanks to "the passions of the collector," is likely to be incomplete, disordered, and irreducibly subjective. What such an archive lacks in order or completeness, however, it will make up for in traces of subjectivity and desire that otherwise would have been lost to the historical record. This is especially important in the case of minority sexualities, because conventional historical traces—marriage and birth records, all the signs that confer recognition on normative relationships—tend to be absent. The passions of the collector often incline toward the queer end of the spectrum for just this reason.[31]

However, as in Benjamin's comparison of the collector with the ragpicker, substantial class differences divide those whose passions encourage the collecting of rare erotica and those who, with lesser means, collect erotic experience, all the better to archive it. It is not coincidental, in Delany's account of pornography, that class—rather than gender, race, or sexuality—remains the most significant category of analysis. When, to take another example, one considers Henry Spencer Ashbee, the Victorian gentleman whose extraordinary collection of pornography became the basis of the Private Case at the British Museum, one sees how he enjoyed, along with economic privilege, a kind of access to pornography that routinely was denied women and the lower classes.[32] Yet while socially privileged in terms of his gender, race, class, and nation, Ashbee, albeit married with children, was not sexually normative in his erotic tastes and practices. His interest in what now would be categorized as BDSM (specifically, flagellation), together with his exceptional commitment to archiving pornography, marks this Victorian gentleman as distinctly queer. Indeed, the practice of collecting pornography, as a kind of sublimated promiscuity that seeks out more and more mediated sexual experience, is always potentially queer, insofar as it resists the monogamous ideal governing heteronormativity.

If access to porn and its archives has been historically an issue of social class, then technological developments during the mid- to late twentieth century have transformed the landscape by democratizing access to the means of representation. Here the relevant case would be Sam Steward, the English-professor-turned-tattoo-artist, whose impressive porn archiving, detailed by historian Justin Spring, exemplifies the passions of the collector.[33] By comparison with Ashbee, Steward appears as more of a collector of erotic experience—even as what distinguishes him in turn from other twentieth-century gay adventurers was the meticulous recording of his thousands of sexual encounters. Like a good librarian, Steward archived those encounters in an index card–based "Stud File" and, when Polaroid technology came along to facilitate amateur pornography, he took snapshots of his men too.[34] Although Steward became one of Alfred Kinsey's most valuable informants, his collecting and archiving were motivated primarily by the search for pleasure. Or perhaps we should say that, in Steward's case, the practice of archiving to preserve and enhance erotic pleasure did not require any pretension to scientific knowledge as its alibi. His porn archive constituted more of an *ars erotica* than a *scientia sexualis*.[35] Ashbee and Steward—both world-class porn archivists, both passionate about BDSM, both queer in their own ways—were divided by differences the most salient of which was *not* sexual identity.

As these examples indicate, the question of class in porn involves at least three dimensions. First, in terms of content, pornography since the Marquis de Sade has repeatedly, almost obsessively, taken differences of social class as its subject.[36] Second, until recently social class was a primary factor in determining access to the archives of pornography. Third, beyond questions of content and access, class has been central to porn's capacity for diagramming otherwise imperceptible forms of social mobility. That, at least, is the claim of Frances Ferguson's *Pornography, the Theory*, a book whose distinctive thesis has not yet been assimilated by the field of porn studies.[37] This failure is attributable in part to how the field tends to be divided between scholars working in film studies and those who approach pornography from other disciplinary perspectives. *Porn Archives* attempts to bridge that divide by including a broader range of disciplinary approaches and by offering a sustained engagement with Ferguson's account of pornography. This volume stages a cross-disciplinary conversation about pornography, with contributions from scholars working in art history, information science, and ethnic studies, as well as in literary, film, and media studies.

The challenge of assimilating competing accounts of pornography is partly a question of disciplinarity. But it is also, as I've been suggesting, a question of technology. Thinking about porn in terms of different media—whether painting, sculpture, print, photography, film, video, or digital—alters the account of porn that is likely to be generated, just as any experience of porn depends on the technology through which it is mediated. Regardless of content, a pornographic image on film cannot be the same as a digital pornographic image, for example. Not only that: critics of pornography face the additional challenge of negotiating an intractable tension between porn as a technology of knowledge (part of the will to know) and porn as a technology of pleasure. Whatever form it takes, pornography is never just one thing. The term *pornography* designates not a single, homogeneous entity about which judgments may be made but a plurality of genres, media, technologies, and conditioning archives. Rather than awkwardly referring to *pornographies*, we have chosen to speak instead of *porn archives*, wishing to acknowledge both the heterogeneity of the category and the conviction that sexual explicitness, in spite of appearances, bears no essential meaning.

## Pedagogical Archives

*Porn Archives* begins with Linda Williams surveying the field of pornography studies that she widely is regarded as having founded. Her assessment, useful as a supplementary introduction to this volume, is critical of the state of the field, which she finds to be lacking much of the scholarly infrastructure that typically supports academic disciplines and subfields. At the heart of the problem is what she calls "the missing archive." From the perspective of film studies, the "lack of preservation of the pornographic heritage is appalling"; it hobbles the field's development. This is a very real problem, although it changes complexion when one considers porn archives from a vantage other than that of film history. In addition to the archive, Williams engages tough questions of pedagogy and critical terminology—questions that remain central to the study of pornography from any disciplinary perspective.

The question of pedagogy is central to the next chapter, which archives a classroom conversation with Frances Ferguson about her book *Pornography, the Theory*. Ferguson situates the issue of institutions in a broader historical perspective by comparing pornography to the eighteenth-century utilitarian classroom theorized by Jeremy Bentham. In so doing, she clarifies the distinctiveness of her own account of pornography while also anticipating the discussion of pedagogy found in several of the volume's chapters. Because Ferguson's account has not been engaged by scholars in porn studies, we wanted to include this interview with her as a way of connecting the implications of *Pornography, the Theory* to wider debates. Pornography for Ferguson, like the Benthamite classroom, constitutes a "utilitarian social structure," characterized by the extreme perceptibility of shifting value assignments as bodies become mobile in a circumscribed space. Elaborating her account in relation to Catharine MacKinnon's critique of pornography as sexual harassment, Ferguson explains how "something can be pornographic without being sexually explicit": what makes it pornographic is not its content but its use in a social situation of inequality. The original way in which Ferguson connects pornography to the nonsexual dynamics of social systems is particularly illuminating for subsequent *Porn Archives* chapters that take up and engage her thinking in different contexts (such as that of disability porn).

In chapter 3, the experimental videographer Nguyen Tan Hoang addresses pornography in the classroom from a specifically queer perspective. By drawing on his own experience as a student making sexually explicit videos, Nguyen concretizes the discussion of pedagogy. His archive of instructional scenes exemplifies how teaching may involve less imitation than initiation — and hence his title's allusion to *The Opening of Misty Beethoven* (directed by Henry Paris, 1976), a hard-core classic of eroto-pedagogic initiation based on *Pygmalion*. Nguyen describes how the roster of teachers named in his title helped him to develop his aesthetic practice of creating "counterpornographies," and how he learned not simply to critique the sexually explicit but also queerly to produce it. Aspiring through his work to "expand the official gay-porn archive," Nguyen crosses sexuality with axes of racial, ethnic, and intergenerational difference in a contestatory fashion that aims to interrogate porn without draining it of heat. By revealing the classroom as a site of something more than institutional discipline, his chapter resonates with Ferguson's account of Benthamite education.

In chapter 4, David Squires extends the focus on education by considering how the presence of pornography in the library "raises an entire set of questions about intellectual freedom, community service, media access, heterogeneous social values, and more-practical concerns about how to manage potentially sensitive collections." This chapter develops the discussion of porn's institutional status by, on the one hand, bringing to bear debates in postwar information science about the preservation of sexually explicit material, and, on the other, considering libraries as imaginary spaces. Building on an analysis of the library scene in Pauline Réage's *Story of O* (where the heroine submits to sexual instruction at the hands of sadistic gentlemen patrons), Squires examines the library as an institution charged with the pedagogical mission to educate its users. This mission expanded to the possibility of sexual education after obscenity law shifted its focus from books to films during the 1960s, thereby presenting libraries with a new set of questions and opportunities. The shift in censorship policy positioned libraries to become privileged institutional sites for negotiating so-called community standards. Drawing on Ferguson's account of pornography as defined not by content but by social use, Squires shows how libraries—like classrooms—actively participate in the social production of knowledge about sex.

## Historical Archives

The degree to which part I considers historical issues suggests just how artificial the separation is between it and part II. Nevertheless, the chapters in "Historical Archives" focus especially closely on particular moments in the history of pornography, beginning with Jennifer Burns Bright and Ronan Crowley's account of the evolution of library policies governing access to sexually explicit material. This coauthored chapter considers the situation of the sexuality researcher who, in today's library context, is constrained to peruse pornography in public. Here the archive is not missing, just peculiarly troublesome to consult, since "the contemporary scholar of pornography is an unwitting heir of old battles for and against sequestration." Tracing the history of these battles at the British Museum Library and the Kinsey Institute, Bright and Crowley demonstrate how conventions of disciplinary space continue to determine the circulation of material among shifting publics and counterpublics. This history is not simply one of expanding access following sexual liberation but instead tells the story of mutating protocols and intensifying regulation—a story, that is, of discipline in the Foucauldian sense. Print pornography, mediated by libraries and hybrid institutions such as the Kinsey Institute, is archived according to disciplinary systems that continue to evolve.

In chapter 6, Loren Glass examines another historically crucial institution that mediated print pornography: Grove Press. Anticensorship victories in the trials of *Lady Chatterley's Lover*, *Tropic of Cancer*, and *Naked Lunch* allowed Grove Press to publish a host of "underground" Victorian titles, including *My Secret Life*, the pornographic autobiography of an anonymous Victorian gentleman. As with the writing of Sade, such works had been previously unavailable to all but a handful of readers. A significant chapter in the history of democratizing access to sexually explicit works, the story of Grove Press involves what Glass calls the "desacralization" of obscenity. By domesticating the Sadean aura, Grove made Sade available to not only a mainstream audience but also the possibility of feminist critique. Glass's history shows how "the dissolution of the sacred category of evil as a descriptor of pornographic texts enabled the secular category of politics to emerge as the central battleground." This process also laid the groundwork for the U.S. reception of Foucault's *History of Sexuality*, whose critique of a censorship model of sex (that is, the repressive hypothesis) invokes *My Secret Life* and Sade as exemplars.

The influence of Foucault's *History of Sexuality* is central also to Joseph Bristow's analysis, in chapter 7, of *Teleny*, an anonymous work from 1893 that Neil Bartlett called "London's first gay porn novel." Showing how *Teleny*'s erudition supports its "concerted defense of homoerotic pleasure," Bristow reshapes our understanding of pornography as a technology of knowledge. Rather than serving the normalizing deployment of sexuality that Foucault saw emerging in the Victorian period, *Teleny* draws on an astonishing range of discourses—scholarly, aesthetic, musical, scientific—in order to articulate a counterdiscursive challenge to the medicolegal pathologization of homosexuality. Bristow's meticulous locating of the novel in its historical and bibliographic contexts enables us to appreciate how powerfully original *Teleny* is. At the same time, he emphasizes that it is not simply cosmopolitan erudition that distinguishes this novel but also its passionate celebration of the "gay phallus," its unabashed pleasure in "the physiological splendor of the ejaculating male organ." In this way, the chapter contributes a historical argument on behalf of the importance of pornographic representation for minority sexualities.

*Image Archives*

The chapters in part III, by focusing on primarily still images in a range of visual media, draw our attention to the heterogeneity of visual archives in which sexually explicit images occur. In chapter 8, Robert L. Caserio contrasts explicit homoerotic art with contemporary digital porn to interrogate the dichotomy between activity and passivity that structures so much of erotic life. Examining the work of Lucian Freud, Francis Bacon, and John O'Reilly, Caserio finds a profound meditation on erotic passivity that challenges the wider culture's commitment to agency and mastery. That commitment was central to the popular rationale for video technology, which emphasized the viewer's privacy and enhanced agency in the viewing experience, thanks to the possibilities of remote-control manipulation of the image. The privileging of agency was also central to feminist critiques of pornography, which argued on behalf of women's agency and control over their sexuality. Given this context, the erotic allure of masculine passivity and, indeed, the queer agency in passivity that Caserio discloses are all the more striking.

By contrast, the next chapter focuses on masculine activity in one of its most hyperbolic guises—namely, gay black porn superhero comics. Darieck Scott shows how the comic form exaggerates particular attributes (whether superhero powers or sexual prowess) far beyond any human proportion, and how exaggeration may perform critical work, especially in a racial context where black men already are caricatured as oversexed and hyperphallicized. Although the hyperbolic muscularity of mainstream comic superheroes makes them ripe for gay appropriation, the gay black porn comics drawn by Belasco, David Barnes, and Patrick Fillion render the protagonists heroic by exaggerating their sexual beauty and allure. The emphasis on black beauty gives these porn comics a utopian dimension, argues Scott, even as they position the ideal reader as nonblack in order to maximize the desirability of blackness. As with other porn archives, these gay black porn comics are not simply showing us sexually explicit content but also teaching us how to look at it.

Another archive that experimented with representations of gay sex—this time through collage—is the subject of chapter 10. Robert Dewhurst unearths the history of *Gay Sunshine*, a San Francisco–based news monthly that ran throughout the 1970s and that, by means of a collagist aesthetic, "sought to assemble a lost archive of queer subcultural and literary history." From its inaugural issue, *Gay Sunshine* subjected the pornographic centerfold to what Dewhurst calls "pornopoetic" collage treatment by mingling and overlaying poems with nude male figures. Dewhurst connects this collage technique, which combines disparate and fragmentary materials, with the practice of queer-archive assembly, which entails pluralistic inventiveness and a "radical global politics of solidarity." *Gay Sunshine*, located in the crucial decade between Stonewall and AIDS, prefigures through its aesthetics the emergence of coalitional queer politics in the 1990s. Together with the other chapters in "Image Archives," Dewhurst's contribution suggests how historical constraints on erotic expression—particularly for gay men—promoted forms of experiment in which representational realism seemed the least important criterion.

Chapter 11, "This Is What Porn Can Be Like!," pursues the question of queer pornographic expression from a female perspective by archiving a conversation between the feminist porn scholar Mireille Miller-Young and the producer-director Shine Louise Houston, whose film *Champion* recently won the Movie of the Year award at the Feminist Porn Awards in Toronto. The conversation affords multiple insights into not only the role of female producers and consumers of pornography but also the impact of new media technologies from a filmmaker's perspective. Houston describes the economic constraints of running a business in the age of Internet porn, which sometimes generate tension between capturing women's sexual pleasure on screen and producing films that work as aesthetic or commercial artifacts. Despite the enumeration of manifold constraints, however, what comes through most strongly in the conversation is that this queer, feminist filmmaker bears a utopian vision of pornography's possibilities for minorities—"*This is what porn can be like!*" Houston and Miller-Young share with the volume's other contributors a determination to take the best examples as representative of the genre, rather than the worst—in other words, to treat pornography on a par with other expressive genres, such as the novel.

## Rough Archives

If the chapters in "Image Archives" focus on queer representations, those in "Rough Archives" focus on primarily heterosexual moving-image porn that falls outside the mainstream. Since these chapters examine pornographic scenarios involving women—scenarios that also typically involve domination or violence—they engage feminist debates about disequilibriums of power in porn more directly than do other contributions to *Porn Archives*. In chapter 12, Lisa Downing intervenes in these debates by considering the snuff film, a genre that epitomizes the radical feminist critique of pornography. Distinct from the missing archive or fugitive archive, snuff constitutes a *fantasmatic archive*—one containing no verifiable instances—that nonetheless performs significant cultural work. Tracking the itinerary of this fantasmatic archive, Downing offers a critique of recent obscenity legislation in the United Kingdom that criminalizes the possession of images simulating erotic death. She shows how Britain's "extreme images" laws entail policing fantasy rather than sexual consent, all in the service of enforcing the majority's erotic norms. If the problem is less censorship than intensifying normalization, then we start to see how categories of sexual identity take a backseat to broader questions of power and coercion.

The next chapter pursues these questions by examining the formal principles at work in the archives of "rough sex." Focusing on *Forced Entry* (directed by Lizzy Borden, 2002), an infamous video by Extreme Associates that was subject to federal obscenity indictment, Eugenie Brinkema shows how roughness characterizes not only the sex in the film but also its atypical formal features. Although it is about as hard core as U.S. porn gets, *Forced Entry* exemplifies not the "frenzy of the visible" described by Linda Williams in *Hard Core* but instead what Brinkema calls a frenzy *at the expense of* the visible, thanks to its idiosyncratic roughening of all aspects of the pornographic experience. This roughening also impacts the pornographic archive, which in its normative incarnation would be smooth, complete, and well ordered. Anticipating John Paul Ricco's claims later in the volume, Brinkema argues on behalf of the ethics of a rough archive, one that does not disavow the roughening effects of time's passage but rather embraces finitude.

In chapter 14, Marcia Klotz investigates BDSM pornography in the context of online interactivity, focusing on the controversial web-based porn studio Insex, founded by the performance artist Brent Scott in 1997 and shut down by Homeland Security in 2005. Probing questions of consent, coercion, and mediated intimacy, Klotz examines the site's experiments with live-feed technology, in which viewers around the world could have a say in what Insex models did. As part of her research, Klotz adopts an interactive methodology and conducts an informal ethnography via online interviews with former site members and models, as well as with the makers of *Graphic Sexual Horror*, a recent documentary about Insex. Like Ferguson, Klotz asks what makes something pornographic when there is no nudity or genital contact involved. Her chapter is also closely in dialogue with Downing's, even as its focus on globalized interactivity anticipates the chapters in the next part.

## Transnational Archives

If Internet technology has contributed to globalization, it likewise has facilitated the transnationalizing of pornography. The chapters in this part examine porn archives beyond the boundaries of the United States, beginning with Ramón E. Soto-Crespo's account of the history of obscenity legislation in Puerto Rico—a history that is closely related, though not identical, to that of the mainland United States. A borderland created through repeated migrations between the island and the mainland, Puerto Rico has a cultural and political specificity that resists the nationalist model on which archival practices conventionally depend. Soto-Crespo argues that migration provides access to pornography at the same time as it problematizes our understanding of the archive. Starting from a description of "el archivo," the stash of old copies of *Playboy* and *Penthouse* that local island boys hid and treasured, this chapter traces the history of pornography in Puerto Rico and its development in the borderlands. The emergence of Boricua porn during the 1990s offered vibrant images of migrant masculinity that displaced Nuyorican representations of ethnic masculinity as "mongo" or impotent. Analyzing this set of transformations, Soto-Crespo makes the case for a theory and practice of archiving that, decoupled from the nation-state, can accommodate cross-border mobility as well as the ephemera of "trash archives."

Chapter 16 extends the focus on Latino porn to Latin America, while also developing Soto-Crespo's notion of "trash archives" via the distinctive Brazilian genre of *pornochanchada*. Focusing on *A b . . . profunda* (Deep ass), a Brazilian parody of *Deep Throat*, Melissa Schindler locates the film in its historical context by delineating the neglected genre of pornochanchada, which was trashy without necessarily being sexually explicit. Expanding to Brazil Hunt's thesis that pornography appears when the masses gain access to new technologies, Schindler shows how "what made pornochanchadas distinctive was that they emerged from the historic and artistic redistribution of power that occurred when, all of a sudden, 'everyday' people had access to the film camera — not just to a seat in the theater." Condemned as trashy because they are associated with common people, pornochanchadas are pornographic less because they depict explicit sex than because they reveal how "low-class" tastes and practices consistently traverse class lines. Schindler argues that, through its trashiness, the despised pornochanchada critiques not only U.S. imperialism in Latin America but also Brazil's own complex social hierarchies. *A b . . . profunda* advances this critique by extolling the anus as a site not of waste or trash but of universal pleasure; in so doing, it puts the *ass* back in *aesthetics*.

The next chapter pursues, in specifically philosophical terms, further connections between pornography and social critique. Elaborating Jean-Luc Nancy's work on ethics, John Paul Ricco makes the case for "pornographic faith" as a matter of putting one's trust in the nakedness of being together, where what is entrusted is the shared exposure to vulnerability and the paradoxical singularity of each other's finitude. He contrasts pornographic faith with the global spectacles of disaster and humiliation that Jean Baudrillard christened "war porn," thereby differentiating two opposed senses of pornography, neither of which depends on sexual explicitness. After the explosion of the Abu Ghraib image archive, it has become imperative to distinguish war porn from other superficially similar pornographic imagery. By elaborating pornographic faith as a mode of resistance to the contemporary biopolitics of bodies, Ricco provides the terms for this crucial distinction, even as his globalized framework makes tangible hitherto unremarked biopolitical connections. The chapter's emphasis on finitude links it to Brinkema's, since both argue for the limits of the archive and point, in fascinating ways, to what in pornography remains unarchivable.

Chapter 18 develops the discussion of war porn by examining websites (such as LiveLeak.com) that circulate as pornography digital images of military violence, mutilation, and bombing. This archive of war-related imagery, generated by gun cameras and increasingly sophisticated surveillance technologies, records actual events whose appeal lies partly in the fact that they have not been staged for the camera and, moreover, are too grisly for public viewing. Prabha Manuratne describes how this imagery is reframed in the language of mainstream porn and consumed by "online communities [that] relish combat footage as a sexual object, even as nations wage war in the name

of abstract ideals, such as God, security, or democracy." Confronting the pleasure of viewing this imagery, she argues that war porn indexes the limits of
pornography by abrogating distinctions between fantasy and reality. War porn
presents real events through an ethnopolitical fantasy that produces libidinal gratification for those who archive and share it. The chapter's focus on
fantasy, desire, and pleasure as transnationally constituted links Manuratne's
account to not only Ricco's but also the next chapter's discussion of pornographic desire across ethnic borders, in the form of foreskin fetishism.

## Archives of Excess

It can be hard to countenance the full spectrum of what gives people visual
pleasure. Although the archive of war porn—like some of the archives analyzed in this part—exists at the outer reaches of pornography, it manifests
certain continuities with mainstream porn in its preoccupation with bodily
anomaly and excess. The chapters in this part show how we think about normative bodies and their sexuality by focusing on the pornography of foreskins, amputees, and underage figures. These chapters get at something central about human desire by looking without blinking at the margins of sexual
representation.

Chapter 19 considers the phenomenon of "foreskin fandom," examining
how a small piece of ostensibly excess flesh has become fetishized in gay porn.
Harri Kalha, Finland's leading scholar of pornography, accounts for this phenomenon by locating it in the culture of circumcision that has overdetermined
the meaning of the male prepuce. Through the lens of Robert Mapplethorpe's
iconic *Man in a Polyester Suit*, Kalha shows how the foreskin, in addition to
being racialized, signifies as natural, untouched, masculine, and desirable,
on the one hand while, on the other, it is cast as foreign, dirty, feminine, and
disgusting. These meanings make it ripe for fetishization, as does the link between circumcision and castration: "Here is a body part that can easily be lost
or has indeed been (partly) lost," Kalha explains. Appropriating the Freudian
model of fetishism, he argues that making a spectacle of the foreskin, as in
some gay porn, works to divert attention from its more politically troubling
connotations. At the same time, however, the development of communities of
foreskin fandom, through pornography and online discussion groups, recasts
fetishism as a collective commitment rather than an individual pathology.

In chapter 20, Steven Ruszczycky tackles what currently may be the most
controversial archive of fantasy in our culture, that concerning the sexuality
of children. Focusing on Matthew Stadler's novel *Allan Stein* (in which a man
seduces—or is seduced by—a teenage boy), Ruszczycky shows how the construction of the pedophile as an identity category works to absolve the rest of

us of any responsibility for these fantasies. Similar to the fictions that child-pornography laws tell about realness and pedophiles, Ruszczycky argues, the fantasies of child pornography may offer "new modes of ethical relation between adults and youths that begin with rethinking one's own relation to what is most troubling about the self." Outlining a history of these fantasies and the legislation surrounding them, the chapter connects child pornography to broader cultural concerns, thus underscoring porn's capacity to crystallize the anxieties and desires of the society in which it circulates. The fact that the U.S. Supreme Court defines child pornography as the documentation of a crime links Ruszczycky's study of this marginal subgenre to questions of evidence and forensics that, as we have seen, remain central to any archive.

Examining the archive of same-sex amputee porn, chapter 21 articulates queer theory with disability theory in an effort to develop their shared commitment to treating anomalous bodies and nonnormative practices as not merely defensible but positively desirable. Curious about the processes through which pornography makes disability sexy, I elaborate psychoanalytic categories other than fetishism to describe such processes. The chapter argues that a Freudian theory of sex reveals not that anatomy is destiny but, on the contrary, that fantasy unsettles anatomy. By encouraging psychic mobility, fantasy has the capacity to undermine identity—as does pornography by prioritizing action over identity. The emphasis on action puts my chapter in conversation with Ferguson, as I try to explain how although her and Williams's accounts of pornography both derive from Foucault, they nevertheless remain sharply distinct in their assessments of the political significance of visibility. Sexual explicitness may be mobilized for widely varying uses, particularly in the realm of disability.

..............................

We are happy to include as an appendix to this collection a bibliography of institutional archives of pornography compiled by Caitlin Shanley. Focusing on institutions worldwide, it provides the most comprehensive listing of archives of sexually explicit material yet published. The bibliography will be invaluable for researchers, not least because many of the university collections listed neither publicize their pornographic holdings nor catalog them in ways that make them readily accessible. Sequestered, disguised, and consequently underutilized, these archives suggest just how much sexually explicit material has been preserved—and how much research remains to be done.

# Notes

1. L. Hunt, "Introduction," 13.
2. Kendrick, *The Secret Museum*, 2–17.
3. Kendrick, *The Secret Museum*, 8.
4. See De Simone, "The History of the Museum and the Collection," 169. Subject to multiple closures, reopenings, and reorganizations, the secret museum within a museum finally became fully accessible to the general public only in the twenty-first century.
5. See Foucault, *History of Madness*, chapter 2.
6. Postcolonialist scholarship has been especially committed to developing this insight, at least since Gayatri Chakravorty Spivak's "The Rani of Sirmur." See also Arondekar, *For the Record*; A. Burton, *Archive Stories*; Stoler, *Along the Archival Grain*.
7. Vismann, *Files*, 12.
8. Foucault, *The Archaeology of Knowledge*, 126–31.
9. On the complex materiality of archival dirt, see Steedman, *Dust*.
10. Derrida, *Archive Fever*, 4n1.
11. In addition to her contribution to the present volume, see L. Williams, "'White Slavery' versus the Ethnography of 'Sexworkers.'" Osborne, "The Ordinariness of the Archive," offers a cognate argument that the primary function of archives is to generate epistemological credibility. In "Dirty Little Secrets," Eric Schaefer provides a useful discussion of the issues involved in preserving and accessing moving-image porn.
12. Several newspaper reports noted that Weiner was known as a "technophile," a term that alludes to his early adoption of social-networking technology in political campaigns but that, in this context, also carries overtones of sexual fetishism. See, for example, Michael Barbaro, "Weiner Admits He Sent Lewd Photos; Says He Won't Resign," *New York Times*, June 6, 2011.
13. See Jan Hoffman, "A Girl's Nude Photo, and Altered Lives," *New York Times*, March 26, 2011. In a comprehensive report, Dena Sacco and her collaborators at Harvard Law School survey this issue, with the aim of assessing the constitutionality of recent child-pornography prosecutions, in various states, that involve teenagers sexting. See Sacco et al., *Sexting*.
14. See "Girl Posts Nude Pics, Is Charged with Kid Porn," Associated Press, March 27, 2009. News reports on additional cases are detailed in Sacco et al., *Sexting*, 7–9.
15. Sacco et al., *Sexting*, 22.
16. One survey of sexting behavior, *A Thin Line: Digital Abuse Study* (conducted in September 2009 by MTV in conjunction with the Associated Press), found that 45 percent of sexually active young people had been involved in one or more sexting-related activities (cited in Sacco et al., *Sexting*, 4). As the incidence of sexting increases, the practice is becoming normalized among younger generations, with digital resources becoming as fully integrated into their sex lives as into other aspects of their lives.
17. Mitchell, *Cloning Terror*, 123–24.
18. The circumstance of pornographic imagery's going viral is exacerbated by the subgenre of bareback porn, which, in some instances, treats one particular virus (HIV) as an object of desire. See Dean, *Unlimited Intimacy*, chapter 2.
19. See Foucault, *The History of Sexuality*, vol. 1.
20. In addition to Arondekar, *For the Record*; and Stoler, *Along the Archival Grain*, see

Cvetkovich, *An Archive of Feelings*; Massumi, "The Archive of Experience"; and D. Taylor, *The Archive and the Repertoire*.

21. Thomas Waugh, among others, has thoroughly documented this fact vis-à-vis gay men. See, for example, Waugh, *Hard to Imagine*; and Waugh, *Lust Unearthed*.

22. Manoff, "Theories of the Archive from across the Disciplines," 10.

23. On the notion of counterarchives, see Foster, "An Archival Impulse"; Merewether, *The Archive*; and the work of Brent Hayes Edwards. On migrant archives, see Lazo, "Migrant Archives." On queer archives, see Cvetkovich, *Archive of Feelings*; Halberstam, *In a Queer Time and Place*; Halberstam, *The Queer Art of Failure*; and Herring, *Another Country*.

24. Lazo, "Migrant Archives," 37.

25. L. Williams, "'White Slavery' versus the Ethnography of 'Sexworkers,'" 128.

26. Brandon Griggs, "Playboy Puts 57 Years of Articles, Nudity Online," CNN.com, May 20, 2011, accessed January 2, 2014, http://www.cnn.com/2011/TECH/web/05/20/play boy.issues.online/.

27. Thanks to Richard Garner for helpful conversation on this topic.

28. An excellent overview of these debates may be found in Cornell, *Feminism and Pornography*.

29. See Delany, *Times Square Red, Times Square Blue*.

30. Wizisla, "Preface," 2.

31. For a discussion of collecting as a specifically queer practice, see Camille and Rifkin, *Other Objects of Desire*; and Herring, "Material Deviance."

32. See Gibson, *The Erotomaniac*.

33. See Spring, *Secret Historian*; and Spring and Steward, *An Obscene Diary*.

34. From an amateur pornographer's perspective, the great boon of Polaroid instant cameras, with their self-developing film, was that this technology, introduced in 1948, enabled the production of sexually explicit photographs without recourse to either a commercial film developer or a home darkroom. Suddenly one could quite easily circumvent both the legal risk of obscenity charges and the practical challenge of developing photographic film independently. I discuss further Steward's archiving practices in "Sam Steward's Pornography."

35. On this distinction, see Foucault, *The History of Sexuality*, 57–73.

36. For exemplary analyses of class differentials in pornography, see Juffer, *At Home with Pornography*; Kipnis, *Bound and Gagged*, chapter 4; and Penley, "Crackers and Whackers."

37. Ferguson, *Pornography, the Theory*.

# PART I

Pedagogical Archives

# 1

# Pornography, Porno, Porn:
# Thoughts on a Weedy Field

Linda Williams

## The Field

Academic fields are gardens that need to be tended. Sometimes they grow and flourish; sometimes they dry up and die. For the last ten years many of us working in pornography studies have labored under the belief that we were building an important field that deserved academic legitimacy. There was often an evangelical fervor about our work. Against the odds, we tried to build a field that would be as much like any other as possible. I want to take a cool look at the extent to which this has actually happened. What would we need to really make such a field instead of, as I think has too often happened, to only gesture toward it?

In 1989 I published my first—and last—single-authored book about pornography: *Hard Core: Power, Pleasure, and "the Frenzy of the Visible."* It was hardly the first book on the topic, but I believe that it was the first academic, feminist book to be interested in the form and history, the power and pleasure, of moving-image pornography. In writing this book I had absolutely no intention of spawning a field. I simply wanted to understand more about these troubling, fascinating, and provoking films, just then turning into the more ubiquitous videos that actually made my study of them possible. How could I understand these pornographies as part of our popular culture, as genres like other film genres? What was their address to us as spectators; what was their history?

I did not, at that time, seek a place for what would come to be called "porn studies" in the academy. In 1989 that seemed unthinkable. However, ten years later, after publishing an updated second edition, I began to think that it might be possible. For me it would be a subfield of film and video studies; for others it might be a subfield of history, art history, anthropology, cultural studies, or the then-developing queer studies. It would be an interdisciplinary field, and it would gain acceptance in the various welcoming places where it could grow and build knowledge.

By 2004, when I edited a volume, titled *Porn Studies*, by other scholars and some of my own students, I was convinced that such a field was not only possible but inevitable. Indeed, the very blunt and familiar title of that anthology would seem to have signaled that such a field had already arrived. Yes, it *was* possible to put aside the "tired debates" between procensorship, antipornography feminism and anticensorship, "sex-positive" feminism. The field that was mapped by my anthology was also mapped by the earlier wide-ranging 1999 anthology *Porn 101: Eroticism, Pornography, and the First Amendment*, and later by Peter Lehman's *Pornography: Film and Culture* (2006).[1]

I look back at my own anthology, *Porn Studies*, because it is fairly typical of the field mapping carried out by these others. But with the vantage of hindsight I now introduce a more critical perspective than the enthusiasm with which I first introduced it. What has flourished and what hasn't? The anthology is purposely long (496 pages), as if to impress with the sheer volume of approaches to all kinds of pornography. The first part attempts to introduce the variety of the field. It seemed important at the time that the field not be limited to the narrow range of heterosexual hard-core films and videos that I had analyzed in *Hard Core*, but that the field could be located in a lot of unlikely places: for example, in the Starr Report on President Clinton's sexual relations with an intern (see the chapter by Maria St. John), or the home video of Pamela Anderson and Tommy Lee—a private video that had "gone viral" on the Internet long before such a term even existed (Minette Hillyer). There is also the example of hard-core Japanese pornographic comics marketed to women (Deborah Shamoon). Finally, this part offers a case study and analysis of amateur online porn sites (Zabet Patterson). If this part succeeds in introducing the variety of pornographies, it perhaps is guilty of ignoring what still remained the mainstream of hard-core heterosexual video pornography, whether obtained on DVD or delivered online, thus skewing the impression of what pornography was in its most dominant form. As we shall see, this is part of futurist rhetoric.

Part II, "Gay, Lesbian, and Homosocial Pornographies," is an attempt to map the boundaries of nonheterosexual pornographies, and it primarily focuses on moments in the history of gay and lesbian pornography. It included a chapter by Thomas Waugh on the homosocial reception conditions of the classical American stag film; a chapter on the culture and aesthetics of all-male moving-image pornography that focuses on a key film from 1977 (Rich Cante and Angelo Restivo); a pioneering chapter on the emergence of lesbian pornography from 1968 to 2000 (Heather Butler); plus a queer reading of a straight work of pornography by a gay director (Jake Gerli). The first and last chapters foreground the importance of the possible queer context for the reception of ostensibly straight pornographies.

Of all the possible subfields of pornography studies, this queer and queering tendency has perhaps flourished the most, although it is telling that the male side of the queer continuum has especially flourished while the female side has not. Although there are lively pockets of lesbian porn making in Denmark and the San Francisco Bay Area, there is not an equally thriving academic field of lesbian pornography studies—at least there has been no equivalent to the earlier groundbreaking studies of gay male porn by the likes of Richard Dyer; or Tom Waugh's history of gay male eroticism in photography and film before Stonewall, Hard to Imagine; or the affecting memoir of Samuel R. Delany, Times Square Red, Times Square Blue; or the chapter on graphic specularity in Earl Jackson Jr.'s Strategies of Deviance; or John Champagne's study in The Ethics of Marginality of the social-cultural context of the reception of gay and straight pornography. Pornography studies is a thriving subfield of history, ethnography, queer studies, and film and media studies, uninhibited by seemingly irrelevant feminist debates. If lesbian pornographies and lesbian pornography studies have been slower to develop, it may well be because they are still suffering from the legacy of those "off our backs," "on our backs" debates.[2]

Two recently published books show the range of diverse and passionate investment in this field. Jeffrey Escoffier's popular account of the rise of gay pornography, Bigger Than Life: The History of Gay Porn Cinema from Beefcake to Hardcore (2009), is an authoritative account of the rise of gay pornography since the seventies—the studios, the stars, the auteurs. Written by an enthusiastic and knowledgeable fan, this book is a model of the genre of popular writing about pornography. Also published in 2009, and proof that this subfield can accommodate a wide range of approaches, is Tim Dean's Unlimited Intimacy, which is about the subculture of barebacking.[3] Here is a scholarly, theoretical contrast to Escoffier's fan history, though in its own way it also is the work of a fan of the community it studies. While Dean's book sometimes tends to read pornography as if it could be the authentic ethnography of a subculture, it is nevertheless a stunningly original contribution. One of the most striking findings of this book is that the most long-standing trope of visible male pleasure—the ubiquitous convention of the money shot—is no longer necessary in a subgenre whose fantasy is the invisible "breeding" of a virus. Dean's central idea that bareback pornography "constitutes a mode of thinking about bodily limits, about intimacy, about power," and that it is also a "valid way of thinking about a virus," is the most provocative contribution to pornography studies that I have seen in recent years (even though it is also the most troubling).[4] There seems to me no doubt that this particular subfield of pornography studies will continue to flourish, for the people who write about it have found these pornographic texts crucial to who they are.

Another, much less popular subfield is mapped in the third part of my anthology: "Pornography, Race, and Class." The class aspect of this part, represented by a previously published piece by Constance Penley ("The White Trashing of Porn"), is complemented in the racial section of this part by two attempts to move beyond the usual complaints about racial stereotypes, to understand their popularity in the pornographic context. The undersexed stereotype of the Asian American male (as discussed by Nguyen Tan Hoang in "The Resurrection of Brandon Lee: The Making of a Gay Asian American Porn Star") and the oversexed stereotype of the black man and woman (as discussed by me in "Skin Flicks on the Racial Border") are the two obvious examples. If pornography is a genre that seeks to confess the discursive truths of "sex," then what happens when racialized bodies are asked to reveal their racialized versions of these truths? What happens, we find, is often a particularly blunt eroticization of the very taboos that remain unspoken in more polite forms of culture.

In these chapters we encounter what many pornography critics consider to be the limit of the serious study of this subject. Daniel Bernardi, for example, writes that "watching pornography is not likely to lead to physical acts of violence such as rape, but it might lead to the perpetuation—or ignorance—of violent ideologies such as racism."[5] Bernardi puts his finger on the reason for the relatively stunted development of this aspect of the field. To even broach the subject is to appear to revel in forms of racism and stereotyping that only degrade the others depicted. Bernardi critiques the field of pornography studies for not doing more with race, while simultaneously scolding those scholars who do discuss race if they do not simply say, as he does repeatedly, that such pornography is beyond the pale, only racist, and without any cultural interest. He thus cites approvingly Richard Fung's criticism of the conflation of *Asian* with *anus* as if that were a fate worse than death—a position that Nguyen's chapter specifically challenges.[6] Bernardi is also one of the few scholars I know of who agrees with the *first version* of Kobena Mercer's famous analysis of Robert Mapplethorpe's nude photos of black men.[7] While Bernardi is careful not to call racist those few who have managed to write about race and pornography in the U.S. context, he does charge that those scholars—for example, me and Mercer in his second version of the Mapplethorpe chapter—are insufficiently antiracist. This brings us back, somewhat uncomfortably, to the same kind of false dichotomy of anti-pro pornography with which feminist debates of the eighties and nineties were so entangled. Indeed, Bernardi describes me as a "radical sex feminist" scholar who writes about "the virtues of pornography."[8] Here we encounter a perennial problem of the field:

to write about pornography with any detail or interest is not to automatically advocate its virtues. It would seem that to be interested in pornography or race—or the intersection of race, class, and gender with their performative identities—is to be cast onto one or the other side of an antiporn-proporn divide that scholarship on pornography, I argue, must get beyond.

A much less contentious aspect of the pornographic field is contained in the fourth part of my anthology: the intersection, as well as the sometimes-rigorous separation, of soft- and hard-core forms of sexual representation. Somewhat unfairly, hard-core pornography has received the lion's share of attention in a field that has a strong relation to soft-core and less graphic erotic depictions. In this part of the anthology, Despina Kakoudaki demonstrates how pinups were deployed for patriotic purposes during World War II, while Eric Schaefer explains the crucial influence of 16 mm film technology in the transition from sexploitation erotica to hard-core, aboveground, narrative features. Schaefer identifies the importance of exploitation and, particularly, sexploitation cinema in the move to hard core. Here again we encounter the opening of an extremely rich subfield developed more recently in books by Linda Ruth Williams (no relation), David Andrews, and Nina Martin, all pointing us toward non-hard-core genres that have been immensely popular, especially with heterosexual couples and straight women.

What I find most intriguing in this work is that, unlike my own hard-core pornography studies of the late eighties and nineties, it has not been seemingly influenced, or its claims predetermined, by the antiporn feminism of the late seventies and early eighties. Scholars of hard core in that era had to situate the "legitimacy" of the pornographic field in relation to a vehement antipornography feminist stance that viewed the genre's explicit sexual representations as the quintessential example of the male objectification of the female. In contrast, the work of Linda Ruth Williams—pioneering a revolution in the academic and feminist study of soft core with The Erotic Thriller in Contemporary Cinema (2005)—needs no such apologia. Nor does David Andrews, who followed with Soft in the Middle: The Contemporary Softcore Feature in Its Contexts (2006). Subsequently, Nina Martin issued her study Sexy Thrills: Undressing the Erotic Thriller (2007).

All of this work asserts the importance of the genre of soft-core erotica, which has a complicated history and legacy adjacent to pornography: the genre has been disparaged both as sex-film manqué (not explicit enough) and as a kind of pornography for women. Linda Ruth Williams calls soft core the cinematic equivalent of "coitus interruptus."[9] While this leaves open the question of whether all sex in movies that is not explicit should be called soft core—since not all of this sex is so prominent or so overtly aimed at arousal—what may be most significant about the study of the soft-core genre is its apparent appeal to both male *and* female viewers. The soft core examined by all of these writers can exist in its own right (as Andrews suggests), but it often simulates sex scenes laced with narrative thrills and danger. Williams, Andrews, and Martin illuminate a genre that frequently borrows from the traditions of the romance and the soap and that is primarily disseminated in the home, but that also links up with the traditions of noir and thriller to create a potent hybrid.[10] The historical category of sexploitation cinema is also flourishing, with new work by Schaefer and Elena Gorfinkel soon to be published.[11]

The final brief part of my overstuffed anthology is "Pornography and/as Avant-Garde." This part posits that the study of pornography and of the avant-garde can benefit from being considered in light of one another. Ara Osterweil examines Andy Warhol's *Blow Job*, while Michael Sicinsky considers the connection between motion study and Scott Stark's highly edited interruptions of the familiar gestures of pornography in his film *Noema*. The avant-garde is not always pornography and pornography is only rarely—as, say, in the work of Warhol, Curt McDowell, Wakefield Poole, Carolee Schneemann, Barbara Rubin, Peggy Ahwesh, and Bruce LaBruce—the avant-garde. Nevertheless, as I have recently argued in *Screening Sex* with respect to narrative art films, there is such a thing as the hard-core art film, and there is also such a thing as hard-core art, and they sometimes interestingly converge. Indeed, Kelly Dennis maintains that something called "Art/Porn" has flourished since the fondling of statues in antiquity through to today's point-and-click interactivities on the Internet.[12]

I do not pretend that the organization of *Porn Studies* maps the entire field of pornography studies. In fact, there is a lot missing in the book—most pointedly, the examination of what started the proliferation of pornography studies to begin with: the mainstream, heterosexual hard core that, subsequent to my book and to Laurence O'Toole's 1998 *Pornocopia*, has been comparatively ignored by all but antipornography scholars. The one exception may prove the rule: the freelance journalist David Loftus introduced a breath of fresh air by interviewing a great many men about how they use pornography.[13] It is a mistake, I believe, to ignore the pornographic mainstream. Both O'Toole and Loftus wrote engaging, informative books, though they are journalistic studies rather than scholarly tomes. Another part of the field that needs further cultivation is the absolutely essential connection between new technologies and the pornographies that often enable them. Here I do not mean the kind of hysterical reaction so typical of studies of Internet pornography but historical and theoretical studies of the intersection of public policy, new technologies, and embodied life by scholars as diverse as Wendy Chun, Eric Schaefer, and Joseph Slade.[14]

The field of pornography studies, as I have so far described it, is thriving in some areas and in need of tending in others. An academic field of study is a branch of knowledge at the college or university level, recognized by learned societies and by academic journals in which its research is published. So what do we need to make pornography studies more consistently excellent? First, we need the kinds of things that one expects to occur in any other scholarly field as a matter of course. Despite all I have just described and despite the place pornography occupies in the public imagination, there is (to my knowledge) no journal of porn studies, certainly no program or academic center for porn studies, and no learned society that promotes porn studies. The Kinsey Institute, which one might think of as a likely place for both archives and scholarly conferences, has not provided these resources. Nor have there been many academic conferences on the topic.[15]

In the absence of scholarly societies, academic conferences, and archives, what we have in great profusion—albeit sometimes the haphazard profusion of weeds—are anthologies. Some of these are essential and field defining, such as Lynn Hunt's incomparable *The Invention of Pornography*; some of them are lively grab bags, such as *Porn 101*.[16] While enormously important and influential, anthologies alone, certainly not my own, cannot sustain a field. What is more, in the absence of more sustained work, they can sometimes indicate a tendency of scholars to dabble—to write the occasional article, or to participate in the sporadic panel, rather than to do the kind of sustained work of individual scholarship that is still the coin of the realm in the humanities.

And here we confront the real problem. There are perhaps only a dozen full-length books that might be said to contribute to pornography studies. I count the books by Steven Marcus, Walter Kendrick, Tom Waugh, Laura Kipnis, Jane Juffer, Joseph Slade, Linda Ruth Williams, Dave Andrews, Eric Schaefer, and Tim Dean. I'm not counting the books by journalists and nonacademics. It is extremely rare for those who write scholarly monographs on pornography to follow that work up with a second book; nor can we blame university presses, which are mostly willing to overcome the difficulty of printing explicit images.[17] If we compare, for example, the robust field of film and video horror, which seems to publish a new book every month, we can sense the difference between a truly thriving field and one that seems more sporadic.

As Andrews has astutely noted, what we seem to have is a field that is always on the brink of emerging but that never quite arrives. Depending on your attitude toward the subject, this can be a cause for alarm or hope; but the constant mode of anticipation is one reason the field remains weedy. Contributing immensely to this problem is the fact of the missing archive, a crucial element necessary for the cultivation of a scholarly field. The lack of preservation of the pornographic heritage is appalling, and we cannot count on the hit-or-miss salvages of the Internet to do the job. Having discussed this elsewhere, I will only say here that the absence of an archive contributes to the absence of serious historians.[18] Sometimes, of course, like any "emerging" field, there is a need to rely upon an outsider, even outlaw, status to invite initial interest. Unfortunately, however, the kind of interest attracted is too often of the passing, what-are-they-up-to and how-far-will-they-go-now sensationalizing kind, and not the academic field-building kind.[19] Antipornography books by feminists continue to be written, but they tend to rehash old antipornography positions and to ignore the role of fantasy.[20]

So what is the bare minimum needed to better cultivate this field? First of all, there should be a range of approaches and branches, a range of sustained publications, a range of conferences and archives, and the ability to transcend, as the "At the Limit: Pornography and the Humanities" conference in Buffalo did, "the stale censorship debates," in order to ask, as this conference asked, "what else is interesting about porn?"[21] In other words, scholarly discussions need to move beyond that overarching divide that animated the interest in pornography in the first place—that is, the debates within feminism about the patriarchal evil or the relatively banal inevitability of this thing called pornography.

### Pornography, Porno, Porn

But there is another problem inherent in the very titles of many of the anthologies I have discussed, including my own and including the one you are reading. In the original invitation to the Buffalo conference, I was asked to craft a paper that would investigate "the ways in which porn studies has challenged us to think differently about our bodies, representation, and sex/sexuality." In the revised invitation to the conference, I was asked to participate in a public forum that could "begin to formulate a conceptual vocabulary for porn studies as a discourse of limits." I'm interested in this "discourse of limits," and will turn to it in a moment, but first let me consider the other part of this call that was taken for granted: the very term porn. In everything I have said so far, I have tended to use what might be called the vernacular approach to the field. I have slid into the habit, which was not initially familiar to me when I wrote the first edition of Hard Core, of calling the subject matter porn. How have we come to designate a field of academic study by this term? Why have we lost the graph in pornography? And when I say we, I must first of all include myself, since my 2004 anthology uses that term.

In my 1989 book on pornography, though I sometimes use hard core as a vernacular synonym for the noun pornography and sometimes as an adjective to distinguish it from soft core (as in "hard-core pornography"), I tend to use the word pornography to signal the focus on explicitness and maximum visibility of sex acts in contradistinction to soft core. But in the 1999 epilogue to the second edition of Hard Core, the more vernacular word porno begins to creep in; for example, I title one subsection of the epilogue "The 'Classical Era' of Theatrically Exhibited Porno." Looking back at my vantage point from 1999, I find that I exhibit a certain fondness for the ambitions of the "classical era," when moving-image pornography told stories and explored sexual fantasies while still aspiring to be more like mainstream films. In the epilogue I slip into the use of both porn and porno to refer to moving-image pornography.[22] Both terms are short and seem to signal a kind of familiarity, as if to say that after ten years of study the object had been with us long enough to have a nickname that signals our new comfort with the genre.

By the time I published my 2004 anthology of writings about the genre, titled simply Porn Studies, it would seem that I had embraced the short term wholeheartedly and was using it exclusively to describe the entire field of study. In fact, I had ceded my original title to the will of the press. My original title, "Pornographies On/scene," would undoubtedly have sold fewer books. For Duke University Press, my wordplay between obscene and on/scene was too supersubtle for a title—too grounded in a necessarily paradoxical understanding of the simultaneous revelation and concealment implied by the slash. My preferred title wanted to signal the historical change that had occurred between an era when all explicit sex was considered obscene and kept (as ob signaled) off scene and the more contemporary moment when the obscene had come on/scene. By connecting the familiar obscene with the less familiar on/scene while stressing the instability of the slash that differentiates what is off or on scene, this title suggested that explicit pornographies still bear traces of their once-forbidden status—of their situation, as the Buffalo conference title puts it, at some limit.

Another reason for the rejection of this title is that the publishing example of combining the idea of academic study with the short, familiar word porn had already been set by Porn 101. Since then we have had a number of books and articles with this combination (Art Porn, Porn.com), all of which have signaled, one way or another, a certain acceptance of the ubiquitous phenomenon. In contrast, the articles or books that wish to signal disapproval of the genre typically use the full term pornography.[23] The very use of the term pornography has thus seemed to implicitly accept an antipornography and even a procensorship position.

In other words, it can be a slippery slope from the defense of the First Amendment to endorsing a priori the value of sexual explicitness as an inevitable march toward progress.[24] Pornographies on/scene are a fact that needs to be recognized. They are not a form of progress or freedom that must necessarily be embraced. The last thing I wanted to suggest with the publication of *Porn Studies*—or the use of that title—was that proliferating pornographies had been brought unproblematically on/scene. What I wanted to convey, and what probably would have been better expressed had I kept the original title, was the inevitability of an ongoing conflict, a perpetual push and pull between on/scenity and obscenity as a part of the neoliberal dilemma of an ever-expanding market for all sorts of sexual representations. And that market now certainly includes the market for scholarly books about pornography.

Contained within my own terminological shift, from *pornography* to *porno* to *porn*, is the dilemma of placing oneself "on the side of" an industry whose main purpose is to make money by producing lifelike sexual fantasies. Though I certainly want to respect the dignity of sex workers and support better working conditions for them, and though I also want to uphold freedoms of speech and the possibility of pornographies that are also art, I do not think it is wise for scholars to conflate our own work of scholarship with the work of the pornography industry—even, I would add, when we might be doing what is called participant observation.

When scholars adopt the language of the industry for the name of their object of study, it is a little similar to film or cinema studies calling itself movie studies or flick studies. The field of film studies has had to work hard to earn whatever respect it now has in the academy, and it has done so by not associating itself too closely with the industry. Pornography studies need to work even harder to disassociate itself from the industry. By this I do not mean that we should avoid industry terms to designate generically significant sex acts. These terms are both useful and often quite eloquent. But when we name the field in which we work, we should be scholars, historians, and critics, and especially good ones, even if we also happen to be fans, "users," or shocked or aroused observers. To be a pornography scholar one does not need to love the genre, but one does need to *know* the genre—its long history, its various theorizations, and its many forms of criticism.

Related to this question of terminology is that of scholarly tone. I once described Steven Marcus as writing the whole of his groundbreaking 1964 study of Victorian pornography—*The Other Victorians*—as if he were holding his nose. I wished to introduce a different tone; not that of the high literary scholar deigning to soil himself or herself with a brief immersion in the materials of the Kinsey Institute, but, in my case, as a film scholar taking pornography as much as possible as a genre like any other. Obviously, tones can be complicated. Behind Marcus's tone of disdain lurked a prurient interest that gave his work an intriguing tension. Both my generation of pornography scholars and the generation that has followed have mostly made a point of not holding their noses and have been willing to admit their own interest, fascination, and personal predilections for certain kinds of pornography.

We have also sometimes described sexual acts in the vernacular rather than hiding behind Latinate terms. In doing so, we have tried to "speak plainly" and not occult our possible attraction to the genre behind a veneer of false objectivity. So, by this reasoning, if *blow job* seems more in the spirit of what you are describing than *fellatio*, then say it. But also consider whether *blow job* is an apt term. Blowing is rarely what one sees done in that particular sex act; in fact, quite the contrary. If you then choose the Latinate term, as I have mostly done, there is still the further problem of knowing how to pronounce it.[25] The core problem is how much one wants to speak from the point of view of a subjective participant in sex acts and as a subjective viewer-user-player of films, videos, and, now, interactive games. Over the last thirty years we have all grown more familiar with pornography, and so we have tried to signal that familiarity, though sometimes at a cost.

The moniker *porn studies* makes a judgment. It implies that the user is not shocked by these objects, these images, these sounds, these soft- or hard-core depictions. It signals that such work is not obscene to me, and for me at least—if not for those of you who call it by its more formal term *pornography*—I approve of bringing it into not only the home, where it has already been for almost two decades, but also the academy. The name implies, like my invitation to the Buffalo conference, that we may already have moved "beyond the stale censorship debates." But have we? If we have moved beyond the old debates of feminist anticensorship and feminist antiporn, we have only moved into new ones—about pornographies online invading the home, about fantasies of death and degradation, about availability to children, about the increasingly "porous interface" between our bodies and our media technologies. I would suggest that we have not moved beyond any limits, that we are destined to remain at some limit in our studies of the many different kinds of pornographies that exist.

I would therefore not agree with Feona Attwood when she worries about "what will happen to the Secret Museum of pornography when there are no more museums to hide it away in. . . . How will the 'secret of sex' continue to be produced once it has been so exhaustively revealed? Can the charge and thrill of a pornography that has for some time depended on its sense of transgression continue to be reproduced in such a context?"[26] My first response to Attwood's argument is to ask: where are the secret or public museums preserving this history? My second is to say that I'm not as worried as she is that pornographies can exhaustively reveal the "secrets" of sex. To think this way is to think of sex as a fixed thing that better and more-pervasive media technologies simply reflect. But this is not the case. There will always be some new limit, shifting borders of on/scenity and obscenity.

I am fully aware that my terminological objection is probably not going to change many habits. Queer folks will probably go on saying *porn* to signal their solidarity with a pornography that has been so important to their coming out. Others will want to signal their lack of concern with limits. Perhaps all I can say is that we should be aware that we have a choice when we name what we study, whether *porn*, *porno*, or the word that still connotes the graphic nature that is so much at issue: *pornography*.

## At the Limit

Watching pornography is always partly a matter of looking for that place where something goes too far, the place that exceeds our personal limits. We might not have a name for what that limit is but, as Supreme Court Justice Potter Stewart long ago declared, we know it when we see it. Limit is the place where we inevitably say, "Stop! This is where I draw the line!" Pornography is characterized by its tendency to provoke the need for such limits. The provocation of the original title for the Buffalo conference, "At the Limit: Pornography and the Humanities," rested partly on the inference that pornography might want to lodge itself as a field in the humanities, as if to say to the humanities: *What do you think of that!* The limit is the place where pornographies seem to need to get distinguished one from another; it is the place where some pornographies, as exemplified by the divine Marquis de Sade or by the fantasy and the practice of barebacking, always seem to invite us to draw the line. Indeed, I would say that the limit, "at the limit," is the place where life gets transformed into death, where Georges Bataille's "taboo observed with fear" evokes the desire that depends on it, and we come face-to-face with something that is beyond pleasure, is dirty, and is perhaps even fatal.[27]

Let me give an example of how the business of pornography negotiates this idea of limits. If I wish to purchase a work of pornographic video from the website of Treasure Island Media (TIM), I must make a prejudgment about my reaction to the sexual acts that may be depicted within. The entry to this site requires me to click "OK" at the bottom of a long paragraph that tells me what I am consenting to. Many of the acts described are highly Latinate. If I click the button, it means that "I am a consenting adult who desires to and legally may view this material; I do not find graphic depictions of the activities listed above or any activities deriving from erotic or sexual attraction or passion distasteful, repugnant or obscene to my sensitivities and, therefore, I freely and so informed waive any right I may have to be protected from 'obscene' material by Title 189, United States Code . . . and any and all other laws of similar nature or intent." To purchase this pornography, then, I have to say in advance that nothing in it will exceed my own personal limit, that I already know that it is not obscene to me. Furthermore, I assent to describing myself as a person who desires to see these mysterious activities, and that, having done so, "I will not act as an informant or appear as a witness in any action taken against TIM."

Now, of course I understand that this is a legal ploy. I will click "OK" because by now I am really curious to know what the words *irrumation* and *urolagnia* mean, but I am partly clicking "OK" precisely because I know that these works may challenge the limits of what I want to see: I may find them *obscene* in the literal sense of that word. In other words, in order to satisfy my curiosity, I have to proclaim myself to be someone who has no limits. This is, at the limit, what the familiarity of "porn studies" does. It implies that everything is okay and misses the point that I want to watch because it may not be. But it is also possible that this disclaimer exists to dramatize a "transgression of limits" in a form that actually has so many rules that there is not that much transgression left. After all, the worse thing that could happen to pornography, as my quote from Attwood suggests, is that it become banal. It is possible, then, that this disclaimer is all about giving me the impression that the work is breaking taboos that are not really broken.

In asking me to give up my limits, TIM may actually, as Damon Young notes, be "instating those limits through its very rhetoric and announcing itself, precisely, as what will go beyond them."[28] This, ultimately, is my criticism of the other Tim (Dean, that is). For in appearing to actually believe in the disclaimer, Dean seems to convince himself that he is doing ethnography on a community through its pornography. In other words, he gives the impression that he believes the fantasy. The video may look like documentary, it may engage real bodies penetrating and being penetrated in all sorts of ways, but it is also an erotic fantasy that depends on erecting the limits it wants to seem to transcend. Pornography on film, video, or the Internet is always two contradictory things at once: documents of sexual acts and fantasies spun around knowing the pleasure or pain of those acts. Pornography studies needs to remember that it must always exist at the problematic site of this limit.

## Notes

1. Elias et al., *Porn 101*.

2. I refer to two historically succeeding lesbian feminist journals: *Off Our Backs*, an antipornography journal that begin in 1970 and ceased publication in 2008, which occupied the position of portraying lesbian sex as positive and natural, and the 1984 "dyke" reply, *On Our Backs*, which not only challenged the antipornography stance of its predecessor and continues today, but in addition morphed into the production of lesbian pornography (through Fatale Video). These lesbian pornographies, in contrast to the more

politically correct gentleness of *Off Our Backs*, celebrated butch-femme, dildo-wielding, and S/M lesbian fantasies. See H. Butler, "What Do You Call a Lesbian with Long Fingers?," 178.

3. Dean, *Unlimited Intimacy*.

4. Dean, *Unlimited Intimacy*, 105.

5. Bernardi, "Interracial Joysticks," 223.

6. Nguyen, "The Resurrection of Brandon Lee."

7. Mercer published an initial article attacking Mapplethorpe in 1987, "Imagining the Black Man's Sex," and then revised his interpretation in "Skin Head Sex Thing." My comments are taken from his revised version of the latter in his 1994 book, *Welcome to the Jungle*.

8. Bernardi, "Interracial Joysticks," 222.

9. Linda Ruth Williams writes, "If hardcore really does it, softcore merely fakes it. If hardcore hangs on the authenticity of the real view (that adolescent shock of seeing people *actually getting off*), softcore holds back, cannot show, kisses but finally does not tell." L. R. Williams, *The Erotic Thriller in Contemporary Cinema*, 269–70.

10. Portions of this section on soft core are excerpted from my review "Studying 'Soft' Sex."

11. See Gorfinkel's "Dated Sexuality" and "Tales of Times Square" and Eric Schaefer's edited collection *Sex Scene*.

12. Dennis, *Art/Porn*.

13. Loftus, *Watching Sex*.

14. Hui Kyong Chun, *Control and Freedom*; Schaefer, *Bold, Daring, Shocking, True!*; and Slade, *Pornography and Sexual Representation*.

15. In fact, the conference at which an earlier version of this chapter was presented is a major exception and only the second I have attended in my career. I'm not counting a conference that I was once invited to host in London at the National Film Theatre, which had planned to have both a conference and accompanying screenings. The screenings were ultimately canceled and the conference itself ended up occurring by private invitation only, thus duplicating many of the features of the Victorian "secret museum."

16. Other anthologies include Attwood, *Porn.com*.

17. See the reprint of the Society for Cinema and Media Studies discussion in Kleinhans, "In Focus, Visual Culture Scholarship, and Sexual Images."

18. See L. Williams, "'White Slavery' versus the Ethnography of 'Sexworkers.'"

19. Perhaps I am here idealizing the gravitas of other more legitimate fields; perhaps I am just saying that I don't want to belong to a club that would include me as its member, or that would elect me as den mother!

20. See, for example, Boyle, *Everyday Pornography*.

21. This is from the invitation to the conference "At the Limit: Pornography and the Humanities," which took place March 26–27, 2010, in Buffalo, New York.

22. L. Williams, *Hard Core*, 298.

23. See, for example, Bernardi, "Interracial Joysticks"; Boyle, *Everyday Pornography*; Cornell, *Feminism and Pornography*; and Dines, Jensen, and Russo, *Pornography*.

24. See, for example, Steven Madison's claim that there is an "elision between advancing toward the new millennium and advancing toward a more open speaking of sex that strongly accords with Modernist notions of progress," in "Online Obscenity and Myths of Freedom," 20.

25. During the first talk on pornography I ever gave, I consistently pronounced *fellatio* as *fellahtio*, until a kind colleague took me aside and corrected me.

26. Attwood, "Reading Porn," 99.

27. Bataille, *Erotism*, 37–38.

28. Young continues: "This is a ploy to bolster the aura around its own product, to produce an authentically shocking and transgressive pornography amidst a sea of banality." Damon Young, e-mail message to author, March 24, 2010.

# 2

## Pornography as a Utilitarian Social Structure:
## A Conversation with Frances Ferguson

*Frances Ferguson visited the University at Buffalo for a conversation about her book* Por-
*nography, the Theory: What Utilitarianism Did to Action. On February 4, 2010,*
*she met with Tim Dean's graduate seminar* The History and Theory of Pornography.

...............................

Tim Dean: Thank you for coming to Buffalo to discuss *Pornography, the Theory.*
The book has been out for a while now—it was published in 2004—but it
seems to me that your argument has not been well grasped or assimilated
among those who study pornography. Some folks have said that it's not really
about pornography. I suspect what they mean by that is that it's not a book
about pornography in the way that we usually think about pornography—but
that's what makes it both difficult and very interesting.

Frances Ferguson: What I'm really trying to do is to distinguish pornography from obscenity and from the debates about obscenity and blasphemy. I
wanted to get away from the idea that pornography is about certain representations that can be made socially acceptable or kept socially unacceptable.
In that understanding of pornography, a particular relation to a certain kind
of pornography enables you to feel as though you have a way of signaling
who you are as opposed to other people. It's a way of treating the question of
speech and representation under the rubric of free speech in a way that consolidates individuals' right to traffic in social capital. That issue is really minimal for me. The question that looms larger concerns the connection between
social representational systems and individuals, particularly the way in which
social representational systems—of which pornography frequently provides
a good example—are distributing relative advantage and disadvantage all the
time. So that's why I link up pornography with relatively or completely nonsexual subjects. There is a dynamic that's being depicted in [Marquis de] Sade,
in [Gustave] Flaubert, or in [D. H.] Lawrence that can plausibly be called

pornographic and that operates in relation to the nonsexual things that we encounter all the time.

Dean: You locate that dynamic also in the classroom. Here we are in a classroom, in a course on pornography. But your interest isn't really in "porn pedagogy"; you're interested rather in how pornography and the classroom both exemplify what you call "utilitarian social structures."

Ferguson: Where we are right now doesn't exactly count as a classroom in the way that I was talking about the classroom in my account of pornography. There I was talking specifically about the Benthamite classroom—the classroom described in Jeremy Bentham's writing on education—because it manages to make regular a tremendously important feature of what goes on continually in public life, which is the constant registration of value. Rather than focusing on the content of education, Bentham is interested in how value is being registered by classrooms in which everyone is being ranked all the time. He's producing a kind of social game that is designed to show value and particularly *relative* value. So what would be a good answer in one situation and would get you to the head of the class wouldn't do so with another group. In these utilitarian classrooms people constantly move from one group to another; each day people walk in and take their seats according to how well they did the last time they were doing math or spelling or something, and then everybody does a kind of rotation after the next exam because their relative place may well have changed.

Bentham based his educational writings and his *Chrestomathia* on the work of Joseph Lancaster and Andrew Bell, and we tend to think of those systems as deeply repressive. Yet one of the things that all the people engaged in them thought of them as doing was creating a situation in which you could have a relatively neutral structure without a substantial layer of authority figures and people playing to authority figures. So the notion of currying favor or being an apple polisher really didn't exist, since you were working with relatively rigid structures that no one could affect by smiling particularly attentively at the teacher.

Dustin Parrott: I have trouble getting rid of the notion of these structures being repressive. The participants in such structures are not starting from an even playing field. They enter into it with different capabilities and different access to certain kinds of understanding to begin with. It seems to me that no matter how rigid or ostensibly neutral the system itself might be, the participants are entering into it unequal to one another.

Ferguson: I can see why that would be an issue if you were talking about a lot of situations prior to the utilitarian classroom and a lot after it. But, in point of fact, the notion of school class is really very important. What these sys-tems—particularly the Lancasterian, Bellite, and Benthamite systems—are doing is trying to pluck people out because they are as equal as it is possible for them to be. They're trying to avoid a situation in which you've got a one-room schoolhouse with an eighteen-year-old studying with a six-year-old. These schools were started as schools for the children of the working poor, and they were the only schools that offered any real education to the sons and daughters of the poor. They're very much opposed to the entire Oxford, Cam-bridge, Rugby, Eton sense of educational privilege, and they stress education in the vernacular instead of in Latin and Greek. So although it is easy for us to feel, at this distance, that they were wildly repressive, in fact I think that there was something genuinely progressive to these structures. These educational systems saw themselves not as placing everyone under surveillance or disci-pline, but as trying to indicate what kinds of things people were capable of— to distinguish one person from another so that you could award social credit.

Now, I think there are real limitations to what Bentham is doing. If I had to characterize his position in a history of social thinking, I'd say that he's like a game theorist who hasn't quite made a move into systems theory. He's doing an excellent job of showing how a game can be deployed, but he doesn't yet have the systems-theoretical approach of someone like [Niklas] Luhmann that will give you a full sense of the difference that the effects of this system entail.

*Parrott:* But if we take these Benthamite social structures and apply them out-side the context of schooling at this particular historical moment, and try to imagine these structures creating the benefits you mention—recognition, validation, etc.—in other settings, does it work? If we think about porn today, we see a proliferation of niche markets (which might be regarded as quasi-Benthamite social forms as you characterize them) that contain a variety of "kinds" of porn—porn that seems to say, "If you don't see yourself (your body, your tastes) reflected in the mainstream, here's something for you." That seems to me good in and of itself, but there's still a hierarchy in the market-place and these specialized forms, when compared to one another, are still subject to differential access and recognition. Within these special structures individuals might be granted recognition and mobility, but once they move outside of those limited realms they are again pushed to the bottom of the social order or shunted off to the side. Doesn't this compromise the power of those structures to offer the benefits you suggest they might offer?

*Ferguson:* The thing that matters to me is the fact that there's still a hierarchy. The production of self-expressing, self-affirming niche markets puts pres-sure on the hierarchy, but it's not going to eliminate the hierarchy altogether.

Parrott: That makes me think of Michael Warner's suggestion that the goal is not to dismantle the public itself, but to make possible a counterpublic, or a reflexive way of thinking about the public, so that there can be a balance or alternative to the majority. And in many ways that's much more realistic than imagining we might somehow dispatch hierarchy altogether.

Ferguson: Everyone knows what it's like to be in a situation in which no one is saying, "We can see exactly what the power structure is here." Nevertheless, you know someone is in a position of power relative to you, and you sometimes know that someone is relatively disempowered in relation to you. What I really like about Bentham is that he's trying to do something with the consciousness of relative advantage and disadvantage that just hadn't been done before. He imagined that you could empower people to think, "I may not be rich, but I can really do math, and I've learned I can really do math in the presence of lots of people who, though they are poor like me, are in a position to see certain accomplishments as the product of this larger social system that is the school." This kind of thinking undermines the world of privilege in which everyone from Oxbridge always gets everything. That's why I have a more positive account of the rise of bureaucracies in England than many people do, because I don't think bureaucracies were just creating mindless paperwork. I think that they were trying to create a space for a non-birth-based system of acknowledgment.

Dean: Your reading of Bentham is very different from the one that we inherit from Foucault's Discipline and Punish.

Ferguson: Yes. One of the most influential readings of Foucault, particularly in North America, says that he was concerned with how a disciplinary society was a neoliberal, essentially repressive setup that made everyone into his or her own parole officer. Disciplinary society created an artificial version of conscience, making people prisoners of the faculty of conscience as they increasingly deployed their sense of social expectations against themselves. Now, it's certainly the case that Foucault is talking about the rise of something like conscience in society when he's talking about the panopticon and discipline; I don't mean to dispute that. But he's also talking about developments that can't be coded onto neoliberalism quite as quickly as many people have done—such as the rise of our ability to evaluate things in the world. Not necessarily to evaluate them accurately, but to feel as though we can gauge how rich someone is, for example, or how prosperous their family was, just from having the briefest of conversations with them.

*Dean:* Part of what is really distinctive about *Pornography, the Theory* is not just that you have a different reading of Foucault but also that you trace deep connections between the educational experiment of Benthamite schools and the rise of pornography in the eighteenth century.

*Ferguson:* I realize that one of the strangest things about this book is that I just don't care about content. There is no part of the book that is interested in sexual content for its own sake. I think it is possible for something to be pornographic without being sexually explicit. An example would be a scenario that occurred in what we'll call real life, in which a music teacher was giving a lesson to a student—it was just the two of them alone together—in a room where there was almost nothing, except a chair on which the teacher had placed a book that was once popular, Alex Comfort's *The Joy of Sex*. This is one of those situations in which the cover of the book, sexually inexplicit as it is, counts as pornographic because there is a kind of conspicuous identification of the student's position relative to the teacher in a way that makes indirect reference to sex.

What's pornographic here is that their actual situation of proximity to one another makes their bodies carry the burden of the physicality of the situation, and the display of this book cover is designed precisely to do that. It's not what's in the book; there is nothing about the book's cover that is offensive—it's just a series of words without any illustration at all. But the application of that book to that particular social situation is an example that illustrates one point of my account of pornography—that it's not "content" as such that's important.

*Dean:* What seems nice about this example is that you've got something that is sexually implicit rather than explicit, and its implicitness has to do with the arrangements of the bodies in the physical space.

*Ferguson:* And the fact that this is a situation in which you are very aware of the inequality between the persons.

*Dean:* So part of what connects pornography with the Benthamite classroom is that awareness of the hierarchy?

*Ferguson:* Yes. But I should make clear that the Benthamite classroom is trying to create a positive production of inequality that counteracts what gets featured as tyrannical inequality in many of the texts I'm discussing—for example, in Sade. One of the key things in Sade is that there are people who are in a position to exercise absolute power over other people; that seems to him like a positive claim that a pornographer wants to make. So if you regard that Sadeian claim as something like the last hurrah of the ancien régime, then you start imagining that there are other ways of doing things. Bentham is particularly important for constantly banging away against what he sees as tyranny. Part of what I try to show is that Bentham was a major political thinker.

Steven Ruszczycky: I want to stay a little longer with your *Joy of Sex* example. Insofar as the teacher's and student's physical proximity to the text in question seems to be an important element in constituting that text as pornography, how does the Internet—where individuals who need not be in the same room can access the same text at the same time—relate to your understanding of pornography?

Ferguson: That's an important question, and it's one that I don't address in the book. People say that there is an unbelievable amount of pornography on the Internet, but by my lights there isn't so much. There is a great deal of sexual visibility on the net, but until there is some way in which one person can be actively harmed by another, it's not going to count as pornography for me. (Harmed or benefited—the effects don't go in just one direction.) There may be erotic videos that have been sent back and forth between people that would become "pornographic" if they had been used to entrap someone or abduct someone, or something along those lines. I can imagine that there could be use of a sexual image from a distance that would count as personal harm or injury, even though it didn't involve people being in the same space. It's a problem for Tiger Woods and John Edwards that there are recordings of things that they've said and done, and that these recordings are being sent to their home. That's an example of a real impact on a person in a way that's related to what I think of as pornography.

Jana Schmidt: The music teacher situation reminds me of a situation of sexual harassment that moves easily from a casual encounter into harassment—as, for example, when you have a group of men showing each other pictures of a naked woman and a woman enters the room. When in your book you describe pornography as sexuality with inequality, and in discussing violence you take up [Leo] Bersani and [Georges] Bataille, I kept thinking of inequality in the specific sense of harassment and female sexuality. Within the utilitarian scheme, the notion of "unsexed" subjects makes sense; but what about inequality in terms of the relations between women and men in pornography?

Ferguson: There are all kinds of inequalities that could be addressed along the lines of the example you mention. I can easily imagine that if you have a group of insistently heterosexual men who were showing images of gay men in such a way as to make a gay man feel under pressure from walking into that room, then you would have a perfect analogue to the case of the woman that you describe. I don't think that any time there is a sexual image shown anywhere that it necessarily has to result in harm to someone; but it's important to register that this is not just a matter of free speech. It's a matter of understanding how particular social environments can become confined enough for you to see how power moves in them.

Nick Mugavero: Thinking about the example you just gave, I wonder if we could draw a correlation between that and, say, the display of religious iconography? For example, there is a crucifix on the wall and someone of another faith comes in and perhaps there is a tension between those two faiths such as to prevent someone from accessing value-altering groups. In that sense, the religious representation shares a lot of similarities with the sexual representation. Would we call that a pornographic display? You're very clear about it not having to have sexual content.

Ferguson: I deliberately didn't lump questions of pornography together with questions of blasphemy for reasons having to do with the fact that we think of religion in terms of beliefs and doctrines. Our model for thinking about religion deals with the differences between one person's belief and another's by trying to create a public space, a generally neutral public sphere, in which—for example, in John Rawls's account—there is an overlapping consensus that will keep the fact of absolutely irreconcilable differences of belief from becoming an issue. What you're describing is a situation in which, say, I walk into a doctor's office and the receptionist says to me, "Have a blessed day"—this is something that happens a lot in Baltimore!—and that comment could be construed as offensive.

I didn't want to get into the whole question of belief because I wanted to avoid a Stanley Fish–style debate about these issues—a debate that makes it seem as if we've all got our beliefs all the time and our conventions are formed by our clustering in belief communities. One of the things that his positions have never really been able to account for is how people ever change anything. He's got such an intensely neoplatonic account of belief that it seems to have existed in all of us before we were born—it's not just a product of our having grown up in particular environments or having imbibed with our mother's milk that we're Democrats rather than Republicans or Catholics rather than Protestants. It's the thing we bring to everything we see. This is a wildly idealist position that totally misses the point about a debate around pornography. It says that it's only pornography if you think it is. That's not true! There are a lot of things that are not written in stone but are nonetheless real and have real social impact. I think that is what one should try to understand, not the ways in which one has beliefs that one is constantly projecting on everyone and finding some buddies to share with.

*Dean:* It's exactly that neoplatonic conception of belief that you're pushing against in your book by looking at situations in which someone or something can change—situations in which the mobility of power becomes very evident (hence the Benthamite school, in which people are constantly playing musical chairs after a test). Doesn't pornography point to sexuality as an arena in which power becomes extremely mobile and things can change?

*Ferguson:* Yes. One of the reasons why Sade is so interesting to me is that he seems to be talking about that to an unbelievable degree. His Justine is an amazing character because she thinks everything is about her belief. She thinks that if she conceives of herself as innocent—as never having wanted any of the effects that she brings about—then she will be absolutely innocent. That's a kind of hyperidealism because it's essentially denying that there is any change effected by what one does.

*Mugavero:* I have a question about Sadeian hierarchies and what you referred to, a few minutes ago, as absolute power. I was reading Elaine Scarry's *The Body in Pain*, where she claims that the vision of suffering is turned into the spectacle of power because the pain caused by torture is so incontestably real that that same quality of realness gets attributed to the agencies that cause the pain. Do you see a correlation between this dynamic of torture and Sade's pornographic hierarchies, especially in terms of the value of a power that is dependent on "extreme perceptibility"?

*Ferguson:* I don't know that I believe in an incontestably real pain or suffering. What interests me about Sade is that even though there is the establishment of a hierarchy in which someone is in a position to take control over someone else, he gives us examples in which power isn't about one person's capacity to control another. I'm drawn to examples such as that of the Girls of the Watch, in *Justine*, in which there are young women who are forced to stay awake and keep watch all the time. The guy whom they're watching is described as having a penis that is almost infinitesimally small; he's just a physical mess, and he sleeps a good deal of the time that the Girls of the Watch are watching him. What's important about this example is that even though physically he's relatively powerless and even though he's asleep, there's a system that is making him head of the entire show. In that circumstance, surveillance consists in being the object of the power rather than having it. I'm really interested in how Sade captures a kind of glamour rather than identifying moments in which we can say, "There's the real suffering!" or "There's the real power!" I like this example because it's a clear oxymoron: a strong guy is really weak, according to a different set of standards outside the system. (And it doesn't rely on the Freudian psychoanalytic scheme to achieve its reversals.)

*Mugavero:* So then what becomes of the possibility of the Girls of the Watch to recognize that the power that keeps them in their relative positions within the hierarchy is fictive? It seems as if it is the very real power that is created by the system that keeps them there.

*Ferguson:* In that particular episode they run away. But you're right about the question of why they are there. The assertion of power, of the man's power, is particularly clear because the Girls of the Watch are not consenting to be there in any way. They're there because they're being compelled to be there and to act in a certain way. So the fact that they can get away means that you're not talking about the same issues of complicity or willingness that might be raised by the Benthamite approach. No one is making anyone go to Bentham's school; this is before English education is universally mandated. I really want to stress that I don't subscribe to a position in which suffering becomes power, or suffering produces some ability to transform your situation. One of the reasons why pornography may be considered part of a systems-theory approach is because it is not just about emancipatory narratives in which we all get together and realize that there are a lot of us and there's only one of him, and we can make a rush for it. The real point of Foucault's disciplinary account lies in getting us to think about something other than emancipatory narratives—getting us to think about what it was like for people to participate in what does not correspond to our idea of freedom and to do so apparently willingly.

*Dean:* Isn't your attempt to get away from this kind of naive emancipatory narrative connected to what you say about "extreme perceptibility"? It's a phrase that you use a lot in the book, and it's clear that the capacity to make something visible is important to your account of pornography.

*Ferguson:* Yes, I'm skeptical that visibility should be aligned straightforwardly with emancipatory politics. As if what you want to do is to have pornography as self-expression and as the promulgation of a community by means of products that align viewers and makers. That's a perfectly plausible line of argument, particularly for people in film, where the place of characters on the screen relative to the members of the viewing audience is so important. For example, I find interesting how Carol Clover describes some of the films she's looking at in *Men, Women, and Chain Saws* as gender benders because they encourage even the men in the audience to start identifying with a woman in a certain position in the film. That's an important account of the way narratives work in terms of reporting positions to viewers in the narratives. But if you're looking at these systems rather than at persons and their points of view, you see that it's possible to talk about something like heightened attention falling on certain things.

Dean: This is what you mean by "extreme perceptibility" rather than, say, ordinary perceptibility or visibility.

Ferguson: Yes. They may be perfectly visible, but the system is operating to give a kind of stress to the visibility—to light things up, you might say. The good version of that is Bentham's idea that these spelling-bee-model exams might enable someone who didn't think particularly well of his or her own abilities to recognize that, gee, he or she was better than anyone else at something—and that would be one way of coming forward into the spotlight. But you can also see how that notion of visibility is manifested in reality television, in all of those shows that now get rigged: the idea is that you take someone who is perfectly unacknowledged—visible, but not acknowledged—and figure out how to deliver a starring role to that person.

Maria Almanza: Would you say that this "extreme perceptibility" works the same way in the novel as it does in film or television?

Ferguson: I'm glad you brought that up, because earlier someone mentioned that in my account of pornography I don't talk about film, only about the novel. My portfolio happens to be eighteenth- and nineteenth-century literature, and I became fascinated by the fact that the word pornography had fallen out of the language between the time of late antiquity and the end of the eighteenth century. Suddenly you have people like Réstif de la Bretonne and Sade using the word pornography when people hadn't been using it for many centuries. That is a question for philology: what was going on that led to the revival of the word, and to a whole new way of thinking about what pornography was? Why did there seem to be a need for a new (or revived) word that would be distinct from sexual explicitness and erotica? After all, we know of no time when erotic literature, erotic painting and drawing, and now erotic film have not existed. But these things are not necessarily pornography, in my view; it's only pornography if you have that power disequilibrium as part of the system that's being set up by the use of the representation. My concern here draws on Raymond Williams's interest in key words; I wanted to add pornography to the list of words that have a distinct history.

David Squires: Before you say more about the novel, I wonder if I can ask how what you're saying now, about the history of the word, fits with Walter Kendrick's history of the term pornography? One of the things that we've been thinking about in this seminar is archiving—we began with Kendrick's The Secret Museum and the excavation of the ruins of Pompeii, which revealed depictions and artifacts that had to be hidden away. As if pornography reemerges historically along with the archive as a place that it can be stored and sequestered.

*Ferguson:* Yes, Pompeii is late Roman antiquity. That's a perfectly compatible account of the revival of the word.

*Squires:* Yes, but I wanted to ask about the principle of exclusion that is integral to your definition of pornography. One of the consequences of putting something in an archive is that certain people don't or can't see it. So, in this case, the institution—or, as you might say, the fabricated social system—itself excludes people by design. I'm struggling to understand how an institution, or its regulatory functions, can be pornographic.

*Ferguson:* That's an important point because one of the big questions that must arise about these social structures is who gets to be in them and who is excluded from them. The reason I was interested in writing about [Lawrence's] *Lady Chatterley's Lover* and the trial of that book is that both *Lady Chatterley* and its trial history revolve around questions of class and access to pornography (or to texts that have been seen as pornographic or obscene). Also, in my account, questions of access to sexuality. Lawrence grasped something that modern social science is constantly talking about—namely, that poor people have less sex than rich people. It's not just that rich people have greater access to archives or that rich people have been able to assemble collections of erotic or pornographic materials because they have the money to buy them and the places to keep them. They also have more-active sex lives. Lawrence is extremely interested in that subject and in a power of sexuality that comes up against a notion of class. This goes back to the issue of altering the power structure that Dustin Parrott raised earlier.

The publication history of *Lady Chatterley* is very interesting in this respect, because the book gets tried twice: it's tried first in the U.S. and then in Britain. Sir Allen Lane, who owns Penguin Books at the time, decides to provoke legal action in Britain, and he does so in a very clever way from a business standpoint. He knows that the book has been cleared in the post-office trial in the U.S. and so knows that it is highly likely to be cleared in the British trial, but he doesn't want to lay out a lot of money—to print a million copies and distribute them and then have them confiscated. He decides to cut a deal with the government office that brings obscenity cases and to get them to agree that the only thing he needs to do is have a few copies delivered to them: that will count as publication. You need publication to trigger the legal question in the first place. He wanted to trigger the legal question because he wanted to make the book accessible and to think of himself as adding this book to a generally available archive. From the beginning Penguin books were supposed to be widely accessible—Allen Lane famously said that they were books that didn't cost any more than a pack of cigarettes, so anybody who had any money can afford them. And he saw himself as taking books worth reading to persons without great financial resources. So you see there have been lots of ways of thinking about the importance of expanding the availability of certain images and texts so that they won't count as a private archive. But ultimately I don't think that the debate about obscenity or blasphemy is the whole story. That debate has basically been won, and there aren't so many places for it to go.

*Robbie Dewhurst:* I'm reminded here of one of my favorite lines in your book, where you say that Flaubert was particularly qualified to capture the utilitarian moment because he was an "archivist of boredom." Can you clarify this relationship between pornography and boredom, or simply say more about pornography and affect?

*Ferguson:* That's a really interesting question, because it gets at the way in which these systems are used to generate a sense of knowing what you're doing and what you want, when you couldn't formulate that sense for yourself. If you think specifically about pornography, you see how it generates the idea that sex sells—you know, just add a dollop of sex to any commercial and you will have automatically made this horrifically dull thing look as if it is appealing. Flaubert is great at recognizing the importance of the agricultural fair, in which cattle are being made interesting, for example. He is able to sense a mechanical production of a representation of value that starts generating interest where no interest was before. There are times when that can seem like a good thing, and then there are times when you think that it's good that we don't have to go around constantly having unbelievably sophisticated moral senses and affective lives.

*Dean:* Are you saying that this capacity that Flaubert exemplifies is specific to the novel as distinct from, say, film?

*Ferguson:* There is something important about the novel as a genre that I wish I had said more about in the book than I did. The novel is important because of free indirect discourse. Free indirect discourse involves the intrusion of observation into the experience of one person who is singular, whose experience is not automatically available to everyone. It's quite different from what an omniscient narrator is able to tell you, because free indirect discourse deploys the distinction between *he looked* and *he saw*. Free indirect discourse is going to say, "He saw." I can look around this room and tell what you're all looking at, but not what you are seeing. It's the rise in the sense that the act of seeing can be treated as if it were visible that makes free indirect discourse so tremendously powerful in the novel and links it with pornography. Free indirect discourse involves a kind of surveillance that is much deeper than any kind of surveillance we are accustomed to thinking of when we think about infrared cameras and speed cameras, because it is really imagining that it can get at your thought. Seeing the importance of free indirect discourse in the novel makes it possible to see the importance of ways of creating artificial faculties for individuals that had not been done before. There had been surveillance involving actual guards from time immemorial. But it's not until you have legal procedures that are applied systematically—that is, without the very arbitrary decisions of very arbitrary people—that you get a sense of a world that was constantly there to be tapped in relation to your personal faculties. The novel is the social-scientific equivalent of a fairly regular system of law: it makes it possible for you to feel that there is a shared social world that proceeds with enough regularity for you to feel that you understand what people must be thinking (whether or not you're in fact correct in your surmises).

Dean: You're talking about historical shifts in ways of seeing—whether of surveillance or heightened perceptibility—but you're also talking about changes in narrative style that alter the relationship between subjects of discourse.

Ferguson: Yes. I should say that in *Pornography, the Theory* I was talking about something like a grammar. I've recently been rereading Émile Benveniste's writings on subjectivity and language, particularly his quite brilliant analysis of first- and second-person pronouns as opposed to third-person pronouns (in the first volume of his *Problems in General Linguistics*). He's describing what you can think of as a more refined grammar than the one we customarily operate with, and he distinguishes absolutely between first- and second-person pronouns, on the one hand, and third-person pronouns, on the other. He says that usually we just go down the list: first, second, and third person, but that's wrong. His point is that we need to think of grammar quite differently from the way we ordinarily do. He's interested in how the first- and second-person forms are linked to each other because you have two persons who are there entering into discourse. They're not just speaking a language; they are entering into discourse in the course of operating the pronouns. That kind of grammatical insight—which doesn't revolve around talking about particular persons and their actual feelings, or the particular content of what they're saying—is tremendously important to me. In the final analysis, what Benveniste is doing with grammar involves a kind of committed abstraction that I wanted to bring to the discussion of pornography. This is why the notion that you can have a pornography that is empty of sexual content, with that *Joy of Sex* book cover, ends up being important for me. That example is all about the I/you grammatical move.

Dean: Is that I/you grammatical move another version of what you're trying to get at in tort law, where people come to have a relationship even without knowing each other?

Ferguson: Yes, and that seems to me implicit in any situation where you have a thing that is seen as a product. Catharine MacKinnon talks about how once something is taken to be a product, it is seen as being able to deliver something. It's not just your idea of it. I think that's a very important point. Seeing pornography as a product that is delivering something other than just the ideas you've had wandering around in your head makes it possible to say that it—this product—may be doing some good for you. But it also may be doing some harm. In so far as you can imagine positive advantages of a product, you must be able to imagine that there may be the same disadvantages that there can be with any product. You may expect your Prius to take you to the grocery store, and part of that expectation involves the requirement that its brakes work so that it doesn't injure you in the course of your using it. In that case, you've got a sense of being able to apply the model of tort law, which is one that says a product has a grammar; it doesn't just exist as essentially a black box. A product has a trackable grammar. That is why Marx imagined there might be products that disclose themselves and give a sense of where all their parts came from.

James Godley: You mention Justice Potter Stewart in your book and his famous line that he knows porn when he sees it. This seems to say that only when the law is an instrument of surveillance can one recognize pornography—and yet it is only by deferring to something outside the law, someone's personal impression, that one can recognize pornography. There's a paradox about the law's grammatical positioning here.

Ferguson: What I'm trying to do is change the sense of the law in that Potter Stewart moment and not regard the law as a kind of antagonist to an individual observer, but rather as a system in which we are all participants and observers simultaneously. Stewart is making a very basic observation that it would never occur to you to take certain things into a courtroom and say, "This is pornography, and there's a problem about it that involves an injury being done to someone." But I take the corollary to his point to be that it isn't just the words or images that are at stake but the use to which they are put—and that's what is really plausible about his position.

Godley: If the law understands pornography in terms of what it's doing, isn't that parallel to what the law itself does more generally, in so far as the law is concerned with what people are doing to each other? As you say about tort law.

Ferguson: The law—and especially the law of torts—doesn't worry about the positive part. It is only concerned with harm; and that's what the very word tort entails. The law always takes things that are broken in some sense—and then we blame the messenger, because the law seems to be about nothing other than dealing with broken things. Insofar as tort law is a way of saying that there is such a thing as a relationship between persons who sometimes haven't ever met one another before, the law is a kind of grammar producing that relationship. It's not exactly an iteration of specific laws that say do this or don't do that. Tort law is not legislation that says in advance that you better not kill someone; rather, it's a law that says even if you didn't mean to kill someone, suddenly you have to look back on your actions and consider a new evaluation of them.

In that sense, the law is giving you a large-scale consciousness of exactly the kind you see in lots of eighteenth-century writing. If you think of Rousseau's *Confessions*, what's novelistic about it is not that it seems to deploy some of the same conventions as lots of novels do, but that it starts working the conscience: "I did something at moment X because I thought it was the right thing to do but, oh, twenty pages on, two years on, I realize I had done something terrible." That's analogous to the way tort law handles actions and products, but it is obviously not identical to it. I think it's remarkable that conscience really works differently in novels from the way it worked before—it involved much less external surveillance, and that's where Foucault's account of discipline comes in. Even when he's not talking about disciplinary systems, it seems to me that his punch line is that conscience becomes a much more important thing than it was before.

*Dean:* Wasn't Bentham also important for rethinking law as well as education?

*Ferguson:* Yes, Bentham was a major political thinker, and he's seen as a guiding spirit of Anglo-American law, because he figured out how to get away from the rather horrible Blackstone-like reliance on custom and translations of custom. William Blackstone, from whom Bentham took classes at Oxford, was giving all kinds of rationales for common law and was constantly defending the fact that anyone who was the chief landholder in the county was automatically a justice of the peace and was in a position to make legally binding decisions about any case that came before him. It's as if we were to take a whole bunch of cases to Malcolm Forbes just because he happened to be a rich man. In the Blackstonian view, the rich had more of a stake in justice because they had property and needed things to proceed in an orderly way. It was that ideological position that Bentham saw himself as opposing, and so he started writing constitutions and defending legislation because he thought these were ways of establishing the rules of the game in advance of the playing, rather than only after the playing. (Of course, it's an important principle of modern law that people can't be held liable according to laws that get passed after the time of their action.) Incidentally, Bentham also wrote one of the first discussions in defense of homosexuality in English, but his essay on pederasty wasn't published until 1978, because he had been so muzzled during his lifetime by his friends.

*Leah Benedict*: I have a follow-up question about tort law and the way that it is set up in your book's introduction. You start with what we could call an acknowledgment of harm that produces an imaginative trajectory of loss, of what a person's future could have been. Then it seems that, conversely, criminal law starts with the imaginative production of an event that may or may not have happened. Are you suggesting in your introduction that pornography moves from tort law to criminal law, from the trajectory of loss or damage to the problem of intent?

*Ferguson*: You're right that I was trying to restrict my discussion to tort law rather than criminal law, because obscenity legislation revolves around criminalizing acts of speech and saying, "You had the intention to do something that would corrupt public morals." Using tort law helped me to move the discussion of pornography away from obscenity and questions of intention. But even with obscenity legislation, there are difficulties proving intention, and then they get into all the problems of distribution—as if to say, "You didn't just keep it under your vest the way someone like Rousseau did when he realized he was a masochist and enjoyed being flogged but just couldn't bear to tell anyone this, and so ended up not being flogged." Rousseau's situation is one that criminal law might be interested in but tort law would have nothing to say about, because tort law is concerned only with the world of effects.

And the reason I'm so interested in the work of Bernard Williams is that he is a moral philosopher who is concerned with noticing what it is that you've done, and thinking, "What would it be like to say I didn't mean to run over that little girl, but I did, and I'll just get on with it?" Williams says that even though you didn't mean to injure her, you ought to feel agential regret: you ought to feel the regret of someone who knows he or she did something that resulted in something terrible for someone else. It's the desire to look at morality not in terms of intention—and criminalizing this intention instead of that one—but in terms of the effects of actions. It really was the case that Rousseau contemplated many more terrible things than he actually perpetrated (although his theft of the ribbon that he then pinned on the servant girl Marion was pretty terrible). You can see how people might be in a position to feel terrible about being annoyed at *x* or *y*, or about having had thoughts of one kind or another, but that shouldn't matter. I'm all in favor of decriminalizing thought. One of the worst things about the move into obscenity and blasphemy is that it really does criminalize thought even when it is saying that we have to legitimize a new kind of thought too, and not let anyone step on anyone else's thought. It's really important to focus on moments when you realize that things you didn't recognize as actions actually are, and what it means to take them up in some way.

Dean: What you're saying here reminds me of Foucault's point, in "The Subject and Power," when he says that "what defines a relationship of power is that it is a mode of action that does not act directly and immediately on others. Instead, it acts upon their actions: an action upon an action, on possible or actual future or present actions." Your book shows us how this works in concrete instances and, indeed, how pornography becomes part of a historical transformation in the mechanism of power relationships. Thank you for writing the book and for having this conversation.

# 3

## The Opening of Kobena, Cecilia, Robert, Linda, Juana, Hoang, and the Others

*Nguyen Tan Hoang*

At the beginning of a gay porn video called International Skin (directed by William Richhe, 1985), a young Asian man named Ken addresses the camera and announces that he is making the porn video as a homework assignment for his film class. The premise of the video rests on Ken's recruitment of his multiracial, "international" friends to have sex on camera for his project. Like Ken, I have often used school equipment and cast my friends for my various art video projects. Making sexually explicit imagery as a homework assignment, as crude and clichéd a porn conceit as that sounds, has in fact constituted the enabling condition for my own art practice. Indeed, it has functioned as a robust response to, and a dialogue with, the work of my teachers. This chapter explores an alternative pedagogy of porn and how it sheds light on feminist and queer aspects of pedagogy more generally. I use my own experience as student and teacher as a case study. Those various homework assignments to make sexually explicit photographs and videos continue to inform my artistic and scholarly pursuits.

Teaching pornography has been couched as a hazardous endeavor. In several anthologies on porn studies published in the past few years, authors of introductory chapters engage in a twofold project: first, they seek to justify and legitimize the scholarly research and teaching of pornography; at the same time, they go on to provide detailed warnings and cautionary tales about the dangers that such a project would entail.[1] For instance, Linda Williams points to the centrality of pornographic discourses permeating American national politics, film and television programming, and public health literature. She coins the term on/scene to mark "the gesture by which a culture brings on to its public arena the very organs, acts, bodies, and pleasures that have heretofore been designated ob/scene and kept literally off-scene."[2] Peter Lehman calls attention to porn's cultural value, its contribution to a better understanding of human sexuality, its role in the development of media technologies, and its importance in film and media history. Conversely, Williams, Lehman, and other porn scholars also highlight the hazards of bringing pornography into the classroom. There are titles and subheadings in book chapters and articles about teaching porn labeled "NSFW" (not safe for work), and the advice is often, "Don't do it without tenure."[3] Henry Jenkins reminds us that "educators have had their reputations destroyed, lost their jobs, and faced legal sanctions for teaching or researching porn."[4]

So while pornography is considered central to cultural studies scholarship, it remains a touchy subject of research and teaching. Professors make themselves vulnerable to charges of sexual harassment and invite the potential wrath of administrators, antiporn activists, religious fundamentalists, and sensationalist news media. Teachers may be accused of promoting pornography, of turning sexually unformed and impressionable students into consumers of porn, or, even worse, turning them into pornographers. For their part, students may receive this education of desire as anxiety producing, traumatizing, or a form of rape. On the one hand, there are the alleged benefits of teaching and learning about what sex is, how to have sex, the diversity of sex acts and sexual identities, and the unruly workings of fantasy. On the other, these benefits are offset by the detrimental effects to the students' and professors' psychological and professional well-being.

Lest I come across as an upstart who naively dismisses these cautionary tales as mere paranoia suppressing the ideals of academic freedom, I want to make clear that I absolutely value and am sympathetic to all of these warnings by more experienced scholars. Indeed, I have been accused of being a pornographer in at least one student evaluation. This evaluation was from an introduction to film class in which I did not teach porn. Registering his or her dissatisfaction with my strict attendance policy and performance as a teacher, the student sought to support the evaluation by referencing my art video work, effectively branding it as pornography. I do not wish to defend myself against the student's assessment of my teaching here. Rather, what I want to note is that the student sought to discredit my qualifications as a teacher largely due to my scholarly publications on pornography and experimental video productions that routinely employ sexually explicit imagery.

I have taught sexually explicit material in another class, an upper-division seminar on Asian American film, video, and new media, focusing on sexual representation. During the first and second meetings, with ample warning, I screened clips of gay porn as well as lesbian porn, and I stated that it is the students' responsibility to review the syllabus carefully, including the films, videos, and readings, before signing up for the course. Interestingly, this happened to be the most successful course I have ever taught. I find myself in a strange position as a gay male professor who teaches sexually explicit material at an all-women's college, a context some might deem a safe space for the discussion of pornography. At the same time, my position as an Asian male teacher also poses a menace to female students (straight and queer), not to mention department chairs and college deans, who see my scholarly research in pornography as a potential threat to the psychic well-being of my female students.

The reason I bring up these teaching incidents at some length is because, although they confirm the cautionary tenor of writings about porn and pedagogy, I want to offer a counternarrative based on my own experience as a student of queer and feminist pedagogy, one crucially centered on learning about sexually explicit imagery. Instead of a moralistic, protectionist, and reactionary context marked by fear, disgust, offense, harm, and trauma, my education in the subject has been enormously enabling, liberatory, and, to use a dated term, *empowering* in my formation as a scholar and artist. For the past twenty years, I have been committed to making sexually explicit imagery—a sort of counterpornography—in my photography and video work. By sharing my trajectory of porn pedagogy, I seek to interrogate the framework produced by conservative forces in constraining our roles as educators. I want to challenge the terms of porn and pedagogy focused around warnings, cautions, discretion, protectionism, phobia, and sex negativity. Teaching porn is different from other modes of pedagogy because it activates bodily reactions from teachers and students, thus highlighting the fact that both are sexual subjects, and that teaching and learning are embodied practices. Protectionism's attempt to separate sex and sexuality from cerebral, intellectual realms is ultimately untenable. A feminist and queer pedagogy of porn challenges hierarchical relationships of pedagogy, expanding and making other kinds of relationships legible—ones I name *intergenerational friendship*. I will have more to say about this concept in the conclusion.

My development of a counterpornography has taken place squarely within the university, from my undergraduate days at UC Santa Cruz to my graduate studies at UC Irvine and Berkeley. The education I received at the University of California required my teachers to take risks, all of them professional, some also personal, in opening themselves up to the pedagogy of sexually explicit material. In turn I have made myself open, and receptive, to their instructions and examples. As my comments about the student evaluation make clear, the pedagogy relation, especially concerning sex and sexuality, is shot through with policing and regulation (on the sides of teachers *and* students). Rather than seeing this process as the result of individual psychological and moral failings, I contend that a technique of shaming powerfully inflects the pedagogy of porn within academic institutions. The following narratives illustrate acts of violent shaming as well as strategies that negotiate and disarticulate those shaming practices.

*The Opening of . . .*

As a sophomore at UC Santa Cruz, I showed nude self-portraits in a student photography show. A viewer of that exhibition wrote in the gallery comment book: "Tell that fag Viet Cong to stop showing his rice dick." As a response to that racist and homophobic epithet, two years later I titled my senior thesis art show "Fag Viet Cong Shows Rice Dick: Reclaiming the Asian Male Body." A viewer of the senior exhibition wrote in the comment book, in Vietnamese: "So you want to shame Vietnamese people. Better watch out for your life. You disgrace my people and country." It was signed, "Santa Ana gangster."[5]

The two terrorizing responses to my art shows highlighted for me the interlocking issues of race and sexuality and their real-life stakes and urgency in my artistic work. The threat in the second comment alerted me to the limited viability of the subtitle of the show: *whose* Asian male body did I seek to reclaim? It is impossible to ascertain what part of the show was responsible for the failed interpellation of the anonymous Vietnamese male viewer—whether he was disidentifying with the appellations of *fag*, *Viet Cong*, *rice dick*, or whether he was rejecting the attempt, or the need, to reclaim an Asian male body via its public display "in a sexual field." Although I had wanted to point to the limits of mere inclusion and to direct attention to the "structuring power of . . . photographic discourses," my project of reclamation ultimately suffered from the strategy of the reversal of stereotypes—namely, of replacing wimpy, asexual, and undesirable with masculine, homoerotic, and desirable. As such, the project's mere privileging of one bad term in the place of another good, or better one, was easily contested and rejected.[6]

*Kobena*

Between the two art shows, I was enrolled in an art history course taught by Kobena Mercer. He was newly hired at UC Santa Cruz and arrived with great fanfare, right after the publication of the landmark queer film anthology *How Do I Look?* (1991), which contains his chapter on Robert Mapplethorpe's *Black Book* (1986), "Skin Head Sex Thing: Racial Difference and the Homoerotic Imaginary." Kobena was the first professor I had in college who made his subject position as a gay black man central to his scholarly work. His presence in the classroom exhibited a mixture of intellectual sophistication and glamour (the sexy British accent that made me and my female friends swoon), but also a strangeness and vulnerability. As a first-generation college student studying art and art history, subjects considered esoteric and extravagant by my immigrant parents, I was giddy with excitement in encountering texts that spoke to my social, political, and aesthetic sensibilities. At the same time, I experienced insecurity about my academic abilities and guilt over my chosen fields of study, as if I were intruding on privileged, forbidden territory. I recognized a similar sense of being out of place in Kobena's presence in the classroom, whether due to his new experience as a teacher or his recent move to America. This teacher's strangeness and vulnerability reverberated with my own.

What further unites Kobena and me in this story—his critical (and to a certain extent, confessional) reassessment of Mapplethorpe's work and my student photo-text projects—is the difficulty in registering our status as desiring sexual subjects, or more precisely, our desiring sexual subjectivity as gay men of color. In an earlier essay in which he diagnoses the racial fetishism performed by the white male subject (Mapplethorpe), Kobena inadvertently effaces his investment, fantasy, jealousy, and vulnerability—in short, his desire from his masterful and, by his own admission, aggressive reading of the photographs.[7] Similarly, in my goal of making Asian men visible as desired sexual objects, I had recourse to an essentializing, and politically right-on, rhetoric of reclaiming Asian male sexual agency, thus attempting to fix the meanings of Asian masculinity. In my I Love . . . photo-text series, presented at my senior exhibition, under a black-and-white ID picture of an Asian man, the viewer is presented with a grammar exercise, a fill-in-the-blank sentence (e.g., "I love _____ computers/cock") or an option to circle the correct vocabulary word (e.g., "I love math/men" and "I love rice/rimming"). On the one hand, the "choices" in these sentences reinforce the incommensurabilities between Asian and homosexual identities. On the other, the stark oppositions also mark a refusal to separate them out, suggesting a resignified embrace of negative racial and sexual stereotypes. To be sure, such a resignification (the "reclaiming" in the show's name) remains unstable. For the anonymous Santa Ana gangster, such a reclamation amounts not to a racial reparation but to yet another instance of racial abjection. This is an abjection that he, in turn, seeks to displace onto me, a self-identified fag Viet Cong who could never be granted citizenship in his country. Like Kobena, I fell into the trap of reading against white gay male desire without recognizing my complicity and subjection within a multiplicity of gazes—for instance, ones that remain steadfastly invested in remasculinizing Vietnamese American manhood.

Cecilia

In a body of experimental videotapes (beginning in the late 1980s) that investigate lesbian subjectivity through popular-cultural narratives, Cecilia Dougherty presents various scenes of her and her female lovers kissing, humping, grinding, fucking, coming—not in any touchy-feely kind of way, but in a down-and-dirty manner. For example, her video Grapefruit (1989) restages John Lennon, Yoko Ono, and the rest of the Beatles as a multicultural, all-lesbian affair. In *Gone* (2001), the lesbian writer Laurie Weeks channels Lance Loud in a loose remake of the PBS documentary series *An American Family* (produced by Craig Gilbert; directed by Alan Raymond and Susan Raymond, 1973).

Cecilia was my teacher in graduate school at UC Irvine in the mid-1990s. Though she never assigned her own work or showed it in class, the other graduate students and I checked out her videotapes from the art department's video library and watched them as unofficial homework. In *Joe-Joe* (1993), Dougherty and her then-girlfriend Leslie Singer both play the gay British playwright Joe Orton as a dyke couple in modern-day San Francisco's Mission District. The video opens with Joe and Joe's visit to their literary agent Peggy Ramsay's (played by the writer Kevin Killian) office to deliver their script for the Beatles. While waiting for him to read it, Joe and Joe excuse themselves to the loo, where they proceed to make out and engage a quickie session of bathroom sex, depicted here in a frank, explicit style.[8]

Watching your teacher have sex on-screen is not only perverse but also startling, scandalous, forbidden, and a little transgressive. This was a uniquely queer pedagogical model: white working-class Irish American lesbian teacher and gay refugee Vietnamese American student—reminiscent of, but not quite the same as, the same-sex teacher-student, mentor-mentee model propagated by gay porn and pulp novels. It was partly through the experience of watching each other having sex on video, me watching her and she watching me, that our queer bond in the classroom was formed. In spite of the differences of race, gender, age, and sexual repertoire, we managed to forge a connection through our desire to see and create new queer images, ones that show who, what, where, and how we get off. The sex-positive, feminist self-determination in her work—far from a sterile, sanitized repertoire of images and acts—is shot through with the messiness of contradiction, power, and pleasure. Even as Cecilia's queer dyke sexual scenarios are saturated with impurity and illegitimacy because they "ape" gay male sexuality, their lesbionic retakes of these scenes serve as catalysts for my own sexual scenarios.[9]

My first video, entitled *7 Steps to Sticky Heaven* (1995), was produced as the final project for her class. It deals with the politics of sticky rice and potato queens in San Francisco, an issue that generated heated debates in the gay Asian community at that time.[10] In between talking-head interviews, I insert sequences of me eating rice and spreading it on my naked torso, as well as explicit scenes of me having rough sex with a white ex-boyfriend and gentler sex with an Asian friend. Following Cecilia's lesbian lead, it was important for me not only to have Asian men talking frankly about sex on camera but to show them having explicit, hard-core sex. The various "steps" indicated in the title of the video pokes fun at self-help literature and its concerns with self-improvement and self-esteem. Indeed, the soft S/M, top-bottom-style sex between the ex-boyfriend and me, shown as an earlier step, is replaced in a later step with frottage and mutual oral sex between me and an Asian buddy. The abandonment of potato for sticky rice suggests a healthy progression from a relationship of negative power imbalance to one of positive mutuality. Yet the fact that I included the politically incorrect sex scene with the white ex-boyfriend at all—not to mention the sequence's dynamic camerawork, quick editing, and the enthusiastic sexual performances—intimates the enduring appeal of interracial sex, even as such activities are disavowed and branded as evidence of racial objectification. Retrospectively, I might rename this method *negation through imitation*, a phrase used by Judith Halberstam to describe Cecilia's exploration of lesbian sexuality through "pirating" the imagery, form, scripts, and objects of heterosexual and gay male texts, but repurposed to fashion a new vision of lesbian desires.[11] In a similar vein, I suggest that far from being a touchy-feely celebration of sticky heaven, *7 Steps to Sticky Heaven* draws on the language of Asian-niched pornographic imagery with its concomitant reliance on white top–Asian bottom positions and the dominance and submission that obtain therein. The sexual, artistic, and pedagogical dialogue between Cecilia's and my videos challenges the commonsense assumption that sex drives a wedge between lesbians and gay men. Furthermore, my learning to make sexually explicit videotapes from a lesbian professor challenges the cliché that poses "lesbian piety" against gay male sexual outlaw.[12] Instead, the lessons she provided constitute a unique, productive form of cross-gender, cross-generational queer initiation.

## Robert

The sense of urgency of making sexually explicit images in Cecilia's videos also informs the work of Robert Blanchon, another professor of mine at UC Irvine. His wide-ranging body of work includes conceptual pieces that poke fun at art-world institutions, as well as irreverent and poignant pieces that deal with his own mortality as an HIV-positive man. It is the latter body of work that had a profound effect on me as a young gay man who had come out during the height of the AIDS crisis. I remember Robert as a sexy, witty, funny, and charismatic teacher, a modern-day dandy with his ascot, cane, and blue hair. He cut a striking figure against the bland architecture of the Irvine campus.

His short video, *let's just kiss + say goodbye* (1995), culls scenes from late 1970s and early 1980s gay porn videos, in particular nonsexual in-between moments that set up and string together the sexual numbers: watching a boxing match on TV with a buddy, complaining about bad prison food, and trying on jockstraps at the sporting-goods store. Backed by the song "Kiss and Say Goodbye" by the Manhattans, the video celebrates and memorializes the pre-AIDS, precondom era of gay porn, its anonymous actors, and a vibrant gay sexual culture on the verge of extinction:

> I'm gonna miss you, I can't lie
> Understand me, oh won't you try
> It's gonna hurt me, I can't lie
> Take my handkerchief and wipe your eyes
> Maybe you'll find, you'll find another guy
> Well let's kiss and say goodbye.

The emotional resonance of these lines is amplified by the video's resignification of the lyrics. The song's recounting of the end of a generic heterosexual love affair is re-scored as a farewell to a gay sexual culture decimated by AIDS. In the place of the male lover's hesitant suggestion that his female lover "find another guy," Robert's video reframes the song's personal appeal as a public address to a gay male collective. The sentimental words are refunctioned as an homage and eulogy to a fast-disappearing homosexual way of life. Yet, this disappearing sexual culture lives on in *let's just kiss + say goodbye*. Robert's archiving of found porn footage works to ensure that the vitality, and loss, of gay sexual culture will not be missed by those other guys who come after him, those who go on to find other guys and create other futures.

This video, along with Robert's other work, demonstrates that any discussion of pedagogy and porn situated in the historical context of the mid-1990s must consider the centrality of HIV and AIDS. My response to *let's just kiss + say goodbye* is a video called *Maybe Never (but I'm counting the days)*, made for my MFA thesis show in the spring of 1996. The video features an endless recitation of *I've never* and *I never* phrases spoken by my Asian American undergraduate friends: "I've never showered with you after hot sticky sex. I never held your hand in public. I've never taken your breath away. I never had the chance to say good-bye. I've never videotaped us fucking on your futon. I've never felt your cum on my face and chest. I never learned how to pronounce your name." These pronouncements are scored with a soundtrack of pop songs containing "never" lyrics, including "I'll Never Love This Way Again" by Dionne Warwick, "Never as Good as the First Time" by Sade, and "Never Gonna Give You Up" by Rick Astley. The video expresses the sense of loss, longing, and desire felt by me and my friends as young people growing up in the age of AIDS. The video's verbal expressions of unsafe, taboo sex acts are coupled, and fused, with romantic regrets and missed connections. And yet, by giving expression to sexual practices considered impossible to act on, and their attendant feelings of vulnerability, disappointment, and regret, the video allows for the enactment of these very gestures, albeit in highly attenuated and mediated forms.

During the quarter I was enrolled in Robert's graduate critique class, his photo spread in the gay porn magazine *Honcho* (September 1995) came out. One of my fellow gay classmates got his hands on the magazine and a group of us pored over it like horny teenagers. In the nine-page spread entitled "Razor Burn," a slim, bleached-blond Robert with a five-o'clock shadow strips off his clothes and proceeds to shave his pubes and balls, looking like a punky youth on the final pages. Robert's porn shoot can be read as his way of asserting his status as sexual subject, as human subject, at a time when social and political forces deemed otherwise. A sense of recognition occurs for me in looking at Robert's porn spread, back then and now: an art teacher with "a deadly virus" reinvents himself as a youthful, desirable pornographic body. A sense of misrecognition occurs for me in looking at Robert's porn spread: an Asian art student makes photographs and videos to counter the view of Asian men as obscene, unworthy of pornographic objectification. While Robert's *Honcho* spread assures his induction into the official gay male pornographic archive, in the nick of time, before his declining health would render his body too legible as sick, diseased, and undesirable, my entry into this public pornographic scenario can only take place via fantasy, on the other side of the page, as a reader, looking on. The closest I come is through my art video practice, my counterpornography. In spite of these differences, both Robert's and my practices seek to expand the official gay porn archive, in his case to contest its exclusion based on HIV status, and in my case on race and ethnicity.

## Linda

My arrival at Berkeley marked a crucial shift in my engagement with sexually explicit material. In my second semester there, I took Linda Williams's graduate seminar Pornographies On/scene. Finally I was able to integrate my long-term interest in making sexually explicit work with the critical studies of the history and theory of pornography. It was in Linda's seminar—with its required weekly screenings where we watched entire porn films, not mere clips—that I first saw such 1970s classics as *Deep Throat* (directed by Gerard Damiano, 1972), *The Devil in Miss Jones* (directed by Gerard Damiano, 1973), and *Boys in the Sand* (directed by Wakefield Poole, 1971). The porn I had seen up to that time had mostly been contemporary gay videos. The class inspired me to take a closer look at the earlier history of moving-image pornographies, both straight and gay, to better account for recent developments, especially the influence of medium formats, such as the VCR and VHS tape, on the production, exhibition, and consumption of porn.

I made the short video *K.I.P.* (2002) while I was enrolled in Linda's class. The source footage comes from a porn video of the early 1980s porn star Kip Noll that I rented from Tower Video in the Castro neighborhood of San Francisco. While watching it at home, I discovered that the tape had been rented so many times that there were numerous glitches and dropouts on it, thus signaling that these were the parts of the video that past viewers considered to be the hottest. My rescanning of specific sequences where the tape breaks down asserts my presence (as a phantom reflection on the television monitor) as one viewer "in line" between many before me and others to come after me. The video screen also reflects my image as an Asian viewer, breaking and entering into a hot porno fantasy, but one that seldom acknowledges my presence and desire. As a gay man who grew up and came out in the age of AIDS, the 1970s holds a mythic status in my sexual imagination. The only visual access I have to what it must have been like is through gay 1970s porn, seen on bad VHS dubs. I am interested in the convergence of video as a highly unstable visual material that inevitably degenerates and the concept of gay male generation, where the important political gains of previous generations are taken for granted, rejected, or entirely forgotten. *K.I.P.* suggests that recording and redubbing old images anew will enable and ensure the archiving of sexual memory and the restoration, and expansion, of sexual possibilities for future generations to come. The imprinting of my own image among the bodies of these white gay men from the 1970s and 1980s registers my desire as a contemporary viewer for these missing men. But it also underscores the need for reimagining a different pornographic history that takes into account another group of missing bodies: an alternative archive where gay Asian men took an active role on and off the pornographic screen.

One important lesson I learned from Linda's seminar was that pornography constitutes a diverse body of texts with complex and uneven histories. My participation in the seminar and the production of *K.I.P.* showed me the importance of historicizing pornographic texts, their specific conditions of production, exhibition, and consumption—thus complicating my ahistorical assumptions about racial stereotyping and the politics of visibility. I also learned from her how to talk about and teach sexually explicit material in a frank, critical, and serious manner. I admire her intellectual risk taking, her tackling of highly charged topics that most scholars would not dare to broach. In her chapter "Skin Flicks on the Racial Border," Linda takes on the volatile question of race and sex in interracial (white-black) porn. In an analysis of the film *Mandingo* (directed by Richard Fleischer, 1975) and its interracial sex scene between a white master and his black female slave, and another scene between a white mistress and the black male slave (the Mandingo of the title),

Linda contends that "in these transgressions of the racial border between master and slave, the recognitions take place through and because of, not despite, erotically charged racial differences."[13] This insight about the "erotic recognitions across racial difference" and power differentials has been incredibly generative for my own work on queer interracial (Asian-white) lust, in such texts as sticky rice–potato queen sexual politics, in experimental diasporic documentaries, bottom-top positionings in the videos of Brandon Lee, and the queer domestic bond between a Filipino houseboy and his white mistress in the Elizabeth Taylor and Marlon Brando vehicle Reflections in a Golden Eye (directed by John Huston, 1967).[14]

## Juana

Recognitions, affiliations, affinities, and alliances across difference as analyzed in Mandingo by Linda and in Reflections in a Golden Eye by me reverberate in the work of Juana María Rodríguez, another professor of mine at Berkeley. The basis of Juana's and my connection, both scholarly and personal, is propped up by our commitments to rethinking racial-sexual subjection: my interest in gay Asian bottomhood and her interest in Latina femme sexuality. We are both deemed inappropriate and excessive for our refusal to have our bottom and femme positions co-opted by racial-sexual political orthodoxies. In my video Forever Bottom! (1999), I exploit the association of gay Asian male bottomhood with femininity, faggotry, and racial abjection. In it I show close-ups of my legs in the air and face pressed against various surfaces as I adopt different bottom positions. A heroization of the insatiable, unrepentant Asian male bottom, the video captures the Asian bottom "taking it" everywhere: on the carpet, in the shower, against the stove, on the lawn, in the backseat, among the trees, at the seashore, and so on. Instead of asserting Asian men's butch top potential, the video criticizes the emplacement of Asian men as feminized, passive bottoms by performing the bottom role excessively, enthusiastically, passionately.

In her chapter "Gesture and Utterance: Fragments from a Butch-Femme Archive," Juana defies the generic separation between theory and practice when she writes: "This essay is about sex. Not the representations of sex on flickering screens or fictional pages . . . ; the sex here is about the performance of a sexual archive brought to life through gesture, utterance and interpretation."[15] Among theoretical references from Michel Foucault, Giorgio Agamben, and Jacques Derrida, she embeds explicit passages detailing raunchy sex acts and orgasmic cries: "The femme scans her eyes downward. The butch grabs his cock. . . . He pushes the tip inside her, she bleeds; he ejaculates, she conceives."[16] Arguing that "sexual acts and sexualized bodies have no meaning outside of those we assign them," Juana posits that queer sex, in this case butch-femme sexuality, has the power to reinterpret heteronormative genders and sexualities.[17]

When I taught Juana's chapter in a queer cinema class, my politically savvy queer students adamantly protested her use of the pronoun *he* to refer to the butch in these sexual scenarios. They insisted that the butch must be identified by feminine pronouns because butches are by definition female-bodied individuals. My students were invested in contesting the binary of male-female genders through their use of gender-neutral pronouns, such as *ze* and *hir*, and making heteronormative sexes and genders strange with their use of terms like *cisgender* and *cissexuality*. The two most vocal students against the labeling of the butch as a "he" produced a safer sex video targeted for female-to-male trans people as their creative assignment. Interestingly, the very role-playing in Juana's text is reenacted in the students' own video.

Over footage of vigorous finger fucking, cunnilingus, and a three-way dildo circle jerk, we see texts such as "butch," "androgynous," and "gender non-conformist" on the screen. The two students' insistence on linking butch with female bodied with the pronoun *she* suggests the need to claim a radical difference from heterosexuality for the butch-femme couple. Yet in their depiction of sex acts playfully connected to identity labels, they bear out Juana's observation that "fingers, fellatio, nipples, assholes, and kissing are texts available for interpretation; names and meaning are assigned, circulated, enforced, toyed with, and transformed but are never absolute."[18] Thus, textual captions "tomboy-femme" and "gender-rejector" accompany a person in jeans finger fucking a person wearing lacy pink panties. "Indecisive" is used to describe two topless individuals making out and humping one another on a dorm-room bed. In another sequence, "boyish" strokes a lavender dildo while watching a sex scene from *Boys Don't Cry* (directed by Kimberly Peirce, 1999). The rejections and refusals of gender naming in the textual labels—in counterpoint to the visual track displaying fingers, breasts, tongues, vaginas, strap-ons, and asses—simultaneously destabilize *and* rely on gendered language and body parts to create the video's eroticism.[19]

## Hoang and the Others

In sharing these various scenes of instruction from my formation as an artist and an academic, I want to reexamine a current trend in queer and feminist pedagogy. At the beginning of the chapter, I discussed the limitations and self-censorship set into play by the discourse of protectionism. This discourse of protectionism rubs up against the erotics of teaching found in feminist and queer pedagogy, as articulated by scholars such as Jane Gallop, Joseph

Litvak, and David Halperin. For example, in the work of Halperin, Gregory Bredbeck, and Ellis Hanson, we encounter the Greek model that draws on Plato's *Symposium* to link pedagogy and pederasty; Plato's text characterizes the transmission of knowledge and culture as one that flows from grown men to young boys. Being filled with knowledge is analogized as getting fucked up the ass—that is, a model based on masculinist hierarchy. As Gallop writes in "The Student Body": "A greater man penetrates a lesser man with his knowledge. The student is empty, a receptacle for the phallus; the teacher is the phallic fullness of knowledge. The fact that teacher and student are traditionally of the same sex but of different ages contributes to the interpretation that the student has no otherness, nothing different from the teacher, simply less."[20] This transmission of knowledge from an older man to a younger one requires the student to passively "put out," surrendering to the phallic teacher's knowledge and wisdom. Alternatively, the feminist model sees pedagogical relationships as a relation between mother and daughter, a nurturing relation that rejects power and hierarchy for recognition and mutuality. Gallop writes: "The woman-to-woman paradigm shows the teacher giving up her authority and its association with distantiation in favor of blurring the boundaries between teachers and students."[21] Both the phallic and the feminist models rest on same-sex, generational, reproductive frameworks, with little to "no otherness" taken into account. In the former model, there is an explicit acknowledgment, and eroticization, of power, but this power only flows one way; in the latter, power differentials are domesticated and disavowed. Neither model adequately considers the negotiation of power across differences beyond the age gap.

In place of these two models, I propose a third: a queer pedagogy that complicates and expands the two gender-segregated relations. I see queer friendship, in its broadest sense, as a paradigm that can account for the various crossings—of race, age, class, gender, sexuality, and generation—that underscore these feminist and queer scenes of sexual instruction. This model is posed in the spirit of queer relationality and kinship that rewrite the scripts of heteronormative sociability and Oedipal dynamics. Following Foucault's oft-quoted statements about homosexuality and friendship, I suggest a deployment of queerness as a modality "to arrive at a multiplicity of relationships."[22] This multiplicity of relationships effectively exceeds state-sanctioned couple forms, resulting in an ethical stance: "A way of life can be shared among individuals of different age, status, and social activity. It can yield intense relations not resembling those that are institutionalized. It seems to me that a way of life can yield a culture and an ethics."[23] Along the same vein, Elizabeth Freeman reminds us of relationships that have been "fundamental to queer life: friendships, cliques, tricks, sex buddies, ex-lovers, activist and support groups, and myriad others."[24] It might be argued that the teacher-student relation is among the most privileged, esteemed, and institutionalized ways of life. However, as my narratives about my teachers illustrate, the feminist and queer studies classroom can potentially depart significantly from the dominant, hierarchical, and professional relationships between teachers and students, mentors and mentees.[25]

I suggest that queer intergenerational friendship captures the richness and complexity of my interactions with my teachers, accounting for recognitions across our respective social differences and antagonisms. In this regard, I have found Jennifer Doyle's work on queer friendship especially generative. She writes, "Friendships between men and women (queer or not) are more often stunted by the absence of feminism than by the absence/presence of sexual desire. In fact with a feminist ethic in place and a queer sensibility, the presence/absence of desire between friends seems less like a spoiler and more like a starting place."[26] In response to some gay male theorists' claim that sex drives a wedge between lesbians and gay men's relationships, Doyle argues for the expansiveness and generosity found in these cross-gender relationships, as opposed to the "stinginess" of heteronormative sociability.[27] In this spirit, we might rethink associations between teachers and students, mentors and mentees, as intergenerational friendships, "regardless of actual age."[28] At the same time that I call attention to the supportive, coalitional, and mutual ties in renaming teacher-student relations as queer friendship (and I am aware that I am glossing over the very real hierarchy and power imbalances that exist), I also want to deidealize friendship itself as a relationship of mutuality, reciprocity, and equality. Heather Love calls our attention to "an alternative trajectory of queer friendship marked by impossibility, disconnection, and loss."[29] Yet in spite of these very real conflicts in friendship, those occasional and inevitable falling-outs, I propose queer friendship as a more capacious model for the pedagogical relation because it makes room for a broader range of affinities, affiliations, and associations than models based on conventional pedagogical reproduction.[30]

Returning to pedagogy and porn, I am in full accord with Linda Williams when she points out that teaching sexually explicit material provides an important venue for students to talk about sex acts, sexuality, and sexual identities in a critical and sustained manner, a venue not available anywhere else in the university.[31] In a related discussion, Clarissa Smith observes that bringing pornography into the classroom enables students to see themselves as sexual subjects and as participants in the production of knowledge about sexuality.[32] Similarly, Earl Jackson Jr. considers teaching sexually explicit texts as part and parcel of our "intellectual integrity" and "moral obligation" to our students because "sexuality [is] central to the formation of . . . [students'] identities and the major reason for their oppression (and their existence as a site of re-sistance) within dominant culture."[33] As these scholars make clear, engaging our students in serious, rigorous study of sexual representation constitutes an important task for us as educators; we perform a disservice to our students, and to our own intellectual and pedagogical projects, if we do our job according to the guidelines of harm maintenance. Numerous queer and feminist writers have noted that the appeal to censorship of sexually explicit material is often complicit with the suppression of nonnormative sexualities. Such suppression affects not only students but teachers as well. To be sure, the risks taken by my teachers made them vulnerable to institutional censure. Yet they readily took the risks due to their desire not merely to challenge conventional pedagogical frameworks but to tackle head-on issues central to feminist and queer art, activism, and scholarship.

As Hanson reminds us, the "pedagogical gaze is panoptical not because the professor is omniscient, but because professor and student are both vulnerable, seen by what they do not see."[34] He goes on to say that such an exposure is consonant with bodily exposure and shame. Instead of deploying shaming mechanisms to corral teachers and students within their respective institutionalized roles, we might use our capacity to be shamed—whether inflected through race, class, gender, age, nation, education, region, or other modalities—as the basis for forging alliances in the coproduction of knowledge about sex and sexuality.[35] The porn archives, visual and literary, material and ephemeral, those that wait to be excavated and others that must be imagined, will be incomplete without the enthusiastic, dedicated efforts of friends, friends with benefits, lovers, artists, activists, producers, performers, fans, scholars, teachers, and students.

## Notes

I would like to express my thanks to Tim Dean, Steven Ruszczycky, and David Squires for their diligent work on the collection. My gratitude also goes to Tim Dean, Matt Pieknik, Cynthia Wu, Mireille Miller-Young, and Linda Williams for helpful feedback at "At the Limits: Pornography and the Humanities" conference held at the University at Buffalo in March 2010. Last but not least, this essay is dedicated to my teachers who taught me about sex and so much more.

1. See Gibson, More Dirty Looks, especially H. Jenkins, "Foreword"; Lehman, "Introduction"; and L. Williams, "Porn Studies."

2. L. Williams, "Porn Studies," 3.

3. "Not Safe for Work? Teaching and Researching the Sexually Explicit" is the title of the introductory article in a special issue of the journal Sexualities (2009), coedited by Feona Attwood and I. Q. Hunter. "Don't Do It without Tenure" is one of their article's subheadings. See Attwood and Hunter, "Not Safe for Work?"

4. H. Jenkins, "Foreword," 2.

5. Santa Ana, California, is located in Orange County in Southern California, home of the largest population of Vietnamese in the United States.

6. My artist's statement regarding this body of work in 1993 reads: "My photo-texts explore the homoeroticism of the Asian male body. Playing off mainstream American media representations of Asian (American) men as wimpy computer nerds, threatening kung fu masters, and ruthless businessmen, I employ the codes of art/fashion/advertising/institutional photography to insinuate the Asian male body in a sexual field. While it is interesting to 'include' Asian men in visual representations traditionally reserved for white men, it is even more important to problematize these culturally-b(i)ased criteria of what constitutes hypermasculine sex appeal and strength. This process involves questioning the structuring power of dominant modes of representation themselves, such as critically and self-consciously employing different photographic discourses."

7. Mercer, "Imagining the Black Man's Sex."

8. Joe-Joe follows the film Prick Up Your Ears (directed by Stephen Frears, 1987) quite closely, but with a crucial difference: the conflation of Joe Orton and his live-in lover Kenneth Halliwell into a lesbian couple, Joe-Joe. This early bathroom sex scene—decidedly a domestic one in an apartment—cleverly riffs on the public-toilet sex that Orton frequently engages in Frears's film.

9. Indeed, the scrolling text that opens the video clearly situates the work as the centering of working-class lesbian culture: "Imagine that we are totally and fabulously popular. Imagine that two young working class lesbians can capture the core of a nation's appetite for humor, can act as our literary conscience, and can do it without selling out. Imagine that the two Joes have their fingers on the pulsebeat of a nation."

10. In the gay argot of Asian American communities, sticky rice refers to Asian men who date other Asian men, while potato queens designates those who date white men.

11. Halberstam, "The Joe-Joe Effect," 361.

12. The phrase lesbian piety is used by Ellis Hanson in his response to Halberstam's critique of his presentation at the infamous "Gay Shame" conference at the University of Michigan in March 2003. See Hanson, "Teaching Shame," 161.

13. L. Williams, "Skin Flicks on the Racial Border," 293.

14. I analyze these texts in my book; see Nguyen, A View from the Bottom.

15. Rodriguez, "Gesture and Utterance," 282.

16. Rodriguez, "Gesture and Utterance," 284–85.

17. Rodriguez, "Gesture and Utterance," 283.

18. Rodriguez, "Gesture and Utterance," 283.

19. This video employs a pornographic vernacular to raise awareness about latex gloves, finger cots, dental dams, and condoms. Far from conjuring up sexual assault and trauma, the use of pornographic conventions constitutes an empowering gesture for these two students. Their video was a hit at the public student screening at the end of the semester. Almost all of the film studies courses I teach include a creative assignment (this could take the form of a single-channel video, an artist's book, a photo series, a PowerPoint presentation, and so on). This is a pedagogical strategy that I bring with me from my days as a graduate student at Berkeley, where professors gave students the choice of making a creative work in place of a research paper, or alongside a critical essay. I firmly believe in the integration of theory and practice; incorporating creative assignments in a critical studies course encourages students to think of themselves as active

producers of culture. Further, it breaks down the stubborn divide between criticism and production that has historically plagued film departments. Most crucially, it expands students' conception of what constitutes critical thinking and intellectual labor: critical studies invariably informs production and vice versa. This is precisely one of the limits I see in the teaching of porn and other sexually explicit material in the university. In Linda Williams's introduction to *Porn Studies* (2004), she cautions against allowing students to write porn screenplays, in order to "create better pornographies" (21). By contrast, I would be supportive of such projects. Although I would not specifically designate it as a required assignment, I would give students a choice of engaging with the material in creative ways other than conventional academic essays.

20. Gallop, "The Student Body," 43. See also Bredbeck, "Anal/yzing the Classroom"; Halperin, "Deviant Teaching"; Hanson, "Teaching Shame"; and Litvak, "Discipline, Spectacle, and Melancholia in and around the Gay Studies Classroom."

21. Gallop, "The Teacher's Breasts," 25.

22. Foucault, "Friendship as a Way of Life," 135.

23. Foucault, "Friendship as a Way of Life," 138.

24. Freeman, *The Wedding Complex*, ix.

25. Halperin makes a salient point about the different aims of feminist and queer pedagogy when he writes: "A successful outcome consists not merely in an improved grasp of theory, method, and application, but in an altered self-understanding, an enhanced sense of possibility, and a transformed relation to one's social, political, discursive, and personal situation." Halperin, "Deviant Teaching," 153.

26. Doyle, "Between Friends," 329.

27. Doyle, "Between Friends," 337.

28. I am indebted to Damon Young for this idea (and phrasing), which was formulated in the mentorship program guidelines we worked on together for the Society for Cinema and Media Studies Queer Caucus.

29. Love, *Feeling Backward*, 75.

30. I am not advocating that teachers and students should become "buddies," or for them to pretend that they are peers on equal footing. Just as one has many types of friends with varying levels of intimacy, one can cultivate different forms of friendly relations with one's teachers or students. In renaming the teacher-student relation as intergenerational friendship, I encourage an explicit acknowledgment of the pedagogical relation as involving an exchange of power and a receptiveness to the other, rather than a one-way hierarchical reproductive mode of interaction. Further, the teacher-student, mentor-mentee relationship, like most kinds of relationships, is always in process, shifting, developing, and changing.

31. L. Williams, "Porn Studies."

32. Smith, "Pleasure and Distance."

33. Jackson, "Explicit Instruction," 137–38.

34. Hanson, "Teaching Shame," 143.

35. This formulation draws on influential theorizing around gay shame in queer studies. See Crimp, "Mario Montez, for Shame"; Sedgwick, "Shame, Theatricality, and Queer Performativity"; and Warner, *The Trouble with Normal*.

# 4

## Pornography in the Library

*David Squires*

Thus, less than twenty-four hours after her arrival, during her second day there, she was taken after the meal into the library, there to serve coffee and tend the fire. Jeanne, whom the black-haired valet had brought back, went with her as did another girl named Monique. It was this same valet who took them there and remained in the room, stationed near the stake to which O had been attached. The library was still empty. The French doors faced west, and in the vast, almost cloudless sky the autumn sun slowly pursued its course, its rays lighting, on a chest of drawers, an enormous bouquet of sulphur-colored chrysanthemums which smelled of earth and dead leaves.

— Pauline Réage, *Story of O*

### A Perverted Library

When Grove Press put out an American edition of *Story of O* by Pauline Réage in 1965, the publication did not initiate a momentous legal battle over obscenity, nor did it face aggressive censorship campaigns. Generally speaking, it did not even shock public tastes or outrage critics. The translation hit shelves in a plain white wrapper that indicated the book's title and its intended audience ("limited to adults") after Grove Press had already engaged in a series of high-profile legal battles over the so-called modern classics *Lady Chatterley's Lover* and *Tropic of Cancer*.[1] By 1965 *Story of O* had accrued the peculiar distinction of winning the Prix des Deux Magots at the same time as weathering a publicity ban in France. Rather than sparking a new round of public debate about literary value and obscenity in the United States, however, the novel's publication typified a historical moment that redefined pornography's relationship to the general public by granting mainstream audiences access to sexually explicit literature. As Eliot Fremont-Smith wrote in his *New York Times* book review the following March, the moment of *Story of O*'s publication "marks the end of any coherent restrictive application of the concept of pornography to books."[2] His review goes on to affirm both artistic vision and art's visibility. "What art is about is *seeing*," Fremont-Smith explains, "which is why art is always at war with those who would righteously restrict the scope or manner of vision."

Pornography also trades in the visual, and efforts to censor it have organized around a will to suppress the visibility of sex. Following Linda Williams's development of the principle of maximum visibility, we can say that straight porn most successfully makes visible women's bodies and men's pleasure.[3] As the epigraph suggests, however, Story of O exemplifies the circumstances in which pornography operates according to a different and distinctly spatial problematic that arises from the mainstream acceptance of so-called obscene printed material. Outlining the spatial dimension will require a shift in critical attention away from questions about how or why we look at sexually explicit materials toward related questions about how or why we organize them as we do. With that in mind, the basic question that begins my investigation is where, if anywhere, in the library do we find pornography?

With the decline of legal censorship and the resulting increase in access to pornography after the Second World War, public institutions in the United States had to reevaluate their relationship to formerly banned materials. Libraries emerged in the later 1960s as a privileged and highly contested institutional space for those reevaluations because the legal changes regulating print culture impacted more than just their moral sensibilities; those changes also impacted the core of their professional practice. Naturally, librarians felt the urgency of legal decisions regarding obscenity, and, within the field of library and information science, debates about collection development began to formalize around the question of pornography.[4] In that discursive context and at that historical juncture, pornography amounted to a problem that raised an entire set of questions about intellectual freedom, community service, media access, heterogeneous social values, and more practical concerns about how to manage potentially sensitive collections.

I do not want to overestimate Story of O's engagement with any of those issues. The library mentioned in the epigraph is hardly central to the novel's development, and, like many libraries of an earlier era, it seems to serve only a select group of gentlemen readers rather than the variously constituted communities at issue for public institutions. However, Story of O's notably unspectacular publication history marks a moment in postwar America when dirty books found their way to public bookshelves without any of the Comstockery that met earlier attempts in the twentieth century to peddle pornography. In the relative calm following the censorship cases pushed forward by Grove Press, during which it published Story of O, a professional debate about institutional practices and responsibilities flourished within the field of library science, eventually incorporating considerations of image and moving-image porn. Although those debates incorporated highly contested watchwords—*freedom, decency*, and *democracy*, to name just a few—the most vocal participants identified their stakes as the life, or death, of the library.

Before attempting to account for those debates and the problems they raise for thinking about the space of the library, it helps to consider how *Story of O* depicts that space within its narrative frame. Brief as the reformulation is, it nonetheless stands as an example of the imaginary formulations that structure debates about libraries. At the same time, it places sexuality squarely within the space of the library and so offers a perspective that needs further development. Doing so will provide the entry point to discussing some of the problems of imagination attendant on thinking about the place of sexually explicit materials in libraries. Taking the library scene in *Story of O* as a point of departure, I also want to suggest that turning attention to the organization of institutions that house, archive, and sometimes lend sex materials can help produce an understanding of pornography in spatial, rather than primarily visual, terms.

As in any sex scene, immanent to the library scene in *Story of O* is an organizational model that puts bodies in relation to one another. Positioned near and stoking the fire, O stands under the bureaucratic authority of her valet, whose physical power over her body derives from his position within an institutional hierarchy. While she tends to the service end of the library's function, he is "stationed" near the stake that symbolizes and at times materializes O's attachment to her submissive role as servant. Jeanne and Monique, who fill a similar if not identical role to O, indicate the bureaucratic nature of the valet's authority by demonstrating its reach over a particular group of servants. Unlike the other two women, however, O's presence clarifies the particularity of the bureaucratic arrangement by emphasizing her newness within the system. The valet takes her to the library so that she can learn to navigate the space according to a sexual pedagogy. In this case, the pedagogical form depends on a sadomasochistic relationship of dominance and submission that teaches O to take the submissive role in serving gentlemen readers. Within twenty-four hours of arriving at Roissy—a Sadean château that inverts liberal-humanist expectations about sexuality—O learns to serve coffee and her flesh in the same gesture of ardent acquiescence to violations of her selfhood. By representing the library as the primary stage of her sexual education, *Story of O* figures it as a space of initiation, learning, and discovery. In other words, it is a social space designed to produce knowledge.

Characterizing the library as a space designed to produce knowledge should not come as a surprise. In fact, leaving aside the sexual content, that characterization might easily align with the stated goals of any public library.

As a quick glance at library mission statements reveals, public libraries task themselves first and foremost with pedagogical goals: to provide patrons with information that will satisfy their educational needs and, more important, to educate patrons about the value and standards of library use.[5] To sustain itself as an active institution, the library depends on teaching people to locate and access the media that it houses, which, in our information-rich age, can require considerable know-how. That pedagogical mission places librarians in a complicated relationship of authority and responsibility to patrons—they must turn patrons into productive library users while accounting for the needs of individuals. The successful library instructor, however, will teach patrons to navigate library systems so that they can satisfy their own particular needs, thereby incorporating themselves into the bureaucratic mechanisms of the institution that make it operate efficiently.

For the sake of clarity, I should emphasize that I do not intend this assessment of the library's pedagogical function to be a critique of institutional power. Of course the library reproduces its values by educating patrons. However, the library that educates patrons about the mechanics of its information systems also gives patrons the power to better navigate those systems, effectively making the library serve them on a more individual basis. Rather than acting as a gatekeeper, the librarian serves as an instructor who animates the relationship between patron and media by making the points of connection more direct. The sexual dynamic of Story of O perverts that instructor role by collapsing the agent of library service and the object of library education into a single body. O plays the pupil (the subject of an educational program) while also maintaining service responsibilities (the agent of custodial duties at the library). The gentlemen readers, on the other hand, maintain their position as patrons (subjects of library service) while also adopting the instructor's authority over and responsibility for teaching O to submit to Roissy's sexual mechanisms. The peculiar organization of institutional roles at the library in Story of O effectively creates a double hierarchy that structures O's sexual education. She finds herself servant to both the library and its patrons, without the librarian's traditional authority to interpret patron needs according to already extant institutional systems. Of course, librarians may often feel so beholden—caught between the demands of the institution and the demands of a patron—but their professional relationship to patrons remains defined by the power and the responsibility to enhance access to institutional services.

One way to understand the retooled and thoroughly bound position that O experiences is to bill it as a consequence of the sadomasochistic program at Roissy. Seen against the backdrop of more conventional institutional bureaucracies, however, the double hierarchy that defines her place in the library tips the relational dynamics in a way that allows patrons' sexual desires to enter a formula otherwise designed to separate them from patrons' educational needs. As both patrons to be served and instructors to be heeded, the gentlemen readers have the opportunity to introduce sexuality as a material concern for O's education. Thus, their desires define the library's use. When they want their coffee and their newspaper, the library functions as a posh reading room. When they want to fuck, the library functions as an orgy hall. Characteristic of pornographic fantasies, Story of O erases the relational obstacles that regulate access to sexual encounters as O learns to place herself at the complete disposal of Roissy's patrons. Perhaps it's an obvious point, but this scene makes no room for the stereotypical shushing librarian. It also obscures the library's collection and so forecloses any possibility for the holdings to mediate O's sexual education. With that foreclosure, the novel imagines one possible reconfiguration of institutional space that would allow for the entry of sexuality and sexual experience.

By foregrounding the relationships between bodies in the library, Story of O unwittingly identifies some of the anxieties of librarianship in a postcensorship age. Will the introduction of sexual materials into the general catalog change the library's institutional program? Will sexual materials in the library change the relationship between librarians and patrons? Will explicit materials encourage sexual harassment in the library?[6] The novel touches on those professional anxieties by depicting a set of relationships common to a conventional library but arranged in an unconventional manner. Where the usual arrangement prescribes an institutional bureaucracy attended to by custodians serving patrons, Story of O gives us a slightly different situation; we find custodians subject to the desire of patrons under the authority of a bureaucratic institution. Notably, the novel presents that reorganization against the backdrop of an image depicting the library as bound by and to death. Oblique sunlight illuminates a bouquet of chrysanthemums that smell of earth and dead leaves. The visual image of a traditional funerary flower combines with the olfactory sense of tilled earth to associate the library with an open grave, while the dead leaves allude to an otherwise absent collection of books. Without explicit attention or detail in the text, the ignored volumes return to their place in the library as a haunting image of their individual folios. More than as an active repository, Roissy's library acts as a burial site animated by sexual activity.

## Dead Collections

If Story of O provides an unconventional arrangement of bureaucratic relationships within the space of the library, its vision of the library as a dead space follows from a much more pedestrian history. Tracing that history, however, leads to a number of entanglements that still need scholarly attention if we hope to unravel them. One of the most obvious problems arises in the distinction between libraries and museums, both of which constitute archival institutions. The two institutions serve different purposes in the contemporary era and, in fact, they have distinct histories. Even so, drawing firm distinctions between the two without the benefit of careful historical analysis may prove problematic. Suffice it to note here that some of the divergences occur in the differences between stacks and galleries, bibliography and archaeology, circulating materials and exhibiting materials.

Despite the differences, libraries and museums have found themselves bound up together or used interchangeably in popular and critical imaginations. At least part of the association derives from the fact that national libraries and museums often were housed together, the most prominent example being the British Museum and Library—two institutions that remained yoked by shared physical space until 1997. The most enduring connection for theoretical associations, however, focuses on the overlap in archival practices. Specifically, cataloging technology acted as a confluence between the institutional development of libraries and that of museums during the nineteenth century. Although institutional catalogs had been in use since at least the end of the sixteenth century, the nineteenth century saw an "unprecedented and still unparalleled interest and activity in cataloging," as Ruth F. Strout explains in her brief survey of cataloging history.[7]

Amid that cataloging frenzy, the word pornography appeared as a new category in the taxonomy of classical artifacts. A number of scholars writing about pornography have explained that the excavation of Pompeii and the many sexually explicit representations preserved there posed a problem for catalogers hoping to take advantage of print media to share archaeology's newest discoveries. In perhaps the most thorough treatment of that history, Walter Kendrick explains that the problem stemmed from anxieties about audience and authorial credibility. Catalogers could not regulate access to their volumes in the way a "secret museum" housing the objects themselves could regulate access to their premises. Motivated by fear that impressionable members of the public might put scholarly material to lascivious ends, catalogers created internal obstacles to dampen the erotic effects of the representations they publicized. Kendrick clarifies that such catalogers would leave text untranslated to "protect" women, children, and the poor. M. L. Barré's French catalog of the Museo Borbonico (1875–77), which housed the objectionable artifacts uncovered at Pompeii, even went as far as miniaturizing some of the more erotic aspects of nude relics.[8]

In addition to what now seem to be drastic attempts at maintaining decorum, Barré also depended on the combination of classification and figurative association to maintain the credibility of targeting a professional audience. The subset of a "pornographic collection" in museum catalogs correlated to a distinct space within libraries where offensive materials could remain hidden from public view. Barré's concern about communicating his intellectual intentions moved him to define his work as scientific, invoking disciplinary authority to give his work a grounding metaphor. More than the seriousness of science, however, Barré's use of analogy provided the lasting characterization of archival spaces as lifeless. He concludes the introduction to the eighth volume of his catalog with this description of his methodology: "We have looked upon our statues as an anatomist contemplates his cadavers."[9] Barré, far from the only writer to associate archives with dead bodies, may have been the first to link the process of cataloging with a process of exhausting the vivacious spirit assumed to inhere in sex materials. Why should the abstract spatial organization of an archive ring the death knell for materials housed in it? For Barré that process of stagnation appears as merely a hopeful justification for his work with obscene materials. He hoped that the statues, robbed of their erotic charge, would not seem like indecent objects of study. As the conceptual link between an archival death and sex materials continues to operate in more recent discourses on pornography, however, Barré's professional anxiety has morphed into anxiety over the loss of sexual allure.

A recent book by Geoff Nicholson exemplifies that anxiety, insofar as it documents the author's ambivalent fascination with the act of collecting and systematizing objects related to sex, especially pornography. In the early sections of *Sex Collectors*, Nicholson articulates his fascination with the social place that pornography occupies. He locates that place quite literally in the trash. Describing his work as a trash collector in Sheffield, England, he tells readers that he and his coworkers were in the habit of rummaging through bins to sort out items of interest. The one thing they could count on finding, apparently, was pornography. It seems that many of the people who liked to look at and read sexually explicit publications did not find them fit for owning. Although not prone to disposing of pornography himself, Nicholson sympathizes with the gesture of dispersing a collection when he explains the hesitancy he feels about sex museums. Both pornography and museums carry the sexual charge of revealing intimate secrets, so long, he suggests, as they are kept apart. When combined in the form of a public sex museum, the process of detaching the sex objects from their primary milieu among cultural detritus and placing the objects on display in a legitimate institutional setting "involves a sort of death. Quite simply, things die when they're put in museums."[10] Nicholson differentiates between private sex collections and institutional, or public, sex museums. For him, the elimination of allure from an object culturally imbued with sexuality has less to do with the accumulation of such objects in physical space than it does with their classification in a taxonomic order. The process of ordering a collection, whereby individual objects become parts of the whole, creates what Nicholson calls a "metonymic displacement."[11]

The concept of metonymic displacement derives from Roman Jakobson's revisions of classical rhetoric and Jacques Lacan's later psychoanalytic readings of Jakobson's formative work.[12] Nicholson, however, cites the literary theorist Eugenio Donato's usage, which posits metonymic displacement as an operation that produces the fiction by which museums sustain themselves as representational totalities. In a chapter on Gustave Flaubert's novel *Bouvard et Pécuchet*, Donato argues that classificatory systems never adequately represent the world, because they attempt to homogenize the irreducible heterogeneity of its constituent parts, displacing the singularity of those parts in the process.[13] The anxiety that Nicholson and Donato share hinges on the perception that a museum's classificatory system mutes the diversity that gives the items their dynamism. For Nicholson, that prior vitality explicitly relates to sexualized objects, which he believes the archive somehow sanitizes. Donato works at a more abstract, generalizable level when he invokes a Derridean problematic to question any claim that would suggest an archive has the power to stabilize the fraught relationship between a singular object and its place in the collection.[14] He argues that an archival institution — including the "Library" and the "Museum," both of which he capitalizes to indicate their prototypical status in his reading — imposes "the impossibility of reaching its order, its totality, or its truth."[15] For him, the museum requires critical demystification because it undermines the value of individual objects and because it disavows the vicissitudes that disrupt classificatory order.

Donato's theory exposes the limit of any archival project that seeks to organize its holdings into an ontological hierarchy. Totalizing systems of classification cannot account for disorder in the form of decay, missing items in a series, the arrival of foreign objects, the potential for a single object to hold various indexical positions, or any of the limitless and unpredictable possibilities that the world may introduce to an archive. He overstates his case, however, when he suggests that a catalog extinguishes the life of its objects by abstracting each item in the series from its own particularity. Of course catalogs abstract particularities. But that process erases the dynamism of a heterogeneous collection only if we misunderstand an object's value as the product of classification. Barring against that misunderstanding, Donato forgets that a catalog not only organizes a collection but also provides access to it. A catalog necessarily opens the collection it orders to the disorder of a world that it cannot replicate. The inability to satisfactorily represent the world according to a spatial arrangement may be, for that reason, the function of an archive's potential rather than its failure. Admittedly, Donato's deconstructive reading of the museum supposes a model archival institution, allowing him to sidestep some of the more practical problems facing archival institutions. That elision underestimates the suppleness of actual cataloging technologies, which often find ways to account for the outside world even if they account for it at the limits of representation rather than through the mastery of representation.

Despite any tendency to idealize catalogs as totalizing technologies, the concept of metonymic displacement helps identify the abstract processes that structure archives as virtual as well as physical spaces. By introducing an *outside* to the understanding of an archive's internal operations, Nicholson and Donato specify the dichotomous configurations that lead to a fantasy of archival space as dead space. In short, they formalize the equivalencies that organize life, sexual allure, and objects on the outside, while placing death, sexual stagnation, and serialized records on the inside of the archive. The inevitable failure of the inside to represent the outside explains why Nicholson, for example, finds sex museums "unsatisfactory and disappointing."[16] They cannot reproduce the excitement of his childhood experience reading girlie mags under the bed sheets or his adult experience recovering pornography from the trash bin, precisely because they create a socially legitimate space for "high-minded speculation about sexuality and culture."[17] Systematized archives and cataloged museums, for Nicholson, confer upon the study of pornography exactly the sort of intellectual authority that Barré hoped to reserve when he insisted that the secret museum's holdings were as cold to him as corpses.

That authority took a long century to accrue over the grave of indecency. Nonetheless, the historical trajectory from anxiety-ridden pronouncements of professionalism at the end of the nineteenth century to the disaffected indifference toward public sex collections at the beginning of the twenty-first century dramatizes the shift in imagination that produced pornography as a body of knowledge, if necessarily a contentious one. Only one of many struggles surrounding the study of pornography, the dialectic between live sex and dead archives animates the critical imagination as it attempts to manage the seemingly self-canceling attributes of sexual materials: their potential to produce pleasure and their potential to produce knowledge. That dialectic animates the library scene in Story of O as sexual education anathematizes books as "dead leaves"; it informs early justifications for cataloging erotic statues as if anatomizing cadavers; it haunts contemporary sex museums that kill the allure of their holdings in order to encourage intellectual speculation; and it also structures recent debates within academic porn studies about the collection, preservation, and transmission of pornographic materials.

*Negotiating the Archive*

Up to this point I have avoided asking the most basic question facing librarians in the age of relaxed censorship following the Grove Press cases: should we collect pornography? Before addressing the factors complicating that question from the institutional end of discussion, I want to elaborate a set of tensions structuring the archive as an imaginary space. Those tensions inform a substantive rift between different perspectives within porn studies. We find, on the one hand, an imperative to archive pornography as an identifiable body of knowledge. On the other hand, the idea that cataloging pornography renders it somehow unpornographic leads to the conclusion that archival projects are doomed to irrelevance, if not failure. To call the rift a debate may be misleading insofar as the perspectives on pornography's relationship to archival conservation hardly speak to one another. Introducing aspects of the discourse on pornography from library and information science will help lessen the gap between positions, in part because library science has produced a sophisticated understanding of the archive that neither idealizes nor forgets its material form.

To understand the most difficult challenge of constituting a porn archive we must move away from deconstructive treatments of representation and taxonomy toward a Foucauldian approach that understands pornography as itself a social structure. Frances Ferguson elaborates that theory in her book *Pornography, the Theory: What Utilitarianism Did to Action* by drawing a parallel between pornography and evaluative social structures developed by utilitarian thinkers, including Jeremy Bentham (whom Foucault famously critiques in *Discipline and Punish*).[18] The main thread of Ferguson's argument develops a positive reading of utilitarianism that suggests that pornography, much like a spelling bee or an athletic competition, undermines identity-based privileges by assigning value to performance within the context of the predetermined rules of the field. Her complex theory of pornography strays from the most familiar definitions, and I cannot do justice to all its nuances here. However, I want to pay special attention to one of the more unusual aspects of Ferguson's analysis—the sidelining of content.

Her avowed disinterest in the subject matter and substance of the books she reads leads her to insist that pornography necessarily eludes the archive. As she explains, during the late eighteenth century, "the content of pornography became less and less important and the development of a context (or environment) that amounts to a representational technology assumed center stage."[19] In other words, pornography emerges as a representational form rather than as a distinct subject. Ferguson argues throughout the book that representations need not cause offense or even involve sexually explicit content to count as pornography by her definition.[20] Rather, a representation must cause some demonstrable harm—usually in the form of sexual harassment—that excludes someone from participating, for example, in workplace or school activities. Can a dirty magazine still cause harm after it's taken out of the office and put into an archive? How do libraries collect pornography if removing a representation from its immediate context changes its status as pornography? While Ferguson may not have any interest in library acquisition policies, her account demands consideration here because it produces a problem for porn studies insofar as it insists on the radical ephemerality of pornography. Defined by the uses to which it is put, pornography cannot be possessed as one possesses a copy of *Story of O*. The pornographic object recedes along with the possibility of pornography as a form of material knowledge.

Ferguson emphasizes historical distance rather than context, but she and Nicholson both remain skeptical about the status of porn in academic hands because they define it against presumably innocuous scholarly interests. As Ferguson explains, the objects of her study, all from centuries past, now seem "distant and inoffensive—in short, historical and/or scholarly."[21] Even without agreeing on what designates pornography as pornography, both writers seem to agree that once a text assumes the pall of scholarly detachment it cannot retain its pornographic qualities. Ferguson diverges from Nicholson, however, when she concludes that the transmission of pornography, from one generation to the next or from one context to another, presents a theoretical *and* a material impossibility. She writes:

> If it doesn't feel contemporaneous, it isn't pornography. Pornography brooks no stance involving historical distance. This is a point made obvious in the way that video stores that specialize in hard-core rentals treat their own stock. Aside from a very small number of "classics," pornography doesn't seem to them worth preserving; the tape is frequently more valuable to them than the images on it, and they substitute new images for old with great alacrity. In that, it seems to me that they are on to something about pornography that scholars like Walter Kendrick miss. When Kendrick talks about a "secret museum" containing historical pornography, he ignores the fact that the difficulty of compiling a museum or archive is not that untold images have been lost under the pressure of censorship. Rather, untold images have been lost because they didn't seem worth saving to some of the very persons who had been their most enthusiastic admirers.[22]

The empirical evidence supporting Ferguson's understanding of the challenges surrounding the creation of an archive goes further than placing pornography on the trash heap—it erases the historical record of pornography.

To understand the space of an archive we must understand the material vulnerability that Ferguson indicates in her example. However, while that example allows for a strong critique of Kendrick's overestimation of censorial power, it trades on an understanding of porn that ignores the institutions—whether courts, libraries, or publishing houses—that earmark objects as pornographic. That blind spot forecloses any account of how those institutions consecrate pornography's scholarly value and, conversely, any account of how pornography shapes institutions. We must stipulate that, even when they coincide with one another, consuming and collecting porn do not amount to precisely the same thing. Despite any presumed indifference on the part of the consumers originally targeted by material culture, archives of all sorts do exist. That said, we should take Ferguson's example seriously because it shows that archives exist at the limits of their ability to represent the entirety of even clearly demarcated fields. Archives are in fact always partial.

For a theorist interested in social institutions, it seems surprising that Ferguson would not acknowledge that, apart from commercial determinations of value, scholarly institutions have decided in the past and may decide again in the future that pornography is worth preserving, even if such institutions operate on a comparatively limited scale. Williams, on the contrary, has not failed to recognize the potential for nor the fact of porn archives. Writing from a very different perspective, with significantly more commitment to porn studies as an academic field, Williams positions the archive as a necessary foundation for the study of an orphaned history of sexuality and American film. Although her disciplinary background determines the context in which she discusses archives, her insistence on the need to archive pornography impacts the developing field of porn studies as a whole. To the extent that it addresses questions of access and administration, Williams's exhortation to conserve touches on key questions for institutional archives regardless of the media any particular collection features. Anyone researching pornography should be generally sympathetic to the archival imperative when she articulates it as a principle of access: "Any archive, even a sex film archive, exists in order to be preserved and for its contents to be made available to those interested in its materials."[23] In contrasting Williams to Ferguson, however, I do not mean to suggest one as a corrective to the other. Instead I intend to draw attention to the different conceptions of pornography that allow for two different understandings of how an archive exists, if it exists at all.

Ferguson's and Williams's theories of pornography share some basic features: they both think of porn as a technology that enforces visibility; they both use Foucault to theorize that aspect of porn's work; and they both think of pornography as essentially representational. Where Ferguson tries to account for how such representations raise questions about the justice of social recognition, however, Williams argues that they mediate between knowledge and pleasure.[24] In Williams's account, pornography becomes the site at which the experience of pleasure and the production of knowledge interpenetrate to form a generative loop. Perhaps the most important difference between the two theories is also the most obvious: film stands out as the primary technology of representation for Williams. Cameras, magic lanterns, zoetropes, kinetographs, kinetoscopes, and other precursors to present-day movies produced a "new larger-than-life, projected film body" that heightened visibility.[25] Film put the body on display in such a way that its movements could be stopped, slowed, played backward, reconstituted, and endlessly repeated. For Williams, then, the document assumes a central role in the development of pornography. Porn must exist in a material form that can reliably repeat, for different audiences in different contexts, the same visual manifestation of bodies.

The centrality of the pornographic document as a mediating technology underpins Williams's interpretation in *Hard Core* of stag films and 1970s mainstream hard-core films. To characterize it broadly, that seminal study sought to stabilize uncertain documents of visual pleasure as a form of knowledge by contextualizing porn's history and its critical significance. In more recent work, she has pursued that project by advocating for the development of pornography archives that will make sexually explicit materials more accessible to scholarship. For example, speaking from the vantage point of the Kinsey Institute, our most extensive archive of sex materials, Williams concludes: "It is no longer enough to be able to view stag films on Kinsey Institute premises at Indiana University in private screenings. The stag film heritage needs the collaboration of scholars and archivists to preserve and study a body of work that has been far too long neglected."[26] Her concluding comments focus on the production of a DVD of those stag films housed at the Kinsey Institute, a project that fell through due to Indiana University's anxieties over copyright. Williams's imperative to archive, then, treats access to the archive in its secondary effect of circulating the materials it contains.

Although vital to the field of porn and film studies, this imperative moves too quickly away from the space and the materiality of the archive itself, which in turn deemphasizes the importance of the technological conditions that produced the movies in question. Part of the advantage of archives and special collections is that they preserve representations in their original material forms even if their original material contexts no longer exist. In doing so, they mark the difference between 16 mm and 8 mm film, vanity publications and commercial publications, collectors' editions and penny papers—distinctions that have been instrumental in reconstructing the history of pornography's institutional reception. The space of the archive also poses another advantage, intimately linked to the materiality of its holdings, in that it reminds us of the vulnerability of any archival project. Archivists cannot define pornography better than anyone else, cannot collect the entirety of whatever they do define as pornographic, and oftentimes cannot catalog everything they manage to collect. Once an archive does enter materials into a catalog (thereby making them accessible to the public), those materials become more vulnerable to deterioration, damage, vandalism, and theft at the hands of the people using the collection. Rather than presenting the greatest challenge to constructing an archive, however, the material vulnerability of its holdings makes apparent one of the ways in which the archive is most alive.

## The Living Library

By suggesting that the archive has living characteristics, I go against the grain of the critical and literary imagination. Instead, I follow the majority of modern library and information scientists who base their philosophy on S. R. Ranganathan's five laws of library science, the last of which proposes that the library is a living, growing organism. As he explains in his foundational treatise, first published in 1931:

> It is an accepted biological fact that a growing organism alone will survive. An organism which ceases to grow will petrify and perish. The Fifth Law invites our attention to the fact that the library, as an institution, has all the attributes of a growing organism. A growing organism takes in new matter, casts off old matter, changes in size and takes new shapes and forms. Apart from sudden and apparently discontinuous changes involved in metamorphosis, it is also subject to a slow continuous change which leads to what is known as "variation," in biological parlance, and to the evolution of new forms.[27]

Ranganathan, unlike most writers theorizing the archive outside of library science, tells us of the vital characteristics of a practicing archival institution and explains how they govern the organization of archival space. As a growing organism, the library does not serve as a stable foundation prior to a field of study. Rather, it gathers in a single physical space objects from various fields foreign to each other and juxtaposes them according to a mutual classificatory order. If that order does not adequately represent a totality outside itself, it provides instead a space wherein society confronts the limits of self-representation and self-knowledge. Librarians in the United States, during a twenty-five-year period of post–Second World War social change, rethought the space of the archive to better accommodate sexual materials, especially pornographic print materials. When collected, those materials testify to the importance of sexuality within the institutions that house them.

The debates among librarians about whether or not to archive pornography depend on a distinction between the library as an institution and the library's holdings. Different conceptions of the institutional role of the library determine what sort of holdings it should make available to the public. As Martha Cornog and Timothy Perper explain in the introduction to Libraries, Erotica, Pornography, librarians have fluctuated between understanding the library as a custodial institution of public tastes and an institution in service of intellectual freedom.[28] While that distinction should not be understood as self-evident or unproblematic, it has nonetheless structured debates about collecting sexual materials. In the wake of decensoring print, the general trend has been a shift toward understanding libraries as serving the interests of intellectual freedom. The problem of pornography, however, has highlighted the limitations of that trend. In 1966, for instance, following several decades of obscenity trials, Kathleen Molz lamented that "librarians have traditionally placed a greater reliance in these matters on the literature of jurisprudence than on the literature of criticism, for pornography is essentially an aesthetic, not juridical, problem."[29] Citing Story of O, among other novels, as an example of "high pornography," she suggests that academic and literary critics have a responsibility to identify the "inherent tawdriness of much modern fiction."[30] Using the rhetoric of artistic taste—as opposed to obscenity, morality, or harm—she concludes that libraries should focus on traditionally valued works of literature rather than subcultural interests.

At about the same time, Dan Lacy published an article arguing that public pressure accounted for the exclusion of pornography from libraries more often than collection policies.[31] Responses to Molz's reservations about standards of literary value can be articulated in the form of a social and ideological argument. For example, in 1971 Bill Katz asked, "Why shouldn't the larger public libraries have a section devoted to pornography?"[32] In answer to his own question, he argues that libraries absolutely should include some so-called controversial materials in the interest of democracy. Shifting tone from the political toward the social, he concludes that collecting pornography "would be a move toward the future before the future caught up with and passed the library."[33] In these formulations, the library constitutes less a reflection or a foundation of the society it serves than an idealized organization of its various factions. The marginal factions either drop out because they don't constitute enough of a demand or, more liberally, they constitute a future audience that the library must serve if it wishes to remain relevant.

One outcome of the intensified debate—within library science as well as other academic, professional, and social fields—was an increase in printed material about pornography. Regardless of the various positions on the matter, a discourse on pornography increasingly came on/scene, as Williams would put it, and libraries could not ignore the growing body of literature. As Cornog and Perper explain, "If public debate exists, then a need to know exists, and that is what libraries are for: to provide relevant material to all sides in the debate."[34] How exactly to provide those materials, however, became the focal point of efforts to rethink the space of the archive. By the mid-1980s, librarians realized that available methods inadequately provided access to the sexual materials that had come into the forum of public debate. In efforts to increase access, they began formulating ways to update cataloging systems and shelving practices to help avoid "bibliocide."[35]

Those efforts, however, had to arbitrate between two competing concerns—the desire to maximize intellectual and physical access while protecting the integrity of their holdings. Much as the imaginary space of the catalog shaped the physical space of the museum in the earliest instances of "pornography" archives, now both Dewey Decimal Classification and Library of Congress Classification dictate the actual shelf location as well as the grouping of books. How a book gets cataloged determines how accessible it will be to people searching for sex materials; whether it falls under erotica or pornography, whether it gets grouped with traditionally pathologized or traditionally normative sexual behaviors, whether it sits next to other books about sexuality, or whether it ends up with the books on librarianship all depend on how the catalog, or the cataloger, inscribes the acquisition. Not surprisingly, different libraries handle the catalog in different ways, sometimes supplementing it with bibliographies or vertical files, depending on the size of the collection, the needs of the library's patrons, and its institutional function.[36]

Despite different approaches to intellectual access, every library has to face similar questions about physical access that recall the infamous Private Case at the British Museum Library and L'Enfer at the Bibliothèque nationale de France. Should sexually explicit materials be segregated from the general collection? If considerations of that question from the eighteenth century to the early twentieth revolved around questions of morality and anxiety about the impressionable minds of ungentlemanly patrons, certainly traces of those concerns showed up in more-recent deliberations over physical access to sexual materials. However, by the mid-1980s, professional discourses focused on the competing interests of convenience for patrons versus protection for the materials.

A remarkable number of librarians met the obligation to collect sexual materials with exasperated objections that such materials inevitably suffer from damage, vandalism, or theft.[37] Their objections were not unfounded. A

1987 survey of what happens when libraries subscribe to *Playboy* revealed that in many cases they experienced negative reaction from staff members who apparently had to retrieve copies from men's bathrooms, clean fresh semen from the pages, and struggle to keep the periodical shelves in order. As one respondent explained, "Paper copies lost much weight in the form of photos of nubile young women. They even mutilated the microfilm. . . . Why? They weren't even in color!"[38] The physical instability of sexual materials takes the forefront in weighing the pros and cons of collecting pornography. Many of the libraries surveyed did continue to collect *Playboy*, but they sacrificed patron convenience by keeping it on reserve behind the circulation desk or by making it available only as a microfiche copy.

That strategy for protecting the holdings follows in a long archival tradition of prioritizing material preservation over circulation. In the case of pornography, however, there is at least one key difference. Responses to the vandalism of sexually explicit materials are inconsistent with responses to the vandalism of other holdings, even though all holdings stored in open stacks remain equally vulnerable. As Cornog and Perper write, sexuality collections in general "pose special problems in security and preservation."[39] In fact, browsing the limited collection of critical works on pornography available at my home institution, I found a copy of *Dirty Looks: Women, Pornography, Power* damaged by a semen stain that prevents interested parties from reading the entirety of Chris Straayer's article on Annie Sprinkle (see figure 4.1). I also came across a copy of Wendy McElroy's book *XXX: A Woman's Right to Pornography* defaced with this defiant counterclaim scribbled over the preface: "LIAR. PORNO IS SEXISM." Less abrasive, perhaps, but equally distracting are extensive marginal comments criticizing every one of Laura Kipnis's claims in the introduction to *Bound and Gagged*. How does one understand the insistent marks of these library vandals, some of which are, admittedly, more immediately legible than others?

While some librarians take such vandalism as an affront to their work as custodians of public texts, critical scholars of pornography might just as easily understand them as acts of protest against their research. Cornog, however, offers a more remarkable interpretation that makes such instances of material defacement speak to the living characteristics of an archive: "Almost by definition, vandalized material is popular material, so much in demand that patrons will transgress the usual rules of the library and society to possess it. Theoretically, at least, librarians should be delighted to possess such items because they draw people into the library. And from that viewpoint, reasonable responses to vandalism are buying more copies (print and/or fiche), making photocopies of popular selections, and restricting the rate or duration or privacy of use through limited circulation or a reserve room sys-

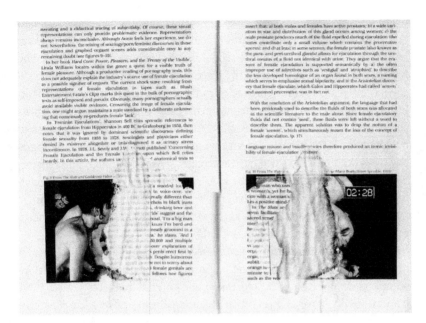

4.1. Damaged pages of Dirty Looks: Women, Pornography, Power, edited by Pamela Church Gibson and Roma Gibson. This copy belongs to the University at Buffalo's Lockwood Library.

tem."[40] In other words, if we accept the aphorism that many hands make dirty books, we can move beyond censorship to considerations of regulation and circulation.[41] Cornog does just that by providing a rationale for increasing the circulation of controversial materials, rather than locking them up, on the practical grounds of increasing the social function of an archive.[42] Equally important for understanding archival space is the ability to read patron use in the marks that readers leave behind them, whether that use amounts to protest, study, recreation, or sexual fulfillment. Just as a cataloging system juxtaposes unlike materials in a single space, the material archive places a semen stain, antiporn sloganeering, and study notes on a plain of equivalency so that each speaks to how readers negotiate, engage, and contest the formal organization of sexual knowledge. Needless to say, the sort of engagement such vandalism represents depends on the material manifestation of an archive.

The space of the archive as a social institution requires both a physical location and material holdings in order to provide patrons with the opportunity to engage to the fullest extent the bodies of knowledge that the archive organizes, not to mention the chance to engage with the other bodies that any archive draws into its space. For that reason, the availability of library materials to physical defacement and decay at the hands of their most passionate readers—what we might judge as their very instability as material—stands as one of the most important features of a living library. This does not begin to answer the question of whether we should or should not archive pornography. Rather, it begins to understand the place of pornography and other sexually explicit materials in the archive as opening toward negotiations of sexuality in a social institution that, by various turns, bears the stereotype of complete asexuality or fantastical hypersexuality.[43] By better understanding the various polemics and institutional contests that have included or excluded pornography from the archive, we will have a stronger sense of pornography's history and a better understanding of the history of the social institutions regulating it. Pornography's place in the archive speaks to shifts and fragments in public opinion at the same time as it speaks to librarians' critical responses to those changes.

In the move from serving as guardians of public decency to crusaders for intellectual freedom in the second half of the twentieth century, archival institutions amount to neither repressive nor progressive forces per se. These institutions do, however, ground the changing ideological terms in a material practice of collection and dissemination that demonstrates the limited efficacy of society's attempts at representing itself to itself. The archive does not, as some suppose, constitute a technology that provides unmediated contact with the past.[44] The archive does, however, provide a unique space in which we can begin to understand the material articulations and contestations that reorder how various social fields produce sexual knowledge. To the extent that institutions heed the imperative to collect porn, whoever uses those collections should heed the correlative imperative to examine the power that the archive has to administer the study of pornography.

## Notes

I owe many thanks for the help and encouragement I received while writing this chapter. Tim Dean offered his astute editorial advice and corroborative anecdotes during every stage of the writing process. Linda Williams provided encouraging feedback during the initial drafting stages. Steven Ruszczycky and Allison Siehnel talked me through some of the thornier theoretical aspects of my research. Finally, Caitlin Shanley patiently entertained my interest in her profession, providing me with a crucial foothold in unfamiliar territory.

1. In 1962 Grove's edition of *Naked Lunch* also went to trial in Boston for obscenity. The Massachusetts Supreme Court reversed the lower court's decision in 1966, lifting a ban on the grounds of the novel's apparent social value. For an account of the legal and literary history of that period, see Glass, "Redeeming Value." My reading of Réage is indebted to his scholarship on Grove Press.

2. Eliot Fremont-Smith, "The Uses of Pornography," *New York Times*, March 2, 1966, 39.

3. L. Williams, *Hard Core* (1999), 48–49. Williams traces the history of hard-core pornography back to the advent of moving motion images.

4. Moore, "Broadening Concerns for Intellectual Freedom." Citing *Story of O* along with several other Grove Press publications as examples of controversial books deemed "to have merit and value," Moore describes a newly felt freedom from concerns about the legality of such books. He writes, "Librarians are recognizing the necessity—and the privilege—of basing selection on critical judgment rather than on satisfaction of popular demand" (311). The opposition between demand and judgment registers a professional awareness of the critical turn toward rethinking acquisition policies in light of deregulation. It also marks a tendency to articulate such debates in terms of taste before access.

5. American Library Association, "Mission & Priorities." American Library Association, accessed March 19, 2014, http://www.ala.org/aboutala/missionpriorities. Almost every library has a mission statement available for patron review. The American Library Association's basic mission exemplifies the field as a whole in its emphasis on fostering librarianship with the intent to "enhance learning and ensure access to information for all."

6. Internet access in libraries has heightened situations in which employees feel sexually threatened. In 2003, for example, a dozen Minneapolis Public Library employees filed suit against their employer for providing patrons with unfiltered access to online pornography. They settled the case outside of court and, as cited in a legal memorandum by Janet M. LaRue, the Minneapolis Public Library acknowledged in a public statement the importance of finding a structural "balance between allowing the public access to lawful materials and protecting its employees" (2). See Janet LaRue, "Library Procedures for Disabling Software Filtering and Unblocking Web Sites," Concerned Women for America, August 25, 2003, accessed March 19, 2014, http://www.plan2succeed.org/.

7. Strout, "The Development of the Catalog and Cataloging Codes," 270. She names *Nomenclator*, published in 1595 by Leiden University, as the first catalog printed by an institutional library.

8. Kendrick, *The Secret Museum*, 16.

9. Barré quoted in Kendrick, *The Secret Museum*, 15.

10. Nicholson, *Sex Collectors*, 33.

11. Nicholson, *Sex Collectors*, 34.

12. For more on the background and development of metonymic displacement, see Dean, *Beyond Sexuality*. Chapter 5, "Bodies That Mutter," offers a concise explanation of how Lacan revised Jakobson's models of metaphor and metonymy to develop "the implications of Freud's account of 'dream-work' in rhetorical terms" (179).

13. Donato, "The Museum's Furnace," 64.

14. Donato's article precedes Jacques Derrida's book-length essay *Archive Fever*. Nonetheless, Derrida's interest in the relationship between memory and representation informs Donato's use of deconstruction to formulate the modern museum as a failed archival project. *Archive Fever* adds that the failure to reconcile memory with an accurate representation of the past conditions the possibility of a future that avoids simply repeating the past.

15. Donato, "The Museum's Furnace," 58.

16. Nicholson, *Sex Collectors*, 28.

17. Nicholson, *Sex Collectors*, 30.

18. Foucault, *Discipline and Punish*, 195–230.

19. Ferguson, *Pornography, the Theory*, 2.

20. This point presents a certain difficulty for understanding what specifies pornography. What, for example, distinguishes pornography from any other method of causing an individual harm? Would prayer in public schools count as pornographic because, as she writes about pornography, it "might be used to deny an individual access to the value-enhancing activities" of the social structure (xvi)? My understanding is that Ferguson's theory would not in fact consider prayer pornographic unless it denied access on sexual grounds, either by salacious innuendo or by hierarchizing bodies according to sexed distinctions. I would argue that despite minimizing the importance of sexual content her theorization of pornography depends on the particularity of sex.

21. Ferguson, *Pornography, the Theory*, 153.

22. Ferguson, *Pornography, the Theory*, 152.

23. L. Williams, "'White Slavery' versus the Ethnography of 'Sexworkers,'" 128.

24. L. Williams, *Hard Core* (1999), 3.

25. L. Williams, *Hard Core* (1999), 45.

26. L. Williams, "'White Slavery' versus the Ethnography of 'Sexworkers,'" 135.

27. Ranganathan, *The Five Laws of Library Science*, 383.

28. Cornog and Perper, "For Sex, See Librarian."

29. Molz, "The Public Custody of the High Pornography," 99.

30. Molz, "The Public Custody of the High Pornography," 100.

31. Lacy, "Censorship and Obscenity," 474.

32. Katz, "The Pornography Collection," 4064.

33. Katz, "The Pornography Collection," 4064.

34. Cornog and Perper, "For Sex, See Librarian," 26.

35. Cataloging can present challenges to access even after materials enter the library system. An anecdote about *Tales of Times Square* illustrates one difficulty: "Although its chapters deal with such topics as stripteasers, prostitutes, and peep shows—in short, the sex industry—LC [Library of Congress] classed it as 974.71, a 'New York' notation appropriate for history and civilization books." The cataloger Sanford Berman describes the mistake as "bibliocide by cataloging" because it effectively obscured the book's content from anyone looking for information about the sex industry. Even still, however, many libraries physically segregate adult materials by placing them in special collections or on reserve. Quoted in Cornog, "Providing Access to Materials on Sexuality," 169.

36. Cornog and Perper, "For Sex, See Librarian," 14. Surveys have indicated that university, school, and public librarians each provide different levels of access to sexual materials. Even within the university, social science librarians tend to be more liberal in their treatment of sex materials than those in the humanities, who in turn tend to be more liberal than librarians in the sciences.

37. Cornog, "What Happens When Libraries Subscribe to *Playboy*?," 149.

38. Cornog, "What Happens When Libraries Subscribe to *Playboy*?," 159.

39. Cornog and Perper, "For Sex, See Librarian," 26.

40. Cornog, "What Happens When Libraries Subscribe to *Playboy*?," 158.

41. Coutt, "Perverted Proverbs," 126.

42. This reading of library vandalism does not advocate for the abandonment of DVD projects such as the one the Kinsey Institute had planned. Nor does it recommend careless gambling with precious materials. An anecdote from Gershon Legman's experience at the Private Case illustrates the outdated and naive elitism such a position would as-

sume. During his time researching at the British Library he met a fellow researcher who walked out of the archive with several valuable manuscripts. In astonishment, Legman asked if they don't check briefcases, to which the man replied, "Anybody who uses the British Museum is *a gentleman and a scholar*." The lesson is that circulating *all* controversial materials without consideration of their value or replaceability would no more contribute to the archive's function than would circulating all holdings in general. See Legman, "The Lure of the Forbidden," 59.

43. For a brief account of the sexy librarian stereotype, see Indiana, "In the Stacks and in the Sack."

44. Kendrick, *The Secret Museum*, 5. Kendrick suggests that the excavation of Pompeii fascinated the British because it offered them "the compelling spectacle of an unmediated vision." That assertion contradicts the history of Pompeii catalogs, which he demonstrates to be highly mediated forms for transmitting sexual knowledge from antiquity to modernity.

# PART II

Historical Archives

# 5

## "A Quantity of Offensive Matter":
## Private Cases in Public Places

*Jennifer Burns Bright and Ronan Crowley*

The British Museum has a strict duty to preserve objects—even pornographic ones—
for posterity. A historic object isn't any less historic because it causes offence, and
the guardians of our cultural heritage can't suddenly start behaving like the Taliban.
So exactly how much controversial material has the museum collected? What's on
Her Majesty's top shelf?
—Tony Barrell, "Rude Britannia"

Pornographic material in the preserve of institutional repositories is an old
battle, not a new insurgency, in the campaign to document cultural memory.
From aficionados of erotica to critics in the field of porn studies, readers face
a number of challenges, not the least of which is the rarity of the undervalued,
often reviled, poorly produced, and ill-preserved materials that constitute the
porn archives. As Patrick Kearney observes, any collector of a "respectable"
modern writer could find copies of just about anything published, had the collector the means; that said, "all the money in Christendom won't produce a
copy of something like *There's a Whip in My Valise* to order."[1] Moreover, because
of policies that withheld such volumes from library catalogs for much of the
twentieth century, the issue is as much one of access and morally guided conceptions of value as it is one of the perceived limits of an institution's mandate
for cultural preservation.

Long before Internet pornography, the Children's Internet Protection Act
(CIPA), and the privacy desk, libraries and museums employed a very different battery of filters to regulate and to organize the pornographic material
that came into their collections.[2] The British Museum Library had its Private
Case, Suppressed Safe, and Cupboard; the Bibliothèque nationale de France
its L'Enfer (Inferno).[3] The Library of Congress maintained a Delta Collection
for dirty books, appending the Greek letter to the catalog cards of such volumes, and the Bodleian Library at Oxford used the Greek letter phi, mimick-
ing, it is said, the sound a reader might make upon discovering them.[4] The

Widener Library at Harvard marked its erotica with the designation "Inferno" (later "I°"), while the New York Public Library opted instead for an approving five stars.[5] The Chicago Public Library, according to one reporter, kept even scholarly studies of sex under lock and key, requiring patrons to "fill out a form designed to convince the librarians you are not a sex maniac."[6] Acquisitions librarians at Trinity College Library Dublin, caught between the Scylla of legal-deposit provisions and the Charybdis of restrictive censorship legislation enacted in the wake of Irish independence—what one commentator defended as a "tiny segregation of a little pornography"—were obliged to apply to the minister for justice in respect of prohibited titles.[7] The surviving import permits carry ministerial seals and stipulate that "the said publications will be placed in a special press [that is, a closet] in the room of the Librarian of Trinity College, Dublin, and will not be issued to readers except with the personal permission of the Librarian."[8]

Few, if any, of these systems and stowaways are still in use. Accession policies vary enormously from institution to institution, and, even within a single repository, the treatment of pornography weaves a tangled history from the warp and weft of political change, advances in library science and archival studies, and Comstockery in all its hues and textures.[9] This chapter focuses on the historical practices that libraries, in particular, employed to moderate access to sexually explicit, restricted items. While holdings that were once cordoned off have now largely been integrated into general collections, the press-marks and shelf numbers of their former confinement serving as curios for the attentive reader, a new set of restrictions has sprung up to moderate the consultation of pornography in the library. Surrounded by other professional readers of rare books and manuscripts, scholars not incurious of their fellows' projects, and monitored by the watchful eye of staff, the sex researcher in the modern library stages the consumption of pornography. Under these conditions, even the most stalwart and sex-positive scholar viewing a stack of explicit images can be distracted, if not intimidated outright, by a system designed, in fairness, to safeguard against the defacement, mutilation, or theft of library holdings. Certainly, the scholar is conscious—indeed, self-conscious—of public consumption of that most intimate of private goods: pornography.

While economic theory divides public and private along lines of rivalry and excludability, the library—in particular, pornography in the library—is the locus of several very different senses of the distinction. Public libraries are generally distinguished from private by being maintained out of public funds and by a catholic policy of access; in the older British universities, however, public library is an obsolete denotation for a library whose inclusiveness extends only to all members of the university. In the United States, by contrast, even private libraries that have been granted Federal Depository Library Program status must allow the general public access to federal government publications. These niceties of internal distinction aside, the institutional library appears irrevocably public when juxtaposed with an individual's "private shelf." For Emerson, a visit to Cambridge Library was the occasion for "renewing the conviction that the best of it all is already within the four walls of my study at home. The inspection of the catalogue brings me continually back to the few standard writers who are on every private shelf; and to these it can afford only the most slight and casual additions."[10] From private shelves of volumes for frequent consultation to the closed stacks of the library, public and private in the study and the institution alike are understood in spatial terms as distinct zones. The boundaries between garret and reading room, closed and open stacks, are porous, continually traversed in the everyday circulation of books, but spatially distinct nonetheless. It is in the institutional treatment of sexually explicit material, however—material often conspicuous for its noncirculation—that the fraught history of the commerce between public and private, the commerce between *publics*, begins to emerge.

This chapter traces the commute of pornography from secluded print material to its highly visible latter-day consultation at designated library desks and Internet portals; such a trajectory, however, is irreducible to the gradual amelioration of benighted social attitudes within a singularly conceived public. Rather, successive phases in the life of the porn archive correspond to discrete publics, each of which has its own activity and duration and, as Michael Warner argues, which "act historically according to the temporality of their circulation."[11] Insofar as the diabolical element common to the Bibliothèque nationale de France and the Widener Library suggests affinities beyond the nature of holdings, such collections can be read as "essentially intertextual, frameworks for understanding texts against an organized background of the circulation of other texts, all interwoven not just by citational references but by the incorporation of a reflexive circulatory field in the mode of address and consumption."[12] Warner notes that "publics have an ongoing life: one doesn't publish to them once and for all (as one does, say, to a scholarly archive)"; in the "ongoing life" of the porn archive, the putatively ephemeral is subject to variously straitened modes of circulation.[13] Even though earlier practices that were intended to stymie the circulation of sexual materials, and that strove to separate the "honest and legitimate" researcher from the "sex maniac," have given way to a broader platform of access, similarly relativistic, culturally shaped notions of propriety and prudery exist today for the documentarian who consults pornography.

Pornography has its place, quite literally, in the library. From the locked cupboards and out-of-bounds cabinets to the sentinels posted at consultation desks, pornography archives are couched in the rhetoric of disciplinary space. This is, at once, field specific as library science and regulatory or normalizing. Spatial dimensions—where pornography is deposited and how it circulates in institutional space—emerge time and again in the discourse surrounding this vexed subject matter, inviting analysis of how space acts to reinforce and to reinscribe traditional moral codes and how readers are affected by making pornography public, by pornographic publics.

As Walter Kendrick, among others, has shown, the taxonomy of sexually explicit material developed precisely in response to the problems of visibility and confinement: what to do with the scandalous finds that were being unearthed at Pompeii in the late eighteenth and early nineteenth centuries.[14] Originally a term for treatises on prostitution (Greek *porne graphia*), *pornography* in the modern sense can be attributed to the whores' guides of the seventeenth century, which parodied handbooks of rhetoric in instructing prostitutes how to traffic in willful delusion and lure customers.[15] By the time of Frederick William Fairholt's *A Dictionary of Terms in Art* (1854), the coinage had gained another nuance of visibility: "Licentious painting, employed to decorate the walls of rooms sacred to bacchanalian orgies, and of which examples exist in Pompeii."[16] Ten years later, a specialist usage became the acceptation when the editors of the 1864 *Webster's Dictionary* picked up Fairholt's definition.[17] "If Pompeii's priceless obscenities were to be properly managed," Kendrick observes, "they would have to be systematically named and placed. The name chosen for them was 'pornography,' and they were housed in the Secret Museum."[18]

In a not dissimilar vein, while obscenity carries first and foremost a legal valence, one widespread folk etymology, the Greek *ob skene* (offstage), circles the same issue of where to house or enact extreme material and actions— relegating violence and sexual atrocity to the wings. Equally, the demotic locution *top shelf* (as in "top-shelf magazines," for one) figures a body of writing in terms of its physical placement out of harm's way, though in the public eye, whether on the bookstand or the library shelf. Given the proportion of open-access collections to closed stacks in any library, invisibility is not, tout court, the grounds for classification as pornography. Rather, the library locates pornography in strictly defined, enclosed spaces, and a library silence surrounds these private cases. Their existence is denied; contents are out of sight; catalogs are off-limits.

The cloistered library has long been cast as a site of illicit or sexualized material in the popular imagination. To the continued consternation of the Vatican, the Holy See is reputed to house the world's largest collection of pornography, squirreled away in its catacomb vaults.[19] Even apocryphal collections, it seems, specify a spatial organization. Others, however, have created their own catacombs. Before 1964, when Trinity College Library Dublin implemented a changeover to an electronic system, the news that a book or journal had been banned in Ireland was greeted with the physical removal of its entry slip from the guard-book volumes of the *Accessions Catalogue*. As late as November 2008, bibliographic records for banned publications were suppressed from the college's public catalog. In 1962, the official guide to the British Museum Library was still misleading readers that "all books held by the Museum could be traced through the General Catalog."[20]

Pornography became a "closed stack" of privacy within the public archive, unreachable by the channels of circulation that normally provide access, but generative of another form of publicity: the public-relations problems that dogged holding institutions. From legal deposit occasioned by copyright legislation to the acquisition of personal collections compiled by a Henry Spencer Ashbee or a Ralph Whittington, pornography in the library is as much an uninvited by-product of the statute books or a consequence of other acquisitions as it is the outcome of systematic purchase or solicitous courting of the book fanciers.[21] When Ashbee bequeathed to the British Museum the library of many thousand volumes that he and his father had collected over the course of seventy years, a clause in his will stipulated that acceptance of the literary works brought with it "about 1000 books in 1600 vols. (exclusive of duplicates) of an erotic or obscene character."[22] The London *Daily Chronicle* chose to ignore the erotica, calling the bequest "one of the choicest 'windfalls' which our great national collection of books has received in modern times." Other accounts from the turn of the century acknowledged the sexual material, even as they glossed over its content with the occluding Latinate and Greek neologisms *facetiae* and *kruptadia*.[23]

A fissure in the project of the national archive, then, the valuation of pornography in the library also carries a telling class inflection. Victorian circulating libraries (Mudie's Select Library and W. H. Smith and Sons foremost among them) insisted on the "Higher Class of Books" for their stock, effectively policing the sexual literacy of their working-class readership.[24] In this instance, "Higher" cut out the top shelf. Pornography was relegated to ancient university libraries like the Bodleian and Cambridge University Library, and to the British Museum Library, all of which, as Lisa Sigel observes, "separated these collections from the rest of their materials through closed stacks under anachronistic call numbers. Even if the vigilant managed to find out about the collections, they could not look at them because of user restrictions."[25] As the erotic material in these closed stacks was not available to the public of library patrons, one might consider it private, but the knowledge of the collection formed a public of its very own. In the Anglophone world, perhaps the most famous of the closed-stack collections is the British Museum

5.1. David Roger, the deputy keeper of books at the British Museum, looks at books in the Private Case. Photograph by Tom King © Mirrorpix (1968).

Library's Private Case (see figure 5.1). Before its official closure in 1990, the Private Case housed works that were confirmed or supposed to be legally impermissible due to the obscenity laws that, prior to 1959, forbade ownership and distribution of pornographic material in Great Britain. And yet a small group of people knew about the Private Case and could use it. One such individual was Alfred Kinsey, who visited the British Museum in 1955 and left deeply disappointed by the confusing cataloging method in place, a method he called "a maze." In this instance, the public of the Private Case required a spatial orientation of privacy: " 'One way of finding anything erotic in the British Museum,' Kinsey observed wryly, 'is to look for anything upside-down or turned backwards. They [the curators] are exceedingly reticent about showing anything.' "[26]

The brainchild of Sir Anthony Panizzi, the fledgling Private Case collection was initially held in a cupboard kept in the keeper of printed books's office. The collection swelled considerably with the acquisition of the Ashbee bequest in 1900 and other donations later in the twentieth century.[27] G. K. Fortescue, keeper of the printed books at the time of the Ashbee bequest, noted to the trustees of the British Museum in his preliminary report that the bequest contained "a quantity of offensive matter which is of no value or interest and which could not possibly be distributed."[28] Some of this material was destroyed, dismissed as both worthless and unsuitable for circulation—two fundamental criteria for inclusion in an open public collection. Such an action was compliant with the national library's mission of individual and societal betterment. Over time the contents of the Private Case, some 3,100 volumes since the 1840s, were made available in a limited fashion to researchers demonstrably motivated by scholarly interest. Without listings in the public catalog that might serve as a finding aid, however, ascertaining precise holdings was a work of scholarship in itself. Libraries' reticence to make public their collection lists thus gave rise to a culture of patron-compiled bibliographies and catalogs, whose importance, Joseph W. Slade argues, is impossible to overstate.[29] The British Museum Library's stonewalling did more than create opportunities for justifying a new practice, offering a virgin territory to the bibliophile with archival interests; the library was also the site of struggles over the constitution and delimitation of an appropriate public for pornography in the library.[30]

Supporters and opponents of censorship in the Private Case drew swords as early as 1890, when Wilfred Ignatius Wilberforce, an offended nephew of a former employee of the library, approached Richard Garnett, keeper of printed books. To Wilberforce's complaint about the purchase of "immoral books," Garnett downplayed the size of the collection and articulated a policy that would hold through to the 1960s: objectionable volumes "are locked up [and] they are excluded from the catalogue and anyone wishing to consult any of them must undergo a cross-examination calculated to deter all but really honest and legitimate research."[31] Submission to cross-examination allowed Havelock Ellis to access Ashbee's collection in the early decades of the twentieth century. However, he shared his frustration with Montague Summers over the inaccessibility of a full listing of the material in the Private Case.[32] In an ironic turn, Ellis's own pioneering *Studies in the Psychology of Sex* became a matter of debate in 1913, as its sexual content placed it beyond public access. This censorship was brought to light in the first public acknowledgment of the Private Case's existence; E. S. P. Haynes, in *The English Review*, demanded that the British Museum Library's holdings be made available. This publicity ushered in a slight spatial reorganization when, in the spring of 1914, some forty-two works were moved from the Private Case to the general collection.[33]

Relegated to the Private Case, Ellis's work, along with that of fellow sex researchers Edward Carpenter and Margaret Sanger, became, like more-conventional pornography, the stock-in-trade of the semiclandestine booksellers who hawked books with sexual themes or suggestive titles through the mail.[34] Mail circulars became a crucial alternative distribution network for medical and psychological research on sex, by means of which dealers sold or lent materials to a narrow public. Advertisements in comic weeklies and trade journals ran under the colors of the rare-books trade, borrowing the legitimacy of a cognate market, and included in their euphemistic reach not merely quasi-pornographic gallantiana and notorious classics with sexual content; works disseminating information about conception and sexual behavior, penned by bona fide medical researchers and anthropologists, also made up the wares of the Victorian colporteur and, in the twenties and thirties, the New York booklegger.[35] Samuel Steward, a longtime collaborator of Kinsey, comments that he was able to purchase Freud's *Beyond the Pleasure Principle* and *The Interpretation of Dreams* from a confectioner in his boyhood home of Woodsfield, Ohio. He traces the provenance of his copy of Ellis's *Studies on the Psychology of Sex* to a traveling salesman, who discarded the volume in the Steward family's boardinghouse "after stealing it from the 'restricted' section of an Ohio library."[36] The integrity of the institutional collection could be challenged by an E. S. P. Haynes, but the delay with which the porn archives were reorganized gave rise to an altogether more punctual sphere of activity in the comic weeklies and trade journals.

Blurring generic categories and piggybacking on perceived value may have suited the sales tactics of the porn dealers; a similar conflation now obtains to the pornographic materials that survive in institutional repositories. In the British Museum Library, former Private Case volumes are issued in the Rare Books and Music Reading Room, to readers sitting at desks usually designated for rare-book consultation.[37] Holdings that formerly epitomized polarized conceptions of worth, prestige, and value—medieval and modern manuscripts on the one hand, and throwaway pornography on the other—are united in the library today by their singularity and fragility. For much of the porn archive, as Lesley Hall suggests, unique survivals belie the extent of original production.[38] Indeed, limited survival has made porn archives of porn libraries.

The British Museum Library, for example, has an incomplete run of the salacious threepenny *Bits of Fun*. Once housed in the Cupboard, the library owns what is perhaps the sole-surviving run of this interwar weekly. At the other end of the spectrum of cultural prestige, among the so-called Z-Safe items—the library's classification for its most fragile and most valuable manuscripts—are some sheets of notes that James Joyce compiled while writing *Ulysses* (1922). One of these sheets contains his verbatim cribbings from *Bits of Fun*, a list of hosiery items prepared for the hallucinatory fifteenth episode of the novel, "Circe."[39] Two documents, then, produced in the summer and fall of 1920, survive in the British Museum Library, each of which has a distinct history of acquisition, accession, cataloging, and storage that corresponds to its putative literary merit and perceived scandalousness but which belies shared textual content.

Indeed, the same year *Ulysses* was published, *The Library Journal* distributed a questionnaire on the subject of "questionable books in public libraries" to thirty-one public libraries and six state library commissions in the United States.[40] While American librarians tended to omit only those titles that had "no permanent informational or artistic value," excusing other objectionable books on the grounds of their difficulty for "the young and immature mind," their Irish counterparts were still resolutely cleaving to distinctions between art and obscenity.[41] In the spring of 1922, a relative of Joyce's called into Trinity College and was told that, although *Ulysses* had been received, the book had been the subject of no little consternation for the library. An assistant librarian informed the relative: "When we ordered a copy we thought it would be interesting to future Irish Students but found it was nothing but a *disconnected* story of gross obscenity and was not art. Had we known it was such a vile production we would not think of allowing it into the Library." He also said that "it was not catalogued and added that it would not be issued unless readers satisfied the librarian that they required it for special reasons."[42] Inasmuch as literary modernism successfully made the commute from the pillory to the classroom, pornography, in however limited a fashion, has begun to describe the same trajectory in recent years. For all the classification distinctions made in the British Museum Library between Joyce's working notes and one pornographic weekly, nowadays the contents of the Z-Safe and the former Cupboard alike are protected from patrons rather than, as formerly, the other way around. Siân Echard, writing of the fetishization of medieval manuscripts in modern archives, identifies such a tension between "the principle of access and the practicalities of implementation."[43] Nowhere is this relationship more forcibly played out than in the *condition* of pornography in the library. For it is the physical state of sexually explicit holdings—often singular witnesses that are faded, foxed, and suffering from edge wear—that increasingly determines scholars' access.

As institutional inertia gave way to pressure from a newly consolidated public of readers and researchers, the issue of access haunted the British Museum Library throughout the twentieth century. That public and its call for access underwent a fundamental shift as Britain, and the West more generally, opened its doors to the sexual revolution in the late 1960s. Scholarship, often the work of independent scholars or those on the periphery of academic institutions, was an important component of this change. Independent scholarship pushed the library out of its entrenched position of moralizing guardian of so-called objectionable books or, at best, of denying the existence of such material. Instead, libraries began to acknowledge the value of these holdings and, concomitantly, to recognize the need to preserve them. An editorial in the British *Library World* from 1922 argued: "We librarians do not like to pose as moralists, but we have no objection to taking upon ourselves the duties of the physician. And as doctors, we can have no hesitation in sterilizing our shelves, in cutting out and casting from us the morbid, neurotic, wrong-headed decadent books."[44] Forty years later, the American *Library Journal* asked libraries "in every state of the union" about the local availability of some twenty fiction titles that "might pose problems in book selection": recently published volumes ranging from Vladimir Nabokov's *Lolita* (first published in the United States in 1958) to Jere Peacock's *Valhalla* (1961). The journal sought to amass a bulwark of evidence against precisely such attempts to remove "'problem' fiction"—a telling redefinition in itself—from library shelves.[45]

The publication of a number of important works on the sexual history of Britain and America, many of which explicitly addressed or saw print only after considerable travails related to access, acted as a fulcrum for this transformation.[46] One of the earliest, Peter Fryer's *Private Case—Public Scandal* (1966), captures the widening rift between institutional policy and public opinion. Fryer argues that the lack of an available catalog for what was, after all, a public resource maintained by taxpayers' money, coupled with onerous application procedures, rendered the Private Case the "public scandal" of his title.[47] As late as 1981, would-be readers still needed a long-term reader's pass and a special application for requests from the Private Case. That year also saw the first near-complete bibliography of the collection in Patrick Kearney's *The Private Case*; Fryer's was a timely intervention in what was becoming a burgeoning field of scholarship. His title emphasizes the act of making public that accompanied growing awareness of the Private Case, an act that for the library was strangely similar to outing. Those who critiqued authority and organized new discourses about the collection formed what in Warner's lexicon would be deemed a print-based "counterpublic," similar to those mobilized by gay or sadomasochistic sexual dissidents.[48]

Library practice lags somewhat behind legislation. Fryer's account corroborates those of other sex researchers who, in the period following the United Kingdom's Obscene Publications Act 1959, were denied access to catalogs of the obscene materials in the Private Case and Suppressed Safe.[49] Although the statute had created an exception for publications that could be shown to contribute to the public good—defined broadly as educational in some fashion—it was not entirely clear why one would need such an education or what exactly it might entail.[50] It is perhaps unsurprising, therefore, that the British Museum Library had to turn to Fryer to assist them with the recataloging process of integrating former Private Case volumes into the general catalog. Complaining of "their willingness to pick [his] brains of such small knowledge, in a notoriously obscure field," Fryer gave voice to his frustration with library staff who drew on the specialized knowledge he had painstakingly acquired "scrap by scrap in the teeth of [British Museum Library] obstruction."[51] In the reevaluation of pornography at midcentury, libraries found that they had alienated the few parties qualified to assess and make sense of the resurfacing collections. Libraries now needed the ascendant cultural capital of their agitated patrons.

This specialized knowledge cannot be underestimated. It would cut through the bibliographic thicket common to pornography and other clandestine writing. Researchers clarified pseudonyms and flattened a Potemkin village of ersatz publishing houses that had been set up to fool the law.[52] Only a few scattered authorities would know, for example, that Margaret Anson's *The Merry Order of St. Bridget* was actually the work of James Glass Bertram, a Scottish bookseller and historian of flagellation; that the first edition was most likely published in London, not York; and that its 1857 publication date was a blind for 1890 or 1885.[53] Yet despite their rehabilitated status, many sex researchers still found in the librarian a formidable bar to research, a figure who denied requests and who demanded letters justifying the need for access. Peter Farrer, who started his research on cross-dressing in Victorian periodicals on the strength of a reference in Ellis's *Studies in the Psychology of Sex*, worked for decades to compile a bibliographic record of correspondence columns in the British Museum Library's newspaper collection, then housed at Colindale. He records with contempt and heartache the "satisfied smirk" on the face of the disparaging staff member who, one day, informed him of the relocation of the newspapers to the main library at Bloomsbury. There they would be kept behind a desk.[54] Kearney, another independent scholar working in his free time, also struggled with access as he compiled his own Private Case bibliography. The British Museum Library initially refused outright to allow researchers to see the Private Case catalog because "it was traditional and thought prudent" to keep readers (even those clearly motivated by professional ends) at a distance.[55] Kearney was allowed to see the catalog only after it had been, as Paul Cross evocatively states, "cannibalised" by library staff—that is, rendered defunct by physically discarding records for individual items as books were reintegrated into the general collection.[56] In the seven years that he worked on his bibliography, Kearney was allowed to visit the Arch room, where the Private Case was housed, on only "one delirious day."[57] Images of cannibalism and delirium lend an exoticism and danger to the space, creating an almost Conradian mystique. As one penetrates deeper into the heart of the pornographic collection, one runs the risk of losing professional detachment.

Even the scholar whom one might expect to champion library patrons' access to erotic materials, Gershon Legman, preeminent pornographic-publishing trade specialist and bibliographer, separated collectors into "normals" interested in the freedom of speech and "perverts" collecting for prurient reasons.[58] The uneasy hybridization of scholar and pervert still lingers—a descendant of the suspicious character who masqueraded as a legitimate researcher in Garnett's day and lingered among the "normals" in Legman's. Indeed, the contemporary scholar of pornography is an unwitting heir of old battles for and against sequestration. Despite earlier policies and theories explicated in the very books housed in the Private Case, which claimed that one cannot be sexually perverted by reading about perversions, the individual scholars working nowadays still do not manage to entirely escape the suspicion that they are somehow prurient, that the very research they undertake is suspect.

The pornography collector suffers, moreover, from what many would consider an excessive drive to taxonomize. Umberto Eco, in his study of catalogs, *The Infinity of Lists* (2009), speaks of bibliophiles who murmur the "catalogues of the great libraries" like a litany, and "read antiquarian bookshop catalogues with the same pleasure as others read thrillers."[59] The bibliographer's singular thrill is the list—what Eco calls the junction of practical and poetic, where function is conquered by the pleasure of listing.[60] For the sex researcher, a catalog of off-limits material often has to stand in for the entirety of the library experience, forcing him or her to make a fetishistic substitution of part for whole. Bibliographies thus represent a vexed yet critical way station in the commute of institutionally housed pornography from seclusion to highly visible consultation. Not without a certain aptness have clandestine catalogs, like the later mailers circulated by the smuthounds, often ended up in the very porn archives they chart.

Conflating the compulsive with the collector-curator, the pornographer with the preservationist, begs the question of what precisely separates the sex researcher from the librarian, beyond the latter's custodianship of the issue desk. As much as Kinsey disapproved of the British Museum's reluctance to display its holdings, he noted that "the curators themselves are not reticent in talking about erotic items."[61] During his 1955 visit he was impressed by the zeal with which employees encouraged wealthy patrons to purchase and donate sexual materials to the British Museum Library. He even had his picture taken with Dr. Eric Dingwall, likely the staunchest Private Case supporter ever on staff at the British Museum Library. "Dirty Ding" Dingwall, who worked in Cambridge University Library beginning in 1915, joined the British Museum Library as a volunteer in 1946 and, as Cross observes, "was more important than anyone else in building up the Private Case" by purchasing items with his own money and donating them to the institution.[62] In the 1950s he also encouraged the Kinsey Institute to donate duplicate copies of erotic works to the library. In turn, when the British Museum Library received the Charles Reginald Dawes bequest in 1964, it retained the Olympia Press publications but passed over a collection of Soho typescripts—semiliterate, mimeographed pornographic fiction—that found a home instead in the Kinsey Institute.[63]

Kinsey, his own books often subject to removal from general library collections, is a rare custodian in the annals of pornography's institutional treatment: a sympathetic and accommodating figure for researchers seeking no small quantity of obscene matter. The institute that bears his name occupies a unique position in the world of pornography. Both a public and private institution, its history reflects the belief that sex researchers ought to be able to conduct pornographic research without government censorship, and yet the hard-won battles that established this entitlement have reinscribed censorious practices in many of the institute's current policies. To fend off negative publicity and in anticipation of lawsuits in response to his groundbreaking *Sexual Behavior in the Human Male* (1948)—litigation that could have tapped the pockets of Indiana University—Kinsey's Institute of Sex Research was incorporated as a separate legal entity in 1947.[64] A private collection that endeavored to protect the erotic library for researchers was thus created under the aegis of a public institution, although, then as now, the general public was not granted access. Kinsey used proceeds from *Sexual Behavior in the Human Male* to finance the institute, and, as a collector and curator, he collected pornography with the same zeal he had exhibited for his gall wasp collection.[65]

Because he had to rely, for the most part, on foreign booksellers who were subject to strict antitariff laws prohibiting obscene material from being sent through the U.S. mail, from 1947 to his death in 1956—a period that Linda Williams dubs "the heyday of the institute's collecting frenzy"—Kinsey faced seizures and legal troubles that created significant financial setbacks for the institute.[66] He defended his entitlement as a scientist to collect sex data under an exception in the U.S. Tariff Act of 1930 that allowed for the importation of "books of recognized and established literary or scientific merit."[67] Initial successes with this rather free interpretation of the statute were cut short by a change of administration. Refusing to bow to suggestions that he either stop purchasing or provide a letter of justification for each volume in each shipment of books he sought to import, Kinsey felt that any compromise with customs officials would "endanger not only his research but the work of other sex researchers" by allowing the government to act as the arbiter of research material.[68]

A precedent in his favor was established in 1957, although this was not until after Kinsey's death and at significant legal cost to the institute. *U.S. v. 31 Photographs* bracketed off the sex researcher as immune to the prurient appeal of erotic material and articulated "a conditional privilege in favor of scientists and scholars, to import material which would be obscene in the hands of the average person."[69] In company with other rulings, most notably *Roth v. United States* (1957), the institute was equipped with the legal sanction to import sexually explicit material.[70] Notably for our purposes, the judgment in *U.S. v. 31 Photographs* also employed a metaphor of containment: obscene material was seen as a biological toxin that needed proper confining. Just as "proposed importations of bacilli of dangerous and highly contagious diseases do not lead us to shut our ports in panic" but instead to "place our faith in the competence of those who are entrusted with their proper use," the presiding judge Edmund L. Palmieri concluded that sexually explicit material could be safely contained by professionals.[71] The perceived danger that such material posed in 1950s America illuminates the rationale behind the closed cases that exist in so many of the nation's libraries. The ruling gave rise, more systemically, to the strict access policies that are still in place at the institute today. Current access guidelines restrict collections to those with "demonstrable research needs."[72] The written request form, another document in the reams of paperwork that constitute the porn archive, is intended to ascertain both a would-be patron's qualifications and intention to use the material for research in sex, gender, or reproduction.

Conditions of access remain a fraught domain precisely because library holdings can no longer be written off simply as a "quantity of offensive matter"; pornography has become a resource to protect. The Private Case, even in its present-day form distributed across the general collection, houses the single extant copy of many now-valuable obscene books. More than one librarian has lamented the mutilated photographic plates or the excised sections of periodicals that rupture the historical record. Access to material with sexual content may thus be limited on conservationist grounds. Samuel Steward's biographer, Justin Spring, to take one example, found that Yale's Sterling Memorial Library restricted access to rare books with sexually graphic content, as they were "frequently stolen or mutilated and therefore were categorized as 'restricted' for their own good."[73] Perhaps only scholars of rare books and manuscript holdings are as systematically separated from their primary sources as researchers of porn archives. Indeed, the latter may well occupy the more isolated position.

"The current problem for institutional collections," as Geoff Nicholson notes, "isn't what to keep, since it appears that everything is worth keeping—the day of the unconsidered trifle is long past—but of knowing how to organize and make sense of what they've got."[74] The Kinsey Institute, in particular, struggles with the idiosyncratic cataloging system invented by its founder, which disregards the form and material of pornographic accessions in favor of their genre and the detailed distinctions among sexual behaviors portrayed therein. Liana Zhou, who heads the Kinsey Institute's library, notes that "the Library simply labels as 'erotica' all materials produced for the purpose of arousing sexual response or which contains sufficient sexually explicit matter to do so."[75] Kinsey's scientific taxonometrics, with their complex system of sexual nomenclature, derived from his training in genetics. This idiosyncratic system was suspended in favor of the Dewey Decimal Classification in the 1970s.[76] Zhou notes that although the Dewey Decimal Classification was able to organize many of the erotic materials under the subcategories of the 800 class, it could not account for such elements of the collection as the "'girlie' magazines, nudist publications, tabloids, underground publications, homosexual magazines, pulp novels, and other publications that are collected by few, if any, libraries."[77] Metadata pertaining to source, provenance, and other identifiers are tracked by an internal filing system, but it is unavailable to the researcher. Certain types of pornography that do not enjoy First Amendment protection or the conditional privileges carved out by Kinsey—pornographic images of children, for one—are also withheld; in a recent interview, the Kinsey Institute was unwilling even to discuss such materials.[78] For these and other reasons, a significant portion of archival materials is unavailable, irrespective of a researcher's credentials.[79]

In the case of the British Museum Library, accessing sexual materials remains a spatially inflected difficulty, even if for entirely new reasons. The desuppression of Private Case volumes—which in the later years of their confinement were held in a "security pen" in a "specially constructed sheet-steel covered cage"—has created a host of access issues related to cataloging quirks and library security.[80] The top shelf has been effectively dismantled, and desegregation means that it is all but impossible to assess the collection from either a historical or current standpoint. With an ever-growing collection, now over 150 million items strong, and a mandate to obtain a copy of every publication produced in the United Kingdom and Ireland, the British Museum Library struggles with the laborious and ceaseless project of cataloging its acquisitions. One consequence of the digital catalog, which currently cannot be searched by shelf mark, is that technology has usurped the role of the keeper of the printed books as censor of pornographic material. If one knows the titles or has Kearney's catalog, works can be requested by volume (in limited batches); the Private Case as a discrete collection cannot be reconstituted using the library's resources, however. By contrast, much of the Kinsey Institute's smaller collection can be searched by call number, providing mappings of the physical arrangements of the stacks, even if users are unable physically to view holdings. "Even though the library has closed stacks for security reasons," Zhou notes, "a well-conducted call number search under any of the classification areas would generate a shelflist of what was included in that portion of the collection."[81] Here is the library shelf without books.

Access, however, still depends on the efficacy and completeness of the indexing and retrieval tools, and, the online public access catalogs (OPACs) notwithstanding, it is common for researchers (in the Kinsey Institute, as in other libraries) to discover that sought-after materials are either not cataloged or are missing. Pornographic films, in particular, pose a number of problems with regard to acquisition, access, and preservation in libraries.[82]

Although digital media promise greater access, policies involving the relatively new public Wi-Fi service at the British Museum Library reveal a further censorious barrier to the researcher of pornographic material. The British Museum Library's guidelines for "appropriate use" of the public Wi-Fi service state that the provision of Internet access does not allow for "the creation and/or transmission of any offensive, obscene or indecent images, data or other material" or "the creation and/or transmission of material which is likely to cause annoyance, inconvenience or needless anxiety."[83] At issue, again, is venue. Once placed on the metaphorical top shelf or housed in a locked cage, sexually explicit print matter is now available, in theory, to anyone who can secure a reader's pass. Downloading or streaming unvetted pornography, on the other hand, is forbidden, irrespective of scholarly intentions.[84] Researchers risk losing access to the collection if they work on audio-visual Internet material in the course of their research or if they create an uncomfortable working environment in the specialist reading rooms wherein pornography is consulted. New policies, a reevaluation of sexually explicit holdings, and the legacy of old restrictions have thrust the researcher center stage. In a twist on Williams's principle of maximum visibility, the seeker after sex knowledge is thus imbricated into the visual field of sexuality, despite his or her scholarly agenda and the changing social mores that have made special applications largely a matter of the past. The very spatiality of the reading room dictates this uncomfortable position. Where maximum visibility "proves elusive in the parallel confession of female sexual pleasure," taking pornography out of the private reading room or secluded carrel and into the glare of public consumption renders mute any outward sign of enjoyment.[85] If researchers respond to sexually explicit material in a manner unbecoming of institutional probity—whether with arousal or, as with much historical pornography, with laughter—they risk their credibility in the counterpublic that has fought for access to such material and defined itself in revaluing it. Affect polices legitimacy; one's scholarly motivations must remain patent within the public forum of the library.

How, then, do we account for the library's stamp on the clichés of the pornographic imagination, whether as the trysting place in much sexually explicit material or as the location of that staple of the genre: the female librarian who, with the deft removal of hairpins and the unbuttoning of a

5.2. Samuel Steward's Stud File. © Estate of Samuel Steward (2011).

shirt, transforms herself into a figure of desire? Although the history of pornography archives is one of collector renegades, individuals who skirt censorship and censure whether to fulfill a private whim or a debilitating compulsion, the accession of these collections to public institutions amounts to more than the pitting of freedoms of expression against reactive, institutional mores and moralizings. Indeed, in some cases, pornography incorporates the very structures of the library.

For example, the archive of Samuel Steward, a pornographic writer and former English professor, was stored for decades in the attic of the executor of his estate. It contains the notes of his alter ego, Phil Andros, a street hustler who penned gay erotica about his experiences, and a carefully curated record of Steward's sexual encounters that includes photographs, artwork, and an extraordinary card catalog. The latter, Steward's "Stud File," organizes more than 4,500 encounters with men from the years 1924 to 1974, with individual notations typed on some 746 index cards and boxed as a library card catalog (see figure 5.2). As Spring notes, the whole is "painstakingly alphabetized, coded, annotated, and cross-referenced." [86]

Erotic memoirs of literary Casanovas in the nineteenth and twentieth centuries abound. *My Secret Life* (circa 1880) and *My Life and Loves* (1922), to take but two famous examples, were saturated with the sort of detail that would ensure their placement in the private cases and closed stacks of the library.[87] The Stud File, a one-off for the most part that did not circulate, amounts, by its very nature, to a private case. Collector and cataloger, writer and reader, Steward interpolated the procedures of curation into his private library, organizing *personal experience* as pornography in an archive of index cards with no retrievable referents (save, perhaps, memory). The Stud File places in time and space not a collection of pornographic books but the collector himself. A key of acronyms and number strings anatomize the physiology of his partners' penises and the varieties of guy-on-guy action. Given that homosexual pornography or records of gay sex were punishable crimes in the United States for much of the twentieth century, most of the acts described in the Stud File were illegal at the time of notation. Steward's symbolic Private Case was kept from public view, like its institutional equivalent, to safeguard its contents— but under a very different mandate of cultural preservation from that in operation at the British Museum Library.

Initially a case history kept for private perusal, the Stud File began as a coded list of Steward's sexual encounters while he was still in high school.[88] By early 1949 he had met Kinsey and, encouraged by the latter's interest in the Stud File as a possible donation to the institute, became much more specific in his notations and dates. The date of an encounter with no less a figure than Lord Alfred Douglas is erroneously placed as "July 1937" in the Stud File, which, as Spring notes, "was impossible since Steward arrived in England only on August 10 and departed on August 19."[89] Thanks to Kinsey's intervention, however, the Stud File offers an invaluable archive of gay sexual experience. Because of its subject matter and the confidentiality rules of the Kinsey Institute, however, it would be unavailable today had Steward agreed to donate it.

The spatiality of counterculture records is always one of closed cupboards, but having closed archives in public institutions may create continuing barriers to social justice. Had it not been for the discovery of Steward's voluminous personal archive in his executor's attic, Spring would have been unaware of this extraordinary and historically significant record keeping. "Despite feelings of great goodwill" toward his biography, Spring reports that the Kinsey Institute could not provide him access to a host of unique materials in the archives, including a partial copy of the Stud File.[90] This particular object, then, represents a complex failure for the researcher. It owes its survival, and continued relevance, to its space outside the disciplinary institutional structure of the library, one that would literally have buried it. Had the Stud File been found in London in the early twentieth century, it might have been discarded as "a quantity of offensive matter"; had Kinsey convinced Steward to donate the card catalog in toto, it would not be available to anyone outside of the institute. Sixty years later, these records remain closed. The Stud File, in recording one little-known man's sexual encounters with thousands of his faceless contemporaries (even if their cocks are described in the exacting code of his notation), frames an institutional quandary that may profitably be placed before all institutions that retain sexually explicit material on their top shelves: how should a mandate of cultural preservation respond to twentieth- and twenty-first-century cultural studies that have an urgent need of increased access to material suppressed decades ago?

Finding a place for pornography in the library was as much the invention of a category of exclusion as it was the sequestering of inimical print material. The turnaround of institutional policy on sexually explicit holdings has seen a dramatic shift in the last fifty years—as recently as 2008, the Bibliothèque nationale de France staged the exhibition L'Enfer de la Bibliothèque, Éros au secret (The Inferno of the library, Eros in secret)—but the commute from seclusion to celebration has burdened the sex researcher, if not the exhibition-going public, with access policies freighted with the hard-won battles whereby the porn archives were constituted in the first place and then made to open up to examination.[91] The rhetoric of disciplinary space is paramount in this formation. In the nineteenth and early twentieth centuries, normalizing imperatives assembled and made sense of a heterogeneous array of print matter; the conventions of another age now hide this vastly expanded material in plain sight.

## Notes

This chapter was presented in part at the Modernist Studies Association convention in November 2010. The authors extend their thanks to Justin Spring and the "Modernism and the Scene of the Archive" seminar participants; to the archivist Lesley A. Hall of the Library at Wellcome Collection (and to the trustees of the Mass Observation Archive, University of Sussex, for the material used herein); to Liana Zhou and Catherine Johnson-Roehr of the Kinsey Institute for Research in Sex, Gender, and Reproduction; and to Assumpta Guilfoyle and Barbara McDonald of Trinity College Library Dublin. Many thanks are also due to the institutions that supported the research: the Office of Research and Faculty Development and the Center for the Study of Women in Society at the University of Oregon and the School of Humanities and the Humanities Center at the University of California, Irvine.

1. Kearney, The Private Case, 66. Though Kearney notes that there is no copy of the volume in the British Museum Library's Private Case, the 1961 edition of There's a Whip in My Valise is listed in another of the library's places of concealment: Cup.358/178.

2. Despite a challenge from the American Library Association questioning its constitutionality (United States v. American Library Association, 539 U.S. 194 [2003]), the Children's

Internet Protection Act of 2000 mandates that schools and public libraries that receive federal funding for Internet access or internal connections must employ technologic protection measures to block or filter access to content harmful to minors.

3. Prior to the commencement of the British Library Act 1972 on July 1, 1973, the national library of the United Kingdom was part of the British Museum. We use the designation *British Museum Library* throughout.

4. Pershing, "Erotica Research Collections," 195; Legman, introduction to *The Private Case*, 17.

5. Ziolkowski, "Introduction," 12.

6. Newman, "The Smut Hunters," n.p.

7. Alfred O'Rahilly, "Alfred O'Rahilly's Reply to H. G. Wells in the *Standard*," quoted in Ashworth, "Clashing Utopias," 277; Hoare, "The Libraries of the Ancient University to the 1960s," 335.

8. Permits to import banned books, 1933–52, are held in the Manuscripts and Archives Research Library at Trinity College (TCD MUN/LIB/15/572–589).

9. Coined in a *New York Times* editorial ("Comstockery," Dec. 12, 1895, 4), *Comstockery* refers to the censorship of works thought to be immoral. Anthony Comstock (1844–1915) headed the New York Society for the Suppression of Vice's antiobscenity crusades, a campaign that resulted in statutory changes in U.S. law in 1873 that made it illegal to transport obscene material through the U.S. mail.

10. Emerson, "Books," 97 (originally printed in *Atlantic Monthly*, January 1858, 345).

11. Warner, *Publics and Counterpublics*, 96.

12. Warner, *Publics and Counterpublics*, 16.

13. Warner, *Publics and Counterpublics*, 97.

14. Kendrick, *The Secret Museum*.

15. James Grantham Turner traces this etymology to link the early novel with the whores' guides *La Retorica della puttane* (1642) and its English adaptation, *The Whores Rhetorick* (1683), arguing that both forms involve the crafting of a character that appeals to the eye of a customer. See Turner, "The Whores Rhetorick."

16. Fairholt, *A Dictionary of Terms in Art*, 348.

17. Among many commentators in the 1980s, Bill Sherk seems to have been the first to consult his *Webster's* (*500 Years of New Words* [Toronto, Ont.; Garden City, N.Y.: Doubleday, 1983], 196). That said, Kendrick's *The Secret Museum* has been instrumental in the widespread circulation of the definition. For a useful run-through of a century's worth of pornography in the dictionary, see Hoff, "Why Is There No History of Pornography?," 39n6.

18. Kendrick, *The Secret Museum*, 11.

19. E. Michael Jones discusses the rumor in more detail in his *Degenerate Moderns* (88–93), crediting its origin to no less a figure than Kinsey.

20. Green and Karolides, *The Encyclopedia of Censorship*, 457.

21. For Ashbee see I. Gibson, *The Erotomaniac*, especially 147, 150, and 152–57. Ralph E. Whittington, a former Library of Congress archivist, sold his collection of pornography and erotica to the Museum of Sex in New York City in 2002. Peter Carlson, " 'King of Porn' Empties Out His Castle: New N.Y. Museum Buys His 30-Year Collection," *Washington Post*, August 24, 2002, C1.

22. This is from the preliminary report, by G. K. Fortescue, to the trustees of the British Museum, concerning the Ashbee bequest, dated October 28, 1900. "Appen-

dix G. Concerning the Fate of the Ashbee Collection," in Mendes, *Clandestine Erotic Fiction in English*, 466–67. In a 1901 report, Fortescue revised his estimate to 2,379 volumes.

23. Quoted in I. Gibson, *The Erotomaniac*, 155. *Facetiae* was a euphemism employed by booksellers to designate not the "funny books" that its etymology suggests but erotica (160). *Kruptadia*, another obsolete trade term, means "hidden things." Fryer, *Private Case — Public Scandal*, 29.

24. Roberts, "Trafficking in Literary Authority," 9.

25. Sigel, *Governing Pleasures*, 174n23.

26. Pomeroy, *Dr. Kinsey and the Institute for Sex Research*, 412.

27. Cross, "The Private Case," 203–5. This article is the first official history of the Private Case. Compiled by an official of the British Museum Library, it was published one year after the Private Case closed. Green and Karolides (*The Encyclopedia of Censorship*, 457) credit Panizzi with the Private Case's invention.

28. "Appendix G. Concerning the Fate of the Ashbee Collection," in Mendes, *Clandestine Erotic Fiction in English*, 466. Mendes traces a semantic shift in subsequent versions of the document that indicate that original materials — and not copies — were destroyed in the six boxes of materials withdrawn from the collection at accession.

29. Slade, *Pornography and Sexual Representation*, vol. 1, 96, 107–13.

30. Warner, *Publics and Counterpublics*, 12.

31. Garnett quoted in Cross, "The Private Case," 205.

32. Kearney, *The Private Case*, 356–57. Kearney includes a facsimile of a 1926 letter from Ellis to Montague Summers that suggests that he use his connections at the British Museum to have the Private Case cataloged.

33. Cross discusses the newspaper debate regarding the withholding of Ellis's volumes and other similar studies, along with the fallout of Haynes's disclosure, in "The Private Case," 210. Haynes's article, in fact the work of several collaborators, was published as "The Taboos of the British Museum Library."

34. A file containing some of these dealers' catalogs was also placed in the Private Case at P.C.16.i.2 (now Cup.364.g.48), as noted by Legman, introduction to *The Private Case*, 49.

35. See, for example, the discussion on books advertised for sale in the threepenny weekly *Photo Bits* in Levin, "How Joyce Acquired 'The Stale Smut of Clubmen.'" One extant example of these rare British lending library catalogs resides in the Mass Observation Archive at the University of Sussex (*Direct Book Supply Co. Catalogue 3A* [London: 1949], n.p. Mass Observation Sex Survey file A.9 16/1, "Advertising and Publications: Published Material on Sex," Mass Observation Archive, University of Sussex, London). See also L. Hall, "Sex in the Archives." The American trade is explored in Gertzman, *Bookleggers and Smuthounds*. *Gallantiana* is the first of five categories of items in which the bookleggers traded (61).

36. Spring, *Secret Historian*, 10.

37. Tony Barrell, "Rude Britannia: Erotic Secrets of the British Museum," *Sunday Times*, August 30, 2009, accessed November 30, 2010, http://www.thesundaytimes.co.uk/sto.

38. L. Hall, "Sex in the Archives," 5.

39. See Crowley, "Dressing Up Bloom for 'Circe,'" 3.

40. Feipel, "Questionable Books in Public Libraries — I," 857.

41. Feipel, "Questionable Books in Public Libraries — I," 858.

42. Joyce enclosed this account by an unnamed Dublin relative in a letter to Harriet Shaw Weaver, dated April 10, 1922. British Library, Add MS 57,346, vol. 2. 1920–1922, f. 96.

43. Echard, "House Arrest," 195.

44. Unsigned editorial, *Library World* 24, no. 10 (1922): 182.

45. Moon, "'Problem' Fiction."

46. Two examples will suffice: I. Gibson, *The English Vice*; and Marcus, *The Other Victorians*.

47. Fryer, *Private Case—Public Scandal*, 134–35.

48. Warner, *Publics and Counterpublics*, 56.

49. Fryer, *Private Case—Public Scandal*, 13; Legman, *The Horn Book*, 11; Kearney, *The Private Case*, 63.

50. Obscene Publications Act, 1959 (7 & 8 Eliz. 2 c. 66, s. 4).

51. Fryer, *Private Case—Public Scandal*, 135.

52. Though from a later period, see Mendes, *Clandestine Erotic Fiction in English* for an accomplished example of such scholarship.

53. Anson, *The Merry Order of St. Bridget*.

54. Farrer, introduction to *Confidential Correspondence on Cross Dressing*, 6.

55. Cross, "The Private Case," 221.

56. Cross, "The Private Case," 221. Kearney discusses his methodology before and after he was allowed access to the library's Private Case catalog; see Kearney, *The Private Case*, 68.

57. Kearney, *The Private Case*, 63.

58. Legman, introduction to *The Private Case*, 40.

59. Eco, *The Infinity of Lists*, 377.

60. Eco, *The Infinity of Lists*, 371.

61. Pomeroy, *Dr. Kinsey and the Institute for Sex Research*, 412.

62. Cross, "The Private Case," 217.

63. Fryer, *Private Case—Public Scandal*, 12.

64. J. H. Jones, *Alfred C. Kinsey*, 593. M. W. Newman reports that Kinsey's studies were not available, for example, to borrowers at the Chicago Public Library. M. W. Newman, "The Smut Hunters." The institute is currently known as the Kinsey Institute for Research in Sex, Gender, and Reproduction.

65. Within five years the institute was valued at over $170,000, housed 13,790 volumes, and had an annual acquisition budget of more than $25,000. J. H. Jones, *Alfred C. Kinsey*, 669–70. An associate of Kinsey, Paul Gebhard, relates experiences of "field trips," during which Kinsey would allot thirty minutes per bookseller in a large network he cultivated, and would quickly evaluate and buy any material related to sex, even if, at times, it was of questionable value. His purchases ranged from conventional book objects to ancient Peruvian artifacts to rooster-head condoms and sadomasochistic gear (668–69). For Kinsey's gall wasps, see Yudell, "Kinsey's Other Report," 80–81.

66. J. H. Jones, *Alfred C. Kinsey*, 669–70; L. Williams, "'White Slavery' versus the Ethnography of 'Sexworkers,'" 109.

67. Section 1305 of the code prohibits the importation of obscene materials. See Stevens, "*United States v. 31 Photographs*"; and Yamashiro, "In the Realm of the Sciences." Stevens miscites the section of the code as 305 throughout.

68. J. H. Jones, *Alfred C. Kinsey*, 672.

69. U.S. v. 31 Photographs, 156 F. Supp. 350, 358 (SDNY 1957).

70. In Roth v. United States, 354 U.S. 476 (1957), the publisher Samuel Roth prevailed against the United States in a landmark decision that redefined the grounds under which literary works could be classified as obscene (and thus made mailable). The decision increased access to previously censored works of literature to the general public, not merely researchers with a stated academic purpose for viewing the material.

71. U.S. v. 31 Photographs, 156 F. Supp. 350, 357 (SDNY 1957).

72. "Using the Library," the Kinsey Institute for Research in Sex, Gender, and Reproduction, Library and Special Collections, accessed on November 30, 2010, http://www.iub.edu/~kinsey/library/use.html.

73. Spring, *Secret Historian*, 409.

74. Nicholson, *Sex Collectors*, 67.

75. Zhou, "Characteristics of Material Organization and Classification in the Kinsey Institute Library," 339.

76. Catalogs were prepared from the mid-1970s to 1982 by G. K. Hall, and an in-house database was initiated in 1980. The catalog became available in part online in 1995, with ongoing efforts to complete the digitization of the holdings. Zhou, "Characteristics of Material Organization and Classification in the Kinsey Institute Library," 350–51.

77. Zhou, "Characteristics of Material Organization and Classification in the Kinsey Institute Library," 343, 346. This system creates myriad divisions within the collection. For example, on Bright's visit to the Kinsey in 2006, the S/M photo collection was housed in sixteen boxes, separated into years from 1885 to 1950, with additional subcategories denoting homosexual and heterosexual acts, flagellation, spanking, sex, bondage, and lone poses.

78. Liana Zhou, telephone interview with Jennifer Burns Bright, September 14, 2010. The institute's historical involvement with child abusers is the subject of the British television documentary *Secret Histories: Kinsey's Paedophiles* (1998), directed by Tim Tate.

79. Confidentiality provisions mean that, even in institutions with explicit missions to disseminate knowledge about sexual behavior, much goes unavailable. Fifty-year-old privacy clauses attached to case histories that were given to Kinsey's associates tie the hands of the Kinsey Institute, for instance.

80. Cross, "The Private Case," 225.

81. Zhou, "Characteristics of Material Organization and Classification in the Kinsey Institute Library," 351.

82. Schaefer, "Dirty Little Secrets," 93–101.

83. "Guidelines for British Library Users on the Appropriate Use of the Public Wi-Fi Service," British Library, accessed on Nov. 24, 2010, http://www.bl.uk/whatson/planyourvisit/wifi/wifiguidelines.html.

84. Tony Barrell, the reporter who wrote the epigraph to this chapter, was not permitted to see the shelves, but he was allowed to talk to library staff about Private Case desuppressions. Barrell, "Rude Britannia."

85. L. Williams, *Hard Core* (1989), 49.

86. Spring and Steward, *Obscene Diary*, n.p. This album of Steward's photography, artwork, and ephemera features an image of the Stud File box and several of the index-card records contained therein.

87. Harris, *My Life and Loves*; and anonymous, *My Secret Life*. Steward also wrote, at the request of Kinsey, an unpublished sexual diary in the tradition of these works. The single-spaced, thousand-page typed manuscript is one of the few records known to exist that chronicles American gay life in the mid-twentieth century. Spring, *Secret Historian*, xiii.

88. Spring, *Secret Historian*, 16.

89. Spring, *Secret Historian*, 102n44.

90. Spring, *Secret Historian*, 409–10. These materials included "nearly all of Steward's photographic contributions to the Kinsey archive, its partial copy of Steward's Stud File, all of Steward's sexual history, his [sadomasochistic] sex film with [Mike] Miksche, and many of his various other contributions to its archive, including his sex calendars." See also Steward, "Dr. Kinsey Takes a Peek at S/M."

91. The exhibit ran from December 4, 2007, to March 2, 2008. Quignard and Seckel, *L'Enfer de la bibliothèque*.

# 6

## Up from Underground

*Loren Glass*

Few books have had a more lasting effect on the study of sexuality in the United States than Robert Hurley's 1978 translation of the first volume of Michel Foucault's *The History of Sexuality*. Arriving on American shores just as the multipronged cultural backlash against the sexual revolution of the late 1960s was gathering steam, Foucault's famous attack on the "repressive hypothesis" forced scholars in the United States, many of them veterans of that very revolution, to entirely rethink the philosophical and political assumptions behind the struggle against censorship that, only a decade earlier, seemed as though it had been definitively, and triumphantly, won. Foucault almost single-handedly inverted our understanding of censorship, proclaiming that the modern era that we had previously seen as "repressed" in fact witnessed "a regulated and polymorphous incitement to discourse" about sex that his short study proceeds to document.[1] Yet Foucault's historical examples of this incitement are notoriously scanty and selective. Indeed, only two of them were available in English at the time: *The 120 Days of Sodom*, by the Marquis de Sade, and the anonymous Victorian autobiography *My Secret Life*, both published by Grove Press in the 1960s. Before Grove published them, it is fair to say that only a handful of American readers would have had any access to these texts.

For Foucault, these two examples of "scandalous literature" are representative of the historical incitement to discourse, despite the fact that, as he himself admits, almost no one read them at the time. *The 120 Days of Sodom* existed only in manuscript form until the Sade scholar Maurice Heine brought out a three-volume limited edition in the 1930s, which would be the basis for Grove's American translation. Correlatively, a mere six copies of *My Secret Life* had been privately printed by its author during his lifetime, only three of which were extant when Grove brought out its edition. These authors may have been motivated by an incitement to discourse, but their discourse had a profoundly restricted audience until after the Second World War. If we adjust our historical lens to understand these texts in terms of readership and access, instead of authorship and production, a somewhat different story emerges.

I will tell this different story, focusing on Grove's acquisition, translation, and publication of these texts, as well as the innumerable other "underground classics" it issued in the second half of the sixties, after the press had rapidly dismantled America's Comstock-era censorship regime with the highly publicized trials of *Lady Chatterley's Lover*, *Tropic of Cancer*, and *Naked Lunch*. As I have discussed elsewhere, Grove achieved this rapid series of successes through the strategic use of expert testimony by academic professionals who could attest to the "redeeming value" of these texts.[2] This testimony in turn supplied the basis for the paratextual packaging—academic prefaces, judicial decisions, and sometimes even trial transcripts—that established the initial thresholds of interpretation of these texts for an entire generation of readers. This process of academic consecration was crucial to the publication of the works of Sade and *My Secret Life*, which were able to enter the literary marketplace of the late sixties without any legal trouble.

Indeed, after his string of remarkably rapid legal successes, Grove owner Barney Rosset proceeded to realize the fears of his opponents by exhuming the entire literary underground of the Victorian and Edwardian eras, massively expanding the readership for an entire canon of texts that had previously only been available at considerable cost through illicit channels. By making these texts available legally and inexpensively for the first time, Rosset rendered these channels unnecessary, permanently transforming the structure of the cultural field and, I hope to prove, preparing it for the intervention Foucault would subsequently make.

One unfortunate effect of Foucault's intervention has been to obscure these conditions of possibility. Foucault's attack on the repressive hypothesis, in other words, has had the paradoxical consequence of repressing the historical transformation effected by its adherents. The so-called end of obscenity may not have been as liberatory as its proponents had hoped, but it did bring about a radical expansion of access to erotic and pornographic materials that had profound cultural consequences for the generation that would form Foucault's core audience in the United States. In order to account for this seemingly paradoxical situation, I deploy Max Weber's theory of the "vanishing mediator," specifically as it is elaborated in Fredric Jameson's classic essay of that name.[3] As Jameson explains it, Weber formulates Protestantism as a catalytic historical agent between medieval Catholicism and modern secularism. Protestantism paradoxically enables this transformation by democratizing access to the sacred, previously confined to monasteries, which in the end had the consequence of freeing up the process of rationalization that had ordered the lives in those monasteries. Protestantism, in other words, enabled the desacralization of the world precisely through democratizing the institutions of the sacred. Grove Press effected an analogous process with obscenity, which under the modernist regime had become the sacralized property of a cultural elite but which Grove made available to a wide mainstream readership.

The vanishing mediator has another function in Weber's schema that is equally pertinent to my argument: the "routinization of charisma."[4] Here, focusing more specifically on the role of individuals in the creation of institutions, Weber theorizes that the prophet serves as a vanishing mediator between the personal charisma of the magician and the institutional authority of the priest. The prophet achieves this mediation by "debracketing" the charismatic authority of the magician, which in turn lays the groundwork for the institutional appropriation of this authority in the form of a priesthood. Correlatively, if Rosset and his colleagues at Grove positioned themselves as prophets of sexual revolution in their campaign to democratize pornography, they were also laying the groundwork for the reconstitution of charismatic authority in the form of academic expertise. Foucault's centrality to academic discussions of pornography is an example of this reconstitution. My narrative, then, is not intended to disprove Foucault's version of the history of sexuality; rather, my intention is to clarify why it emerged when it did, and why it proved so compelling to an entire generation of American academics.

Sade was among the most sacralized and charismatically invested writers when Grove began, in the mid-1950s, to import the latest avant-garde literature from Paris into the United States. Sade's writing had been situated as the secret subterranean source of the amorality of modernist aesthetics since Charles Baudelaire, but it had been unavailable legally in both the Francophone and Anglophone worlds until the postwar era. Indeed, its unavailability buttressed its mystique during the era of modernism, when simply having read Sade indicated membership in an exclusive club. As part of its effort to popularize modernism, then, it was inevitable that Grove would publish Sade in the wake of its string of successes in the courts. Unsurprisingly, Rosset's interest in the "divine Marquis" went back to the very beginnings of Grove, when Rosset published in May 1953 a carefully sanitized selection of Sade's writings, chosen and translated by Paul Dinnage as a sort of "anthology-guidebook." The book is prefaced by Simone de Beauvoir's now-classic article from Les Temps Modernes (Modern times), "Must We Burn Sade?" Grove's selections followed on Edmund Wilson's lengthy New Yorker article of 1952, "The Vogue of the Marquis de Sade," which deprecated the hagiographic bias of the foundational Sade scholars Maurice Heine and M. Gilbert Lely (whose biography of Sade Grove would later publish in translation) but praised Beauvoir's more measured essay as "perhaps the very best thing that has yet been written on the subject."[5] Wilson declined to write an introduction for the volume, but he agreed to let Grove use his article in their promotional efforts. This small volume sports an untranslated epigraph from Baudelaire's *Journaux intimes* (*Intimate Journals*) exhorting the reader, "Il faut toujours revenir a de Sade, c'est-a-dire a l'homme naturel, pour expliquer le mal" (It is necessary always to return to Sade, which is to say, to natural man, for an explanation of evil); features selections in which the more explicit portions remain untranslated as well; and concludes with a chronology and bibliography compiled by Dinnage; the book anticipates the scholarly seriousness with which Grove would publish Sade in the sixties.

In the same year that Grove issued these sanitized selections, Austryn Wainhouse, using the baroque pseudonym Pieralessanddro Casavini, published his unexpurgated translation of Sade's novel *Justine* with Maurice Girodias's Olympia Press, soon to become notorious as publishers of the Traveler's Companion series of English-language pornography. Girodias would initially publish in Paris many of the authors, including Jean Genet, Samuel Beckett, and Henry Miller, that Grove would later bring to the United States. Over the next decade Wainhouse, a Harvard graduate on leave (permanently, it would turn out) from his doctoral studies at the University of Iowa, translated a variety of Sade's writings for the Traveler's Companion series under this pseudonym. These translations became the foundation for the massive three-volume two-thousand-plus-page edition of Sade's work that Wainhouse and Richard Seaver assembled for Grove in the mid- to late sixties, after the risk of censorship had been eliminated by the series of successes with D. H. Lawrence, Henry Miller, and William S. Burroughs. Seaver, along with Wainhouse, the Scotsman Alexander Trocchi, and the South African novelist Patrick Bowles, was a founding member of the Merlin collective in Paris in the fifties, an association of English-speaking exiles who produced the short-lived literary journal *Merlin* while also translating and writing, under a variety of pseudonyms, pornographic texts for Girodias's Traveler's Companion series.[6] At the time, Seaver was a doctoral student at the Sorbonne working on a dissertation about James Joyce and building his collection of rare editions of the work of the Sade. In 1959 he returned to the United States to work as an editor at Grove, a position he held for the entirety of the sixties.

Seaver had initially envisioned a one-volume edition, but Wainhouse convinced him to adopt the more ambitious three-volume plan. In the June 1965 issue of Grove's groundbreaking magazine the *Evergreen Review*, Seaver set the stage for the imminent publication of the first volume with an article entitled "An Anniversary Unnoticed," juxtaposing the much-publicized 400-year anniversary of Shakespeare's birth with the unacknowledged 150-year anniversary of Sade's death. For Seaver, Sade was as important as Shakespeare, and his article placed him in the company of Baudelaire, Gustave Flaubert, Émile Zola,

Joyce, Lawrence, and Miller as great writers whose books have outlived their initial condemnation to become literary classics. Seaver further reminded his readers that "Swinburne, Baudelaire, Lamartine, Nietzsche, Dostoevsky, Lautréamont, and Kafka . . . kept one or more of Sade's major works at hand, to read and contemplate."[7] His ultimate hope was that Sade would be made available to more than these "fortunate few," and his collaboration with Wainhouse did indeed ensure that this democratization of access was achieved.

Grove's edition of Sade, which remains the most ambitious and comprehensive English translation of that author's voluminously repetitive work, is particularly noteworthy for the extensive paratextual apparatus incorporated into the texts. As Seaver wrote to Wainhouse in 1965, the intention of all this paratextual material was "to convince the censors (or judge) that we are serious about this business, that we have spent a long time preparing this work, which is a work of considerable scholarship."[8] The first volume (1965), which includes *Justine* and *Philosophy in the Bedroom*, along with other minor works, features a forty-eight-page chronology of Sade's life and an extensive bibliography of primary and secondary work. It also includes two scholarly introductions, one by Jean Paulhan, the postwar Parisian man of letters whose membership in L'Académie française is prominently noted on the front cover, and one by Maurice Blanchot, the French novelist and literary theorist. Paulhan compares Sade's work to "the sacred books of the great religions," while Blanchot makes a "discreet request, addressed to all Sade's publishers present and future: when dealing with Sade, at least respect the scandalous aspect."[9] The back cover quotes Baudelaire ("It is necessary to keep coming back to Sade, again and again"), Algernon Charles Swinburne ("this Great Man to whom I am indebted"), and Guillaume Apollinaire ("the freest spirit that has ever lived"), among others. Thus the Sadean dialectic of the sacred and the scandalous is simultaneously recognized and compromised by the scholarly seriousness of Seaver and Wainhouse's paratextual apparatus. As with the great avatars of Protestantism, Seaver and Wainhouse inaugurated the process of desacralization by democratizing access to the sacred.

The second volume (1966) — most of which is taken up by what Seaver and Wainhouse call Sade's "masterpiece," the wildly explicit and unfinished comprehensive catalog of sexual atrocities practiced by an incestuously constituted circle of libertine aristocrats upon a carefully selected harem of boys and girls at an isolated chateau, *The 120 Days of Sodom* — includes two introductions and a revised translation of Beauvoir's "Must We Burn Sade," which proclaims that Sade "deserves to be hailed as a great moralist" along with the Sade scholar Pierre Klossowski's "Nature as Destructive Principle," an excerpt from his seminal study *Sade mon prochain*, in which he notes that Sade's work resembles "the analysis of evil for evil's sake which we find in Saint Augustine's *Confessions*."[10] And indeed it was the moral implications of Sade's work, particularly in their ambiguous relationship to contemporary American liberalism, that would most concern Seaver and Wainhouse, who dedicate this second volume "to the memory of Maurice Heine, who freed Sade from the prison wherein he was held captive for over a century after his death, and to Gilbert Lely, who has unselfishly devoted himself to this same task of liberation and restitution." The back cover quotes prominent American academics praising the publication of the first volume, including Wallace Fowlie ("a courageous publication"), Henri Peyre ("an event of importance in American publishing"), and Harry T. Moore ("it is highly important that we have this authentic and definitive edition"). The third volume, published in 1968, features only the massive novel *Juliette*.

This extensive paratextual apparatus describes a migration from European to American protocols and centers of consecration and moral deliberation. Sade begins as the dirty secret of Francophone modernism, lauded by such luminaries as Baudelaire, Apollinaire, Georges Bataille, and Blanchot but generally unavailable to the common reader in French or English until after the Second World War, when every distinguished French publisher, including Jean-Jacques Pauvert, Les Éditions de Minuit, Éditions du Seuil, and Éditions Gallimard, began to bring out Sade's work, along with biographical and critical appraisals, such as Beauvoir's and Blanchot's. Then, with Olympia Press and the Merlin collective as a conduit from France to the United States, Grove in effect domesticated the Sadean aura, first through the herculean scholarly efforts of Seaver and Wainhouse, and then with the imprimatur of established Francophile academics such as Fowlie and Peyre. Grove's Sade, in other words, represents an inevitable culmination of the canonization of European modernism in the American academy.

Sade also represents the apotheosis of a belief in the subversive power of writing that was ironically vitiated by the unopposed publication of his work. The biographical and critical material incorporated into the Grove Press volumes all emphasize that Sade did not truly begin to write until he was imprisoned, and that his obsessive writerly regime during his lengthy incarcerations can be understood as a vengeful assault on the system that condemned his behavior. The very materiality of this writing is fetishized by Grove's edition in the form of facsimiles of his script on the paste-down endpapers of all three volumes (see figure 6.1), facsimiles of letters from Seaver's private collection, and a copy in the introductory chronology of the first volume of the order of the minister of the interior forbidding Sade access to "pencils, pens, ink, or paper." As Beauvoir's essay affirms, once Sade was imprisoned, "a man lay dying in captivity, but a writer was being born."[11] Sade's interest, then, lay less in his libertinism—although his biography has proven to be of perennial

6.1. Marquis de Sade's handwriting was reproduced for the paste-down endpapers of the three-volume Grove Press collection of his writings, *The Marquis de Sade*.

interest to scholars—than in his obsessive efforts to explain and justify it in and through writing.

This fetishization of writing correlates with a conviction about what we might call the effectivity of reading. In his account of translating Sade, published in the *Evergreen Review* in 1966, Wainhouse affirms that "sometimes it happens that reading becomes something else, something excessive and grave; it sometimes happens that a book reads its reader through."[12] In their translators' foreword, Seaver and Wainhouse elaborate: "Whether or not it is dangerous to read Sade is a question that easily becomes lost in a multitude of others and has never been settled except by those whose arguments are rooted in the conviction that reading leads to trouble. So it does; so it must, for reading leads to nowhere but to questions."[13]

For Seaver, these questions involved both the metaphysical and historical extensions of the problem of evil. The "Publisher's Preface," which follows the translators' foreword and was also written by Seaver, confirms: "Now, twenty years after the end of the world's worst holocaust, after the burial of that master of applied evil, Adolph Hitler, we believe there is added reason to disinter Sade."[14] Using the vocabulary elaborated by John Peters in *Courting the Abyss: Free Speech and the Liberal Tradition*, one can understand Sade as an "abyss-artist" whose entire philosophic and aesthetic program is based in moral negation, and Seaver and Wainhouse as "abyss-redeemers" who "recognize the peril of the fiery deluge but believe that (vicariously) fathoming hell's lessons justifies the risk of the descent and trust that enlightenment will follow their forays."[15] The constant coupling of the principles of liberty and evil in the proliferating metadiscourse about Sade in the sixties inserts Grove's publication of his work into the postwar crisis of liberalism, which had been forced by the Holocaust and the atomic bomb to face the nihilism that had always shadowed liberalism's individualist ethos.

Seaver succeeded in getting Sade's anniversary noticed in the precise terms he intended. One month after his article appeared, the first volume of Grove's edition of Sade was reviewed by the Hunter College French Professor Alex Szogyi for the New York Times: "One hundred and fifty years after his death in 1814, it is perhaps ample time for the Marquis de Sade to be welcomed into the public domain. For a world conscious of its own absurdity and the imminence of its possible destruction, the intransigent imaginings of the Marquis de Sade may perhaps be more salutary than shocking."[16] Szogyi goes on to praise Grove's "generous, handsome, critical edition, beautifully printed with two major essays on the Marquis's work." He then concludes with the question: "May we not see his work as an immense plea for tolerance in a false and antiquated society?"[17] This oddly unselfconscious juxtaposition of an absolute evil analogous to Hitler or the atom bomb and an absolute liberty dedicated to the tolerance of any and all deviance and desire epitomizes the paradoxical image of Sade that was propagated by Grove's paratextual efforts. Sade was simultaneously a symbol of the evil that humanity had recently proven itself capable of and the freedom it purportedly aspired toward. Seaver perceived this paradox more acutely than Szogyi and significantly thought it could only be resolved through making the work widely available. As he notes in his Evergreen Review article: "Which is he: devil or saint? Or perhaps both? Obviously, it is impossible to know until the doors are at last flung open and his works made available to more than the fortunate few."[18]

Elisabeth Ladenson notes in her wonderful study, Dirt for Art's Sake: Books on Trial from Madame Bovary to Lolita: "The idea of Sade as the incarnation of liberty was to have a great deal of staying power." Focusing on the popular cinematic renditions of Sade that followed upon the mainstream publication of his work, Ladenson concludes that Sade "has become a sort of libertine Dalai Lama, dispensing wisdom and preaching personal liberation through the shedding of sexual and social inhibition."[19] But this Sade could only emerge once he had been purged of the aura of evil that partly legitimated reading him in the first place. Both Sade and his modern avatar Jean Genet (also published by Grove) entered the American literary marketplace in the sixties as avatars of evil, and their evil was frequently framed in explicitly religious terms, as is evident in the title of Sartre's massive study *Saint Genet*, the English translation of which was published in the United States in 1963. However, as Hannah Arendt's discourse on "the banality of evil" indicates, this religious framework was residual, and the successful integration of Sade's work into the American literary marketplace in the end diminished the satanic aura associated with it.[20]

The back covers of all three volumes of Grove's *The Marquis de Sade* specify along the bottom border that "the sale of this book is limited to adults," and certainly another crucial reason that Grove was able to issue these volumes without legal interference was its invention of an "adult" category of literature in the sixties. In 1966, the year that the U.S. Supreme Court took up the case of Putnam's publication of John Cleland's notorious *Memoirs of a Woman of Pleasure*, Grove formed the Evergreen Club specifically for distributing its more controversial titles to adult readers. The events are related. Putnam's case had been appealed along with *Mishkin v. State of New York* and *Ginzburg v. United States*, and the Court issued a split decision on March 21, 1966, exonerating Cleland's book but affirming the guilty verdicts in *Ginzburg* and *Mishkin*. The reasons for this split illuminate the success of the Evergreen Club. While *Memoirs of a Woman of Pleasure* was issued by a reputable publisher, Ralph Ginzburg and Edward Mishkin were pariah capitalists who had marketed their wares on the margins of the legitimate publishing industry. In affirming the guilty verdicts, the high court determined that it "may include consideration of the setting in which the publications were presented as an aid to determining the question of obscenity."[21] While this logic was maligned at the time, it also marked the inception of a theory of "variable obscenity," which would displace the more absolute definitions with which the Court was struggling at the time. And by far the most consequential application of the doctrine of variable obscenity was the legal distinction between minors and adults that Grove would help to install in the literary marketplace during this era.[22]

Thus, even though the split decision in 1966 put Mishkin and Ginzburg in jail, it provided Rosset, whose reputation was at its peak, with the opportunity to move in on their turf, legally and profitably exhuming the entire literary underground of the modern era. Indeed, Grove almost single-handedly transformed the term *underground* into a legitimate market niche with a campaign in 1966 to encourage readers to "Join the Underground" by subscribing to the *Evergreen Review* and joining the newly formed Evergreen Club. By specifying its audience as "adult," by continuing to emphasize its literary reputation, and by marketing its explicit materials through the institution of a book club, Grove was able to turn the Court's developing variable-obscenity logic to its advantage. Rosset dealt in much the same wares as Ginzburg and Mishkin, but the combination of Grove's literary reputation and the restricted audience enabled by the club prevented him from suffering their fate.

In the opening months of 1966, "Join the Underground" appeared in full-page ads in prominent venues such as *Esquire, Ramparts, New Republic, Playboy*, the *New York Review of Books*, and the *Village Voice*, and on posters throughout the New York City subway system. Grove also distributed tens of thousands of free stickers to subscribers, which began to appear on public benches and in public bathrooms across the country. The press's full-page ad in the *New York Times* opens by provocatively specifying its target demographic: "If you're over 21; if you've grown up with the underground writers of the fifties and sixties who've reshaped the literary landscape; if you want to share in the new freedoms that book and magazine publishers are winning in the courts, then keep reading. You're one of us." The ad proceeds to chronicle how Grove spearheaded this transformation, from the court battles over Lawrence and Miller to its promotion and publication of the Theater of the Absurd and the French new novel. Then, in order to entice the audience expanded by Grove's efforts to join the club and subscribe to the magazine, the ad offers a free copy of one of three titles: *Eros Denied* by Wayland Young, *Games People Play* by Eric Berne, and *Naked Lunch* by William Burroughs, which Grove could then describe as "an authentic literary masterpiece of the 20th century that has created more discussion, generated more controversy, and excited more censors than any other novel of recent times."[23] The campaign was a big success, as more than fifteen hundred new members joined the club from the *New York Times* ad alone.[24]

Buoyed by this success—circulation for the *Evergreen Review* had nearly doubled from 54,000 to 90,000 in the first half of 1966—Grove commissioned Marketing Data Inc. that summer to distribute a survey to *Evergreen Review* subscribers. The survey established that the *Evergreen Review*'s typical reader, according to an article in *Advertising Age*, "is a 39-year-old male, married, two children, a college graduate who holds a managerial position in business or industry, and has a median family income of $12,875."[25] Rosset and the managing editor Fred Jordan promptly mounted a follow-up campaign, proudly trumpeting that *Evergreen Review* has "a collection of readers who are better educated than *Time*'s; better off than *Esquire*'s; and holding down better jobs than *Newsweek*'s."[26] It would be to these well-paid and well-educated readers, adjacent to and clearly interested in the countercultural communities that remained the magazine's core constituency, that Grove would channel much of its catalog in the later 1960s, a catalog that was increasingly ballasted by pornography and erotica exhumed from the Edwardian and Victorian undergrounds, much of which Rosset acquired when he purchased the under-the-counter cache of a bankrupt Midtown bookseller for six thousand dollars in

1966, and all of which was made available through the Evergreen Club in the ensuing years.

After Sade, the most notorious and voluminous example of this underground literature was the eleven-volume anonymous autobiography *My Secret Life*, which documents the sexual exploits and escapades of a Victorian gentleman whose identity has never been established with certainty. *My Secret Life* had already achieved a certain visibility with the publication of Steven Marcus's groundbreaking study, based on his research in the Kinsey Institute's archives, *The Other Victorians* (1964). This book devotes two full chapters to the extremely rare manuscript and provides the terminological foil for the first part of the first volume of Foucault's *History of Sexuality*. Grove in turn would make extensive use of Marcus's book in its packaging and promotion of *My Secret Life*, including offering it at a reduced price to Evergreen Club members who purchased the massive autobiography.

As with its publication of Sade, Grove's approach to *My Secret Life* was assiduously scholarly. The preface extensively quotes from *The Other Victorians*, paying special attention to bibliographic description and detail and concluding that "in the interest of preserving the authenticity of a document of great importance, which until now has been available only to a very few scholars, it was deemed best to make as few changes as possible."[27] The lengthy introduction, written by the former Kinsey Institute archivist and bona fide eccentric Gershon Legman, then opens with the significant claim that "bibliography is the poor man's book collecting."[28] Legman's introduction is forbiddingly fastidious, lengthily laying out the little-known history of the surviving bibliographies of erotic literature and putting forth his theory that the author of *My Secret Life*, known in the text only as "Walter," was actually the erotic book collector and bibliographer Henry Spencer Ashbee, also known as Pisanus Fraxi, whose bequest of his collection to the British Library formed the nucleus of its notorious Private Case. Grove's massive box-set two-volume hardcover edition runs to well over two thousand pages, supporting Legman's contention that *My Secret Life* "is not only the most erotic but also . . . the *largest* autobiography ever published."[29] The set ends with a forty-two-page subject index that includes such interesting entries as "Balls, men's felt by me whilst fucking"; "Energetic buttocks in fucking"; and "Privy seat, a little girl fucked standing on."

If the publication of Sade was understood as the disinterment of the underground of Enlightenment rationalism, the publication of *My Secret Life* was understood, with Marcus's study providing paratextual authority, as the exhumation of the underworld of the Victorian novel. As the preface favorably recaps: "One of the most interesting aspects of *My Secret Life* is the way in which it relates, and adds a new dimension, to the Victorian novel." It goes on to cite Marcus's contention that "it adds considerably to our understanding of the Victorian novel if we read it against such scenes as those represented in *My Secret Life*, if we understand that the Victorian novelists were aware of such scenes, and that their great project, taken as a whole, was directed dialectically against what such scenes meant."[30] The preface concludes by citing a review of Marcus's study, which affirms that *My Secret Life* "is the other side of the Victorian novel, what Dickens and Meredith and George Eliot and Thomas Hardy were obliged to leave out. And if only for this reason . . . it should be published as soon as possible."[31]

However, reviewing *My Secret Life* for the *New York Times*, the Cambridge University professor J. H. Plumb, agreeing that Grove's publication "helps to adjust our vision of 19th-century England and Europe," warns that it is "only a fragment of evidence" and that Marcus "has only scratched the surface." He concludes that "in the 19th century, industrial society was creating new patterns of living, not only economic or social but also sexual. And we ought to give to the Victorians the close attention that we give to savage and primitive societies. The material abounds."[32] Over the next five years, Grove would make sure that this material became available not only to scholars but to the general public, bringing out an entire catalog of underground "classics" under a series of new imprints, such as Venus Library, Zebra Books, and Black Circle. Between 1966 and 1971, Grove brought out such titles as *The Boudoir: A Victorian Magazine of Scandal*, whose back cover claims, "circulating from hand to hand, this daring assortment of exotica was at one time enjoyed only behind closed doors. Now, at last, it can be read by all"; *Forbidden Fruit*, whose jacket copy informs us that "the recent 'discovery' of an entire body of underground Victorian and Edwardian literature . . . has given us a new perspective on life in that luxuriant era"; *Green Girls*, which the jacket copy attributes to "the Annals of the Victorian Underground"; *Gynecocracy*, celebrated as the "First American Publication of the long-suppressed Victorian classic"; *Harriet Marwood, Governess*, which the jacket copy describes as "redolent of the exquisite patchouli in the works of those unknown delineators of the strange and delicious bizarreries of the outwardly upright Victorians"; *The Lustful Turk*, billed as "a classic example of the Victorian Age's underground novel"; *A Man with a Maid*, which is extolled as "one of the most famous underground novels of Victorian England"; *The Modern Eveline*, which "offers yet another fascinating description of life and love among the not-so-stuffy English aristocracy around the turn of the century"; *New Ladies' Tickler; or, The Adventures of Lady Lovesport and the Audacious Harry*, billed as "one of those extraordinary books from Victorian times in which the characters absolutely refuse to be unhappy"; *The Pearl*, a complete reissue of "The Underground Magazine of Victorian England," which "flourished on the subterranean market until December, 1880, when it vanished as mysteriously as it appeared"; and *Sadopaideia*, which "may well rival *My Secret Life* as an important literary discovery."

All of these titles sold well—alongside Sade, Genet, and other more notorious authors—through the Evergreen Club, many were prominently reviewed, and a number of them were bestsellers. Indeed, on June 29, 1968, *A Man with a Maid* and *The Pearl* were numbers 2 and 3, respectively, on the *New York Post* bestseller list. This popularity significantly contrasts with the prior limited availability, and indeed collectability, of most of these titles, which Grove frequently emphasized in its jacket copy and in its promos for the book club. Thus *The Memoirs of Count Alexis* is billed as an "extraordinary volume—limited to only 700 copies in its privately printed original edition"; *The Abduction of Edith Martin* is billed as a "relentlessly faithful reproduction of a privately published erotic classic, limited in the early 1930's to an edition of only 250 copies"; and *"Frank" and I*, one of the many flagellation novels Grove reissued, is billed as "originally published in 1902 in an edition of 350 copies for private subscribers." *My Secret Life*, largely unavailable when Grove brought out their popular edition, epitomized this shift from private to public circuits of distribution, which transformed the publishing industry by eliminating the need for a literary underground.

By the late sixties, the Evergreen Club had become a primary supplier of pornographic texts, including illustrated sex manuals, legal-advice books, erotic-art catalogs, and gay porn. The club reissued the complete Olympia's Traveler's Companions series and began featuring package deals such as an "erotic dozen" with titles like *Young Anal Daughters*, *The Incest Lovers*, and *Anal Babysitters*. Grove also set up a separate Evergreen film club for distributing both experimental and pornographic film after Rosset's landmark succes de scandale in 1968 with *I Am Curious (Yellow)*. One Evergreen Club brochure announces: "Now! For the first time ever . . . A Historic 'Blue-Film' Festival Right in Your Own Living Room!" Another trumpets: "The Most Famous Actress of Our Time Will 'Go All the Way' for You—In Your Own Room!"[33]

Grove's forays into pornography were highly profitable, enabling the press to purchase an entire building on the corner of Mercer and Bleecker Streets, with a private elevator for Rosset, who was now a national celebrity, prominently profiled in *Life* magazine as "The Old Smut Peddler" and in the *Saturday Evening Post* under the title "How to Publish 'Dirty Books' for Fun and Profit." The *Life* profile, significantly, focuses on Rosset's forays into film, which it calls his "new four-letter word."[34] The author Albert Goldman summarizes Rosset's plan in prophetic terms:

It's time to scale the movies down to human proportions. The moving picture camera today is just a very expensive typewriter. A Hollywood director can go home, like the young writer used to go home from the ad agency, and knock out a very good movie for $50,000. It's possible to take that movie and squeeze it into a cassette videotape the size of a book. And then one evening, when the kids are in bed, you can slip that cassette into your TV set and, without getting dressed or driving the car, you can watch *Tropic of Cancer* or *The Story of O* right in your own living room—where the censor can't go.[35]

Rosset's plans anticipate with uncanny accuracy the direction the porn industry would take in the seventies and eighties, as videocassettes, and then the Internet, enabled a privatization of consumption that would make pornography into a legitimate billion-dollar industry.

But Rosset would not reap any profits from the transformation he prophesied. As I've detailed elsewhere, on April 13, 1970, a group of women led by the feminist Robin Morgan, who had been employed as an editor at Grove (ironically, she worked for Seaver), occupied its offices, demanding union recognition and asserting that Rosset had "earned millions off the basic theme of humiliating, degrading, and dehumanizing women through sado-masochistic literature, pornographic films, and oppressive and exploitative practices against its own female employees."[36] In that same year, Kate Millett published her groundbreaking feminist manifesto *Sexual Politics*, in which Grove Press authors Miller and Lawrence figure as "counterrevolutionary sexual politicians."[37] Grove responded by publishing essays by second-wave feminists in the *Evergreen Review*, including excerpts from Vivian Gornick and Barbara Moran's foundational 1971 anthology *Woman in Sexist Society* and an essay by the *Evergreen Review* contributing editor Julius Lester entitled "Woman—The Male Fantasy."[38] But the seventies were unfriendly to Grove, as its countercultural constituency fragmented and the publishing world continued to conglomerate. Rosset had to cease publication of the *Evergreen Review*, and in the early eighties he was forced to sell the press to Ann Getty, who promptly fired him. His last significant acquisition was Kathy Acker.

Grove's exhumation of the underground had two profoundly significant consequences. On the one hand, the desacralization of pornography enabled the emergence of the full-blown industry that exists today, and that would become the central target of feminist critique. The end of obscenity, in other words, precipitated the politics of pornography, casting a crucial historical sidelight on Catharine MacKinnon's polemical claim that "obscenity law is concerned with morality, specifically morals from the male point of view. . . . The feminist critique of pornography is a politics, specifically politics from women's point of view. . . . Morality here means good and evil; politics means power and powerlessness."[39] What MacKinnon crucially doesn't recognize is the degree to which the "moral" struggle of the sixties laid the groundwork for the political critique of the seventies and eighties. The end of obscenity made these texts available for critique—both Andrew Dworkin and Angela Carter use Grove's *The Marquis de Sade* in their important feminist studies of pornography—and in addition the dissolution of the sacred category of evil as a descriptor of pornographic texts enabled the secular category of politics to emerge as the central battleground.[40] Indeed, one could argue that Grove's elimination of the threat of censorship enabled the terminological shift from obscenity to pornography that MacKinnon thematizes here.

MacKinnon, of course, is a college professor, and the other significant consequence of Grove's exhumation of the underground has been the installation of academic expertise as a crucial charismatic weapon in this political battle. And, in a very significant sense, Sade is a primary source of this charisma, which has been so successfully routinized in the contemporary academy. As Frances Ferguson affirms in her important study *Pornography, the Theory*, "the twentieth century has embraced Sade's writings with an enthusiasm so intense that it once appeared that writing about Sade was almost a predictable stage in establishing an intellectual career; what the writing of pastorals and epics had classically done to demonstrate poetic seriousness, writing about Sade did for writers like Blanchot, Bataille, Beauvoir, Barthes, Lacan, and Foucault."[41] If the charismatic authority of these French intellectuals was established through their knowledge of Sade, then this charisma was, in turn, routinized in the American academy by its embrace of their work, which has informed so much of the study of sexuality in the United States since the eighties.

The domestication of Sade was a necessary prelude to the consecration of Foucault in the United States. By the seventies, Foucault had moved beyond his own Sadean apprenticeship: he wrote prominently of Sade's foundational historical significance in "A Preface to Transgression," originally published as part of the journal *Critique*'s "Hommage à Georges Bataille" in 1963, and in the classic conclusion to *Madness and Civilization*, originally published in 1961.[42] But his apotheosis in the United States would have to wait until the end of obscenity, when Sade would become as familiar to a generation of American academics as he had once been to a coterie of French intellectuals.

## Notes

This chapter derives from my book, *Counterculture Colophon: Grove Press, the Evergreen Review, and the Incorporation of the Avant-Garde* (Stanford, CA: Stanford University Press, 2013). It is reprinted with permission of the publisher.

1. Foucault, *The History of Sexuality*, 34.
2. Glass, "Redeeming Value." For a detailed account of the "end of obscenity" by one of the lawyers central to Grove's campaign, see Rembar, *The End of Obscenity*.
3. Jameson, "The Vanishing Mediator."
4. For Weber's original formulation of this important concept, see *On Charisma and Institution Building*, 48–66.
5. Wilson, "The Vogue of the Marquis de Sade," 173.
6. For an excellent history of Olympia Press, see de St. Jorre, *Venus Bound*. See also Campbell, *Exiled in Paris*, 36–80, 122–80.
7. Seaver, "An Anniversary Unnoticed," 54.
8. Letter from Richard Seaver to Austryn Wainhouse, March 16, 1965, Grove Press Collection, Syracuse University Special Collections Library (GPC hereafter).
9. Paulhan, "The Marquis de Sade and His Accomplice," 10; Blanchot, "Sade," 38.
10. Beauvoir, "Must We Burn Sade?," 40; Klossowski, "Nature as Destructive Principle," 66.
11. Beauvoir, "Must We Burn Sade?," 14.
12. Wainhouse, "On Translating Sade," 51.
13. Seaver and Wainhouse, "Foreword," *The Marquis de Sade: Justine, Philosophy in the Bedroom, and Other Writings*, xii.
14. Seaver, "Publisher's Preface," xxii.
15. Peters, *Courting the Abyss*, 86.
16. Szogyi, "A Full Measure of Madness," 4.
17. Szogyi, "A Full Measure of Madness," 22.
18. Seaver, "An Anniversary Unnoticed," 54.
19. Ladenson, *Dirt for Art's Sake*, 229, 234.
20. Arendt, *Eichmann in Jerusalem: A Report on the Banality of Evil*.
21. "United States v. Ginzburg," in *Censorship Landmarks*, edited by Edward de Grazia (New York: Bowker, 1969), 485.
22. The seeds of the shift from absolute to variable definitions of obscenity can be usefully tracked across two influential law review articles: see Lockhart and McClure, "Censorship of Obscenity"; and Lockhart and McClure, "Literature, the Law of Obscenity, and the Constitution." See also Heins, *Not in Front of the Children*. The constitutionality of a different standard of obscenity for minors was affirmed by the Supreme Court's ruling in Ginzburg v. New York, 390 U.S. 629 (1968).
23. "Join the Underground," *New York Times*, March 13, 1966, 21.
24. Letter from Richard Seaver to Harry Braverman, January 14, 1966, GPC.
25. "'Evergreen' Digs into Underground Appeal, Finds 'Sold Out' Types Really Dig Its Copy," *Advertising Age*, July 25, 1966.
26. "Do You Have What It Takes to Join the Underground?," GPC.
27. *My Secret Life*, xviii.
28. *My Secret Life*, xxi.

29. *My Secret Life*, xlviii.

30. *My Secret Life*, xvi.

31. *My Secret Life*, xviii.

32. J. H. Plumb, "In Queen Victoria's Spacious Days," *New York Times*, January 1, 1967, 26.

33. "Private Invitation . . ." From Vertical File—Erotica Dealers (United States) (20th century 1960–1979)—Grove Press. Kinsey Institute for Sex, Gender, and Reproduction.

34. Goldman, "The Old Smut Peddler," 50.

35. Goldman, "The Old Smut Peddler," 49.

36. Robin Morgan quoted in Gontarski, "Introduction," xxvi. For further detail see Glass, "Redeeming Value."

37. Millett, *Sexual Politics*, 233.

38. Gornick and Moran, *Woman in Sexist Society*; Lester, "Woman—The Male Fantasy," *Evergreen Review*.

39. MacKinnon, *Feminism Unmodified*, 147.

40. See Carter, *The Sadeian Woman and the Ideology of Pornography*; and Dworkin, *Pornography*, 70–100.

41. Ferguson, *Pornography, the Theory*, 76. On the significance of the "routinization of charisma" for the rise of theory in the American academy, see Guillory, *Cultural Capital*, 176–265. Guillory's principal example is Paul De Man, but he offers his model as applicable more generally to all the figures who were canonized as inaugurators of theory during this era.

42. Foucault, "A Preface to Transgression"; and Foucault, *Madness and Civilization*, 282–85. See also Abbeele, "Sade, Foucault, and the Scene of Enlightenment Lucidity."

# 7

## "A Few Drops of Thick, White, Viscid Sperm": Teleny and the Defense of the Phallus

*Joseph Bristow*

Ever since the mid-1980s, when Winston Leyland and John McRae produced their influential, if divergent, editions of the anonymous 1893 novel *Teleny*, their research has thrown invaluable light on a rare fin-de-siècle work that celebrates sexual intimacy between men.[1] In its most climactic scenes, sperm ejaculates with luxuriating, if not melodramatic, abandon: "The slit gaped," the narrator recalls in a representative passage, "the tiny lips parted, and the pearly, creamy viscous fluid oozed out—not all at once in a gushing jet, but at intervals, and in huge, burning tears."[2] No sooner had these modern editors brought such striking episodes to notice than the British writer Neil Bartlett stressed the historical value of *Teleny*'s brazen eroticism. In his view, *Teleny* commands our attention because it counts as "London's first gay porn novel."[3] The description is apt given *Teleny*'s depiction of an atmospheric nighttime world that, similar to "every large city[,] has its peculiar haunts— its square, its garden"—for public sex; such "trysting-places," we learn, are where the protagonist is cruised by "a brawny man" who "clenched his powerful fist, doubled his muscular arm at the elbow, and then moved it vertically hither and thither for a few times" (85). The novel appears, Bartlett writes, "to relate our story, in our language, because it seems that this text—hidden for so long and part of our dark, private world, [is] speaking a pornographic language which seems hardly to have changed at all."[4] Bartlett's statement stands at the center of a thoughtful memoir that explores the powerful links between late Victorian and late twentieth-century gay men's metropolitan experience.

By comparison, according to Ed Cohen, in an essay contemporaneous with Bartlett's memoir, *Teleny* is not so much a fundamentally historical as explicitly political document. The novel, Cohen asserts, is "one of the most articulate defenses of same sex love to be found in late-Victorian fiction."[5] Cohen's comments remind us that this previously little-known work has special importance because it appeared two years before Oscar Wilde was imprisoned for committing acts of "gross indecency" prohibited by the eleventh clause of the United Kingdom's Criminal Law Amendment Act (1885). For reasons that have at times puzzled historians, the Radical MP Henry Du Pré Labouchere added this amendment, which prosecuted all sexual contact between males (even in private), to the passage of a law largely aimed at raising the age of consent in order to prohibit the sexual trafficking of girls.[6] To be sure, fresh inquiries suggest that what the homophile campaigner John Addington Symonds called "Labby's inexpansible legislation" rendered unambiguous what was already implicit in earlier statutes.[7] But *Teleny* seems highly responsive to this all-encompassing 1885 law because it addresses the powers of intimidation that the amendment bestowed upon members of the public and the press. At one point, the protagonist, Camille Des Grieux, recalls that he received a threatening missive that read: "If you do not give up your lover T[eleny] . . . you shall be branded an *enculé* [bugger]" (110). Such bullying proved terrifying because there was always "the occult hand of an unknown enemy . . . always uplifted against you, and ready to deal you a mortal blow": "a single word uttered against you in the street by a hired ruffian, a paragraph in a ranting paper by one of the modern *bravi* of the press, and your fair name is blasted for evermore" (112). Since the Labouchere Amendment was understandably nicknamed the "Blackmailer's Charter," it is hard to avoid the political potency of Des Grieux's fears.

There is no question that *Teleny* contains some of the most unabashed homoerotic writing that emerged, against the odds, in an era when legal prohibitions on male homosexuality in Britain became more formalized than ever before. Published in a limited subscribers-only edition, the novel was aimed at a small but defiant group of readers who could at last take pleasure in a sexually arousing narrative that refused to consign the man-loving phallus to shame. Yet on each orgasmic occasion, *Teleny* does more than hyperbolize the "tears" that issue from the "tiny lips" of a decidedly emotive penis. Time and again the narrative represents the joys of sexual arousal by paying precise attention to the physiological splendor of the ejaculating male organ:

> Our fingers hardly moved the skin of the penis; but our nerves were so strained, our excitement had reached such a pitch, and the seminal ducts were so full, that we felt them overflowing. There was, for a moment, an intense pain, somewhere about the root of the penis — or rather, within the very core and centre of the veins, after which the sap of life began to move slowly, slowly, from within the seminal glands; it mounted up the bulb of the urethra, and up the narrow column, somewhat like mercury within the tube of a thermometer — or rather, like the scalding or scathing lava within the crater of a volcano. (94)

Nowhere does this glorified phallus, which had been subject to legal inter-diction and medical pathology at this time, show evidence of deficiency or disease. Instead, its life-giving fluid spurts forth in a well-versed scientific vocabulary that expresses sexual health, not sexual abjection, most often through recourse to the incomparable sensitivity and strength of this part of the gay male body.

*Teleny*, however, goes to even further lengths to celebrate the wholesome "sap" that explodes from the urethra. This sensual narrative draws on an im-posing repertoire of cultural allusions that pays homage to the long history of men's intense desire for their own sex. In its scenes of torrid intimacy, it is not uncommon to find Des Grieux quoting the "eager and impassioned tender-ness" that Percy Bysshe Shelley discovers in the statues of Emperor Hadrian's male lover, Antinoüs.[8] Nor is it odd to discover Des Grieux's object of af-fection, the Hungarian pianist Réné Teleny, advising him against indulgence in "real blasphemy to the Mysian god" (106). In similar fashion, these men-loving men comment on "imitations of the libidinous Pompeian encaustics" that they find in the dandyish artist Briancourt's studio (122). Ubiquitously in *Teleny*, we encounter a shrewd, if not erudite, intellect situating the male characters' same-sex yearnings in a far-reaching tradition that links rebel-lious romantics like Shelley to classical writers such as Plato. Unquestion-ably, *Teleny*'s wealth of cultural references, not to say its expansive knowledge of music and informed understanding of modern science, suggests that this work sought to lend scholarly authority to its impenitent portrayal of gay sex.

The swelling "sap of life" that erupts throughout *Teleny* has a larger pur-pose, one that reaches beyond the novel's ostensible aim: to gratify the small group of subscribers who derived sexual pleasure from the first edition. The bibliographical research of James G. Nelson and Peter Mendes has revealed that *Teleny* also had a serious, altogether scholarly, ambition. The work be-longs to a notable development in bookish erotic writing that had for some time been the primary interest of the maverick publisher Leonard Smithers. As Nelson writes, toward the end of summer of 1891 the twenty-nine-year-old Smithers, who originally trained as an attorney, courageously set up a partnership with Harry Sidney Nichols; the two men moved from Sheffield to London, where they "established themselves in a well-appointed rare-book shop and separate printing business in Soho, then the center of the porno-graphic trade."[9] The store provided a commercial outlet for the erotic works that Smithers and Nichols had previously issued, in collaboration with the explorer and ethnologist Richard Burton. Smithers's inspiration to build this kind of list was Burton's privately issued, unexpurgated ten-volume "plain and literal translation" of *The Book of the Thousand Nights and a Night* (1885–86). Several years later, Smithers became Burton's publisher. In 1890 Smithers printed fifty copies of the "Terminal Essay" that Burton appended to *The Book of the Thousand Nights and a Night*. In the foreword, the editor announces that the book "has been produced for private circulation among Scholars and Students of Sexual Psychology."[10] The term *sexual psychology* points to the seriousness that Smithers applied to Burton's work during a period when medical specialists were pursuing inquiries into eroticism.

Throughout his comprehensive Orientalist account of the extent of pederasty within the Mediterranean and Middle Eastern regions he called, after Petronius, the "Sotadic Zone," Burton rails against a late Victorian "age saturated with cant and hypocrisy."[11] He was appalled that such double standards obliged editors to bowdlerize English translations of classical writers such as the scurrilous Roman poet. Smithers's initiative to bring out this exclusive run of the "Terminal Essay" in turn encouraged Burton to work closely with him. With Smithers's aid, Burton ensured that a fully annotated translation of the Latin *Priapeia* appeared, as did *Teleny*, in the list devoted to the Erotika Biblion Society, which took its name from the comte de Mirabeau's erudite revolutionary pornography. This edition of the *Priapeia* for the first time gave its select audience access to faithful renderings of its ninety-five phallocentric poems. Further, Burton's and Smithers's exacting glosses in this edition of five hundred copies enabled readers to grasp such phenomena as infibulations, as well as Latin slang for sexual parts and erotic practices.

Yet it was not only the scholarly distinction of the Erotika Biblion Society's list that mattered to Smithers; he also stressed his desire to produce volumes that "all true Bibliophiles will appreciate, covet, and hoard."[12] This was the case with the subsequent four different editions of Burton's *Thousand and One Nights' Entertainments*, which Smithers issued between 1894 and 1897. Smithers wanted, above all, to maintain high production values so that this scholarly work was "freed from the burdensome restriction of being kept under lock and key, and to take its place on the library shelf alongside Cervantes and Shakespeare."[13] His determination to print fine editions of sexually challenging literature did not stop there. He boldly followed in the footsteps of Henry Vizetelly, who had in 1888 suffered three months' incarceration for publishing a translation of Emile Zola's *La terre*. In 1894 Smithers published English editions of no fewer than six of Zola's fictions, including Ernest Dowson's translation of the novel that landed Vizetelly in jail. Smithers showed similar daring by sponsoring Wilde after the Irish writer suffered disgrace. Upon Wilde's release from jail in May 1897 (when he exiled himself to the Continent, traveling incognito), Smithers was the only publisher to lend the maligned Wilde firm support. At Smithers's behest, Wilde's *Ballad of Reading Gaol* (1898), which carried an elegant design by Charles Ricketts, passed into seven editions before the publisher went bankrupt, seventeen months before the author's early death in November 1900. Smithers's business folded when he had cultivated a list of gifted decadent authors, including not only Dowson and Wilde but also Aubrey Beardsley.

Since the 1930s critics have at times been tempted to associate Wilde's name with *Teleny* because of a questionable "Notice bibliographique" that bookseller Charles Hirsch included in the French translation of this work. Hirsch claims that when he ran the Librairie Parisienne in London in 1890, he received a visit from a "man of forty years, large, fairly podgy . . . who wore on his wrist a row of thin gold bracelets garnished with colored stones" (171).[14] Seldom, Hirsch says, did this gentleman come to the bookstore alone: "Distinguished young men who appeared to me to be writers and artists usually accompanied him" (171). In the past, Hirsch states, he had sold this customer—whose identity he did not know at the time—several works. One of these volumes was the picaresque romp *Sins of the Cities of the Plain* (1881), featuring the infamous male prostitute Jack Saul. On this occasion, however, the unidentified gentleman asked Hirsch to hold on to a thin notebook stamped with a wax seal that a friend would collect from the bookseller at a later date. As it turned out, since this document was picked up from and deposited at the store three times, Hirsch's curiosity was piqued. And so he leafed through two hundred pages of manuscript. "What a curious mixture of various handwritings, of erased parts, omitted, corrected or added pages by different hands," Hirsch recalls (172). From this evidence Hirsch infers that the "extra-licentious production" that awaited collection was a so-called round-robin text by diverse hands evincing a far wider array of cultural reference than one might typically find in a modern work of erotic fiction (173). In particular, Hirsch observes that "quotations and passages from the Holy Books" were so many that he wondered if a "clergyman completely imbued with theology" had a role in writing it (172–73).

Hirsch proceeds to observe that several years afterward he discovered the edition that Smithers had issued "clandestinely in two volumes in a run of 200 numbered copies at the price of five guineas" (173). When he consulted this rare find, Hirsch learned that the action had been clumsily transplanted from London to Paris. Later still, when he spoke to Smithers about these conspicuous changes, he ascertained that Smithers had transferred the setting to Paris because the publisher did not want to "shock the national pride of [the] English subscribers" (174). Hirsch claims that the 1934 French translation is based on the original manuscript before Smithers took his editorial pen to it. Moreover, Hirsch adds that it was some time before he realized that the man who first left the manuscript at the Librairie Parisienne was none other than Wilde. Apparently, Hirsch subsequently delivered a parcel of books to Wilde's finely decorated home, at Tite Street in Chelsea, where he discovered that "some of the bizarre furnishing, tapestries, and ornamentation corresponded rather closely to the descriptions . . . in *Teleny*" (174–75).[15]

Hirsch's "Notice bibliographique" inspired both the Gay Sunshine Press and the Gay Men's Press to impute that Wilde counts among the coauthors of *Teleny*, since their editions feature the Irish writer's image on the cover. Certainly, *Teleny* shares some references with Wilde's *The Picture of Dorian Gray* (1890; revised 1891)—the novel that angered a small but vocal group of journalists, one of whom believed it dealt with "medico-legal" matters made notorious by the recent homosexual scandal known as the Cleveland Street affair.[16] The most notable echo arises from the moment when an "elaborately-illustrated edition" of the Abbé Prévost's *Manon Lescaut* (1731; revised 1753) captures the attention of Wilde's protagonist.[17] In chapter 8 of *Teleny*, Des Grieux reminds readers that Manon Lescaut is his "namesake's mistress," since in Prevost's novel the character Des Grieux pursues a headstrong, and ultimately tragic, affair with her (137). But despite the allusions *Teleny* shares with *The Picture of Dorian Gray*, especially to homoerotic classical figures such as Antinoüs (whose presence in queer writing during this period extends well beyond Wilde's oeuvre), there is little in *Teleny* that equals Wilde's inimitable style. Even if, at one point, Teleny declares that "sin . . . is the only thing worth living for" (53), this is not as adept as the following observation by Lord Henry Wotton, whose elegant phrasing casts a homoerotic spell over his protégé Dorian Gray: "Sin is the only color-element left in modern life."[18] In any case, the authorship of *Teleny* remains obscure because the manuscript to which Hirsch refers has never surfaced. As a result, modern editors have had to decide which of the 1893 or 1934 editions should be taken as copy-text. This point is made all the more complicated by the fact that where Smithers is supposed to have shifted the action to Paris, Hirsch in turn translated the English text into French in the name of restoring the London setting.

These questions about the authentic text of *Teleny*, not to say Wilde's involvement in it, can prove distracting.[19] If one point emerges from the allusions to works such as *Manon Lescaut*, it is that the narrative moves with considerable ease between England and France. That the manuscript of *Teleny* was transferred to Paris and translated back to London says much about the cross-Channel milieus in which homosexual men of a certain class enjoyed sexual contact with one another. No matter the degree to which the topography of the novel does or does not conform to the distinct homosexual geographies of these two great European cities, it remains the case that the narrative is equally comfortable referring to Alexandre Dumas *fils*, Voltaire's *Zadig*, pre-Raphaelite poetry, or *Paradise Lost*. In other words, the novel assumes cosmopolitan knowledge of English and French cultures and idioms, as well as deep acquaintance with the classics and the King James Bible.

More to the point, the fact that diverse hands produced this work under the auspices of the Librarie Parisienne on Coventry Street ("two streets from Lisle Street," as Bartlett observes, "the home of Jack Saul") speaks to the cultural intermixing that was central to the sexual sociability represented in the novel, which blends keys elements of the homoerotic subcultures of London and Paris.[20] Correspondingly, the desire to share sexual experience in a sociable manner between gay men is written into the very structure of the work. From the outset, Teleny is based on a principle of narrative intimacy, which begins with Des Grieux's unnamed but implicitly queer interlocutor making the following request: "Tell me your story from the very beginning . . . and how you got to be acquainted with him" (3). Framed in this manner, Teleny situates its readers in close proximity to the anonymous main narrator so that we remain privy to Des Grieux's recounting of his romance with the Hungarian virtuoso. Instead of demanding a confession, in the interrogative method through which a doctor or lawyer might wish to extract information from a homosexual subject, the narrator serves as a confidant whose promptings encourage us to recognize Teleny's magnetic attractiveness: "Was there any peculiar dynamic quality in his eyes?" (5). As we can tell from both its publication history and narrative technique, Teleny marks a point of convergence between men who wish to share knowledge of a homoeroticism that not only crosses the Channel but also recognizes that in either Paris or London it can and should be possible for men to have sex with one another, in ways that are culturally literate, not constitutionally degrading.

As several critics have shown, Teleny unfolds a romance that helps us to understand not only the breadth of erotic practices worthy of the Priapeia but also an urgent desire for gay men to have freedom to enjoy both public sex and domestic bliss. Scholars such as Matt Cook have turned to Teleny to inquire into what he calls the "topographical foreplay." This is dramatized in a narrative that features scenes of gay cruising that could "map . . . readily on to the Embankment and Embankment Gardens in London" or the "roped-off area between place de la Concorde and the Allée des Vieves in Paris."[21] Meanwhile, Sharon Marcus stresses that one of the most significant aspects of the novel is its concentration on the wish for "domestic privacy, with its promise of a couple's merger and communion," which toward the end of the story the two main characters manage to sustain for some time.[22] "Neither of us accepted," Des Grieux recalls of his love affair, "any invitation to whatsoever entertainment where the other was not also a guest." "Had our union," he adds, "been blessed by the Church, it could not have been a closer one" (138).

Yet in a politicized work that is populated by such a broad repertoire of cultural references, it is surprising that readers have seldom looked as closely as they might at the reasons why Camille Des Grieux takes his first and last names from two tightly connected French novels. We have already encountered the first: the Abbé Prévost's *Manon Lescaut*, which had by the 1890s been adapted for the opera by Daniel Auber, Jules Massenet, and Giacomo Puccini. The second is *La dame aux camélias* by Dumas *fils* (1848) (often known simply as *Camille*), in which the extravagant consumptive prostitute Marguerite Gautier avidly reads the tragic tale of her eighteenth-century French debt-ridden predecessor, Manon Lescaut, who dies in exile somewhere between New Orleans and Charleston, held in the arms of her ever-faithful Des Grieux. Both Prévost's and Dumas's narratives provide notable points of reference when it looks as if Teleny might desert Des Grieux; the musician asks whether his partner "think[s] it necessary to sacrifice" himself "like the 'Dame aux Camellias' or Antinoüs . . . on the altar of love" (152). Since this intense relationship ends in heartbreak soon after Des Grieux discovers Teleny's sexual betrayal in painful circumstances (Des Grieux espies his mother receiving sexual favors from the musician for paying off his debts, an episode followed by Teleny's suicide), the narrative evidently wishes to affiliate itself with, and correspondingly transform, a French tradition of highly emotive and widely popularized courtesan romances.

The famous novels of the Abbé Prévost and Dumas *fils* are hardly the only literary writings that help shape an erotic novel that becomes increasingly cluttered with heterogeneous literary allusions. The multifarious references range from a quotation from Dante Gabriel Rossetti's "The Card-Dealer" (in which the pronoun is noticeably changed from female to male) and a comment on Longus's *Daphnis and Chloe* to *Othello*, *Hamlet*, *King Lear*, "Merlin and Vivien" from Alfred Tennyson's *Idylls of the King*, Laurence Sterne's *A Sentimental Journey through France and Italy*, Algernon Charles Swinburne's "Garden of Proserpine," and two widely reprinted poems on nostalgic themes by Charles Lamb and Walter Savage Landor. The final page of the novel draws attention to the passage in the Old Testament where Zophar, Eliphaz, and Bildad believe that Job suffers because he must have sinned to cause God's wrath. The very last quotation in the story, which figures Teleny as a modern-day Job, comes from the King James Bible: "His remembrance shall perish from the earth, and he shall have no name in the street" (Job 18:17). Such quotations, which at times appear to reflect the coauthors' individual predilections, reveal that on almost every page *Teleny* goes out of its way to anchor its often feverish romance in ancient and modern literary genealogies that aim to add resonance—if not cultural legitimacy—to the tragic tale it recounts.

The allusiveness of *Teleny*, however, does more than simply culminate in the Book of Job to characterize the heroic plight of the ultimately lovelorn Des

Grieux. The ensemble of cultural, literary, and religious allusions belongs to a cabinet library that also includes several interrelated works of late nineteenth-century cultural and scientific inquiry, ones that inform the novel's concerted defense of homoerotic pleasure. To begin with, the differing subtitles of the 1893 and 1934 editions draw careful attention to fin-de-siècle scientific analyses of somatic delight among men-loving men. In the Erotika Biblion Society's volume, the work is subtitled *The Reverse of the Medal—A Physio-logical Romance*. The "reverse of the medal" is the literal translation of the French idiom for the flip side of the coin; the French term, *le revers de la médaille*, which is quoted in the opening chapter, is Parisian slang for the anus or, as one of the characters puts it, "the back side" (13). By comparison, Hirsch's translation of the final part of the subtitle, *Étude physiologique* (Physiological study), serves to characterize this novel more accurately as a work written in full knowledge of French studies of perverse sexuality rather than a romance whose passionate intensity is oriented more toward the tradition of the Abbé Prevost and Dumas *fils*. This picture deepens in complexity when one sees that the exceptional neurology of the homosexual phallus in this story has its basis in the types of extrasensory perception that the Society for Psychical Research had been exploring for more than a decade. These subtitles therefore put critically into reverse the emergent scientific case study that often took the pathological "pederast" and "sodomite" as its object of scrutiny. By contrast with the sexological *études* that gained such prominence in France during this period, *Teleny* offers its alternatives by looking at studies of telepathy and music: areas of inquiry in which *études* variously relate to bodily and psychic affirmation, potent creativity, and, when the two connect together in this narrative, phallic pleasure.

The prospectus that Smithers circulated among potential subscribers to the 1893 edition helps to elucidate these points. In his study of clandestine erotica, Mendes reprints Smithers's prospectus, in which the publisher states that *Teleny* is "based to some extent on the subject treated by an eminent littérateur [John Addington Symonds] who died a few months ago."[23] The recently deceased Symonds, who made his mark as an authority on ancient Greek literature and the cultural achievements of the Renaissance, had done perhaps more than any of his literary contemporaries to provide public visibility for patterns of male same-sex desire, whether in Plato's dialogues or Walt Whitman's "Calamus" poems. Symonds's poetry, too, explores homoerotic themes, as we see in "The Meeting of David and Jonathan" (1878), which *Teleny* at one point implicitly evokes. This poem recalls the famous biblical verse where Jonathan declares to David: "Thy love to me was wonderful, passing the love of women" (2 Samuel 1:26). In Symonds's rendition of these men's intimacy, Jonathan addresses his beloved in a histrionic Victorian idiom:

Darling art thou called,
Darling of all men, Darling of the Lord,
But most my Darling—mine.[24]

As Smithers knew, the work by Symonds to which *Teleny* clearly refers is the impassioned *Problem in Modern Ethics* (1891), which takes "Medical Psychologists and Jurists" to task for their "vulgar errors."[25] Especially offensive to Symonds in this privately published study are the findings of Ambroise Auguste Tardieu, whose medical accounts of male homosexuality (in Symonds's words) are "devoted to describing what he believes to be the signs of active and passive immorality in the bodies and persons addicted to these habits."[26] According to Symonds, it proves "horrifying to think that a person, implicated in some foul accusation, may have his doom fixed by a doctrinaire like Tardieu."[27] Such "erroneous canons of evidence" had much to do with the ignorance of the judiciary when sentencing men tried for homosexual misdemeanors.[28]

By the time *Teleny* appeared, Tardieu's work had become a notorious point of reference in debates about the corrupted physiology of the practicing male homosexual. In his influential *Études médico-légale sur les attentats aux moeurs* (Forensic studies on sexual offenses), which underwent six revisions in the twenty years after its first appearance in 1857, Tardieu writes: "The dimension of the penis of the individuals who engage in sodomy are either very thin or very voluminous."[29] As William A. Peniston observes, "in the most extreme cases" Tardieu "believed that the emaciation of the penis resembled that of a dog's."[30] In neo-Lamarckian fashion, Tardieu insisted that while the active sodomite's behavior led to bestial deformation and urinary illnesses, the same was equally true of the passive pederast, who suffered numerous medical problems. Worse still, such diseases—whether "the infundibuliform deformation of the anus" or the "extreme dilation of the anal orifice"—put the sodomite on the path toward criminality. "Not only," Peniston remarks, "was the sodomite a health risk to himself and his partners, but he was also a danger to society."[31] Tardieu, who was attached to the Hôpital Lariboisière in Paris, remained the leading French authority on this topic for many years.

Yet, as Symonds shows, Tardieu's once-influential pronouncements had not passed unchallenged. In this regard, Symonds draws attention to the 1889 *Handbuch der gerichtlichen Medicin* (Handbook of forensic medicine) by J. L. Caspar and Carl Liman, who "approach the subject with almost equal disgust, but with more regard for scientific truth."[32] Modern historians, however, have revealed that Tardieu had even earlier critics, including his successor at Lariboisière, Paul Brouardel. More to the point, Tardieu came under attack in Jean-Martin Charcot and Valentin Magnan's 1882 study, "Inversion du sens génital et autres perversions sexuelles" (Inversion of the genital sense and other sexual perversions), which belongs to what Michel Foucault sees as the growth of "abnormal syndromes valid in their own terms rather than symptoms of a disease."[33] Yet as Robert A. Nye emphasizes, Charcot and Magnan's adaptation of the new psychological vocabulary of *sexual inversion* hardly liberated the gay phallus from Tardieu's understanding of its distended forms. From these doctors' perspective, inversion corresponded with other perversions, especially fetishisms, which were "the consequences of masturbation or sexual exhaustion."[34] Nye stresses that commentators who made use of Charcot and Magnan's findings assumed "the same connections between these sorts of perversion and functional impotence."[35]

Nowhere in *Teleny* is the man-loving penis either misshapen or impotent. In chapter 4 Des Grieux roundly dismisses "a modern medical book" that states that "the penis of the sodomite becomes thin and pointed like a dog's" (48). As Des Grieux says, there is no question about the healthy "bulky head" of his or his friend's glans (49). Much later, when Des Grieux consummates his passion for Teleny, his knowledge of the *Priapeia* informs his description of his lover's luscious genitals: "My lips were eager to taste his phallus—an organ which might have served as a model for the huge idol in the temple of Priapus, or over doors of the Pompeian brothels, only that at the sight of this wingless god most men would have—as many did—discarded women for the love of their fellow-men. It was big without having the proportion of an ass's; it was thick and rounded, though slightly tapering; the glans—a fruit of flesh and blood, like a small apricot—looked pulpy, round and appetizing" (98). In this passage, the penile "tapering" relates to aesthetic elegance not habitual deformation; Des Grieux celebrates the tip of this well-proportioned organ almost as if it were a still life. Yet all too typically in *Teleny*, the narrative defends the gay phallus by elevating men's attractiveness to men over men's desire for women. Such excerpts appear after readers have witnessed the "really loathsome" spectacle of two physically repulsive female prostitutes (the one a "consumptive girl," the other a "flabby hog") practicing tribadism (44, 41). Moreover, the praise of the "pulpy" glans comes after the double rape of a virginal chambermaid. This young woman takes her life after a young coachman follows Des Grieux's attempt to deflower her. The coachman thrusts his "good-sized turgid phallus" inside her, where "it jut[s] forth its sappy seed" while rending her hymen in two (76). As these horrifying episodes show, *Teleny* exalts the superior beauty, sensitivity, and classical distinction of the man-loving penis by depicting women's bodies as either wholly abhorrent or the natural objects of a man's "limber weapon" (77).[36] In no respect can Des Grieux's experiences of the female brothel to which he is taken as a young man or his sexual assault on the chambermaid compare with his adoration of Teleny's phallus, which is associated with not only physical health and sensual delight but also aesthetic experiences that transcend the flesh.

At the same time that Smithers's prospectus alerts us to the links between *Teleny* and Symonds's critique of Tardieu, it also provides some insights into the reasons why phallic pleasure belongs to a cultural world in which Hungarian music arouses the most achingly pleasurable erections in Des Grieux. "The subject," Smithers writes, "was recently treated in a largely-circulated London daily paper, which demonstrated the subtle influence of *music and the musician* in connection with perverted sexuality."[37] Although the newspaper source that Smithers mentions remains obscure, the mechanism through which music induces homosexual eroticism is clearly detailed in *Teleny*. Throughout this "physio-logical romance," the "blood vessels" of Des Grieux's phallus are "strongly extended and the nerves stiff, the spermatic ducts full to overflowing" (17). His erection, which intensifies when the exchange of glances with his lover runs like an "uninterrupted current" of electricity between them, is not just the result of a sexual pickup (18). Such ideas, which focus attention on telepathy, have a firm basis in some of the inquiries conducted by the founders of the Society for Psychical Research in the early 1880s. "There was," Des Grieux informs his listener, "a strong transmission of thoughts between us. This is by no means a remarkable coincidence. You smile and look incredulous: well, follow the doings of the Psychical Society, and this vision will certainly not astonish you any more" (57). Such telepathic communication begins once Des Grieux hears Teleny perform. Immediately, Des Grieux experiences an Orientalist vision that embraces an Arab world that stretches from the "luxuriant loveliness" of the Alhambra to the "sun-lit sands of Egypt[,] . . . where Adrian stood wailing" for Antinoüs (6). Later Teleny will disclose to Des Grieux that he, too, had reveled in this Orientalist sexual fantasy: "Do you believe in the transmission of thought?," he asks the man who will soon become his lover (15). As Pamela Thurschwell has observed, it is no accident that "Teleny's very name conjures up tele-communications as well as his telepathic connection to Des Grieux."[38]

Moreover, Teleny's name evokes *le style Hongrois* that became central in nineteenth-century discussions of Romani music that many commentators believed aroused the most emotive, natural, and, by extension, erotic responses. Noticeably, the telepathic electricity that connects Des Grieux and Teleny intensifies when the virtuoso performs his Hungarian *tsardas*: a style of rapturous music that "quite differs from our set rules of harmony" (5). Such music, we learn early in the novel, has "gorgeous fioriture," which is "of a decided Arabic character" (5). The tsardas, once it impresses its charm upon the listener, "ever thrills" the "nervous organization" (6). Des Grieux's praise of the "latent spell which pervades every song of Tsigane" (i.e., the Roma) derives from the exhilarating contrasts that this music achieves as it moves from the "soft and low andante" that evokes "the plaintive wail of forlorn hope" to the "prestissimo" that culminates in "a paroxysm of mysterious passion" (6).

Such observations bear strong resemblances to remarks that Franz Liszt in 1881 had elaborated in *Des bohémiens et de leur musique en Hongrie* (Gypsies and their music in Hungary). Liszt's study sums up a body of thinking about "gypsy" music whose untamed emotions characterize a "Hongraise": "In these melodies the delirium of an extreme joy and the feeble languor of a motionless apathy follow one another quickly. . . . The result is that they always impart to one another the effect of contrast in all the different phases to which oscillations between orgy and disgust are bound to give rise."[39] Such music, Liszt contends, arises from an unfettered culture whose "inspiration [is] fired by an incessant *desire*."[40] If, in his prejudiced view, the Jews suffer from an imitative desire to assimilate to Gentile culture ("the Israelites have never produced anything really new"), the "gypsies" regard "authority, law, rule, principle, precept, obligation, [and] duty" as "insupportable."[41] Liszt's idealistic line of thinking is clear to see in Emily Gerard's travel writing, dating from 1888, where she describes a tzigane player: "Sometimes, under the combined influence of music and wine, the Tziganes become like creatures possessed; the wild cries and stamps of an equally excited audience only stimulate them to greater exertions. . . . It is then that the Tzigane player gives forth everything that is secretly lurking within him — fierce anger, childish wailings, presumptuous exaltation, brooding melancholy, and passionate despair."[42] Wild pleasures of this kind make it seem as if the Hungarian musician has power of "drawing down the angels from heaven into hell!"[43]

Gerard's exuberant description is quoted at some length in Herbert Spencer's "The Origin of Music" (1890), an article that engages with arguments about the sexual foundation of music deriving from Darwin's *Descent of Man* (1871). "I conclude," Darwin observes, "that musical notes and rhythm were first acquired by the male or female progenitors of mankind for the sake of charming the opposite sex."[44] Spencer, who rejected Darwin's hypothesis, turned to Gerard's account of the tzigane to claim that such impassioned performance stemmed from an "overflow of energy" that might in some, though by no means all, instances be amatory.[45] Accordingly, Spencer found much to fault in *The Power of Sound* (1880) by Edmund Gurney. Gurney was a leading member of the Society for Psychical Research who explored the "mighty associational elements connected with the primæval use of musical sounds under the influence of sexual emotion."[46] Gurney appealed to the nervous organization of the body to explain a vital evolutionary development not just in music but also in poetry. In particular, he studied the energizing ways in which the "outflow of nervous energy which often gives to ordinary emotional expression an expansive delight unknown to our silent meditations, has its current filled, by means of rhythm, from the deeper and wider sources of our whole nervous organisation."[47] When we realize that the "thought" of Teleny acts upon Des Grieux's "nerves as an electric current" (92–93), we can also conclude that the novel has in mind the first major work by the Society for Psychical Research, *Phantasms of the Living* (1884), with which Gurney was involved, where we are told that "electricity affords . . . a singularly close parallel to telepathy."[48] Not surprisingly, Des Grieux's electrifying vision, as the tsardas accelerates in tempo, climaxes in orgasm: "The hand was moved up and down, slowly at first, then fast and faster it went in rhythm with the song[;] . . . some drops even gushed out—I panted" (7).

Such intense pleasures, however, come at the highest price. Des Grieux, as we have seen, ultimately cannot compete against his mother when it comes to maintaining Teleny's material needs. Teleny's ensuing suicide certainly reveals that the homosexual male body can prove extremely vulnerable when struggling to live a sexually uncompromised life. Elsewhere the novel reiterates this point in a very different, if equally terrifying, episode, which results in a gay man's needless death. In chapter 7, the wealthy Briancourt welcomes Des Grieux and Teleny into his lavish home, whose furnishings ("soft Persian and Syrian divans") amplify the Orientalism that the novel frequently evokes when depicting the orgiastic "Sodom and Gomorrah" of male homosexual pleasure (122). Here, in rooms that bear some resemblance to the Turkish and Middle Eastern decorations of Leighton House, they meet a Western soldier known generically as "the Spahi"; he joined the Spahis, the French army's light cavalry regiment based in North Africa, so that he might "see what new pleasures Algiers could afford him" (125). A sexual athlete, the Spahi yearns to have a bottle inserted into his anus: "Quicker—further in—let me feel— let me feel," he cries, as the instrument of pleasure excites "all the nerves of his body" (134).

Just after the Spahi's "phallus squirted out a few drops of thick, white, viscid sperm," he makes a "slight shivering sound"—a sound that is, as the partygoers spectating his pleasure quickly discover, the result of the bottle breaking inside his rectum: "The handle and part of it came out, cutting all the edges that pressed against it, the other part remained engulfed within the anus" (134–35). At first glance, it might appear that this devastating scene aimed to titillate the readership of a narrative that contains equally brutal episodes, including ones that express extreme sexual contempt toward women. Such incidents might imply that the resplendent viscosity of the sperm that issues from the phallus in *Teleny* is the least defensible component of a work that trades, with much disappointment, in what Bartlett calls "vitriolically misogynist, heterosexual phrasings when it wants to eulogize the sole object of its devotion, a man's cock."[49] Similarly, as Chris White observes, this "entirely incidental and casual" episode provides a depressing instance of the use "of the Oriental to construct images and practices of illicit sex," not least because this figure—who is noticeably "given no name, only the title of his military occupation"—"is expendable and expended by the experimentation of a group of westerners."[50] Yet to view *Teleny* largely as a work whose main aim was to fashion scenes of female rape and Orientalist sodomy for an audience eager to experience homoerotic arousal fails to characterize some of the other purposes that motivate its constant appeal to the strength of the gay phallus. If we concur that this frequently scholarly novel takes such a rebellious stand against authorities that wish to pathologize the music-loving sodomite, we may well be left wondering why the bottle breaks inside the Spahi's rectum. Why does this terrible act occur? As we quickly find out, one of the participants in this party is a doctor ironically nicknamed Charlemagne. This medical man immediately orders his instruments to see if he can save the soldier's life. Even though the doctor is able to extract pieces of glass, he knows that "an inflammation might take place in the pierced parts of the intestines" (135). Thus he urges the injured man to visit a hospital, and it is clear that Charlemagne—despite the authority and professional expertise associated with his moniker—will not accompany him. "What," the soldier says, "go to the hospital, and expose myself to the sneers of all the nurses and doctors" (135)? Unable to turn to the medical care he needs, the Spahi goes back to his lodgings, finds a revolver, and shoots himself.

In the end, this drastic turn of events indicates that it is not the anal and penile pleasures of homosexual men that remain indefensible. By rallying as much cultural and scientific authority as it can to legitimate men's love for other men, *Teleny* points an instructive finger at the medicolegal establishment. As this distressing episode reveals, what cannot be defended are the "vulgar errors" of physicians and jurists, including the author of "the Blackmailer's Charter," along with physicians such as Tardieu, Charcot, and Magnan. At a time when science inspired *Teleny*'s coauthors to imagine that the homosexual pervert might inhabit a supersensual body (one whose propensity for aesthetic pleasure was intimately linked with his telepathic prowess), it remained the case that legal and medical judgments ensured that his healthy anus and penis, when these organs should command greatest respect, were deemed fit for nothing less than death.

## Notes

My thanks must go to Laure Murat for advice on aspects of the French language and to Elizabeth C. Miller and William A. Cohen for their responses.

1. The two editions are the anonymously authored *Teleny: A Novel Attributed to Oscar Wilde*, edited by Winston Leyland (1984) and the one attributed to Oscar Wilde and others, *Teleny*, and edited by John McRae (1986). These two editions vary in the copy-text they follow. As I explain, the 1893 edition is set in Paris, while the 1934 French translation locates the action in London. Leyland claims that his edition "is the first unexpurgated version in English based on the original manuscript" (17). By assuming that the information provided in the "Notice bibliographique" signed by bookseller Charles Hirsch in the 1934 French translation can be trusted, Leyland restores the setting of *Teleny* to London and changes "personal and place names, short phrases and sentences, etc., back to their original form" (17). By comparison, McRae disputes the authority of the French translation and reprints the 1893 text, which appeared from the Erotika Biblion Society under the Cosmopoli imprint issued by Leonard Smithers. I discuss some of the more salient details of the bibliographical history of *Teleny* later. As both Leyland and McRae point out, three previous editions of the novel, issued between 1958 and 1975, are incomplete or inaccurate.

2. Caleb, *Teleny*, 94; subsequent page references to *Teleny* are from this edition and appear in parentheses in the text. The editor, Amanda Caleb, follows the 1893 text published by Smithers. Her annotations are more extensive than McRae's.

3. Bartlett, *Who Was That Man?*, 83.

4. Bartlett, *Who Was That Man?*, 83.

5. Cohen, "Writing Gone Wilde," 805.

6. See F. Smith, "Labouchere's Amendment to the Criminal Law Amendment Bill." Smith contends that Labouchere inserted the amendment to overturn what he saw as poorly drafted legislation.

7. Symonds, "To Havelock Ellis," 3:587. Charles Upchurch clarifies the ways in which the 1885 act made official the already implicit legal prohibitions against male same-sex intimacy. See Upchurch, *Before Wilde*.

8. "The mouth and molding of the chin resembled the eager and impassioned tenderness of the statues of Antinous": Shelley, "The Coliseum," 1:168. See Caleb, *Teleny*, 8.

9. Nelson, *Publisher to the Decadents*, 3.

10. The editor's foreword reprinted in Nelson, *Publisher to the Decadents*, 318.

11. R. Burton, "Terminal Essay," 192.

12. Quoted in Nelson, *Publisher to the Decadents*, 44.

13. Quoted in Nelson, *Publisher to the Decadents*, 42.

14. Caleb includes a translation of Hirsch's "Notice bibliographique" in her edition of *Teleny*, 171–75. For an excellent discussion of Hirsch's involvement with *Teleny*, see chapter 7, "*Teleny*, the 1890s, and Charles Hirsch's 'Notice bibliographique,'" in Colligan, *A Publisher's Paradise: Expatriate Literary Culture in Paris, 1890–1960*, 212–44.

15. The interior of Wilde's home was decorated by E. W. Godwin, and its style was not in the manner detailed in *Teleny*. Critics of *Teleny* tend to concur the furnishing mentioned in the novel implicitly allude to the Orientalist decoration of the artist Frederic Leighton's home, which I mention later in the chapter.

16. This is from an unsigned notice in the *Scots Observer*, July 5, 1890, 181, and is reprinted in Beckson, *Oscar Wilde*, 75. There is some possibility that the author is Charles Whibley. The notice also remarks that Wilde's novel is fit only for "outlawed noblemen and perverted telegraph boys," which recalls the scandal linked to Lord Arthur Somerset, who fled the country after police officers became aware of his visits to a male brothel

on Cleveland Street, London, where young men employed in a post office offered sexual services.

17. Wilde, *The Picture of Dorian Gray*, 35, 208.

18. Wilde, *The Picture of Dorian Gray*, 32. In the 1891 text, this line reads: "Sin is the only real colour-element in modern life" (192).

19. No evidence has yet arisen to suggest that Wilde met Smithers before July 1897; Wilde informed his friend, Robert Ross, that he found the publisher "very intoxicated but amusing" at Dieppe. Holland and Hart-Davis, *The Complete Letters of Oscar Wilde*, 919.

20. Bartlett, *Who Was that Man?*, 102.

21. Cook, *London and the Culture of Homosexuality*, 122.

22. Sharon Marcus, "At Home with the Other Victorians," 133.

23. "Prospectus" for *Teleny*, in Mendes, *Clandestine Erotic Fiction in English*, 252.

24. Symonds, *Many Moods*, 155.

25. Symonds, *A Problem in Modern Ethics*, 9–15.

26. Symonds, *A Problem in Modern Ethics*, 23.

27. Symonds, *A Problem in Modern Ethics*, 25.

28. Symonds, *A Problem in Modern Ethics*, 25.

29. Tardieu, *Études médico-légale sur les attentats aux mœurs*; quoted in Peniston, *Pederasts and Others*, 53.

30. Peniston, *Pederasts and Others*, 53.

31. Peniston, *Pederasts and Others*, 54, 55.

32. Symonds, *A Problem in Modern Ethics*, 23.

33. Charcot and Magnan, "Inversion du sens génital et autres perversions sexuelles"; Foucault, *Abnormal*, 310.

34. Nye, *Masculinity and Male Codes of Honor in Modern France*, 112.

35. Nye, *Masculinity and Male Codes of Honor in Modern France*, 112.

36. It is worth noting that *Teleny* is not entirely consistent in its misogyny. Later, in the densely allusive chapter 8, Des Grieux declares: "No man is ever able to madden a woman with such overpowering lust as another tribade can. . . . The quintessence of bliss can, therefore, only be enjoyed by beings of the same sex" (147). This discrepancy is probably the result of the divergent sexual attitudes of the novel's coauthors.

37. "Prospectus" for *Teleny*, in Mendes, *Clandestine Erotic Fiction in English*, 252.

38. Thurschwell, *Literature, Technology, and Magical Thinking*, 34.

39. Liszt, *The Gipsy in Music*, 2:317.

40. Liszt, *The Gipsy in Music*, 1:111.

41. Liszt, *The Gipsy in Music*, 1:40, 68–69.

42. Gerard, *The Land beyond the Forest*, 2:123.

43. Gerard, *The Land beyond the Forest*, 2:124.

44. Darwin, *The Descent of Man and Selection in Relation to Sex*, 2:336.

45. Spencer, "The Origin of Music," 453. Spencer discusses Gerard's account on 468.

46. Gurney, *The Power of Sound*, 195.

47. Gurney, *The Power of Sound*, 444.

48. Gurney, Myers, and Podmore, *Phantasms of the Living*, 129.

49. Bartlett, *Who Was That Man?*, 83.

50. White, "The Metaphors of Homosexual Colonialism and Tourism," *Victorian Literature and Culture* 23 (1995): 5, 6.

# PART III

Image Archives

# 8

## Art and Pornography:
## At the Limit of Action

Robert L. Caserio

Scholarly attention to activity and passivity in erotic life has tended to be absorbed by debates about gender contrasts, or about sadism and masochism. When the foremost debate in the late 1980s — between antipornography feminists and anticensorship feminists — was resolved in favor of anticensorship, the resolution neutralized the contrasts (in discourse if not in fact) between genders and between active and passive sexual dispositions. The active-passive dyad was especially superseded: its place was taken by affirmations of a happy interweave of power and pleasure in pornographic picturings of sex, and in sex itself. Sadism and masochism each lost its edge, as did the contrast between active and passive erotic biases. The neutralizing supersession has been maintained. But is it possible that the foreclosure of contrasts — of contrasts and not simply of differences — has been premature, and that a divide between activity and passivity continues to be culturally and erotically formative, even though other contrasts (between male and female, between sadist and masochist) might seem less so?

Linda Williams's indispensable histories of visual pornography illustrate the absorption and the subordination — if not the neutralization — of the significance for sexual experience of active and passive leanings. For example, Williams's *Hard Core* (1989) unfolds a sequence whereby pornography progresses — not in any simple way, to be sure — toward challenging "the viewpoint of the phallus."[1] The penultimate challenge concerns "power, pleasure, and perversion," a trinity of terms that heads the chapter on S/M porn.[2] The chapter cogently argues against studies wherein "activity and passivity have been too rigorously assigned to separate gendered spectator positions with little examination of either the active elements of the female position or the mutability of male and female spectators' adoption of one or the other subject position and participation in the (perverse) pleasures of both."[3] Once past these "problematic" contrasts, therefore — and, one must suppose, once past their reification by the producers of pornography as well as by the culture that produces the producers—active and passive phenomena are admitted to be elements in the erotic mix, and hence in the pornographic repertory, but without having any centrality for analysis or experience.

That, at least, would seem to be the conclusion of *Hard Core*. Nevertheless, in her later book, *Screening Sex* (2008), Williams suggests, or implies, that a technological and media revolution in the production and dissemination of porn—the pornographic and sex-hunting practices called into being by the Internet—might provide an occasion for further thought about the status of action in desire and in pornography. In a discussion of interactive sex simulators that concludes *Screening Sex*, Williams attests: "Sex Simulators turn the involuntary confession of pleasure that is the money shot into a cybernetic performance that I can command and control."[4] "The involuntary confession of pleasure" is a euphemism for orgasm, and ejaculation is also a euphemism, albeit unavowed, for passivity, surrender, loss of control. Antithetical to loss of control, the sex simulator invests its user with masterful command. Williams describes a typical experience with the interactive sex simulator: "[It gives] a closeness that puts me right up against [the object of desire's] genitals either through the body of an avatar whose gestures I control or through an ability to move all around the sexual activity."[5] Williams respects this voluntary rather than involuntary pleasure, accepting that "it is also an activity that can put [her] increasingly in the place of the film director, choosing acts, scenes, interactions. It is an ideal of connectivity and relation." "But is it 'having' sex?" she asks.[6] Her question hints at a limit of acceptance, even though the question is a taking-off point for claiming, and affirming, that "an ideal of connectivity and relation" inheres in sex, whatever its variety. The enhanced agency of the director-like porn consumer appears, as Williams sees it, to be an ideal in itself, one whose realization the technological revolution in pornography promises to bring ever closer to achievement by enhancing rather than limiting a person's power of action.

Enhancement of a person's power of action is likely to strike us as more valuable than limitation of it. Even in regard to pornography, which defers action via a substitute, do we not prefer being in the driver's seat, considering our ability to initiate and direct our actions (and those of our desired object) preferable to a passive relation to them? I see a habitual cultural value assigned to enhanced agency in Williams's attention to "command" and "control," and her involvement of them with eros. Inasmuch as we continue to favor the enhancement, the divide between activity and passivity in our address to erotic experience is not as superseded, or as neutralized, as we might assume—or want it to be. I am about to examine three visual artists whose work solicits erotic response—indeed, the photomontages by one of them depend on the incorporation of images clipped from gay-porn magazines.

Despite the solicitation, however, and as an essential part of the solicitation, the work foregrounds passivity. The foregrounding suggests a value in the shared capacities of eros and art to limit or undo a person's power of action.

The limitation or undoing does not bring *activity* and *passivity* into an alliance whereby the terms can be understood as synonymous or interchangeable. Even the strongest argument (after Williams's) for the synonymy of the terms—Zabet Patterson's "Going On-line: Consuming Pornography in the Digital Era" (2004)—does not foreclose the possibility that we might yet have to keep them distinct.

Patterson focuses on amateur cyberporn sites that give users twenty-four-hour access not just to sex but to every aspect of the lives of the "amateur." According to Patterson, such access changes the user's status in relation to the active-passive contrast. You, the user, "are present to the space [the amateur] is in . . . more directly than in conventional narrative film (pornographic or otherwise) because you are solicited as a participant in this space," Patterson writes.[7] "But you necessarily," Patterson continues, "experience the situation and its pleasure in a thrown and almost robotic state, comfortably deprived of the necessity of action." However, should this deprivation of action become uncomfortable for "you" (by which she means the user or viewer), the amateur claims that she or he is really the one who is waiting for the viewer to "do" something. The anxiety about "action" is transformed into what Patterson calls *interpassivity*, a term she borrows from Slavoj Žižek's *The Plague of Fantasies* (1997). To grasp Patterson's invocation of interpassivity, we must "understand that in Web-based amateur pornography, viewers are witnessing an abolition of the spectacular . . . through a collapse of subject and object and of the poles of activity and passivity."[8] Thanks to that collapse, as the other person—the amateur—"perform[s] *in the place of* the viewer," the viewer comes to enjoy "not necessarily the impulse toward masturbation, but precisely the experience of seeing, and having, someone else enjoying." The enjoyment, surprisingly I think, outdistances eros as well as the active-passive polarity: "Critically, . . . in amateur porn, the enjoyment is not just sexual. . . . This further extends the concept of interpassivity and its relationship to sexual pleasure because . . . secondary activities become primary. . . . The sexual activities are somehow less important than the other activities." For example, the amateur "eat[s] sushi, bak[es] cookies, and buy[s] pizza with and for" the viewer.[9] Does the gist of these quotations not recover—and make primary— the pornography user-viewer's agency and action, no less than the amateur's? As the user-viewer's enjoyment outdistances eros, it gives way to the user-viewer's identification with "activities" and with the "performer." The identification thus slips away from the synonymy between action and passivity that is intended by interpassivity. Moreover, Patterson aligns interpassivity with work. On the one hand, the term is a directive agent: "The term . . . pushes us toward a different understanding of the type of work that goes on in looking at Internet pornography." On the other hand, the phenomenon turns the viewer from passive spectator into active worker: "In this scenario of interpassivity, we are pushed toward being conscious of pleasure as itself a type of work."[10] While "the scenario" is said to do the pushing, so that the viewer is made passive, one might claim that the pusher is first and last the directive user-viewer, whose ultimate identification with the performer consolidates what the user-viewer wants in the way of action when going online to begin with. Despite Patterson's intentions, perhaps interpassivity best designates a scenario wherein an interval of passivity facilitates two all-determining actions: an initial purposeful search for erotic satisfaction and sooner or later a resolved, hence actively achieved, possession of it.

If I question Patterson's formulations, it is also the case that I want to describe a phenomenon that she and I share a pursuit of. Despite what we share, however, my contrarian impulse means to propose how difficult it remains to come to terms with passivity, whether it be erotic or otherwise. Even as we search out passivity, a compensatory rectification of it in the name of action apprehensively looms in our theorizing—lest we lose the name of action! It should be noted that Žižek's version of interpassivity is less targeted than Patterson's at equilibrating action and passivity, and less concerned about preserving passivity (or passion, for that matter) as a form of activity. That is partly a result of Žižek's use of his neologism to apply to more than amateur cyberporn, and of his equation of interpassivity with an essential psychological—and Jacques Lacan-inspired—misprision: "You think you are active, while your true position, as embodied in the fetish [discussion of which motivates Žižek's introduction of interpassivity], is passive."[11] Indeed passivity, not activity, is for Žižek the dark unconscious core of selfhood. Only erroneously can the self identify with its actions or with an other who seems to be "doing" things for it. Interpassivity is a form of disavowal, involving what is "unbearable": not being active through another but being passive through another. Being passive through another makes one into an object, rather than a subject. "So what is unbearable in my encounter with the object," Žižek explains, "is that in it, I see *myself* in the guise of a suffering object." He writes, "In interpassivity I am decentred in a much more radical way than I am in interactivity, since interpassivity deprives me of the very kernel of my substantial identity."[12] And what is this kernel? "Inert passivity," Žižek says.

The very tonalities of Patterson's and Žižek's uses of interpassivity suggest how widely contrastive are their addresses to it. The contrast testifies to the still unsettled bearing of passivity in our experience. The artists and artworks to which I now turn are, I think, more likely to corroborate Žižek's rather than

Patterson's claims about an essential human undergoing—indeed an essential "suffering"—of passivity, but readers will read and judge for themselves. At the very least, with appropriateness to the present volume, the artists suggest the possibility that Internet pornography has antecedents in art as well as in the most commonplace erotica; that there might be a similarity among artists, pornographers, and pornography seekers and users; and that simultaneously, despite similarities, visual art in evoking eros might distinguish itself from pornography inasmuch as the former does not disavow the passivity that, if Žižek's Lacanian perspective is correct, underlies "active subjects." The pornography seeker and user surely is an active subject, inasmuch as he or she yearns for action and is impatient for it.

The work of the contemporary American artist John O'Reilly, whose life and career span the era between the Second World War and the present day, produces Polaroid photography-based montages that are visual stagings of the debates and possibilities I've just canvassed. His montages characteristically involve gay porn with reproductions of art icons, so art history speaks in his implicit engagement with activity and passivity. A typical O'Reilly assemblage is the Polaroid montage *Undershirt* (1993). It excerpts from Diego Rodríguez de Silva y Velázquez's *Los borrachos* (*The Drunkards*) the head of Velázquez's luscious-lipped boy Bacchus (he is crowned with grape leaves), and collages it next to a cutout from a gay-porn magazine. This cutout shows a lesser-lipped, sweet but smart-alecky boy, wearing only a white undershirt, his spread knees at the viewer's eye level and his crotch sporting a formidably lengthy erection, quirkily bending to the viewer's right. The two boys appear to hug each other, as if art history were a wedding or at least an embrace between great art and gay pornography—or as if it should be. It is a tentative wedding, because the enticingly fresh face of Bacchus looks dreamily up and away to the viewer's left rather than at the porn boy beside him, whereas the photographed boy's face dreamily smirks without looking at the Velázquez, and his succulent-like member tends in an opposite direction. Will the two frames of reference, art and pornography, not come together after all? On what terms, other than by mere willful splicing, might they merge? O'Reilly enlists "classic" art to address those accumulating questions, but he has an implicit relation with a more immediate tradition. So in following him I must involve his appeal to art in the past with a more present history. The relevant, present history is exemplified by Lucian Freud and Francis Bacon. In Freud, Bacon, and O'Reilly a meditation on erotic passivity appears to be central.

Exposition of the meditation might well begin with Freud's *Man Posing*, an etching from 1985–86 that displays a naked man on a sofa, his wide-apart knees and thighs constituting the central horizontal line of the picture.[13] What response does *Man Posing* solicit from a viewer? The man has a hairy torso, and the lines of the etching communicate his fine body hair to every part of the picture; similarly, the soft rondures of his thorax and limbs communicate with the buttoned upholstery of the sofa, which is torn open at one end—the openness a rhyme for the vulnerability and receptivity of the figure. If we say that *Man Posing* asks us to see the etched lines merge with the man's body hair, so as to equate art and living excrescence, or that it asks us to consider art's etchings and our skin as equal upholsteries on which we rest, then we have yet to look at what in the etching is impossible not to face, dead center: the prominently bulging genitals, the perineum, the cleavage of the buttocks beneath. With what feeling or thought are we to face this soft center of the picture—a center that, by its prominence as well as its softness, endows an absence of erection with a paradoxical potent passivity?

The question feels all the more pointed, and an answer all the more in suspense, with *Painter and Model* (1986–87), which transposes into paint the etched figure in *Man Posing*, only reversing the directional lean of the model and straightening one of his knees. The female painter in the picture, to the left of the man on the sofa, has downcast eyes, as if to avoid the sight of the same cynosure that *Man Posing* opens to us—as if to tell us, whose eyes are as active as Freud's, that we must baffle stirrings of desire, or at least of tenderness, for the flesh in the painting, lest we become overactive in relation to it. The eyes in the painting that are open, the man's eyes, are recessed in an intensity that might precede or follow arousal; and there is a complicated conjunction between the tube of the penis and the tubes of paint at the painter's feet. Is the paint that is the artist's smock, and the smock that is the painted canvas, a disseminated ejaculate? Is this a picture of coitus interruptus, or of intercourse already achieved, or a painting of an annunciation: announcing an immaculate intercourse—immaculate because action is in suspense?

Whatever the picture models, Freud's eyes surely are not immaculate, despite the alibi of innocence afforded by the abashment of the cross-gendered painter in the picture. Doesn't the painter outside the picture, Freud himself, solicit in the viewer an entry point for arousal—an entry point for activating command of at least one of its lures, which is the one that the female painter is not regarding? She regards the paint, of course; and the naked man regards an invisible intensity that is not genitally located. But Freud and the viewer are head-on to the genitals and the perineum. Whether or not the confrontation is to activate desire or to pacify or make passive the very desire it solicits remains a matter of suspense.

That Freud's head-on suspenseful looking or desiring is his characteristic habit can be seen on the basis of an early pen and ink drawing from 1943: *Boy on a Bed*, which can't be ruled out as an image that haunts Freud's reclining male nudes. Here there are two drawings in one, one atop the other. In the top picture a nude boy poses frontally (he is postpubescent, as his hairy armpits make clear), his legs are spread toward the viewer, and his genital zone is as central as it is in the etching and painting of forty years later. The bottom picture is a detail of the top, but at a different moment. In the picture on top the boy's arms are raised; his hands are behind his head. The bottom picture shows the boy's right fist having moved to his penis, which he now is grasping; his fist, his testicles, his perineum, and the inner outlines of his thighs are given a close-up prominence. Because the boy's hand entirely covers his penis, hiding as well as expressing masturbation, the perineal area becomes especially salient, in itself and as a visual synecdoche of the boy's penis and manual action, even of what he might be fantasizing about. Moreover, in the movement from the top drawing to the bottom, Freud refocuses the viewer on a point of potential entry, as if offering a reminder of the viewer's capacity for penetration, if only by the eye. The eye is made active master of the boy, even as the boy practices his own mastery of fantasy.

A mastering penetration—the "classic" sexual action, for multiple males— would seem to be more alluring than a passive receptivity to penetration. Freud's famous painting Naked Man with Rat (1977–78) shows a naked red-haired man lying on a sofa, his face a rictus of pain, his thighs splayed, his genitals at the picture's center, his right forearm crossed over his pallid abdomen, and his right hand grasping a black rat. This nude is perhaps a picture of fantasy—a very specific one. It is impossible to see Lucian Freud's painting without thinking of his grandfather's "Rat Man" case. The original Rat Man fantasized a pleasurable anal penetration by his father but repressed his fantasy, censoriously expressing it as a horror of experiencing anal torture by a rat. The vulnerably open legs of the man in the picture, complemented by alignments of perineum, glans, rat tail, and rat's head, revive the fantasy of Sigmund Freud's patient. If that original fantasy is being communicated to a viewer, it is not surprising if the viewer reacts adversely. The viewer—whether male or female, considering what appears to be at issue—won't be inclined to empathize with such transfixed proneness, or with any receptivity toward it; the viewer will feel more identification with the naked man's defensive left palm, raised by the side of his face in an apotropaic gesture, than with the man's spread knees, which are queerly contrastive to the left arm's groping resistance. The upraised palm, the upraised forearm, and the panicked or tortured facial expression argue the presence of a will to act—to call a halt to, to actively master, invasion and submission. Yet the picture shows a will to action undergoing incapacity. It is as if Lucian Freud and Žižek converge here—as if Freud were painting the unconscious passive core of selfhood, in relation to which the active life is a fantasy, and action only a relatively powerless gesturing.

Although O'Reilly, as we will see, evokes passivity no less intensely than Freud, he appears to be more at home with invasion and penetration, whether they be construed in erotic terms as a kind of desired or desirous passivity or in terms of an intercourse between art and pornography. In a Polaroid montage series called *Occupied Territory*, O'Reilly collages photographs of heads from a Second World War portrait album of German soldiers, bodies lifted out of gay-porn magazines, and canonical art. *Occupied Territory* #12—*Eigner* (1995) shows the face of a helmeted soldier attached to a porn magazine's photo of a voluptuously muscular, hirsute, long-limbed body on a bed of rock, the model's right hand touching, and about to toy with, his flaccid penis. If this soldier represents the occupying army, then the background, which is a Jean-Baptiste-Camille Corot landscape, means that the naked soldier has wandered into art and fallen languorously asleep there.[14] A painted Corot shepherd is coming to find him. Will the shepherd be a David, and act murderously, when he discovers this sleeping gigantic representative of the occupying forces? But who occupies, or preoccupies, whom? Art already occupies the erotic territory. What comes next strategically in the way of advances, and from what side of the border between territories?

O'Reilly jokes with us, but he is also profoundly serious. It is easier to joke about canonical art discovering pornography in its territory, or about pornography being surprised by an incursion of art, than to think through what is going on when one invades the other. As an attempt to think it through, at least in terms of the constellation of terms and artists here, I enlist the myth of Apollo and Marsyas. The story of the master artist-god and the bestial pretender to art has often been told: Apollo emerges the victor in an art contest to which he was challenged by the satyr. When Marsyas loses the contest, his skin is forfeited to the god, who supervises the flaying of the defeated challenger. The myth allegorizes, according to Renaissance exegesis, mastery of animal life by reason and art—and also mastery of body by soul. How does this apply to O'Reilly? Klaus Kertess has discovered that O'Reilly saw Titian's *The Flaying of Marsyas* (figure 8.1) in 1991, and that the painting, in which O'Reilly recognized multiple affinities, had an immediate impact on O'Reilly's montage *War Series* (1991–92), wherein O'Reilly indirectly registers his responses to the Gulf War.[15] O'Reilly, I propose, reworks the myth by redirecting its allegory about mastery toward a meditation on action and passivity. Apollo is a masterful figure because his power of action has no limits—the submissive suffering undergone by the aspiring but artless animal body is antithetical to the god's boundless agency. O'Reilly imagines a contest between the figurehead of masterful art and agency, Apollo, and the satyrs of gay pornography—beings for whom a metamorphosis from passivity into exalted action is only a dream.

It turns out that Freud's and Bacon's artworks are also caught up in the

8.1. Titian (Tiziano Vecellio), *The Flaying of Marsyas*, 1570–75. Oil on canvas, 212 × 207 cm. Archbishop's Palace, Kromeriz, Czech Republic. From *Titian: Paintings and Drawings* (Vienna: Phaidon Press, 1937).

myth of Apollo and Marsyas, at times explicitly evoking it. A further comment on Titian's version of the myth might make clearer how it resonates among the three latter-day artists. Richard Wollheim has laid out an extraordinary analysis of *The Flaying of Marsyas*. He makes several leading points. He says that Titian's posing of the satyr's inverted body and his handling of paint, "in connecting the body so powerfully with suffering, retain[s] [a] connection between the body and vitality."[16] "This Titian does," Wollheim writes, "when he presents . . . massive suffering . . . as the supreme occasion on which man can, through his determination and the straining of body, wrest activity out of passivity." The warrant for Wollheim's claim is his reading of the satyr's "great haunted eyes [in which there is] a totally unexpected look of acceptance— acceptance triumphant over suffering."[17] To this unexpected reversal of the satyr's significance in his contest with the god, Titian adds another. Wollheim continues: "Apollo, pressed up against the great hulk of his prey, stares into the exposed flesh with such intensity as to suggest that his desire is *to envelop himself in the creature that he dismembers.* . . . In Titian's painting the penetration of victor into victim is . . . envisaged. There is to be a merging of bodies."[18]

Wollheim leaves the gist of the last-cited sentence — "there is to be a merging of bodies" — in suspense. Brilliant as his reading is, its logic, perhaps in solidarity with Marsyas, does not have its feet quite on the ground. What does it mean to speak about *penetration, victor,* and *victim* if those entities are as intermingled, as mutually absorbed, as Titian's Apollo is absorbed by the satyr's body? How exactly does activity get "wrested," or wrestled, out of passivity? If such interminglings or metamorphoses do occur, do the semantics of the intermingling, including that of *penetration,* not signify an absorption of action by passion and passivity? Wollheim's reading of the painting prefigures Patterson's interpassivity—understood as a collapse of the difference between action and passivity—inasmuch as he considers Apollo suddenly immobilized, unexpectedly fascinated by what the "amateur" does. But of course what the amateur does is suffer, and accept it; and what the god might be doing in enveloping himself in the flayed creature is discovering another version of "the inert passivity which contains the density of [his] substantial being."[19] The resonance of the Marsyas myth in Titian's work leads us to the myth's resonance for visualizations of eros in the work of Bacon, O'Reilly, and Freud.

Photographs of abattoirs are familiar in studies of Bacon, in part because they represent the archive of photographs and reproductions that served as the artist's working models. He would not paint from life, even though, through a blatant pun, the slaughtered pigs evoke the artist's name and hence suggest a life study, not a still life. One often-reproduced photograph in Bacon's possession shows a butcher cutting open a pig carcass hanging by its feet; other hanging pig carcasses are in the shot.[20] It is customary to connect such photographs with the right-hand panel of Bacon's *Three Studies for a Crucifixion* (1962). The panel shows a bloody, dangling animal carcass, but the carcass has a human face, hanging upside down but appearing to strain upward, its jagged-toothed mouth open as if gasping for air, or screaming. Despite the photographs, the origin of this "crucifixion" might be the artist's knowledge of Titian's Marsyas. That strung-up figure, half animal, half human, crucified by the artist-god is, at least, no less likely an inspiration than the strung-up animal. That Bacon has painted a dog, ready to lap up the victim's blood, at the bottom of the panel is relevant: Titian shows a dog lapping up the satyr's blood. I suggest that Bacon's art is largely a screen image for a contest with Apollo. The contest varies the Marsyas myth because Bacon often wages the competition on Apollo's ground rather than on the satyr's. That is to say, Bacon apparently aims to rival the god's penchant for flaying, as in a characteristic study of lovers, the triptych *Three Studies of Figures on Beds* (1972).

The coupling figures in the left and center panels of the studies include a man, but we are unsure about the gender of the other; one of them is belted or gartered; the limbs of both are outlined, but they are also smeared together. The effect of the painting is to make one see a nakedness that is different from what being unclothed means. It is as if the inwardness of the merger of bodies is stripped bare, the very transfer of bodily fluids is under scathing examination. In relation to the writhing, leaking victims, the artist-god keeps a masterful distance. What he sees is chilling, hence is antipornographic, despite his view of intercourse. In relation to the erotic dissolve of sexual coupling—certainly a blur of the difference between action and passivity—the action that masters the dissolve, recovering it from its indeterminacy, is painting. The painter thereby dominates erotic fate. Or perhaps he "gets off" by dominating it? An erotics of domination, shared by every pornography seeker and user, inasmuch as pornography makes its consumer feel that he or she is mastering an erotic lack, might be the one remaining element of pornography in Bacon's picture—or in front of it, where the painter handles his brush.

Yet if we accept Wollheim's version of Titian, and catch an echo of Marsyas in Bacon, we can see that Bacon also inhabits the figures in the painting and the satyr figure in the myth. The white seminal spatter at the bottom of the canvas hints—interpassively, to be sure—at a collapse of distance between mastering artist and resigned goat. The artist is erotically mixed up with the painting; he is a commanding soldier passively surrendered to intermingling absorptions. The hint of the collapse of distance between master painter and erotic subject changes to explicitness if we consider anew Bacon's renowned relation to the nineteenth-century photographer Eadweard Muybridge. The debt of Bacon's *Two Figures* (1953), a blue spectral picture of a bed in which one humped male figure covers another prone beneath him, needs no reproduction: it is thoroughly familiar, as is its basis in Muybridge's 1887 sequence of stills, *Wrestling, Graeco-Roman*.

Might one see Muybridge as an Apollonian master who exerts a rivalry with animal motion, stripping its skin, tearing off its self-deceiving cover? After all, animal motion does not exist in devitalized strips; it exists that way only as a result of an intervening technology, and in the eye of the master of the technology. Martin Harrison's *In Camera, Francis Bacon* (2005) briefly links skin and film with Muybridge and Bacon but only reasserts a commonplace: that Bacon's painting copies the films or skins of camera motion. Bacon copies those skins on his Apollonian side, to be sure. But Bacon also moves painting back into Marsyas's position. He does so as if to prepare for the penetration of the sufferer by the act of a god—but on the sufferer's terms and not the god's. Bacon's version of the wrestlers in *Two Figures* is based on Muybridge in order to reverse the camera. *Two Figures* reanimates the stills. Putting the strips back together, the painting deprives Muybridge's male beauties of their Greek-inspired comeliness: it withdraws from the erotic master eye what the master eye demands for arousal. In the painting the heads of the figures are side by side yet also intermingled, not actively striving against each other for the goal of mastery as the heads and bodies of the wrestlers do in the photography. And into the grimace that is visible in the painted conjunction Bacon infuses an equivalent for what Wollheim notes in Marsyas's "great haunted eyes": an expression that might be accepting of and laughing at pain as well as expressing it.

The ambiguity and doubleness of the grimace draws a viewer closer, in absorbed perplexity; and no reproduction of Bacon's work conveys the indeterminate expressiveness in the actual canvases. Despite the uncertainty, however, it is an expression of vulnerability that is achieved by Bacon's reanimation of film-stripped skins. Whatever the compound of intermingled elements, and despite Bacon's return of the photographic stills to the fluidity of motion, a yielding of action-centered elements to the pathos of passion informs the composition. Pathos similarly informs the series of portraits of anonymous "men in blue" from the early 1950s. The portraits have been interpreted by critics either as satires of businessmen or as preparatory studies for Bacon's hysterically screaming popes.[21] Neither view is fully responsive. The paintings, especially *Man in Blue IV* and *Man in Blue V*, evoke the blurred first stirrings of personal and erotic interest; as with the development of an intimate relation, they require a viewer's nearness to them if an integration of features or of characteristics is to develop. The required nearness intimates a merger of bodies that supersedes rivalrous wariness and will to mastery; it changes a definite distance between viewer and viewed into an indefinite but absorbing proximity. Pornographic impulse and structure—that is, if they depend on willed control (such as the interactive-sex-simulator joystick)— are baffled.

In *Hard Core* Williams cites and paraphrases Rick Altman's "idea that a genre can undergo 'semantic shifts' which take on entirely new subject matters. . . . Although a new semantic element may be triggered by historical phenomena, it cannot enter a genre except through accommodation to already existing syntaxes."[22] Following Williams, Patterson, and Žižek—as well as questioning them—I have been hypothesizing one of those semantic shifts. Eros is ancient, so an entirely new subject matter is not at issue. But an already-existing syntax—of couplings, of differences between activity and passivity, of differences between art and pornography, of the pornography seeker's will to enable baffled powers of erotic action—has been suggesting a curious semantic reversal, one that is underwritten by ancient mythical themes. In the light of the latter-day artistic evocations of Apollo and Marsyas, I propose that the pornography seeker and viewer-user becomes the equivalent of the Apollonian mastering agent: after all, Patterson's interpassive subjects are oriented toward thwarting constraints that might inhibit their activity, even if and when they let "amateurs" "do it"—do whatever!—for them. In the curious descent of idealized agency in the work of the artists, the divine figure, who in the past represents the most idealized version of human action as a form of domination over its objects, now ranks with a lower order of being, in part because the godlike will to domination has been metamorphosed as a vulgarity. A pornography industry catering to mass demand promises every consumer a piece of the action, especially through the enabling neo-divine magics of Internet technology. Anything that occurs interpassively—at least in a sense that is not identical with Žižek's interpassive—flatters the pornography viewer's sense of the power of his or her pleasure.

The Internet pornography industry, whether professional or "amateur," along with its subsidiaries (i.e., the autopornographic self-advertising hookup sites), are indeed sites of power and pleasure. And their intention is to increase the operative power of erotic action for any willing subject. Meanwhile, at the border of art and pornography, in the work of Bacon, Freud, and O'Reilly, the satyr—to speak parabolically—absorbs the god. In their work, that is to say, the satyr incorporates the god's refinement but does not take in the god's insistence on being a master and on actively mastering lack. The satyr, who in the myth represents a creature lacking substance, now suspends Apollonian will; it is the god who is strung up by his heels. That is why, if one accepts Titian's picture as a prefiguration of a semantic-mythological-iconographic reversal engendered by historical contingencies, Wollheim seems wrong to claim that in Titian's painting Marsyas's massive suffering "wrest[s] activity out of passivity." The suffering appears instead to obstruct activity's domination, to diffuse it into forms of passionate undergoing. Freud, O'Reilly, and Bacon repeatedly picture the diffusion.

If this diffusion disrupts pornography, it nevertheless becomes a new lure for eros, one that can even wrest elements of pornography into alliance with it. Bacon's beautiful *Study from the Human Body* (1949) shows the back of a white male torso standing amid, and also hesitantly entering, a field of blue-black strips or stripes that, constituting the body's environment, figure Muybridgean flaying. The passive resistance of the back and the buttocks to the strips are a white equivalent of Marsyas's suspended endurance. The very blankness of the figure perhaps solicits eros by the figure's movement into a depth to which it is drawn beyond actively directive, explicitly articulated lineaments of desire. As for O'Reilly, the more fleshed-out lineaments—at least as O'Reilly employs them from gay pornography—don't necessarily add up to customary pornographic bait. There is nothing immediately sexy that meets the eye in O'Reilly's *To Patrick* (1975–97) #22 (figure 8.2) even though the picture is blatantly evoking a sex act. But what act, what action? A back-eyed or back's eyed view, O'Reilly playfully answers; it is also a play on the "annuit coeptis" that tattoos the promiscuous back of the almighty U.S. dollar. Simultaneously, the Polaroid montage portrays the art divinity—a master painter's

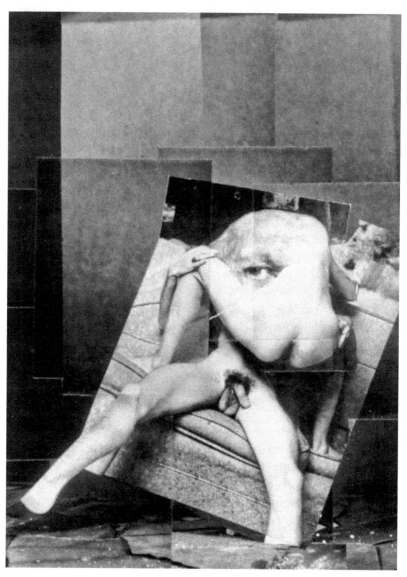

8.2. John O'Reilly, *To Patrick (1975–97) #22*, 1998. Polaroid montage, 8 3/4 × 6 7/8 in. Collection of Tom Morrissey. Image courtesy of Miller Yezerski Gallery.

painted eye—absorbed into, and hungrily nosing, a figure whose right fore-leg ends in a goat's hoof.

There is indeed, as Wollheim says, a merging of bodies. Possibilities of merger in O'Reilly suggest a broad expanse of erotic novelty, not filled with made-to-order figures or poses, even at the moment O'Reilly enlists made-to-order gay poses. But that which is ordered by the will seeking sexual "action" is undone by O'Reilly's assemblages because they throw sexual will off-balance, or redirect its aims. Predicting similar possibilities of undoing the will to action, Bacon's *Study of a Nude* (1952–53)—a full-length back view of a man with his arms raised over his head and his hands together as if he is preparing to dive into uncharted waters of figuration—likely alludes to one of Thomas Eakins's bathers from *The Swimming Hole* (1884–85). But Bacon's diver also might be said to be hanging from his wrists, as Marsyas often does in visual depictions of his punishment. When O'Reilly adapts this figure that harks back to Bacon and Eakins, the adaptation takes on darker possibili-ties of bodily and sexual diving. Number 27 of the *To Patrick* (1975–97) series shows on its right side the back of an ivorine nude stripling bending forward, his head against or amid the strips of light that come from Bacon. The nude appears to be masturbating himself while undergoing a fucking by a standing figure composed of, and also cloaked by, contrastive black strips. The black figure stands between the youth and the viewer. The youth's white diving back, plunging forward into Apollo's light in order to facilitate penetration from behind, appears to submit to an ultimate master. Still, although the master fills the picture with an appearance of doing, the master is composed only of charred paper or Polaroid detritus, of an abject skin, itself a token of some-thing that has received and has suffered action more than it has acted.

To say so is not to regret the loss of action. For those who surmise the loss as incompatible with the democratization of enablements, or irresponsible to increased agency, a last suite of pictures, modulating into an upbeat note, might provide some compensation. On the left-hand panel of Bacon's *Double Portrait of Lucian Freud and Frank Auerbach* (1964), Bacon's full-body portrait of Lucian Freud participates in the Apollo-Marsyan dialectic. The painting sus-pends Freud over a blood-bright ground, assigns him a goatish face, and commingles penile- and buttock-like shapes and colors with springy goatish legs. The spattered paint reminds one that the canvas is a skin detached from Freud's body. The portrait is not without sprightly expressiveness, however. In response, Freud takes up Bacon's mythic suggestion of Freud as a satyr, albeit with a contrastive emotional tone. Freud's self-portrait *Painter Working, Reflec-tion* (1993) splices Apollo (the edge of the painter's upheld brush becomes a knife) and Marsyas (the shoes, the painter's only clothing here, change the painter's feet into hoofs). The master artist-god is overshadowed by the satyr, however, or absorbed into the human animal, made passive-eyed in relation to him, as the spectator of the portrait must be. For the fierceness of the picture and the stance it portrays melt its aggressive Apollonian menace into a defeated being's pathos; the very density of the paint suggests the inhibition of the artist's will, the arrest of his action, by his medium.

In the light of Freud's splice of Apollo and Marsyas we can come to Freud's *Naked Man on a Bed* (1989–90) without having to repeat the puzzled, emphatic disgust of previous responses to Freud's representations of flesh. In regard to this particular picture, in 1994 Arthur Danto, reviewing Freud's work in *The Nation*, comes to a limit point of his own critical brilliance. He notes the painter's realism that extends even to "the cleft between [the naked man's] buttocks [that] clearly shows an anus as natively brown as Courbet's splayed female vagina is pink."[23] He goes on to note that the figure "looks like he could have used a bath. . . . The naked body smells of sweat, urine, bodily discharges, cheap perfume, deodorant, dirt." Danto concludes that it is "the ultimate humiliation to be stripped" in the way that the naked man and other figures in Freud are.[24] Danto forgets the stripping of Marsyas and the semantic reversals that the myth can initiate. Freud's naked man mimes Marsyas's bent arm and crooked elbow, recalling one's attention to the satyr's perplexed eyesight; the foot, half-stripped of a sock, makes the sock a counter for the satyr's skinning. Of course, Freud has upended and further splayed Marsyas so that we must peep into a bodily domain of vulnerable passivity: perineum and anus. Is the arousing of action in the offing? Is that what disturbs critics of this image? Danto masters the image by way of his Apollonian distinction between the naked and the nude; and the critic's mastery does not leak, surrendering nothing, not a drop of sweat, to eros. That Freud might be representing, as Bacon and O'Reilly also might be, a passive openness that allures eros yet suspends agency, leaving agency out of the picture or subordinating its drive for importance, receives no consideration.

Wollheim in reading Titian recollects that Dante in *Paradiso* calls on Apollo to invade him, to take him out of himself so that he will be passively receptive to inspiration, as when, Dante says, Apollo tore Marsyas out of the sheath (*della vagina*) of his limbs (*membra sue*).[25] O'Reilly's *War Series #24 — Lt. Killed in Action Germany 1945 Age 23* (1991) (figure 8.3) poses a response to one's wonder about the relation of the upended Marsyas to arousings of action and to manipulations *della vagina*. On the montage's upper left we see a photographed document of armed action: a battle for mastery. The penetrating digit of a Christ Apollo that O'Reilly borrows from Giovanni Bellini might seem to replicate the masterful rifle in the battle zone (which also is in the rear of the picture). But the appearance of masterful penetration is contravened by the passivity of the penetrator. Apollo/Christ has already been absorbed into

8.3. John O'Reilly, *War Series #24—Lt. Killed in Action Germany 1945 Age 23*, 1991. Polaroid montage, 8 7/88 × 11 15/16 in. Collection of John Pijewski. Image courtesy of Miller Yezerski Gallery.

the crucified animal Marsyas. As he probes and opens the male he grasps, his art-historical face wears an expression of ecstatic receptivity. The expression puts masterful aggression in a subordinated place. This picture perhaps better articulates Wollheim's attempt to read out of Titian a nonaggressive merger of victor, victim, and penetration. It takes another merger, that of O'Reilly's merger of art and pornography, to show how both can be on Marsyas's terminally passive side, following the track whereby the assertive action of Titian's Apollo (and of Marsyas's initial challenge to the god) comes to the point of surrender.

The merger and the surrender do not always need to be taken lying down. In O'Reilly's *An Early Morning* (1997) (figure 8.4), Marsyas is on his feet, fully erect, and supports Apollonian light and refinement. Has Vermeer's letter-reading young woman in the upper world received the letter from the satyr below? Or is he reading a love letter from himself, written by her as him to him as her? Her arms emerge from his ribs, making him Adamic. But she is the phallic signifier, belonging to a preoccupied upper world that does not think how much it absorbs the lower one, despite the intermingling of the two. The

8.4. John O'Reilly, *An Early Morning*, 1997. Polaroid montage, 8 3/8 × 6 11/16 in. Collection of Klaus Kertess. Image courtesy of Miller Yezerski Gallery.

intermingling, we might say, is the artist's object lesson for us about how genders are not the contrastive, or even the differential, things that prejudice burdens them with being; we also might say that the intermingling interpassively neutralizes the active-passive contrast. But the intermingling is also a result, as in O'Reilly's assemblage, of tearing: it is a torn entity, and the tear is not neutralized. The torn entity can remind viewers of their own torn entities, of their not being in control of eros, even though their eyes, desire, and lust have willed to see, master, and enact their object.

Earlier I claimed that passionate undergoing can lure pornography into an alliance with passivity. The claim, and my tracing of modern handling of the iconography of Apollo's flayed scapegoat, is not intended to be ahistorically generalized. Maybe pornography does not express a predominating mastering impulse wherever or whenever it appears; maybe it is an ally of domination only in our contemporary national culture, where passivity is always passive aggression, and where promotion and flattery of everyone's so-called agency is a daily requirement. I understand and respect the urgency for many of us of enablement and agency. Nevertheless, to make a supreme value of agency presents problems of its own, and it worries me because it especially seems to corroborate a triumphalism that saturates American culture. And then, after all, we already do have considerable agency in our ordinary daily lives. Something else might be required of us. *Pace* Patterson's "amateurs," at Internet hookup sites—if only to judge by Craigslist.org or Muscle.com—the requirement of agency seems to pervasively determine the sites and their users. The demands-cum-commands of the sex seeker who also is an autopornographer make such a fuss that it is hard to distinguish a search for sex from a temper tantrum.

On a lower frequency, however, or at a lesser volume, and underneath the self-picturing Internet seeker's striking of poses, pornography might speak more about passivity, in the way that O'Reilly and Bacon and Freud identify with eros, with what might be even more sexy than masterful demand. The artists' merging of art and pornography suggests that the most arousing pornography, the purest, whether we find it in the raw or in O'Reilly's fusions, positions eros as an opening to positions, rather than any taking of them. Male openings, and their representation, matter here, because they are, as it were, culturally most off-base. If pornography and art when they embrace each other suggest a receptive passion that doesn't take an assertive stand (penile stands are not prima facie assertive), what might a fuller recognition of nonassertion at the heart of eros signify for domains where eros is at a distance? Could there be political inspiration to be derived from Marsyas's side of the picture?

## Notes

1. L. Williams, *Hard Core* (1989), 247.
2. See L. Williams, *Hard Core* (1989), 184–228.
3. L. Williams, *Hard Core* (1989), 205.
4. L. Williams, *Screening Sex*, 316–17.
5. L. Williams, *Screening Sex*, 321.
6. L. Williams, *Screening Sex*, 322.
7. Patterson, "Going On-line," 113.
8. Patterson, "Going On-line," 116.
9. Patterson, "Going On-line," 119.
10. Patterson, "Going On-line," 117, 118.
11. Žižek, *The Plague of Fantasies*, 115.
12. Žižek, *The Plague of Fantasies*, 116.
13. Permission to reproduce Lucian Freud's work for this chapter was refused by the artist via his legal representative Goodman Derrick LLP, London, and after the artist's death again was refused by Goodman Derrick LLP. For reproductions of all works discussed here see Bernard and Birdsall, *Lucian Freud*. Images of Freud's work also can be viewed on the Internet.
14. Francine Koslow Miller identifies the background as a reproduction of Corot but does not specify a particular painting. See Miller, "John O'Reilly's Assemblies of Magic," 174.
15. Kertess, "Crucifictions," 11.
16. Wollheim, *Painting as an Art*, 26. My allusion to the Renaissance exegesis of the Marsyas story is indebted to Wollheim, *Painting as an Art*, 324.
17. Wollheim, *Painting as an Art*, 326.
18. Wollheim, *Painting as an Art*, 327; emphasis added.
19. Žižek, *The Plague of Fantasies*, 116.
20. See Cappock, "The Motif of Meat and Flesh." Reproductions of the abattoir photographs are on pages 323–25. Permission to reproduce Francis Bacon's work for this chapter was made impracticable by production requirements set by the artist's estate. For reproductions of works by Bacon discussed here, see Cappock, Harrison, Schmied, and Steffen. Images of Bacon's work can also be viewed on the Internet.
21. See, for example, Harrison, *In Camera, Francis Bacon*, 106; Schmied, *Francis Bacon*, 18–21; and Steffen, "The Representation of the Body," 205.
22. L. Williams, *Hard Core* (1989), 183. The reference is to Altman's *The American Film Musical* (Bloomington: Indiana University Press, 1987).
23. Danto, "Lucian Freud," 101.
24. Danto, "Lucian Freud," 102, 103. Danto is contrasting "nakedness" in Freud to "nudity" in artistic tradition.
25. Wollheim, *Painting as an Art*, 326.

# 9

# Big Black Beauty: Drawing and Naming the Black Male Figure in Superhero and Gay Porn Comics

*Darieck Scott*

Here is a fragment of a story you've heard many times even if you never listened to it, a fact you know even if you rarely consider it. This is Markus Ram—a porn star, in case the phallic drag name didn't alert you—responding to a question in a collection of interviews of gay porn stars, the same question the interviewer asks all his subjects: "What primary skills or attributes do you feel you bring to the porn star table?" Ram replies, "I think of this question as what makes me unique as a porn star. The first thing is, and this may sound funny, my humanity. So often I have seen black models portrayed as nothing more than a big black dick stereotype. I've never been into that personally and wasn't about to start in my fledgling porn career. I wanted to show a black guy who could do and be much more than the stereotype. Smile a little—show some realness in my acting—and try to show that I'm a nice guy who likes to fuck and get fucked."[1]

Though Ram's *nomme de cinéma* perhaps belies his wish to avoid being over-identified with his penis, what Ram's statement recognizes is the likelihood—call it a fact—that when the body on the screen in a porn film is black and male, the dick is what you seek and what you see. Or as Frantz Fanon puts it: "As regards the black man everything in fact takes place at the genital level."[2]

You know this, and if you have not paid attention to the tendencies in porn representation and reception that Ram notes or only done so in moments of swiftly squelched discomfort, it is not because you are "a racist"—a designation that often seems to me uselessly nondescriptive except in the case of persons who make racism their profession, like Nazis or many Republican politicians. It is because hyperconsciousness of differences in skin color and physiognomy, and the assignment of hierarchies of value according to those differences, is a filter currently operating in your brain for processing sensory data: a filter you imbibe with language and mother's milk from the social world that makes you *you*. When such a fundamental filter gets pointed out by stories like Ram's, by facts like these, of course it might make you uncomfortable enough to conveniently stop paying attention to it. Worse, paying attention might blunt the achievement of your erotic and sexual pleasure (which, as one who sets a high philosophical and moral value on such achievements, is to me no small loss).

Ram, with all the intelligent fierceness that living as a black body and knowing you are always at risk of becoming a black *figure* endows, trumpets his humanity as his contribution to porn—and he must know that viewers' confirmation of that contribution is a quixotic quest rather an accomplishment.

Can we find some porn where Ram's figure gets to be something other than a big black dick (BBD), and where we still get to have our pleasure, some place where the black male figure is more or other than his BBD, but (to enunciate the collective in masculine terms for no other reason than symmetry) where our dicks still get hard? I think we can. In other worlds, parallel universes, places lacking our four dimensions but nonetheless imbricated with our reality, tethered to it: and through fantasy, a faculty that wholly creates these other-dimensional worlds and partly creates our own. What is race in comics—blackness on a two-dimensional, black-and-white, gray scale, or colored-in plane? Something we play with; someplace where the *figure* we imagine to be real in the world is entirely and inescapably the figure we know isn't real at all, but that makes us come anyway.

### Big Black Monster

This chapter examines imagery of black male characters as implicit or explicit superheroes in pornographic comics. Rather than framing these depictions with reference to pornographic comics in general, I approach this imagery from a direction that, for a few moments at least, allows us to see something other than the big black dick, or rather, to see unexpected qualities such as heroism, softness, beauty, and humanity attributed to that appendage and its bearers. This is the vantage gained from reading gay-porn comics as they converse with the genre from which these cartoons derive their visual codes: mainstream superhero comics.

Black male characters are of course relative rarities both in the corpus of gay erotic cartoons and in mainstream superhero comics, and it is this double deficit that the images and texts I examine attempt to address. These images work both within and against the usual assumptions of hypersexuality, monstrosity, and criminality that shape visual representations of black men in Western culture, and they represent black male *beauty* as a form of superheroic power and the black male body as a fantasy object of desire.

The black male figure is generally now described in cultural analysis as operating according to a kind of erection-castration paradox (to put the matter in vaguely Freudian terms). The figure is thus contradictory, at once hypermasculine and feminine. The powerful allure and threat of the figure's insistent phallic preening is also an index of its bearer's degraded social status, its position as object prone before an observing subject who fears, desires, and potentially controls it. The two, degraded status and potential power, are inextricable from one another.

We can detect this paradox clearly enough in the curious phenomenon of the black male comic book superhero. The fantasy of power inherent to the superhero genre seems to falter when the hero is black: either the reader ignores it—turning away, refusing to notice—or the black superhero figure's power and heroism are distorted to more closely resemble the black male figure's usual threat (erection) or his weakness (castration), or both.

Jeffrey A. Brown's *Black Superheroes, Milestone Comics, and Their Fans* (2001) argues that while the extreme hypermasculinity of male superheroes in comic books (armor plated, bloated musculature, varying degrees of invulnerability, and so on) presents various kinds of potential anxieties for comics' (mostly male) readership, these anxieties are generally well managed within the conventions of the genre, as these hypermasculine characters become touchstones for collective fantasy. The management of these anxieties does not work as well when the superhero is a black male, a figure already overdetermined in Western cultures as an exemplar of extreme, out-of-control physicality. "If comic book superheroes represent an acceptable, albeit obviously extreme, model of hypermasculinity," Brown notes, "then the combination of the two—a black male superhero—runs the risk of being read as an overabundance, a potentially threatening cluster of masculine signifiers."[3]

Implicit in Brown's analysis is the observation that the paradigmatic comic book superhero is in important ways *conceptually* white: if the hero isn't white, then the hero is an exception, a different case, since part of what defines the hero is his whiteness (or rather, the ink, color, or digital process indicating the character's "white" skin tones). The names of black superhero characters once they do arrive on the scene in the 1960s and 1970s exemplify the underlining and emphasis on the *difference* of blackness in the comic-book world. The fact that comic strips are a visual medium means that the creators' drawings and color will prompt a reader to *see* that such a character is black.[4] But with the early black superheroes, comic book creators often took the tack of also choosing a character name denoting blackness, as though offering instructions to the colorist who would enter the production process well after the drawing and writing were completed—for example, Black Panther, Black

Lightning, and the 1970s black Wonder Woman's name was Nubia. The early naming of black superheroes indicates, then, that superheroes are by definition white.

The conventions of representation that provide the ground for superhero comic book literacy thus retain as a lingering effect the unacknowledged white supremacist or Eurocentric physical-aesthetic assumptions at work in the establishment of the genre in the late 1930s and 1940s, when Superman and Captain Marvel burst onto the pop culture scene. The black male superhero disturbs or fails to comply with assumptions established in the genre's infancy; he is not entirely legible within those conventions. The black male superhero's "potentially threatening cluster of masculine signifiers" might account for the commercial underperformance of titles centrally featuring black superheroes: they generally don't sell very well relative to the majority of white-superhero titles, and no title centrally featuring a black superhero has yet had the ongoing commercial presence of Superman, Batman, Captain America, and so on. Due to the "overabundance" of signifiers coalescing around a black superhero figure, readers are not quite able to see, or are resistant to seeing, black superheroes, and readers are not able to take these superheroes on board as they do with Spider-Man and Superman. Brown's argument thus applies the erection-castration analytic, which cages the black male image in most cultural discourses in which he appears. Here in the realm of the consumption of black male superheroes, which is the consumption of images and narratives of fantasy, the black male figure, because he is ultra-masculine and yet without masculine power, is both a spectacle (because he is different and cannot but shout his difference to all before whom he appears) and invisible (because he is different and the filters dictating what can be recognized do not recognize the peculiar data of his presence).

The character Blade provides an example of how these matters get knotted up in the practice of conceptualizing and presenting a black superhero—one that, in this case, has enjoyed a notable spike in popularity and attention in the last fifteen years (though as of yet no title that was not either a miniseries or canceled for lack of sufficient sales). The vampire-hunting part-vampire Blade was the lead character in a three-movie film franchise starring Wesley Snipes (*Blade* in 1998, *Blade II* in 2002, and *Blade: Trinity* in 2004). Blade was originally a supporting character—and nemesis—of Dracula in the 1970s Marvel series *Tomb of Dracula*, written by Marv Wolfman and drawn by the great Gene Colan. Blade was in his first incarnation a more or less normal human being. Faintly redolent like so many black characters in 1970s superhero comics of the blaxploitation film icons Shaft and Superfly, Blade wore a short brown peacoat and green goggles. Blade's raison d'être was a vengeance mission: a vampire named Deacon Frost had killed Blade's mother, and he was determined to eradicate the species from the earth (Frost's name itself hints at the way the character became implicitly racialized in contradistinction to Blade). As the star of the series was its heroic antihero Dracula, Blade's mission did not, of course, succeed. When *Tomb of Dracula* came to its end after about seventy issues, Blade sank into comic book limbo with it.

In the movie franchise and in comic book revivals inspired by the films' success from the late 1990s onward, Blade became what the comic character had fought furiously not to be, a vampire-human hybrid, whom, in the revamp, Frost had created by biting Blade's mother while Blade was in utero. The filmmakers and Snipes chose a number of visual and behavioral alterations in order to impress upon viewers Blade's heroic status—as well as his Otherness, his not-human hybrid *difference*, which was, as it turned out, the primary source of his power and heroism, more so than vengeance and the pursuit of justice. Blade's look was transformed: the brown leather jacket and green pants and goggles became sexy tight leather pants and a flowing cape-like black leather duster coat; the original Blade's 1970s afro became, curiously, an almost equally outmoded 1980s fade (the revamp appeared in 1998, at a time when the afro, in fact, was cresting in its comeback) with a widow's peak growing ever more severe with the release of each subsequent movie; and Blade's persona, previously voluble and unconvincingly hip during the talky thrashings he administered to the evil undead, became a badass, his face always stony or clenched in an inexpressive-to-angry expression, and his speech laconic and replete with growls and grunts; plus he had big muscles, and big fangs.

In figures 9.1 and 9.2, from one of the short-lived comics inspired by the movies, we can observe the way that Blade's superhero image steps into the narrow range allowed to the black male figure, and how the authors of his look attempt to parlay that figure's tendency to signify threatening difference itself, and thus to appear in various discourses as alien, nonhuman, or animal, into a constitutive aspect of Blade's superhero power. Blade's new look emphasizes his being other than human. By contrast, the paradigmatic superhero Superman, whose being nonhuman is also the source of his power, looks not only human but like a human paragon.

The emphasis on Blade's vampire nature in his *look* can be said to tap into the menagerie of grotesque images commonly used to elicit audience discomfort in the horror genre. In this respect Blade takes up an aspect that the other paradigm-setting superhero, Batman, was originally meant to exemplify (though in Batman's case with only occasional success throughout the character's long history)—that of being frightening, presumably to his ene-

9.1. "Duel at Dawn: Part 7," *Blade* 1, no. 6 (May 2000): 12. A muscular and scarred Blade in frayed costume, his face scored with lines, emerges from wreckage to do battle with a demon.

9.2. "V3s," *Blade* 2, no. 4 (August 2002): 17. A shirtless Blade awakens from a nightmare that taunted him with reminders of his inhuman status. Note this version's disfigured animalistic brow and eyes, and the character's peculiar cranial markings.

mies but also, in the thrilling way of horror, to his readers. But this representational tactic is given a particular twist in Blade, in that it is the black male body—always already borderline monstrous—that is the badass hero Batman exemplifies. Blade is a hero who is visually as or even more terrifying and more potentially productive of nightmares and horror than the vampires he hunts.

In the movies, especially the first entry, most of the villains, including Frost (played by slim seraglio-eyed Stephen Dorff), are dressed chicly in nightclub attire and bright colors, and they look more or less like the attractive young white people usually cast as victims in a slasher flick. (Frost in the comics is a white-bearded old man drawn wearing a shapeless robe.) Snipes, whose good looks and smoldering on-screen sexiness have made him more than adequate to play romantic and heroic leads on several occasions, is in the film's reconceptualization of the comic book character a different genre of black male body, one that is the site of discomfort, and perhaps of horror. Contrast this set of depictions with, say, Buffy the Vampire Slayer, where the cleverness of the conceit lies in the idea that a type of character who is usually a victim in horror stories, and has a body the image of which corresponds with physical weakness and sexual desirability, becomes the powerful hero.

The comic book images actually push this representational tactic further, as though making up for the lack of audible growls in Snipes's on-screen performance with elaborate visual disfigurements. Thus, the post-1970s *popular* Blade is both the monster of whom the audience is horrified and the hero who slays the monster; his figuration at once capitulates to and exploits the familiar erection-castration paradox.

Blade's problem might well be that as a black figure, he's confined by the history that produces blackness, a history that a range of shorthand cultural references renders into a history of defeat and loss and suffering.[5] We might surmise that part of what makes Superman work is that he's a product of imagination that arises alongside the post–Second World War triumph of U.S. military and economic dominance and the country's arrogant international exportation of its cultural products: in that sense, the triumphs of superheroes in the fight against evil on the comic book page are secured in the readers' imaginations by the perceived political, economic, and military triumph of the nationality (and people or race) of which the hero is a *super* representative. In such a context, it's difficult to pose even an edgy antihero character like Blade, even in the postintegration, hip-hop era where black male cultural icons from Muhammad Ali to Snoop Dogg to Barack Obama are not uncommon, because by simple dint of the character's blackness he is tethered to a history in which triumph has by and large not been secured in reality or in the readers' imaginations (black triumph almost always gets produced as precarious in narratives that tells such a story, as Obama particularly demonstrates).

Blade is a *super* representative of a historically subordinated or defeated group, or, at least, a group that is so perceived. How can comic book creators, fantasy purveyors, and we who consume their creations as templates for our own fantasies imagine a powerful black hero who is triumphant given such a history? And if he is truly powerful, why does he not use his power to transform the history he lives through to effect justice for his people? There are two ways to solve the problem: such a hero has to not be noble in his intentions (i.e., he has to be shady and quasi criminal, as one of Marvel's most famous black heroes, Luke Cage, originally was), *or* he has to be a victim en route to the acquisition of his powers, so that his history recapitulates that of the people whom he represents, and the operation of that history thus remains undisturbed. Blade, like Superman, is an orphan who is superstrong, fast, and always able to heal from injuries, and who makes himself into a hero by fighting against evil. Yet this triumphant, powerful, and even, in fantasy or ideological terms, paradigmatically *American* position is for Blade the result of a curse (a vampire bit his mother and/or murdered his father, depending on the version of his origin). What this speaks to is that in addition to the surfeit of signification that attends the black image, there is also the problem of *imagining a black* hero in comics when white supremacy is or has been the actual order. Creators are tasked with thoroughly or convincingly imagining black triumph — and often can't, or just don't.[6]

Little wonder, then, that Blade has to be a monster to make him work. Here, in comics as elsewhere, the historical and culturally sedimented truth of white-supremacist domination over black people becomes a stumbling block even to the *imagination* of black characters possessed of power.

## Beauty and the Superhomohero

Is part of what works to undermine the black superhero's popularity and his puissance in the fields of imagination what Markus Ram observes, that the figure of the black male is obscured by the penumbra of darkness — or light — thrown off by the big black dick?

The role of the BBD in mainstream superhero comics is of course subtextual; you never see Superman's penis, or any other hero's. But homoeroticism is a significant subtext in mainstream superhero comics; and it is one (itself multilayered) element among the unsettling "cluster" of signifiers from which most comics fans flee, having become inured to repressive readings or failures to read in which the genre has educated them. Thus, what at once links and complicates the familiar paradigms of black male imagery as they play out in superhero comics is an unacknowledged element in the superhero comic genre: the homoeroticism (or the homosocial that cannot be disentangled from homoeroticism) that is very likely a part of a mostly male readership enjoying the adventures of muscular male superheroes as spectacle.

A key ideal mined in superhero comics is physical beauty. The heroes are rendered as more sexy than reality and as gorgeous specimens. There are plain or ugly people running about in Metropolis and Gotham City — they just usually aren't heroes. We can think of Lex Luthor, whose baldness is a sickly egghead contrast to robust Superman's full head of hair and the spit-polished S-curl dangling over Supe's forehead like a taunt to all those for whom the Hair Club for Men had not yet been invented, and also of the equally bald but far nastier looking Dr. Sivana, enemy of the original Captain Marvel, another early hero; or later in comics history, we can think of the biggest villain in all Marvel Comics, the Fantastic Four's nemesis Dr. Doom, who is so disfigured (a twisted face to conveniently reflect his twisted sadistic mind) that he wears an iron mask that isn't very pleasant to look at either. Ugliness belongs to the villain; and in that sense part of the hero's heroism is, precisely, his beauty. It is in this context that we find a black male superhero like Blade, who is horrifying and unpretty, as villains are.

The creators and consumers of gay erotic cartoons have had an ongoing love affair with superhero comics and acknowledge the (homo)eroticism of superheroes with motivated gusto. Felix Lance Falkon, an early observer of underground gay-themed graphic work, comments: "The interest in the muscular physique as a subject for homoerotic artwork . . . can be attributed to several sources. . . . [One] major cause . . . is the proliferation of comic book superheroes—Superman and his myriad of descendants—in costumes that usually revealed every line of their musculature. . . . Regardless of the intent of the artists, . . . the comic book heroes do much to establish clean-cut musculature as a virility symbol among adolescent boys, and even more important, to establish that symbol in pictorial form—as a *drawing*."[7] The emphasis on the *drawn* aspect of this work bears a bit of meditation. Thomas Waugh, a seasoned critic of pornographic photographs and pornographic cartoons, argues that porn comics are a fantastic, *nonindexical* genre of representation: "Graphics offer a richer spectrum of fantasy than do indexical images like photographs, often in inverse proportion to their importance as documentary evidence."[8] Part of what is fantasized about in such works are other worlds, parallel realities of cooler sexier realness, in which madly contortive sex of the sort the characters get to have with men as gorgeous as the characters are is readily abundant. In erotic comics, beauty stimulates desire, but it is possible to read these desires as having a political resonance at the same time as they are erotic (and perhaps, at least potentially, the politics are part of their erotics). Waugh observes that the gay erotic cartoons he's collected from before Stonewall "usually have a utopian dimension," and he concludes that "in some sense, non-indexical eroticism can be more utopian than the indexical variety."[9]

## Big Black Beauty

We *need* the utopian here—we need a place that isn't actually there, a way of seeing what we can't actually see, which is to say a different filter than that which is normally and normatively in operation—so that we may see something else, other possibilities. We need the utopian because, contrary to black cultural-nationalist rhetoric from the 1960s, black often isn't beautiful in a world where aesthetics is an arm of the hydra of white supremacy.

The weight of a long history of associative linkages produced in philosophy, literary rhetoric, stage and screen performances, and the language of everyday encounter has meant that on a certain level, the notion of black beauty is a conundrum, a challenge and an exception if not an oxymoron. The classical world's slowly arrived at decision that truth produces beauty (a thing or idea is beautiful because, or insofar as, it's truthful) becomes, much later, the romantic poet Keats's somewhat sophomoric reformulation of this notion in the closing lines of "Ode to a Grecian Urn." The romantic ideal, "'Beauty is truth, truth beauty'—that is all/Ye know on earth, and all ye need to know," becomes a suggestion that the good are beautiful and the bad are ugly—a point of view we certainly know to have been harnessed by, and to have arisen alongside, the development of white-supremacist, racist thought and practice in the very conceptualization and establishment of the grand and glorious West. Though all of this is less true than it was *because* of the cultural interventions of Black Power rhetoric as it accompanied the relative success of battles for political inclusion of black folks in the United States and the decolonization of African nations, the blackness-equals-ugliness (or at least unprettiness) equation has not been eradicated from cultural consciousness and cultural practice.[10]

The equation retains potency, not least in that realm where individual psyches and collective cultural production meld to designate the range of possible and probable sexual or romantic partners. In the worlds of gay men—a thoroughly modern world, which has arisen more or less alongside that of the relatively new black-is-beautiful counterregime—this legacy has given rise to the phenomenon of the "snow queen"—a (usually) black gay man whose supposed or proclaimed primary sexual and romantic interests are in white men. The only element I wish to draw from debates and discussions of this phenomenon for use here is an insightful comment by the self-proclaimed snow queen and acclaimed filmmaker Isaac Julien (though Julien's is a self-proclamation that reveals a complexity in the phenomenon that users of the term rarely admit, or even wish to know), who observes: "In fact in this Western culture we have all grown up as snow queens—straights, as well as white queens. Western culture is in love with its own (white) image."[11] Julien's comment is of course to state in a (somewhat) different context exactly what Fanon says when he declares that there is only one destiny for the black man, and it is to become white.[12]

This is where fantasy demonstrates not only its pleasures, however complicated those frequently are, but its uses, equally complex. In Monica L. Miller's discussion of the history of the black dandy and black male sartorial self-presentation, she quotes the artist Yinka Shonibare (born in London, raised in Lagos), "who has 'found beauty one of the most radically subversive strategies to counter Eurocentric hegemony on the use of beauty.'"[13] Shonibare says that he wants his art, which attempts to articulate beauty to Africanity and blackness, to operate like poetry—which is to me to say he desires his work to operate like metaphor, in the production of unexpected conjunctions between disjunct and apparently incommensurable or contradictory concepts, things, descriptions. This then is one way that a *black beauty* signifies, as *poetic*, as unexpected, as inventively, creatively conjoining supposed opposites, calling attention to its operation as a representation and pointing toward transformative responses to it and the world in which it exists. To fantasize, to represent blackness in terms of beauty, is potentially to endow the black figure with a value that its figuration usually operates to mitigate. It is perhaps to endow that figure with a kind of power—though such power, as we'll see, has to be framed in a particular way.

## Black Stripped

To see how the power of black beauty might be represented, let's look at some negotiations of the limitations of the black male figure in pornographic comic strips of the cartoonists Belasco and David Barnes, whose work almost exclusively focuses on black characters, and Patrick Fillion, whose images are multiracial. All of these strips feature explicitly erotic black male superheroic figures or actual superheroes. In these images, the *beauty* of the characters — a fundamental characteristic, too, of mainstream male superheroes, but not generally acknowledged in fandom or deployed as a plot or thematic device — is emphasized, though it is also true that their beauty is bound up with, or at least cannot be extricated from, familiar racist images of black male hypersexuality.

The porn-comic genre is meant to sexually arouse, and Belasco's, Fillion's, and Barnes's presentation of the characters as objects of desire as well as figures with whom to identify—sites for the reader to sexually fantasize, like porn in any medium—renders them, within the terms of the genre, analogous to the hero in superhero comics. While references to the superhero genre can be located in visual codes and construction of narrative in some of these cartoons, the visual strategy of black beauty and sexual desirability as power comes into particular focus where the black male character is explicitly a superhero or hero. Whether the black superhero is a reference providing a foundation for how we read the porn comic or the porn comic protagonist is explicitly a black superhero, in fictional worlds where what would be a battle in mainstream superhero comics becomes the sexual act in sex comics (or the sexual act becomes the conclusion of a truncated version of such a battle), the black male character's beauty is itself a form of *power*, not unlike super speed or laser vision.

It should be noted that how we recognize, feel, and assess the presence and operation of *power* in the context of a pornographic gay male comic already illustrates the ways in which that concept must always, understood properly, be seen as relative in a scale of measurement that also designates the not-powerful, and that therefore the content of power is not absolute but malleable, that in the blink of an eye the subject is subjected and an object too. These characters (again, points of identification as well as objects on the page to be desired or to prompt as-if fantasies of possession of them) are black male figures with big black dicks, and thus ultramasculine in a way that confirms the common linkage between the black male body and threatening (as well as desirable), violent masculinity. At the same time, that they are black male figures means the erection-castration paradox is in play, and the characters are — in the parlance of English-speaking adolescents of all ages — "pussies" as well as human-shaped apparatuses for BBDs. And at the same time, since these representations are of all-male sexual worlds, another doubling is functioning. Leo Bersani describes this when he tells us that gay male fantasies both work to establish and disestablish masculinism; such fantasies worship at the altar of phallic masculinity but also never cease to feel the appeal of masculinity's violation (insofar as to be penetrated — as a male figure in a gay male fantasy can be, and often will be — is to become or to risk becoming nonmasculine or feminine).[14]

That these paradoxes and confusions of signification should be at work in a supposedly simple genre where penises are enormous and where conventions of representation satisfy the wish for power with the fantasy of shooting lethal rays from one's fingers or eyes is curious, to be sure. But it points to the way that exaggeration and caricature — which is in large part the work of the comics genre — are useful forms of analysis and revelation, and it underlines as well the heterogeneity and plasticity of what *appears* as though it is a rock-solid element of our human reality, like blackness.

Belasco is probably the most prominent of gay male comics artists whose work features black men. In addition to the big, glossy collection of many of his strips — *The Brothers of New Essex: Afro Erotic Adventures* (2000) — his strips, poster art, and illustrations have been appearing in black gay publications such as GBM, porn magazines, and ads for clubs and events, and as cover art for editions of James Earl Hardy's popular *B-Boy Blues*, since the early 1990s. A fan of cartoonists such as Tom of Finland and the Hun, Belasco, a commercial artist, hungered for "more imagery exploring a wider range of African American men" than he saw in those artists' work, or in popular culture generally.

Belasco's primary protagonist is Boo, a broad-shouldered, sculpted-physique, earrings- and baseball-cap-wearing Apollo who would today likely be called, appreciatively or not, a thug. One of Boo's forays, in the strips "Boo: Pleasure 'n Pain" and "Hard Knox," finds Boo whisked off to a subterranean all-but-magical place, where a band of black men whose clothing looks as though it were inspired by Earth, Wind and Fire album covers practice BDSM and have captured him so that he will perform for their pleasure. Boo, heroically, endures his spankings and other trials but gets the sexual better of his fellow performers, and he eventually defeats the wizardy warlocky master, precipitating a general revolt among the captives and s/m brethren against the (ugly) master's cruelty. Boo, the captors, and captives all have a lot of fun in the bargain.

Another strip, "When the Master Commands," features the character Oasis, an exotic dancer and "the most scandalous brother in New Essex!" This strip takes the superheroic subtext of Boo's adventures a step further. Belasco's homage and debt to Marvel Comics is evident in the strip's opening (figure 9.3), which is like the splash page of a 1960s or 1970s Marvel comic, surrounding a large-panel rendering of the "hero" with text that enumerates his various "powers"—the primary puissance being, as is evident by Belasco's rendering of Oasis nude and erect, his immense sexual attractiveness. "Hard of body, head and dick, watch as Oasis gets in way over his head (both of them) in his first spine-tingling, pulse-pounding, dick-throbbing adventures!!!!" This list of noun-gerund adjectives is familiar to any reader of Marvel Comics in the 1960s and 1970s, as its adrenaline-pumped style is pure Stan Lee, the creator (along with artists Steve Ditko and Jack Kirby) of so many heroes now perhaps better known from their appearances in movies, such as Spider-Man, the Fantastic Four, the X-Men, the Avengers, Thor, and the Hulk. (Note that Oasis sports a flattop haircut, a bit less 1980s and early 1990s retro than Blade's, but close.)

Oasis, after starting a melee at the strip club because the club patrons became obstreperous in their zeal to sample his wares, gets fired. Needing work, Oasis answers an ad for a sex worker willing to play out the fantasies of a recluse who lives in a suburban mansion. Once he's arrived at the mansion, Oasis is told to wait naked for the "master's" arrival, whereupon the lights are doused. Oasis slips and falls hard in the darkness, and he awakens to find a shadowy figure licking him all over and generally having his way with him—treatment that hits Oasis's "hot spots." Oasis wonders whether his assailant, who's wearing a "strange body suit," is black. A panel shows the mysterious man's hands, partially gloved, grasping Oasis's buttocks, and a thought balloon lets us in on Oasis's sex-worker-cum-rape-victim thought process: "He's got some big-ass hands! I wonder . . ." Then on to the next panel we see Oasis's body pressed up against a shadowy body-shape next to him and two very swollen erections, with the text: ". . . I was right. Big-ass dick, too! He's black." The bodysuit in shadow with penis unsheathed proceeds to force a blow job from Oasis and soon showers Oasis's face with lovingly detailed tendrils of ejaculate—which upsets Oasis, who was more or less fine with the

9.3. Belasco, "Oasis: When the Master Commands," in *The Brothers of New Essex*, 136. This is the cartoonist Belasco's erotic version of a traditional Marvel Comics–style superhero splash page, featuring the sexually irresistible Oasis, poised to embark on an adventure.

forced fellatio but finds the unexpected cum facial to be disrespectful. But no matter: Oasis falls asleep, muttering, "Everything is blurry . . . Your . . . dick . . . was . . . DRUGGED?!"[15]

With his strange bodysuits and sleep-inducing powers, Mr. Big Black in the Body Suit clearly bears the hallmarks of supervillainy. But he's a porn supervillain, revealed to be black by his fulfillment of black-man-is-a-big-penis cultural conjuration—and he's all the more so since the nearly full-body sheath makes him something of a walking black phallic symbol. When the master finally reveals himself in the light, he is in fact attired in a form-fitting face-concealing bodysuit replete with spikes running along the head, shoulders, ass, and crotch. He tells Oasis, "I wasn't always the master. I was taught by the first master"—the picture of whom on the wall, we see, is a ringer for Oasis. Now the master wishes to teach Oasis to be a master, as he himself was taught—a task that involves Oasis's elaborate submission, since his brief for the evening is to navigate "the maze of temptation" in the catacombs beneath the mansion. "If you can navigate your way out without succumbing to its carnal pleasures, i.e. cumming," the master warns, "you will be released. . . . However, if you fall prey to lust and spill your seed, you lose and will be mine to do with as I please."[16]

Oasis then prepares himself for his heroic task by donning his own version of superhero togs (figure 9.4). This skimpy costume, more Wonder Woman bathing suit than Superman long johns, is a curious development, since Oasis will not need clothes to have sex. It serves to underline the strip's conscious reference to superhero comics. Oasis then has sex of various configurations with several of the catacombs' lusty denizens—one-on-ones and a three-way, getting expertly sucked, getting brutally fucked, and imperiously fucking others—a quick set of herculean labors. He triumphs over each of the men by making them ejaculate with his superior sexual skills and overwhelming allure, while he successfully manages his (black and) blue balls.

At the end of the strip, Oasis finally confronts the master himself, who reveals that his supervillain suit has been adapted to transform him into a human vibrator ("The former master, my beloved Demitri, left me an array of tools to handle young bucks like you")—underlining the master's transformation into a walking big black dick (figure 9.5). After he and Oasis fight, the master tries to fuck Oasis into submission. Oasis finds the pleasure of the master's suit-powered thrusts to be so intense that he risks dying "from ecstasy," but resourceful Oasis turns the tables, and, applying techniques of "erotic suffocation" in which his sex skills have made him proficient, he chokes the master into unconsciousness. But in addition to defeating the evil master, Oasis also has other interests, and he continues to ride the big black cyborg dick. "This dick feels sooo goood!" he cries, in a panel that shows us Oasis's penis in the foreground, larger than his head and dripping with precum, though it is the master's unseen penis that is being spoken of—and Oasis comes, at last (figure 9.6).

Oasis's ejaculate, like the rest of him, is superhuman; its mysterious properties are such that contact with the master's bodysuit seems to fry the suit's system—so we see from the electric lightning-like lines frizzing around the master's splayed limbs in the panel where Oasis sprays over him. Thus the defeat of the master is complete: Oasis's ejaculate, his sexuality, is *power*, almost bearing a divine valence in the universe of superhero comics, where lightning and electricity are frequently the province of gods and mutants. According to

9.4. Belasco, "Oasis: When the Master Commands," in *The Brothers of New Essex*, 158. Oasis, having accepted the challenge of navigating the villainous Master's Maze of Temptation, girds for sexual battle by donning a mask and skin-tight (though scant) attire. The single-page panel completes the citation, and explicit erotic revision, of the superhero-comics visual tropes hinted at in figure 9.3.

the rules of the game as first established, Oasis's ejaculation was to seal him into submission and defeat; but the tables are turned. The master who was once not a master and learned submission to become a master falls, while the captive hero defeats his captor and gains his freedom, breaking the cycle of mastery and submission, through "losing"—though losing is orgasm, and it is by means of the glory of Oasis's sexual skills and his Helen of Troy–like inducement of maddening desire (the property of his beauty) that his triumph has been achieved. The borderlines between masculine-penetrator, feminine-penetrated, between domination and submission, master and slave—and of course the inescapable reference of these terms, in a context where black char-

9.5. Belasco, "Oasis: When the Master Commands," in *The Brothers of New Essex*, 169. In the final confrontation, the villainous Master reveals that his skin-tight ebony-black bodysuit includes a large electrified dildo/penis.

9.6. Belasco, "Oasis: When the Master Commands," in *The Brothers of New Essex*, 172. Oasis triumphs by turning the Master's attempted rape into an occasion for his own orgasmic pleasure. The electric zigzag lines in the final panel showing the Master's electrocution also indicate the nigh-godlike power of Oasis's ejaculate.

acters appear, to the history of slavery in the Americas—are all crossed and blurred, even as each piece of them is touched upon and stroked for Oasis's pleasure and, presumably, for the fantasizing pleasure of the reader.[17]

Patrick Fillion is a white Canadian cartoonist whose work has been widely reproduced in a variety of venues where illustrations of sexualized male figures appear—anthologies of gay art, beautifully produced monographs, and a wide array of porn magazines. He is also the creator and impresario of a line of comic books, Class Comics, featuring lavishly illustrated stories of gay male characters. (Class Comics publishes the work of a number of creators.) The characters Fillion has created include callboys, cops, strippers, aliens, demons, and, most prominently, a plethora of superheroes bearing names like Naked Justice. A blurb on the back of one of his collections calls Fillion,

9.7. Patrick Fillion, "Creature of the Night," *Boytoons: The Men of Patrick Fillion*, no. 2 (June 2004): 11. Fillion's vampire figure sports inhuman fangs and "evil" eyebrows not unlike many versions of the superhero Blade, but here these features distinguish the character as an erotic fantasy.

accurately in my view, "the Stan Lee of gay erotic comics." The surprise—if we compare Fillion's universe to that of gay male porn films and of mainstream superhero comics—is how frequently black male characters appear: a lot. In fact one of Fillion's hardcover collections of illustrations is called *Hot Chocolate*, and it is exclusively devoted to his drawings of black men. We can see in figure 9.7 Fillion's homage to and transformation of the Blade figure—not only the erect big black dick, flying free as though winging on its own, but Blade's clearly vampiric features nonetheless rendered as nonmonstrous, as softened from the hard angles of the Marvel comic into a combination of masculine jawline and soft, prettifying facial features. Likewise, in figure 9.8 you

9.8. Patrick Fillion, "Dark and Dangerous," in *Hot Chocolate*, 38. Fillion's romantic fantasy is one of many in a collection "dedicated to the Beauty, Dignity, Strength, Intelligence and Power of the Black Man."

can see that while Fillion's black men are always sporting outsized members (again, often larger than the characters' heads!) in an apparent fulfillment of the reduction to BBD that Markus Ram decries and that figurations of Blade conceal behind images of fright and horror, they are also illustrated as *beautiful*, via soft lines and the rendering of dreamy, romantic, happy expressions. (It must be noted that *all* of Fillion's characters, whatever their race or species, have penises longer and fatter than even Tom of Finland's.)

One of Fillion's stable of superhero creations is a character called Space Cadet: like many of Fillion's heroes, he's gloriously good-looking and hugely endowed, and (unlike the majority of Fillion's heroes) he's also black, with blond hair. In his earliest appearances as a secondary character—and sex partner—in the adventures of Naked Justice (a red-headed solar-powered hunk whose lover was Ghostboy, a Latino), Space Cadet wore an ungainly fishbowl helmet and sported a laser pistol and seemed to have the vague power set of a classic mainstream hero like Adam Strange, one of the many "spaceman" creations inspired by the Cold War competition for space flight in the

9.9. Patrick Fillion, cover of *Rapture #3*. Fillion's superhero Space Cadet is attacked and fondled by Vallan the satyr, with apparently rapturous results for Space Cadet.

1950s and 1960s. But later Space Cadet moved to center stage, getting his own series, and he doffed the helmet and acquired new, jazzier powers involving "radiation bursts" shot straight from his fingers and eyes. Arguably his chief power, though, is to be such a delectable bottom that he attracts the attention of horny villains and interlopers. On the cover of *Rapture #3* (figure 9.9) we see that though his costume is torn from his body as a result of some foregoing violence, his expression is one of, well, rapture, as he's fondled from behind by a demonic satyr who appears to have his penis deep up Space Cadet's backside. In the pages of the issue we discover that the satyr, Vallan, has been spying on Space Cadet to determine whether or not he's powerful enough to serve as a champion in Vallan's realm, which is menaced by Baron Von Phallus. Space Cadet's subsequent voyage to the land of the satyrs finds him constantly being fondled, molested, and mounted. (He's stripped of his costume almost immediately—satyr customs and immigration at work, evidently.) The voyage also finds him constantly being called "the dark one": as in, "The dark one is glorious! What a magnificent warrior's physique he possesses!"; "We could play with the dark one"; and "Forgive us, my lord. . . . We could not resist the beauty of the dark one!" Though Space Cadet complains that the satyr, fairy, and centaur folk he's supposed to champion (but who've been busy having their way with him while he's comatose) should call him by his name (Byron) rather than "dark one," the very next line has Strider, the king of the centaurs, replying: "As you wish, dark one."[18] Later King Strider hits the double, saying: "You truly are a Nubian prince, dark one." Space Cadet replies, "Okay, fine . . . you can keep calling me 'dark one' . . . if you kiss me." The text caption after the two kiss makes the language of Strider's dialogue its own. Fillion writes, "Strider swoops Space Cadet into his arms, hungry to get at the Nubian hero's rigid member."[19]

Byron, needless to say, does not hail from the ancient land of Nubia or its present-day national locations: the descriptive refers to his color, his race, and his heritage. Thus, Space Cadet's highly fuckable loveliness is black fuckable loveliness—and we see this, too, when he faces the villain Icecap. Icecap has been lured to come out of hiding by the smell of Space Cadet's free-hanging cock and wastes no time verbally highlighting what we can see, which is the two characters' racial difference. (Indeed, Icecap's whiteness is so unrealistically extreme that the confrontation seems to be between villainous ice people and heroic sun people, as though plucked from a simplistic version of a 1990s Afrocentric fantasy.) "Oh, groovy! It's my favorite fudgesickle!" Icecap taunts. "I've missed you! You're the tastiest chocolate sundae I've ever had, you know!"[20]

The insistence here on language that does the unnecessary work of racial marking—and that makes the superhero-supervillain fight a racial confrontation—seems at first to be only another iteration of the practice that began with the racialized naming of heroes in the 1960s and 1970s. From this point of view, the conceptualization and depiction of an erotic black superhero figure differs between Belasco and Fillion along predictable lines, insider black versus outsider white. But there are (perhaps surprising) resonances between the two, similar methods of reconfiguring the black male image to achieve a beautiful black male superhero, such that the view from inside blackness to black beauty is not, as it turns out, altogether different from the outside view.

For one thing, Fillion's use of Nubian takes up (and eroticizes) naming that has its most recent provenance in popular Afrocentric parlance (the putative ur-heritage of black folks being "the original Nubian"). Second, Fillion dedicates his volume Hot Chocolate—which, by the way, probably features as many if not more distinct black male characters as appear in Belasco's corpus—in these words: "This book is dedicated to the Beauty, Dignity, Strength, Intelligence and Power of the Black Man." Key here is the definite article, though it remains lowercase: "*the* Black Man"—an appellation designated from a position outside blackness or black communities, but that of course also has its uses enunciated from inside, as in this comment in Belasco's foreword to *The Brothers of New Essex*: "The stories in this book only scratch the surface of the kinds of erotic tales I have in my head to tell. Luckily, there are other artists such as . . . David Barnes who have taken up the task of providing stories and imagery that explore the sexuality of *the black gay* (or same-gender loving . . . take your pick!) *male*."[21] All of this is on one level a demonstration of how the discourse of racialization has worked in the case of African diasporic slavery and its aftermath—a hodgepodge of peoples naming their heritages with a variety of different names get called *black*, are forced to internalize this name, and later assert their presence, designate their historical experience, and demand redress for injustice using the names and terms they have acquired, the names that were central instruments in their subjugation.

A strip by David Barnes, whom Belasco names as his cotraveler, provides an illustration of how this circuit of naming is also a circuit of ways of looking, and of ways of conceiving, fantasy. One of Barnes's characters is Raheem, described in a splash page thusly: "He's part black, part Puerto-Rican, he's young and full of cum . . . He's a homeboy, he's a playboy . . . He will rock your world. . . ."[22] In "At the Gym," Raheem rocks the world of the lucky folks who happen to be present when he goes to exercise. While the story turns entirely on Raheem's appeal, Barnes's style is less hyperreal in the Marvel way than Belasco's and Fillion's; it is instead more sketch-like, calling you to fill out the missing dimensions with your own imagination. Raheem's beauty is thus perhaps not as aesthetically apparent as Boo's, Oasis's, or Space Cadet's—rather it is established by the other characters' responses to him.

In this vein the culminating panel of figure 9.10 draws attention: who are the two voyeur characters, extreme right and left, in the panel? Neither plays any other part in the story or has any other dialogue; the old man appears here and nowhere else, and the young guy has appeared watching Raheem's shorts bulge, and he appears again after the cum-shot panel standing around watching. (There's a considerable amount of *watching*, it seems, when black male characters are in the center of the porn comic, since Vallan watches Space Cadet, and Oasis gets observed at different times in his story, by the master and his servants or captives.) The two observing Barnes characters are white and the sexual performers are black, and this of course is underlined by the younger man's line, which spills out of the borders of the panel: "God, I love black men!"

Why are these white characters included? To establish the response Raheem garners, his power over men. The fact that they are voyeurs rather than partici-

9.10. David Barnes, "At the Gym," in *Meatmen: An Anthology of Gay Male Comics*, vol. 21, edited by Winston Leyland (San Francisco: Leyland Publications, 1997), 63. Raheem Ramos's sexual prowess in the gym showers inspires an ecstatic response from a white observer in Barnes's cartoon.

pants might be a nod to the reader, a way to represent us in the story so that, as promised, Raheem rocks *your* world. But it is surely significant that these voyeurs, and by extension perhaps *you*, the reader, are white. The line, which is so necessary to include that it spills out of the panel in order to be part of the story (such spillage occurs only one other time in the nine-page strip, when the sound effect of Raheem's penis getting erect is too much to contain), confirms the beauty, desirability, and lovability not just of Raheem but of Raheem and Aaron (the character Raheem has sex with) as representatives of black men in general—Raheem as *the* black man. And in the world in which, as Julien contends, we are all at least a bit of a snow queen, the beauty of the black male figure is most firmly established by—and might well require—the construction of a white viewer recognizing it, even in a fantasy created from a position supposedly in blackness or within black communities.

Granted, Belasco, Barnes, and Fillion come from different racial positions as they create their fantasy figures, but once they enter the discourse of fantasy, visual and textual, and once that discourse shapes them as much as they shape it, what is the degree of difference between them in how they *see* the black figure? How truly different are Belasco's and Barnes's conceptualizations from Fillion's? In Belasco's Oasis story, the villainous master, sheathed in a black shadow suit, identified as African American by the size of his dick felt in the dark, and hyped up by the suit to be a human vibrator, is the BBD. Oasis is the black *beauty*, who also has a big dick: one value (beauty) becomes visible in part because it is broken off and distanced from a more exaggerated—and, in typical binary fashion, less attractive (the suit isn't cute)—and problematic value (the überdick), which must come along with the black male figure. Oasis ejaculates—in symbolic terms, he is able to summon his own vital energy, the stuff of his genetic being, and it saves the day for him though he has been told to keep it in check in order to survive—while riding the big black dick, which is a creation of the suit, and which is thus artificial in the story, as a way of pointing to its chimerical nature in reality. Just as for Barnes and Fillion, for Belasco too there has to be a position *outside*, as it were, from which blackness can be valued as beautiful and desirable: An outside-black or nonblack position must be shaped within the narrative, and be shaped by the flow of tableaux, for *seeing* black beauty, because the domination of ways of seeing and valuing in a snow queen world would make such beauty otherwise invisible, or conceal it beneath the more familiar veneers of monstrosity and threat.

The dictates of the snow queen world mean that the *difference* of the black figure is inescapable, a given: blackness will be an object in the eye of dominant discourse, and it will be alien, though it can also, with effort, be a beautiful object, a gorgeous alien. Thus, when Markus Ram is asked in the interview with which I began this chapter whether problems with the hiring and depiction of black porn actors in film would disappear if there were more black-owned or black-operated studios, Ram replies: "I don't think it matters who runs the studios."[23] And what we see here suggests he may be right.

There is an analytic lying behind my reading that I've preferred not to foreground, and I'm going to keep it tamped down, except for this one moment, in order to illuminate further the complex kinds of responses and effects of visual and narrative representation such as we're observing in these porn comics. The analytic is of course psychoanalytic theory, and I turn here very briefly to a definition of *phantasy* (the spelling of the word preferred in psychoanalytic theory outside the United States because its derivation from the German *Phantasie* encompasses a broader sense of both the contents and the creative activity of imagination, rather than the reduction to whimsy and triviality that often occurs with *fantasy*) in Jean Laplanche and Jean-Bertrand Pontalis's *The Language of Psycho-Analysis* (1973). "It is not an *object* that the subject imagines and aims at" in phantasy, they note, "but rather a *sequence* in which the subject has his own part to play and in which permutations of roles and attributions are possible. . . . The primary function of phantasy [is as] the *mise-en-scène* of desire."[24]

I take this formulation of fantasy's function as the mise-en-scène of desire to mean that fantasies not only provide the stage settings and roles for the playing out of desire's fulfillment, but that they establish—they create, psychically—the structure which sets desires in motion, which makes desire possible or recognizable as desires. These desires themselves actualize a subject-object relation even if their objects are not clear or singular: what is significant is an apparent separation between the perceiving and receptive consciousness and something or things which that consciousness perceives in relation to what must then thereby become its own "self."

Presumably any number of desires are at work for which a black superhero fantasy provides the mise-en-scène. I want to suggest that among them what is being structured and set in motion is a desire *for* blackness in its beauty, for blackness *itself* as a tangible, consumable object. Blackness cannot become such an object unless its consolidation also renders us the fantasizers, through participation in the artist's fantasies, as also thereby separated from blackness, whether or not we "are" black. We are then as readers all positioned as *nonblack* desiring blackness in these strips.

This returns us to the Julien formulation that we are all snow queens and to why it probably doesn't matter much who runs the porn studios. But here we are snow queens (whose melancholic attachment to a blackness that our very entry into a racialized world required us to abject) who turn around to greedily imbibe that blackness from which we have been alienated. Of course, the likely *outside* available—in a snow queen world—is the white position that sees blackness (and creates it) as different, whether beautiful or ugly. And then insofar as the image, flat on the page, two-dimensional, is the gateway to and the frame for this fantasy, is not the produced experience, however fleeting, one of *having* the privileges of whiteness (rather than "being," and perhaps rather than performing, white)? Which is in part to have the position of being unobserved observer, to enjoy an unmarked presence and momentary plenitude only experienced in relation to a *necessarily* (for the process of attaining white privilege to work) idealized blackness: an experience which is perhaps only ever fulfilled—only ever consummated—in fantasy.

This is a good news, bad news observation: Such effects we can see as utopian, because they model for us a reality in which a certain kind of privilege—an erotic privilege, a privilege to eroticize and enjoy—becomes common. Linda Williams makes an analogous observation in writing about depictions of interracial lust in porn and in the mainstream film *Mandingo*. She notes that such depictions regularly exploit racist stereotypes in order to create pleasure for all viewers: "The excitement of interracial lust—for both blacks and whites—depends on a basic knowledge of the white racist scenario of white virgin/black beast. But the pleasure generated by the scenario does not necessarily need to *believe* in the scenario. Rather, we might say that there is a kind of knowing flirtation with the archaic beliefs of racial stereotypes. . . . The pleasure of sexual-racial difference once available to white masters alone are now available to all." Williams adds "though not equally to all," which of course is the bad news that is easy enough to see, since we find here limits that we likely don't want even to utopian *imagining* in our fantasies: limits that appear in the narrowness of a conceptual structure, of a widely held cultural phantasmatic, that cannot find any more free, empowered, connected to pleasure position than that of "white."[25]

This analyzes and describes our inescapably racist or race-informed ways of looking and erotic fantasizing. But before we fall too far down the deep, deep well of this particular despair, I would like to point out that even where we have to be interpellated into something like whiteness to see and desire black beauty, we are at the same time seeing the conjunction of supposedly disjunct elements. These comics are also initiating a process of building a (black) beauty with properties that render it an ideal in the Kantian sense, a rule unto itself.

There is another layer to the achievement of the representation of black beauty, subtending the apparently necessary construction of an outside-black or nonblack viewership, a layer that Oasis's villain, even in his relative ugliness, helps us recognize. This is the way in which the black male figure can be or is beautiful via its operation as a surplus, an excess, a double. We can discern the valuation of the surplus in an element of homosexual desire, which might not from a certain vantage be love of the *same* so much as it is love of *more*—that is, I love dicks, it is not enough that I have one, I have to have in whatever way possible many, many more. For Belasco and Barnes, creating from the point of view within a social position identified as black, black is or becomes gorgeous, loved, revered, but as *more* than their own, as an excess of blackness that appears in their creations in the mode of exaggeration: the master villain in the Oasis story. Or blackness appears as a transcendent value, a cobbling together of meanings that cohere into something like the divine. And by *divine* here I mean to designate by way of nominative placeholder something that does not exist or cannot be measured in the human scale, something that is consummately a *figure* acknowledged to be larger than life (a dick that's *that* big or cum that's like lightning) and operating as a container for a variety of aspirations, desires, and wishes: *the* Black Man to whose "Beauty, Dignity, Strength, . . . and Power" Fillion dedicates his work,[26] and the generalized "I love black men!" ejaculation that arises from watching two black men fuck and that overspills the boundaries of the page.

It is this black beauty as excess and surplus that, of course, a medium steeped in the fantastic, as comics are, is particularly primed to explore. Markus Ram wants, rightly enough, to be measured and seen in the human scale. In this his name is little help. But perhaps his embrace of such a name's cartoonish quality, which puts him in line with an industry practice that in its big-wink over-the-topness seems to gesture just as fondly toward the wild world of superheroes as gay porn comics do, also tries to make use of what porn comics revel in but what the documentary conceit of film porn (it's *real*) seems to mitigate: unreality, as if, exaggeration, the elements of big-F fantasy. And perhaps his superheroic name concedes that it is in those elements that the power of the black male figure lies.

## Notes

1. Keehnen, *Rising Starz*, 249.
2. Fanon, *Black Skin, White Masks*, 135.
3. Brown, *Black Superheroes, Milestone Comics, and Their Fans*, 178.
4. This involves a not-uncomplicated series of illustrative choices for the artist. Note, for example, the peculiar cross-hatchings denoting shadow or melanin that Charles Schulz chose to place around the edges of Franklin, the only black character among the round-faced philosophizing *Peanuts* characters. See my discussion of this matter in the context of Los Bros. Hernandez marvelous comic *Love and Rockets*. Scott, "Love, Rockets, and Sex."
5. I have discussed this matter at length in *Extravagant Abjection*. See especially the introduction.
6. There is, after all, Quentin Tarantino's *Inglourious Basterds* solution: you're creating fantasies, so why not make the reality you create have a history that diverges from our own? This was a problem faced by creators of Superman during and after the Second World War. There were issues where Superman beat up Hitler and essentially won the war. But later references to the war either rewrote comic book history to accommodate actual history, erasing Superman from the 1940s to begin his existence later or devised elaborate explanations of Hitler's possession of a powerful magical weapon that prevented Superman from landing in Festung Europa—since of course Superman's second big weakness after kryptonite is magic.
7. Falkon with Waugh, *Gay Art*, 59.
8. Waugh, *Out/Lines*, 20.
9. Waugh, *Out/Lines*, 20, 21.
10. Toni Morrison's first novel, *The Bluest Eye* (1970), explores the psychic weight of

the history of the association between blackness and ugliness against which "black is beautiful" rhetoric intervened, and the destructive effects of that ingrained linkage on a black community in Ohio. Speaking in an interview of her conception of the novel, she says: "This is . . . mid-sixties. Most of what was being published by black men were very powerful, aggressive, revolutionary. . . . And they had a very positive, racially uplifting rhetoric to go with it, some of which was—all of which was stimulating—but some of which I as an older person thought, wait a minute. One of which was, you are my black queen, black is beautiful. And I thought, yeah: but why so loud? Then I thought, wait a minute, they're gonna skip over something, and no one's gonna remember that it wasn't always beautiful. No one's gonna remember how hurtful a certain kind of internecine racism is. . . . When I wrote The Bluest Eye, it was about that. Before we all decide that we are all beautiful and have always been beautiful, let me speak . . . for some of us who didn't get that right away." Toni Morrison, "Toni Morrison Talks About Her Motivation For Writing," December 4, 2008, accessed May 5, 2009, http://www.youtube.com/watch?v=_8Zgu2hrs2k.

11. Julien, "Confessions of a Snow Queen," 82.

12. Fanon, Black Skin, White Masks, xiv.

13. M. Miller, Slaves to Fashion, 266.

14. See Bersani, "Is the Rectum a Grave?," 222.

15. Belasco, The Brothers of New Essex, 145, 146; ellipses in the original.

16. Belasco, The Brothers of New Essex, 156; ellipses in the original.

17. See chapter 5 of Extravagant Abjection for an analysis of S/M erotic fantasies' references to the history of slavery in the Americas.

18. Fillion, Space Cadet #1, 6, 4, 8.

19. Fillion, Space Cadet #1, 18, 19; ellipses in the original.

20. Fillion, Rapture #3, 5.

21. Belasco, foreword to The Brothers of New Essex, n.p.; emphasis added; first ellipses added, second ellipses in the original.

22. Barnes, "Raheem," 103; ellipses in original.

23. Keehnen, Rising Starz, 248.

24. Laplanche and Pontalis, "Phantasy (or Fantasy)," 318.

25. L. Williams, "Skin Flicks on the Racial Border," 302.

26. Fillion, Hot Chocolate, 3.

# 10

# Gay Sunshine, Pornopoetic Collage, and Queer Archive

Robert Dewhurst

Publications that . . . perpetuate the stupid haggling over whether or not "gay" is an appropriate word or whether or not a naked body is fit material for the expense of printer's ink . . . are not newspapers in the sense of actualizing the right to free press.
—Nick Benton, "Who Needs It?"

With these words of editorial introduction, Nick Benton launched the inaugural issue of San Francisco's vintage queer newspaper, Gay Sunshine, in 1970. Adorned with an oversized cover illustration of a winged, pantless, and priapic fairy descending toward the reader, and boasting a content that included items as various as a dispatch from a gay inmate at Soledad Prison, an alert to look out for cops posing as cabbies at local bars, an interview with Huey P. Newton, a first-person lesbian memoir, and a pornographic centerfold of poetry, this issue of Gay Sunshine announced the arrival of a new moment in gay small-press print culture.[1] While only one outpost on an entire network of fugitive "radical movement" rags that appeared in the immediate wake of the 1969 Stonewall riots in New York City, Gay Sunshine would make, over the course of its decade-long run, a uniquely visionary contribution to both queer print culture and American literary history at-large—and one that has yet to be critically documented. Collocating activist communiqué with literature, essay, and pornography across forty-six newsprint issues (followed by a final book issue), Gay Sunshine developed a startling typographic and editorial aesthetic of collage as it sought to assemble a lost archive of queer subcultural and literary history.

Although recent years have witnessed the emergence of a small but enthusiastic critical discourse on midcentury American small-press culture—particularly around the history, personalities, and presses of the punkish mimeograph revolution of the 1960s and 1970s—little consideration has yet been given to the parallel, overlapping, and divergent history of the free gay press.[2] Divergent because, as Judith Halberstam has persuasively argued, more than a degree of phenomenological specificity can fairly be ascribed to something we might call "queer temporality."[3] Post-Stonewall and pre-AIDS, *Gay Sunshine* and its contemporaries across North America (e.g., *Body Politic* in Toronto, *Fag Rag* in Boston, the *Furies* in DC, and the *Gay Liberator* in Detroit) inhabited a particularly precious moment in queer time-space and themselves constitute an archive of a lost queer past. While contemporary queer theorists such as Halberstam and Lee Edelman have read AIDS-inflected queer time under the infamous epithet (lifted from the Sex Pistols) of "no future," these community papers of the 1970s testify to the existence of an earlier, similar but substantially different, sense of queer temporality. In the pages of *Gay Sunshine* a marked sense of "emphasis on the here, the present, the now" most certainly comes across, but it is one determined by the exciting affective potentia of community building and political action rather than the trauma of a virus.[4]

Publications like *Gay Sunshine* existed under a different set of historical conditions than their contemporaries in the mimeo scene and deserve their own narrative. Among the post-Stonewall newspapers, *Gay Sunshine* merits particular attention for its broad editorial scope, its long print run, and its wide circulation (which reached an international scale in the hands of editor Winston Leyland). *Gay Sunshine* took the project of community building to a metalevel, frequently serving as a theater of commentary and debate about the current state of gay-press subculture and delivering occasional editorials on the topic that took the form of histories of the present.[5] Although *Gay Sunshine* is a quintessential artifact of the celebratory identity politics that characterized the emergent gay-rights movement in the post-Stonewall era, the newspaper forged a unique aesthetic of collage that seems to have anticipated the anti-identitarian energies of the shift to a queer politics in the 1990s. *Gay Sunshine*'s simultaneous editorial accents on a politics of radical solidarity and on research in gay lifestyles and literatures past, present, and international manifest an impulse to bring together disparate phenomena that do not necessarily belong together according to the logics of identity or similitude. If "form is never more than an extension of content," as Robert Creeley would have it, then *Gay Sunshine*'s collagist aesthetic may be understood as a typographical strategy that provided a queer form for the paper's radical editorial vision.[6]

### Pornopoetics

One of the striking implications of reviewing *Gay Sunshine* in the present day is the importance of literary culture to gay-community formation during this period, which the paper makes plainly visible—a relation that seems to have diminished significantly in the digital age with the advent of online networking technology. *Gay Sunshine* was an important publishing venue for poets in the New American tradition (born out of Black Mountain College, the San Francisco Renaissance, the New York School, and the Beat scene), and the newspaper's most effective collages often took the form of poetry centerfolds. Creatively drawing upon a certain set of historical relationships—between pornography and the modernist avant-garde (an association normally worked out in courtrooms), between modernist aesthetics and collage (inaugurated by Pablo Picasso and Georges Braque around 1912 and later imported into poetry by T. S. Eliot, Ezra Pound, Gertrude Stein, and Louis Zukofsky), and between the form of the centerfold itself in the pornographic press and content that is the most explicit or exciting—these centerfolds literally juxtaposed poems with visual pornography.[7] *Gay Sunshine* thus forged a new tabloid form of small-press poetry publishing that may be called *pornopoetic*—a form that, in its purposive use of a paratextual surround to enhance and shift the total aesthetic effect of any given group of poems, may best be understood through the emphases of modern textual criticism. *Gay Sunshine*'s pornopoetic collages literalize Jerome McGann's metaphor for the innovative use of page spaces as entire compositional fields that was pioneered by small, modernist poetry presses; McGann writes that in such publications "meaning was most fully constituted not as a conception but as an embodiment."[8] By actually typesetting poems within and around visual depictions of bodies blissfully fucking, *Gay Sunshine*'s collages orchestrate a striking collaboration between poem and page that adds a visceral new layer to the meaning of small-press "embodiment" in this context.

Setting a precedent it would maintain throughout its entire print run, the first issue of *Gay Sunshine* opened wide to a centerfold featuring a series of very short poems by Paul Mariah, cut up and pasted within a large collage of candid and posed photographs (nudist hippies sunbathing on a beach, two men kissing, a couple laid down in a statuesque missionary position), whimsical romanticist drawings (including a self-portrait by Rembrandt), and a pinup-style celeb cutout (Mick Jagger in a bulging bodysuit) (see figure 10.1). This potpourri of visual information overwhelms the semantic content of the poems themselves, whose edges are trimmed ornamentally to emphasize their heterogeneity from the rest of the spread, even as that content is amplified and projected at the reader by this erotic paratextual surround.

The poems in Mariah's collage—short one-offs revved mostly by jokey sex puns (e.g., "my greatest asset, / as a lover . . ." and so on)—might be relatively unremarkable on their own, but the entire page effects an absorbing and exuberant visual reading experience that recalibrates the total readerly effect of

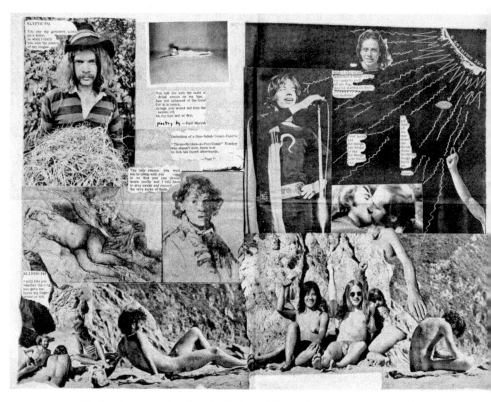

10.1. Untitled poem and collage by Paul Mariah. *Gay Sunshine* 1 (1970). © The Literary Estate of Paul Mariah; used by permission. Image courtesy of the Poetry Collection of the University Libraries, University at Buffalo, the State University of New York.

the poems into something much more than the sum of their syllabic parts. Jagger's androgynous sex symbolism is rendered even queerer by Mariah's campy recontextualization of his flamboyant arena-rock stage presence, just as the lines "your hands / say / the things / you forget / to say" take on an unexpected layer of meaning within the cut-and-paste environs of the centerfold. Beyond the queer sensibility of the collage as a form, the evident DIY aesthetic of Mariah's centerfold also recalls Guy Debord's imperative to seize and *détourner* spectacular materials in a society inundated with a white noise of bourgeois visual information and advertising. Mariah does not simply make use of found materials but effectively appropriates, repurposes, and recodes images for his own ends. As Debord writes, "*détournement* is the antithesis of quotation."[9]

Mariah, who himself founded the historic gay literary magazine (and press) *Manroot* in 1969, remained a mainstay of *Gay Sunshine*'s pages until 1974. Local San Francisco poets like him would soon find a community of peers in the newspaper's pages that today reads like a cross-country who's who of the New American poetry, and beyond: Antler, Joe Brainard, William Burroughs, Dennis Cooper, Larry Eigner, Allen Ginsberg, John Giorno, Robert Glück, Harold Norse, John Wieners, and Jonathan Williams all would become contributors to the newspaper.[10] A subsequent collage by Mariah, published lengthwise along the entire back page of *Gay Sunshine*'s second issue, would wonderfully explicate the newspaper's emerging pornopoetic collage aesthetic, and perhaps helped prepare readers for the decade of *Gay Sunshine* poetry to come. Casting the iconic civil-rights image of a silhouetted raised fist against a repetitious backdrop of male asses, Mariah's collage makes a visual pun on the notion of fisting to emphasize the mutual coextensivity of poetry, politics, and pornography (see figure 10.2). The text of the poem itself does nothing but hammer the conceit home, and in the register of romantic love, no less. It begins:

I want you to know
how it feels
to have a fist
the size of a poem
up yr ass.

Moreover, by so blatantly repurposing such an iconic symbol of black nationalism for a politics of queer rights, the page makes a vivid comment on the newspaper's emphatic politics of interracial, interclass, and intergender solidarity.

Although Mariah's first collage appears without attribution, his second is signed as follows:

Paul Mariah
Poem & Collage
Sept. 1971
San Francisco.

Besides asserting that the poem and collage were conceived together by the artist as a single work, Mariah's signature also indicates the way in which *Gay Sunshine* organized the very possibility for its contributors to conceive and publish such large-format intermedia work. Given the experimental aspect of the newspaper's collages in general, and the tutorial quality of Mariah's fisting one in particular, this back-page spread is especially compelling when read within the context of Michel Foucault's remarks on fisting as an "innovative" twentieth-century practice. The biographer David Macey has suggested

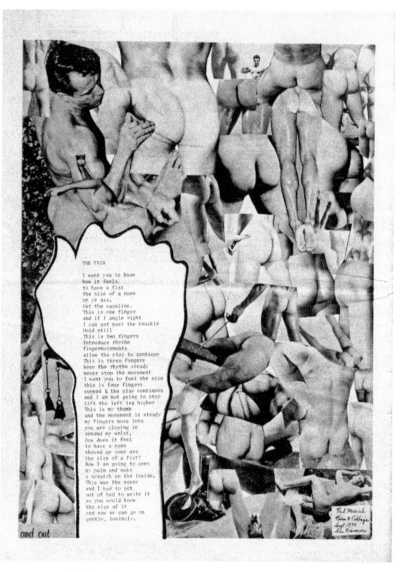

10.2. Poem and collage by Paul Mariah, "The Figa." *Gay Sunshine* 2 (1971). © The Literary Estate of Paul Mariah; used by permission. Image courtesy the Poetry Collection of the University Libraries, University at Buffalo, the State University of New York.

that Foucault was the unnamed "French *savant*" cited in Edmund White's *States of Desire* as declaring that "fist-fucking is our century's only brand-new contribution to the sexual armamentarium," and the critic David Halperin has noted how significantly such an invention of a new pleasure testifies "to the creative potential of a gay praxis."[11] When questioned about fist fucking in a 1982 interview, Foucault emphasized precisely this creative dimension of the phenomenon:

> Well, I think what we want to speak about is precisely the *innovations* those practices imply. . . . I don't think that this movement of sexual practices has anything to do with the disclosure or the uncovering of S&M tendencies deep within our unconscious, and so on. I think that S&M is much more than that; it's the real creation of new possibilities of pleasure, which people had no idea about previously. . . . We know very well what all those people are doing is not aggressive; they are inventing new possibilities of pleasure with strange parts of their body—through the eroticization of the body. I think it's a kind of creation, a creative enterprise.[12]

However genuine an invention of the twentieth-century fist fucking is (aestheticized descriptions of the practice, at least, seem to appear in the works of Geoffrey Chaucer and the Marquis de Sade), Foucault's notions about the emergence of the practice in the 1960s and 1970s powerfully reveal the ways in which *Gay Sunshine* crystallized a gay-movement ethos that articulated the invention of novel literary, political, and sexual practices as coextensive enterprises. Just as fist fucking represented a breakthrough for the degenitalization of sex and for the creation of new possibilities for pleasure, *Gay Sunshine*'s pornopoetic collages expanded the horizons of where meaning and content might be found on a page in a literary journal, and they expanded the range of pleasures such a page might offer. Looking at the poetry collages in the newspaper, it is easy to imagine "nonliterary" uses the pages might be put to, which would traditionally be coded as illicit in the vaunted realm of aesthetic experience.

Not all poetry spreads in *Gay Sunshine* took the single-author, photomontage form of Mariah's: for many issues the newspaper ran centerfolds that powerfully combined a group of poets' work with explicit drawings by Brainard, for example, and after the sixth issue Leyland himself often did triple-duty as the paper's editor, designer, and collagist. But throughout the course of the paper's run, other *Gay Sunshine* poets often adopted the form to run pornopoetic experiments of their own, accepting a newfound compositional permission extended by the publication. I have focused on Mariah's first two collages to begin at the beginning, so to speak, and to establish collage as an exemplary formal feature of *Gay Sunshine*'s pioneering content (keeping "content" and "form" here on the Möbius strip of indistinction asserted by Creeley's classic formula). Going back further, a glance at Mariah's first collagist appearances in *Gay Sunshine*, taken alongside an earlier appearance of his poetry (from the same "klyptic" series) in the pre-Stonewall Los Angeles–based gay lit mag ONE, provides a striking lesson in the determining effect of typography and textual environment on the creation of small-press literary meaning. There, Mariah's short stanzas are presented on a stark white page with the same minimalist, austere layout one might find in the aesthetically conservative *Sewanee Review* or *Kenyon Review*. Next to his *Gay Sunshine* collages, Mariah's appearances in ONE look downright bleak—not to mention incomplete.

### Subcultural Context

*Gay Sunshine* radically expanded the space opened up by early homophile literary periodicals such as ONE and the *Mattachine Review* by carrying forward and synthesizing divergent tendencies that were immanent in other small-press productions of the 1950s and 1960s in the Bay Area. *Gay Sunshine's* collages bear a genetic resemblance to the artist Jess Collins's 1950s "paste-up" experiments (see figure 10.3), for instance, or might be productively read alongside the poet Robert Duncan's evocative notion of "grand collage."[13] A list of tabloid precedents for *Gay Sunshine's* pornopoetic collages would include the *Berkeley Barb* and the Haight-Ashbury-centered *San Francisco Oracle*. The *Barb*, one of the counterculture's groundbreaking and paradigmatic underground papers, was founded in 1965 and quickly captivated a cult readership by combining radical civil-rights journalism with startling sexual content—usually in the form of a large classifieds section that included personal ads as well as ads for mail-order pornography and novelties. Similarly, the *Oracle*—a large-format underground paper that released twelve issues in a short burst from 1966 to 1968—forged an aesthetic that ran to the hippie end of the countercultural spectrum but celebrated a distinct sense of Beat fan culture also evident in *Gay Sunshine*. The *Oracle* printed a lot of poetry, often with a typographical surround amped up to keep pace with the dazzling psychedelic visuals that decorated every issue. (As an aside, it's worth noting here that Leyland claims the title *Gay Sunshine* is partially a reference to the LSD experience.)[14]

An East Coast precedent for *Gay Sunshine's* pornopoetic designs is Ed Sanders's infamous New York City mimeo, *Fuck You: A Magazine of the Arts*, which ran for fourteen issues between 1962 and 1965. *Fuck You* broke important ground for offbeat queer publications with its wildly unorthodox aesthetic of "total assault on the culture." In a recent catalog essay published to coincide with an exhibition of queer zines at Printed Matter in New York City,

10.3. Untitled "paste-up" by Jess Collins, circa 1950s. © The Jess Collins Trust; used by permission. Image courtesy of the Poetry Collection of the University Libraries, University at Buffalo, the State University of New York.

the curator A. A. Bronson identified the radical significance of Sanders's cottage industry for the prehistory of queer zine culture: "[Queer zines] seem similar to the underground newspapers of the 60s. Or the mimeographed journals of the poetry scene in New York in the 60s. . . . We should almost be including Fuck You: A Magazine of the Arts as a queer zine."[15] Although Fuck You sometimes boasted ribald editorial copy that rather shocks given the politically correct standards of today (e.g., "Girl Friday young lady snapping pussies needed for various FUCK YOU/press projects—proofreading . . . grass weighing . . . editorial prick-riffing"), the magazine did indeed assert a free-form sexual politics that was anything but heteronormative.[16] Fuck You was an earlier publishing venue for many gay poets who would later appear in Gay Sunshine (Duncan, Ginsberg, Wieners, and others) and was never shy to push the envelope of homoerotic pornopoetic representations: witness in figure 10.4 the magazine's actual marketing, for instance, of a "John Wieners' Orgasm Tonic," for which an advertisement appeared in Fuck You's July 1965 issue.[17] (Notably, Wieners himself would go on to decoupage extraordinary porno-poetic collages for his final opus, Behind the State Capitol: Or Cincinnati Pike—published by Fag Rag's offshoot imprint Good Gay Poets in 1975, and clearly influenced by the aesthetic of these gay-community newspapers.)

## Queer Archive

One way in which Gay Sunshine stands out from its genealogical surround of precedents and peers is the paper's sustained editorial commitment to queer-archive assembly. I suggested how the collagist nature of Gay Sunshine's poetry spreads provides a powerful metaphor—beyond the actual cut-and-paste designs of the newspaper—for the newspaper's vast and solidarity-based political repertoire. Now I would like to suggest that this metaphor can be extended even further, both to figure the unique shape of the paper's multifarious archive and as a heuristic into understanding the capaciousness and complexity of queer archives in general. Moreover, the very notion of the archive provides one additional and literal means to read some of Gay Sunshine's pornopoetic spreads.

It would be difficult to overstate either the priority or scope of Gay Sunshine's queer-archival commitments. Extending well beyond its efforts to maintain itself as a vital publishing venue for innovative contemporary gay poetry, Gay Sunshine's archival aspirations were also manifest in a vast series of extensive interviews, historical essays, internationalist special features, and photo-essays that graced the pages of the newspaper throughout the entire course of its run. Gay Sunshine went through three distinct editorial permutations: a first period during which the paper was published by a collective loosely

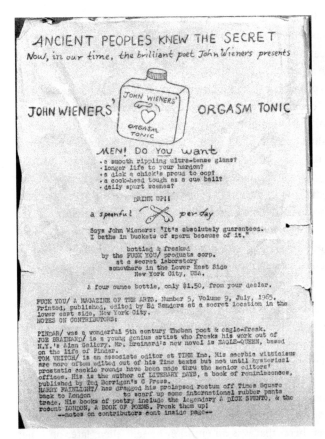

10.4. Advertisement for "John Wieners' Orgasm Tonic." Drawing by Ed Sanders. Originally published in Fuck You: A Magazine of the Arts, July 1965. © Ed Sanders, 1963–2013; used by permission. Image courtesy of the Poetry Collection of the University Libraries, University at Buffalo, the State University of New York.

affiliated with the Berkeley Gay Liberation Front and that included, among others, Benton, Gary Alinder, and Konstantin Berlandt (issues 1–5, 1970–71); a second period after the dissolution of this collective in early 1971, during which the publication was "resurrected" by a second collective coordinated by Leyland and including Mariah, Morgan Pinney, Tony DeRosa, and others (issues 6–15, 1971–72); and a third period during which Leyland took over editorial duties exclusively, acting, in his own words, as a "one-man band" to publish the newspaper—now restyled Gay Sunshine: A Journal of Gay Liberation or simply Gay Sunshine Journal—until the end of the series (issues 16–47, 1973–82).[18] Leyland was a former Roman Catholic priest who left the church in 1968 after being censured for sermonizing against the Vietnam War. As

*Gay Sunshine* transitioned into Leyland's hands upon his arrival in Berkeley in 1970, the newspaper quickly transcended its presumed purpose as only a local or activist publication, and increasingly became a formidable international newspaper of the arts.[19]

*Gay Sunshine* is probably best remembered today for its legendary interview series, a regular feature of the newspaper in its *Gay Sunshine Journal* incarnation that eventually resulted in two perfect-bound anthologies (*Gay Sunshine Interviews*) published by Leyland in 1978. Even an abbreviated list of names included among the roster of *Gay Sunshine* interviewees is striking: Ginsberg, Wieners, Burroughs, Christopher Isherwood, Gerard Malanga, Gore Vidal, Tennessee Williams, and Jean Genet all gave interviews to the paper. *Gay Sunshine* interviews were incredibly extensive (Ginsberg's was edited down for publication from seventy-eight typed pages); they asked questions other publications would never risk, and very often sought to uncover new pieces of information for an accumulating queer archive. A segment of Allen Young's conversation with Ginsberg, for instance, runs like this:

> *Young:* You've referred to Whitman and Edward Carpenter, and in some of your poems you mention Garcia Lorca. For me it was a very recent discovery that these famous writers were gay like myself, that I had this bond with them. I'm curious as to how you made this discovery?
>
> *Ginsberg:* Lorca's "Ode to Walt Whitman" speaks of "the sun singing on the navels of boys playing baseball under the bridges," which is an image of such erotic beauty that immediately you realize that he understood, that he was there; that was an emotion he felt. Then, later on I met somebody in Chile who knew him and said that he'd slept with boys. . . . I don't think there's any written biographical history.[20]

In seeking to retrieve a history of queer literature, *Gay Sunshine* was carrying forward a project inaugurated in the pages of its earlier homophile-movement precedents. The historian John D'Emilio notes that the pre-Stonewall *Mattachine Review*, for instance, "produced a major bibliography with more than 1,000 entries," while its lesbian contemporary, *Ladder*, "printed articles ranging from biographical portraits of literary figures such as Radclyffe Hall and Walt Whitman to explorations of homosexuality in European history and in non-Western cultures."[21] Nevertheless, *Gay Sunshine* carried this archival impulse to a new extreme and historical depth—and did not stop at the level of bibliography or anecdote.

Alongside the newspaper's interest in documenting more "public" (though often protectively coded) forms of gay culture like literature, *Gay Sunshine* interviews were also concerned to archive more "private" aspects of the interviewees' lives, and often asked candid questions about matters—like sexuality—traditionally understood as personal and outside the realm of public discourse. Elsewhere in the Ginsberg interview, for instance, Young has the poet describe in detail his relationships with Jack Kerouac and Peter Orlovsky. Similarly, when *Gay Sunshine* interviewed Burroughs, the interviewer pursued a line of questioning that ran like this: "Could you tell us something about your own past and present sexual encounters?" "And when you say 'boy,' do you mean an actual boy?" "Is the Arab world's concept of a homosexual quite the same as in the Western world?" And so on.[22]

Literary discussions like the one with Ginsberg about Lorca and Whitman were typical of *Gay Sunshine* interviews, and of a piece with a series of literary-critical essays that very frequently appeared in the newspaper not only to review the latest gay literary anthologies and volumes but also to recover primary evidence of a lost gay literary past. With titles like "Russian Gay Literary History: 11th–20th Centuries," "The Gay Novel: An Historical Overview," "Ganymede in Renaissance Literature," and "Gay Male Sensibility in Poetry since 1945," such essays were very much in the spirit of *Ladder*'s earlier features and quickly became a familiar aspect of the paper's general content.[23] Similarly, questions like those put to Burroughs on queer life in the Arab world were not infrequently the subject of extensive essayistic histories and reports in the paper: titles here include "Mexican Gaylife in Historical Perspective," "An Historical Study in Indian Homosexuality," "Man-Boy Love in the Far East," "Sodomy among Native Americans," "Gay Life in Lima," and "Ass Fucking Past and Present."[24] This emphasis on foreign culture highlights what Charles Shively, the editor of *Fag Rag* and a frequent *Gay Sunshine* contributor, would call the publication's "3rd world perspective"—an impetus that would reach its fullest expression in separate special issues on Latin America and Brazil.[25] Again, *collage* serves as a term that not only describes the innovative typography seen in *Gay Sunshine* but also figures the newspaper's pluralistic aesthetic, archival, and academic commitments, as well as its radical global politics of solidarity.

A less frequent aspect of *Gay Sunshine*'s archival enterprise manifested as photo spreads that would sometimes appear in the paper in place of the poetry centerfolds. Showcases of images taken by individual photographers, the photos in such spreads tended less to the fine-artistic than to the documentary end of the aesthetic spectrum. A feature in the twenty-fourth issue of *Gay Sunshine* by the photographer David Greene, for instance, was simply titled "Photographs of My Gay Friends." Reminiscent of the genre of documentary portraiture that occasionally attends subcultures with highly distinct dress codes like early punk or hard-core music scenes, but *without* that sense of vibrance or visual distinction in place, Greene's photos are casual portraits of his friends around the city. An unexpected kind of normalcy emanates from these images, as though the point were not to assert these subjects' status as exotic or Other, but simply to document the fact that Greene's own queer community *existed*. Such portraiture recalls the art historian David Deitcher's remarks on the desire for discovering "evidence of a past that is hard to find."[26] In a candid essay about his own longing to discover homosexual content in found, sexually ambiguous portraits of male friendship from the nineteenth century, Deitcher observes how:

> all too often, the historic traces of same-sex love consist of entries in police records and court documents, or stigmatizing evaluations by psychiatrists, psychologists, and criminologists. . . . Resistance compels the queer historian to unearth precious traces of that past, and to disseminate them in the form of previously untold stories of men and women, some of whom succeeded and some of whom failed to live with and act upon their forbidden love. Through such acts of recuperation, the queer historian helps to ensure the continued availability of that past as a source of validation and connection for more or less isolated individuals in the future.[27]

*Gay Sunshine*'s deliberate showcasing of work such as Greene's can be understood as a form of present-tense engagement in the kind of historical labor Deitcher describes. The imperative tone of Deitcher's comments matches the radical-political register of many *Gay Sunshine* editorials and helps make legible the degree to which work such as Greene's—and in general the practice of queer archiving itself—should not be mistaken as anything other than a strategic and principled form of resistance.

Just as collages combine disparate and fragmentary materials, queer archives have had to be historically inventive in taking up their unorthodox project of documenting subcultural and ephemeral phenomena, emotions, and lives. Ann Cvetkovich has recently written a useful history of the Lesbian Herstory Archives in Brooklyn and the Gay and Lesbian Historical Society in San Francisco, among other archives. Her book highlights the unique set of problems queer archives have had to concern themselves with solving, as they labor to collect materials that are primarily ephemeral, to improvise storage and maintenance in the absence of available public spaces or funds, and to negotiate with more orthodox institutions like public libraries for exhibitions. Cvetkovich notes how modern queer archives such as these are one of the legacies of Stonewall, preserving for public access "materials that might not be found in libraries or other public institutions, such as pornographic books, short-run journals, and forms of mass culture that are objects of camp reception."[28] *Gay Sunshine*'s efforts to retrieve evidentiary bibliographies, research essays, and photographs of past and present gay cultures are nothing if not spirited enactments of this post-Stonewall archival impulse. The inclusion of pornography on Cvetkovich's list of archival objects is interesting, not just because porn may be especially ephemeral but because porn shares with queerness a kind of analogical relationship to archiving itself, in the sense that both have always been constituted, at least partially, through processes of siphoning and exclusion.

Judith Halberstam has also written about the way in which the specific aspiration to archive ephemera—and thus bridge two terms that would seem to be, by definition, opposed—places the queer archive in a unique set of circumstances. When discussing the specific challenges posed by archiving subcultural ephemera associated with the riot grrrl movement of the 1990s, Halberstam argues:

> The notion of a [queer] archive has to extend beyond the image of a place to collect material or hold documents, and it has to become a floating signifier for the kinds of lives implied by the paper remnants of shows, clubs, events, and meetings. The archive is not simply a repository; it is also a theory of cultural relevance, a construction of collective memory, and a complex record of queer activity. In order for the archive to function it requires users, interpreters, and cultural historians to wade through the material and piece together the jigsaw puzzle of queer history in the making.[29]

Like pornography (completely pervasive, but simultaneously subterranean and ephemeral), queer subculture poses a special set of challenges to the archivist—but ones that may be approached as either debilitating or enabling, depending on one's perspective. For Halberstam, the difficult project of queer archiving represents an opportunity to retheorize the very idea of the archive, and to test the boundaries of what an archive can do. In Halberstam's view, queer archivists should abstract beyond the traditional image of the archive as a brick-and-mortar library (or, as in the case of the Lesbian Herstory Archives, a privately owned brownstone), and approach the archive as a "floating signifier" set to the project of archiving the fluidity of queer life itself. Halberstam's own image for this different kind of archive is curious—the jigsaw puzzle, an image not very far afield from the art productions found in so many of *Gay Sunshine*'s pages, and one that effectively suggests the collagist nature of queer-archive work. But while collage may be an apt metaphor for queer archives in general, it's crucial to recognize that collages such as Mariah's—unlike Halberstam's jigsaw puzzle—not only offer a possible metaphor for queer-archive assembly but themselves *are* a kind of archive. A final reason that I take collage to be a queer form is because collage, in the spirit of détournement suggested earlier, offers marginalized authors a means to improvise self-representation from found materials when the mainstream culture provides them with none.[30] Just as *Gay Sunshine*'s historical features and interviews metaphorically collage an accumulating queer archive from historical fragments, certain of the paper's poetry collages are themselves—in addition to being striking from visual and literary standpoints—literal archives of queer lives and "collective memory."

## "A Magazine Is a Society"

If *Gay Sunshine*'s special brands of journalism, lit crit, photo-essay, and collage sought to bring historical communities and identities into visibility and representation, the extent to which the newspaper itself actually *forged* a community should not be underestimated. After forty-three issues *Gay Sunshine* culminated in a major tenth-anniversary double issue (which was followed by one last tabloid issue, number 46, and a final book issue, number 47) before Leyland retired the newspaper to pursue full time the more permanent format of perfect-bound books, which he had begun publishing in 1975 under the imprint Gay Sunshine Press. For the anniversary issue Leyland asked longtime readers and contributors to write in with their own memories and takes on the history and accomplishments of the paper. The published responses effectively verify the poet Jack Spicer's fantastic axiom that "a magazine is a society," and they highlight the degree to which *Gay Sunshine* organized the possibility for a particular national queer "radical movement" readership to come into existence.[31] Steve Abbott, a Bay Area poet and publisher of the seminal New Narrative magazine *Soup*, wrote a particularly revealing memoir for the occasion. Abbott's articulate self-reflection on *Gay Sunshine*'s formative influence on his life powerfully demonstrates the way in which the newspaper's archival politics and aesthetics cooperated to create a vital and coherent sense of community in the present. His statement merits quoting at length:

> When I first became aware of *Gay Sunshine* in 1970–1, I was organizing anti-war work in Atlanta, Georgia. The impact it had upon me, along with documents such as Carl Wittman's *Gay Manifesto*, was immediate and phenomenal. I'd long been aware of my own homosexual feelings but had felt they were a private concern to be subordinate to other political work. Here, at last, were arguments that up-front homosexual liberation was equally important and complementary to the women's and Black liberation movements.
>
> I was also then a columnist for the campus newspaper at Emory University where, the year before, I'd been student government president. In a column I will never forget, I made my "coming-out" a public event. Over the next two years I helped organize Atlanta's Gay Liberation Front and, for a year, was the Gay Lib editor of *The Great Speckled Bird*. I vividly remem-

ber the first National Gay Liberation Conference in Austin, Texas, where I was able to meet several members of the Gay Sunshine Collective whose writings had influenced me so much.

Over subsequent years, Gay Sunshine continued to provide crucial information and support toward my own formation as a Gay person and a poet. . . . The Allen Ginsberg interview was particularly influential to me as were pioneering essays on the traditions of homosexuality in the Middle East, Russia and Japan. I began to see how writers and poets were often at the forefront of the Gay movement in all countries, and when Winston [Leyland] accepted my first poem for publication, brief as it was, I felt I'd received an important stamp of approval. . . . Many of the writers whom I now consider friends—Aaron Shurin, Robert Glück, Dennis Cooper, Robert Peters, Ian Young, to name just a few—I first met and corresponded to as a result of their work in Gay Sunshine books, anthologies, and of course, the journal itself. Mao Tse Tung is credited with saying "Without a culture, there can be no army." Without Gay Sunshine, there would not have evolved the strong sense of Gay culture and community I feel proud to be a part of today.[32]

Abbott's narrative is not unlike others shared in the issue, and he tells a particular version of a coming-out story perhaps only possible in the moment of the 1970s. By Abbott's own account, Gay Sunshine radicalized his already far-left politics with its fundamental assertion that sexuality was a legitimate site of struggle and should be included within a full repertoire of solidarity-based civil-rights politics. This single revelation prompted an entire reevaluation of his own life, resulting in a turn toward gay-community organizing and demonstration, publishing, correspondence, art production, and eventually a move to San Francisco. Abbott names the Bay Area friends he connected with because of Gay Sunshine, and his later role in the city's New Narrative scene offers an opportunity for reflection on the material, unforeseen effects that small-press publications self-generate: although Gay Sunshine stopped publishing as a newspaper just as New Narrative was a nascent literary movement, one wonders whether that community would have ever manifested as such had not Gay Sunshine organized the possibility for its existence.

Curiously, Abbott's story also unwittingly opens onto another moment that wonderfully illustrates Deitcher's description of the queer archive as a source of connection for individuals in the future. In a piece commissioned for performance in 2009 by Michelle Tea's Into the Streets program for the National Queer Arts Festival—for which Tea sent artists and writers into the archives of San Francisco's GLBT Historical Society to riff on or enact pieces of local queer history—the poet Eileen Myles delved into back issues of Gay

*Sunshine* and came up with a prose story in which she rewrote her own queer autobiography from a gay-male perspective. Myles's first-person "memoir" inhabits a character much like Abbott, who flees his dreary suburban Massachusetts existence after discovering a Wieners poem in *Gay Sunshine*, busing the same week to San Francisco to meet and fuck one of the paper's editors.[33] Myles's fictional memoir, like Abbott's actual one, can be read as exemplary of what Cvetkovich calls an "archive of feeling," for its recognition that cultural texts such as *Gay Sunshine* function not only as repositories of information but also "as repositories of feelings and emotions, which are encoded not only in the content of the texts themselves but in the practices that surround their production and reception."[34] Myles's contemporary reanimation of *Gay Sunshine* highlights the way in which the queer archive's documentation of ephemeral and often personal materials opens opportunities for affective self-recognition across generational (and gender) boundaries. Similarly, the story tunes into the real way in which *Gay Sunshine* produced a queer geography all its own—one coordinated around a scattered national readership, but with a particularly strong social gravity around San Francisco that literally pulled people into the orbit of the Bay Area. True to Halberstam's own definition of queer geography, *Gay Sunshine*'s unique production of space decentered traditional notions of body- or person-based spatiality for a community-based model that located "sexual subjectivities within and between embodiment, place, and practice."[35]

This expansive social force of *Gay Sunshine*, so aptly summed up by Spicer's axiom, is furthermore intelligible as what Michael Warner describes (in a formulation serendipitously suited for Spicer) as "the magic by which discourse conjures a public into being."[36] If, as Warner has it, "the key development in the emergence of modern publics was the appearance of newsletters and other temporally structured forms oriented toward their own circulation," then *Gay Sunshine* is exemplary of Warner's notion of a "text counterpublic"—a kind of public that comes into being only in relation to the circulation among strangers of texts that seek to radically challenge and transform dominant public-discourse norms.[37] The specifically *counter*public performativity of *Gay Sunshine*'s self-fashioned discourse is registered in D'Emilio's remarks on earlier homophile magazines, which anticipated and laid essential groundwork for this aspect of *Gay Sunshine*'s project by "inventing a form of public discourse . . . [wherein such] magazines became a kind of laboratory for experimenting with a novel kind of dialogue."[38]

The extent to which *Gay Sunshine* organized a textual counterpublic highlights the degree to which queer archives—like literary or pornographic magazines—not only are documentary enterprises, but are also profoundly generative. As the novelist Richard Hall puts it in his remarks for the anniversary issue: "It may well be that GS and Winston Leyland have invented gay culture."[39] Over the course of a decade, *Gay Sunshine* did not just gather a group of disparate, existing materials and persons into the pages of a newspaper; rather it forged a distinct and particularly compelling vision of gay history and present-tense politics. Although *Gay Sunshine* and its pioneering contemporaries have yet to receive the kind of literary-historical attention they merit, they brought a small-press queer counterpublic into existence whose presence and effects far exceeded the 1982 date of *Gay Sunshine*'s final issue. While *Gay Sunshine*'s particular sense of its queer time and place now speaks from a bygone era, the newspaper devised important typographic and archival strategies that could later be witnessed in the pages of other West Coast magazines, such as Dennis Cooper's *Little Caesar* (Los Angeles, 1976–82) and Abbott's quite collagist *Soup* (San Francisco, 1980–85), and are visible today in contemporary lit-sex zines, such as Hedi El Kholti's *Animal Shelter* (Los Angeles, 2008–) and Evan Kennedy's *The Swan's Dirty Rag* (San Francisco, 2010–). Although literature and pornography—just as collaging and archiving—are normally conceived as distinct enterprises, *Gay Sunshine* and its descendants stand as powerful illustrations of the way these phenomena erotically mingle, and indeed may be read as metaphors for one another, when the context is queer.

## Notes

1. Selections from *Gay Sunshine* are anthologized in book format in the two-volume collection *Gay Roots*, as are many of the newspaper's interviews in the two-volume collection *Gay Sunshine Interviews*, both published by Gay Sunshine Press. These volumes do not reproduce the original typesetting or imagery from the newspaper, nor have the newspapers been archived online in facsimile. I accessed the newspapers at the Poetry Collection of the University Libraries, University at Buffalo (SUNY), which holds a complete run of the series. My thanks to Poetry Collection curators Michael Basinski and Jim Maynard for their perennial warmth and hospitality.

2. For recent histories of the mimeograph revolution, see Clay and Phillips, *A Secret Location on the Lower East Side*; and Kane, *All Poets Welcome*. Also see Jed Birmingham and Kyle Schlesinger's wonderful journal devoted to the genre, *Mimeo Mimeo*. For exceptional discussions of the cultural history of queer printing, see Bronson and Aarons, "AA Bronson Interviews Philip Aarons"; Herring, *Another Country*; Meeker, *Contacts Desired*; and Nelson, *Publisher to the Decadents*. For some historical commentary on Boston's *Fag Rag*, see Moore, *Beyond Shame*.

3. See Halberstam, *In a Queer Time and Place*.

4. Halberstam, *In a Queer Time and Place*, 2.

5. See, for example, Winston Leyland's op-ed "Gay Radical Press: 1972," 5.

6. Creeley's aphorism, formulated in a letter to Charles Olson, became a founda-

tional precept of the New American poetry after Olson emphasized it in his 1950 essay, "Projective Verse."

7. For a discussion of modernist writing, the courtroom, and the legal discourse of "obscenity," see Glass, "Redeeming Value." For a robust discussion of collage as the fundamental aesthetic principle of modernist writing, see Antin, "Modernism and Postmodernism" and "Some Questions about Modernism."

8. McGann, Black Riders, 46.

9. Debord, The Society of the Spectacle, 145.

10. The absence of women in this list is conspicuous, and programmatic rather than an oversight. Although Gay Sunshine maintained express solidarity with lesbian liberationists—and often did so in the form of printing essays and journalism by queer women—the general priority of the paper is succinctly expressed in the phrase that appears on the cover of issue 7 (from 1971): "A male paper of gay militancy." On one occasion Gay Sunshine did publish the pioneering New American queer poet, mimeo publisher, and community organizer Anne Waldman.

11. Halperin, Saint Foucault, 92–93.

12. Foucault, "Sex, Power, and the Politics of Identity," 165.

13. As a recent exhibition curated by Michael Duncan and Christopher Wagstaff for the Crocker Art Museum in Sacramento makes evident, Jess was the leading figure of an entire circle of artists and writers who were experimenting with collage in the Bay Area at midcentury; others in this group included Helen Adam, Wallace Berman, Robin Blaser, Ernesto Edwards, Fran Herndon, Lawrence Jordan, Patricia Jordan, and Eloise Mixon. See the catalog for this excellent exhibition, An Opening of the Field: Jess, Robert Duncan, and Their Circle. For Duncan's notion of "grand collage," see his 1968 preface to Bending the Bow, as well as The H.D. Book, where Duncan writes: "The great art of my time is the collagist's art, to bring all things into new complexes of meaning, mixing associations" (58–59).

14. Leyland, introduction to Gay Roots, 17.

15. Bronson and Aarons, "AA Bronson Interviews Philip Aarons," 10.

16. Fuck You: A Magazine of the Arts 7, no. 5 (1964): 6.

17. Bernadette Mayer's complaint about Ted Berrigan's East Coast mimeo "C" (1963–66) indicates just how novel Fuck You's anarchic aesthetic was, and helps to variegate our sense of mimeo culture: "What I objected to was the way poetry was published in 'C' and other magazines; it was always a certain kind of poetry, surrounded by white space, seen as precious, pretentious maybe. I wanted to remove poetry from that context and just let it be, surrounded by conceptual art, anything but that precious feeling that you get from many magazines" (quoted in Russo, "Poetics of Adjacency," 132). For a strong critique of the masculinist homosociality that prevailed in postwar poetry communities, see Davidson, Guys Like Us.

18. Leyland, introduction to Gay Roots, 18.

19. For an interview with some members of the second collective, see Gay Sunshine 10 (1972). For convenience here I have opted to use only the shorter title Gay Sunshine throughout.

20. Ginsberg, interview with Allen Young, 5.

21. D'Emilio, Sexual Politics, Sexual Communities, 111.

22. Burroughs, interview with Laurence Collinson and Roger Baker, 11.

23. These articles may be found in Gay Sunshine issues 30, 22, 19, and 44/45, respectively.

24. These articles may be found in *Gay Sunshine* issues 26/27, 26/27, 38/39, 38/39, 40/41, and 24, respectively.

25. Shively, letter to *Gay Sunshine*, 3.

26. Deitcher, "Looking at a Photograph, Looking for a History," 23.

27. Deitcher, "Looking at a Photograph, Looking for a History," 23–34.

28. Cvetkovich, *An Archive of Feelings*, 242–43.

29. Halberstam, *In a Queer Time and Place*, 169–70.

30. My thanks to the editor of *Animal Shelter*, collagist and cultural presenter Hedi El Kholti, for helping me to see this point.

31. Spicer, "Poetry and Politics," 157.

32. Abbott, letter to *Gay Sunshine*, 4. My thanks to Kaplan Harris for drawing my attention to Abbott's statement. Harris quoted from the *Gay Sunshine* anniversary issue in a talk presented for Margaret Konkol's Small Press in the Archive lecture series at the University at Buffalo Poetry Collection, "After ~~Language Poetry~~ New Narrative: Innovation & Its Social Discontents," on March 17, 2010.

33. Myles, "Gay Sunshine, 1971."

34. Cvetkovich, *An Archive of Feelings*, 7.

35. Halberstam, *In a Queer Time and Place*, 5.

36. Warner, *Publics and Counterpublics*, 105.

37. Warner, *Publics and Counterpublics*, 94–95.

38. D'Emilio, *Sexual Politics, Sexual Communities*, 114.

39. R. Hall, letter to *Gay Sunshine*, 5.

# 11

## This Is What Porn Can Be Like!
## A Conversation with Shine Louise Houston

*Mireille Miller-Young*

*Mireille Miller-Young visited San Francisco for a conversation with the porn producer and director Shine Louise Houston. On April 29, 2010, they met at Houston's home to discuss her award-winning feature film* Champion *and her independent porn company, Pink and White Productions. Houston had planned to attend a screening of* Champion *in Buffalo, New York, the month prior but had to cancel. The following is an excerpt from a longer interview with the author and Shine Louise Houston. The transcript was prepared by Jade Petermon.*

...............................

**Mireille Miller-Young:** Thank you for having me over. We were disappointed that you couldn't attend our conference in Buffalo last month, "At the Limit: Pornography and the Humanities." But we were very happy for the opportunity to screen your latest film, *Champion*; as a fan of your work, I was excited to see it. The movie has been out for a while now, since 2008, and has been well received. There seems to be a consensus that it's your biggest cinematic achievement thus far. How do you understand the film's success?

**Shine Louise Houston:** There are two sides to that issue: the professional side and the popular side. All three of my feature films made the festival circuit when they were released, but this one got Movie of the Year at the Feminist Porn Awards in Toronto. It's doing well in professional venues. On the popular side, most people who write or blog about it are very positive, claiming it as something new in pornography. But it doesn't sell that well. I have to say, though, to me it's not something new; it's just going back to seventies porn. That era of porn has been an important touchstone for me.

**Miller-Young:** Do you mean that cinematic quality was higher then?

**Houston:** Yes, both in terms of the cinematic quality and the thoughtfulness of filmmaking, the movies were better. Of course you have to wade through bits of misogyny and racism here and there, but on the whole they were more interesting movies. One of my favorites from the seventies is called *Score*. It's a really well-done bisexual film with an interesting, odd story line. It has compelling characters. It incorporates nonconsensual sex in a good way. It's devious and funny and a little dark. I look at that and think, *This is what porn can be like!*

Technology has had a huge impact on the porn industry. Video, for instance, made a big difference. In the eighties and nineties, when video was everywhere and nobody knew how to light for it yet, you can see a divergence away from the quality of filmmaking present in the mid- to late 1970s. There are some gems in the eighties, but generally the creativity didn't approach the previous generation of films. But if we look back at seventies porn, why can't we follow its example? *Champion* is my first attempt to do that.

Miller-Young: In addition to impacting production, video transformed everything in terms of the consumption and privatization of viewing porn. The seventies is a very interesting period for me as a historian of pornography, especially of black women's performance and representation. Searching the archive of black erotica I found a woman named Desiree West. She was a major actor in the seventies. She wasn't as famous as Vanessa Del Rio, but she performed with John Holmes and did a number of provocative films. *SexWorld* is one you might know.

Houston: I haven't seen *SexWorld*, but I know the poster.

Miller-Young: It's an interesting example because it created an interface between desegregation and the sexual revolution. The SexWorld that gives the movie its title is a laboratory for exploring sexual fantasy. One of the experiments pairs a bigoted white man with a black woman as a way of showing him that his sexual desires run deeper than his prejudices. Even if flawed, the movie was an exploration of racialized sexuality that was uncommon in popular media before then. In the 1970s, black women were using pornography as a performative site to do a lot of new things. You begin to see certain actresses subverting their own performances, for example. I always wonder how those performances get recorded. Could you talk about what is important to capture in terms of the cinematic? Does it offer a space to use multiracial actors to explore desire in different ways?

Houston: I stick to the technical aspects. I've learned that the less I think about the sex, the better I can capture it. In a philosophical sense, if I try to spearhead racial content consciously, I'll always miss the mark. When I formulate cinematic ideas around race, gender, and representation, I superimpose too much of my own shit on the sex and I miss my goal.

So instead I look at the technical problems. Like, what happens when we use this specific focal length? What does it do to these people when I shoot the sex from this angle? If it doesn't work, I try to shoot the sex in a different way. I don't direct the sex. I don't tell them what to do. It's all about the process and trying to stay invisible. For the Crash Pad Series, I don't book the actors to avoid enacting my own personal biases. It's not like I'm not conscious of race and gender. It's just that there are so many layers in my brain. That's why I'm a visual person.

Miller-Young: I'm interested in the point you just made about expressing your ideas through the kinds of shots and angles as well as the depth, space, and time. It reminds me of the scene from your third film, In Search of the Wild Kingdom, featuring the two transmen of color, Will and Papi. There was an amazing shot from below looking up at Will's face. It was my first time seeing a transman in porn with such depth. His face was really well framed, and rarely obscured. I loved that. But I wonder about the choices you make in creating shots like that. Do those technical decisions express something about sex or gender or intimacy or racialized desire?

Houston: There is a big distinction, a line drawn in the sand even, between Champion and Wild Kingdom. I think my decisions and my learning curve took a huge leap after Wild Kingdom. This is the critical artist speaking, but I would say the first three movies are shit. I was surprised that people liked my first porn, The Crash Pad, so much. It must be empty out there if that has become a cult classic! The sex is hot, but now I think the series is crap. I wanted to have more fun with my next try, Superfreak, but I was sick. I had a one-hundred-and-three-degree temperature throughout the entire shoot. We slashed several scenes that I wanted to do, and instead I built it around just one scene.

I got a bit closer with Wild Kingdom. It's a mockumentary about a documentary film crew trying to film real lesbian sex, but we had some technical issues. I hated the lighting in that room and we didn't have enough time for set dressing. We shot the film in just six days, which caused problems during the editing process. But I really did like some shots, for example that shot of Will. I loved Will and Papi as a couple. They had amazing sex, but I was disappointed that I couldn't capture it the way I wanted. Around that time a friend of mine said to me, "You're close." I agreed, but I wasn't getting something; something was wrong.

Miller-Young: Did you figure out what exactly?

Houston: For one thing, we were shooting scenes at a ninety-degree angle, sometimes face and sometimes crotch. One of my friends pointed out that fucking was a conversation, so we started shooting it like dialogue. And ever since I've cut sex scenes like a conversation. It worked. I finally figured out how to translate that experience.

It wasn't as if the performers weren't giving great performances. We weren't missing the mark on casting. It was a technical problem. When we started thinking about it like a technical problem, I could see the beauty on the screen. So now we have rules: thou shalt not zoom, thou shalt not slow pan, thou shalt have a fixed focal length. If you want a closer shot, you have to get closer!

Later we worked out a system for moving around a couple without crossing lines or breaking the flow of their scene. That was the big breakthrough and we saw the results for the first time in *Champion*. We were doing it in the Crash Pad Series for a while but we really figured it out in *Champion*. Also for *Champion* we used a 35 mm lens adaptor, which gave us a more cinematic aesthetic. I decided I wasn't going to spend two thousand dollars on an adapter just yet, so I built one instead. I finally felt like, *ah, there's the pretty!*

We consistently got more pretty and more intensity between couples in *Champion*. Even still, there are some people who don't like my style. One guy on the Pink and White Productions forum wants to see scenes cut between tight shots and full body shots. I don't like that, though, because it flattens the whole experience. I stay tight on purpose.

*Miller-Young:* Does that approach add depth or intimacy?

*Houston:* It adds intimacy, and it's easier to get interesting compositions. I always come back to the technical questions.

*Miller-Young:* Now that you are explaining it, I see the difference between *Champion* and the other movies. There is more consistency, focus, and a kind of a single plane that's different than a series of perpendicular shots. I think people picked up on the effect of that single plane when we screened your film in Buffalo, but they expressed it in a different way. The men in particular wanted to know why the scenes were so long and why they featured multiple orgasms. In a lot of porn, gay and straight, the scene ends after a man comes. But in your films, the actors keep coming and coming! Is the length of a scene a technical problem? If you don't direct the sex, what kind of directions do you give to get the pacing you want?

*Houston:* I just ask them what they have in mind. Honestly, before we start I'll say, "Give me an idea of what you are going to do." And that's it!

*Miller-Young:* I wonder then how you edit the sex scenes? *Champion* moves through the dialogue and the fighting sequences really fast, but the sex scenes are long. Are the edits preserving the sex as it unfolds? Or do they change the duration of sex?

Houston: Here's the business side of directing—if you want to sell a movie, it has to be somewhere around eighty or ninety minutes. So, yes, I have to cut parts. In fact, my scenes are considered short by industry standards. A fifteen-minute scene is a short scene. I hate that the last scene in *Champion* is twenty-two minutes. There was so much stuff—about two hours of fucking—that I had a hard time editing it down.

Miller-Young: I want to ask about that scene. Some people seemed to think it was a little anticlimactic because it lacked the screaming and yelling. They were surprised after the ultraorgasmic moments of the earlier scenes.

Houston: It is anticlimactic. I was bummed about that. Dallas was supposed to be running the scene. Dallas is definitely toppish and that character was top in the ring—the sex was supposed to reflect that. It was also supposed to be about Dallas's orgasm, and I really tried to cut it to make sense to me, but it turned out more balanced. Dallas had a hard time cumming on film. Instead there was a great moment when Syd takes the lead and does an amazing squirt. I had to cut that, though, because the scene wasn't about Syd. Ultimately it was my least favorite scene because it didn't work how I wanted it to work.

Filming *Champion* raised a lot of questions about how to make porn. On the one hand, we asked ourselves, what is the narrative structure of an adult feature? But on the other hand, we were thinking about what sells. Well, on the business side, I needed four and a half sex scenes and couldn't go over two hours.

Miller-Young: Why did you cut the squirting?

Houston: Because Dallas was supposed to be more dominant in that sex scene.

Miller-Young: But they were trading in that scene.

Houston: Yes, the top-bottom dynamic wasn't as strong as I had hoped.

Miller-Young: If you edited to keep the consistency of a dominant-submissive narrative, that raises a question. How do you balance between giving people the freedom to do whatever they want and at the same time working toward a final product? I mean, if you're trying to capture real sex, you have to deal with the fact that sometimes people just don't come, or don't come in the way you want. This approach necessarily changes the money-shot formula, which insists on a climactic visualization of male pleasure. In straight readings of porn's history, the fundamental problem has always been trying to capture women's pleasure on-screen. It sounds like the dominant-submissive dynamic helped you manage that problem in *Champion*, but then it also introduced new challenges. How do you prioritize trans pleasure, for instance?

*Houston*: Do you mean the editing process or the shooting process?

*Miller-Young*: Both, or either. Is it important for you to cultivate trans pleasure? Is it important for you to show women's pleasure?

*Houston*: Of course, that's the whole purpose. But if we're talking about orgasms specifically, there *are* scenes where one person comes and the other person doesn't. That can be hot. But let me clarify the process: We shoot a lot of raw material. The narrative comes out when we start editing that material and piecing it together. We worked that way for the Crash Pad Series especially, and I learned a lot from that process of experimenting with the edits. So much so that I started new projects just so I could explore new things. But as far as my personal ethics and standards on set, it's important that people do what they're going to do. I want them to control the on-set experience as much as possible, so that it is pleasurable, but I don't give up control in the editing room. Sometimes those standards come into conflict and I'm slightly disappointed with the final product, like the last scene in *Champion*. All I can say is that it happens.

*Miller-Young*: Do the performers ever feel like they didn't deliver?

*Houston*: Some people get bummed if they don't come. I had one performer apologize! But it was still a good scene and, anyway, talking about goal-oriented sex, sometimes the goal is something other than orgasm.

*Miller-Young*: I'm still fascinated by the freedom you give performers, partly because in mainstream hetero porn there is pressure for women to fake it. Why don't you ask people to fake it? If you need to consider market demands — four and a half sex scenes in ninety minutes — why not just direct the sex? Is there some kind of political, aesthetic, or artistic rationale for only shooting real orgasms?

*Houston*: I don't want to watch people having fake orgasms. I've watched a lot of porn with fake orgasms. It's always laughable! I spoofed that kind of porn in *Wild Kingdom*. That movie expresses my sentiment—it's ridiculous, it's silly, and I don't want it on my set. Of course, someone I'm shooting could fake it on their own. There have been times when I decided, hmmm, *I'm not going to ask*.

Also, there's a rationale on the business side because we have a smarter audience. Especially in Internet porn. Probably 50 percent of the people who visit our website are women, so you have to think about who is watching my movies. I keep my audience in mind, but I still come back to what got me started—I make movies that I want to see. That way, at least, I know one hundred other people who will want to see it too. Not everybody will want to see what I want to see, but a few people will.

*Miller-Young:* The popular conception of women as porn consumers is that they usually want an elaborate fantasy, something that emphasizes a story line and deemphasizes hard-core sex. But you think that women consumers want to see authenticity in porn? What is your reading of the female consumer?

*Houston:* I think the idea that women just want fantasy is bullshit. Maybe soft-core fantasy hit a particular market in the eighties, when Candida Royalle and other folks were producing porn for women and couples. But then I think about the generations that are coming up now. We've played with sexuality and power so much since the eighties that this generation is a bit savvier about separating sex from sentimentality. I think the popularity of the Crash Pad Series is that it works around this premise: it's just fucking! We don't need a love story, or any elaborate story line, because hard-core fucking is just sexy. However, I do want porn to be pretty in a way that I don't think it generally has been since video took off in the eighties. All the beauty left and, as I already mentioned, part of my mission is to bring it back.

*Miller-Young:* But even if your movies move through the dialogue quickly to focus on the sex scenes, the narrative is still an important aspect of the quality of your work.

*Houston:* It is. I came out as a narrative filmmaker after college. I went to San Francisco Art Institute, where they take a very experimental approach to making movies. It's a cheesy story, but my commitment to narrative came while I was watching *The Matrix*. It made me realize that I want to tell a really good story. Now my goal is to find the intersection between telling a story and capturing really hot sex. The next movie I make is called *Snapshot*. It's a kick-ass suspense thriller. But before I can make it there are some structural changes that I have to make to my business.

*Miller-Young:* I'm interested in the business side of pornography. One aspect of my research investigates the political economy of specific businesses within the structure of the adult-entertainment industry. Black men have been directing for a while and, compared to black women, have had an easier time getting their projects financed and distributed. When I started the research in 2002 there weren't any black women directing! Now that there are, I'm interested in how people like Vanessa Blue, Diana DeVoe, Venus Hottentot, and you do it. Can you tell me how you have been able to raise capital, learn the industry, and get distribution?

*Houston:* A friend of mine started an online group for local porn makers. I met Tony Comstock there and he asked me to help him find models and equipment. I didn't know who he was, but I said, *sure, why not?* So I helped him get a location and equipment, then worked as his production assistant. In the middle of the shoot two of his investors show up—one was Christophe Pettus from Blowfish. So Tony introduced us and later I showed him a short demo I'd made by myself to raise money. But the whole thing was a mess. The optical drive on my new computer went out, so I couldn't burn him a disk. Instead I dumped it to tape and in the process erased the sound. I was sweating bullets while he traded his attention between the demo and his e-mail. I was sure I'd fucked up the deal. When it finished, though, he asked: "How does seven thousand dollars sound?" It sounded great! That's how the partnership with Blowfish started, and before we finished production on *The Crash Pad* Christophe offered to pick up the total budget and distribution—about eight thousand dollars. That's what it cost to do the first volume. We made the next three movies with Blowfish, too, but now are moving toward self-funding.

*Miller-Young:* Pink and White is your own production company but Blowfish is the distribution company?

*Houston:* Yes, they were coexecutive producers and distributors.

*Miller-Young:* Making a movie is one thing, but getting it out there is the hard part. How has distribution affected your business?

*Houston:* Here again technology is changing the industry. Business is moving toward the Internet. People still buy DVDs, but companies have a new angle on how to distribute and sell. The next movie that I make will screen at festivals before it goes to DVD. That way it will reach a larger market of people who, after seeing it, might want the DVD. But in terms of online business, I do much better with the single Crash Pad Series website than I do on all my movies combined.

*Miller-Young:* That's surprising, considering the widespread recognition you received for *Champion*.

*Houston:* Yes, but it's an indication of how people watch porn. Plus, our online presence means we're becoming a force in the industry, for good.

*Miller-Young:* A force for good!

*Houston:* For good because the industry is very hard on smaller businesses. I should explain the way this works. I'm simplifying, but basically digital distribution for video on demand can happen in two ways. They buy content for a flat fee or they'll offer a contract that, on the high end, pays 20 to 25 percent to the content creator. Honestly, I'm really tired of other people making more off my content than I do. That's one reason I'm starting a project called Point of Contact, which will act like a sort of hotbed for producers. We'll provide a tiny bit of micro financing; they upload the content to our website. We edit and distribute it; they get 40 percent lifetime royalties. And we'll stream content for a few people in Australia or Germany who cannot run their own websites for legal reasons. Basically, our percentage covers processing and bandwidth. Content creators get the rest of revenue and, even though we're not making a profit, it helps us in other ways.

Miller-Young: You benefit just by having more material on your site?

Houston: Yes, because it brings more traffic from other sites, it lowers credit-card processing costs, and it makes bandwidth cheaper.

Miller-Young: Let me make sure I understand: the software required to watch video on demand is owned by other companies, even if you have it on your site? Unless you have your own they take a huge cut?

Houston: They take 80 percent! That's why we're building our own software.

Miller-Young: Clips4Sale does that?

Houston: Clips4Sale now offers payout percentages but video-on-demand companies like SkinVideo will take your content for a flat fee and make money off it forever. Sometimes they'll give you 10 percent or 11 percent, but even porn stars who have clips on their own sites only make about 20 percent of the total sale.

On-demand companies like AEBN and Hotmovies.com: those are the big names, and they'll give you up to 25 percent. We got 25 percent because we have a name. Imagine what they are doing to other people! It's possible to create software for video on demand yourself, but some producers get reamed up the ass by these companies because they don't know the technology or are afraid of technology.

Miller-Young: I want to ask the porn stars I talk to about this issue. Why do they choose to use certain sites and what are they getting out of them? I think sometimes it's just easier, especially if they are not technologically savvy.

Houston: They do have benefits. The companies can be helpful. If you want a particular wording, for instance, they will accommodate your requests. Or maybe it breaks a price point for some people because those sites have a lot of traffic. But I wonder why some people who have the means don't develop their own technology. I find that power lies in owning the technology; it lets you control your own business.

It is true that people aren't making money like they were ten years ago, but there is another wave of development that's coming along on the Internet. There's a certain level of value in new venues, you just have to find the untapped markets.

Miller-Young: Earlier you said that 50 percent of your web audience is women. Is that also the target market for your films?

Houston: It's hard to tell from the information that we get from our management site, but it seems like a lot of straight men and a lot of queer folks like it.

Miller-Young: How do you cull the data on gender and sex?

Houston: We just get names and locations, which is why it's hard to tell. A lot are men, but they could be trans guys. Some names are gender neutral. The vocal people are always queer folks, but I'm sure there are lots of lurkers.

Miller-Young: That's interesting because it raises a question that is key to porn's, and queer folks', place in the world: who else is paying attention? Who is watching porn without, ostensibly anyway, belonging to its audience? The idea of lurkers hints at the possibility of censorship, but even beyond legal censorship, I wonder if the politics of respectability has affected you.

Houston: At one point, yes. I had just turned thirty or thirty-one and wasn't sure what to do with my life. I was working retail at the feminist sex shop Good Vibrations and wanted something else but couldn't decide what. Learn to make furniture? Go back to painting? I'd always wanted to learn about film, so maybe that? Somehow all the doors opened in the film direction, so I decided, *Okay life, if this is where we're going, let's go.* I didn't set out to make porn. But I met Tony and Christophe and one thing led to another; I made *The Crash Pad* and it sold like crazy, then I made another and another and here I am — known for making porn.

Miller-Young: Did your family resist your decisions along the way?

Houston: No, my mom was supportive. She's pretty much my family and was happy that I owned my own business. Generally, though, I was surprised at how much encouragement I received. That might be a Bay Area thing, I don't know, but everywhere I went people were supportive. Of course, I was careful about who I told.

Miller-Young: That's great! My mom felt like she'd worked too hard to have her daughter doing a PhD on porn. Obviously it's different for academics, or even directors, than it is for performers, but I find that we all worry about the stigma of being associated with porn. For directors specifically, I wonder if other people ever accuse you of exploiting your performers?

*Houston:* I got that question a lot in the beginning, but I think that as a community we are moving past it *because* more people are talking about their experiences making porn. One thing I found helpful in answering that question, though, was to highlight problems in the industry at large. For example, I'd point out that on set I always treat people with respect. I pay people as best I can. I only work with performers doing it because they want to do it. I never ask people to do anything they wouldn't normally do. We don't do fluid swapping activities. So, no, it's not exploitative. As I've always said, we use our voices to counteract the voices speaking for us, whether as queer folk, women, or trans folk. By creating new images, we create new voices.

*Miller-Young:* The representation of sexuality and desire is something older performers talk about often. I interviewed some black actresses active in the eighties who were, for the time, sex radicals. They explored their sexualities through sex with multiple partners and that sort of thing. And they always told me they wanted to see people who looked like them and acted out their fantasies. Today the primary interest seems to be making money and surviving this economy, at least for the women entering the mainstream hetero market. I'm curious about the women in your films. Who are they? Are they doing other kinds of sex work or just part of the queer community in the Bay Area?

*Houston:* It's a cross section. Most are amateurs; some have never done porn before. For some it'll be the only time they do it, but others want to get their feet wet and start with me—a few people who have gone off to do more and more. The Crash Pad Series and Pink and White Productions are kind of incubators in that way.

*Miller-Young:* I think it's great that you provide a space where people realize something about themselves—whether they are consumers or performers—and so I hesitate to ask about the negative side, but I wonder if other black women have ever confronted you or criticized your work?

*Houston:* Only white people have. Maybe it's white guilt. But the only folks who ask me why there aren't more brown people on the site and have issues around power dynamics and skin color are white people. I don't know why that is.

*Miller-Young:* Is it a feminist conflict between the antiporn versus prosex positions? Or are second-wave feminists responding negatively to your movies?

*Houston:* There are lines between ages and social positions within feminism, and they definitely determine responses to my work. Older women tend to have more problems with it. I always watch who walks out during my films and it's usually older folks.

*Miller-Young*: What sort of problems?

*Houston*: I'll give you an example from a great thread on my site. It was weird, and you'd have to read it to understand all the reasons why, but for one, it conflated body issues with the commodification of queer culture. Just like anticapitalist critiques, if you believe that all economic exchanges in a capitalistic society lead to commodification, then you'll always have a problem with my business—or any business for that matter. But I don't believe that commodification necessarily causes body issues. As I said before, one reason I make porn is to change the images available to folks, although that does require selling images.

Abroad, though, it's a different critique. In France and London people wanted to know why, in *Wild Kingdom* and the Crash Pad Series especially, I perpetuated the stereotype of black women as butch, or, more generally, as masculine. But that's not the stereotype in the United States. Here we have a stereotype of black women as hypersexual—in some cases asexual, but more often hypersexual.

*Miller-Young*: I agree that the stereotype is of a hypersexualized black woman, but also a butchy black woman that is supposed to remind us that *real* femininity is white femininity.

*Houston*: Exactly. I got that question two or three times in different ways.

*Miller-Young*: Has your work generally been received abroad in different ways than it has been in the U.S.? Are Europeans fascinated with you in a different way than people are fascinated with you in North America?

*Houston*: I'm not sure I can answer that, but I will say that I felt like people in Berlin were starting from the same place that I was—more so, anyway, than people in France or London. People in both the U.S. and Canada seemed to perceive a conflict between queer politics and feminism, which is interesting because when in Berlin, where they host the PorYes Feminist Porn Awards, people consistently interchange *queer* and *feminist*. Which makes some sense; they are interchangeable in some ways. To take an example from science, we have string theory and we have M-theory. Both look at the same thing but from a different angle. So if you look at one, two, three, four, five different waves of feminism, you see that queer theory incorporates, or at least responds to, all those various influences.

*Miller-Young*: I want to come back to the question of influence, especially in regards to the new direction that *Champion* is taking your work. You said that seventies porn has been an important model, but there must be other influences as well.

*Houston:* Well, I was studying *Raging Bull* a lot before writing *Champion,* which was fun, so why not go with it?

*Miller-Young:* There are shots from *Raging Bull* in *Champion?* Is that why you incorporated mixed martial arts, or were you influenced by the popularity of Ultimate Surrender, sexual wrestling competitions?

*Houston:* Neither, actually. Syd really is a kick boxer and I was watching Martin Scorsese, so the two things converged. You have to pay homage to your heroes. Hitchcock was also an inspiration. I owe a lot to Scorsese, Hitchcock, the Wachowskis, the Coen brothers, and Jim Jarmusch. I got ideas from all of them. Who knows? Maybe I'll be the Jim Jarmusch of porn.

*Miller-Young:* What about porn directors?

*Houston:* I don't know about directors, but as I said before, *Score* made an impression. I watch a lot of gay porn. I thought Wash West's movie *The Hole* was a smart parody of *Ringu.* I watch all the movies Paul Thomas does for Vivid Entertainment. I've seen a lot of Chloe Hoffman's stuff, which tends to be pretty good for mainstream porn. She was my first porn crush.

*Miller-Young:* How do you see yourself in relation to other women directors who have started their own companies, particularly people like Bella Donna or Tristan Taormino, who is especially vocal about queer sexuality?

*Houston:* I can't compare notes that way because I'm hypercritical of myself. I have to work with blinders, which is good and bad. I think being competitive with others in the industry is a good thing and a bad thing. It can be inhibiting. For example, I watched some of Maria Beatty's early movies, which draw on surrealist and noir-ish aesthetics. Even without putting her on a pedestal, I felt like she was the person to beat. But our work is very different, so it wasn't an especially productive fixation. On the other hand, I was having problems with narrative when I saw Anna Brownfield's movie *The Band;* it's a punk-rock love story. She got it, so seeing that helped resolve my own difficulties.

*Miller-Young:* Well, you're certainly carving out your own space in porn. I'm grateful for everything you do and for talking to me about it. Thank you.

# PART IV

Rough Archives

# 12

# Snuff and Nonsense: The Discursive Life
# of a Phantasmatic Archive

## Lisa Downing

This chapter takes as its subject the discursive deployment of an urban myth, an imaginary object: the snuff film. This phantasmatic object has produced a wealth of media speculation, has been the linchpin of political and legal argumentation, and has been a sensational plot feature in numerous novels and films.[1] The idea of snuff marks the nexus of a set of cultural fears and fascinations that cluster around fantasies about extremity, the exceeding of limits, and the exercise of violent power in the service of eroticism. The term *snuff film*, coined by the poet and rock lyricist Ed Sanders in a book on Charles Manson's cult killing spree of the late 1960s, was used to refer to the video recordings that the killers allegedly made of their crimes.[2] *Snuff*, in the sense that we understand it today, rose to prominence in the popular imagination with a set of media stories that circulated in the United States during the 1970s about the rumored existence of a genre of pornographic films, thought to be made in South America, which culminated with the female performer being murdered—"snuffed out"—on camera.[3] This media speculation galvanized antipornography feminists, who espied in the rumored phenomenon of snuff an actualization of their contention that pornography is the graphic representation of violence against women. It takes to the logical extreme the slogan Robin Morgan would coin in the 1980s, "pornography is the theory; rape is the practice," since the violation of female personhood becomes a literal annihilation in the imagined snuff formula.

Capitalizing on the media furor over the purported existence of snuff films, the producer Allan Shackleton bought *Slaughter*, made in Argentina in 1971 by Michael and Roberta Findlay. *Slaughter* is a film inspired by the Manson family killings that depicts the homicidal spree of a group of young male and female bikers operating in thrall to their cult leader, Satán. Shackleton then tacked on to the end of this film a final sequence, which appears to be behind-the-scenes footage, of the director kissing and fondling a script girl on camera before mutilating and finally killing her by means of a bloody evisceration.

The composite film, *Snuff*, was released in commercial cinemas in 1976. Marketing of the film suggested (without stating outright) that this was a "real" snuff movie, deploying taglines including the xenophobic legend: "The film that could only be made in South America . . . where life is CHEAP!" The furor that accrued to *Snuff* provoked an increased swathe of feminist activism and media interest, with pickets and demonstrations outside cinemas that screened the film.[4]

The question of the generic definition—of both *Snuff* and *snuff*—is a fraught one. According to Eithne Johnson and Eric Schaefer, the assertion that *Snuff* would have fulfilled the criteria for a snuff movie had the killing not been proved to be fictional is erroneous, since they claim that *Snuff* fails to deliver on the generic demands of the porn film, of which snuff is a subgenre. They argue that *Snuff* has less in common with commercial hard-core films, such as *Deep Throat* (directed by Gerard Damiano, 1972), that were contemporaneously playing in cinemas than with films belonging to the exploitation movie subgenres known as ghoulies (featuring gore) and the roughies or kinkies (featuring simulated gruesome death and kinky sex).[5] The main link with pornography, for them, lies in the fact that "the distributors for *Snuff* attempted to capitalize on the cross-over success of feature-length hard-core pornography by choosing mainstream release over the more restricted exhibition circuits of drive-ins and grindhouses." The result of this choice of screening venue was that "*Snuff* defied easy categorization."[6]

The FBI, which investigated the murder allegedly committed in *Snuff* in response to the outcry it prompted (and found it to be a fake), established a provisional definition of a snuff movie: a film in which a person who is shown alive at the beginning of the footage is killed on-screen and shown dead by the end. The film must have been created for the purposes of producing sexual arousal (i.e., constitute pornography), and it must be commercially distributed.[7] Thus, the capacity of "pornography" to signify as a closed generic category becomes crucial for the North American legal definition of snuff. According to this arguably arbitrary definition, a commercial narrative film containing simulated snuff elements, such as *Hostel* (directed by Eli Roth, 2005), does not meet the definition, since no one is really killed. Neither does a video made by a murderer of his or her own killings produced for personal viewing (even though the alleged Manson tapes of just this kind provided the term *snuff*), since such a film would not be made for commercial distribution. Nor, for that matter, do the clips that have recently gone viral on the Internet showing real deaths, such as those from war zones, because, although they depict death in the raw and may be claimed to fuel a sensationalist or even sexual appetite for extreme images, they do not meet the commercial definition of porn. Moreover, for Linda Williams, in *Hard Core*, "the mistake that reads Snuff's violent horror as pornography demonstrates the need to be clear about what kinds of violence and what kinds of perversion do operate in contemporary hardcore commercial film pornography."[8] Violent material may not be pornography, and pornography may be apparently violence- and death-themed without being snuff. Many accounts of pornography, then, accord import to the generic markers that define it, reifying the category either legally or philosophically or both—even when these taxonomical markers are built on shaky ground, given the difficulty of establishing intention, in this case the intention to arouse.

Thus, the snuff phenomenon needs to be seen as a set of cultural fantasies and anxieties without a proper object, in that any critique or analysis of snuff is based on a wholly phantasmatic corpus (and often a shifting series of definitions). Writings about snuff inevitably say more about the culture that dreams snuff than about the production of any film that may or may not meet the definition. My insistence on the absence of a stable object, and the concomitant wobbliness of arguments based on a denial of this absence, is not intended to downplay the ethically troubling nature of the *desire* to bear witness to actual murder for sexual titillation (the collective wishful belief in the possibility of snuff) or the cultural misogyny that casts the victim (in these imaginary snuff scenarios) as a disposable young woman. Rather, it is to acknowledge the ways in which using phantasmatic material as empirical evidence inevitably skews arguments about pornography.

## Feminism, Snuff, and Censorship

Johnson and Schaefer point out the extent to which fears about snuff color much procensorship writing about the dangers of pornography: "Despite the mythic status of the snuff film[,] . . . [it] remains an ominous presence in the polemics of traditional foes of pornography and antipornography feminists. In the absence of an 'original' snuff text, the disciplinary thrust of the antiporn narrative demands simulations that can be taken to instantiate the trajectory from sex to death that allegedly characterizes the pornographic."[9] Yet many such antiporn critiques go further than drawing assumptions about the meanings of, and potential repercussions issuing from, images of simulated violence. Not only do they take the existence of snuff porn as given but also they often posit a communal viewing memory, as if we can all reliably know what is at stake in a snuff image. Avedon Carol, an anticensorship feminist, explodes this myth, commenting that "a number of anti-porn writers claim they have seen a real snuff film—yet when we read their descriptions, we recognize the ending of the movie Snuff itself."[10] One example she gives is of a leaflet produced by Campaign Against Pornography that describes "disemboweling [sic] woman"—the method of murder employed in *Snuff*—"as if it were an entire genre within pornography."[11]

Jane Caputi, in arguing that the imaginary of sex crime is a feature of not only the lives, fantasies, and actions of serial murderers but of the modern culture that is fascinated by them, writes: "The core assumption of the Age of Sex Crime is the equation of 'sex' with the male mutilation and murder of a woman. So too, the essence of pornography consists in the conditioning of male arousal to female subordination, humiliation, objectification, pain, rape, mutilation, and even murder. It is largely because of pornography that members of contemporary culture can see the torture of women and think *sex*."[12] "Murder" is inserted as one of a range of violent practices to which men routinely submit women within pornography. Having staked her theoretical claim about the ways in which this alleged pornographic content conditions the culture, she goes on to illustrate her argument—erroneously—with the "evidence" of snuff: "It is in that quintessential pornographic product—the 'snuff film'—that the wavering dividing line between patriarchal fantasy and patriarchal reality purely dissolves. In these films an actress is told that she will appear in a scene of simulated murder, but then, with the camera running, the woman is actually tortured, murdered, dismembered. Here, clearly, the image not only potentially elicits the act, but is absolutely inseparable from the act."[13] It is an irony that in describing the dissolve of the "wavering dividing line" between reality and fantasy, Caputi's own line between theoretical exposition and factual evidence blurs. Without an actual snuff movie to draw upon and submit to careful analysis, the argument relies for its power on its devastating rhetoric and totalitarian tone.

In *Only Words*, the lawyer Catharine MacKinnon argues, in the context of the constitutional law of the United States, that pornography should not be protected as free speech under the First Amendment. For her, it is more than representation; it *is* violent action (as pornography in this logic coerces, uses, and abuses members of the sex class—women—in the actual making of pornography, and then leads to the acts of violence and degradation that are committed against other women within a patriarchal culture that is saturated with pornographic imagery). Thus, pornography enacts a sociosexual transubstantiation. MacKinnon's arguments also operate as if the existence of snuff movies is a given (indeed, she claimed to be aware of some extant examples, but refused to furnish evidence or provide details).[14] She writes: "Only for pornography are women killed to make a sex movie, and it is not the idea of a sex killing that kills them."[15] The fact that she cannot substantiate her claim that women actually *are* killed for pornographic films is subordinated here to the greater polemical point and legislative aim for which the presumption of the existence of snuff is deployed: "Snuff films cast a light on the rest of pornography that shows it for what it is: that it's about the annihilation of women, the destruction of women, the murder and killing of women—in which murder and killing are just the end point that all the rest of pornography is a movement towards."[16] While not everyone—not even every feminist—would agree with the radical-feminist assertion that pornography is the graphic depiction of rape, as the concept of consent in a heteropatriarchy is rendered meaningless by the power differential between men and women, the argument can nevertheless be backed up with illustrations, as many forms of sexual penetration (that may be redefined as rape within this logic that precludes consent as meaningful) are in ample evidence in porn. But basing the argument for porn's inherent violence on the (non)example of snuff movies must inevitably fail to convince at any level other than that of metaphor or passionate hyperbole, as what is stated cannot be seen.

In a radio interview conducted by Larry Josephson with Andrea Dworkin for American Public Radio in 1992, snuff films are again invoked as the limit case for adjudicating the harm done by pornography and the justifiability of the legislation toward which Dworkin and MacKinnon were working.[17] This time, however, Dworkin's concern is not with insisting that snuff films are out there in number (though she does claim that two men are in prison in California for having made one), but rather that the validity of the libertarian argument against censorship in any form needs to be tested against the hypothetic case of the snuff film:

> Dworkin: I want to know what you want to do about the snuff films. You tell me.
> . . .
> Josephson: I would certainly punish people who make snuff films or who use children in pornography.
> Dworkin: Yes, so then what would you do about the film?
> Josephson: I guess I would say, first of all, that it has not been proved that there's a connection between viewing those films and committing the acts that they depict.
> Dworkin: So you would protect the film?

Dworkin pushes Josephson to take a position on the prohibition of certain types of material, rather than simply criminalizing the producers of the hypothetical snuff film:

> Dworkin: I am asking you, what would you do about a real snuff film?
> Josephson: Oh that's easy, that's easy. Then the people who made it are criminals because they murdered somebody.
> Dworkin: The film. What would you do about the film?

*Josephson:* I would say. And you're not going to like this. I would say that I'm with Justice Blackmun. I'm a First Amendment absolutist; I do not believe that the government should prohibit the viewing or the speaking or the showing of anything, in spite of the fact that some people may be offended, and some people may be psychologically damaged.

*Dworkin:* Be offended? We're talking about an industry being built on human blood. This is not being offended.

*Josephson:* I don't think that *Penthouse*, for example, is built on human blood.

*Dworkin:* I'm trying to be very specific.

*Josephson:* You're drawing a very extreme example.

*Dworkin:* No, I wrote down the example that you gave me. You brought up the example of snuff and I'm trying to get from you, okay, you don't think there should be any laws about any pornography. I'm saying to you, okay, Larry, let's say you're right. And the only issue that we have here is suppose somebody makes a pornography film in which a woman is killed as a sexual act. Now, what would you do about the film because under American law right now that film is protected speech. I think that's wrong.

Dworkin's comment reveals that it was the interviewer who introduced the topic of snuff films as a test case, not the radical feminist falling back on a privileged straw man of the pornography wars. Nevertheless, her implication that there may actually be a whole industry "built on human blood" risks making the same sleight of logic between ethical hypothesis and factually inaccurate assertion as Caputi and MacKinnon in the examples discussed earlier. The urgent issue of violence against women, within and outside of the porn industry, is not served—and is, in fact, repeatedly sidelined and undermined—by the obsessive recourse to the singular trope of the snuff movie, that overdetermined and emotive trigger term that ultimately fails to work as the most effective argument for the existence of cultural misogyny or as an indication of the realities of exploitation within porn.

## Simulation, Stimulation, and the Law

I have discussed the extent to which antiporn discourses about snuff have tended to take for granted its status as "really" existing, often enabling opponents to dismantle arguments simply by refuting the truth of this claim. The discussion of snuff, then, centers on ontology. And the ontology of snuff is dependent on a literal relationship between representation and reality. A snuff film exists only if the person who appears to be killed can be proven to have died (we have seen that the title of *Snuff* is revealed as a lie when the directors are able to present their "victim" unharmed—at least according to the FBI criteria). Yet, in certain recent legal contexts, the condemnation of the fact of depicting a real crime on camera for sexual titillation takes a backseat to the policing and criminalization of fantasy. In 2008 the Criminal Justice and Immigration Act was passed in the United Kingdom by the Labour government.[18] Part of this act involved criminalizing the possession of "extreme pornographic images." A pornographic image is here defined as "of such a nature that it must reasonably be assumed to have been produced solely or principally for the purpose of sexual arousal." Extreme images are defined as "grossly offensive, disgusting or otherwise of an obscene nature." These images are further defined as depicting in "an explicit and realistic way" a range of practices, including real or simulated acts of bestiality; serious injury to a person's anus, breasts, or genitals; and—most pertinent to the topic under discussion here—"an act which threatens a person's life" and "sexual interference with a human corpse." The final criterion is that "a reasonable person looking at the image would think that any such person or animal was real."

The mere *appearance* of reality here precludes the necessity to establish whether a violent crime against a person has been carried out and visually documented.[19] In defense of the act (which was forcefully opposed by members of the Liberal Democrat Party and widely supported by Labour and the Conservative Party), one Conservative peer, Lord David Hunt, declared: "We are targeting . . . material not on account of offences which may or may not have been committed in the production of the material, but because the material itself . . . is to be deplored."[20] It has been claimed that the act moved the legal emphasis away from the conditions under which such material was made (possible abuse to those depicted or the fact of a crime having taken place) and on to the possession and distribution of material, for a practical reason. This was to avoid the prosecution having to "prove that the events being depicted had actually taken place—that a person's life had actually been taken or that a life-threatening injury had been inflicted; in short, that a very serious crime had taken place."[21] If it doesn't particularly matter whether a death is really a death or not for the prosecutors, it certainly matters whether porn is really porn (in the terms of the legal definition), and—more crucially—whether the acts portrayed in the said porn are sufficiently deviant to be assumed to fail to turn on the moral majority.

In his article on the culture of surveillance created by recent UK law, with particular reference to the Extreme Images Act, Julian Petley argues that the insistence within the law on appearance rather than fact—on the "reasonable person" being convinced by the verisimilitude of a representation—can open the way for a range of material beyond niche porn (such as horror-film footage and stills and art photography) to be criminalized. He uses the analogous example of how, in upholding the law concerning the indecent images of children, photographs by the artists Robert Mapplethorpe and Nan Goldin have been targeted and suppressed.[22] What is at stake in this law, then, is clearly the issue of policing the boundaries of acceptable sexual practices and of taste. Mainstream commercial pornography is not criminalized, even if it can be argued by some to bear messages that are distasteful, misogynistic, or hateful, because the "disgust" that features in the wording of the law has to be the disgust felt by that "legal fiction," the "reasonable person"—which is no more than an ideological construct.[23] Niche pornography depicting simulated death (what I am calling *snuff-play porn*), such as the simulated necrophilic imagery featured on the U.S.-hosted website Necrobabes (now illegal to access in the United Kingdom), on the other hand, is criminalized because enough "reasonable persons" can be assumed to find it unpleasant. So too are photographs and videos made by private individuals depicting certain consensual acts, with one or more partners, for their own pleasure or that of a group of friends.[24]

Opposition to the extreme images law has been pursued by a number of British civil liberties groups, which continue to campaign for its repeal. Among these, Backlash has included on its website a series of personal testimonies and longer essays by women talking about their sexual identities and preferences, defending the type of pornography criminalized by the act, and explaining their relationship with it.[25] "Emerald" self-identifies in the following way: "I myself get off on rough sex." Asked how she describes her sexuality, she writes: "One of the first ways I would describe my sexuality is individual and personal. That is, it is mine, and no one else's. . . . Just as each individual is, each individual's sexuality is unique." She goes on to question the definition of both violence and pornography used in the wording of the law: "Who is it exactly that is determining what 'violent' porn is? For example, I myself would hold that any filming of true non-consensual sex or violence would not be something I would even consider 'pornography.' It would simply be illegal violent acts that happened to be taped." "Jane Clarke," a self-identified "dominant woman," concurs: "Materials featuring children, animals, necrophilia are already banned and for good reason. There cannot be consent in these activities. I cannot see how this law will possibly reduce harm through the possession or potential illegality of possessing 'extreme' adult pornography. Realistic depictions of acts are, as stated, depictions. They are not real. Extreme adult pornography featuring depictions of acts of these are just that—realistic depictions."

Other women talk about the distinction between commercial "violent" pornography and images made for personal use. "K," who describes herself as "sexually submissive," writes: "One of my favorite umbrella organizations is Kink (http://www.kink.com/) who provide various fetish-based or 'violent' pornography sites. It is clear there that all activities are consensual, as is frequently shown in the 'after portion' where they interview the participants." "Emma," who is "heterosexual and use[s] bondage and sadomasochism as part of [her] sex life," also focuses on the issue of consent, but she comments that "BDSM images are consensual and are mostly posed by people who are within the scene, unlike commercial pornography, which is often posed by women who are driven into it by economic necessity. BDSM erotica is a celebration of the sexuality of the models." Whether images are being accessed from commercial sites such as Kink's or produced by "scenester" amateurs, the accounts seek to differentiate extreme porn from either acts of depicted (nonconsensual) violence or mainstream commercial pornography, neither of which feature the "after portion" to which K alludes. These are images that usually show the participants who have featured in the violent scenes smiling and relaxing after the shoot—a guarantor of the lack of harm perpetuated during the filmed activities (a guarantor that would, of course, be irrelevant to the possibility of arrest for those possessing the "extreme images" under the UK legislation, given the lack of interest regarding whether or not anyone actually died).

Another commenter, "Rosalee," relates the question of pornography and harm to issues of feminism and oppression:

I believe the government should abandon these proposals altogether and instead attempt to get to the root of the real causes of rape, domestic violence and sexual assault. They should allow porn generally to become more acceptable so that when real instances of abuse and coercion occur, the victims of this will find it easier to come forward and complain about it. They need to recognize the difference between real violent crime and consensual acting out and depictions of violent fantasies. The crucial difference is where the acts are consensual, no one is being abused or killed and the woman (or man) who appears to be the victim remains ultimately in control.

Many of these women's testimonies question the apparently unassailable realities of what pornography is as defined by legislation. They emphasize the necessity of pleasure and consent in the making of any image that they would deem pornographic, which they put in opposition to an image of nonconsensual violence that would simply be a record of a crime. While these first-person accounts by women certainly contribute to dismantling the notion that apparently violent acts and forms of representation appeal only to men, or are always oppressive to the individuals depicted, most of the statements draw on liberal arguments of individual freedom, pleasure, and the protection of the private sphere as counterarguments to the law (exemplified in the description by Emerald of her sexuality as "personal," "individual," and "unique"). As "truth" statements about the nature of their sexualities, and about the liberating experience of using BDSM pornography, these testimonials present the very kind of confessional accounts that Michel Foucault identified as symptoms of a repressive hypothesis-driven culture.[26] A structural analysis that examines the networks of power relations operating under the surface of this law is needed too, and it is this kind of analysis to which Rosalee gestures. The radical-feminist condemnation of heterosexual, mainstream pornography as oppressive to the class "women" (an argument that is largely ignored by both the liberal classes and the social conservatives) needs to be juxtaposed with an understanding of this law and the biases that underlie it as oppressive to the class "sexual minority" or—in more pathological terms—the class "pervert" or "paraphiliac." Images that Hunt and company do not find, or at least would decline to admit to find, arousing are delineated as actively harmful, whereas the multimillion-dollar business of depicting and selling images of women performing patriarchy-approved sex acts are not. The difference between the two in aesthetic or philosophical terms is, perhaps, only a matter of taste. However, the difference between the two in ethicopolitical terms is a matter of the operation of what a Foucauldian would term *normativity*.

### Some Concluding Remarks

Laura Kipnis devotes much of the first chapter of *Bound and Gagged*, her thoughtful analysis of the role of pornography in contemporary North American culture, to a discussion of the case of Daniel DePew.[27] DePew, a gay man who shared violent fantasies about underage boys with a number of apparently like-minded strangers on online forums, was approached by an undercover police officer and inveigled into meeting up to discuss these fantasies in person. When he and the man known to him as Bobby met in a hotel room, DePew was encouraged to expatiate upon the idea of kidnapping a boy for the purposes of making a snuff film, in which DePew would be the executioner. Although DePew, who had never committed any act of pedophilia, did nothing but *discuss* the fantasy, he is now serving a term of thirty-three years in prison. For Kipnis, this case perfectly describes the extent to which violent fantasies do not belong only in the minds of the "sick" individual or the mass media that demonizes sexual outsiders. Rather, "governments have them [violent fantasies] as well, projecting them onto the citizenry."[28] She continues, "Daniel DePew's catastrophe was that his particular fantasies happened to coincide with those of the government and criminal justice system."[29]

The significance of the snuff movie—an imaginary artifact—may lie in the ways in which it taps into a series of interrelated cultural fears, sometimes uniting those from radically opposing political and ideological viewpoints (radical prochoice feminists, right-wing Christians, and dirigiste micromanaging governments). Snuff functions not as the ghost of something that once was but rather as the phantasm that harbingers a becoming. Concerns about the pornification of culture and its effects on the sexuality of couples, about threats to the innocence of "our children," and about the increasing "extremity" of online "mainstream" commercial pornographic depictions reach saturation point in the specter of the snuff movie.[30] The fantasy of the snuff movie serves to conjure up for us a commercial venture in which the "torture porn" aesthetic of recent narrative films such as *Hostel* escapes from the bounds of fiction and erupts into the real, or a vehicle in which the violent imagery and destructive language that some commentators espy in certain types of (increasingly mainstream) heterosexual pornography are made literal.[31] Yet the fantasy also draws attention away from actual social phenomena and focuses instead on a ghost that is persistently haunting discourse.

Just as Kipnis's example of the way in which cultural obsessions with pedophilia and snuff—favored fantasies of the authorities—fueled the entrapment of DePew, so the United Kingdom's 2008 legislation criminalizing snuff-play imagery reveals the technologies by which hegemonic power persecutes that which falls outside of the mainstream. The forty-year history of using *snuff* as the byword for the metaphorical meaning and logical outcome of all pornography by antiporn commentators needs to be seen as a straw man that genuinely risks detracting attention from careful analyses of the ideological investments of the privileged in protecting some types of (commercially viable) material and (societally conformist) subjectivities while demonizing "aberrant" others.

## Notes

I am grateful to the Leverhulme Trust for the award of a 2009 Philip Leverhulme Prize that provided the research leave that enabled me to complete this piece of work. I would like to thank Julian Petley for helping me to locate a copy of his published work that was invaluable for writing this piece and Tim Dean for suggesting relevant material and for being an unfailingly tolerant and understanding editor. This chapter is written from the point of view of a feminist who is anticensorship while being sympathetic to some of the arguments of radical feminism regarding the structural inequalities of hetero-patriarchal culture that make it impossible to regard either the meanings or the conditions of (heterosexual) pornography and prostitution as neutral or free of power imbalances. Further, my perspective is that of an advocate for cultural and legal acceptance and depathologization of sexual paraphilias and nonnormative sexual practices. It is while embodying this difficult yet fruitful tension between liberal and radical-feminist sensibilities, and between an allegiance to feminist concerns and an abiding fidelity to other sexualities' rights issues (that are entirely dismissed by, and seen as incompatible with, certain branches of feminism), that I have wrestled with the arguments made in this piece.

1. Narrative films borrowing from the genres of pornography and horror that use the snuff-film phenomenon as part of their subject matter and, in some cases, form include *Peeping Tom* (directed by Michael Powell, 1960), a film that presciently predates the heyday of the snuff-movie phenomenon, in which a murderer films his victims in their death throes; *Hardcore* (directed by Paul Schrader, 1979), in which a man who is trying to liberate his daughter from the porn industry has to sit through an apparent snuff movie in order to determine if his daughter is its victim; *Mute Witness* (directed by Anthony Waller, 1994), which features a mute makeup artist who stumbles across the filming of a snuff movie in the studio where she works; and *Tesis* (directed by Alejandro Amenábar, 1996), in which a disturbed young male film student is the maker of snuff films in which the protagonist, a masochistic young woman, ends up inadvertently starring. For more, see N. Jackson, "The Cultural Construction of Snuff."

2. The term is used in Sanders's book *The Family*. See Kerekes and Slater, *Killing for Culture*, 7.

3. See, for example, Johnson and Schaefer, "Soft Core/Hard Gore"; and Stine, "The Snuff Film." Also see the television episode "Does Snuff Exist?," directed by Evy Barry, from the series *The Dark Side of Porn* (first aired in the United Kingdom on Channel 4 on April 18, 2006).

4. For a feminist indictment of the film, see LaBelle, "Snuff."

5. Johnson and Schaefer, "Soft Core/Hard Gore," 48.

6. Johnson and Schaefer, "Soft Core/Hard Gore," 41.

7. See Barry's episode "Does Snuff Exist?" from *The Dark Side of Porn*.

8. L. Williams, *Hard Core* (1989), 194.

9. It is an error to believe that the polarized debates regarding pro- and anticensorship belong to an earlier age of feminism. Recent lectures and publications by the radical feminists Gail Dines and Sheila Jeffreys demonstrate the currency of such discourse, while the proporn activism and writing of, for example, Susie Bright, provide a counterpoint. And as much feminist debate now takes place online in the form of blogs, the liveliness of this issue is attested to by the wealth of posts in the past five years about pornography, attracting hundreds of comments from both sides of the debate, on radical feminist sites such as I Blame the Patriarchy and Rage Against the Man-chine.

10. Carol, "Snuff," 128.

11. Carol, "Snuff," 128.

12. Caputi, *The Age of Sex Crime*, 164.

13. Caputi, *The Age of Sex Crime*, 168.

14. See Strebeigh, "Defining Law on the Feminist Frontier": "In lectures, she often refers to pornography as a continuum on which the end point is 'snuff.' For years, rumors about 'snuff films' in which women or children are killed as part of the sexual experience, have been dismissed as fiction. MacKinnon, however, increasingly believes they exist. People have begun coming to her with stories about their experiences, she says, often as children, of being coerced to appear in films in which victims were killed. She declines

to give details." "Equal: Women Reshape American Law," accessed July 31, 2010, http://www.equalwomen.com/nytmagazine1991.html.

15. MacKinnon, *Only Words*, 15.

16. MacKinnon, *Only Words*, 15.

17. The transcript is available on Dworkin's website: "Modern Times Interview of Andrea Dworkin with Larry Josephson: Radio Program, American Public Radio, 1992," accessed July 31, 2010, http://www.andreadworkin.com/audio/moderntimes.html.

18. The full text of the relevant part of the law can be found on the "Criminal Justice and Immigration Act 2008" page of the National Archives website legislation.gov.uk: http://www.opsi.gov.uk/acts/acts2008/ukpga_20080004_en_9#pt5-pb1.

19. For more on the fetishization of the "real" in these pornography debates, see Downing, "Pornography and the Ethics of Censorship."

20. Hunt quoted in Petley, "Pornography, Panopticism and the Criminal Justice and Immigration Act 2008," 425.

21. Hunt quoted in Petley, "Pornography, Panopticism and the Criminal Justice and Immigration Act 2008," 426. Given that the legislation came about as the result of the efforts of Liz Longhurst, the mother of a murdered woman, Jane Longhurst, whose killer, Graham Coutts, had been in possession of a large collection of Internet pornography depicting sadomasochistic imagery, especially images of erotic asphyxiation, the defense of the law on the grounds of deplorable taste rather than the commission of offenses (issuing from, if not featuring in, the pornographic product) may appear somewhat inconsistent.

22. Petley, "Pornography, Panopticism and the Criminal Justice and Immigration Act 2008," 427. On the difficulties of interpreting the status of confiscated images and the danger to civil rights implicit in this, see Petley, " 'Snuffed Out.' "

23. Petley, "Pornography, Panopticism and the Criminal Justice and Immigration Act 2008," 425.

24. For a frequently updated blog detailing progress and outcomes of the cases that have so far come to court under this law, see Backlash at http://www.backlash-uk.org.uk/wp/?page_id=497.

25. Backlash, "Women's views on the proposal," accessed July 31, 2010, http://www.backlash-uk.org.uk/womensviews.html. Cached version of the webpage available at http://web.archive.org.

26. Foucault, *Histoire de la sexualité*, 1.

27. Kipnis, *Bound and Gagged* (1998).

28. Kipnis, *Bound and Gagged* (1998), 8.

29. Kipnis, *Bound and Gagged* (1998), 13.

30. For the effects on the sexuality of couples and threats to the innocence of children, see Paul, *Pornified*; on increasing extremity, see Dines, *Pornland*.

31. Dworkin opens *Pornography* with a now-infamous description of the "beaver hunters" image, which depicts a naked woman strapped, spread-eagle, onto the car hood of the "hunters" as a captive trophy. Gail Dines discusses the language of Internet gonzo pornography in which women are reduced from sentient citizens to objects. She quotes one website that writes: "Watching the transition from civilian to cumbucket is an amazing thing to watch" (*Pornland*, xx). And, on an "anal suffering" site, the women are described as "totally fucked up" and "destroyed" (xxi).

# 13

## Rough Sex

*Eugenie Brinkema*

For all I know there may be porn films featuring violent rape scenarios,
but I haven't seen any.
—Edward Buscombe, "Generic Overspill"

This chapter is a polemic for letting roughness take its toll. Let roughness
work over, break up and coarsen, agitate and make irregular or uneven or
jagged, cruelly choke and casually decimate, do a rude violence to, even, yes,
*destroy* a bit: bodies, in sexual practices; film form, in explicit representation;
and, prey of this volume, the unwieldy archive of pornography itself.

The rough is the approximate, the estimated, the premature; it arrives too
soon. The rough is indistinct, imprecise, and sketchy: rough drafts; the rough
cut of a film; shaggy, rutted, or disturbed; uncultivated; untrimmed; vague.
Unformed, ill-formed: what debases or degrades the clarity of form. Partial
and incomplete, perhaps abraded or ground down, or with edges showing.
Marked by aperture and irresolution, roughness undermines finality and closure. Discontinuous, asymmetrical, then disjunctive. But also brutal, also
mean, also cruel and unfair. Unedited, overlong, not shaped, lacking boundaries or hard, firm lines, wide and diffuse. It is Georges Bataille's *informe*: "a
term that serves to bring things down in the world. . . . What it designates
has no rights in any sense and gets itself squashed everywhere, like a spider
or an earthworm."[1] The not-smooth of material. The raw aberrance of things.
Difficult, also hard, also, even, nearly impossible. Both violence (he roughed
him up) and freedom (we roughed it), erotics (he roughed me up) and the
harsh grueling (we roughed it). Unrefined, crude, with a lack of style, primitive and disheveled, the coarse and underground, the hairy, the ugly. All dis-
tractions, every detour, interruptions, irrelevancies: deliberate roughness is a
form, and it forcefully recuperates the low-budget roughness of pornography
as a mantle, claiming, exploiting, and elaborating it as an aesthetic.

This chapter analyzes rough sex as a narrative conceit and metaterm for profilmic gestures in the controversial 2002 pornographic feature film *Forced Entry*, by the production company Extreme Associates.[2] Run by the husband-and-wife team Rob Black (given name: Robert Zicari) and Lizzy Borden (given name: Janet Romano), Extreme Associates is known for methodically violating the contents of the infamous Cambria List, the self-regulating recommendations agreed to by most of the mainstream U.S. pornography industry.[3] The company's outré fare includes a series called *Cocktails*, in which women are face-fucked until they throw up and then, in turn, are forced to drink the amalgam of spit, vomit, and semen; *Fossil Fuckers*, in which middle-aged to elderly women have sex with young men; the *Slap Happy* gonzo franchise, each picture consisting of a series of short takes in which Alek James Hidell grabs women by the hair, makes them deep throat him until they gag, vomit, or are exhausted, and then intermittently slaps them or holds their noses so they cannot breathe; and so forth. This chapter uses *Forced Entry* to think through rough sex in pornography as a formal principle; it then deploys that typology of roughness in order to consider what possibilities the wildly not-smooth might bring forth for reappraising the very notion of a pornographic archive.

My argument is that documented, profilmically real rough sex or representations of diegetic rough sex produce formal complications for pornography (and it should go without saying that representation and action are not the same thing, though they blur here). Rough sex renders rough form, a form that is ill-formed and unformed, which becomes approximate and uneven and interrupted, a form that is worked over and absolutely wrecked. *Rough sex*, as I employ the phrase, is not a subgenre of niche-targeting pornography; nor is it reducible to an itemized list of performed or documented acts determined in advance (*bukkake*, hair pulling, spitting, slapping, punching and bruising, face-fucking or choking, piss play, bondage, ass-to-mouth contact, degradation, rape, torture); nor—certainly—is it invoked as an outer limit of pornographic propriety or epithetic charge related to issues of consent, censorship, or obscenity. *Rough sex* betokens, rather, the way in which a sexual and bodily violence that is also a narrative violence (which, in addition, is a profilmically real, albeit a priori contractually delimited violence) becomes an aesthetic formal disruptor. Roughness is a forceful, generative way in which bodies taken to their limit complicate and make rough the formal language of pornography.

## Broken Riven Forms

*Forced Entry* is one of the infamous "federal five" films that, after a six-year legal battle during George W. Bush's "war on porn," landed their producer (Black) and director (Borden) in a federal prison on obscenity charges.[4] It is also the film featured in the *Frontline* episode "American Porn," in which the PBS crew filming the taping of the third rape scene (of the Extreme Associates contract girl Veronica Caine) walks off the set because they could not determine consent.[5] The film is organized around the conceit of a serial rapist and killer who is obsessed with the serial killer Richard Ramirez (a.k.a. the Night Stalker) and who commits the crimes documented in the film as a homage to him. *Forced Entry* opens with the double foyer of a large house, an eighteen-year-old virgin home alone, and a doorbell signaling an outside presence: a man is lost, he needs directions, and at the moment the girl is distracted—against all wise counsel, she takes a call in another room—he maneuvers through the barrier that was never fully closed against him, fulfills the destiny that an open door signals, and enters. The first segment involves the rape and suffocation of this girl; the second involves a second assailant and an unseen videographer documenting the rape and shooting of a pregnant woman (and her dog); the third involves the abduction of a stranded woman, and her sexual assault and murder by knifing. In the second and third diegetically video-recorded segments, the homage to the Night Stalker takes the form of a second-person address to the camera: "This is for you, Richard." A homosocial network of imitation and desire circulates through these addresses, with the attacker redirecting allegations of forced pleasure from the victim to Ramirez himself: "Do you like this, Richard? You like what I'm doing to her, Richard?" The inspirations for the homage are made explicit, including Ramirez's affection for the band AC/DC, invoked in *Forced Entry* with the omnipresent AC/DC hat worn by the assailant; the Satan worship for which Ramirez was notorious, evoked in the film's mise-en-scène; and the fact that, prior to his arrest, Ramirez was identified on the street, pursued, and beaten by several men who held him until the police arrived. At the end of the Extreme Associates film, the killer is spotted and chased; in this version, the men on the street kick him to death, with a postmortem blow struck by the journalist dogging the killer after he announces the breaking of the fourth wall: "This is a dead killer. This was *Forced Entry*."

The visual language of *Forced Entry* troubles to an extraordinary degree the understanding of pornography offered by Linda Williams in her canonical treatment of the genre, *Hard Core: Power, Pleasure, and the "Frenzy of the Visible."* Williams's central claim is that pornography is obsessed with the problem of the visibility of female pleasure: "Hard core desires assurance that it is witnessing not the voluntary performance of feminine pleasure, but its involuntary confession"—the "frenzy of the visible" of her title.[6] This is a difficult argument to make in regard to *Forced Entry*: no women have orgasms, and the actresses' corporeal energy is consumed with crying, pleading, screaming, and struggling. Williams, in fact, identifies only three possibilities for how

264  EUGENIE BRINKEMA

roughness is figured in pornography: as highly ritualized sadomasochistic play; as rape converted into ravishment in order to preserve a woman's pleasure despite herself; and a shift, during the period of second-wave feminism, to a structure in which rapes are the nodal negative against which good, affirmative sex is positioned.[7] None of these models is adequate for accounting for *Forced Entry*.[8] At no time do the codes of the film suggest a rape that is inching toward seduction or converted, over the duration of the assault, into ravishment: cries of pain and violation, "you're hurting me" and "I'm scared," and visual signs of resistance remain constant. The women fight, whimper, and cry; they refuse and wail; they close their legs and try to get away; and, in the end, each is murdered. There is not a single act of nonforced sex in the entire film or any instance of female pleasure, either in complicity with or against the will. While it would have been generically and logistically feasible to have had any of the victims engaged in other kinds of sexual acts prior to being attacked, the excerpting of the forced entries into the body is purposeful and polemical—and the roughness of the sex in the film, both narratively and profilmically, is absolute. Nor can one read *Forced Entry* through scholarly work on S/M. The film is not composed of elaborate rituals of theatrical, contractualized play; nor does it explore and exploit the pleasures of roles, boundaries, performance, and limits. Unlike the tightly delimited, often scene-restricted *contract* of S/M, rough sex relies far more on a model of blanket *consent*, one that is largely open, broad, and related to the conditions of possibility for the event (which cannot fully be determined in advance). There is no question that *Forced Entry* is an antipornography feminist's nightmare; but that is not to say that rough sex in the film (or elsewhere, for that matter) is sheer unregulated violence—it does have its own conventions. What is so remarkable, then, about *Forced Entry* is the way in which rough sex in the film causes film form to *violate* these very conventions. Rough sex, in other words, despite having its own formal logic, can and will precisely rough up this formal logic; it is an always potentially self-cannibalizing set of conventions.

Williams's three models for rough representation cannot, as I've argued, account for *Forced Entry*. Rather, this film is about force and it is about entry—and those concerns are very different matters altogether. *Forced Entry* is less film than formal principle as violent machine: the film visually, temporally, narratively, and pornographically asks what it is to force an entry, to break into something, to make it jagged where once it was smooth, to puncture what was once closed and whole. The drive to make visible involuntary confessions of the body does not entirely disappear in *Forced Entry*. However, it is redirected into spectacles of a body moved against its will—not toward wet arousal, but toward the effects of violence on skin and embodied space. The film is obsessed with its own title, ever attempting to make visible the effects of unwilled opening. Neck and throat muscles register brutal, hard, and sharp throat-fucking with bulges on the side of the body, distended pumped cheeks, and stabbed gullets visible through the skin. Hair becomes matted with stress and sweat. Extreme close-ups reveal how the pubic mound swells and strains during vigorous penetration; the bullied anus is vast after assault, and, in the third attack, the buttocks are taped open to display this gaping and reveal the violence done to rings of tautness. Also preserving this drive for visibility—the impulse to reveal interiority or to skin the body (what Tim Dean calls hard core's interest in "the mysterious privacy of the insides")—is, in the third attack, an overspill of vomit following violent deep-throating.[9] These effects are all signs not just of a body moved but also of a body prodded and distended, stretched, pounded, and contused. The secrets confessed are not those linked to fantasy and pleasure but those of the objectality of the body. Rough sex is a way in which the body is returned to meat, the head made hole, the limp malleability of skin reduced to elasticity and scarlet. Rough sex brings out the effects of force on the brute materiality of flesh, effects that are ever in excess of their cause.

The violence is rendered in flashes and bits: the girl is crying because the man is slapping her; he punches his finger into her and then drags her upstairs by her hair. The pleasure of the male body is made manual, reclaimed by hands that force open and stretch orifices and an oral machine that hurls cunt-laced invective and sputum. In the opening segment of the film, the assailant spits on and in the girl's mouth; slaps her, hard and repeatedly; and, despite her protestations of "I don't know how," he slams her face onto his penis, demanding cruelly: "Who controls your mouth?" The elicited speech, controlling the output of the mouth, is given its reverse image, its pornographic negative, in a recurrent gesture of the man, hands on either side of the girl's head, grabbing the edges of her lips and stretching their fibers horizontally, distending the orbicularis oris, baring gums and rows of teeth, turning the oral cavity into a thin black slit. The monstrous pose, a slight half frown, is held for a duration against the countervailing twitchings of the body; for variation, he may spit into the opening. Face (head) reduced to face (plane); mouth to line; skin to angle (and indeed, the industry refers to this gesture as *fish-hooking*). I am not being glib—this film takes seriously one reading of the injunction in Giorgio Agamben's *Means without End*: "Inasmuch as it is nothing but pure communicability, every human face, even the most noble and beautiful, is always suspended on the edge of an abyss. This is precisely why the most delicate and graceful faces . . . look as if they might suddenly decompose, thus letting the shapeless and bottomless background that threatens them emerge. . . . Be only your face. Go to the threshold. Do not remain the subjects of your properties or faculties, do not stay beneath them: rather, go with them, in them, beyond them."[10] *Forced Entry* takes a cavity, turns it into a grimace, a pure visibility at the threshold of visibility. Agamben's notion of gesture, which he puts at the center of (all) cinema, is also, and more troublingly, operative here: "What characterizes gesture is that in it nothing is being produced or acted, but rather something is being endured and supported."[11] Rough sex in *Forced Entry* demands that, like roughed-up bodies, the text must also suffer something—flesh and form do not produce anything, they simply are called upon to endure the taxing of their limits.

...............................

*Forced Entry* takes the form A B A′ B A′ B-a″-B C, where each A involves scenes of attack containing profilmically real sexual acts, with subsequent iterations involving different victims and different permutations of attackers (while the central serial killer paying homage to Richard Ramirez remains constant); B involves Rob Black's turn as a tabloid journalist breathlessly reporting on the rapes and murders after each takes place, and occasionally involving communication with the media-courting killer; and C is the final scene, in which, after assorted other men have been arrested, two civilians chase the killer on the street and kick him to death. The segments of the film that are denoted with prime and double prime marks signal that those scenes were diegetically framed as being filmed with a video camera during their commission; so, for example, the second attack, which begins with a woman on a sofa cooing to her dog that she is going to have a baby, is framed by doubled white frames and a REC in the upper-left-hand corner of the screen as two men grab her and toss aside the dog; the remainder of the attack is mediated through this conceit. Finally, the lowercase, double prime *a* stands for a fourth attack, which is peculiar for several reasons: it is mediated through the tabloid journalist, but doubly, as both an image that has been previously recorded and framed diegetically, and is now, as an object sent to him through the mail, being played back and watched, by him, on yet another screen; it also is the sole segment not to feature the serial killer, who has been present in each of the previous three attacks, but instead features the variation of an unknown man (hence the lowercase letter); and, as denoted by the primes, it is abruptly terminated in the middle of a sexual act and before either male orgasm or the murder has taken place. It is the most peculiar of all the segments; I will return to it.

I articulate the large-scale composition of the film because, on its surface, *Forced Entry* would appear to conform well to one of the strongest claims Linda Williams makes about the form of pornography: that it is marked by structural alternation, with the hard-core sex scenes functioning like the song-and-dance numbers in the classical musical, relieving tedium, expressing the ineffable, and providing extraordinary, even magical, counterpoints.[12]

The some-A-then-some-B form of the film, and the predictable three hard-core scenes, might seem to follow suit. However, in place of an *alternation* form, *Forced Entry* follows a roughed-up model that privileges *interruption*. Pornography is highly teleological; because male orgasm, canonically depicted through the visible shot of ejaculate, is the profilmically actual moment (and coded representational signal) that the sexual episode is over in conventional pornography, that aim rules all, and its visual achievement provides closure. Pornography is not a genre marked by aperture; despite the proliferation of variations on any original title, it is not a sequel form generated through cliff-hangers: one knows what is going to happen—which is the source of pornography's simultaneous capacity to arouse and to bore.

This aspect of predictability may be illuminated by reconsidering an account of fantasy that has been highly influential in film studies. In their description of fantasy as not "the object of desire, but its setting," Jean Laplanche and Jean-Bertrand Pontalis write that "the subject, although always present in the fantasy, may be so in a desubjectivized form, that is to say, in the very syntax of the sequence in question."[13] The visibility and finality of the money shot in the vast majority of pornography suggests that one form that the syntactical subject occupies is the durational arc leading to a period, the suspension before arrival at a semicolon. Fantasy is for resolution and certainty, with forms of doubt and uncertainty requiring displacements of the assurance of the teleological.[14] This investment in telos means that pornography is obsessed with the aesthetics of continuity. Williams's argument that pornography alternates sexual and narrative numbers may be apt for most features, but this alternation is ultimately smooth and smoothable, suturable, reconcilable to a narrative of history. Segments that are subject to the overriding logic of alternation, while discontinuous on a metastructural level, internally have a high degree of coherence and progress toward closure.[15] Porn scenes are almost never marked by internal irresolution (indeed, bodily resolution is the point, and is made as visible as possible).

My contention is that formal alternation is not a sustainable model once rough sex enters the picture. Alternation suggests a predictable pattern (the pleasures of classical pornography and the musical require this predictability). *Forced Entry*, despite its broad segments and silly interludes, is riddled with internal interruptions that make the segments that ostensibly alternate so unstable and fragile that the feature's reliance on self-contained units to juxtapose falls apart. The film's large-scale form is not gonzo's frame-to-frame fucking without respite, nor does it hold up stable bounded segments of hard core to alternate with narrative relief or tedium. *Alternation*'s root *alternare* suggests "to do one thing after the other."[16] That narrative segments of most pornographic films appear by turns, taking turns, and waiting for (their) turn suggests that the alternation model is recuperable for other narratives about relations to the other: relations predicated on mutuality, balance, deferral. To come after the other, to wait for the other to have or take its turn—one should make explicit the ideology of the term *alternation* when deployed for pornographic analysis: it suggests not only a balanced and evenly predictable form, but also a balanced sexual egalitarianism—liberal turn-taking in bed can also be imputed to the word.

The discourse of turns suggests, furthermore, a stable register of participants: for Williams's argument to be sustained requires the neat and certain separation of hard core from narrative segments, that one will definitively be able to tell the difference, and that a bleed between the two will not take place. Alternation's parity requires a kind of formal good faith: that what is alternating is consistent and coherent, stable and centered enough to mark its difference, to wait its turn, to reappear straightforwardly. Preeminent model for a suturable structure, alternation is another name for a tidy sense of history, a history marked by telos and linearity, a will toward closure, improvement, and progress that everywhere reeks of modernity. In a way, classical pornographic features partake of the grand Western narratives of equity and symmetry, the drive toward improvement and linear progress, means that lead to certain ends, and the efficacy of action.

*Forced Entry* thinks otherwise. It is marked by a refusal of turn-taking, an other conscripted to the desire of the one, violent inequity, nonegalitarianism, and, finally, an invasion of the hard-core segments into the ostensibly nonsexual narrative segments in the odd penultimate scene. Interruption's *interrumpere* is a breaking in, "to break asunder," a disjunction and breach in continuity; it suggests breaking apart, breaking up, breaking off.[17] It involves rupture and dissimilarity, a corruption of smoothness. Instead of a relation through turn-taking and mutual deferral, it involves the interpolation between, the interposition among, the introduction of difference, and a structural commitment to sending form off in new directions in place of returning to a form of the same. Rough form renders a self-interrupting text. Every sexual instance in the film (more broadly, every corporeal encounter) is predicated on violence and violation, and the film formally bends to the demands issued by roughness and its related terms—resistance and struggle; entry but also its refusal. In place of *alternatus'* "one after the other," *Forced Entry* explores what happens when the two things taking turns are not equal participants, when one of the turn-takers is, in fact, being made to participate against her will. Instead of one after the other—sexually or structurally—it is one, and then one, and then one, taking, and taking, and taking. In the film, interruption manifests formally in several ways, but it always derives from the film's principal investment in rough sex. Roughness interrupts the form of the film and interruption roughs up the text in four primary ways: (1) temporal disjunctions, (2) visual difficulty, (3) interruption and the category of the unrecorded, and (4) failure and aperture. I will discuss each of these forms of roughness in turn, and then explore how they complicate the film's central problematics of force and entry.

Formally, temporal disjunctions begin right away: after the assailant enters in the first section, the virgin returns to a now disconcertingly empty foyer. At her realization that something has gone wrong, he rushes in from another space and grabs her, begins slapping her. But between her realization and the first assault, the screen flashes pink and black strobes of the shot, diegetic seconds before, of him entering the house. These flashes are intercut with a quick shot of a female face covered with some sort of white fabric— retroactively this brief image will have announced in advance the plastic garbage bag that will suffocate the girl after she is repeatedly raped. The flashing images with an indeterminate status do not merely signal a fracturing of the diegesis; they also produce strange leaps in time—backward by seconds, forward by minutes, even hours. The effect is to announce of this girl: she will die. As far as the film is concerned, she is already dead. (Indeed, perhaps she is figured as so rapeable precisely because she is marked for death; if this is the case, then the film's temporal form will have colluded in marking her thusly.) The formal violence this effects is striking: in place of pornography's or the slasher film's building suspense toward a wet bodily climax of either semen or blood, the end is determined and presented in advance and imported in order that there be no doubt, neither suspense nor suspension. The slackening of the film's long-form time, rendered through the quickening of its local time in the startling flashes, breaks up time, even evokes something akin to Freud's famous account of trauma and temporality in *Beyond the Pleasure Principle*: that the intensity of images constitutes external stimuli that are so powerful they puncture the psyche's protective barriers; or, the excitations are internal to the film, and in place of breaking in, they are breaking out, erupting and escaping the film. The temporal discontinuities render the victim one who is murdered before she is raped; the form conscripts both spectator and victim to a certain forward progress that will end certainly in death, and conscripts death to the visual language of necessity. The flashes break up but also confirm time: they are the future inscribed onto, and broken into, the present. The temporal intrusion of the future certain death removes contingency, wonder, or doubt; it adds, therefore, a corporeal pathos to the struggles of the victim, to her body's registering of the effects of violence.

The formal strategy of interrupting the scene with these flashes continues. Minutes into the attack, which has moved upstairs to the girl's parents' bedroom, at the protestation "you're hurting me," the image flashes to the girl's face over a toilet—which, in the first instance, is too vague to be readable but retroactively will be the final degradation of the rape: he will piss on her face and in her mouth. These flashes pose the question of whether the future is fantasmatic, but with each passing diegetic minute, the stability of their predictive power is inscribed more legibly. Like a traumatic repetition, the moment of entry into the foyer is replayed; it is the image most often flashed, occurring numerous times in the first segment and quite late into the rape. At the man's question without a possible answer—"Do you want me to get rough with you?"—the reply of the entry into the house covers over, but also determines, the forcible entry into the body. This query defines the assailant's bad faith and the temporal irregularity of the first attack. The asking simultaneously obliterates the second person to whom it is addressed, annihilating through the violence of its content the subjecthood of the addressee who could produce an I or assent or refuse any language of *want*. Furthermore, the query arrives well after the attacker has already gotten rough, which suggests yet another temporal loop: as though the future could be restarted at that moment, as though one could define this moment as the one from which henceforth violence will occur. It is a question that imagines a victim can answer, and that imagines time can start over; it is therefore an entirely fantasmatic question. The operative energy of this impossible, self-annihilating question is ultimately directed at the text: that which, in its wake, is conscripted to roughness is the form of the film that increasingly breaks down and comes apart. After everything—the anal penetration, the face-fucking, the spitting and the slapping—he ejaculates, urinates on her face, and asks a curious question: "Do you know who Richard Ramirez is?" It is the first invocation of the conceit that will define the film; it is simultaneously an address to victim and to spectator. The aggressor grabs a white plastic garbage bag and covers the girl's head, and at the image of her face distended and bent, but also preserved and mummified, also whitened into its death mask, the thirty-minute scene concludes exactly as we knew, twenty-nine minutes prior, it would.

While the first of the three main attacks breaks up the diegesis visually and breaks into the narrative temporally—thus rendering rough form a matter of the unsmoothening of linear time—the second segment pulls roughness inward to the possibility of the visuality of violence in the context of pornographic representation. Specifically, if the first segment asks how a fairly uncomplicated pornographic image might be put into a narrative of violence and a roughed-up form, the second segment bends in its pornographic commission to the problem of rough sex. Resistance, refusal, violation—these become formal aesthetic doctrines that interrupt, block, and undermine the principle of maximum visibility that is the ontological promise of pornography. The second segment opens with a woman on a sofa, nuzzling her little dog, cooing to it anthropomorphically that she is pregnant and going to give it a little sibling. The image is oddly small, the aspect ratio of a photograph or embedded television screen, and tinted sepia; it therefore suggests the possibility that this image is, at some indefinite later time, being rewatched by an unnamed viewer—its color tint reeks of prelapsarian calm, even nostalgia. The image fades to black. Flash: a bright blue screen announces "VIDEO" in the upper right quadrant. (Do not forget that this means "I see.") Then appears the full image, consisting of two internal white square frames within which is a flashing red "REC" in the upper left corner. Two men charge, grab the dog, and toss it away, put a gun to the woman's head. They slap her breasts, and at her plea for mercy, her plea that she is pregnant, they hit her—hard—in the stomach, saying: "Are you pregnant? Are you pregnant? Huh? Not anymore." Held down, she is kicked, punched, slapped, and stepped on. Over the thirty-minute scene, her body will be mapped and purpled. This segment consists of little more than a pregnant woman, partially undressed, getting beaten up; while sexual penetration of mouth, vagina, and anus is a part of that broader assault, most of the scene's duration is composed of slaps and punches, strangling and struggle. The true visual subject of this segment is the woman's resistance, or, rather, the specificity of the juxtaposition of pornographic hard-core convention with her wild physical confrontation.

This resistance is something totally other than rape representation's flailing hands, familiar from painting, sculpture, and film; it operates far more like a block to or assault on the genre itself. For a rape converted to a seduction or ravishment is entirely available for complicity with the cinematic image. Indeed, the close-up of an unclenching fist or any number of terrified eyes that relax into lids of pleasure takes place over—indeed, the conversion occurs through the mediation of—the image. Likewise, a rococo sadomasochistic scene is a visual gift. But a rape that narratively remains a rape—in the context of a genre premised on the wide-open exposure and visibility of the naked, opened, stretched, and exposed body—is a visual disaster. The image in the second segment of Forced Entry is continually marked by a frustration of the visibility of the female body. The actress struggles to keep her legs closed at every turn. The angles her pressed-together knees form as they pivot on the hard doubled lines of her clamped-tight calves and thighs are not an obstacle to be one time overcome, or a single barrier to be broken. Those legs are self-healing wounds, catastrophically absorbing the two aggressors' efforts to apply force. "Open your fucking legs!": This is the order of the film, voiced by the assailants, a collusion between rape drive and representational drive. Early in the attack, at the moment of a successful wedge between those locked knees, the woman reaches her hand down and, in a remarkable gesture, covers her vulva. This protective motion radically countermands pornography's imperative for maximum visibility—at the instant the "meat shot" that defines hard core is violently pried from the body, it is masked. (In fact, it is such a refusal of the generically mandated visibility that it therefore suggests an unnerving realism, that it might be the instinctive act of the woman playing the victim of the attack—a strict divide of actress's body from victim's body, when both end up contused, is impossible, and while broad issues of consent are not the issue here, small corporeal flinches may well be. Rough sex constitutively poses that disconcerting nonseparation.)

This resistance is not overcome. It renews itself. It breathes kinesthetic energy into the scene, a scene constituted around the force of resistance under the pressure of resistance, and not resistance's overcoming through force. Forced to put her mouth on a penis, she keeps stopping, closing her lips. In extreme close-up, we see the consequence of this corporeal refusal— a penis slips out of the woman's clenching body: Static; Slap. Blue screen. *Open your fucking legs.* She covers her vulva, again. Covers her mouth with a manicured hand. The frustration of visibility is absolute. No sex act continues without visual and temporal interruptions, none continues for more than a few long seconds before either her struggle or the film's editing breaks in to interrupt whatever act is struggling to take place. *What are you stopping for? Suck. Don't stop. Suck the dicks.* She runs out of the frame—is dragged back in. They shove her out of the frame and pull her back in. Violence's order: "Open your mouth." The diegetic videographer, articulator of his own weak resistance, voices doubt about the victim's pleasure, concern about the likelihood of legal repercussions, and, articulating another failure and difficulty regarding entry, worries of a fist, "I don't think that's going to fit." *Open your goddamn fucking legs.* Against her struggle, very late in the scene, the damning charge: "You're fucking fighting too much." The target of this accusation remains ambivalently suspended between actress and character, between subject and body, and poses the question: Who should not fight this much? It is levied at least as much at those extraordinarily willful knees as any choice-making agency. They close tight, the pale fleshy stems cross.

This resistance is a formal principle; it involves tension and blocking and makes the text into a self-interrupting one, rendering an irregular, halting rhythm of force and refusal for each act of struggle. The pornographic demand is complicit with the violent one: *Open your mouth.* The vectors of force that move and pry, close and bend, interrupt the smoothness of the sexual congress, and each act simultaneously blocks and removes the visual target of the pornographic aim. Bodily refusal confronts pornographic demand: the violent struggle for entry to the body becomes a formal problem for visibility itself. A *no*, after all, is more than an interruption in the great long "and yes I said yes I will Yes" of unbound pornographic utopianism (with apologies to

Molly Bloom); a *no* is an absolute obliteration of resistancelessness. It introduces a limit at the instant of its attempted transgression. Refusal inserts a difficulty into the film because its corporeal end is the squirming disruptor to a visual availability that is the analogue and consequence of sexual availability. In other words, it is visibility of and into the body that is conscripted to a diffuse entry by force in the filming of the second rape sequence. The forcing open of legs and mouth in the second segment, then, is as much a forced entry of light into recesses as organs into cavities. The men struggle for that opening and either delay or do not even bother to do much with the opened body once it has been made available. Rough visual form is this interrupted and uneven image, an image that is the visual consequence of the rough sex in the narrative and profilmically. In place of Williams's "frenzy of the visible," *Forced Entry* is in a state of visible frenzy; rough sex pushed to this limit privileges the frenzy, but at the *expense* of the visible. The consequence of this formal struggle to "get in here" is explicit: it is a struggle to the death.

Forced entry is the consequence of the demand for entrance meeting corporeal resistance. That the struggle to force an entry is not singly overcome—nor ever converted into an affirmation that negates that struggle—means that the dominant gesture of the attack is the repetition of the demand for entry meeting the refusal of that demand. Forced entry, as such, then, is not raised to the status of a singular assault or event: it is cause and consequence of the repeated refusal of the demand to *open*. It is therefore a law that includes the certainty of its own violation. One only forces open that which has closed against entry each time; isolating the forcing of the entry captures the instant of the passage between open and closed, an attempt to open what was closed, but it is because it is closed that that opening must be forced. This pulsing of violent possibility is a bodily, but also a formal, problematic. The vitality of movement that is the hallmark of pornographic cinematic representation—the body moved against its will in orgasm—is here sustained by a vitality against being opened up. It enlivens but also breaks up the form—makes it struggle to take place.

This interruption on the level of visual access becomes a more radical cinematic problem in the flashing blue screens that punctuate the already-punctuated scenes of assault. This metainterruption or structural interruption of the interrupted and blocked image consists in the introduction of the category of the unrecorded as a visual and temporal device for fracturing the diegesis. Blue screen is a phenomenon of VHS playback; the quick intercut images of a blue screen reading "VIDEO" or "STOP" are a marker of a divergent temporal scheme in which the previously recorded footage is being watched at a later time by an undetermined viewer. In contrast, the two mise en abyme frames, with the flashing "REC," are meant to signal the temporality of the live recording of the footage, coincident with the time of the attack. One line of time coincides with that which occurs after the murder, therefore it is a record of the final minutes of an already-dead woman; the other documents the minutes beforehand, when any outcome is still possible. Blue screen, like static (which also flashes periodically), is unrecorded videotape; the second segment of Forced Entry consists of an uninterrupted linear attack that is rendered for the film by a highly parsed and fragmented series of shots, often very brief, juxtaposed with unrecorded tape. This is an obvious point, but one worth making explicit: The unrecorded, as the state of the pure potentiality of video documentation, is what is effaced in continuity editing and in the classical cinematic form to which, as much as any blockbuster, the vast majority of pornographic features strictly conforms.

The reminder that footage is filmed, that it is framed — that the temporality of the unrecorded covers over the profilmically continuous action — is the traditional purview of the avant-garde. For any genre in which the profilmically real is significant (and for pornography, it is more than significant; it is sustaining and essential), that the unrecorded should repeatedly appear is striking. What those blue screens achieve is a roughening up of the smooth state of recording and replaying the attack; what they and the shots of static generate is a space for the attack to fail to appear except as marked by that failure. This is a pornographic feature that — for all the extreme close-ups of penetration, leaving no razor bump or bruise or wet, soft fold unexplored — is also riddled with absences, with gaps, and with things that do not present themselves to vision. That the blue screen and static are associated with problems of unrecorded tape *during playback* at some later time suggests furthermore that this footage is multiply opaque, for, of course, we also do not know who watches this image, for whom this video playback is riddled with segments of unrecorded tape. The viewer could be the law. Or it could be Ramirez. The rough footage could condemn. It could arouse.

The constant addresses to multiple recipients — to Ramirez himself; to the videographer, "Are you getting all this?" — also interrupt the continuity of any sexual act, continually break into the image with a close-up of the assailant's face. The main attacker falls toward the camera at one point, pushing the woman's face so close that the image blurs, screaming, "Say hello to Richard!" The combination of moral reluctance and technical ineptness in the figure of the videographer — an exaggeration, if also literalization, of a low-budget production reality familiar in pornography — means that the camera is often too far from its imagistic target or that it wanders on an upward tilt, capturing a dirty white ceiling. "Get in here, man" is the constant directorial order from the serial killer; and with this order, the camera itself is called upon to participate in a form of forced entry, a forced proximity to the violated body.

However, the technological agent of capture has to be called to this role again and again, as though magnetically repelled from the bruises and the roughness. The camera and its operator keep retreating from the scene; each time, it is demanded that it, and he, return, get closer. *Get in here and get this. Open your mouth. Push that fucking little baby out.* Assailants and film are obsessed with issues of entry and exit as moments of transition and passage. Entry is the site of anxiety, but it is also the ostensible site of erotic investment.

What does it take to get in, to get the image, to enter the scene? In the second segment, the almost breathless monologue that links together the image between gaps of unrecorded blue and static is constituted by a parallel series of commands. The main assailant divides his time between barking orders to the pregnant woman and to the diegetic videographer. They are the same command. *Open your legs. Get in here and get this.* The demand to "get in here" is a demand for access: to the woman, for her body as meat, and to the camera, for the image as property. The demand is also the rapist's archival drive. The aim in *Forced Entry* is not to rape and kill but to document the raping and killing as a homage to a figure who is himself created through serial-killer celebrity culture and mediated technologies. *Get in here, man. Get in here and get this.* The violence of archival desire—that *getting in here and getting it* is as apt a description of cinematic inscription as it is of fucking and scarifying—subtends those seemingly pleasant discourses of sexual and archival life-giving preservation.

A roughed-up form does not end or ends too soon; it is riddled and fails. One of the most peculiar aspects of the final, fourth, odd attack in *Forced Entry* is that it arrives in medias res, departs at the wrong time, and appears where it does not belong: in the B section of the alternating form, in the midst of a narrative scene that is meant to be separate from the hard-core segments. That the logic of rough form should culminate with an unwise and unwelcome structural entry of hard core into the narrative interludes suggests the degree to which entry and roughness are tied up with each other. The fourth attack is a hard-core scene that does not wait its formal turn; bypassing alternation's patience, it interrupts the narrative segment and is interrupted and prematurely aborted in turn. The abrupt termination and lack of sexual or formal closure in this scene suggests how rough form dissolves the propriety of even those internally coherent segments. Once a film follows an interruption logic in place of an alternation logic, both the sanctified preserve of an asexual narrative and the sanctified telos of hard-core culmination are subject to forms of force, cruelty, and departures from internal rules. In the final segment depicting sexual attacks, after the reporter puts in the video and presses the play button, we see him seeing the image first, his face registering horror. The image that the film cuts to is marked, as in the second attack, with two embedded white squares framing the image, a blinking red REC in the upper left corner, and a white cross at the dead center of the image; unlike in that segment, this conceit continues throughout the entire attack, framing and simultaneously blocking the image that takes place within and underneath it. Forced entry in this attack takes the familiar form of repetitions of tongue into mouth, his foamy spit into her mouth, his penis into her mouth. But there is also a new violation. The new assailant demands of the woman that she tongue, lick, and suck his anus: the order arrives as he lowers his pants and bends backward toward her face, occasionally grabbing her hair and forcing her toward his anus. Her face and tongue disappear into his intergluteal cleft. The violation and the demand is for the aggressor to be penetrated anally by the unwilling other. This reversal radically complicates the question of entries in relation to the other. Here the force is in the imperative for her to *enter him.*

After the episodes of forced analingus, each requiring repositioning and accompanied by new demands, the scene turns to fellatio—and then abruptly ends. The film concludes with a segment that does not end; the man's orgasm does not arrive; the attack and footage stop too soon. This scene does not resolve. Rather, it aborts at the moment of its complication, which is to say, it continues indefinitely, is archived in its commission. Entry itself is the point of this scene—not resolution or telos. Another infamous production by Extreme Associates, the *Slap Happy* franchise to which I alluded earlier, is likewise marked by compelling formal problems of interruption, usually due to the exhaustion or gag reflex of the women being throat-fucked, slapped, and choked. However, in other ways, formally those films are very ordered and structured; indeed, the conceit is a tight repeating spiral, each segment containing the neat and finite end familiar in gonzo of ejaculate on the face signaling *fin.* Teleology, the signature of pornography, remains king. Even in the barebacking pornography that Tim Dean analyzes—in which transgression requires internal, which is to say invisible, ejaculation—what Dean calls the "reverse money shot" of ejaculate streaming out of an anus indicates that an end was reached, that orgasm took place.[18] *Forced Entry*'s departure from this mandate is a striking transgression of generic law; the frustration and incompletion and premature ejection (of the videotape) is the roughest cut of all. Mid forced analingus, mid oral sex, before orgasm, before a killing—the final scene has no frame. As with the attack that continues behind the punctuating flashes of static and blue screen in the second segment, this attack persists well after the cut. The generic departure is remarkable for its commitment to formal interruptibility over maximum visibility.

However, the final scene makes perfect sense if regarded in another light. For it is entry as such that is the obsession of this film. It hews to its title. The problematic of entry is what is taken to its conceptual limit in the final, nonteleological scene, wherein violence reverses itself to imagine a forced conscription to *enter*, not the state of having been *entered*. This last assault re-imagines how force could be deployed for entry independent of direction and bodies, which is to say autonomous of who or what is entered. With the conscription of the victim's tongue into the anus of the final assailant, entry as a gesture is made the agent of force, and entry can go both ways as a pure form of force.[19] If one can be forced to enter, then passivity and penetrability are delinked, and it is entry as the state of passage, a crossing and point of collapse between subject and object, that is subject to force's unruly labor. This reversal preserves the strangeness that entry, as something between bodies but conscripting both, carries with it. While entry as such can be made visible through its effects on skin, forced entry requires that entry be refused and requires the repetition of that refusal. Paradoxically, to demand that entry be ever available to be deployed for force requires that entry never become entrance or entered, that entry retain its quality of being a timeless positionless point of passage and transition yet to arrive.

Jean-Luc Nancy's "L'intrus" ("The Intruder"), a lyrical meditation on his heart transplant, would seem worlds apart from *Forced Entry*, but its opening reminder is immensely helpful here:

> The intruder introduces himself forcefully, by surprise or by ruse, not, in any case, by right or by being admitted beforehand. Something of the stranger has to intrude, or else he loses his strangeness. . . . If, once he is there, he remains a stranger, then for as long as this remains so—and does not simply become "naturalized"—his coming does not stop: he continues to come, and his coming does not stop intruding in some way: in other words, without right or familiarity, not according to custom, being, on the contrary, a disturbance, a trouble in the midst of intimacy.[20]

*Forced Entry* does not try to obliterate the strangeness of the intruder; it lets that figure remain at the threshold of forcing entry indefinitely. What the intruders are are signs of their strangeness; not converting the rapes to a seduction, never having entered but always in a state of forcing entry, they remain outsiders, markers of that pure force. In other words, the film does not accept them. For home and for body: what is strange is what remains strange once on the inside. Rough sex lets the intruder retain his strangeness on the level of rough form. It is the force that attaches to entry that ensures that the strangeness of the intruder does not recede. Force, in other words, is linked not to being entered but to the violence of entry as it is made available to circulate among, irreducibly not belonging to or incorporated by, multiple parties, including the pornographic text itself.

The form of rape is *diacritical*, to borrow Saussure's term for the differential structure of the signifier; rape cannot take place alone or on the level of the one.[21] Rape requires an other. There cannot, however, be an irreducible gap between the one and the other; its force requires a point of contact. The other must remain other and otherwise, but the two must relate to each other in their difference—that relation is here called entry. Forced entry is the point of intersection of two connected but different terms—it remains necessarily unassimilable to both. Put in a stronger formulation, forced entry remains outside of either party so that the interior moment of contact—what entry breaks into and thus establishes—takes place at all. Entry is the ephemeral possibility of bodies crossing and bleeding into each other; it and its force belongs to neither party. The interiority of entry is registered in the exteriority of the formal interruptions and displacements, and, therefore, forced entry poses the question of an entry that is not assimilated or assimilable, that remains perpetually strange, foreign, other, unwelcome, violent, and that is also therefore perpetually entering, re-creating the intrusive moment of the force of the initial entry. The film restages an enduring entry in the act of enduring entry on the level of the textual body by breaking up, by remaining fragmented and rough, approximate and uneven. Narrative resistance produces failed entries: visually blocked entries, digits and phalluses that slip out, are squeezed out, so that entry is required yet again, and yet again. The entry may have to take place infinitely—the aporia of the final violent encounter is the suspension without resolution of this ever-arriving entry that is always yet to take place, in which the strangeness and unwelcomeness of the intruder is preserved and not reabsorbed.[22]

## From an Abandoned Archive

The subject of this volume is the archive of pornography, an archive that is unwieldy, approximate, and pocked at present—ever at risk of failing to even constitute an archive. There is simply too much, and much of it is lost; or it is underground or produced by amateurs; or its material is poorly preserved or it is irregularly and unevenly preserved; perhaps it has been seized. Porn scholars return to anxieties about the missing archive and the problems that attend an archive that is not properly constituted, the barrier to disciplinary organization and rigorous academic attention. A smooth archive is the only one worth having, goes one argument; it needs to be strong and whole, glassy and hard. Do not let the archive remain anarchival, uneven, and unfinished; resist its disorder. It is comprehensible why those invested in creating a space for pornography studies in the academy would argue for the need to constitute an archive that documents and preserves that which may then be studied—to find what seems missing. But what does it mean to argue for a smooth porno-graphic archive? What losses are entailed in insisting on the elimination of loss?

Every archive is, by definition, called upon to be a good archive, which is to say a continuous and robust archive, one that does not lose or leave behind its membership. The bad archive (the one that loses or decays, that degrades or forgets—in other words, the archive that is mortal) is precisely what the ar-chive is called upon to remedy and distinguish itself from. The archival stands for the fantasy of all that is imagined it is possible to make smooth: memory, time, history, bodies closed tight. The drive to make pornography archival, in other words, is the drive to ensure that the archive as it exists leaves behind and disavows its roughness. But the sketchy archive, the one that is difficult to traverse—while unpleasant for a scholar to enter—is the one that I think we require. When I call for a rough archive, it is worth being explicit on the con-sequences: membership will go missing; objects of study may disappear, thus rendering impossible forms of iterable scholarly labor and frustrating trans-historical communication; disciplinarity will not be able to constitute itself around notions of canonicity, shared or central texts, or discourses of same-ness, the generic. The smooth pornographic archive conforms to the alterna-tion form of one after the other, after the other; but a rough archive is all inter-ruption, which is to say that no membership is privileged as coming first, and in turn weaker archival members may be done violence to, may be silenced, may disappear. It is a risk; the violence of these losses is real, and the loss of a scholarly object is a loss that is irretrievable and absolute. The rough archive is the one that embraces this destruction and loss, that tarries with the finitude that also attends objects. But it is a risk that is in keeping with the promise of roughness: in the irregular and uneven can be glimpsed a limit at the moment of the possibility of its destruction and transgression.

Why do we even speak of the archive? Why is archival desire so strong? One can imagine that we would not fantasize the archive if the brute fact of the body were not itself so vulnerable to roughness and destruction and destruc-tion's effects. There is no archive without vulnerability to the effects of rough-ness on flesh—as Derrida phrases it in *Archive Fever*: "There would indeed be no archive desire without the radical finitude, without the possibility of a for-getfulness which does not limit itself to repression."[23] Time is rough on mem-ory, and roughest on bodies. So we build and cultivate and desire archives that are smooth and level, substantial and secure. And we thereby imagine that we can defend against the roughness that is decay and loss, imagine an antidote to forgetting's pockmarks, dream of a clean and even and unshak-able collection of objects that will never be destroyed by finitude. Embracing the rough archive suggests letting those other values—the sketchy, early and unformed, uneven, irregular, incomplete, approximate—inform that which archivism defends against. Let memory remain ragged. Let history remain interrupted and uneven. Let bodies, their openings and entries, remain difficult, even fail. Embracing an entropic archive that does not try to deny finitude requires attending to the limit that finitude places elsewhere, on being. Like rough sex, a rough archive celebrates and exploits—without mourning—the sad limits of flesh.

Sex is rough on a body—or it can be. Rough sex is rough on form. Pornography gives us a rough idea of what sex is like, and, like rough sex, a rough idea of what sex could be. In turn, the rough archive, though partial and uneven, even failed and destroyed—meaning *the archival that does not archive*—gives us an archive that, in the energy of being constituted, retains its strangeness so that it can generate new forms of what might be. The intruder must retain his strangeness in order to remain the intruder; likewise, the rough archive lets its membership fail to be incorporated by the archival but remain perpetually in the gesture of becoming part of the archive. The archive's entries remain in a state of being ever about to enter the repository, without being determined by it, without having been archived.

Pornography is certainly rough on an archive. It is too unwieldy, there is too much, and it is heterogeneous; it is difficult; things are misplaced, unaccounted for. But do we admit that roughness, or do we try to smooth it out? It is the question asked each time; it is the very question that force and entry pose. My contention is that a certain kind of pornography—and all its rough and violent edges—can teach the humanities how to think with the form of roughness. Let roughness take its toll. Resist the urge to make it steady and complete, to theorize away or write over the value of roughness—to turn its violence into just another kind of bad commodity and want critique to somehow repair it. The archive pocked and riddled and stained—and, yes, even missing—teaches us how to tarry with the rough without fixing its broken edges. This is an ethical maxim: one must not obliterate the strangeness of the intruder by incorporating intrusion, thus annihilating the very force one would contemplate.

## Notes

1. Bataille, "Formless," 31. See also Bois and Krauss, *Formless*, which explores Bataille's *informe* in relation to contemporary art practices. The authors follow Bataille in figuring the formless as neither form nor content, but as an operation.

2. Choice of language when writing about pornography is a deeply fraught issue: any choice is studied and polemical, and risks being either overly medicalized or overly sexualized, overly authoritarian or overly casual; in this case, as well, my language risks collusion with the discourses of violence in the text. I have therefore chosen, when de-

scribing the body, to usually remain as flatly anatomical as possible, in the hope that a bland precision conveys the multitude of other possible terms. Direct quotations transcribed from the film provide an alternative linguistic landscape. The one but important exception: *fuck* is an exceptional word, with cognates suggesting striking, and the vigor and force of its linguistic impact refuses any alternative.

3. At minimum, *Forced Entry* violates these items on the Cambria List: "No shots with appearance of pain or degradation; No facials; No spitting or saliva mouth to mouth; No peeing unless in a natural setting; No forced sex, rape themes; No degrading dialogue." The entire list is available at the website for the PBS *Frontline* episode "American Porn" (2002), accessed March 19, 2014, http://www.pbs.org/wgbh/pages/frontline /shows/porn/.

4. The *Frontline* episode is cited, by both sides, as one of the reasons for the obscenity charge; footage for the documentary shows Black bragging about the extremity of his pornographic productions and, to some degree, daring law enforcement to shut down the company. See Janelle Brown, "Porn Provocateur," *Salon* (June 20, 2002), accessed March 19, 2014, http://www.salon.com/2002/06/20/lizzy_borden/; Dean, *Unlimited Intimacy*, 137n51; and Gray, "What, Censor Us?" See also Martin Amis, "A Rough Trade," *Guardian*, March 17, 2001. Between federal seizure of the materials and the defendants' plea bargain, a version of *Forced Entry* was released containing a preamble by Rob Black—a mix of claims about the film to come, marrying sensationalistic warnings and a disavowal of its verisimilitude, admonishing the viewer not to "get too freaked out." This framing device is a nod toward a vibrant history of similar warnings in exploitation cinema, but watching this version with the knowledge that indeed prison time was at stake in the film that is to come adds an element of pathos to the tongue-in-cheek counsel.

5. "American Porn," *Frontline*, program no. 2012 (original airdate: February 7, 2002), produced and directed by Michael Kirk.

6. L. Williams, *Hard Core* (1989), 50. Williams continues, "The animating male fantasy of hard-core cinema might therefore be described as the (impossible) attempt to capture visually this frenzy of the visible in a female body whose orgasmic excitement can never be objectively measured. It is not surprising, then, that so much early hard-core fantasy revolves around situations in which the woman's sexual pleasure is elicited involuntarily, often against her will, in scenarios of rape or ravishment."

7. In these early 1980s films, Williams writes, the rapes "do not show women learning to enjoy their coercion; instead the rapes violate their bodies and wills. While the rapists in each film enjoy performing the rape, and while at least some viewers may enjoy watching the depiction of the act, what is emphasized is the anger, humiliation, and pain of the female rape victims. In both cases rape represents the unsuccessful, bad sex to which the films' other numbers respond. These films . . . forcefully present sex as a problem and propose to find better sex as the solution." L. Williams, *Hard Core* (1989), 166. Shaun Costello's 1972 film *Forced Entry*, about a PTSD-suffering Vietnam vet who feels compelled to stalk, rape, and murder women, in many ways conforms to this utopian model of answering "bad" sex with "good" sex: the first extended hard-core scene is a mutually satisfying, consensual one, with which the later violent rape scenes are contrasted.

8. Edward Buscombe suggests that violent rape scenarios are not reconcilable with pornography; reading *A Dirty Western*, he writes: "Although the plot is based on rape the film cannot summon up any conviction in its portrayal. . . . All the time, you feel, it's on the verge of jettisoning the rape plot and just getting on with the sex action." Buscombe,

"Generic Overspill," 30. A similar, influential study, which claimed that the hard-core pornographic feature "rejected violence almost entirely," is Slade, "Violence in the Hard-Core Pornographic Film."

9. Dean, Unlimited Intimacy, 111.

10. Agamben, "The Face," 96, 100.

11. Agamben, "Notes on Gesture," 57.

12. L. Williams, Hard Core (1989), 130–34.

13. Laplanche and Pontalis, "Fantasy and the Origins of Sexuality," 26.

14. See, for example, Dean's work on uncertainty, transmission, and barebacking porn. Dean, Unlimited Intimacy.

15. Like Williams, Aydemir argues for the importance of alternation form to pornography; see Aydemir, Images of Bliss, 110–12, 147–48.

16. Oxford English Dictionary, 2nd ed., s.v. "Alternate."

17. Oxford English Dictionary, 2nd ed., s.v. "Interrupt."

18. See Dean, Unlimited Intimacy, 131–38.

19. The omnipresent AC/DC hat worn by the assailant in the first three attacks is a textual homage to the hat Ramirez left at the scene of his first crime, and a nod toward his famed love of the metal band. Given that I am arguing that unidirectional aspects of entry are put into question with this final scene, it is worth noting that AC/DC is also a slang term for bisexuality, evoking electric current and the notion of "going both ways."

20. Nancy, "The Intruder," 161.

21. Saussure, Course in General Linguistics.

22. This obsession with problems of entry may be why Forced Entry pivots on the second segment involving the narrative conceit of a pregnant victim: it is the scene that most radically articulates the formal problems that sustain the entire film. Pregnancy involves visible proof that the body has been previously entered; it stands for, and registers, a body already in a state of breach. The entry into this body, which is marked as enterable — but also marked temporally by the past tense of having been entered — functions as the terrain on which the struggle for entry autonomous of bodies but as a pure form of force may occur.

23. Derrida, Archive Fever, 19.

# 14

## "It's Not Really Porn": Insex and the Revolution in Technological Interactivity

*Marcia Klotz*

### Bondage Porn: The Really Bad Stuff

Internet bondage pornography appears to have finally come into the public spotlight in 2013, with the Sundance premier of the documentary *Kink*, produced by none other than the utterly mainstream James Franco, the cuddly star of *Oz the Great and Powerful* (Sam Raimi, 2013). The documentary showcases the production team, housed in the San Francisco Armory, that produces Kink.com, a site that features various BDSM fantasies, naked wrestling, sexual machines, and other fantasy material. In an interview, Franco discusses how he became fascinated with Kink.com while shooting a different film in the same building, when he was offered a chance to view a video being made: "It was very interesting because the dynamic in front of the camera was very different from what was happening off camera. It was a BDSM scene of a girl in a cage, and very intense, but off-screen it was surprisingly warm and cooperative, with everyone as a willing participant. I thought I'd like to explore this, and I'm sure a lot of other people would, too."[1] I found myself fascinated by this same discrepancy after I first learned of the world of bondage pornography about three years ago, having heard of a documentary called *Graphic Sexual Horror* (2009), which chronicled the rise and fall of Insex, the first web-based bondage-porn studio. The film was screening in many U.S. cities at the time, but there were no plans for it to show in my hometown of Portland, Oregon. So I contacted the directors, and one of them, Barbara Bell, generously sent me a DVD. She and I entered into an ongoing conversation about the film, and over time became friends. I organized a screening of her documentary for a small group of local bondage-porn models and subscribers to the Insex website, and we discussed it. In the following months I met with two producers of local bondage-porn websites, and I participated in a private online forum of Insex fans from February to June 2010. My questions revolved around how this extreme pornographic form is experienced on both sides of the camera. What makes it work, and what distinguishes it from other genres of pornography?

In its contemporary form, bondage pornography is a medium dependent on the existence of the web, and as such did not yet exist when Linda Williams wrote Hard Core (1989) twenty years ago. Bondage porn comes closest to the genre she discusses under the title of "amateur sadomasochism," distinct from more mainstream varieties of what she calls "violent porn," in that the pain and discomfort represented on film here are not simulated, nor is there an overarching fictional narrative to contextualize the various scenes. Amateur sadomasochism, Williams writes, boasts no recognizable titles and is generally unavailable to a mainstream audience. Relying on an underground distribution system, it works with low budgets and exclusively focuses on "highly ritualized forms of violence and domination enacted on the body of the woman."[2]

While the bulk of Hard Core challenged the feminist condemnation of porn, amateur sadomasochism constituted the single genre for which Williams seemed willing to concede that the radical feminists might be right: "There is in fact every reason to worry about the potential abuse of hard-core violence, since the very conventions of pornography work to enforce a realism similar to that of documentary film. In a genre [pornography] that has often staked its all on visible evidence of the involuntary convulsive experience of pleasure, the ultimate perversion could be the displacement of a hard-to-see pleasure onto an easier-to-see, and apparently similarly involuntary, response to pain."[3] Amateur sadomasochism thus became a kind of scapegoat in the book, the sole genre legitimately burdened with the sins that feminists had lain at the feet of pornography as a whole. This was the really bad stuff, Williams conceded, but she was quick to point out that the vast majority of pornography was not like this.

Williams's distaste for sadomasochistic porn has set the tone for the intervening twenty years in academic writing. This is especially true when women are depicted in submissive roles and men as dominants, which remains normative for the majority of scenes produced and marketed in the industry, although one can find every imaginable gender combination.[4] I know of no scholarly work within porn studies that tries to redeem sadomasochistic pornography in any form; it is second only to child porn as the worst of the worst. Like child porn, it has also been the target of censorship campaigns. These have historically focused less on the possibility of real violence occurring on the set, which is what concerned Williams, than on the danger that it might inspire real, nonconsensual acts of violence. As Lisa Downing discusses in her contribution to this volume, fears of copycat violence inspired a ban against the downloading of "violent images" in the United Kingdom in 2008, following a successful campaign led by Liz Longhurst, the mother of a woman murdered by a man whose computer held images and videos depicting erotic strangulation. In effect, the United Kingdom's decision rewrote Robin Morgan's pithy theorem for the twenty-first century: violent porn was the theory; murder was the practice.

The question of abusive violence, whether on the set or in the viewers' responses, has long framed outsiders' discussions of sadomasochistic pornography. As I began talking to those on the inside of this world, however, I quickly learned to avoid using the word *violence* altogether. It sometimes made people angry. As one participant put it, "This has nothing to do with violence at all. Violence is about *hurting* somebody. Nobody here wants to inflict any real damage on anybody else. What you want—what you're trying to do—is to give them the ride of their life."[5] Without exception, everyone I interviewed for this chapter—both producers and consumers of bondage porn—expressed a paramount interest in both the physical and psychological safety of the models. They rely on the presence of a safeword to guarantee that the model can always call off a scene whenever she or he feels unsafe. (At Insex, the standard safeword was *unh-unh*, chosen for its ability to be articulated even when the model was gagged.)

This leads to a paradox, however: bondage pornography makes visible the very real suffering of a body in pain; its appeal has everything to do with the fact that what we see on the screen is not staged. Yet those who practice and consume bondage pornography eschew violence they define as real. It might be useful to situate this paradox in relation to horror cinema, especially as the relatively recent term *torture porn* for certain films in that genre explicitly thematizes their erotic appeal.[6] In bondage porn, the suffering flesh is real; in horror films, the constraints, pain, and blood are simulated. But the *fantasy* presented in horror is by definition nonconsensual, and the viewer's pleasure has everything to do with imagining *real* damage being inflicted, or at the very least threatened. There are no safewords here. The audience is thrilled in a manner that might more authentically qualify as sadistic, or masochistic, as the case may be, because it oscillates, as Carol Clover richly illustrates, between a truly terrified victim and her or his murderous and deranged persecutor.[7] Horror films are about violence; bondage porn is about sexuality.

About sexuality, that is, but not necessarily about *sex*. I will have more to say about this distinction. Simply put, though, bondage porn does not revolve around the scopophilic pleasure of watching two or more people fuck on camera, as is the case in more mainstream pornographic genres. Instead, our focus remains riveted to a single subject, the model, as her body is disciplined: constrained, pained, pushed to its limit, and then at last released, often in orgasm. We watch as she is overwhelmed by a world of physical sensations, but these are not limited to the zones Freud dubbed erogenous. Absolutely any body part—feet, back, hair, sinuses, gums, *anything*—can serve as the vehicle through which her body will become agitated, excited, and aroused. Sometimes the excruciating nature of her experience is mediated through psychological factors, when she is humiliated, or confined in a claustrophobic space, or submerged in a tank filled with leeches. Whatever the nature of the ordeal, she submits to it *voluntarily*, and the viewer watches, cheering her on, wondering how much she can take, how far she can go.

## P. D. and the Birth of Insex

It is no exaggeration to say that today's genre of bondage pornography is the invention of a single individual: Brent Scott—known as P. D. on the set. He started out as a performance artist, teaching at the University at Buffalo, SUNY, and Johns Hopkins. After being denied tenure, he launched a new porn site called Insex in 1997, dedicated to maximizing the interactive possibilities newly available on the web. The site's offerings consisted in nonnarrative vignettes that began with a model, almost always female, fully clothed, stating her age and verbally consenting to participate in what was about to happen. For the next three hours, she would be placed in increasingly elaborate forms of bondage, as one restraint after the next was added, increasing her discomfort. The final three hours were devoted to intense pain, administered with canes, floggers, electricity, needles, and so forth. Throughout the scene, cameras remained focused exclusively on the model. "Handlers," those men and women who tightened the knots and administered the pain, remained fully clothed and tended to stay outside the shot, often cropped so that one could see, for example, only the arm swinging the cane. After the model had taken all she could endure, the handler would bring out a vibrator. Usually the model had to request, sometimes beg for, permission to orgasm. After she did (often ejaculating), all restraints came off. The show concluded with a second interview, in which the bruised, still-naked model, giggly, trembling, and more often than not somewhat incoherent, responded to questions about how she experienced different parts of the scene.

P. D. described his goal in developing this scenario in these terms:

> The phenomenon that happened at Insex that was unusual or totally unique was the explicit goal of trying to give the girl an orgasm, to create a sexual drama for the girl. The emphasis was on the girl, on her predicament, her state of mind, not on mine. The gradual increase of the ordeal . . . builds up a kind of acceptance of it. Endorphins, and also adrenaline. And all of these excess hormones in the body would create a state of euphoria. And

then, you couple that with orgasm, and you create a kind of ecstatic experience, tantamount to something religious. That was the money shot: the glassy-eyed, euphoric state that you would see on their faces at the end of a show.[8]

What P. D. is describing here is a very different kind of money shot from that of more mainstream porn. Even on the rare occasions when he did have sex with those models with whom he was romantically involved, his orgasm was never the central focus, nor was it a problem if he failed to get hard, which sometimes happened. Instead, the woman's pleasure—under greater scrutiny here than ever—was displaced onto pain, discomfort, and fear, an ordeal she had to endure before the orgasm that would release her could attain the ecstatic quality that P. D. was seeking.

One element that distinguished Insex from the amateur sadomasochism that preceded it was the aesthetic seriousness P. D. brought to his work from his background in performance art. Since the 1970s, a number of performance artists have integrated masochistic practices into their art in aesthetically interesting and challenging ways: Chris Burden, Bob Flanagan, Vito Acconci, Marina Abramović, Rebecca Horn, and Gina Pane spring immediately to mind, to name only a few. To my knowledge, however, P. D. is the only one to run the equation in the other direction, to move from performance art into the serious production of hard-core porn for a nonmainstream audience. The result was a breathtaking variety of aesthetic representations, as visually stunning in their attention to color and composition as they were disturbing in the scenes depicted. P. D. suspended women from hooks in shiny red latex bags. He submerged them in cages in murky amber water. He restrained them in medieval metal stocks, suspended them in cramped iron cages, and crucified them. A number of viewers told me how exciting they found Insex in the early years; they never knew what to expect on the site from one week to the next. As Cyd Black described it, "What preceded Insex was pretty standard: red ball gag and white clothesline wrapped around [the women] in a haphazard fashion. These images were totally different. There was something serial-killer-esque about them. They were bound in really uncomfortable positions. It was hot. Even if these girls were consenting, which I learned afterwards of course that they all were, they were not 'acting.' Once a scene was under way these girls were taking full part in it."[9] Black's distinction between consenting and acting gets at the heart of the contradictory nature of reality that distinguishes bondage porn from horror cinema. The welts and bruises we see here are real, as are the screams and tears. But the powerlessness of their position is feigned; they could end the scene at any time.

Trained in software programming and digital editing, P. D. pioneered the technology to create a new kind of pornographic text in the mid-1990s, the live feed, with which he supplemented more traditional weekly postings. During live feeds, members did more than view scenes in real time; they could also type in messages to be read aloud in the studio via "Victoria," that bizarrely flat, disembodied female voice known to Mac users. At first the technology could allow only a small number of members to participate in the conversation, but over the years live feeds were able to accommodate more and more real-time participants. Viewers commented on what they were seeing and suggested modifications to scenes, and at the end, models frequently had to ask members for permission to come. A number of members described how thrilling it was to see their suggestions enacted; they remembered in vivid detail suggestions they had made more than a decade ago that P. D. had enacted. "Demon," who watched from Germany, described the experience as akin to flying alongside a pilot who lets you take over the plane at six thousand feet: "You don't need to know how to get the plane off the ground or land it, but, for a few minutes, you're in control." Viewers trusted P. D. as the final authority; he would only enact those suggestions he found safe and appropriate, and he would stop when the model had taken enough.

On the other side of the camera, the spectators' presence also introduced a kind of protection to the scene. In Graphic Sexual Horror, P. D. tells his interviewer that part of his inspiration to make this kind of pornography had come from stage performances he had attended in Japan as a young man, where kimono-clad women were dragged onto the stage and tied up in elaborate restraints: "The thing that impressed me about the Japanese was this sense of spectacle, of show. It was not done in private, in the bedroom. It was as if this violent subject had to be witnessed by many people, in order to give it some legitimacy, or a sense of safety." Insex re-created the structure of the erotic, ritualized spectacle that P. D. had witnessed in Japan, remaking it in a virtual medium. The mediated nature of the relationship between the handlers and the model also facilitated the viewer's access to the model's experience—her "sexual drama," to use P. D.'s words. Her orgasm was not shared with anyone else; P. D. and the other handlers—both male and female—barely touched her. Their interactions with her were always mediated through instruments, at first through restraints, whips, dildos, cattle prods, needles, and all the other implements of torture, and then, finally, through a vibrator. As the handler's body distanced itself from the model's, she or he became more available as a proxy for the spectator's own engagement with the scene, especially when enacting the viewer's request. In stepping back, the handler opened the model up to the viewing public's access.

One live feed that took place in the spring of 2004 illustrates this principle brilliantly. P. D. linked the message board to a device that translated Victoria's words into electric current that traveled from electrodes taped to a model's nipples to a copper dildo on which she perched. As the studio reverberated with a bizarre computerized singing that sounded like an electronic Gregorian chant, viewers could see their own keystrokes transformed into direct physical sensation—less euphemistically, pain—moving in waves through the model's body.[10]

This same model (912), when interviewed in *Graphic Sexual Horror*, describes a conversation she had while working at Insex: "I confided in my sister what I was doing, what was going on, and her first response was, Oh my God, you're in porn! And I said, No, it's not porn. It wasn't just people taking off their clothes, people having sex to make a buck. It was something really different, something more intense, something more real, more genuine. And I felt honest in my heart that I could say . . . that it wasn't porn." How are we to make sense of this statement? If we define pornography as nonsimulated sex on film, then the question becomes: what is "sex"? A woman, perched on a metal dildo, writhing as waves of electricity course through her body, dictated by the keystrokes of distant viewers: to call such a scene "sexual" is to stretch the concept to the breaking point. But that, as Leo Bersani argues, may be precisely the place where sexuality comes most clearly into focus. Bersani points to Freud's observation that every intense emotional experience, including terror and pain, invokes a sexual response. From here, Bersani generalizes, sexuality becomes "that which is intolerable to the structured self," or that which shatters us.[11] The mystery of sexuality lies in the fact that we don't try to escape from the shattering; instead we long to repeat and intensify it. To limit our understanding of sex to its reproductive function, to the genital relations between two different people, is to deny its radical dimension. Any real investigation of sexuality, Bersani argues, "leads to a massive detachment of the sexual from object specificity and organ specificity."[12] Insex enacted that detachment to an extent greater than I have seen in any other genre of erotic representation. The only consistent element from one week to the next was the drama of sexual shattering; the road that led to that goal could pass through any anatomical location, or it could be staged through any realm of experience. Viewers understood this point. As one viewer told me, "Everything that happened at Insex was sexual. Even the opening interview. It was all sex; all of it."

## The Insex Forum and the Question of Consent

In opening up a line of communication between the studio and its members, Insex also created a venue where viewers from around the world could meet one another. They started an online fan forum, where they discussed recent shows, posted their own images, shared fantasies, and became friends. Some traveled internationally to visit one another; some visited P. D. and the studio as well. The community that formed here was immensely important to all of the members with whom I have communicated, coming, as it did, well before the advent of other online BDSM sites, such as FetLife. For those who previously had kept their sexual interests in the closet, the discovery of a community of like-minded people was revelatory. Descriptions of this discovery have a similar flavor to those of gays and lesbians from small towns recounting their first experience of metropolitan queer life in the pre-Stonewall era. Although the George W. Bush administration closed down Insex in 2005, the members' forum lived on, nourished by the friendships that had formed among members and by new material appearing online every week from a host of bondage-pornography sites inspired by Insex and adopting many of P. D.'s ideas. (Kink.com is the largest and most successful of these.)[13]

Curious about Insex fans and their motivations, I asked Bell if I might be able to join the members' forum, or at least to read what was posted there. She passed along my request, and soon I was contacted by a man who identifies himself as "Rope," a long-term Insex member who lives in France. He asked about my academic interests and what my paper might be used for, and then took the issue to the forum's executive council. They decided that the best way to protect their members' privacy was to launch a separate forum just for me, where anyone who wanted to answer my questions could participate. We built up a considerable archive over the next several months, mostly discussing Insex, but also trading opinions about lots of things: relationships, sex, sadomasochism, religion, politics. I don't know how many people read those postings, but there were probably about twenty who contributed, and eight who posted regularly. Although the pool was too small to tell me much about the 35,000 people who watched Insex in its heyday, the forum gave me a good sense of the core community. As our conversation progressed, I became fond of them.

Most of the viewers who communicated with me think of themselves as dominant, though one identifies as submissive. The majority were men. Their own experiences with sadomasochism span a wide range. One has been active since he was a teenager, and has been married to a submissive woman for thirty years, with whom he *plays* (a word he detests) quite actively. Others have never had any real-life experiences in BDSM — other than participating in live feeds. When I asked what they liked about Insex, everyone mentioned the realism of the shows:

Rope (France): What I liked in Insex? It was true, the tears were true, nothing was fake. This feeling is very related to Live Feeds, no cheating possible. Not being a fan of pain, I found in Insex what I've always looked for in my partners/victims/subs (choose the word you want): extreme feelings (Fear, Anguish, Pain, Shame, Hate, Love, etc.).

*Mayfair* (Spain): What I liked about Insex was this feeling—once I had found it—that this was *non plus ultra*, the top of the top, la crème de la crème. Nothing was ever going to go above it, and for a variety of reasons nothing ever has. . . . Insex had this mixture of intensity, image, iconography, and helplessness of the models which I really liked.

*Ethan* (United States): It was far more real than any other videos I'd ever seen, more extreme and more artistic. The initial exposure was a shock of recognition: "At Last! Yes—THIS is IT!" in terms of depiction. I used to look very much forward to the day of the week that the new video would be posted. Then when the Forum got started, and the live feeds began, I was even more satisfied. I had found my community. These were intelligent and emotionally alert and sensitive people.

I joined the discussion forum at just the moment when *Graphic Sexual Horror* was first made available to the members. Most of our conversations in the coming months revolved around the documentary, which both celebrates P. D.'s creativity and provides an unflinching critique of some of his dealings with the models. *Graphic Sexual Horror* is a deeply ambivalent documentary; I found it a perfect text around which to focus my conversation with the fans; the film asked many of the difficult questions for me. Bell's own participation in the forum helped to keep that critical voice alive, and also articulated an insider's perspective into the workings of the studio. Both Bell and her collaborator, Anna Lorentzon, worked at the Insex studio for a period of time before making the documentary. Lorentzon was a camerawoman for years, while Bell, whose SM-themed novel, *Stacking in Rivertown*, had caught P. D.'s attention, was commissioned to write and direct a narrative feature film that was shot at the studio but never released.

On camera, P. D. speaks with a candor and comfort level that clearly comes from knowing the filmmakers well. Interviews with the eccentric, entertaining staff members and with numerous models develop a sense of the excitement in the studio. The film conveys the mood of a vibrant and edgy artistic production, with P. D. at its epicenter. If he had a new idea at two in the morning, everyone had to get up to try it out. Restraints, hoods, and costumes were remade over and over to fit his exact specifications; he tried them all on personally before putting them on the models. The Insex studio comes across as something akin to a theater troupe or a dance company, with a brilliant, emotionally volatile, and slightly deranged director and choreographer at the center who brooks no compromise, and who is perfectly happy to work his company members until their feet bleed or they collapse in exhaustion on the stage. It's a familiar narrative, from biographies of Fred Astaire and George Balanchine to narrative fictions like *Fame*. But these are not dance or theater performances. P. D. did not demand the equivalent of a learned discipline like dance; his models were asked instead to suffer in public and to deliver a kind of openness to the gaze, an availability to a very specific form of intimacy. In the documentary he says: "You might say I got to know these people, I got to know these women, very intimately. And how often do you get to say that, I mean, unless it's as a lover, which already clouds it or fogs it. But to examine them as subjects, really, as crude as that may appear, for the site, was really a hell of a way to look at a person." P. D. wears many hats at once here. He's intimate—like a lover, but not a lover. He's a scientist, examining the models as subjects of knowledge, testing and experimenting on them. He's a director, trying to orchestrate a particular performance, to instantiate a specific aesthetic vision with each scene. And most importantly, the film stresses, he's an employer, with a whole lot of money to throw around.

In the process of making *Graphic Sexual Horror*, Bell says, she and Lorentzon came to realize that they had to treat money itself as a major player in the story they were trying to tell. As the site became successful, P. D. began giving bonuses to women whose performances he found especially moving, sometimes thousands of dollars for a single day's work. For women not accustomed to those kinds of wages, as most were not, the money became a strong motivating force. Less generously, it became a coercive factor. The question of its function constitutes the central focus of *Graphic Sexual Horror*. P. D. himself is impressively self-critical about the influence the money had on him:

> The drive to make this business work turned me into some kind of a monster, probably. I'm sure that paying these girls the kind of money that I did, . . . I absolutely assumed that they had to do what I wanted them to do. . . . I tried to rationalize it too. I mean, that's not unlike what you'd see in any job situation; you don't want to pay them if they're not going to work. But in this situation it's compressed into a five-hour span of time. And there's an urgency implicit in that. She wants that money. So you proceed, you start marching down this path, where I have my needs; it's a business.

Monetary coercion played a role both on and off the set. P. D. sometimes asked women to engage in bondage play with him when the cameras were not rolling, in order to "find inspiration." Some models said it was not clear what the consequences would be if they declined.

On the set the promise of a monetary bonus for a strong performance, along with the prospect of an invitation to return for another session, created a powerful disincentive to use one's safeword. The model known as "1201," an articulate and insightful speaker, offers a compelling description of its function.[14]

> Ultimately it became . . . that I was coming back for the money. I would have said that I was coming back for the challenge, but I wasn't; I was coming back for the money. And it wasn't like I was dependent on it. But I'd never seen myself as someone making one thousand dollars a day, or five thousand dollars in four days. . . . I was in school and I was waiting tables, and I was never in debt. And I would just go shopping or do something totally irresponsible with it. It was fun. It gave me a sense of what having a lot of money was like.

1201 is one of the angriest models interviewed in the film. She tells of a scene in which she was anally penetrated for the first time. The pain was excruciating, and she now thinks she should have used her safeword, but instead she continued. Moreover, she repeatedly returned to Insex afterward. Now she wonders why. While she doesn't dispute that she gave her consent in the moment, she now believes she did so for all the wrong reasons.

Even more troubling for most viewers of Graphic Sexual Horror is a recorded live feed with a young woman known as "S4." In negotiations before the scene began, S4 had listed slapping as one of her "hard limits"—something she was not willing to do under any circumstances. With the cameras rolling, however, a member suggests that P. D. slap her face, and he does. He could be deliberately violating her hard limit, but it seems more likely that he simply forgot about it, his attention split between overseeing the production, pleasing the members, and interacting with S4. She responds with surprise and outrage delivered in a childlike voice; she appears on the verge of tears. In response, P. D. loses his temper. The documentary devotes four full minutes to the exchange that follows, in which P. D. initially tries to call off the scene, but S4 eventually prevails on him to continue.

A retired professional dominant who saw the film with me became furious with P. D. at this point, condemning him as unprofessional and emotionally unsafe. The two models who had worked with him, on the other hand, were more sympathetic. He clearly made a mistake and lost his composure here, but given the extreme stress level of the studio, they found that understandable. And in the end, they pointed out, S4 got her way; P. D. gave in and continued. They criticized the filmmakers for devoting so much time to this exchange, believing it would prejudice the audience against Insex, and against sadomasochism in general.

For her part, Bell says she was not trying to smear P. D. by devoting so much time to the live feed with S4. In a filmed interview, she explains why she found the scene crucial to the film's message:

> You've got things on both sides. P. D. wants to give his members what they want because there's all this money involved. And then you've got this model, and I don't know what's going on for her because I didn't talk to her after this, but there's clearly a tussle going on, and everybody's mad at P. D., but nobody, neither one of them are really addressing the situation. She's not really saying no. She doesn't really want to. She's trying to find that place where she can make it go on, but he'll stop crossing her limit. And he doesn't want to admit that he's done something that he agreed he wasn't going to do.

The question of consent here is of paramount importance; P. D. cannot admit that he has violated the model's consent, because to do so would be to trespass on the sacred boundary that separates the sadomasochistic encounter from abuse. But the need to please his viewers, to maximize his profit, makes him forgetful. For S4 as well, the fear of losing her pay for the day may well have motivated her desire to continue the scene. In the members' forum, Bell stressed that none of the models she ever met had relied on studio money to survive. But when it was offered to them, and in such extraordinary sums, it became nearly impossible to turn down, no matter what they had to go through. Bell's point is thus not to condemn bondage pornography, or even P. D.'s actions, lost as he is in his own enthrallment to the immense profitability of his business. She is arguing instead that the intense focus on consent demanded by such extreme forms of bondage is inevitably corrupted by the power of money.

The men on the forum were less concerned with the coercive pressure of payment than with the film's allegations that P. D. had coerced models into getting tied up off camera and after hours. As Demon summed it up: "Sex after work = sexual harassment; paid play after work = to be negotiated between the parties; Play and/or have sex with me or don't come back = unjustifiable behavior." Rope responded that any woman who shows up in a porn studio knows that she will have to have sex, both on and off camera. Why were we holding bondage porn to a higher standard? Bell and I both objected vigorously; even if such coercion may be ubiquitous in the industry, it's still morally wrong, just as repugnant here as anywhere else.

Yet it was Bell—the filmmaker who brought these allegations to light in the first place—who articulated the strongest defense of P. D. If we take the videos he made at Insex seriously as an art form, she argued, we must understand his need to work with his medium to find inspiration and to try out ideas before putting his creations on stage. This might sound cynical. If we see after-hours bondage as an indulgence of P. D.'s personal desire, it clearly exemplifies sexual harassment. But if we view it as an artwork, dependent on the unique personality, abilities, and limitations of each model, whom he needs to get to know in order to try out ideas (as a choreographer might with a dancer), the stakes change. It all depends on how we define this work, and the nature of the pleasure the artist-pornographer takes in it.

On the forum we also debated the limits of consent, but from a different angle than Bell's discussion of the coercive power of money. I noticed that when models told me the hard limits they had first laid out in their negotiations with P. D., their subsequent work with him almost always pushed precisely those limits. This wasn't the simple violation that S4 experienced, based on a momentary lapse on P. D.'s part; I'm talking about a slow, deliberate attempt to push the model in precisely the direction she said she did not want to go. Bell corroborated my impression in an interview: "I don't know if P. D. does it on purpose, but every model we interviewed said that P. D. will try different methods to push against those hard limits. And that was my experience also in watching him. That is where he is going to get a reaction and it will create spectacle."

This tendency worried some of the forum members. Ethan wrote, "We are clearly walking along the Edge here, and it bothers me." Rope, however, was less troubled. For him, pain, bondage, even orgasm, are never an end in themselves but only a means to something else—a deep emotional experience or psychological transformation. To get there, he has sometimes practiced what he calls "consensual nonconsent" in his relationships. His wife, Yooki, confirmed this approvingly. As an example, he told me that Yooki used to have a phobia of cats. Over a period of years, he exposed her to them while she was tied up, or sometimes simply threatened her with cats, until she overcame her phobia. That kind of experience requires a deep knowledge of one's partner, Rope stressed; it can happen only in a long-term relationship. "He knows me very well," Yooki agreed.[15]

This kind of experience is quite different from what happened at Insex, of course, where P. D. seldom worked so extensively with a model as to establish the kind of deep trust Rope is describing. But Rope said the reason he liked the shows was that P. D. worked on a similar principle as his own; P. D. often took the model to the edge of her greatest fear. Princess Donna, who worked for P. D. as both a model and a handler, says in the documentary: "He wanted what was happening on camera to be real, and he wanted that to be your real dynamic. So he wanted you to really be scared, and really be uncomfortable." Model 62, also interviewed for *Graphic Sexual Horror*, believes that this tendency was what made his work unique: "One of the reasons P. D. got such amazing content . . . is that he can make a girl, while she's still consenting to it, do things that she would never have otherwise done."

This statement gets to the heart of what P. D.'s fans loved about his show, and what his critics, including many within the sadomasochistic community, detested.[16] Many practitioners of sadomasochism insist on fully consenting, point by point, to everything they plan to do, spelled out in minute detail before anything happens at all. Jay Wiseman's SM 101, for example, offers a sixteen-page questionnaire that tries to list every conceivable bodily interaction that might occur, and he advises players to fill it out together before the scene begins (a process he says will take anywhere from forty minutes to two hours).[17] There is a spectrum among practitioners about how thoroughly to elaborate consent in advance, and Insex lies on the other end of that spectrum from Wiseman, closer to Rope's consensual nonconsent. We might think of this as the volitional equivalent to the "shattering" experience that Bersani locates at the heart of sexuality, but here affecting the coherence of the subject, rather than the body.[18]

But if we can't rely on a form of contract theory to separate real violence from this kind of erotic play, where else might we draw a line? One participant framed an answer in terms of temporality, saying that real abuse has the goal of breaking down the subjectivity of the abused person, while erotic simulations of violence aim at the opposite, trying to strengthen the bottom. This response posits the ethical dimensions of sadomasochistic play as oriented toward a future moment in which the submissive will look back on what happened and find a benefit in it. Real torture has no such relationship to the future of the victim. Sometimes one *wants* to be forced into something from which one shrinks in fear. Volition is a porous field, not localizable in a single temporal moment.

This invocation of a future moment in which consent *will have been given* for that which is happening now is the obverse of the regret discussed earlier, when the model realizes her consent was misplaced, given not for the "challenge," but "only for money." One never knows in advance whether or not one will have consented in the future to what one is about to do. As Elizabeth Freeman argues, "Sadomasochism is a, perhaps *the*, set of sexual practices that most self-consciously manipulates time."[19] This temporal manipulation takes many forms; it embraces the deliberate postponement of gratification that so fascinated Gilles Deleuze in Leopold von Sacher-Masoch's work, as well as the fantasy restaging of historical trauma that Freeman herself discusses, or even the magical transformative potential of the future-anterior tense that Lynda Hart relies upon to cast SM as a means by which incest survivors sometimes heal from past traumas.[20] What all of these have in common is a form of shattering that disperses the subjectivity of the self along a temporal dimension, not quite knowing who will be there to pick up the pieces in the future.

This is not to reduce the kind of erotic play that took place at Insex to a form of therapy—facing down fears to overcome them (like Yooki's cat phobia). Neither is it a variation of athletic or military training—a "toughening up" of the submissive. There may well be a specific kind of physical pleasure involved in confronting fear (people spend good money to jump out of planes, after all), and basic training is not without its erotic appeal, as Claire Denis richly illustrates in Beau Travail (1999). Insex had something to do with both of these modes of pleasure, but it exceeded them by explicitly eroticizing the experience and representing it within the framework of a pornographic text. In the process, Insex also transformed pornography, moving away from the depiction of two bodies trying to stage their physical pleasure for a camera that can never quite get inside that experience. Here the focus was on one body, one woman, in it all alone, caught up in the experience of shattering, radically isolated from everyone and everything around her. Paradoxically, it was precisely her isolation that generated a specific form of intimacy with the viewers. Those objectifying numbers that served to identify them notwithstanding, "the models—nude, beaten, gagged, whip-marked—were respected, admired, and in some cases loved," according to Ethan. Rope agreed: "I felt love for so many of them." That love spilled over to the other members of the forum as well, an intimate community founded on the erotic experience of sharing in the isolated shattering of the model, experienced by people likewise isolated before their computer screens, scattered around the globe.

## Notes

1. Marlow Stern, "James Franco and Co. Discuss the BDSM-Porn Documentary 'Kink' at Sundance," Daily Beast, January 21, 2013.

2. L. Williams, Hard Core (1989), 197.

3. L. Williams, Hard Core (1989), 203.

4. A number of writers have defended heterosexual, gender-normative SM practices outside the porn studio, however. See, for example, Hopkins, "Rethinking Sadomasochism"; Newmahr, Playing on the Edge; and Weiss, Techniques of Pleasure.

5. Telephone interview with Barbara Bell, August 10, 2010.

6. The term torture porn first came into vogue in 2005 as a description of Saw (directed by James Wan, 2004) and its sequels, Hostel (directed by Eli Roth, 2005), and the Grindhouse double feature (directed by Quentin Tarantino and Robert Rodriguez, 2007).

7. See Clover, Men, Women, and Chainsaws.

8. Brent Scott did not respond to requests for an interview. All of his citations here are my transcriptions of interviews in Graphic Sexual Horror (directed by Barbara Bell and Anna Lorentzon, 2009).

9. Cyd Black, an Insex handler from 2003 to 2005, was interviewed in *Graphic Sexual Horror*.

10. Cell feed from 912 recorded on April 18, 24, and 31, 2004, and posted on May 22, 2004.

11. Bersani, *The Freudian Body*, 38.

12. Bersani, *The Freudian Body*, 41.

13. The closing down of the site, as described in *Graphic Sexual Horror*, is a fascinating story in its own right. Insex was never brought to court; antiobscenity legislation was never invoked. Instead, the Bush administration invoked the Patriot Act to motivate the banks that carried the Insex account to close it down, on the grounds that Insex was funneling money to terrorist organizations (these allegations were never substantiated). Unable to process money transfers, P. D. was forced to abandon the site. He eventually launched two new sites to replace it, Infernal Restraints and Hard Tied; he now posts weekly articles on both, along with regular live feeds.

14. P. D. began using numbers for specific models, rather than names, after one woman who worked with him went on to mount her own website with her boyfriend, using the notoriety she had gained from working at Insex in a competing venue. The numbers, generally based on the date when the woman first interviewed with him, were intended to ensure that the reputation they gained at his site would always indexically point back to Insex.

15. Rope's anecdote reminded me of a story that my retired dominatrix friend once told me about one of her clients, a wizened but muscular marine, tough and taciturn, who had been a prisoner of war for many months in Vietnam. He wanted her to immobilize him in a straitjacket, and then slowly to lower a hood over his head, just as he had been hooded for most of his captivity. The restraints were necessary because he feared that without them, he would forget where he was and try to kill her. It took months of lowering that hood, bit by bit, to the point where his panic interrupted the session. Finally, after more than a year, she managed to drop it successfully down to his chin. He stopped coming to her after that.

16. When I approached the Portland Leather Association to see if they would be willing to sponsor a screening of *Graphic Sexual Horror*, followed by a discussion with Barbara Bell, their executive committee flatly refused. They did not want to give the impression that they in any way condoned the kinds of things that happened in the Insex studio.

17. See Wiseman, SM 101.

18. Bersani, "Is the Rectum a Grave?," 218.

19. Freeman, "Turn the Beat Around," 39.

20. See Deleuze, *Masochism*; and Hart, *Between the Body and the Flesh*.

# PART V

Transnational Archives

# 15

# Porno Rícans at the Borders of Empire

*Ramón E. Soto-Crespo*

If you browse the adult section of the website for TLA Entertainment Group, you will find a list of destinations where the entertainment company is not allowed to ship its products.[1] Among the listing of countries, such as Austria, as well as U.S. federated states such as Utah, you'll stumble on the denomination "U.S. possessions and territories"; this category includes Guam, the Virgin Islands, Puerto Rico, and the Marianas Islands. To those localities delivery is "completely restricted." When I first discovered this information, it helped to make sense of the dearth of pornography in Puerto Rico when I was growing up there during the 1980s. The history of pornography in the Spanish-speaking Americas markedly differs from its history in the Anglophone world. Only recently have we seen sexuality being addressed openly and without inhibition in Spanish American countries. The same interest is seen in recent examinations of sexuality and ethnic identity in urban and other border regions with large Latino communities in the United States. Yet even in recently produced fictional and anthropological accounts of Spanish American sexual cultures — such as Carlos Ulises Decena's *Tacit Subjects* (2011), Héctor Carrillo's *The Night Is Young* (2002), and Antonio Marquet's *El crepúsculo de la heterolandia* (Heteroland's zenith) (2006) — the question of porn is almost entirely absent.

This chapter addresses that absence in the historical record by articulating the significance of porn in the cultural production of the U.S. borderlands. Specifically, I examine the emergence of porn in the Puerto Rican borderlands of the 1990s and the way it displaced the 1970s cultural production of colonized masculinity that mainland Puerto Rican communities had disseminated with Nuyorican poetry. I make use here of Michel Foucault's theory of the archive as "the law of what can be said, the system that governs the appearance of statements" within a culture.[2] I bring to bear on the discourse of mainland Puerto Rican communities a marginalized visual discourse that challenges the central tenets of its national-colonial discursive parameters. Borderland porn as a visual discourse challenges the rules of formation that govern what can and cannot be said and what can and cannot be represented. The shift in representation from the 1970s to the 1990s is important given that cultural production shifted from poetic modes of expression to a multiplicity of media, including borderland porn. At the same time, the temporal borderland figured prominently in Foucault's engagement with the archive: "The analysis of the archive . . . involves a privileged region: at once close to us, and different from our present existence, it is the border of time that surrounds our presence."[3] In order to make explicit these cultural shifts in the production of porn in the borderlands, I follow John Champagne's recommendations for critical inquiry, by emphasizing the historical, social, and cultural conditions of pornography, rather than textual analyses of individual porn films.[4]

I employ a double methodology. First, I use personal accounts to describe how experiences of porn affect a borderland subject and influence new aesthetic and political subjectivities in the U.S. mainland. In this way, I combine the growing-up narrative conventions that are typical in the field of Latino studies with an emphasis on experiences of pornography, a component that is missing from Latino scholarship. Indeed, Latino studies as a discipline has shown very little interest in pursuing this line of inquiry. I want to bring the fledgling field of porn studies together with Latino studies to help fill a gap in each. Hence, second, I revisit in a nonagonistic way issues left behind by the U.S.-centered field of porn studies. While porn studies seems keen to move beyond discussion of obscenity, I want to examine the history of antiobscenity legislation in places that are within U.S. jurisdiction but that do not necessarily follow in rhythm or pace the development of porn on the U.S. mainland. I am referring here to those geopolitical areas usually understood as borderlands. Originally designating the geographical region of the U.S.-Mexican border, borderlands as a key concept of Latino cultural studies refers to any region where "two or more cultures edge each other."[5] This chapter reflects on the significance of porn as a generative cultural form in the U.S. borderlands.

## A Brief History of Obscenity Law in Puerto Rico

Life as an adolescent in Puerto Rico during the early 1980s was challenging, given how limited access was to porn. With the Internet not yet available and with no access to print pornography, my only sources of visual stimulation were television shows, the underwear section in the Sears Roebuck catalog, fashion magazines, anatomy books, posters of Charlie's Angels, and neighborhood friends. For the most part, the last one kept my hands full. Friends provided vintage porn magazines that were the occasion for circle-jerk sessions, cock-fighting matches, cock-docking rituals, and distance-shooting competitions. With these contests in ejaculation, the more we practiced, the better we became. As with a ballistic missile, angle and arch were key to withstanding gusts of island wind.

We relied on old issues of *Playboy* and *Penthouse*. The magazines that were used for inspiration were kept in a storage house, or barrack, that once had been our playground and later became the local boys' SWAT team headquarters. This clubhouse was a fort guarding our local porn archive—*el archivo*, as we used to refer to it. El archivo consisted of an old wooden trunk that we filled with loose items and trinkets; at the bottom of the pile we hid the magazines under a black plastic cover to make it look like the trunk's bottom. We even had a secret entrance to our porn archive. A back window was always left unlocked and we would climb the fence, hold ourselves from a corner of the roof, and swing our bodies through the wooden window. We performed these acrobatic moves in seconds. Unsupervised, we would perform our daily visits, collectively crossing the borders of the world around us.

I suspect that our porn archive had been supplied by one of my friends. His father was in the U.S. Army and, unbeknownst to him, his "patriotic" activities provided our direct line to porn. He could easily purchase adult magazines at the shop inside the U.S. military base, since it was under federal jurisdiction. Of course, the post office and the federal buildings were also enclaves of U.S. jurisdiction on the island, but those agencies did not sell pornography. At the time, I was unaware of the political maneuvering by states for limiting access to pornographic material. But I had already realized that if I wanted porn, I had to leave the island—or at least move away from its political autonomy and its highly effective legal jurisdiction. In the early 1980s, pornography was available only in those island enclaves that belonged to the federal government.

On June 4, 1980, Puerto Rico's legislature approved Law 97, which amended articles 112, 117 A, and 117 B of the penal code. Those were the articles addressing crimes related to obscenity. Article 112 based its definition of obscenity on the infamous case *Miller v. California*, in which, on June 23, 1973, the Supreme Court ruled that obscene materials did not enjoy First Amendment protection. In *Miller v. California*, the Court revised the test for obscenity previously established in legal precedents such as *Roth v. U.S.* (1957) and *Memoirs v. Massachusetts* (1966). The Legislative Assembly of Puerto Rico embraced *Miller's* approach for determining obscenity, particularly its new emphasis on preserving "community standards." As a result, by 1983 the flow of pornographic material from mainland to island had stopped and the last porn theaters had been closed. Three years of vigorous prosecution by the Department of Justice had eliminated 98 percent of pornographic material and the places to obtain it.[6] Hence, my teen years in Puerto Rico coincided with the state's crackdown on porn. In its antiporn crusade, the Puerto Rican state exceeded precedents established on the U.S. mainland, with the exception, of course, of the state of Utah. By the time I left the island in 1986 for college, my desperation to update those porn magazines that we had treasured in our clubhouse archive was at an all-time high.

During the 1990s, with the development of the World Wide Web, Puerto Rico attempted to extend to Internet porn the laws that had been successful in controlling video and print pornography. Yet by the 1990s the movement to abolish porn in Puerto Rican society had diminished dramatically. Ironically, the best hope for limiting the spread of porn online depended on the U.S. government; in Puerto Rico, those forces opposed to online porn awaited legal resolution at the federal level. On June 26, 1997, the U.S. Supreme Court decided in *Reno v. ACLU* that provisions of the Communications Decency Act were unconstitutional because it suppressed free speech. The new ruling represented a challenge to local forces that were clamoring for federal regulation. As an example of federalism, the Supreme Court's decision closed the door on creative but misguided ventures by a wayward island legislature.

*Condom World: A Brief History of Borderland Two-Way Traffic*

"Condom World is not an amusement park," clarifies an online article. I must admit that I'm unsure which audience needs this clarification — Puerto Ricans on the island who travel en masse every year to Walt Disney World, Epcot Center, Sea World, and every other amusement park that can be fitted into the no-sleep-back-to-back-see-everything-at-once frenzy, or the typical mainland tourist who plans every detail of a vacation and might imagine that Condom World is an amusement park in Puerto Rico. In reality, Condom World is a chain of porn shops that started to encroach on the island during the early 1990s. These small establishments specialize in the sales of condoms, oils, sex toys, and a wide selection of adult videos. They advertise heavily in one of the more widely distributed newspapers on the island, El vocero (The voice) — a savvy decision, given that El vocero does not waste ink on euphemisms. Reporting with punch and bite, this newspaper is known to sensationalize the worst crimes and scandals that sweep modesty-bound Puerto Rican society. Bold red ink is used on the front page to emphasize some brutal killing that took place the night before. I remember bright-red headlines stating bluntly: "Chopped Up for Loose Lips"; "Machete Sliced One in Two, Tripe Everywhere"; and, my all-time favorite, "Maimed but Smirking."

Needless to say, El vocero was an extremely popular daily paper that made a big hoo-hah of accidents, crimes of passion, and gang violence. Given its circulation and impact, any advertisement would be read, talked about, and dissected by small reading communities everywhere on the island and in Puerto

Rican enclaves on the mainland. Whenever Condom World announced the opening of a new store, it triggered an avalanche of letters in opposition. El *vocero* served not only as a disseminator of news but also as a galvanizing agent for conservatives, leftist patriots, and church groups. A July 11, 1999, headline in the *Orlando Sentinel* captures one of these moments: "Condom World Causing Outrage in Puerto Rico." The article clarifies: "The groups Pro-Life Association and Morality in Media held a protest along with some church leaders recently in front of the 2-month-old Mayaguez store and called on police to investigate their claims that the store sells illegal pornographic products."[7]

I should come clean by stating that I have never been to one of Condom World's many stores. However, I was introduced to one while watching the film *12 Horas* (12 Hours, directed by Raúl Marchand, 2001), which narrates the story of three female protagonists enjoying a girls' night out. As part of their itinerary of events for the evening, the women visit one of the stores in order to restock on oils, gels, and massagers. In the film the porn shop is referred to as La tiendita (The little store). The scene provides a thorough view of the merchandise available for purchase as the protagonists draw attention to the more outrageous DVDs and magazines. The camera provides close-ups of printed scenes of *bukkake*, donkey dongs, prego sex, MILF, grannies, daddies, and more. The popularity of *12 Horas* among mainstream audiences, owing to its tragicomic plot, allowed viewers to take a peek inside a porn store, thus making them complicit in the marketing of adult merchandise. If the film mocked the uptightness of Puerto Rico's legislators and their antiporn sponsors, this move was softened by the patriotic sentiment surrounding the film's release. Given that the film industry barely exists in Puerto Rico, the public generally welcomes with pride any Puerto Rican film that manages to get produced. Local patriotism cushioned the impact of suddenly being dragged into the forbidden space of a little porn shop.

Not having lived through the glorious spread of porn shops on the island, I must admit that for me Condom World has an aura of incongruity as an institution that comes from elsewhere. Research reveals that Condom World has its roots in return migration: a corporate chain with its origins in the U.S. mainland, Condom World subsequently expanded its operations to the island. From Hartford, Connecticut, to San Juan, Puerto Rico, and other urban areas, Condom World maps the Puerto Rican borderland; that is to say, it marks the territory of Puerto Rican communities on both sides of the Atlantic Ocean. Condom World, in all its semiotic significance, is the perfect gift that mainland Puerto Rican communities could bring back to an overpopulated island. Having one of the highest population densities in the world, Puerto Rican society has long resisted family planning because contraception has tended to be understood as a form of capitulation to U.S. imperialism. In *Reproduc-*

ing *Empire* (2002), Laura Briggs argues that this complicated connection between reproduction and imperialism stems from the decades of the 1920s and the 1940s. We should make clear that, from 1898 to 1951, Puerto Rico was a colony of the United States. During that colonial past, the 1920s and the 1940s featured two dramatically different types of colonial administration on the island.

The 1920s witnessed the neglect of U.S. Republican governments and their appointed governors. This decade also marked the beginning of a series of failed attempts by local constituencies on the island (with limited help from the mainland) to establish eugenic methods. The most salient was the attempt to sterilize Puerto Rican women living in the rural countryside.[8] Mainland influence was minimal, given that federal regulations on interstate commerce prohibited the traffic of items related to sexuality or "vice."[9] The 1930s saw a politicized labor force on the island and a nationalization of Puerto Rican politics in favor of independence from the United States. The 1940s witnessed New Deal administrations attempting to redress the damage caused by previous Republican governors. By the time the 1940s came, the greater majority of the population had been politicized, and the most radical protofascist, pronationalist elements of the political spectrum argued vigorously that any alteration of Puerto Rican society had the hidden intention of limiting the traditional role of the Puerto Rican family. The mainland passage, the great migration to New York in the 1940s, became understood in this framework.[10] Migration and attempts by the commonwealth state to address the pernicious issue of overpopulation were confronted with accusations of cultural genocide by a Puerto Rican Left that condemned the breaking apart of the greater Puerto Rican family. As Briggs points out: "The charge of genocide was leveled at modernizers by nationalists, who contended that the modernizers wished to end Puerto Rican existence within a generation by limiting fertility."[11]

Briggs's research heavily relies on the analyses of the historians Annette Ramírez de Arellano and Eileen Suárez Findlay. More important for us here are Findlay's historical findings in *Imposing Decency: The Politics of Sexuality and Race in Puerto Rico, 1870–1920*, which elucidates a consistent trend in Puerto Rico's relationship with the metropolis. The form of relationship remains unchanged despite the political transfer that took place in 1898, when the island stopped being a Spanish colony and became a U.S. possession. Findlay explains how the connection in contemporary politics between decadence and the U.S. mainland had its roots in the relationship forged by the island's political culture vis-à-vis the emerging liberal trend in Spanish politics.[12] Her study documents how conservative elements of the local bourgeoisie formed alliances across borders to maintain standards of decency on the island. As might be expected, conservatives argued that liberal ideas stemming from the Spanish metropolis represented signs of imperial decadence and decline.

It is not surprising that the Catholic Church has been one of those institutions that consistently opposed any alteration in traditional Puerto Rican family structure. Even after the formation of the Associated Free State of Puerto Rico in 1952, we see the church plotting against the rapid modernization of the island that took place under the leadership of Governor Luis Muñoz Marín. In 1960 the Catholic Church formed its own Christian Action Party, in opposition to what it saw as socialist practices of birth control promoted by Muñoz Marín's government. An election year in Puerto Rico and in the United States, 1960 saw for the first time the church actively intervening in secular politics on American soil. This activity coincided with the election campaign of John F. Kennedy, soon to become the first Catholic president of the United States. In Puerto Rico the priests threatened to excommunicate those who voted in favor of Muñoz Marín's party, because they opposed his modernizing neo-Malthusian political ideology. In *Muñoz Marín vs. the Bishops* (1998), the historian Maria Mercedes Alonso explains that when the Christian Action Party lost the elections, the result tarnished the prestige of the Catholic Church in Puerto Rican society. It also demonstrated a shift in Puerto Rican society, where a constitutional secularism would shortly come to dominate unchallenged. The proindependence party adopted the Christian Action Party's position and strongly opposed modernity and mainland "decadence" (birth control, pornography, and so on). Their leaders would charge that Muñoz Marín's assault on the traditional Puerto Rican family took the form not only of birth control measures but also mass migration of Puerto Ricans to the U.S. mainland. The proindependence faction would interpret the mainland passage—the migration of thousands of Puerto Ricans to New York City—as a state strategy designed to render barren the island as a site where the Puerto Rican nation-state could grow.

Comprising sons and daughters of an overpopulated island, these mainland Puerto Rican communities have decided to bring home not only hybrid culture but also porn and condoms—a uniquely effective way to contain the demographic explosion. Thus Condom World takes the form of a materialized forbidden fantasy inside an insular community that continues to disavow its extreme population growth. As such, Condom World and its products are imagined as an American malaise that is spreading on the island a decadent culture found only on the mainland. For those antiporn segments of the population, assimilation to American modernity means the pornification of Puerto Rican culture.

*Porn Migration: Boricua Porn and Nuyorican Poetry*

Pornography is, for me, a medium for understanding the movement of crossing borders. The day after arriving at college, in 1986, I went straight to the university bookstore and purchased a copy of *Hustler* magazine. My desire for this particular graphic medium started when I visited college during the summer for preregistration week. After I'd registered for classes, I went to the bookstore where I would be buying my textbooks, and there I saw that porn magazines were readily available for anyone's perusal. Shocked, excited, and perturbed, I could not take my eyes off the magazine section where they were displayed. In the novel *When I Was Puerto Rican*, Esmeralda Santiago ponders the guava that she encounters in a supermarket in New Jersey, telling the reader that the fruit represents a longing for her tropical home. If, for Santiago, the guava signifies the tropical island of her childhood, for me the opportunity to buy porn was an extra incentive to move to the mainland. *Hustler* was no guava, but after a preregistration visit to my college campus, I had to return to the mainland to get it.

In *The Birth of Biopolitics* Foucault argues that "migration is an investment; the migrant is an investor"; thus, at the time I believed that I was investing in my erotic future.[13] *Hustler* set me on a path of discovery that culminated in what I thought was a structural impossibility: Rícan porn. Around 1997 I discovered the compilations *Rican Gang Bang* (uncredited, 1997), and *Rican Sizzle Gang Bang 2* (uncredited, 1997), but they were disappointing performances. Soon after, I discovered videos such as *Chico con leche* (Ron Rico, 2002) and other amateur videos with themes that emphasized the Bronx thugs phenomenon, including *Papi and Chulo* (Ron Rico, 2003). The Bronx thugs phenomenon played on the gang affiliation motif, with the fantasy of typical street-gang members having sex with their young recruits in an initiation theme or gang members playing rough with some accidental street victim.

But my favorite porn videos became *Boricua* and *Boricua 2*, different from the gang-bang and the Bronx thug videos, because they showed amateur video of solo performances. These videos, available only via direct order from the supplier, were not produced by established studios such as Falcon, Mustang, or Titan, and they did not have credits. The Boricua videos played on the fantasy of an ordinary young Rícan man jerking off at the end of a working day in his small tenement apartment. The solo genre performed the fantasy of tenement reality, by contrast with the gang-bang genre, whose underlying fantasy is not ordinary life in a public-housing unit but rather the fear of violence that may erupt under certain circumstances. The Boricua videos dispelled the gratuitous signs of ethnic prejudice by getting rid of gang colors, street-wear dress codes, and all references to physical violence. As predecessors to what can be seen today on Xtube, these videos depicted young, nominally straight Rícan men relaxing in what could be their own apartments. As solo appearances, these performances were less showcased than, for example, the hyperstylized Bel Ami 101 solo series (where all the models and settings are perfect by conventional standards). There was something dangerous and incredibly exciting about watching a well-endowed straight Rícan playing with himself in a tenement apartment. Not only was this a sight that I had never seen but it also offered a glimpse into a sexual fantasy. Zabet Patterson's insight that "the central frisson in amateur porn lies in its articulation of a certain proximity to the life of the spectator" rings true in the case of borderland porn production.[14]

Circulated via mail in VHS tapes, these videos captured for viewers the erotic dimension of Rícan masculinity. More important, these X-rated gems provided an account of the life of mainland male Rícans that somehow managed to make visible that which had remained out of sight on the Caribbean island. There were no Latino or Puerto Rican male performers in the magazines that were part of the porn archives of our youth. By contrast, these videos focused on ordinary Rícans as "porn stars" of some sort; they showed "'real bodies' experiencing 'real pleasure,'" as Patterson puts it.[15] As performance pieces these videos challenged what could and could not be represented in adult media.

The stars of these tapes were not your typical Nuyorican performers who had become notorious in the 1970s. Poetry was not their forte. Unlike the Nuyorican poets—whose performances testified to the trials and tribulations of the Puerto Rican community in New York City—these videos were testimonials to a Porno Rícan male subjectivity in the borderland. Poetry and theater had been this community's preferred medium of literary expression. During the 1960s and 1970s, Nuyorican poetry had become an intellectual and cultural movement for those of Puerto Rican descent who lived in New York City. These street poets had been successful in transforming the meaning of *Nuyorican* from an insult into a term signifying a new urban poetic form. However, by the 1990s the literary impact of this poetic enterprise had waned, and we witnessed the rise of the new Latina coming-of-age novel. At the same time, technological innovations made available to many the capacity to chronicle their lives in visual form. Even as Nuyorican poetry was the established medium of contestation that used the language of the Latino subject's social emasculation, these videos were chronicling new modes of being Rícan by providing testimonies of a male eroticism thriving in barrio life.

Nuyorican poetry made an impact in the literary world by mobilizing new symbols of ethnic masculine identity in the borderland, combining criticism of the Puerto Rican migrant with a critique of the effects of U.S. imperialism on urban communities of color. For example, the title poem of Miguel Algarín's *Mongo Affair* (1978) depicts the flaccid (*mongo*) cock of the Rícan migrant in the diaspora:

mongo means bloodless
mongo means soft
mongo cannot penetrate.[16]

This image of impotence is likewise found in Pedro Pietri's *Puerto Rican Obituary* (1973), where the theme of docility, understood in terms of flaccidity, once again shows its deflated, ugly head. Puerto Rican nationalist politics have interpreted the lack of revolutionary spirit against U.S. imperialism as docility and therefore as assuming a passive role due to impotence (flaccidity). In this context, Nuyorican poets were reactionary poets. Nationalist at heart, they were unable to appreciate the impact of life in the mainland as transformative for Puerto Rican communities.

For example, Nuyorican poets seemed unaware that mongo was a reaction to the emergence of the female breadwinner as a result of changes in workers' employment. American companies preferred to hire women over men because they considered women more reliable employees who would work for less money. Mainland Puerto Rican men, no longer able to find jobs, contended that the unemployment benefits they received made them impotent. Algarín asserts as much in *Mongo Affair*:

that even the fucking a man does
on a government bought mattress
draws the blood from his cock, cockless, *sin espina dorsal*, mongo that's it!
a welfare fuck is a mongo affair![17]

The concept of a male homemaker was simply abhorred as an indication of flaccidity or failed masculinity. These canonical texts drew the parameters of Puerto Rican discourse on the mainland, establishing a straight connection between political and sexual impotence, and their condition as colonial subjects. For these poets, it seemed inconceivable that the perceived impotence was the manifestation of a truncated machismo, or the drastically shortened power of a long tradition of patriarchy.

Given this Nuyorican context, I marveled at the image of a "Rícan porn cock" on the screen as testimony that there was a loophole in the morality claims regarding male borderland impotence. On display was the proof of a massive erection and the corroborative image that a welfare cock could produce a "vibrant gush of Rícan jizz." If not all were mongos, there was still hope on the mainland. As a beacon of hope, the fully erected Rícan porn cock became emblematic of a breakthrough in colonial pessimism. They were no

longer mongos. Mongos were a political myth. Uncut and well fed, those amateur performers made my purchase of those VHS tapes the best investment
I could make in the creation of a *trash archive*, that is, a Rícan porn archive in
the American borderlands. At its heart, this trash archive emphasizes the political and artistic innovations of a visible and virile Porno Rícan borderland
subject.[18] As Horacio N. Roque Ramírez explains, these newly formed archives
of desire, which intersect multiple and excluding spaces, amount to critical
acts of documentation "for marginalized communities constantly involved in
struggles for visibility, political identity, and space."[19]

I see these Porno Rícans' performance as providing an erotic pleasure that
specifically transgresses the taboo of a mongo subject.[20] By representing the
inconceivable, a Porno Rícan, these videos transgressed both the island's ban
on porn and the mainland Nuyorican viewpoint of a colonially depleted Rícan
subject. An archive of this sort substantiates Rodrigo Lazo's claim that Lati-
nos "are still moving . . . into migrant archives that will ultimately displace the
subjectivity that sustains the project."[21] Of course, even when displacement
of a national and mongo identity by a borderland Rícan identity is a welcomed
crossing, there is always the danger of getting trapped in the world of "pornotopia."[22] For Linda Williams, pornotopia is the name for that state of mind
where the performative reality created by media such as porn is confused with
everyday reality. Yet, at the same time, we can argue that the erection of a welfare cock in a Rícan tenement represents a bold departure from the condition
of hopelessness and misery that dominated the discourse of Nuyorican poetic
subjectivity during most of the 1970s and 1980s.[23] As an alternative to the
Nuyorican mongotopia of the previous decades, the Rícan pornotopia rises to
the occasion of imagining an affirmative futurity. If, as the critic Jorge Duany
argues, Puerto Ricans are a "nation on the move," then the raw material that
documents this tale of crossing borders must also account for the creation of
new forms of archiving movement.[24] The Porno Rícan archive represents one
innovative way of telling the tale of border movement.

## The Future Is Porno Rícan

In what is considered a classic text of Latino criticism, Ilán Stavans argues
that the Latin phallus is a "tyrannical" phallus: "The phallus remains an all-
consuming image for Hispanic society, whether as the absent, animating
presence in the *repressive* culture of machismo or the furtive purpose of the *repressed* culture of homosexuality."[25] Recently, he suggests, we have witnessed
an opening in the midst of this tyranny with the writing of Reinaldo Arenas,
José Donoso, Severo Sarduy, and others who have challenged the totalitarian
silence that has dominated eroticism in the Spanish Americas. But they had to

migrate in order to do so. Manuel Puig and Arenas are examples of persecuted writers who had to migrate from their homeland in order to be able to speak without fear about their sexuality. Puig had to migrate from a dictatorship-run Argentina, and Arenas dictated his autobiography while living in New York City. They point to migration as key to the production of those foundational texts that constituted the first generation of sexual memoirs coming from the Spanish Americas. This first generation wrote outside the nation. They exceeded the parameters of national signification and were able to articulate in writing a cultural critique of the tyrannical phallus. Writing from exile, they started a process of democratizing the phallus by contesting its monopoly of meaning.

Puerto Rican porn, prosecuted rather than exactly persecuted, could flourish only on the mainland and thus needed to be taken across the Atlantic to the island. I see in Boricua porn an opening in the domain of Nuyorican flaccidity. What we might call, after Stavans, the borderland phallus challenges the singular meaning that had been operating until then on the mainland. This is an opening that is at once on scene and off island.[26] The parameters of Boricua porn exceeded not only the limits drawn by a long history of obscenity laws on the island but also the models of borderland representation used by the founding writers of a mainland Puerto Rican community. Nuyorican poetry, ruled by the mystique of a lost nationalist "tyrannical phallus," misconstrued this opening. Bound to a master-slave dialectic, Nuyorican poetry was able to interpret the Nuyorican phallus only as signifying lack. By contrast, Boricua porn shows us that there is an impetus for constructing democratic spaces. Not exactly a beacon of freedom, nor a typical celebration of a macho phallus, Boricua porn showed on scene that which until now seemed to exceed Puerto Rican representations of sexuality. Porno Rícan gay male sexuality attained visibility at the borders of empire. There, in the on-scene spectacles of the borderlands, Puerto Rícan subjectivity traveled away from the fictional boundaries of its insular condition. Boricua porn showed us that migration is an investment in an erotic future and that it can no longer remain nameless. Moving beyond the barren quality of past self-understandings, the future looks bold, endowed, and (why not?) Porno Rícan.

## Notes

1. "TLA Gay," accessed March 12, 2014, http://www.tlavideo.com/gay-adult/3.
2. Foucault, The Archaeology of Knowledge, 129.
3. Foucault, The Archaeology of Knowledge, 130.
4. Champagne, "Stop Reading Films!"
5. Anzaldúa, Borderlands/La Frontera, i.

6. In "Pornography and 'the Popular' in Post-revolutionary Mexico," the critic Claire F. Fox describes the complicated relation between the Mexican state and the production of pornography in the Mexican context. Her historical analysis shows the shortcomings of the porn industry even in a country such as Mexico, which has the largest film industry in Spanish America. Because of this long-lasting cinematic tradition and its proximity to California, Mexican cinema has always maintained itself at the vanguard of Latin American cinema; only Brazil rivals its levels of cinematic innovation (146).

7. "Condom World Causing Outrage in Puerto Rico," *Orlando Sentinel*, July 11, 1999, http://articles.orlandosentinel.com/1999-07-11/news/9907090411_1_puerto-rico-condom-mayaguez.

8. In *Colonialism, Catholicism, and Contraception*, the Puerto Rican historian Annette B. Ramírez de Arellano explains that at every turn Puerto Rican women's "emotional superactivity" sabotaged these attempts to control population growth.

9. Ramírez de Arellano explains the legal complexity that made impossible U.S. involvement in Puerto Rican society for the purposes of birth control measures. Her study also depicts the many failures of local initiatives in their attempts to tackle population growth. See Ramírez de Arellano, *Colonialism, Catholicism, and Contraception*.

10. On the literary and political history of the mainland passage, see Soto-Crespo, *Mainland Passage*.

11. Briggs, *Reproducing Empire*, 19.

12. Findlay, *Imposing Decency*, 10.

13. Foucault, *Birth of Biopolitics*, 230.

14. Patterson, "Going On-line," 111.

15. Patterson, "Going On-line," 116.

16. Algarín, *Mongo Affair*, 86.

17. Algarín, *Mongo Affair*, 86.

18. I make use here of the category of trash archives as a collection of what Scott McCracken calls "despised forms," because they articulate that which is forbidden to be said and seen by the rules of national and identity discursive formation. See McCracken, *Pulp*, 1. I also follow Pierre Bourdieu's assessment of "aesthetic judgment" in his work *Distinction*, where he explains aesthetic judgment as neither natural nor disinterested but as a disguised method of class and national differentiation. See Bourdieu, *Distinction*, 485–500. On trash aesthetics, see Cartmell et al., *Trash Aesthetics*; and Olster, *The Trash Phenomenon*.

19. Roque Ramírez, "A Living Archive of Desire," 116.

20. My reading of the Nuyorican mongo subject and the Porno Rícan subject is indebted to Linda Williams's discussion of the eroticism of the racial border. See L. Williams, "Skin Flicks on the Racial Border," 299. In my account, however, the border is not racial but rather lies between national and borderland frameworks for understanding Puerto Rican identity.

21. Lazo, "Migrant Archives," 37.

22. L. Williams, "Skin Flicks on the Racial Border," 300. The term *pornotopia* first appeared in Marcus, *The Other Victorians* (2009), 266–86.

23. I am refraining here from going as far as Sandra Quinn does in her analysis of the Puerto Rican porn video *The Last of the Boricuas* (directed by Lamonte, 1994); she argues that porn has "the power to subvert the dominant order." I don't claim an inherent power

in porn for subverting the dominant order, but rather an interesting historical junction where porn happens to be produced at the right place and at the right time to enable a crucial shift in the matrix of Rícan visibility. Quinn, "The Last of the Boricuas," 221.

24. Duany, *The Puerto Rican Nation on the Move*, 2.

25. Stavans, "The Latin Phallus," 238.

26. *On/scene* is a term developed by the porn studies founder Linda Williams as a way to mark "both the controversy and scandal of the increasingly public representation of diverse forms of sexuality *and* the fact that they have become increasingly available to the public at large." See Williams, "Porn Studies," 9.

# 16

Butts, *Bundas*, Bottoms, Ends: Tracing the
Legacy of the *Pornochanchada* in A b . . . *profunda*

*Melissa Schindler*

All of the films that we made were "porno" something or another. Everything was
"porno." . . . It was a way for the advertising to pre-determine the viewing public,
because calling it "porno" meant the elites wouldn't go.
—Claudio Cunha, quoted in Nuno Cesar Abreu, *Boca do Lixo*

In 1984 Álvaro de Moya made a feature-length hard-core parody of Gerard
Damiano's *Deep Throat* (1972) under the pseudonym of Gerardo Dominó. The
film, entitled A b . . . *profunda* (Deep ass), playfully suggests that the location
of the Brazilian woman's clitoris is not in her throat but instead "na bunda!
. . . no ponto . . . no rabo . . . no cu!" ("in the ass! . . . the bum . . . the tail . . .
the asshole!").[1] A b . . . *profunda* often seems as if it's a direct copy of its U.S.
inspiration, frequently translating the latter's English dialogue directly into
Portuguese and restaging many of its scenes, down to specific acts of cunnilingus and particular cum shots. Given A b . . . *profunda*'s fidelity to *Deep Throat*
in both structure and dialogue, we might characterize Moya's film as an unabashed copy: an attempt to capitalize on its progenitor's success, or, in a
more generous reading, as a testament to *Deep Throat*'s pivotal role in the history of film pornography.

Yet this hard-core spoof hardly pays homage to *Deep Throat* and Damiano;
to say that A b . . . *profunda* simply parodies *Deep Throat* does not suffice. Despite the numerous similarities it shares with *Deep Throat*, A b . . . *profunda*, in
fact, engages far more with a forgotten genre of Brazilian film from the 1970s
that is rarely sexually explicit, except in name: the *pornochanchada*. And as the
film title's clever ellipses make evident—A b(unda) profunda—the clearest clue
to this lineage also happens to be A b . . . *profunda*'s most visible metaphor: the
butt. The figure of the ass encapsulates the film's incisive parody. The campy
humor so often characteristic of parody is perhaps the most clearly defined
feature of the pornochanchada, second only to the genre's association with
the "bad taste" of the masses. Therefore, the ass in A b . . . *profunda* creates

both a literal and a figurative link with the aesthetic sensibilities of the popular classes.

Why privilege the ass, and how is this link not simply an offensive stereotype? After all, the ass is quite often identified as a part of the human body that produces trash—waste material that we are meant to remove as quickly as possible. It is the literal end of the digestion process. Figuratively, the ass symbolizes society's excrement: the trashiest, seediest, most obscene sections of the population. For A b . . . profunda, then, to herald the ass as the site of pleasure par excellence is to transform the ass into a place that is both productive and creative, highlighting it as the origin of a valuable commodity. Had Moya simply wanted to copy Deep Throat, he would have followed its example by focusing on the "deep" orifice most associated with consumption. Instead, he redeems the rump. And as he encourages us to find value in the ass, so too does he reveal the inherent value of those elements of social life so often written off as trashy.

Steeped in artistic traditions that date to the beginning of Brazilian film history, A b . . . profunda employs what I am calling an ass-thetic, or an artistic approach meant to disrupt the social order and decompose notions of class, national, and gender difference.[2] The film neither celebrates nor demands that we tolerate waste; such gestures would deny the waste within every one of us. The irony of A b . . . profunda's ass-thetic lies in the fact that it is an ethos that uses confusion to make its message explicit. In deconstructing social hierarchies, it eliminates divisions—literally mixing us up with one another. Yet even as A b . . . profunda is marked by confusion, it is also rather explicit—and not because it contains images of sex. Instead, it is explicit because it makes clear and evident the truth of social, rather than sexual, relations. A b . . . profunda is "pornographic" but not because it's pornography (in other words, not because it depicts sex acts).

Here it's important to note the dual meanings of to make explicit with respect to hard-core pornography: that is, "to make visible" and "to make clear and obvious." According to Linda Williams, Deep Throat's "frenzies" of hypervisual and explicit sex attempt "to perceive the different 'truth' of women's pleasure."[3] The film glorifies the money shot as the signifier of all pleasure. Deep Throat purposefully depicts explicit (visible) sexual relations and is, in turn, inadvertently explicit (clear) about gender and power relations. Conversely, through employment of the ass-thetic, A b . . . profunda actually subordinates the depiction of explicit (visible) sex to the communication of its explicit (clear) message about social relations: the message that so-called popular tastes and practices consistently cross lines of class, gender, and nationality. More taboo than its vivid sex scenes is how the film repeatedly diverts our attention from the sex taking place on-screen to the actors performing it (and not because those individuals are remarkably well endowed or extraordinarily beautiful). In truth, even if A b . . . profunda contained absolutely no explicit sex scenes, the elites still wouldn't go because in more than one way the film claims that they share the tastes of "the masses." So it's the film's privileging of the second definition of to make explicit that qualifies the film as pornographic.

The proof of this alternative understanding of pornographic lies in tracing the film's connection to artistic, historical, and cultural influences that do not portray explicit sex.[4] Those influences converge in A b . . . profunda's assthetic. In addition to Deep Throat, I include the following on the list of A b . . . profunda's progenitors: the pornochanchada; a decades-old artistic tradition of cultural cannibalism; the historical relationship between the Brazilian film industry and those of other countries, most notably the United States and Italy; and, finally, the Brazilian cultural and political history of the 1960s and 1970s, during which time the censoring arm of the national military regime exiled many of the country's artists. Several scenes from A b . . . profunda show how its inherited ass-thetic destabilizes and confuses existing social hierarchies. The film's focus on sexual desires — especially on so-called tacky, abnormal, or trashy fetishes — exposes high culture's habitual repression of its own trashy (and otherwise unsexual) inclinations. In short, the film reminds us that we are, all of us, burdened with asses (some of us liberated by them), and in so doing, it points out just how ludicrous is the pretense otherwise.

Paving the Way to A B . . . Profunda:
Cultural Cannibalism and the Pornochanchada

If we are to understand how A b . . . profunda owes more to genres, styles, and forms of cultural production that are not sexually explicit than to the sex-explicit film it parodies directly, then we need to begin by examining those genres and styles in greater depth. As I mentioned, rather than being marked by an aesthetic of graphic sexuality, the film instead expresses an ass-thetic, which strives to take apart social hierarchies through debauchery, parody, play, and seediness. For those familiar with recent Brazilian intellectual history, this ass-thetic must seem to resemble the cannibalist aesthetic developed by Brazilian writers and filmmakers throughout the twentieth century. Within the history of cultural cannibalism, two specific moments are of note: one in the 1920s and one in the 1960s. In the 1920s, a modernist writer and critic, Oswald de Andrade, fronted a movement that redefined the image of the indigenous man into an anthropophagus — a cannibal. In his "Manifesto antropôfago" (Cannibal manifesto), Andrade reappropriates the colonial depiction of indigenous Brazilians as cannibals on behalf of Brazilian art. Following Haroldo de Campos, a literary critic and member of the concrete poetry movement of the 1950s and 1960s, the indigenous man who had been cast as a *noble* savage became a *bad* savage in Andrade's conception: one who threatened the enlightened European.[5]

For Andrade, the anthropophagus symbolized the essence of Brazil and Brazilian art, which incorporated (*cannibalized*) the work of non-Brazilians. Returning again to Campos's interpretation of Andrade, the figurative work of cannibalism does not imitate; it digests an archive of European cultural images. Just as we cannot understand histories of Europeans without considering how the anthropophagus preserved and mutated them via ingestion, we also cannot understand European literature without evaluating its presence in the stomachs of Brazilian or Latin American literature. The same is true for Europeans. In other words, Andrade deconstructs the imperialist and racist notion that Europe, Europeans, and European literature are more enlightened than Brazil, Brazilians, and Brazilian literature. But even more than that, he claims that European literature would not exist without its gestational period in the figurative stomachs of the Brazilian cannibal. The hallmarks of Enlightenment thought, once used to distinguish between colonizer and colonized, become the intellectual property of the colony in the "Manifesto Antropôfago." Andrade writes, "I asked a man to define Right. He told me it was the guarantee of the exercise of possibility. This man was named Galli Mathias. I ate him."[6] This aesthetic negates the possibility of an individuated self. We are composed of those whom we have consumed.

The second significant moment in the development of an aesthetic of cultural cannibalism happened in the 1960s, when symbolic anthropophagy was reborn through *tropicália*, concrete poetry, and *cinema novo*, as each of these movements experimented with mimicry, recombination, and hybridity.[7] Campos calls the aesthetic of concrete poetry one of "devoration." It is the taking apart and reassembling of another entity, an act that catalyzes the recomposition of the self. In both Andrade's description of a cannibalist aesthetic and that of Campos's aesthetic of devoration, we see how consumption (ingestion, devouring) constitutes a *productive* process. Rather than being an act of passive assimilation, consumption is instead an act of recombination. Certainly, for the way that it parodies *Deep Throat* and unapologetically plagiarizes a number of cinematic genres that preceded it, *A b . . . profunda* uses an ass-thetic that undoubtedly is part of the cannibalistic tradition elaborated by Andrade and Campos.

In fact, the resemblance between *A b . . . profunda*'s ass-thetic and the reappropriation of the folklore about indigenous Brazilian cannibalism extends to the work of the legendary Brazilian film director, critic, and scholar Glauber Rocha. In a now-famous essay entitled "An Aesthetic of Hunger," Rocha posits 1960s cinema novo as a genre whose "hunger" is a "violent" and tragically "original" approach to neocolonization.[8] According to Rocha, the films that were made during this time depicted truths about life in Brazil, Latin America, and other countries generally under neocolonial rule. In contradistinction to North American and European films in which characters were generally sated and luxuriating in life's riches, cinema novo made visible Brazilians' hunger. Yet this aesthetic is not one of passivity or entirely victimized hunger; it is rather, as Rocha says, an "aesthetic of violence." Here Rocha redefines the colonizer's image of Latin America as a passive consumer of European art into one in which the region is active. Importantly, however, the action of the hungry is not *reactionary*, a depiction that too closely resembles colonial views of indigenous peoples; according to Rocha, the "violence [of the Latin American] is not his primitivism." The aesthetic of cinema novo rests on a violence born of the stomach, not "of hatred just as it is not bound to the old colonizing humanism."[9]

The ass-thetic I am describing, so evident in films like *A b . . . profunda*, might seem to be a continuation of the modernist discourse of cultural cannibalism begun by Andrade in the 1920s. And in many ways, the two are linked, as *A b . . . profunda*'s use of parody constitutes an inherent, if not explicit, embrace of mixture and hybridity. That said, *A b . . . profunda* much more overtly characterizes itself as lowbrow than did, say, the films of Glauber Rocha, through its use of crass humor and tactless—or artless—displays of sexual acts. The combination of humor and sex actually aligns the film more closely with the pornochanchada, a film genre of the 1970s that intellectuals, musicians, and filmmakers of the 1960s (including many who took part in concrete poetry, tropicália, and cinema novo) either ignored or despised. For that reason, it's useful to reflect on how this ass-thetic, although indebted to theories of cultural cannibalism to some degree, actually differs from them. Or perhaps, more important, it's worthwhile to think about how redefining our notion of the pornographic reveals a link between the avant-garde and the lowbrow.

Both Rocha's aesthetic of hunger and the ass-thetic I propose characterize film as an ingestive and creative process whose products cannot sustain notions of distinction, distinctiveness, and individuality. But let me belabor the point: *A b . . . profunda* unabashedly locates itself in the ass, not the stomach. According to Rocha, cinema novo shoved the truth of Brazil's hunger in the faces of Europeans and Americans, but it also, and with equal importance, made Brazilian hunger known to Brazilians themselves. "The Brazilian does not eat," Rocha writes, "but he is ashamed to say so."[10] Thus "An Aesthetic of Hunger" is as much an attempt to enlighten Brazilian masses as it is a declaration meant to disabuse Europeans of the impression of Latin American life as "strange tropical surrealism." Herein lies the difference between an aesthetic of hunger and an ass-thetic. Rocha sets out to "make the public aware of its own misery"—to awaken it—but *A b . . . profunda*, like the pornochanchada, evidences the public's awareness of its own degradation, poor taste, and offensiveness.[11] Not only that, the film depicts people happily indulging their bad tastes. In positing the ass as a site of the production of pleasure, then, a film like *A b . . . profunda* demonstrates how pornographic material is not society's excrement, leftovers, or waste. It is not the place where "good" people refuse to go, but instead is the place where everyone, in fact, is.

The cannibalist aesthetic, the aesthetic of devoration, the aesthetic of hunger: all three of these theoretical interventions rely on a taking back of the figure of the cannibal. He who was once slandered by European histories—denounced for his supposedly barbaric practices (literally his "bad taste")—is now celebrated. While it's true that this aesthetic tradition lauds anthropophagy as productive, it nevertheless maintains the distinctiveness of the cannibal. In contrast, *A b . . . profunda*'s ass-thetic carries on the tradition of locating value in formerly shameful habits, but it does not single out the individuals who espouse those habits—not even to celebrate such individuals. Instead, it implements the consuming cannibalist gesture with the goal of implicating an entire field of cultural production in shared distastefulness. No one escapes. The film does not posit an audience made of the masses needing to be enlightened to their own hunger, but rather an audience quite aware and unapologetic of its desires. The film mocks the elitist who tries to distinguish his tastes from the shameful desires (hunger) of the cannibal by making the former inseparable from everyone else.

Despite the conceptual similarities that connect *A b . . . profunda*'s ass-thetic with the twentieth-century tradition of cultural cannibalism, it's unlikely that the artists and intelligentsia backing the latter would have approved of the connection. After all, the film explicitly identifies itself with the pornochanchada, a forgotten but extremely popular and successful film genre of the 1970s, and one that many of the cinema novistas publicly disdained. Rocha himself denounced the pornochanchada as "audiovisual prostitution," citing as justification the genre's use of actors' scantily clad bodies to make a profit.[12] The film critic Jean-Claude Bernadet is less condemnatory of explicit sex, but no less so of the pornochanchada, whose "real failure . . . is not the fact of its being porn, but the fact that it's hardly porn at all. More preferable to any such approaches, to these superficial methods [like the pornochanchada], is simply to show masculine and feminine organs doing what they are able to do."[13] That critics locate the pornochanchada somewhere between banality and prostitution is a sign of its perplexing affect, just as it is a reason for articulating the genre's distinctive ass-thetic.

Even if exploitation and banality were unique to pornochanchadas—which, of course, they aren't—that would not mean that those who produced the films did not employ the same devouring aesthetic that Rocha and Berna-det see as so promising in the work of cinema novo. As I will explain, porno-chanchadas explicitly named *chanchadas* as their predecessors, and chanchadas themselves were steeped in the tradition of carnival. Just as carnival inverts hierarchies and subsequently subverts power derived from them, so too does devoration methodically undermine the power of the enlightened self. In chanchada films, the music, dancing, parades, and general spectacle of car-nival feed directly into (if not inspire) the visual aesthetic of the films. Porno-chanchadas emerge from a compilation of aesthetic approaches; they also preserve different elements via consumption. But what made pornochancha-das distinctive was that they redistributed power, both historically and figura-tively, so that suddenly "everyday" people had access to the film camera—not just to a seat in the theater. The pornochanchada ass-thetic, inherited by films like A b . . . *profunda*, is marked by its explicit identification with the tastes of the masses.

Given the pornochanchada's heavy influence on A b . . . *profunda*, and par-ticularly since high culture and the avant-garde of the 1960s so fervently re-nounced any relationship with it (resulting in a relative dearth of publications about it), the genre bears some explication here. The term *pornochanchada* first came into use in Brazil in 1973. The term itself is very simply parsed: *porno* refers to "pornography" (or, rather, in Portuguese, *pornografia*), and *chanchada* to a prior Brazilian film genre. According to both Stephanie Dennison and Randal Johnson, chanchadas were musical comedies of the 1930s, 1940s, and 1950s that took their inspiration from Italian films of the same name, as well as from Hollywood musicals screened in Brazil during that period. Chan-chadas were quite popular among the film-going public, and they repeated many quotidian themes with which their mass audiences seemed to iden-tify. Likewise, pornochanchadas were thought to contain the same types of themes and tropes as chanchadas—for example, campy or lowbrow humor (slapstick), music and musical numbers, chase scenes, identity confusion, an episodic structure, and a set of stock characters—with the only difference being that pornochanchadas promoted themselves as erotic films. Their story lines revolved around sex: how to get it and how to have a lot more of it.[14] Yet pornochanchadas contained barely any sex or nudity. By box-office standards, pornochanchadas were enormously popular. Aside from a brief period known as the Bela Epoca (1908–11), the era of the pornochanchada, along with por-nography made during the 1980s, constitutes the most successful period of Brazilian cinema in terms of both the number of films made in Brazil and the number of tickets sold.[15]

That said, Bernadet's aforementioned allusion to the "failure" of the pornochanchada is not uncharacteristic of the genre's critical reception. For a number of reasons, voices representing various political and cultural camps denounced pornochanchadas. As Nuno Cesar Abreu points out, the term was pejorative from its very inception. Not only did it allude to the campy humor and mass appeal associated with the chanchada but it also bore the "stigma" of eroticism. This type of film was "marked by its appeal to 'popular tastes.'"[16] The connection to quotidian audiences and themes was further strengthened by the fact that a large percentage of pornochanchadas were made in an area of São Paulo known as Boca do Lixo (literally, "mouth of trash"). Generally, the directors, producers, and actors of the films lived, partied, and worked in this neighborhood. Sometimes referred to as Brazil's Hollywood, Boca played host to a variety of inhabitants who participated in the creation of the films, along with actors and filmmakers. Marcel de Almeida Freitas argues that what makes the pornochanchada a true public genre is less that it *depicted* everyday people and more that it was made and consumed by such people.[17] The films were produced rapidly and at low cost and, as a result, critics called them "mal realizados" (poorly made).[18]

In one sense, Boca begat the pornochanchada. Importantly, however, this type of film emerged in tandem with what many consider the most oppressive military regime in Brazilian history. Pornochanchadas, writes José Avellar, "were born [in the moment when the censor was born], they were reared and educated there, and they learned to speak the same language."[19] In 1969, five years after a military coup, the operative government put laws into place that created a national censor. But the relationship between the film industry and the government dates back to the 1920s, when producers appealed to the government for help in creating some space in the national market for national films. Foreign competition, particularly from the United States, threatened to crowd out Brazilian films.[20] This didn't just mean that U.S. films did better in the box office. Rather, as there was no internal production of the equipment necessary for filmmaking, it was cheaper to import ready-made foreign films than to buy products necessary for making one of your own.

During the decades that led up to the military dictatorship, the existing governments experimented with the creation of various protective measures, ranging from the institution of import taxes to the creation of national art programs (in radio, film, and, later, television) to the establishment of O Ministério da Educação e Cultura (the Ministry of Education and Culture, MEC). This organization was responsible for institutionalizing short government-sponsored newsreels and promotional videos that were exhibited before every feature-length film. Such newsreels were made internally and thereby supported the Brazilian industry. But of course distributors and exhibitors were also a part of that industry, and so the business interests of one set of citizens conflicted with those of another. Taxed imports hurt distributors even as they were meant to protect artists and producers. In 1969 the MEC formed Embrafilme, or Empresa Brasileira do Filme Nacional (Brazilian National Film Company), which funded film production. Embrafilme would later be associated not only with the stringent censorship of the 1970s but also with pornochanchadas.

The pairing of Embrafilme and pornochanchadas is odd for complicated reasons that point to the challenges of defining the pornochanchada genre. For the most part, Embrafilme did not fund "actual" pornochanchadas—that is, the ones coming out of Boca between 1969 and 1978. The producers of the paulista films (i.e., from São Paulo, specifically Boca) generally procured their own financing. Embrafilme and Boca coexisted somewhat peacefully until 1975, when the former began to distribute films, putting itself in competition with the independent producers and distributors of the latter. So on the one hand, Boca never really aligned itself with Embrafilme. On the other hand, it existed—or, rather, thrived—under heavy censorship at the same time that Embrafilme did.[21] What's more, both of these production centers owed much of their success to another law instituted in 1969, which required movie houses to screen a certain percentage of national films every month.[22] The cinemas had to meet the quota, which meant that someone had to make movies that could be shown. That these films made it through the censor, itself a manifestation of the oppressive tactics of the military regime, marked them as tainted and despised according to the silenced cultural avant-garde.

The avant-garde and intellectual elite had significant cause for such antipathy. As in many other places in the world, the 1960s in Brazil saw the rapid growth of cultural and artistic revolutions. As I mentioned, cinema novo, tropicália, and concrete poetry were three avant-garde impulses that blossomed in the 1960s. Each of these movements was invested in the structural rearrangement and recombination of existing styles.[23] Often, participants of these movements also worked as university professors or wrote for scholarly publications. The military government of the late 1960s quashed this cultural and artistic work, which was aggressively political and invested in mobilizing the public to revolt.[24]

The logic behind denouncing the pornochanchadas is perhaps as follows: if they and the films produced by Embrafilme made it past the censors, the content of such films must have somehow pleased or placated the officials. Whereas many of the revolutionary artists of the 1960s had to flee the country in order to escape harassment from the military regime, the makers of pornochanchadas meanwhile participated in a burgeoning and successful national film industry—something to which filmmakers had aspired for decades. If tropicália and cinema novo had to be stamped out because they promoted transgressive politics, what could possibly be transgressive about the art that survived? Hence Bernadet's condemnation of the genre: the pornochancha-da's only revolutionary promise lay in its potential to say something graphic about sex. But it never did that. Worse yet, many critics argue, pornochancha-das were unabashedly racist, sexist, homophobic, intellectually and artisti-cally vapid, full of stupid and tacky humor, cheap, and poorly made.

What to do with a genre, then, that is not graphic enough to be porn but is condemned for many of the same reasons as porn? If there's virtually no nudity or sex acts, why label it "pornographic" or associate it with porn? It is, in fact, the ass-thetic of pornochanchadas that renders them pornographic. They make no attempt to conceal their trashy themes, bad acting, poorly writ-ten scripts, and shameless plagiarism. According to Avellar, these films oper-ate under an "aesthetic of the Censor," which means that they molded them-selves into products that both met the censor's restrictions and opposed its presence.[25] For Avellar, that these films were "mal acabados" (badly made) manifested the widespread malaise and disenchantment experienced by a people subjugated to oppressive rule. He neither refutes the notion that pornochanchadas are trashy nor offers new interpretations of films that are historically disregarded for being poorly executed. He instead prefers to his-toricize that poor quality as a symptom of oppression.

But in what is ultimately a confirmation of an elitist view of popular cul-ture, Avellar ignores two very important aspects of the genre's history. First, pornochanchadas were not "born" with censorship in 1969; they employ decades-old narrative and cinematic tropes, such as those used by Brazilian and Italian chanchadas, musicals, stock characters, and parody. More impor-tant, he implies that the aesthetic and the affect of pornochanchadas are in-voluntary on the part of the artist and the consumer. Both, in his description, are passive agents who resign themselves to producing and paying for non-sense because censorial chains permit them nothing more.

The military regime was undoubtedly oppressive, and pornochanchadas certainly evoke a trashy aesthetic that often renders them nonsensical, but the senseless logic of that aesthetic is not simply a symptom by which we can measure the hopelessness and apathy of Brazilian society. Avellar seems to say that pornochanchadas signaled a resignation on the part of the people. He suggests that as the government oppressed the people and attempted to pro-mote, internally, the image of a homogeneous, healthy, happy, and productive nation, viewers of pornochanchadas meanwhile insisted on watching trashy movies. By going to bad movies that were themselves characterized by a lack of productivity, spectators were, in fact, behaving "badly."[26] Pornochancha-das achieved unprecedented levels of national production and sales.[27] Despite their popularity, however, their legacy is virtually nonexistent, both nationally and internationally.

It seems that the question of the pornochanchada aesthetic is intertwined with the genre's relationship to the label imposed upon it, as well as with its elision from cinema histories. That is, for any number of reasons, calling a film a pornochanchada identifies it as "bad." But pornochanchadas made no attempt to conceal their poor quality. More significantly, an adult public went to see them knowing the films were bad. Avellar accurately depicts a public capable of identifying and analyzing the art it saw; unfortunately, he does that public a disservice by claiming that the messages and aesthetic of the art itself only existed because of and in conversation with the censor. If, initially anyway, the films couldn't have been thought of as bad since they contained little sexually explicit content, and if they weren't illegal, what badness drew audiences in numbers?

Enjoying and supporting pornochanchadas wasn't simply about resisting the government-imposed image of a good and orderly Brazilian society. Rather, it was the fact that their plots didn't make sense; that the costumes and people looked funny; that one could trace the visible seams of the films' production; that they were being made around the corner by people who sometimes didn't know how to make movies; that, paradoxically, they overtly parodied, mimicked, and assimilated every other type of film, including their own—these qualities ultimately meant that pornochanchadas did not allow people to suspend disbelief. People saw themselves in what took place on the screen just as surely as they saw themselves in the actors and directors, who were also their neighbors and peers.

The trashy or bad aesthetic of pornochanchadas is pornographic insomuch as it exposes the collusion between audience and film. Such movies disintegrate the screen, thereby showing us actors and viewers mixed together on both sides. The breakdown of the film screen—where the screen functions as a dividing line between film and audience—signals a similar dissolution of other supposedly distinct entities like Brazilian and American, foreigner and national, high and low culture, high and low class, trash films and the avantgarde, men and women, and so on. Thus, watching a pornochanchada served a realist rather than an escapist function. And the reality confronted in viewing such films existed long before the oppression of censorship and the presence of the military regime.

Due purely to its sexually explicit content, A b . . . profunda cannot be called a pornochanchada. It is, after all, a direct replica of a hard-core pornography film. Despite its almost absurdly obvious similarities with Deep Throat, however, Moya's movie is more pornochanchada than it is pornography. Just as the film makes obvious its place within the legacy of cultural cannibalism—regardless of whether that inclusion is welcome—it also manifests its undeniable connection to the pornochanchada. Like pornochanchadas, A b . . .

*profunda* parodies a successful U.S. blockbuster; it incorporates many of the motifs and themes common to pornochanchadas, and it reiterates their preoccupation with the lives and concerns of the working class.[28] In short, *A b . . . profunda* inherits the pornochanchada's ass-thetic of mixing and its embrace of trashiness and lowbrow humor. In its use of the symbol of the ass, this movie manifests the aforementioned effect of crumbling societal distinctions between audience and film, actor and enacted, low and high culture.[29] Just as it demands that we acknowledge the ass as a place where pleasure, rather than waste, is produced, it also claims that a host of other asses are not simply expendable elements of society. They, too, are productive.

In *A b . . . profunda* the sexually explicit imagery becomes an artistic device for forwarding the film's socially explicit messages. The depiction of sex acts on the screen is an application of the film's larger ass-thetic. In other words, the sex takes a backseat. Sex also took a backseat in pornochanchadas. They have been attached to pornography not because they contain sexual images—they generally do not—but because they employ an ass-thetic that explicitly breaks down distinctions. Indeed, eliminating any and all sexual content in a pornochanchada effectively created a negative space on-screen: a gaping hole, if you will, where everyone knew sex was taking place. We might argue, then, that the gesture that the pornochanchada makes toward its always already elided sex acts has the same effect on the audience as do *A b . . . profunda*'s most explicit sexual numbers. In each, sex is the mechanism for conveying a more explicit truth about social interaction, namely, that so-called bad taste isn't only vulgar (in both senses of the word).

There are moments from *A b . . . profunda* that illustrate the pornographic ass-thetic that it shares with pornochanchadas. In my analysis of each of these moments, I point to the way in which the film cannibalizes major scenes of *Deep Throat* in order to produce new visions of existing cultural hierarchies. If, as Nuno Abreu argues, "parody is a self-deprecating proposal[,] . . . a declaration of inferiority, but one that also has a cannibalist attitude—the 'devoration' of the colonizer whose power cannot be contested," then, in theory, *Deep Throat* would seem to represent the colonizer that *A b . . . profunda* devours.[30] Given the historic hegemony of the U.S. film industry, reading *Deep Throat* as the colonizer rings true—on the surface. Yet *A b . . . profunda* is not only interested in subverting U.S. power. It takes on a host of other analogs for the colonizer, many of which never appear in *Deep Throat*. In the tradition of the pornochanchada, *A b . . . profunda* employs a particular brand of parody motivated by "a radical attitude of appropriation," meaning, in this case, that it is just as likely to devour Brazilian films and themes as it is foreign ones.[31] The film uses the metaphor of the ass to destabilize various iterations of the colonizer. By focusing on the trashy end of uncontested power, A b . . . profunda undermines authority's claim to legitimacy.

## Undermining the Men of A B . . . Profunda

Viewers who are familiar with *Deep Throat* will find it easy to follow A b . . . profunda, even if they do not speak Portuguese. The parody is a faithful mimic, following *Deep Throat*'s structure and even retaining some of its original dialogue. At the suggestion of a friend, Linda (played by Teka Lanza), seeks the help of a medical doctor because she derives no pleasure from sex. After helping Linda solve her problem, the good doctor employs her as a nurse and sends her out on several home visits to "assist" men. Interestingly, while the premise of A b . . . profunda would appear to make the character of Linda the focus of the plot, if we are to look at how A b . . . profunda dethrones a number of figurative analogs for hegemonic power, it actually makes more sense to examine her male counterparts instead. They are indeed the overt focus of the film, though certainly not because they represent the so-called norm. Whether it be Dr. Jung or any one of Linda's four clients, who indulge in a range of quirky sexual practices, the men in this movie quite literally take the cake, as most of the consultation scenes feature food.[32] By exposing the aberrant sexual practices of businessmen, military leaders, and doctors, the film successfully disintegrates hierarchal distinctions at the same time as its parodic arm "dissolve[s] and pulverize[s] the cinematic imagination."[33] What A b . . . profunda visits on its characters through disclosure of their ass- and trash-focused sexual tastes, it simultaneously visits on its spectators through the illustration of such tastes on-screen. Herein lies the crux of the ass-thetic. The film does not condemn the spectator for having bad taste. It lauds the spectator for it by revealing such taste as shared.

Jung, played by Jaime Cardoso, is the first male character named and developed in the film, and from his very first scene, the film undermines any claims to distinction he might base on being a doctor. Initially, Jung turns to U.S. films for the solution to Linda's sexual problem, but finds this won't do the trick. "I've seen this film," he remarks. "It's called *A Garganta profunda. Deep Throat.* Your clitoris is in your throat!" Not only is U.S. pornography unable to teach Linda how to alleviate her sexual frustration, it also cannot train Jung how to help patients like her. When that line of reasoning fails, he muses: "It must be another movie . . . like a Hitchcock film." He turns to Linda and, as though he were beset with the task of solving a Hitchcock-inspired mystery, he puts his hands on his hips and demands, "*Where* is your clitoris?" The frustrated Linda promptly turns over on the bed and buries her face in a pillow, at which point Jung has a revelation. All of a sudden it makes perfect sense to him that her clitoris would be in her butt. "It's the national preference!" he exclaims.[34]

If the explicit, hard-core sex of films like *Deep Throat* intends to make visible a "truth"—to produce irrefutable knowledge—of women's desire and satisfaction, then *A b . . . profunda* anticipates Williams's critique by manifesting the uselessness of that knowledge in the hands of what is arguably the West's truth-seeking poster boy: the medical doctor. Since U.S. film dominated the Brazilian market, to posit all knowledge derived from such films as ultimately useless is to trouble that domination. Instead, Jung echoes Andrade's cannibal, claiming an innate Brazilian knowledge, in this case, of female pleasure. Jung reassures her: "The Brazilian woman is not prepared to receive just anyone. It's just Brazilian men who know how to do it. I am the newest generation of a dark race, and that's what gives me the ability to 'help' women in this way." Here Jung upstages Western medicine by drawing on the authority of a colonial stereotype: the hypersexualized indigenous male. In the tradition of Andrade's cannibal, Jung reappropriates the label "dark race" and advocates the use of "natural" resources, like sexual prowess.

Yet *A b . . . profunda* makes a habit of pulling the rug out from underneath its recently empowered male figures. Jung's attempts to "fool" Linda into sleeping with him are undermined by her apathy and willingness to let him do whatever he wants from the start. The film plays with this notion of coercion as the doctor repeatedly exposes his own plan to bed Linda under the flimsy guise of a medical examination. For instance, having already decided that the clitoris of a Brazilian woman would "of course" be in her butt, Jung echoes the question in *Deep Throat* that initially and purportedly leads Dr. Young to his discovery of Linda Lovelace's erogenous throat. "Tell me," Jung purrs, "when you have sex, where does it feel the best?" Before she can answer, he speaks over Linda, insisting: "It's not in your throat—no, it's in your tush!" When he actually gives her the space to deny his discovery, he again ignores her response and becomes even more excited by her "virgin ass." He confirms his suspicion through an inspection of her rear end, of which the camera has a close-up view. The irony of the "discovery," however, is that neither the close-up of Linda's vulva nor of her anus actually affords the film watcher (and, we must assume, Jung) a view of anything remotely resembling a clitoris. How could he even tell?

In *Deep Throat* Young's obvious lack of expertise seems to heighten his "victory" over Lovelace. Supposedly, the plot depends on his convincing her of his theory even as both she and the audience know his intentions. But Teka Lanza, who plays Linda in *A b . . . profunda*, never acts innocent and naive enough to make such a hoax believable. Instead, Jung looks the fool as he expends a great deal of energy trying to outmaneuver a person who already seems ame-nable to taking his suggestions. So as Linda is the butt of Jung's joke, Jung becomes the butt of Lanza's joke. Everyone involved in the scene, including its audience, gets mocked at one point or another. Likewise, the actors and audi-ence mock one another: the audience laughs at the bad acting, and the actors laugh at the audience for watching a film they knew would be poorly acted. The "bad" acting (whether that means inappropriate, ill fitted, silly, overdone, mimetic, trashy, and so on) constitutes part of the ass-thetic of both porno-chanchadas and A b . . . profunda. Not merely the symptom of low-budget por-nography, the bad acting in this film contributes to its cultural significance. The man meant to epitomize omniscient power is an absolute joke, to the audience and to himself.

If A b . . . profunda's ass-thetic means to destabilize (neo)colonial power, then its iteration of Deep Throat's soda-drinking scene appropriately stages an overt attack on U.S. imperialism. This scene, in which Linda and a few other nurses are meant to fix Alberto Quilomba, who has sworn off sex as a result of his fixation with Coca-Cola, gives new meaning to Randal Johnson's claim that "Brazilian viewers . . . have been weaned on foreign films."[35] Both Qui-lomba and his abode are outfitted in Coca-Cola products, and the whole sce-nario alludes to foreign influences on the national film industry and on other aspects of Brazilian culture. Ultimately, Quilomba is healed not through a curative cum shot or even through anal sex but, as Linda tells us, when he "no longer wants to drink Coca-Cola" and "only wants cachaça." Here drinking cachaça functions as a euphemism for performing cunnilingus.[36] In this mo-ment, the film calls for a return to an innate Brazilianness. But as other sexual episodes do, the Coca-Cola scene posits Brazilianness as always already com-promised by that which has influenced it (Italianness, Americanness). The Quilomba episode brings together two essential notions of "the consumer" vis-à-vis the ass-thetic. Quilomba is a consumer in the market sense, clearly—too won over by the way products are sold to him to recognize their psycho-logical impact. His consumption is literalized in the physiological sense as well, insomuch as he ingests food. The film raises questions about what hap-pens to both consumer and product postingestion, and it refutes the notion that consumption constitutes an act by which one party is always eliminated rather than a process by which one or both parties are always incorporated. How do we consume culture, and vice versa? How are we sexual consumers, and vice versa?

The Coca-Cola scene exemplifies what the film does more generally: it makes collaborators out of people who "aren't supposed to" commingle. Coca-Cola consumers in the United States merge with Brazilian consumers as Linda's "victory" over U.S. market hegemony exposes the fallacy of an essentialized U.S. (and Brazilian) cultural and artistic production. A b . . . profunda and pornochanchadas "station[ed themselves] firmly at the bottom of the sociocultural class of being," not only by deriving their themes and content from the interests of the masses but also by opening film production to the masses.[37] Boca do Lixo upset the notion that resources go into the mouth and come out as nothing but trash. Instead, it demonstrated that the ass is a site of production. It's not the waste itself that we fear looking at, but rather the fact that waste comes out of its own creative process.

Much like the diagnosis scene with Jung, Quilomba's cure initially seems to herald the return to an innate Brazilian masculinity. But these men never actually convert into the epitome of the Brazilian man. Linda assumes that role, and it is her ass-centric understanding of sexual desire that equips her to do so. She encourages clients to explore their sexual appetites regardless of whether or not they are supposedly in bad taste, much as the film encourages the audience to eschew hegemonic or elitist art. Yet even though the film derides and laments foreign influences, it hardly leaves dominant Brazilian identity unquestioned. Thus, even as it lodges an attack against the neoimperial United States (for whom "the people" is Brazil and the global South), it simultaneously denounces Latin American government and the national elite (for both of whom "the people" refers to the popular classes). The film levels a nuanced critique of neoliberalism, symbolized by foreign corporations like Coca-Cola, one that might seem to exonerate Brazil by positing a Brazilian product (e.g., cachaça) as the antidote to that which has gripped men like Quilomba. Folded into this barbed attack on the United States, however, lies an equally vicious commentary on Brazilian politics of the twentieth century and the ailing masculinity—or deluded male figure—that symbolizes such nationalism. Not only that, but the film also unsettles said figure without simply replacing it with another that is similarly dominant and patriarchal.

Therefore, when Jung sends Linda off on her third case, to treat General Flores, the dictator of an unspecified Latin American country, her "task" is to reorient the wayward military man so that he concentrates on her ass and leaves "the people" in peace. Flores's scant clothing mocks the stereotypical attire of a leader: he wears virtually nothing—just accessories (complete with military medals dangling from his body hair). Sex begins with fellatio, but the group of nurses quickly entices him into performing cunnilingus by holding nondescript red, green, and yellow flags parallel with their labia. There are absolutely no traditional cum shots in this sequence. Instead, after screwing both girls from behind as they grasp hold of a pasture fence, Flores gets the equivalent of cum in his face when the girls rub pieces of a "viva la revolución!" cake all over him. In some respects, Spanish-speaking Flores represents Latin American dictators from countries other than Brazil. Yet even if the scene means to mock regimes of neighboring countries or, perhaps, to sneer at U.S. filmic representation of a ubiquitous Latin American political identity, it nevertheless recalls a public affect regarding the country's then-recent internal military history.

Screened a mere six years after the so-called *abertura* (opening) of the cinema and only three years after the first explicit film could be shown, this scene must have appeared relatively scandalous to Brazilian audiences. Indeed, amid all of its hyperbolic and admittedly pejorative stereotyping of "the" Latin American leader, the film raises interesting conclusions. First, it is absurd to think that a moral and politically upstanding public must be divorced from sex and eroticism. Thus when Jung tells Linda that the goal of her visit to Flores is to get the general to "deixa o cú do public dela em paz" (to leave the public in peace; literally, "clean"), he plays with the language of morality so often leveled *against* supposedly pornographic material. If anything, the "cleanliness" of state-censorship campaigns created an ailing state that needed to be reenvisioned. The scene also forwards a conclusion about the way in which we construct meaning about ourselves through our depictions of sex as well as through actual sexual encounters. Such moments ought to be restorative—curative, even. That restoration, however, is hardly ever about servicing individual needs, at least not in A b . . . *profunda*. Linda and her fellow nurses function as proxies for the heterogeneous public as they smear cake—a signifier of phallic power, like the money shot—all over Flores. So the mutual and reciprocal satisfaction of a brand of sex that tailors itself to the needs and desires of its participants replaces the model advanced by movies like *Deep Throat*. There is still a money shot, but the actors perform it in a way that renders everyone's pleasure visible.

## Conclusion

A b . . . *profunda* is its own type of frenzy. It is chaotic and excessive. It takes the parody too far, even as the acting seems half-baked. In many moments it doesn't explain itself—though, at the same time, it is a parasitic plagiarist, refusing to conceal its artistic, political, and social influences. It wants to confuse you, and more than that, it wants to confuse you with everyone else. Like A b . . . *profunda*, "the *pornochanchada* functioned as a chaotic self-criticism of the Brazilian people," but, in truth, both cast nets much wider than just Brazil.[38] Pornochanchadas tap into a longer filmic and artistic tradition based on the deconstruction of divisions between supposedly distinct entities, be they national affiliations, genders, classes, and so on. This does not mean that pornochanchadas somehow escape stereotype. Indeed, the debates over the nature of their content continue, though those conversations remain limited so long as the films themselves are considered beyond the purview of scholarly study or are simply unavailable to the wider viewing public.

What's more, in spite of the parallels I have drawn between sexually explicit pornography and the pornochanchada, the nature of their relationship demands much further exploration. In its use of an ass-thetic, A b . . . profunda keeps the pornochanchada (and chanchada) traditions alive, but it is equally and unapologetically indebted to Deep Throat. The pornochanchada director Carlos Reichenbach rather problematically points out: "Popular cinema [in Brazil] was ruined by the American porno film."[39] Similarly, in 1984 the famed pornochanchada and pornography director Ody Fraga wrote an editorial about the demise of production in Boca. He says, "Worst of all is that these saviors—these 'sexually explicit films'—imported or national, commit a fundamental error: they are not authentic, or truthful, nor are they real pornographic films. They're just immoral films. . . . Actually, you could condemn them for this: the popular masses feel as though they have been removed from the cultural production of cinema by the industrialization of this singular type of film."[40] For Fraga, the essence of "the pornographic" as a category does not lie in the mere display of sexual images. But as the history of the tenuous relationship between Boca and cinema novo suggests, what makes something pornographic is also not necessarily the fact of its being transgressive or revolutionary. Ultimately, the pornographic is best understood as that which makes us face aspects of ourselves and our communities that we would otherwise refuse to acknowledge. As such, the pornographic ass-thetic of films like A b . . . profunda make obvious the reciprocal relations of inclusion between film and audience, a reciprocity that breaks down (or symbolizes the breakdown of) analogous distinctions in other aspects of life. For better or worse, Boca production bears the fingerprints of the masses and it, like A b . . . profunda, is motivated by a logic of persistent confusion. In the end, the clearest aspect of A b . . . profunda remains its refusal to be clear and explicit about anything but its pornographic relationship with "the people."

Notes

1. Unless otherwise noted, all translations from Portuguese to English are mine.
2. I am indebted to Tim Dean for pointing out this rather ideal homonym.
3. L. Williams, Hard Core (1999), 110.
4. Parody often inspires close, critical readings of two texts. Yet part of my claim is that an analysis of how A b . . . profunda engages with Deep Throat would elide the former's interaction with a wide range of twentieth-century artistic interventions, not to mention reify U.S. film as well as reduce A b . . . profunda to the status of just another pornography.
5. Campos, "The Rule of Anthropophagy," 8.
6. Andrade, "Manifesto antropôfago," n.p.

7. Tropicália was a short but monumentally successful movement most famously associated with Brazilian music, but also included theater, film, and literature, that grew popular at the end of the 1960s. The tropicália (tropicalism) aesthetic recalls Gilberto Freyre's lusotropicalism, an early twentieth-century notion that celebrated a racial hybridity supposedly functioning as a "great equalizer" in Brazil. Tropicália did not portray Brazil as fundamentally equal, but it did employ an aesthetic of mixing in the service of giving voice to Brazilian masses. Likewise, cinema novo, most notably associated with the film director Glauber Rocha (also associated with tropicália), was an avant-garde film genre that sought to reconnect film with the popular. The films of cinema novo often revisited Europeanized versions of Brazilian history in the attempt to awaken Brazilians to what the country had inherited from imperialism.

8. Rocha, "An Aesthetic of Hunger," 70. This text is widely anthologized and easily accessible through the Internet.

9. Rocha, "An Aesthetic of Hunger," 70.

10. Rocha, "An Aesthetic of Hunger," 70.

11. Johnson and Stam, Brazilian Cinema, 71.

12. Assunção, "Relações oblíquas com a pornochanchada em 'P III: Duas vezes Ela' de Paulo Emílio Sales Gomes," 199.

13. Assunção, "Relações oblíquas com a pornochanchada em 'P III: Duas vezes Ela' de Paulo Emílio Sales Gomes," 198.

14. On the chanchada, pornochanchada, and Brazilian cinema history, see R. Johnson, The Film Industry in Brazil; Johnson and Stam, Brazilian Cinema; and Shaw and Dennison, Brazilian National Cinema.

15. Abreu breaks down pornochanchada production in the following way: 1970–75, the establishment of censorship laws to the government's entrance into the distribution market; 1975–81, Boca and the pornochanchada fall into "agony" and succumb to pressure by making what we might call soft-core pornographic films; and 1981–86, hard-core pornography and the death of the pornochanchada. Abreu, Boca do Lixo, 8.

16. Abreu, Boca do Lixo, 21.

17. Freitas, "Entre Estereótipos," 22.

18. Abreu says the genre was viewed as a "cinema mediocre," and that it occurred "on the margin" of the practices of academics, the vanguard, and the media. Abreu, Boca do Lixo, 22.

19. Avellar, "A teoria da relatividade," 67.

20. According to Randal Johnson, "technological and economic dependence marked the development of cinema in Brazil from its very inception." In 1924 Brazilian actors and filmmakers had already sought state intervention on behalf of the national industry. By 1929, Johnson notes, Brazil constituted the fourth-largest overseas market of U.S. films, importing about half the films (in linear feet) as the respective UK and Australian markets, and almost as much as Argentina's. During the 1940s, not even 5 percent of films screened in Brazil were Brazilian in origin. Finally, Johnson tells us that "in 1960, the American industry controlled at least 50 percent of all screen time in every Latin American country except Mexico, where the state owned major studios and exhibition circuits." By then "American films occupied 70 percent of screen time in Brazil." See R. Johnson, The Film Industry in Brazil, 21.

21. Though Embrafilme wasn't the government censor, it was nevertheless a government organization, and the films it produced were guilty by association. Because porno-

chanchadas were virtually the only other films made during that time, their creators were suspected of being in league with the censor as well as Embrafilme.

22. This law was not unprecedented, as government-instituted screening quotas had existed for several decades. But it significantly increased the requisite screening time and dictated screening schedules.

23. Tom Zé's 1973 record *Todos os olhos* usefully connects the music of tropicália and the ass-thetic made possible because of the pornochanchada. One could easily mistake the cover art for the record as a marble in a woman's mouth, meant to look like an eye. It is, in fact, a marble in Zé's asshole. There is an echo of Bernadet's criticism of pornochanchadas here: use nudity for something "productive" and it's not crass. Had the marble not been there—had it just been a close-up of Zé's asshole—would it have been as readily accepted?

24. The body responsible for this censorship was known as Divisão de Censura e Diversões Públicas (Agency of Censorship and Public Entertainment). According to William de Souza Nunes Martins, the agency "was directly connected to the Federal police" and "functioned like an executive agency of coercive politics." It had the power to censor a film in various ways. It could require that producers cut scenes or change titles, and could prevent a film from being exhibited until it made such cuts, which it did—often. Each film required a separate clearance for overseas exhibition in addition to the one it needed for national screenings. Indeed, getting national clearance was much more difficult than getting the equivalent go-ahead for international markets. The agency concerned itself primarily with the "morality" of the Brazilian public, and "films that contained scenes of sex and nudity could be cut and restricted to viewers above 18 years-old, but normally they were freed for export [without those restrictions]" (34, 39). For the agency, "proper" morality was part of "national security," and law number 5536 in particular enabled the censors to mark films with indelible classifications, which of course had ramifications in terms of exposure and profit (31). These censorship laws existed until 1978, when the government announced that it would lift the restrictions. Critics have called this the *abertura* (opening) of the cinema. Souza Nunes Martins, "As múltiplas formas de censura no cinema brasileiro."

25. Avellar, "A teoria da relatividade," 84.

26. Avellar, "A Teoria da Relatividade," 85.

27. The promiscuous application of pornochanchada makes it difficult to determine an official count, but scholars indicate that more than seven hundred films were made in the 1970s. In the 1980s hard-core pornography dominated national production. See Abreu, *Boca do Lixo*; and Johnson and Stam, *Brazilian Cinema*.

28. Pornochanchada parodies almost always played with the idea of crossing national lines that is inherent in the remaking of foreign films. For instance, *Jaws* became *Bacalhau* (Codfish), a common ingredient in many Brazilian and Portuguese dishes. The dependence of U.S. cinema on its foreign markets is not unlike the dependence of European literature on its gestational period in the stomach of the cannibal. Fully digested, the motifs remerge in *A b . . . profunda* in a new form. Consider the vignette in which the main character, Linda, visits the owner of a pizza parlor. The scene is marked by the use of physical humor that was frequently employed in chanchadas, and the characters engage in a food fight that eventually "cures" the patient's sexual dysfunction.

29. I rely here on Pierre Bourdieu's *Distinction: A Social Critique of the Judgement of Taste*. Bourdieu demonstrates that "good" taste in art (i.e., culturedness) is always learned or

acquired. So-called higher classes retain hold of privilege (i.e., make distinctions between themselves and lower classes) by insisting on their distinctive, natural taste. In the same vein, Abreu shows how the upper echelons of the Brazilian film industry distinguish themselves by identifying certain genres and styles as "badly done" or done "in bad taste." See Abreu, *Boca do Lixo*, 145.

30. Abreu, *Boca do Lixo*, 150.

31. Abreu, *Boca do Lixo*, 63.

32. During two of her consultations, Linda throws food in the men's faces: in one, a pizza, and in the other, a cake. Yet another scene re-creates the scene of Coca-Cola fetishism from *Deep Throat*.

33. Abreu, *Boca do Lixo*, 62.

34. This phrase, *É a preferência nacional!*, is quite famously connected to a supposed national appreciation for rear ends.

35. R. Johnson, *The Film Industry in Brazil*, 7.

36. Cachaça is a Brazilian alcoholic beverage made from fermented sugar and is similar to rum. This analogy of course recalls the centuries-long production of sugar that took place in Brazil and was made possible by the labor of enslaved Africans. Moreover, it points to the early presence of Coke in Brazil and Latin America more largely, where it existed as both a product and as a company (with factories and distribution chains).

37. Penley, "Crackers and Whackers," 312.

38. Quoted in Abreu, *Boca do Lixo*, 172.

39. Reichenbach quoted in Abreu, *Boca do Lixo*, 134, 136.

40. Fraga, *Filme Cultura*, 112; which is quoted in Abreu, *Boca do Lixo*, 136; my emphasis.

# 17

## Pornographic Faith: Two Sources of Naked Sense at the Limits of Belief and Humiliation

### John Paul Ricco

In this chapter I operate as a symptomologist, in the sense that Gilles Deleuze, in describing his early work on masochism, distinguished symptomology, "or the study of signs," as "a kind of neutral point, a limit" separate and perhaps prior to etiology (the study of causes) and the therapeutic (the application of a treatment or remedy).[1] Drawing the outline of symptoms is as much the work of the artist or writer, Deleuze tells us, as it is of the doctor or clinician, with the difference being that here I will end up focusing less on signs than on signals—those gestures, steps, or winks that pass without signifying—so as to draw out the path that is signaled by the passerby in passing.

My discussion draws upon a range of recent work in contemporary Continental philosophy on religion and spectacle, ethics and the pornographic, that includes Deleuze on judgment, belief, and infinite debt; Jean-Luc Nancy on the vestige and faith; Jacques Derrida on the econo-theological and the autoimmunity of community; William Haver on violence; and Jean Baudrillard on war porn and the politics of humiliation.[2] Taken together, they enable us to think about the ways in which bodies—simulated and real, virtual and corporeal—are always very much on the line and, biopolitically, are caught up in the death throes of a post-9/11 globalicity; and they enable us to theorize pornographic faith as a double resistance to this econotheological world (dis)order.[3] A symptomology of bodies then, as the study of their sense in passing and in all directions at once, outlines a trajectory that is less a body's movement cloaked in meaning than it is of a body's sense as naked. Naked, because sense is always shared, and as Nancy has reminded us, in our co-existence we are exposed to an inappropriable outside. So we must no longer continue to speak in terms of *a* body, let alone of *the* body, but instead of bodies as the multiplicities that they are, *in and as* their nakedly shared singularity. It is this that renders all bodies pornographic, and so to put one's trust in this nakedness of being together, that is, of being without a world-beyond and without transcendence or what I theorize as *naked sharing*, is what it means to have pornographic faith.[4]

Accordingly, I propose pornographic faith as a way to theorize a double resistance to the loss of meaning and sense making in the world. Following Nancy, this senselessness is precipitated by the death throes of monetary ontology (i.e., global market capitalism) and nihilistic theology (i.e., apocalyptic rapture and jihad). Resonant with yet distinct from Max Weber's notion of the "disenchantment of the world," this new globalized equivalence of catastrophes according to Derrida takes the form of a crisis of credit (religious credo or belief, and fiduciary credit, at once) that, in turn, produces a new species of humiliated subject whose existence is reduced to an unpayable debt and the relentless exposure to surveillance in the name of "security."[5] In other words, pornographic faith would be the incessant resistance to (1) the appropriation of the pornographic by militarized neoliberalism, including as the spectacle of humiliation that, following Baudrillard we will call war porn, and (2) the securitizing of trust and the infinitizing of judgment in the wake of a seismically temperamental theological-fiduciary system of belief. In effect, what pornographic faith opposes are the two principal forms and forces of socialpolitical preemption today: general equivalency or commensuration (consensus) and speculated and projected horizons (system of belief).

..............................

As an amalgam of the words *global* and *Latin*, and as a rephrasing of *globalization*, *globalatinization* is the portmanteau that Derrida coined in order to name the contemporary econo-theological world order, which he defines as "this strange alliance of Christianity, as the experience of the death of God, and tele-technoscientific capitalism," which, he goes on to describe, "is at the same time hegemonic and finite, ultra-powerful and in the process of exhausting itself."[6] It is this oscillating counterrhythm of power at odds with itself that will be so critical to our understanding of war porn.

For as one of the principal mechanisms of globalatinization, *war porn* does not simply refer to images of spectacular destruction deployed either by or against the society of the spectacle; it is also the name that we give to the society of the spectacle's telecinematic staging of its own image death.[7] From George W. Bush declaring the end of major combat operations in Iraq, on the deck of the USS *Lincoln* on the first of May 2003 (just three months after the war began) to the photos from Abu Ghraib prison, to the torture and disaster porn that streams through multiplex cinemas, the study of war porn enables us to understand the ways in which the society of the spectacle sadomasochistically administers shocks to its very own afflicted powers and is the source of never-ending banality and pleasure that does not undermine but, to the contrary, advances—libidinally—consensus as the hegemonic system of political belief.

Asking along with Derrida, "is this not the madness, the absolute anachrony of our time, the disjunction of all self-contemporaneity, the veiled and cloudy day of every day," I would like to propose that the formula that I just put forth enables us to begin to outline a response, facing a host of symptoms the extent of which perhaps still remained unimaginable thirteen years ago. Yet perhaps only if we remain surprised at just how cloudy September 11, 2001, turned out to be, given that we are constantly called upon to remember it as strikingly sunny and clear in its late-summer light. For as Nancy has so aptly put it, on that fateful day in September the God of holy war and the God of the U.S. dollar collided into each other.[8] In immediate response and in direct correspondence to the symbolic targets that had been hit, two things went into overdrive: globalized capital and neoliberalism (World Trade Center towers) and the militarized war machine (the Pentagon), with image spectacle as the mechanism that at once hinges the two together and conceals their ties to each other.[9]

...............................

In both my theorization of pornographic faith and my deployment of the notion of war porn, I heed Derrida's warning, since I wish to avoid producing what he calls "a self-assured discourse on the age of disenchantment."[10] For although we might be duly tempted to speak of integrated pornography in the same way that Guy Debord, in *Comments on the Society of the Spectacle*, speaks of a globally "integrated spectacle," nonetheless and for reasons that hopefully are readily apparent, we would not want to speak of a "pornographic zeitgeist," as Paul Taylor does in a recent article on Baudrillard and the pornographic barbarism of the self-reflecting sign.[11]

Yet even without resorting to the notion of a pornographic zeitgeist, we cannot help but hear in *war porn* a symptomatic resonance with a range of phrases used these days—*torture porn, techno porn, law porn,* and, yes, even something called *flower porn*—in which the semantic force of each is predicated on the sense of porn as the marker of a contaminating string of qualities and attachments: indulgent, gratuitous, uncontrollable, hedonistic, and violent. We might take porn to be a *force multiplier*, as this phrase has entered economic and military discussions these days (in order to refer to a factor that is added to dramatically increase the effectiveness of the calculating instrument that is being used).

...............................

While by virtue of being included in this collection, my chapter is situated in the discursive context of pornography and its critical theorization, it is nonetheless not consigned to any one of the various representational images and genres that constitute pornography and the pornographic, recognizing that while all or at least the majority of pornography presumably tries to be pornographic, not everything pornographic (*res pornographos?*) is reducible, representable, or instantiated in the form of pornography. In theorizing what we might call the *pornographic outside* as the exteriorizing affective force from which pornography draws its power and erotic sense, my discussion is located at the limits of pornography.

The pornographic, as ethico-aesthetic-political comportment, disposition, and technique, is then less a question of image than it is a matter of *vestige*. Vestige in the precise sense that Nancy has theorized it as the drawing and outlining of coming, in passing—including the coming in passing of any body in the withdrawal and departure that marks its exposed singularity and naked sense.[12] To say—as Nancy does—that the vestige is what remains in and as the withdrawal from image "is also," Nancy writes, "to say that the sensible is the element in which or as which the image effaces and withdraws itself. The Idea gets lost there—leaving its trace, no doubt, but not as the imprint of its form: as the tracing, the step, of its disappearance."[13] As the trace, trail, or path that is not "the imprint of its form," the vestige is what we might call a nonindexical trace, and the pornographic vestige, as such a trait, does not insist upon the rendition or return to (of) a body, extraordinary or otherwise (e.g., image, portrait, signature, identity, incarnation). It is, in this way, the inassimilable remainder of any archive.

Further, Nancy reminds us that the Latin *vestigium* means the sole of a foot or shoe (combining the corporeal and equipmental at once), yet given its status less as the imprint of the form (of a foot or shoe) than as the trace of its disappearance, we are encouraged to take the vestige not as the footprint but rather as the footfall or tread—the stepping of the step, if you will.[14] So while all of this will inevitably lead us to recall Wilhelm Jensen's story of Gradiva, and the desirous pursuit of her ever-elusive footstep on the part of the young archaeologist Hanold in Pompeii, we nonetheless must measure the distance between this archival fever to capture the instant of the step, and the nonfetishistic exposure or access to sense in passing, that barely leaves an impression, let alone an artifact, relic, or image.[15] Once again, I wish to affirm that of the pornographic as vestige, there can be no archive and no religion.

The pornographic is that which is at once unappropriable and shared right at, between, and among bodies—the opening up and staging of instances of eco-social corporeal dissensus. Pornographic faith then is the leap that happens between us. An ethical *de-cision* in which *decision* is understood—again following Nancy—as an "opening separation." This is the spacing (not to be confused with the abstraction of space, or the property of spatiality) that is no place other than around us, a perispacing that our bodies stage and share as the coexposed things that they are. In other words, pornographic faith traces the withdrawing and retreating outline of our corporeally shared and nakedly concealed open and exposed separation. Therein lies the naked sense of pornographic faith.[16]

........................

To the extent that faith entails a nonexceptional watching as opposed to a spectacular speculation, it is the exposure to a nonindebted futurity, and to the extent that it is without debt, it stands the chance of having done with judgment. For as Deleuze explains in his important essay "To Have Done with Judgment," judgment establishes the economy for systems of exchange and of belief, and it is the mechanism that ties them together. It is in this sense that we can speak of the doctrine of judgment underlying any econo-theological order, built according to the twofold structure of infinity of debt (as the perpetuation of the unpayable) and immortality of existence (as the survival of the debtor). Given that, as Deleuze makes clear, "it is the act of postponing, of carrying to infinity, that makes judgment possible," then belief is a matter of placing one's trust and hope not in any final judgment or even that which is still to come, but in a futurity of perpetual postponement that strips the future of everything except judgment.[17] Deleuze describes the effect of feeling as though one is in a dream, in which, as he writes, "nothing is left but judgment, and every judgment bears on another judgment."[18] In other words, the futurity of belief is even more than a really bad infinity. In terms of our earlier discussion of trust, we might conceive of judgment and debt, in their various fiduciary and theological forms, as the rendering infinite of the exposed vulnerability that is trust, and of trust being reduced to its contractual securitization and taken-for-grantedness. Effectively, this is the appropriation of trust for the purpose of preemptively appropriating the future by being infinitely indebted to it, through the mechanism of the promise. For as David Hume tells us, "Promises are 'a bond or security,' and 'the sanction of the interested commerce of mankind.' "[19] These are the signs of a permanently broken bond of trust that marks a decisive shift from entrusting to indenturing.

Although not mentioned by Deleuze, this is also exactly the Christian economy of love and faith presented by Søren Kierkegaard in his book *Works of Love* (1847). Based upon an infinitizing and pure mimetic economy of "like for like" that entirely structures one's (inward) relation to God and hence to the world, Kierkegaard professes a conception of love that is entirely predicated upon an "infinite debt which it is impossible to repay."[20] It is debt that is the motor that propels this infinitude, and just as represented in Deleuze's critique, it entails a perpetual postponement, although for Kierkegaard, less the postponement of judgment that, he argues, occurs at each and every moment of our lives than the postponement of any final repayment. Philosophically opposed to externality and the worldly, the sensuous and corporeal, and anything like suspension, pause, interruption, or the momentary—like the syncopation of a step or wink—life is hereby defined as one big IOU.[21] Turning this into a Cartesian-like maxim, Simon Critchley (seemingly by way of its endorsement) summarizes this conception: "To be is to be in debt—I owe therefore I am."[22] For Kierkegaard, it is the urban dweller who, "in the noise of life . . . perhaps does not discern God's or the eternal's repetition of the uttered word; he perhaps imagines that the repayment should be in the external or in an external mode; but externality is too dense a body for resonance, and the sensual ear is too hard-of-hearing to catch the eternal's repetition."[23] The critical undoing of much of this will need to wait another forty years for *The Gay Science* (1882) and *On the Genealogy of Morals* (1887), among others of Nietzsche's texts.

Nowadays—since 9/11 and the more recent global financial crisis—rather than infinite debt and immortality of existence being sustained through economies of exchange, be they monetary and commodity or symbolic and gift based, debt now takes the form of an infinite accumulation of simulated wealth, and the survival of the debtor is phantasmatically sustained each time that death is screened as just another special effect. Both share the phantasm as object of desire, and together as modes of belief place all of their trust in a future that has been preemptively appropriated through various spectacular forms of speculation, whether financial or spiritual.

*Porn*, as the current suffix de jour and even more so in its ostensible replacement of the 1970s-derived suffix *gate*, can be further understood as marking a syntactical shift from the kind of political scandal that has usually ended with some form of legal-juridical sentence to a scandal that not only extends well beyond the political realm but, more pressingly, is seemingly less and less likely to be redressed and brought to some presumably just end. "Frozen scandal" is the way in which Mark Danner describes this production of infinite deferral of judgment, designating it as "our growth industry."[24]

My objective is to consider the effects of this shift, in which scandal has become the spectacular ground and horizon of judgment nowadays, and one of the principal mechanisms for "the act of postponing, of carrying [judgment] to infinity."[25] By serving as the motor and fuel of judgment, but also as the growth industry of our time, scandal not only produces humiliation as spectacle, it has also transformed spectacle into its own humiliating form of infinite judgment. The question that we raise and face is: how do we not resign ourselves simply to being humiliated spectators of the next sequel in the death throes of the econo-theological that is war porn? In the current schema, when "nothing is left but judgment," subjectivity becomes abjectly constituted against the seemingly unsurpassable horizon of humiliation.[26] In this sense, and riffing on the title of Susan Sontag's last book, I might have titled this chapter "Regarding the Humiliation of Others."

..............................

It is from Baudrillard's short yet lacerating article "War Porn" that we derive not only one of the most appropriate names for the self-inflicted death throes of the society of the spectacle but also the means by which to comprehend humiliation as the binding agent of an escalating series of events from 9/11 to today.[27] The word *escalating* is deliberately chosen here since what is in question and at stake is precisely a question of scale, in a number of senses of the term, which include the hyperbolic and spectacular, the widespread and integrated, and the mundane. Of course the question of scale is always at issue in discussions of globalization, but when, as Baudrillard argues, the accompanying violence is not (or not only) dispossessing or exploiting but humiliating, it is that much more difficult to take its measure, especially given the ways in which that humiliation is generated through various modes of digital mediatization. This humiliating violence, operating as it does through a mutually reinforcing and twofold process of criminalization and eroticization, has the intended effect of making one look (and hence feel) bad, and also in turn a little less human. This points to other ways in which to think of the posthuman, although those attendant discourses and debates are ones that I will not be able to engage with in the context of this chapter.

Originally published as "Pornographie de la guerre" in *Libération* on May 19, 2004 — less than a month after the release of some of the photos taken at Abu Ghraib prison in Iraq by the television news show *60 Minutes* on April 28, 2004 — Baudrillard's article critically traces the symbolic linkages between the images of the destruction of the World Trade Center and the photos from Abu Ghraib. The article opens with this paragraph: "World Trade Center: shock treatment of power, humiliation inflicted on power, but from outside. With the images of the Baghdad prisons, it is worse, it is the humiliation, symbolic and completely fatal, which the world power inflicts on itself — the Americans in this particular case — the shock treatment of shame and bad conscience. This is what binds together these two events."[28] The antinomies underlying his argument here are ones that had structured Baudrillard's thinking since the early years of his career, namely: semiotic order versus symbolic exchange and simulacrum of violence and death versus real violence and death. In terms of the historical events and scenarios under discussion here, the arguments are that the United States only has access to simulated violence and death; that the telecinematic immediacy of the terrorist attacks on 9/11 proves this point; that the torturous violence that took place at Abu Ghraib was not only in answer to the humiliation suffered on 9/11 but, in the precise form of torture being staged for the digital camera, was as self-humiliating for the United States as it was actually torturous for the prisoners; and that in those photos from the prison, "the excessiveness of a power [designates] itself as abject and pornographic."[29]

By boldly asserting that "those who live by the spectacle will die by the spectacle," it would seem that Baudrillard is raising the stakes beyond humiliation, toward death, so as to point to the futility of seeking the kind of shelter that war porn is imagined to provide.[30] And yet two paragraphs later he raises the stakes even higher, by stating that in the aftermath of the humiliation of 9/11, there will be those—the ones living and dying by the spectacle—who will "want to answer to it [death by spectacle] by even worse humiliation—even worse than death."[31] What exactly does he mean here by a humiliation worse than death?

Well, first of all, I think we can relieve ourselves of any concern that Baudrillard is operating with some imagined catalog of forms of humiliation in which death is evidently not listed as the most extreme or ultimate form (there's death, and it's humiliating, but there are experiences even more humiliating than death). Instead, he is arguing that—in the mode of revenge taken by the society of the spectacle—death and a belief in the transcendental that is the ground and horizon for having no fear of death are morbidly and symbolically humiliated.[32] As Baudrillard writes:

> Thus the other will be exterminated symbolically. One sees that the goal of the war is not to kill or to win, but abolish the enemy, extinguish (according to Canetti, I believe) the light of his sky.
>
> And, in fact, what does one want these men to acknowledge? What is the secret one wants to extort from them? It is quite simply the name in virtue of which they have no fear of death. . . . It is in that name that they are inflicted with something worse than death. . . . Radical shamelessness, the dishonor of nudity, the tearing of any veil. It is always the same problem of transparency: to tear off the veil of women or abuse men to make them appear more naked, more obscene.[33]

These are attempts to strip the body bare of everything, including death, as though to deny the life of a body of its very own death and to pornographically render it bare.

............................

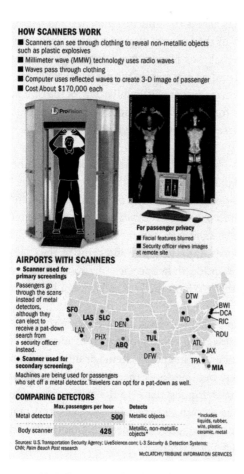

17.1. This information sheet on how scanners work explains: "Computer uses reflected waves to create 3-D image of passenger." © McClatchy-Tribune Information Services. All rights reserved. Reprinted with permission.

Based upon Baudrillard's indefensible assertion that "forced nudity is in itself a rape," we can register the violence photographically recorded in the concrete corridors and prison cells of Abu Ghraib, and we can begin to draw lines of connection from those instances of humiliating violence to the "underwear bomber," and from there to the hues and cries in response to the virtual forced nudity or rape by the full-body image scanners currently being installed at security checkpoints in airports around the world (see figure 17.1). What these sites and scenarios share in common is a digital-mediatic and biopolitical production of nakedness through the at-times brutal and often humiliating transparency of the exposé in which the subject is rendered criminally offensive simply because of a sexual force that is believed to be located solely in its body, lying dormant and waiting to be exposed.

This regime of humiliation is an exact denial of the nakedness that is the "substance" of the spacing that is shared between us as bodies. For if being with or being together is the only way in which to think about ontology, and in turn, if ontology can only be thought of in and as its bodily sense, then what lies between us, as the substance of this "with" of being together, is nothing but nakedness, to which we are always exposed, together. As Nancy has theorized it, "the between-us, whenever it takes place, is always the between of nakedness. This doesn't mean that only nakedness allows us to be between us." This is exactly what war porn denies, and instead insists upon—in the form of forced nudity—as the means of ensuring a collective sense of security. It refuses to accept that (as Nancy goes on to say) "when we are between us—when this happens—we are naked."[34] To put one's trust in this nakedness of being together, or what I refer to as naked sharing, is what it means to have pornographic faith.

If we agree with JoAnn Wypijewski's analysis of our sexual-political times, about which she argues, "like the terrorist, the sex offender is a new category of human being," then all discussion of the various contemporary alliances between technoscientific calculation and telecinematic consensus (one version of which is war porn) must take account of the ways in which, over the past decade, the sex offender and the terrorist, as two of the new forms of life, have been jointly incubated and together are made to suffer a humiliation that, following Baudrillard, is worse than death.[35] This is a vengeful rendering of bodies as at once sexual offending subjects (and thereby pejoratively cast as pornographic) and the objects of sexual offense (as bodies stripped bare). Hence Derrida's description of double rape as the new cruelty that, he writes, "would thus ally, in wars that are also wars of religion, the most advanced technoscientific calculability with a reactive savagery that would like to attack the body proper directly, the sexual thing that can be raped, mutilated or simply denied, desexualized—yet another form of the same violence."[36]

And yet, as Jonathan Schell discusses, this new cruelty is a reactive and a proactive form of savagery, in that it purposefully uses torture as the means to forcibly extract information that will fulfill (albeit falsely) the image of the political future that has been made preemptively.[37] For instance, torture was used prior to the Iraq War as a way to create the mythical narrative connections between al-Qaeda and Saddam Hussein and between Hussein and weapons of mass destruction and to create justifications for the war. So in addition to torture being that which can generate scandal, it might be said that a certain geopolitical drive for the scandalous has become one of the principles used to justify the use of torture. As Schell puts it: the war produced torture, but torture produced the war. The use of torture to shore up preemptive decisions to wage a preemptive war with the expressed purpose of preventing future terrorist attacks: let's call this the Rumsfeld doctrine of judgment.[38]

........................

As Derrida pointed out many years ago, and well before this recent series of events that in fact has only further proven his prognosis, there is an autoimmunity within these campaigns to secure a community's immunity, such that one must think of community as *com-mon autoimmunity*, the attack on its own immunity, security, or, simply, belief system.

This includes attacks on the community's own sense of futurity, or, to put it in a slightly different and perhaps more accurate way, the community's sense of futurity is that which is always under attack. The global war on terrorism then must be understood as both a perpetual chronopolitical and geopolitical appropriation of the future as that which is terrifying and terrorizing. The sense of futurity offered by war porn is a traumatizing futurity, specifically in the way that it enables, through its spectacular exploitation of images of one's own future destruction, a foreseeing of what is catastrophically unforeseeable. The unavowable elation and jouissance of media playback of images of catastrophe, along with the allayed terror through voyeurism of these very same images of terror, might lead us to speak of the community of pornographic autoimmunity. This is a community with no sense of future other than the one that it is spectacularly made to be consensually agreed upon and believed in as a disastrous future already foreseen.

........................

I want to distinguish this negative sense of a nonhorizon of knowledge from one that is more positive by presenting two images of futurity, both of which find their symbolic site in the towers of the World Trade Center. I discovered the first thanks to Derrida—in the published version of his dialogue with Giovanna Borradori, titled "Autoimmunity: Real and Symbolic Suicides." The second image, as counter to the first, came to mind while I was reading this particular footnote of Derrida's.

This first image of the towers is one that Derrida derived from an article by Terry Smith on architecture after 9/11, that he in turn derived from Joseph B. Juhasz's 1994 essay on the architect Minoru Yamasaki.[39] In Derrida's work, the World Trade Center is described as a mythical port to the transcendent and as a target of terrorism, as a symbol of the suppression of open systems and therefore as a cataclysmic terminus, and finally as an imminent sepulcher of the nonresurrected undead echoed in its own twinned ghostly presence. Der-

17.2. The aerialist Philippe Petit balances himself as walks along a steel-cable wire between the two World Trade Center towers in Manhattan on August 7, 1974. Petit is shown here facing the South Tower, as he steps away from the rooftop of the North. The rooftops of both towers were still under construction at the time of this amazing feat of precipitous faith. Still from *Man on Wire* (directed by James Marsh, 2008).

rida goes on to ask, "How can one not 'see' these two towers without 'seeing' them in advance, without foreseeing them, slashed open? Without imagining, in an ambiguous terror, their collapse?" Indeed, what would be such a countervision to this prevision, one that does not foresee the towers as the inevitable site of a violent and catastrophic future—as nontraumatizing and nonterrorizing?

There exists just such an image and event, one equally justified in its description as a heist and an instance of illegal trespass, a coup that was more "de théâtre" than "de grâce." And so an aesthetico-poetic form of criminality or combat should have been the point of reference for Karlheinz Stockhausen, instead of the artistic honor that he so idiotically bestowed to the terrorist acts of 9/11.[40] Like 9/11, this event was also wholly fed by what Derrida describes as "an entire technocinematographic culture and not only the genre of science fiction," and it also entailed years of planning and plotting before it was successfully pulled off. I am referring to the vision of the towers that the French aerialist and street performer Philippe Petit had at the time their construction was announced, and that was realized after their completion: to walk across a tightrope suspended between the two towers (figure 17.2).

Operating without ground or horizon, without reason or belief, his was a singular and spectacular event of trespass, right along the edge and the line of finitude and the law, a temporary suspension and hiatus across an inappropriable space between. His was the body as step, gait, and passage of the one who passes, the passerby, and since bodies are always, as we say, "on the line" in biopolitical regimes, it matters how that line is drawn and how in that act of drawing it is traversed. One of Petit's accomplices admits in *Man on Wire* (directed by James Marsh, 2008): "Of course, we all knew that he could fall. . . . We may have thought it but we didn't believe it." Such a keeping of faith outside belief, as precisely that which cannot be kept, is the step (if not the leap) of faith that happens between us in the ethical decision that is the spacing of bodies in their shared separation. Not simply with other bodies but also with inorganic things (tightrope, balancing rod) and elements and haecceities (wind, cold). Between the high wire suspended without a safety net below and each exacting step extends the gait or leap of faith that does not obey the moral imperative that one must have a body, while at the same time pursuing the Spinozian principle of pleasure that asks what the body can do, precisely thanks to what it cannot know. This is a radical exposure to finitude—beyond knowledge, the thinkable, and the avowable. For whereas the paradigmatically unsayable statement is "I am dead," the unavowable statement that is expressed throughout life is neither "I am going to die" nor even "I will have died," but rather "I am dying." The dying man is then the falling (but not "fallen") man. The man on the wire suspended between the two towers of the World Trade Center knows this, and it is this knowledge that remains unavowable (but not unexpressed—quite the contrary) in each and every step he takes. For at each step and every step there is a suspension or hiatus, an interruption and a loss, and this is what Petit has now come to share with all of those others who stepped out from the office windows of one of those same twin towers on the morning of September 11, 2001.

Hauntingly, this includes the figure of that single falling body, seemingly posed (almost choreographically poised) in its descent, as captured in the widely reprinted photograph taken on the morning of September 11. The identity of the person remains unknown, inconclusive, and as a figure has come to be known simply as "the falling man" (see figure 17.3). We might think of him as the one who executes what Immanuel Kant in *Religion within the Bounds of Bare Reason* and what Friedrich Heinrich Jacobi in his letters to Moses Mendelssohn on Baruch Spinoza refer to as the "salto mortale" (i.e., "breakneck leap, heels over head; more literally, 'leap of death,' i.e., a leap that risks all").[41]

As the body of the utter fool of pornographic faith, the image of the falling man resembles the portrait of the famous schizophrenic Louis Wolfson, who, as presented by Deleuze, "knows how to cross the limit [and who] accedes to new figures. Perhaps Wolfson remains on the edge, an almost reasonable prisoner of madness, without being able to extract from his procedure the

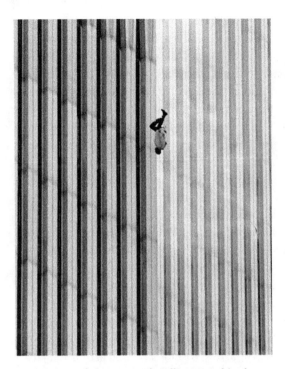

17.3. Commonly known as *The Falling Man*, this photograph by Richard Drew shows a man falling from the North Tower of the World Trade Center on September 11, 2001. His body bisects the two towers. Everything to the right of his vertical line is the South Tower. AP Images/Richard Drew.

figures he scarcely offers us a glimpse of. For the problem is not to go beyond the bound of reason [we might add: naked or otherwise], it is to cross the bounds of unreason as a victor."[42] "This is why," Deleuze goes on to tell us, "Wolfson keeps saying 'paradoxically' that it is sometimes more difficult to remain slumped in one's chair, immobilized, than it is to get up and move farther on."[43] In the end, in seeking a victorious figure, Deleuze found in Wolfson only an unproductive psychotic prisoner, unable to recognize that in his very own written transcription of Wolfson's statement stepped an elliptical figure who traced a line of nonknowledge that, as the line drawn by the tightrope wire, supports the extended periodicity of existence and presents itself as the naked sense that crosses "the bounds of unreason."

...............................

What is needed in order to recognize this particular strangeness is what Nancy calls "naked confidence, of confiding nakedness," defined as placing one's trust in that which is "exposed, exhibited, fragile, uncertain, but also, precisely, exposed, shown, manifested, in its disconcerting and troubling strangeness, the strangeness of the most ordinary encounter as much as of the most unavowable bond."[44] This is what Nancy means when, in his essay "On a Divine Wink," he writes that "the signal of the passerby is, then, nothing but his or her footfall. It is not a signalization or overarching signage" but the step that in its arrival is "suspended between its onset and its absence."[45]

The step (*pas*) opens up a gap in reason just as it opens up a gait in one's walk, and what passes through (or by) is a signal that is not of signification but of the spacing within meaning (i.e., its exemption and withdrawal— *différance*) that is sense's naked exposure. In its unavowabilty it is even less than an indexical trace—such that our hero here is not Jensen's Hanold but perhaps the poet in Stéphane Mallarme's "The White Water Lily," who, as Jacques Rancière recounts, "makes a short boat trip in order to see a lady who is supposed to be staying somewhere along the river in the neighborhood. As he approaches the place where he believes her to be, he hears the faint noise of footsteps that might be the sign of the presence of the invisible lady. Having enjoyed the proximity, the poet decides to preserve the mystery of the lady and the secret of their 'being together' inviolate, by silently departing without either seeing her or being seen by her."[46] We might say that in retreating from the sound of the footsteps, the secret that is shared between the poet and lady is held in naked confidence, and the faith that he has in its preservation is one that might only be characterized as pornographic.

Our final scene comes from Jean Genet's "The Tightrope Walker," which opens with images of the walker loving the wire, through an erotic and at times sexual rapport—and not only while walking across it but even at night, when it is curled up, in its box, like a sleeping dog. More than a fetish object, the wire is here envisioned as possessing a soul and, hence, feelings. It dances by responding to the walker, given that it is responsible for his sustained suspension. The leap of faith taken by the tightrope walker is beyond any calculable (mathematical) reason (i.e., the Kantian conjunction of concept and intuition through which he or she trusts that the technophysics of the rope, tension, tensile strength, gravity, and so on will support him or her with each and every step), but instead arises solely out of and beyond intuition (hence the "leap") in not knowing what it is that supports the rope in its syncopated suspension and response to each step. In the affirmative response to Nancy's question ("that which founds, that which supports, must it not 'itself' be insupportable?") lies an entire ethos of presentation, as a naked sense or faith in the withdrawal, loss, and finitude that we impossibly share together.[47] This is the proper "object" of trust and faith and love, precisely to the extent that it remains inappropriable. As Nancy enables us to understand, and as with

Thomas Aquinas's example of smoke to fire, the step's tread, footfall, and perhaps even something like its scuffmark are not the form or image of the sole of the shoe or foot (the footprint is an indexical sign or iconic image or an idea of the shoe) but its vestige or signal: "He who signals in passing is the passer himself. The passer passes, and in order to pass, is someone. Someone who passes, is but the tread of the passing, not a being who would have passing as an attribute."[48] The step of the passerby is the signal remains of the step in its withdrawal and retreat, in its stepping as always a "stepping out of," as when stripping, disrobing, denuding, and thereby divesting the body of its clothing (vestments, *vêtements*). Beyond the bounds of reason and unreason, knowledge, belief, and the idea, this is naked sense, including the sense that our bodies are—that existence itself is—vestigial. The affirmation of this involves placing one's trust solely (vestigially) in the vestige (remainder); which is to say in the withdrawal and retreat of the step (vestige). Neither the securitized ground of militarism nor the securitized horizon of religion, this is an exposure to the vulnerability and precariousness of existence itself. Pornographic faith is consecrated to this step or leap.

## Notes

I wish to thank to Tim Dean, Steven Ruszczycky, and David Squires for their valuable feedback and editorial acumen, as well as for the outstanding conference that they organized, "At the Limit: Pornography and the Humanities," where an earlier version of this chapter was presented. Over the past few years, I have also greatly benefited from the exchanges I have had with students in my undergraduate seminar "Capital, Spectacle, War," at the University of Toronto. This chapter is dedicated to them. A longer version of this chapter is part of a monograph that I am currently working on titled "The Outside Not Beyond: Pornographic Faith and the Economy of the Eve."

1. Deleuze, "Mysticism and Masochism," 132.

2. Deleuze, "To Have Done with Judgment"; Nancy, *Dis-enclosure*; Nancy, *Noli Me Tangere*; Derrida, "Faith and Knowledge"; and Haver, "Really Bad Infinities."

3. Ontologically speaking, bodies *are* the outline of this limit and line, and thereby all bodies are pornographic.

4. For further discussion see the chapters "Naked Sharing," and "Naked Image," in my book *The Decision between Us: Art and Ethics in the Time of Scenes.*

5. Nancy, *L'Équivalence des catastrophes (Après Fukushima)*; and Derrida, "Faith and Knowledge."

6. Derrida, "Faith and Knowledge," 51–52.

7. This repetition through the remake and sequel of the same apocalyptic disaster narrative in contemporary American film (of which the latest versions have been provided by the director Roland Emmerich) could be perceived as the historical flip side to the first half century of American cinema, about which Gilles Deleuze says: "The American cinema constantly shoots and reshoots a single fundamental film, which is the birth

of a nation-civilization, whose first version was provided by Griffith." Deleuze, *Cinema 1*, 202.

8. "On September 11, 2001, we witnessed the collision, in the symptom and symbol of the clash, between the United States (summarized in the name, heavy with meaning, of 'World Trade Center') and Islamic fanaticism, two figures of absolute value that are also—not surprisingly—two figures of monotheism. On the one hand, the God whose name is inscribed on the dollar, and on the other, the God in whose name one declares a 'holy war.' Of course, both Gods are instrumentalized" (Nancy, *The Creation of the World; or, Globalization*, 39).

9. In this respect my discussion has been greatly informed by Retort, *Afflicted Powers*.

10. Derrida, "Faith and Knowledge," 100.

11. Debord, *Comments on the Society of the Spectacle*, 8–11; and P. Taylor, "The Pornographic Barbarism of the Self-Reflecting Sign."

12. Nancy, "The Vestige of Art."

13. Nancy, "The Vestige of Art," 96.

14. Nancy, "The Vestige of Art."

15. Freud, *Delusion and Dream*. For a discussion of Jensen's story and Freud's own reading of it, see Derrida, *Archive Fever*, 83–101.

16. The notion of faith operative here is close to the "honour" that Haver has brilliantly presented as the virtue of the queer pornographic life and, along with my own theorization of naked sharing, begins to align itself with the ethics involved in Judith Butler's philosophy of precarious (but not "bare") life. See Butler, *Frames of War*; and Haver, "Really Bad Infinities."

17. Deleuze, "To Have Done with Judgment," 127.

18. Deleuze, "To Have Done with Judgment," 129.

19. Hume quoted in Baier, "Trust and Antitrust," 246.

20. Kierkegaard, *Works of Love*, 352, 173.

21. Kierkegaard, *Works of Love*, 352, 177.

22. Simon Critchley, "The Rigor of Love," *New York Times*, August 8, 2010, accessed March 22, 2014, http://opinionator.blogs.nytimes.com/2010/08/08/the-rigor-of-love/?_php=true&_type=blogs&_r=0.

23. Kierkegaard, *Works of Love*, 352–53.

24. Mark Danner, "Frozen Scandal," *New York Review of Books*, December 4, 2008, 26–28.

25. Deleuze, "To Have Done with Judgment," 127.

26. For what has proven itself to be a truly prescient discussion of the extension and exhaustion of belief in contemporary political economy, driven by opinion polls, consumer surveys, market testing, and data mining, see chapter 13, "Believing and Making People Believe," in Certeau, *The Practice of Everyday Life*.

27. Baudrillard, "War Porn."

28. Baudrillard, "War Porn," n.p.

29. Baudrillard, "War Porn," n.p.

30. Baudrillard, "War Porn," n.p.

31. Baudrillard, "War Porn," n.p.

32. Gayatri Spivak argues: "There is neither mourning nor execution without imagining the transcendental, and the transcendental, when imagined, has cultural names."

Spivak, "Terror," 88. In the post-9/11 era, some of those names are American neoliberalism and the war on terror, and militant Islam and jihad.

33. Baudrillard, "War Porn," n.p.

34. Nancy, A Finite Thinking, 40.

35. Wypijewski, "The Love We Lost."

36. Derrida, "Faith and Knowledge," 89.

37. Schell, "Torture and Truth."

38. For an excellent critical analysis of Donald Rumsfeld's role and responsibility in the Iraq War, the U.S. policy on torture, and other political and moral atrocities, see the following articles: Danner, "Rumsfeld's War and the Consequences Now"; Danner, "Donald Rumsfeld Revealed"; and Danner, "Rumsfeld: Why We Live in His Ruins."

39. Terry Smith, The Architecture of Aftermath; Juhasz, "Minoru Yamasaki."

40. See Anthony Tommasini, "Music; The Devil Made Him Do It," New York Times, September 30, 2001.

41. This definition is part of translator Werner Schrutka Pluhar's explanatory note on salto mortale. Kant, Religion within the Bounds of Bare Reason, 134n312.

42. Deleuze, "Louis Wolfson," 20.

43. Deleuze, "Louis Wolfson," 20.

44. Nancy, "The Confronted Community," 30.

45. Nancy, "On a Divine Wink," 119.

46. Rancière, The Emancipated Spectator, 51.

47. Nancy, The Discourse of the Syncope, 9.

48. Nancy, "On a Divine Wink," 115.

# 18

# Parody of War: Pleasure at the Limits of Pornography

*Prabha Manuratne*

The worst is that it all becomes a parody of violence, a parody of the war itself, pornography becoming the ultimate form of the abjection of war which is unable to be simply war.
—Jean Baudrillard, "War Porn"

LOL! Every time I see this vid I cream in my jeans. How can I hold back at the sight of dead sandniggers?
— "RabidMarsupial2," comment on LiveLeak.com

On October 29, 2009, Sri Lankan police drowned a young man who, according to eyewitnesses, had been throwing stones at trains and passing vehicles while dancing on the main highway in central Colombo.[1] The incident took place near Bambalapitiya beach, where the twenty-six-year-old retreated as the police approached. Instead of detaining him, the police chased the unstable man into the Indian Ocean with long clubs, and he eventually drowned. This episode of violence — committed in public and recorded and broadcast by the private television channel TNL — occasioned a few regional news stories and generated online commentary. Emerging at the confluence of naturalized violence and electronic media, the video marks an important phase in the transformation of Sri Lanka's postwar public sphere. What interests me here, however, is the video's reception outside Sri Lanka. Captured from the TNL broadcast and posted to online social platforms, the grainy video of a man pleading for his life has attracted thousands of viewers without the least connection to Sri Lanka's political situation. Why would an English-speaking audience take interest in a Sinhala newscast? More than anything intrinsic to the video, the online platforms hosting and providing access to it supply extratextual context that invites the answer that certain audiences take pleasure in watching scenes of real violence.

Consider a particular repost: user "anurag_kati" from Lucknow, India, shared it on LiveLeak.com along with a short description that condemns the attackers.[2] LiveLeak.com, a video-sharing website that evolved from Ogrish .com, traffics mostly in shocking, sometimes illicit footage recorded on camera phones, camcorders, and military surveillance tools. The website's moderators, the founders of Ogrish.com, have a history of featuring grisly uncensored violence alongside advertisements for hard-core pornography.[3] Perhaps because of the confluence of war footage and entertainment news, videos posted on LiveLeak.com rarely attract solicitous comments. Despite the critical description posted by anurag_kati, for instance, other users from the United States, United Kingdom, and Australia responded in the comment section with glib notes such as "shark food now." The cheeky tone indexes an analogous form of pleasure elicited by the digital promulgation of images now known as war porn. This chapter explores the growing digital archive of so-called war porn by turning to several websites dedicated to storing and disseminating images from the U.S.-led wars in Iraq and Afghanistan. Rather than focusing attention on the content of the images, I emphasize the technological apparatuses that frame the content in such a way that organizes a community of users who engage with the war footage and with one another. User comments, integral to those apparatuses, play an important role in taking stock of the pleasures produced by war porn. As the second epigraph suggests, the vocabulary that these websites have generated for responding to graphic images of war violence goes well beyond smart-alecky one-liners to invest videos that have no sexual content with explicit eroticism.

I begin with the video originating from Sri Lanka in part because it first invited me to ponder the possibility of deriving pleasure from representations of violence unencumbered by the artifice of fantasy and fiction. However, the video also serves as a useful starting point because the video's global circulation dramatically highlights how quickly digital archives can cross the national boundaries that have historically defined their usage. And yet, even as documentation of police brutality in Sri Lanka found its way onto computer screens around the world, familiar national and ethnic boundaries determined viewers' responses in predictable ways. Apparently, the relative ease with which we transmit pornographic images using digital technology does not short-circuit persistent forms of nationalism that continue to contextualize reading practices. My description of war porn here follows Frances Ferguson's insight that "we are likelier to learn something about 'prevailing community standards' from seeing what counts as pornographic for those communities than we are to identify examples of pornography by announcing what 'prevailing community standards' are."[4] That websites such as Live Leak.com, Ogrish.com, and GotWarPorn.com, along with the communities they foster, often assimilate video footage of uncensored violence as pornographic opens onto the question of what prevailing standards they develop to assess pleasurable images. Describing the standards that determine what is or is not pornography, as Ferguson insists, means describing *"objects in context."*[5]

Despite war porn's relatively recent emergence, the context in which it flourished is already waning as online archives meet state censorship and the conditions of production—U.S. military presence in Iraq and Afghanistan—diminish. Already much of the material in question is inaccessible. Similarly, public debate has subsided about the most notorious example of war porn—photos from the Abu Ghraib scandal. Yet as new technologies continue to interface the relationship between mass consumption and war, the task of understanding violence-derived pleasure is as urgent as ever. This chapter aims to take up that task by bringing the nascent field of porn studies to bear on the cultural and conceptual phenomenon of war porn. While many of the smartest critiques of U.S. human rights abuses over the past decade have grappled with the murky significance of war porn, they tend to invoke pornography as a clear signpost designating collective Western shame or perversion. Working against that tendency, I contend here that we cannot fully understand the significance of war porn as a genre without foregrounding pornography's status as a pleasure-inducing representational form.

## The Emergence of War Porn; or, Abu Ghraib as Archive

The 2003 invasion of Iraq set the stage for a new genre of explicit imagery known as war porn. The U.S. military took over the Abu Ghraib prison and, as the world learned in the spring of 2004, began torturing detainees.[6] Military personnel used various techniques to degrade and humiliate prisoners, the most famous of which Joanna Bourke described in the *Guardian* a few days after the scandal leaked: "A woman ties a noose around a naked man's neck and forces him to crawl across the floor. Uniformed people strip a group of hooded men, then laboriously assemble them into a pyramid. Men are forced to masturbate and simulate fellatio."[7] Her descriptions correspond to photographs that have circulated widely since 2004. The descriptions themselves, formulated to conjure both Abu Ghraib and stereotypical S/M porn, have circulated widely as well. Bourke, a historian of rape, was the first critic to publicly denounce the photographs taken at Abu Ghraib as pornographic. More specifically, she insists that the "obscene images have a counterpart in the worst, non-consensual sadomasochistic pornography."[8] As she explains it, pornography provides an aesthetic cognate to the Abu Ghraib photographs. The similarities reveal "our society's heart of darkness," a heart she reads as transforming sexual violence into a bonding ritual. By equating the Abu

Ghraib photos with nonconsensual pornography, however, Bourke goes further than comparing aesthetics to argue for a legal judgment. The burden she places on pornography is not just the representation of violence but also the act of rape — hence, torture.

Calling the Abu Ghraib photos "highly pornographic," Bourke hoped to make a political point of countering the George W. Bush administration's attempts to avoid the designation of "torture." Pornography and torture are both "evil" in her argument because they undermine a baseline of respect for others. In an even more influential article for the New York Times, Susan Sontag makes a similar gesture. Critiquing a distinction that the then Secretary of Defense Donald Rumsfeld drew between abuse and torture, Sontag correctly insisted of the photographs: "That they count as torture cannot be doubted."[9] Where Bourke argued that the photographs documented acts of torture, however, Sontag cannot doubt that they — the photographs — constitute a form of torture. Just as pornography depends on the confluence of sexual action and representational technology, Sontag argues that the Abu Ghraib photographs "seem part of a larger confluence of torture and pornography: a young woman leading a naked man around on a leash is classic dominatrix imagery."[10] What might have amounted to sexual abuse becomes torture, without a doubt, because, as with pornography, it is played out for the camera. The staging, the posing, the hammy gloating, and the swapping of images all contribute to the horror that Sontag attributes to the photographs — as well as their pornographic character.

Unlike documentary photojournalism that attempts to stand outside warfare in order to better perceive it, the photographs taken at Abu Ghraib prison are necessarily embedded in the act of waging war. Taking a picture is tantamount to torturing a prisoner when the photograph means to humiliate and dehumanize the individual forced to pose for it. That photography has become a technique of war, at least in certain instances, leads the theorist Jean Baudrillard to conclude that the images produced at Abu Ghraib resisted classification or assimilation as a type of information. As the product of a specific violence, he argues, the images continued the war effort at the same time as they crystallized the West's unconscionable exercise of power. "The whole West is contained in the burst of the sadistic laughter of the American soldiers," he wrote in a short article titled "War Porn." "This is where the truth of these images lies; this is what they are full of: the excessiveness of a power designating itself as abject and pornographic."[11] Where his English-speaking peers noted pornographic imagery, Baudrillard added the Abu Ghraib photos to the category of pornography because they follow a logic of maximum visibility.[12] The photographs exposed the bodies of Iraqi prisoners while simultaneously exposing their bodies to excessive military power. The images also, by circulating widely, exposed aspects of the Iraq invasion that the United States preferred to keep hidden.

For those writers and pundits struggling to come to terms with a new genre of war imagery in the months after Abu Ghraib, one point allowed for general agreement: inexpensive digital cameras and electronic communication created the conditions for the scandal. For both Baudrillard and Sontag, at least part of what makes the Abu Ghraib images pornographic is the sense that the soldiers intended them for mass consumption. Why else give the camera a confident thumbs up? Perhaps Baudrillard best captures the tension between virtual and real when he describes the whole situation as "a parody of the war itself[,] . . . a grotesque infantile reality-show."[13] Staging scenes of torture at Abu Ghraib allowed soldiers to produce a visual document of their work that they could then e-mail around the world to friends, family, and media outlets. The staging process also overlaid the scenes with a theatrical quality that—for Bourke, Sontag, and Baudrillard—imbued the images with abject, hence pornographic, qualities.

The political Right refused to call what happened at Abu Ghraib torture, but readily accepted the photographs as pornography and, in fact, recommended treating them the way the Meese Report of a generation earlier recommended the Ronald Reagan administration treat sexually explicit materials. The Republican senator John Warner, for example, suggested extending the ban on images of U.S. casualties to cover any further photographs or videos from Abu Ghraib. "I feel it could possibly endanger the men and women of the armed forces," said Warner after seeing a slide show of eighteen hundred Abu Ghraib photos. He concluded that they "should not be made public."[14] This way of thinking suggests that to protect the war efforts from public scrutiny and potential security breeches, all images of the war should be monitored, regulated, and if necessary censored. Calling them obscene tied the images to a juridical precedent that prescribes censorship. Meanwhile, the cultural Right attacked everything from MTV and Howard Stern to same-sex marriage and gay porn for depraving young Americans such as the soldiers working at Abu Ghraib.[15] That war crimes so easily folded into a critique of American sexual culture marks the ambiguous political strategy of describing the Abu Ghraib photos as war porn.

Much of the vitriol over the Abu Ghraib scandal, gushing from the Left and the Right, raised pornography as the representation of perversion for which the United States should be ashamed. Academic studies of the Abu Ghraib photographs have been just as quick to associate them with sexual perversion and shame. Elissa Marder goes so far as to suggest that the soldiers who participated in the abuses might be seen "as human embodiments of shame."[16]

While affirming the war crimes committed by the United States as a national shame feels intuitive, the move to condemn them so resolutely—and in *just the right way*—might correlate to a desire to pinpoint excesses of power. To establish the Abu Ghraib photographs as perversions of power would, reason dictates, implicate the power structure that produced them (whether that structure is the sex-soaked cultural imagination or a sexually permissive military policy).[17] With the benefit of a little more historical distance, Judith Butler critiques the bipartisan and transnational condemnation of the photos as pornographic. The conflation of torture and pornography, she argues, leads to a confused moralism that fails to make a strong ethical injunction against specific forms of brutality. What emerges from the designation *war porn*, she writes, "is a presumption that pornography is fundamentally defined by a certain visual pleasure being taken at the sight of human and animal suffering and torture."[18] Butler rejects such an adverse definition of pornography as a sort of scapegoating that renders certain kinds of sexual exchange objectionable. It is not normatively defined sexual perversion that we should condemn, she writes, but "the exploitation of sexual acts in the service of shaming and debasing another human being."[19] Although critical of the tendency to equate pornography with shame, Butler moves just as quickly as her interlocutors to find the proper form of outrage for the Abu Ghraib photos.

My contention here is that outrage, although an understandable initial reaction, does not go far enough toward formulating a critical insight into the apparent sexual appeal of violent imagery from the war in Iraq. Any ethical mode of looking at the Abu Ghraib photos should require a candid attempt to contemplate their value within a particular social context before condemning the photos, their producers, or their viewers. Contrary to Butler, then, I prefer not to separate the intermingling of sexual pleasure and exploitive power connoted by the term *war porn*. Even if we could ignore the fact that the soldiers producing these violent images call them war porn, her attempt to recuperate pornography incorrectly implies a form of pleasure unpolluted by power. Nonetheless, Butler makes explicit what those reviling the perversity of war porn have only hinted at—pornography aims to please. If the emergence of war porn pushes us no further, it offers a striking pass through "*perpetual spirals of power and pleasure*" that Michel Foucault describes in the first volume of *The History of Sexuality*.[20] If modern power relations proliferate pleasures, perhaps we should not be surprised to find that humiliating political Others takes on sexual significance in the form of photographic representation.

Even a cursory glance at the cultural Right's response to Abu Ghraib evidences the way that staged images of real torture evoke pleasure. In her *New York Times* article, Sontag quoted Rush Limbaugh responding to one of his listeners, who compared the abuses to a fraternity prank: "Exactly my point. This is no different than what happens at the Skull and Bones initiation, and we're going to ruin people's lives over it[,] . . . because they had a good time."[21] If convincing the likes of Limbaugh that Abu Ghraib and a fraternity party represent disparate social situations remains a paradigmatic political challenge of our time, war porn forces us to acknowledge that "a good time" is part of the pleasure that a particular community shares. As undignified as it may sound, the example correctly indicates the emergence of a community that collectively enjoys consuming images of real violence.

*Fantasizing Reality*

Limbaugh's response echoes many of the comments made by viewers of war pornography. By dissociating the images from their provenance on the battle-field and recontextualizing them within the field of social media, consumers of war porn transform the meaning of combat imagery by forming online communities that value particular aspects of that imagery. P. W. Singer, the author of *Wired for War*, compares the pornification of war footage to a professional basketball highlights reel: "The strategy, the training, the tactics, and so on all just become slam dunks and smart bombs."[22] With regard to the people circulating these pictures and videos, however, the appropriate referents are cum shots and smart bombs. Importantly, however, the videos that Singer has in mind are not those produced at Abu Ghraib during the early years of the war in Iraq. Rather, he describes surveillance footage of a drone attacking anonymous Iraqis from the air. Unlike the Abu Ghraib files, nothing here echoes classic dominatrix imagery. Nor does the mise-en-scène strain the line between virtual and real events, as do the staged Abu Ghraib photographs. The appeal of much war porn depends on its claim to authenticity, authorized by no less than the secretary of defense, who expressed surprise and embarrassment that U.S. soldiers let these videos leak.[23]

On the other hand, people viewing such videos on LiveLeak.com feel no need to express embarrassment. A recent video clip showing U.S. Marines urinating on dead Taliban fighters in Afghanistan mortified the Barack Obama administration, but viewers on LiveLeak.com delighted in the footage. "Ha ha ha . . . how does it taste you dirty camel fuckers!? lol," wrote one person. Another confessed, "i like to piss in allahs mouth after i rape his ass."[24] That responses moved so quickly to the language of sexual fantasy suggests that war porn is exactly the right name for this emergent genre of video meme. Devoid of sexual content, and in many cases barely corporeal, these videos nonetheless elicit sexually explicit responses, raising a difficult question: *what makes videos of real violence pleasurable?* While the spectacle of violence in feature films has long served as entertainment, the prevailing wisdom has suggested that such pleasurable affects rely on flamboyant cinematic artifice. In fact, feminist pornography scholars have made a sharp distinction between the potential of deriving pleasure from actual violence and the more common pleasure of fantasizing about violence.[25]

In her canonical study *Hard Core*, Linda Williams takes up the question of violence in pornography as a problem of cinematic realism. Realist theories of cinema based on André Bazin's seminal essay "The Ontology of the Photographic Image" understand photographic images as more than mere depictions. Because the technology registers physical impressions of the world, Williams explains, theories of realism regard photography as manifesting the world itself. Such an understanding of moving images has led critics astray on more than one occasion. As Williams recounts, the 1976 film *Snuff* (directed by Roberta and Michael Findley) convinced "naïve realists unfamiliar with generic conventions" that its final scene documents an actual murder.[26] Despite the naïveté, however, Williams warns against dismissing the outcries that forced the New York City district attorney to investigate the film. Responses to the *Snuff* hoax index more legitimate concerns about the possibility of pornographic films documenting real sexual violence. Taking sadomasochistic porn as the genre most likely to do so, however, Williams convincingly argues that "violence, aggression, and pain become vehicles for other things—for staging dramas of suspense, supplication, abandon, and relief that enhance or substitute for sexual acts."[27] Crucial to her distinction between documentary violence and pornography is the fact that porn stages a fantasy rather than emulating—much less recording—reality.

If we understand pornography, even seemingly violent pornography, as premised upon a contractual agreement to stage sex, then the performance and solicitation of pleasure relies on the construction of fantasy. The disjunction between pornographic fantasy and violent reality has played a key role in defending pornography against behaviorist assumptions that people imitate whatever actions they enjoy watching. The phenomenon of war porn, however, complicates this distinction. Of course, most of the people watching videos of military engagements featuring high-tech weapons have no opportunity or ability to emulate what they see (any more than most people interested in triple anal videos could try *that* at home). More important for understanding the pleasure involved in watching war porn, however, is that despite featuring only the "highlights" of war, it nonetheless features authentic violence, death, and suffering. Substituting surveillance footage for dramatized fantasy, war porn *re-presents* reality—an actual war—as an occasion to fantasize about any number of scenarios, but most especially about the sexual gratification of annihilating perceived enemies.

Much war porn actively constructs a particular narrative fantasy of killing political Others that sustains a sexually explicit desire for violence. The second epigraph, for example, comes from the comments section of a video titled "Insurgents Attack Foiled" on LiveLeak.com that U.S. soldiers confiscated in Iraq after a short skirmish with militants.[28] (Apparently, cameras have their place within the insurgency as well.) The video begins in a tranquil field. One masked man diagrams plans to attack a military bunker occupied by U.S. soldiers as a group of about ten other masked men follow his explanation. At the three-minute mark, the camera cuts to a desert highway framed from inside a pickup truck. The video follows the attack as it degenerates until just past the four-minute mark, when the cameraperson falls to the ground. At that point a screen of text appears, reading: "THIS IS WHAT HAPPENS IF YOU FUCK WITH US." The rest of the video—about seven minutes—comprises still images taken from the perspective of U.S. soldiers, followed by a final caption reading: "IF YOU WANT SOME COME GET SOME BITCHES." The slideshow of dead bodies functions as what filmmakers call the "money shot," a memorable sequence ensuring a movie's success. In pornography, the money shot is synonymous with the cum shot, because it evidences the male pleasure that porn promises to arouse. In this context, images of dead combatants evidence the violence that war porn promises to make visible.

If the video itself does not signify ejaculatory pleasure in any clear terms, the responses help clarify the particular narrative fantasy that the video constructs. "LOL! Every time I see this vid I cream in my jeans," writes RabidMarsupial2. "How can I hold back at the sight of dead sandniggers?" This statement bespeaks the sexual meanings that the video generates at the same time as it provides a sense of how the video loops viewers into a racialized fantasy of domination. The first caption puns on the audience's assumed nationality by situating "US" as both the United States and, emphatically, us not them. Both captions retroactively establish the gazing subject as part of a righteously violent collective. But the viewer does not take pleasure in mere violence. His statement emphatically specifies "sandniggers" killed by "US" as the main turn-on—a specific death, and the end to a specific narrative. The pleasure of watching the video hinges on its authenticity, as comments make clear. Viewers repeatedly articulate excitement for watching footage created by real insurgents recording their own deaths. A rare glimpse at militant planning—what one commenter calls "the cherry on top"—paired with the failed execution of those plans allows a little crude editing to spin a complex narrative of national supremacy. The fantasy of dominating political Others bleeds into a desire for witnessing the real violence of their annihilation. Only the most candid of cameras sustains such a desire, while only the most candid of language appears apt to express the pleasure of watching authentic bloodshed.

## The Look of War, the Word of Porn

If viewers use explicit language to report on their experience of pleasure, the act of writing must generate that pleasure. Comments play an integral role in constructing the narrative fantasies of war porn, so much so that without them war porn could not exist. At LiveLeak.com, the comments are especially crucial for narrating pornographic fantasies because the website actively excludes much of the most explicit content popular at other websites featuring war porn, including Ogrish.com and the now defunct Nowthatsfuckedup .com. LiveLeak.com reserves the right to remove gory videos glorifying death, for example, and does not allow hard-core pornography.[29] Having precluded the most controversial imagery available, the comments section at LiveLeak .com bears an added responsibility for featuring contentious, and often bellicose, theatrics. Quite often such theatrics acknowledge the absence of gore and visible results of violence. For instance, user "PIMPCO225" of Houston, Texas, complained of one video featuring marines in Iraq: "Wow, another video of soldiers shooting guns with no footage of what they are shooting at. Great video Dronetek. U suck."[30] Here the pleasure of sarcasm and insult displaces the desire to see explicit violence. Insults directed at other comments often repeat and redraw nationalist fantasies proffered by the video in question. Without referencing the video at all, for instance, a British commenter aligned himself with the U.S. Marines by dismissing critical comments from other users. "Thankfully, the comments by the French and the Canadians can be safely ignored as being totally irrelevant," wrote "thecleaner001." "Who exactly cares what a French man or a Canadian thinks or says."[31] Perhaps the comment protests too much, however, since its author cared enough to remark on the French and Canadians in a public forum.

The nationalistic fervor in comments tends toward sexually explicit jingoism when they address non-Western political Others, further specifying the ethnopolitical positions of power that comments assume. The explicit language, however, overwrites the competing racialized and gendered discourses in favor of emphasizing the pleasure derived from an imaginative experience of dominance. Another short clip showing a clear U.S. victory, this time due to the intervention of a helicopter, generated several responses that demonstrate this process clearly. One viewer from Fayetteville, North Carolina—home to the major military installation Fort Bragg—articulated his experience from the battlefield: "The best feeling in the world is to know there's some kind of air power above, that chopper lit those haji's up with some hellfire, and the tank at the end was fuckin unloading on something or somebody, allah akba pussy's!"[32] The superlative adjective qualifying the viewer's experience of military reinforcement finds its match in the erotic pitch of a phallic tank "unloading" on the feminized and racialized opponent. Coded with patent pornographic imagery, the comment moves quickly from describing an experience of war to describing a particular video clip, and finally to confessing a sexual fantasy of dominating political Others.

Another, even more pronounced comment borrows language from bestiality sites to dehumanize Arabs and Muslims more generally. "Those pig fuckin,opium smoking,heat stroked idiots really think there going to win against a modernized army," wrote "Yakuza-Irezumi." "Too bad there going to be having sex with 72 PIGS in allahs all gay sex house." The racial slurs *pig fucker* and especially *camel fucker* have circulated widely since 9/11 to refer to Arabs. Here, however, set against the U.S. Army and placed in a sort of bordello, the slur *pig fuckers* takes on a particularly pornographic tone. Writing a fantasy of sexual perversion simultaneously defers heterosexist anxiety over the all-male bonding common to a war's front lines and supplants the scene of war with a scene from pornography. By dissociating the casualties of war from their original context, these comments inscribe war porn as a palimpsest that overlays power relations with sexual fantasies. Judging by the prevalence and specificity of such comments—along with many others that describe "very sexy" war porn videos arousing "raging hard-ons"—the iteration of pornographic language generates much of the pleasure it also describes.

The online interfaces enabling such complex exchanges among viewers, videos, and comments also organize them as a community-driven archival practice that allows access to war porn. As with most archival practices, this one presumes an interested audience. Whereas the Abu Ghraib files became public only after various unintended audiences deemed them depraved, hence pornographic, the videos at LiveLeak.com came "on/scene" for consumption as pornography without any moral condemnation.[33] That the majority of comments evaluate war footage in terms of how "good" it is, (i.e., how much violence and destruction each video displays) confirms the unified enjoyment that viewers experience. This community shares no inclination to shrink from the violence of war. Quite the contrary, users who upload videos can trust that excessive, graphic violence will attract more views and more praise. Unlike the examples I've given, many of the comments do abide by LiveLeak.com's rule against racial slurs. Even those, however, depend on the consolidation of ethnopolitical allegiances for establishing a communal appreciation for images of dead Iraqis.

The economy of acclaim guiding dissemination of war porn was most evident at the very first war porn website, Nowthatsfuckedup.com. Chris Wilson of Lakeland, Florida, began the business in 2004 as a typical amateur-pornography website.[34] By his own account, military personnel made up a large portion of his membership, which became a problem when credit card companies started blocking charges from "high-risk" countries such as Iraq and Afghanistan. He resolved the dilemma by granting soldiers access to the website's pornographic content in exchange for images from the war. By September 2005 the site displayed 244 graphic war images and videos alongside graphic sex images. At the same moment as the Abu Ghraib images were causing a scandal, Nowthatsfuckedup.com was attracting 130,000 unique viewers per day.[35] Lynndie England's infamous thumbs-up in the Abu Ghraib photos seems to suppose a sympathetic audience, but the soldiers submitting images to Wilson's website had a guaranteed community of enthusiasts. Other members of the military often compared notes while supportive civilians cheered them on: "Many thanks to the USA soldiers who are over there kicking ass and wasting these towelheads!"[36]

After several investigations, Nowthatsfuckedup.com finally came down in April 2006. Since then Wilson and others have turned the case into a civil-liberties cause. A far less interactive website, Unseenwar.com, has reposted many of the gory images without any of the amateur pornography. The tone of Unseenwar.com is also very different. Operating under the slogan "They won't show you. We will," the website subsumes the pornographic language familiar to LiveLeak.com and Nowthatsfuckedup.com within a more high-minded argument about First Amendment rights. Similarly, the Office for Contemporary Anarchy in Oslo created an "anti-war book" featuring many of the notorious images from the original website along with member comments.[37] In both cases, the often violent photographs submitted by military personnel find themselves decoupled from the context of amateur porn. Yet they still carry their original captions, which indicate the pornographic structure framing their public reception as mass media. Even under the banner of political activism the images betray the entertainment value that war pornographers assign to them. An image of a dead man with his brains spilling out, for instance, comes with this explanation: "Head shot of a Haji who does not understand the rules of dodge ball."[38] As with user comments that make sarcastic jokes at the expense of victims of violence, such captions efface the tragedy of a violent death to express pleasure at seeing the gruesome results of war.

Despite attempts to reorganize the images from Nowthatsfuckedup.com for morally justifiable purposes, the original conditions of their dissemination leave a trace that confuses the distinction between enjoying war violence and protesting it. Even Wilson's attempt to catalog war porn separately from amateur porn on the original website—to protect people who "get sick easy or have a problem with dead terrorists"—fell into disarray on several occasions.[39] One post from June 2005 mixes war and amateur porn with three images displaying the results of an improvised explosive device (IED) and one image of a naked woman lying on the floor. In December 2004 a soldier posted a JPEG file titled "toe_popper_824" that shows the veins and muscle pouring out of a woman's injured leg. Four gloved hands hold the leg up as the woman lies on an examination table, revealing her genitals to the camera's eye. The person posting the photo admitted some uncertainty about the photo's status in the caption: "Not sure if this goes here or in one of the nudie forums. She stepped on a land mine."[40] That confusion notwithstanding, paired with a subject heading that reads "Nice puss/bad foot," the caption clearly directs viewers' responses by circumscribing the image within the context of pornography. Any tragedy inherent in the image takes a backseat as textual clues emphasize the pornographic online context over the represented scene's context in a field hospital. By directing viewers' line of sight to her vulva before her wounded leg, the text inscribes violence and suffering as pleasurable viewing.

Wilson's archive of war porn at Nowthatsfuckedup.com was unique for attracting so much media attention and for featuring exceptionally gory images. The majority of war porn currently online, however, features very little bloody content. The videos hosted at now-defunct GotWarPorn.com, for instance, ran closer to the video Singer describes in *Wired for War*: surveillance footage filmed by gun cameras, aircraft pilots, and drones. Rather than featuring detailed images of mutilated bodies, GotWarPorn.com mostly showed phantom-like figures filmed from above, scurrying for cover to avoid being shot by the gun and the gun's camera. Like the images collected at Nowthatsfuckedup.com, however, the surveillance videos bear text that situates them within more familiar genres of sexually graphic pornography. One user, for example, described a video titled "Better Than Maxim" as "Rockin' A-10 war porn! Lots of music and lots of money shots rolled into a neat nine minute package. You could do worse with the next nine minutes than watch lots of jihadis meet their virgins." Another user punned on pornographic slang with the title to a video of tanks: "Mastering the Bush: Here's Some Playboy Style War Porn of the MK 44 Bushmaster II in Action. . . . What a Mean Gun." A third description warned viewers: "More Playboy war porn; this is a short 13 second clip of an A-10 at an airshow. . . . Very graphic, very Hustlerish. . . . I debated about putting it up, but . . . I just can't get enough of that sound. Brrrrrrrrrrrrt!"[41] The pornographic references used to describe videos without any well-defined bodies communicate and construct the libidinal pleasures they offer. The descriptions cue viewers to experience images of weapons, aircrafts, and warships as sexually gratifying.

The emphasis on military machinery rather than dead bodies corresponds to the way GotWarPorn.com cataloged its videos. The classification system looked very much like mainstream pornography websites such as Xnxx.com that divide videos into sections ranging from "Anal Sex" to "MILF" to "Vintage Porno." In place of sex acts and sexual identities, however, GotWarPorn .com substituted artillery and tanks, including 30 mm Bushmaster, A-10 Warthog, AH-64 Apache, Sniper, Vintage, and Virtual. The only categorical reference to flesh was a section called "Bodies." In this case, however, the referent is a song by the metal band Drowning Pool. Popular among fans of war porn, "Bodies" featured in many compilations of combat footage at GotWarPorn.com, all of which were collected under the Bodies category. Although the band has resisted interpretations of the song as violent, the repeating line "Let the bodies hit the floor" seems tailor-made to accompany images of anonymous silhouettes collapsing in crosshairs. That the military used the song at the Guantánamo Bay detention camp to psychologically torture Mohamedou Ould Slahi makes the song all the more befitting for war porn.[42] The song's breakneck drum beat, distorted guitars, and screaming vocals create a kinetic soundtrack for otherwise distant, impassive, grainy, and repetitive clips. As with the textual apparatus that constructs war porn as sexually stimulating, the music enlivening surveillance footage works to transform tedium into a narrative rhapsody about the pleasures of violence.

If the majority of war porn appears monotonous without the support of an external framework of fantasy, then that is yet one more characteristic it shares with mainstream pornography. Far from provoking uninterest, however, the boredom of watching pornography can arouse an experience of profuseness that lends itself to confessions of pleasure. As Ara Osterweil explains, boring films "return us to our bodies, impregnating us with apprehension, imagination, and desire. When we are bored, our minds are saturated with thought."[43] The phenomenon of war porn lays bare a saturation of thought that imbues unerotic images of war with sexual significance. War porn thus operates at the limit of pornography, where fantasy no longer finds its correlative in a depiction or performance. Unlike other instances of pornographic violence— S/M porn, for example—war porn does not give viewers a staged presentation secured by contractual agreement. If conservative feminists tend to perceive pornography as misogynistic violence waged by men against women, then war porn implies a prevailing pleasure in watching others, any other, suffer violence. And when the representation of violence leaves no question as to its actuality, concerns about the performers' safety and consent fall away. Partly because it does not involve performers, war porn opens onto an entirely different set of questions. Here I have shifted the analytical focus to fans of war porn in order to elaborate particular conditions determining their experience of pleasure at the sight of real violence.

The key web platforms for collecting and circulating war porn show that online communities relish combat footage as a sexual object, even as nations wage war in the name of abstract ideals, such as God, security, or democracy. The images at websites such as LiveLeak.com, Nowthatsfuckedup.com, and GotWarPorn.com attract comments that situate the pleasure of war porn at the convergence of jingoistic and pornographic discourses. More than anything immanent to the images, however, that pleasure relies on the technological context of online social forums. Video descriptions, user comments, and rudimentary editing techniques align to construct complex fantasies about Arab casualties. That fans of war porn invariably define those injured as "insurgents" is but one aspect of the multifaceted narratives that fantasize a marriage between annihilation and penetration; "fucking up insurgents" joins with and encompasses "fucking insurgents." Just as warlike foreign policy regularly requires racial stereotypes and hierarchies for ideological sustenance, so an aggressive process of marking ethnopolitical difference sustains war porn.[44] The self-affirming pleasures enjoyed by online consumers of war porn, while deserving of critical suspicion, are no more or less abject than the war that produced the novel subgenre of pornography. Perhaps Freud's consolatory remarks on the First World War still apply: "Our mortification and our painful disillusionment on account of the uncivilized behaviour of our fellow-citizens of the world during this war were unjustified. They were based on an illusion to which we had given way. In reality our fellow citizens have not sunk so low as we feared, because they had never risen so high as we believed."[45] Such an acknowledgment would, at least, allow discussions of war porn to address the sexually explicit responses to war violence as communicating genuine pleasure. As troubling a recognition as that may be, it begins with the axiom that power is pleasurable.

## Notes

1. For a complete account, see Panini Wijesiriwardena, "Sri Lankan Police Forcibly Drown a Young Tamil Man," Work Socialist Web Site, November 11, 2009, accessed March 13, 2014, https://www.wsws.org/en/articles/2009/11/slkl-n11.html.

2. Anurag_kati, "Sri Lanka: Bambalapitiya Disturbing Footage of a Mentally Challenged Man Forced to Drown," October 31, 2009, accessed March 13, 2014, http://www.liveleak.com/view?i=318_1256972501.

3. Ogrish.com has undergone numerous changes since coming to prominence in 2002 for posting graphic images of the September 11, 2001, attacks. When LiveLeak.com went public in 2006, it attempted to package itself as more socially conscious and politically correct than Ogrish.com, emphasizing its mission to promote citizen journalism. Thus, it "only accept[s] graphic media that contains sufficient factual background information and/or media that contains news value." Nonetheless, much of the content

and advertising feature sexually suggestive images. See http://www.liveleak.com/faq (accessed March 13, 2014) for more information on the website's uploading policy.

4. Ferguson, *Pornography, the Theory*, 8.

5. Ferguson, *Pornography, the Theory*, 8.

6. The Abu Ghraib prison is located twenty miles west of Baghdad and is now called Baghdad Central Prison. For a fuller account of the Abu Ghraib scandal, see Hersh, *Chain of Command*.

7. Joanna Bourke, "Torture as Pornography," *Guardian*, May 6, 2004.

8. Bourke, "Torture as Pornography."

9. Sontag, "Regarding the Torture of Others."

10. Sontag, "Regarding the Torture of Others."

11. Baudrillard, "War Porn," n.p.

12. For more on the principle of "maximum visibility" in porn, see L. Williams, *Hard Core* (1999), 48–49.

13. Baudrillard, "War Porn," n.p.

14. For more on the effort to contain images of U.S. casualties, see Michael Kamber and Tim Arango, "4,000 U.S. Deaths, and a Handful of Images," *New York Times*, July 26, 2008. For more on Abu Ghraib as a public relations problem, see Matt Welch, "The Pentagon's Secret Stash: Why We'll Never See the Second Round of Abu Ghraib Photos," Reason.com, April 2005, accessed March 13, 2014, http://reason.com/archives/2005/04/01/the-pentagons-secret-stash.

15. For a critique of the cultural wars surrounding the Abu Ghraib scandal, see Frank Rich, "It Was the Porn That Made Them Do It," *New York Times*, May 30, 2004.

16. Marder, "On 'Psycho-Photography,'" 242.

17. Critics have linked the sexually charged torture at Abu Ghraib with Raphael Patai's analysis of Islamic sexual honor in *The Arab Mind*. For more on the military's use of Patai's analysis, see Hersh, *Chain of Command*, 38–39.

18. J. Butler, *Frames of War*, 88.

19. J. Butler, *Frames of War*, 87.

20. Foucault, *The History of Sexuality*, 145. Here I am indebted to Tim Dean's useful rereading of the Foucauldian thesis that pleasure is inextricable from power. See Dean, "The Biopolitics of Pleasure."

21. Quoted in Sontag, "Regarding the Torture of Others."

22. Singer, *Wired for War*, 320.

23. See Sontag, "Regarding the Torture of Others."

24. Kami Pmln, "Marines Urinating on Dead Soldiers Taliban," LiveLeak.com, January 11, 2012, accessed March 13, 2014, http://www.liveleak.com/view?i=5e9_1326333857. For more on the diplomatic crisis provoked by the video, see Graham Bowley and Matthew Rosenberg, "Video Inflames a Delicate Moment for U.S. in Afghanistan," *New York Times*, January 12, 2012.

25. For more on this distinction, see Kipnis, *Bound and Gagged*. The first chapter on *The United States v. Daniel Thomas DePew* is especially relevant.

26. L. Williams, *Hard Core* (1999), 194. For more on Snuff, see Lisa Downing's contribution to this volume.

27. L. Williams, *Hard Core* (1999), 195.

28. "Insurgents Attack Foiled," LiveLeak.com, accessed March 13, 2014, http://www

.liveleak.com/view?i=6ofd7b9937#comment_page=3. The comment quoted was posted October 5, 2009.

29. See LiveLeak.com's FAQs for more information on its rules. It also reserves the right to remove comments featuring racial slurs. It is difficult to tell whether or not the site ever enforces such rules, however, because racial slurs and glorifications of death appear frequently.

30. PIMPCO225 commenting on video by Dronetek, "From the Source: The US First BN 6th Marines/Charlie Co. return fire after being attacked at outpost Utley in Ramadi July 2006," September 5, 2007, accessed March 13, 2014, http://www.liveleak.com/view ?i=coa_1188905339&comment_order=newest_first#comment_page=3.

31. Thecleaner001 commenting on video by Dronetek, "From the Source: The US First BN 6th Marines/Charlie Co. return fire after being attacked at outpost Utley in Ramadi July 2006," September 5, 2007, accessed March 13, 2014, http://www.liveleak.com/view ?i=coa_1188905339&comment_order=newest_first#comment_page=3.

32. IRAQI_TRANSLATOR_USMC, commenting on "US Soldiers and Apache Engage Insurgents after Getting Hit by an IED and Small Fire—Iraq," accessed March 13, 2014, http://www.liveleak.com/view?i=18c_1207265582.

33. Linda Williams coined the term on/scene to underscore the fact that formerly off-scene expressions of sexuality have become common in the public sphere. See L. Williams "Porn Studies."

34. For more on Nowthatsfuckedup.com, see Jeffrey C. Billman, "The Most Depraved Site on the Internet," Orlando Weekly, October 6, 2005. Although the Polk County Sheriff's Department confiscated the website's URL and prosecuted Wilson on obscenity charges, some of the images are available online.

35. Zornick, "The Porn of War."

36. Thomas Kvam, ed., Nowthatsfuckedup (Oslo: Office for Contemporary Anarchy, May 17, 2011), 84.

37. See www.nowthatsfuckedup.org for a printable PDF of the book, Nowthatsfuckedup. Accessed April 18, 2011.

38. Nowthatsfuckedup, 54.

39. Nowthatsfuckedup.com, accessed through web.archive.org on March 26, 2012.

40. Nowthatsfuckedup, 146.

41. All quotes taken from GotWarPorn.com, accessed through archive.org March 13, 2014. A10 Warthog, http://web.archive.org/web/20110815234238/http://gotwarporn .com/labels/A-10%20Warthog.html; Bushmaster, http://web.archive.org/web/20110812 031434/http://gotwarporn.com/labels/30mm%20Bushmaster.html; Bodies, http://web .archive.org/web/20110817104156/http://gotwarporn.com/labels/Bodies.html.

42. Inquiry into the Treatment of Detainees in U.S. Custody: Report of the Committee on Armed Services United States Senate, 110th Cong., 2nd session, November 20, 2008, 139; available at https://www.fas.org/irp/congress/2009_rpt/detainees.pdf.

43. Osterweil, "Andy Warhol's Blow Job," 453.

44. For a classic account of the role race plays in expansionist foreign policy, see M. Hunt, Ideology and U.S. Foreign Policy.

45. Freud, "The Disillusionment of the War," 285.

# PART VI

Archives of Excess

# Fantasy Uncut: Foreskin Fetishism
# and the Morphology of Desire

*Harri Kalha*

Most of my readers will know the photograph *Man in a Polyester Suit* (1980) by Robert Mapplethorpe (figure 19.1). It was part of the artist's Z Portfolio, which he also published in the form of art books: *Black Males* (1983) and *Black Book* (1986). The "black" portfolio was conceptually linked with Mapplethorpe's previous work, portfolios known as X and Y, respectively, consisting of S&M imagery and flowers, all presented in a clinically documentary yet highly aestheticizing style of black-and-white photography. It was thanks to these portfolios that Mapplethorpe rose to international prominence as a visual artist; at the same time, he became a bone of contention for pornography debates, particularly in the United States. These controversies have been studied from varying viewpoints by scholars such as Judith Butler, Richard Meyer, and Linda Williams.[1] I will therefore not dwell on this aspect, intriguing as it is to any scholar interested in the concept of obscenity. Instead, I propose to focus on a minor detail that many scholars would perhaps overlook as irrelevant. For our *Man in a Polyester Suit* possesses something that has yet to be touched upon in critical commentary, something that has remained literally *ob-scaenus*: that small masculine difference, the foreskin.[2]

In the United States of its day, *Man in a Polyester Suit* was a scandal of sexuality as well as a scandal of race, but it was also—or so I wish to suggest—a little big scandal of the foreskin. Whether Mapplethorpe intended so (and my gut feeling is that he knew quite well what he was doing), he made, in this poignantly unsettling photograph, a spectacle of the foreskin. I sense some wrinkling of brows: why fuss over such a marginal detail? Does the foreskin matter—does it, indeed, mutter? In order for us to understand what the foreskin might have to say, we must begin by alienating it—we must trace the route of its alterity, which is also the tangled dynamic of its fetishization.

The foreskin or prepuce, while intimately familiar to millions of people (including to me, a Finn), enjoys a dubious status in the United States, where

19.1. Robert Mapplethorpe, *Man in a Polyester Suit* (1980). © The Robert
Mapplethorpe Foundation. Used by permission of Art + Commerce.

penises tend to be circumcised, due to a hygienicistic ideology that emerged
in the early 1900s. When speaking about foreskins in the American context,
we thus automatically invoke its dominant conceptual counterpart: circumcision. This is already expressed in the term that has come to describe men
like me: *uncut men*—a term that is redundant if not somewhat absurd in the
European context (for example, such a term is unknown to my native Finnish). The term, in itself banally descriptive, nevertheless has a sexualized ring
to it: more often than not it describes the properties of a porn star, a hustler,
or a man seeking or being sought for sexual contact.

It was while working at Columbia University as a visiting scholar fourteen
years ago that I first discovered that a penis such as mine could have novelty
value. It didn't take too much Chelsea barhopping to realize this; after all, the
classic "Do you come here often?" could easily be followed, or replaced, by a
casual but eager, "Are you uncut?" This, as it happens, was the early heyday
of the East European porn phenomenon of "Bel Ami boys"; and thanks to the
wonders of fantasy, I—an almost East European, an almost boy (I was actually

in my thirties)—seemed for some to fit the bill quite nicely. But the scenario wasn't all unambiguous. My American partner, upon first seeing my dick in the flaccid state, exclaimed: "What's that? That looks weird!" He had never before witnessed a foreskin up close and personal.

I was equally surprised to find, back in Europe, how unaware even scholars of gender and sexuality were of the prevalence of circumcision in the United States. I don't think a short account of its history will do the American reader any harm, either. My basic thesis is, after all, that without acknowledging the culture of circumcision, it is impossible to understand why the foreskin could be spectacular any more than scandalous—or why it could be savored as a sexual delicacy. Why, indeed, the foreskin might be a relevant object of analysis. The main ideological milestones in the history of modern circumcision in the United States were the so-called masturbation mania of the late nineteenth and early twentieth centuries and carcinophobia, a similarly obsessive concern with cancer later in the twentieth century. Initially championing circumcision as a tempering "cure" for the social malady of masturbation, American medical science went on to employ the practice in its battle against cancer: the scientific eye thus focused first on vague social pathologies and then on bacterial theory in its rejection of the foreskin. In the course of the twentieth century, the latter justification morphed into a general hygienicism. Paradoxically so, for the more modern life became the less use there was for such a persistent hygienicism. Today, few Americans seem to know what were once—let alone are now—the medical grounds for circumcision, which remains a prevalent practice. (It wouldn't surprise me if 80 percent of my male American readers were circumcised.)

Perhaps my circumcised readers would agree with a certain Willard Goodwin, a medical doctor who sought to justify the ideal of circumcision on "aesthetic" grounds, grounds that to me seem rather dubious but could well make sense to someone from a different cultural background. "[Circumcision] is a beautification," Goodwin wrote, for the circumcised penis "appears in its flaccid state as an erect uncircumcised organ—a beautiful instrument of precise intent."[3] It seems that the uncut penis failed to visually disclose its "precise intent" and hence didn't appear beautiful enough to the medically enlightened eye. Here, an attitude of modern functionalism merges with gender ideology to celebrate the sturdy—phallicly and futuristically invested—"erect" shape, which was thought to occur as a by-product of the operation. What did a man need all that soft, sensitive skin around his tool for? Thanks to the wonders of circumcision, penile morphology could be imagined, more to the point, as less "feminine."

In the course of the twentieth century, the practice of circumcision was established to the extent that doctor Benjamin Spock's popular *Baby and Child*

*Care* (in its 1957 and 1968 editions) strongly recommended the operation for all American wieners, for the simple reason that it made boys feel "regular."[4] Normalcy became the key concept in midcentury America, and where there is normalcy, normativity is never far away. The foreskin thus became irregular—dysfunctional, queer, and peculiar, even somewhat repulsive. As it happens, mainstream America now seemed to be in tune with traditional Judaic teachings: as the Talmudic dictum went, "the foreskin is disgusting."[5]

## Fanning the Foreskin

The foreskin might be disgusting to some, but it has also become a sexual delicacy savored by aficionados. While a keen interest in the uncut is most evident in gay porn, it also figures in other forms of popular culture, as well as the everyday situations I alluded to, not to mention actual sexual scenarios—hetero- as well as homosexual. The pornographic agenda of the foreskin has been championed by several web pages and magazines, such as *Skins, Uncut,* and *Foreskin Quarterly,* which dispense current pornography as well as wisdom on medical questions. In many instances, it is difficult to separate pornography from aesthetics, education, and politics. Many patrons of websites devoted to foreskin imagery comment on the empowering and sexually stimulating effects that the "hot pictures" had on them. Pornographic imagery can thus become part and parcel of "restoration politics" or anticircumcision activism, blurring the borders between the realm of pornography proper—that is, pornography created just for (illicit) kicks—and that of identity politics. Thus acculturated, pornography's "antisocial" nature breeds community, be it in the form of politics, connoisseurship, or fandom.

At the time I started writing this chapter, the American porn industry's "it" foreskin belonged to one Remy Delaine, the Australian-born porn star and cover boy of *Unzipped* magazine's first issue in 2006. Having just been elected Man of the Year by Raging Stallion Studios, Delaine also graced the current covers of *Blue* magazine and *XXX Showcase.* Frisky Fans Video Lounge, an Internet site boasting more than seven hundred film reviews, was quick to report about the sensational new kid on the block. The piece was titled "Thick 'n Creamy French Dish"; here's a little tidbit to show how casually porn speak morphs into showbiz jargon: "New pornstar Remy Delaine carries a dark, powerful sexual magnetism which hums in his movies. . . . 'This [winning the title of Man of the Year] was a complete surprise for me!' exclaimed Delaine as he retracted his foreskin. 'I work hard at making my scenes as good as they can be, and working with the Raging Stallion crew is very easy. . . .' Delaine carries an amazing, thickly-hooded cock. Striking French-Arab looks and powerful eyes make him truly a worthy selection for Man of the Year."

Another editor of the same website was so taken by the actor that he composed a limerick:

There's a Frenchman down under who's hung.
He once inhaled bouillabaisse in his lung.
His foreskin is thick,
which the boys like to lick.
They simply just stick out their tongues.[6]

So Delaine is described deliciously, ambiguously, and multipunningly as "a Frenchman Down Under"; he is seen as sporting the looks of a "French Arab"—indeed one of his starring vehicles was a bit of colonialist exotica called *Arabesque*. (I will return to the thematic of ethnicity and race shortly.)

As for the general relevance of foreskin for pornography, the website Fore skin.org listed 148 porn films that refer more or less explicitly to the *foreskin* in their title. Apart from these films, about a hundred more are cited in which the foreskin plays a part, although the title doesn't directly reveal this (examples of the latter would be Bel Ami and Remy Delaine films). Another website, Movie Monster, offers 289 films in its uncut category. Not exactly marginal, then, this marginal phenomenon. The movies' names are as telling as they are amusing. Apart from the more ordinary *Foreskin Fantasies*, *Foreskin Forever*, *I* [♥] *Foreskin!*, *Uncut Club* (parts 1–6), and *Uncut* (parts 1–12), we find one witty pun after the other: *Uncut Gems: Diamonds in the Raw*, *Boys with a Hood*, *Hooded Stranger*, *Under the Hood*, *Hoods (Totally Uncut)*, *Hoods and Helmets/Uncut Studs*—*Cut Buds*, *Dick in a Turtleneck*, and *Bareback Mountain: The Raw Truth*. And, finally, one of my own favorite titles, *Club Mandom 1: The Blue Collar Cheese Factory* (see figure 19.2).

## Topographies of Desire

I will refrain from analyzing *Club Mandom 1* here, for the cover and title are expressive enough to deliver my point. You might consider the cover image as a kind of subconscious to the *Man in a Polyester Suit*. The film gives us another floppy, sloppy, uncut cock, this time whipped out of a pair of blue jeans and enhanced by a functional ornament (the cock ring), which underscores both the bulging naturalism and its underlying circular geometry. The title itself poignantly articulates a topography of desire: desire's highly troubled, productive relation to the lowly concept of dirt; desire is framed in terms of transgression and class society.[7] The description of the "story line" is rather grotesque, so I'll quote an excerpt:

*Club Mandom* is subtitled *Blue Collar Cheese Factory* because [Tom] Caserta [the producer, director, editor, and star of the film] doesn't merely suck dicks

THE ULTIMATE FORESKIN FANTASY

19.2. Tom Caserta produced, directed, and starred in *Club Mandom 1: Blue Collar Cheese Factory* (Bijou Classics, 1990). As the cover promises, the movie features uncut cocks with an abundance of smegma. The open denim trousers signal the working-class status of the anonymous men who visit Caserta's glory hole.

with foreskin, he relishes and savors the cheesy schlongs of working men. This ain't no pristine skin flick; everything that comes along with the extra flop of skin that covers a penis head is highlighted here and it's explicit. Each and every one of the scenes features lots and lots of smegma—gooey, creamy flecks of cock junk. . . . If this tape sounds a little severe for you, there's always *Club Mandom 2*, an oral celebration of funk-free, circumcised packages.[8]

This is the wisdom of pornographic discourse: foreskinned cocks are presented as both gross and hot, suggesting that hot always already harbors a healthy dose of grossness. The carnivalesque rhetoric that savors dirt and pigging out—relishing "cheese," "cock junk," and "funk"—suggests a fantasy of subliminal transgression. But in terms of fantasy—the fantasy of unlimited intimacy, you might say—the idea of cheesy schlongs works its magic, even to the extent that the audience of hard-core devotees needs to be cooled down with a "cleaner" alternative, a part 2. Ironically, this sequence invokes a temporal logic: from uncut to cut, from original filth to aestheticized filth. Thus, the producers of Club Mandom end up giving us, in spite of themselves, an allegory of acculturation, with "funk-free" suggesting not just cleanliness but social coherence and normalcy. (I will return to the notion of acculturation toward the end of the chapter.)

So, harking back to the Mapplethorpean foreskin, we begin to see how thin the line between spectacle and scandal can be. We also see how right the anti-pornography crusaders were: Man in a Polyester Suit, too, is undeniably "dirty," incredibly pornographic—and very hot. (It took a dyed-in-the-wool moralist to whiff this out while we were naively admiring the cool grisaille textures and Neusachliche composition.) To be sure, Mapplethorpe's photograph is an utterly dubious, helplessly obscene image—hence all the more relevant as a cocksure artistic statement of its era. But let's linger a while on the queer symbolics that the 1980s moralist was so adept at speed-reading. The very concept of "uncut" comes saturated with notions of liminality and alterity: the foreskin, while representing a curiously foreign morphology, also bespeaks "nature," fantastic unfetteredness, the social dimensions of which are an imagined lack of civilization, lower-class status, or symbolic dirtiness—a symbolics that is only sometimes played out in literal terms, as in Club Mandom.

As it happens, the factor of race prominently figures in circumcision statistics as well as the Mapplethorpe photograph. According to a study made in 1997, 81 percent of white male U.S. citizens were circumcised, while the same went for only 65 percent of African Americans, and a mere 54 percent of Hispanic men.[9] In metropolitan centers like New York City, popular lore links Latino masculinity in particular with uncut morphology. Thus we have items like the flier for a New York dance club from a few years back: PapiCock: The Uncut Version (figure 19.3). The title refers, of course, to Hispanic men, while the punny subtitle and a strategically placed circle (neatly framing the "private" parts that are covered with white briefs) plays with the tacit knowledge about the uncut nature of Latin members. Thanks to the wonders of cropping, we do not see the model's face—just a torso of naturally dark, taut flesh, and what is at most the hint of an emerging goatee.

Again, a more literal (though no less potentially campy) representation is provided by pornography proper, in a film entitled simply and appropriately Fantastic Foreskin! (figure 19.4). The cover image applies "sophisticated" means—photo(shop)montage and enhanced perspective echoed by the spectacularizing typography—to underscore the bluntly "fantastic" nature of the Latin foreskin, which comes displayed in a realistic and suggestive tautology of three uncut cocks. A rather typical product of the Latino Fan Club, the film features rugged and smutty urban types that might fit the typological

19.3. This is a promotional poster for New York dance-club event. "PapiCock: The Uncut Version" plays on the double meaning of uncut to advertise an uncensored lust for Hispanic men with foreskin.

category "thug" (at least if they weren't so into gay performance). All in all, the preputial semiosphere manifests its essential flexibility, as modern foreskin fantasies run the associative gamut from the down-home rural to urban modernity, where foreskin explicitly plays on the symbolic of ethnic and social transgression (not least so if we take, as I do, the main clientele for this type of film to represent the white upper-middle class). In any case, we see how the melting pot worked its magic with respect to WASPs and Jewish men, while creating new, "irregular" minorities to function as objects in a fetishistic economy of desire.

19.4. The cover image for the Latino Fan Club's *Fantastic Foreskin!* (directed by Brian Brennan, 2006).

## Fetishism beyond Freud

Talking about fetishism calls for some justification, for in theory—at least in Freudian theory—the male organ itself is poorly suited for fetishization proper. (For Freud, the sexual fetish functions mainly as a substitute for the male sexual organ.)[10] Due partly to Freud's own scientific fetish and his literary drive to narrativity, the highly creative notion of fetishism has been formalized into a normative account centering around a gender-determined "primal" scene. One does, however, recognize a more general structural validity to his theory, and it is this structural model that inspires me to pursue the Freudian path. Scratch the rigidity of the mother-son dyad, then, and replace the fear of castration with a more general sense of bodily anxiety, and you have the situation at hand. Fear of castration is here abstracted, because it is rendered so concrete, minute: here is a body part that can easily be lost or has indeed been (partly) lost. Castration is only partial, hence all the more symbolically potent. The master castrator is culture at large—a modern, superegoistic, patronizing society that marches to the beat of hygienic functionalism.

To my knowledge, Freud doesn't elaborate on this particular aspect in his writings. However, an American psychiatrist, Joseph Wortis—who studied with Freud in 1934 and kept a diary of his student-analysis sessions—provides a bit of rare insight here. Wortis refers to a discussion that indicates that Freud was quite aware of a fetishistic dynamic vis-à-vis foreskins: "I discussed [with Freud] a case history of a homosexual that I had just received from [Havelock] Ellis: the subject was narcissistic . . . , [and he] had been circumcised for medical reasons at the age of eleven and was only interested in uncircumcised boys. Freud explained the case very aptly, said it was a transparent case of fixation at a certain age, that the homosexuality was here closely associated with the narcissism, and the subject really wanted his former self back again."[11] My point here is not to take psychoanalysis at its word—the insistence on narcissistic fixation, indication of healing therapy, et cetera—but simply to see how Freud's insight into the dynamics of "perversion" enabled him to envision a queer scenario of foreskin fetishism—avant la lettre, a good half century before the phenomenon reached any kind of cultural prominence, let alone the kind it has today.

Though Freud's comment was indirect and made in passing, we can easily think along Freudian lines without Freud. The foreskin—aside from being just a delectable body part *an sich*—might be understood to function as a kind of nostalgic safeguard against the idea of mutilation and vulnerability, as well as any potential memory traces of trauma. (If even this strikes the reader as too literally psychoanalytical, please bear with me, for I do believe this structural model will help understand what might be going on behind the pornographic scenes.) In more general terms, fetishism refers to "the investment of separate body parts or portions of raiment with voluptuous sensations," so that sexual interest is focused on "the one part abstracted from the entire body."[12] The pornographic eye tends to zoom in on specific body parts—so much so that speaking about fetishism in the context of pornography seems somehow redundant. Desire is so keen on seeking surplus value from its objects that highly specific properties acquire mythical importance—not just size, then, but various aesthetic specificities also matter here. Pornographic desire is by nature—which is of course to say "by culture"—particular. It tends toward specification, even pickiness; it is by culture drawn to the curious and the foreign. Desire, to be sure, always seems greener, more uncut, on the other side of the fence.

Still, I think it safe to say that many (if not all) circumcised men also share a sense of trauma or loss: a sense of having been unlawfully touched upon and severed—by medical ideology, by modern society. (Hence we have another English term that would be redundant for most Europeans: *intact*. In America, foreskinned men are increasingly referred to as intact—that is, whole, un-scathed, not impaired.) The reference to Freudian castration theory should thus neither be taken too literally nor too abstractly, for the thought of an operation performed in early childhood may well be imagined as a traumatic event, one that can retroactively trigger an anxious dynamic of "fetishistic" attachment.

To shed light on such a dynamic, here are some statements by circumcised men collected on a website devoted to the issue:

"I think of myself and other circumcised men as amputees."

"I think of myself as existing in two parts: my missing foreskin and the rest of me."

"I feel like half a man."

"I feel that my father betrayed me by letting my mother have me circum-cised against his wishes, and I've always sensed that deep down inside he rejected me because he saw me as damaged."

"I wanted to be a girl when I was a child because I knew that girls weren't circumcised."

"I used to think there were two kinds of boys: circumcised boys like me and real boys."

"When I was a child, I prayed I would get my foreskin back in Heaven."[13]

The attention of circumcised men may thus turn to the foreskin of others, not simply because they are Other (as in "opposites attract") but also as if to gain some kind of solace or assurance—treating the other man's foreskin as a nos-talgic keepsake or memento of that which they too once had but were forced to give up. There is also an interesting sense of gender ambivalence that hovers around the statements: though the foreskin itself could be deemed symboli-cally feminine, here we have men who feel just "half a man"—something apart from "real," "intact" men—because of the operation.

My theorizing here does not, of course, assume the mechanisms of desire and disavowal involved to be conscious ones. However, while the erotic-emotional investment in the foreskin can be explained by simple curiosity, it yet seems to "lean" on a fantasy of originality and a painfully nostalgic image of integrity or inviolability: "I too once had one and ought to still have one."[14]

This, of course, is a distinct variation of the classical scenario of *Verleug-nung*, which Freud used to describe the denial that some boys expressed when seeing female genitals (they claimed to see a penis).[15] Instead, here is the horror of too much to see that ignites anxiety; this is a realization sparked by the other male body, inspiring the sudden realization of a potential personal lack, as the *nichts zu sehen* becomes a fact of one's own male body (rather than the nothing-to-see that Freud attributes to the female body). Where exactly, then, does desire figure in? Let's look at some more statements by circumcised American men:

> "From the moment I learned what circumcision was, and that I was circumcised, I was very angry. I learned about it around age thirteen which was when I started masturbating. I fantasized about having a foreskin."

> "I masturbate two or three times a day, always to the same fantasy: the image of my foreskin as it would look and feel now, had it not been cut off when I was born."

> "The only reason I'm gay is that I was circumcised when I was a baby. I feel deprived. It's only with an uncircumcised man that I can have a foreskin."

> "I have a good sexual relationship with my wife, but I'm also turned on by foreskins and have had several uncircumcised lovers. Would I still have been gay if I hadn't been circumcised?"

> "I was circumcised early in life, and I remember when I was about six a boy showing me his penis with a foreskin. I was fascinated and have been ever since. Over the years at school, in showers I have seen many uncircumcised men but have never touched one. I would like to and I would like to engage in 'docking' when a man puts his foreskin over another [my] penis."[16]

Again, far from pondering whether or not circumcision can actually lead to queerness, the point here is to take seriously the anxieties linked with the experience of circumcision, and the relation of such anxieties to the complex workings of desire—desire that by culture seems always already prone to perversion (as Freud so persuasively argues).

Sometimes these accounts by circumcised men seem too good—too appropriately queer—to be true, and it remains impossible to tell whether these are simply cases of life imitating art (namely, the art of psychoanalytic reasoning), examples of clever political rhetoric (against circumcision), or what have you. In the Q&A section of a website devoted to the issue of masturbation, a (self-identified) thirteen-year-old boy writes: "I'm the only boy in my gym class with foreskin on my penis. I get teased about it a lot, although I like the feeling when I masturbate. Some of the guys asked me to show them how I slide the skin back—they all laughed, but a couple of them got erections while watching me. Do you think they are just jealous?" Another young uncut man, fifteen years old, expresses his worry over rumors around school about women refusing to have sex with uncut guys. "Is this true?" he asks.[17] Thus, the foreskin is culturally saturated with images of desire as well as rejection and disgust, even, importantly, all at the same time. Apropos, some readers may recall an episode of *Sex in the City* where the ladies make a humorous fuss about one of Charlotte's dates, an uncut guy who is likened to a Shar-Pei, the fashionably wrinkly dog with the endless layers of loose skin (a pet that has been severely cultured to look so "natural"). Or the episode of the Americanized British talk show *The Graham Norton Effect* (which aired in Finland on January 27, 2007), where Norton's guest RuPaul "happened" to mention an English friend who has "one." Norton—himself an Englishman—then turned knowingly to the audience and remarked grimacingly, "Oh, the trashcan has a lid." (RuPaul went on to add that this friend could stuff up to eighteen marbles inside "it," and, oh, what a money shot it was when he let them all drop!) Thus we have, in the best carnivalesque manner, imagery both gross and fascinating, referencing actual dirt as well as the dirty world of pornography, a.k.a. the sideshow.

Fetishism, at least in its traditional Freudian form, is always informed by an economy of ambivalence: desire is, by culture, "warped"—or enhanced or enriched, depending on how we wish to judge it—by various insecurities and inconsistencies, defenses, denials, and displacements. Typical moments of disavowal play in: I know his is really no more authentic than mine; I know this little difference doesn't matter, but . . . ; I haven't experienced circumcision in a traumatic way, yet. Thus the foreskin devotee expresses a conflictual stance vis-à-vis the object of desire. He admits and denies the naturalness of the foreskin, admits and denies that the extra skin is quite comme il faut, admits and denies that it is "more pure" than his own hygienicized, cultured, and functional penis. But most of all he admits and denies that there is something dubious and foreign to the foreskin, something quite distasteful, even—for isn't this exactly what the normative hygienic ideology that advocates circumcision teaches him to think? It is precisely this kind of desiring dynamic that my reading of the foreskin should help us conceptualize: desire deeply implicated in and complicated by ambivalence—indeed feeding off this very ambivalence, and interweaving potential disgust and denial into desire's intricate workings.

### Discomfort to Desire, Culture to Nature

Now that we have been lured into the realm of the alien(ated) foreskin—that mark of alterity that both fascinates and troubles—we can see even more clearly how the spectacular nature of the foreskin must have played out in *Man* in a *Polyester Suit*. The photograph, carefully staged and cropped by Mapplethorpe, invokes a multiple paradox through the juxtaposition of a covering suit (i.e., culture) with the uncovered cock (i.e., nature) — "uncovered," paradoxically, because covered with skin. In the American context, this black cock can be understood to represent a state of (at least) double dishabille — a dick twice undressed — precisely because it is covered by skin: because it is untouched, left in the natural state. The fact that it is a black man attached to the foreskin further complicates our reading. If the juxtaposition of suit and flesh (with the bright spot of a white shirt accentuating the contrast) represents a kind of oxymoron, *black uncut* becomes somewhat of a redundancy, thanks to the stubborn linkage between blackness and nature in the white Western imagination. Through such symbolic tautology, the image points to the fantasies (and, initially, fears) once displaced onto the black body: fantasies of an imagined natural state — a body bursting, as it were, from its seams.

The British black critic Kobena Mercer, precisely inspired by Mapplethorpe's photographs, has offered us a poignant analysis of the racial-fetishistic logic at play.[18] Mercer looks at *Man in a Polyester Suit* and quotes Frantz Fanon's text from 1970: "One is no longer aware of the Negro, but only of a penis; the Negro is eclipsed. He is turned into a penis. He is a penis."[19] The foreskinned cock — which Mercer overlooks as a British, presumably uncut, man — is naturally draped or "veiled," covered by a hood. It shows plenty, but leaves at least as much to the imagination, and for our dirty minds to savor. Steeped in ambivalence, such a cock can always be uncloaked one more time. The thematic of teasing layers (skin upon skin, fabric upon fabric) is accentuated by the gray textures and the contrasting sartorial culture of the suit, being as formal as daywear gets: a neatly buttoned-up three-piece men's suit, what is more, one made of synthetic material (the antithesis of nature). The photograph was, after all, not named *Man in a Suit*, but *Man in a Polyester Suit*.

As those of us who experienced the 1970s remember, polyester does not "breathe," but this suit-clad man yet manages to breathe through his fly. It is as if the cock wants out of its severe cultural frame, refusing to stay in line. "Nature" is here represented not simply in the black cock with its large pulsating vein but even in the (labia-like) opening of the white shirt and hem of the vest, which itself seems to consist, curiously, of two layers. The photograph thus recalls not just the dominant medical functionalism of its era but Freud's ponderings on "man's discomfort in civilization" (*das Unbehagen in der Kultur*). The art of sublimation, represented here by the neatly cut, snugly fitting suit, provides slim consolation for the person living under the pressures of civilization.[20] Perhaps Mapplethorpe was depicting a cultural paradox: despite the suit (i.e., civilization), the skin tends to preside — it is fore, comes before other things, as a preconceptual presumption, a relic of the transgressive, "dirty" body.[21] In any case, the idea of sublimation here conceptually mirrors the art of circumcision, as both come to express a form of cultural (dis)illusionism.

Moreover, the image activates an intriguing temporal dissonance: while the attire is modern, the cock remains thoroughly archaic. "Desire always proceeds toward an extreme archaism," writes Roland Barthes, whose own relation to foreskins was far from unambiguous. Though Barthes, as we know from the publication of his *Incidents*, had a soft spot for Arabs (and Islam and circumcision go hand in hand), the Sicilian youths captured by the German photographer Baron Wilhelm von Gloeden inspired in him some poignant rumination. Describing the sloppy archaism of Gloedenian trade, Barthes makes it a point to note: "Uncircumcised are what they are, and one sees only that."[22] So, despite an abundance of punctual delicacies ("the rather dirty peasant hands" and "worn feet that are none too clean"), the foreskins steal the show.

My reference to Barthes is not just about dropping names—even though Barthes had an eye for foreskin![23] Recalling Gloeden's photography together with Barthes's paradoxical notion of desire's archaic progression helps to explicate the sense of temporal disarticulation that looms around foreskin fantasies, engendering, as these older images do, a severely *nostalgic* sense of et in Arcadia ego.[24] It is as if the foreskin (even for Barthes, who is likely to have sported one himself) comes to stand in for gross and desirable alterity, an alterity expressed in terms that confuse both temporality and physiognomy. Photographed in the early 1900s, the musty-kitschy classicism of Gloeden harks way back to the ancient world. Thus we have a curious chain of backward glancing: me looking at Barthes looking at Gloeden looking at classical antiquity, with each temporal leap somehow enhanced by the presence of a preputial archaism.

All this tempts me to frame the foreskin in terms of the critique of normative futurism that has been recently labeled the "antisocial thesis." Particularly when viewed in the American context, the foreskin does indeed come to represent antisociality (in the structural sense articulated by Lee Edelman).[25] For surely the foreskin disturbs "knowledge" and rational coherence: it refuses the principle of progress and rebels against modern functionalism—against medical normativity, against conceptual unity and social cohesion, sanitization, and normalization that are still today marketed under the banner of reason.

Displacing the modern anesthetic phallus, the soft, floppy, wrinkly, sensitive foreskin suggests not just symbolic gender ambivalence but a potential space of jouissance beyond progressive culture (indeed, *gender* here seems only a stand-in for normative culture). Of course, the conceptual model of antisociality evoked here is based on structural situationality: in other words, the foreskin, more or less "natural" or neutral in its original context (like that of the Gloeden photographs, where the semiotic of the foreskin becomes a kind of hindsighted premonition), is rendered queer and excessive by way of the antagonistic logic that governs normative sociality. The visual examples I have chosen—from pornographic art to the art of pornography proper—all attest to that disruptive jouissance, a queerness that seems always to emerge to undo "civilized" culture.

That this jouissance quickly turns into a culture of its own right attests to the allegorical logic of redemptive acculturation that we have already witnessed in instances ranging from foreskin fandom to restoration politics. The recent book Un*/Cut, an artsy-pornsy coffee-table book featuring hyperaesthetic photographs of foreskinned dicks, provides a case in point.[26] Bringing together the traditions of scopophilic hoarding and modern photographic art (were they ever completely separate?), this volume, featuring a hundred or so flashy close-ups of foreskin after photogenic foreskin (with just a couple of circumcised cocks thrown in for measure), would surely have tickled the fancies of nineteenth-century students of the body and sexuality—not to mention the likes of Gloeden or Barthes. The book begins with a foreword by Jim Eigo (an American journalist), which to me recalls Freud's musings on das Unheimliche (the uncanny): "In [these] pictures the penis attains the dark, sinuous, shuddering beauty of a great fairy tale, one that lodges in the memory. And as with a fairy tale, the emotions stirred are deep, disruptive, conflicting, thrilling, primal and in the end irresistible. Often these wayward members, whether asleep or rearing their heads, recall handsome, powerful animals, the penis a species of its own, or a form of vegetation, or a feature of the landscape, some out-cropping of rock. (A cherished few appear so tender that the viewer just wants to protect them.)"[27] As we go from forbidden fruit to gay eye candy, we witness the emergence of new communities of desire—of shared fetishism and "aesthetic" connoisseurship—that channel what may initially be little more than perverse, antisocial, unheimliche manifestations of the drive. I take this to be an effect of what Edelman calls "the irony of irony's relation to desire": foreskin fandom emerges to accommodate desire's social tendency, to turn an extra profit of meaning on what was initially mere jouissance—or a simple piece of soft skin.[28]

*The Foreskin Next Door*

Having noted earlier the implication of racial alterity in the dynamics of desire, I wish to briefly elaborate on that argument, so as not to cater to a simplistic, stable understanding of the notion of alterity (as in black, Latin, and so on). As I indicated, European males, however "white," are by no means exempt from the economy of desire described here. Some of the most successful pornographic production companies of the last fifteen years—Kristen Björn and Bel Ami, to name just two of the best-loved ones—both benefit from and inspire foreskin fandom. This is not to say that these companies are explicitly advocating the pleasures of foreskin fetishism, or even that their films and photography would knowingly center on that body part. Rather, we might think of the foreskin in these images as a kind of Barthesian *punctum*: relating to the prickly foreskin is a matter of reading, and as such it requires some initiation or sensitization to obtuse cultural meaning.[29]

Clean and white as the Bel Ami boys are, uncircumcised is what they are also, engendering yet another subcategory of alterity—that green grass that we are so naturally drawn to—one that reflects global and transnational as well as intra-European cultural hierarchies. A brief look at a variety of Bel Ami postcards (published in the form of very popular postcard books by Bruno Gmünder) will give an idea how the foreskin—always emphatically represented and not just casually depicted—accentuates the naturism that is Bel Ami's obvious trademark.[30] These books show how the foreskin spices up the myth of originality—of Eastern European ethnic alterity, of Slavic sexiness— that this particular variant of transnational porn thrives on. *Green* is indeed the key word here: the locations are conspicuously green; the young'uns are green; everything is natural, woody, rustic, and archaic. All this "organicism" bespeaks an unsoiled, idyllic arcadia—an arcadia that one (when attuned to the critical mode) suspects has precious little to do with the everyday realities of the mainly Slovakian men posing as porn stars.[31]

Take, for a more concrete example, the advertisement for the Bel Ami DVD *Get Lucky with Lukas* (published in *Unzipped* magazine in November 2002—see figure 19.5). Here the photograph makes sure that Lukas Ridgeston's natural wonder is visible despite the erection that is taking place. The foreskin is thus depicted "in action," emphasizing both the head of the penis in a process of revelation and the skin itself, its versatility (how fascinating, the mechanism of preputial sliding). Upon closer inspection of Bel Ami photographs featuring Ridgeston, one notes the recurring semiotic theme: the foreskin "in action," and, by the same token, as just "half a foreskin." This peekaboo effect is something that most of the images considered here attest to or at least hint at: from *Club Mandom* to *Fantastic Foreskin!*, from Bel Ami to the "art photography" of Un*/Cut, we are presented with the virtual *photogénie* of the foreskin.

Ironically enough, this semiotic of preputial upward mobility seems to mimic an evolutionary movement away from nature, meeting the modern culture of circumcision halfway, as it were: in the ambivalent imagination— hardly literalized at the level of consciousness—of circumcised consumers.

19.5. This advertisement for the Bel Ami DVD *Get Lucky with Lukas* appeared in *Unzipped* magazine in November 2002.

Here the semiotic of movable parts may well be more of a semiotic of removable parts—representing the best of both worlds. From the vantage point of fetishism, what such images give us, essentially, are allegories of disavowal. Again, fetishism seems to manifest its key dynamic here: fantasy can function as a safeguard against alterity; making a spectacle of a particular body part may in fact turn the gaze away from some of its disturbing aspects.

The cult of Ridgeston's natural wonder reached its apex in 2000. In May of that year, *Unzipped* published the following news item: "Had enough of the Bel Ami boys yet? I didn't think so. You just can't read enough about Lukas Ridgeston, and I just can't write enough. So in a bit of news that should elate fans worldwide, it's reported . . . that a Ridgeston dildo is now in the works. Actually two, and who more deserves to be replicated twice? One was molded with his foreskin retracted; the other has a retractable foreskin that took a full year to develop."[32] So again we have, bizarrely enough, the best of both

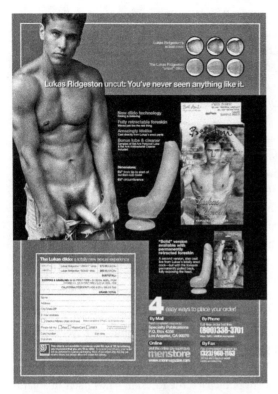

19.6. Advertisement for Lukas Ridgeston dildos, with a cutout order form in the lower left-hand corner, appeared in *Unzipped* magazine in March 2001.

worlds, this time in the form of two dildos: one "realistic" (read: fantastic) foreskinned one, and another for those who might find the foreskin a bit much.

An ad published ten months later (figure 19.6) displays both products plus Ridgeston himself, again at half-mast: "Lukas Ridgeston uncut: You've never seen anything like it."[33] On the upper-right side of the ad we are given photographs of the foreskin (both the original and the plastic one, six images in all) in action, of course. That is, in various stages of retraction—of retro-action, we might say, for there is again something distinctly retro about the foreskin thus represented. (While writing this chapter I checked whether the product was still available: at the time the uncut version—selling for $69.99—was sold out, whereas the solid version—selling for ten dollars less—was still available. We can deduce from this that foreskins sell very nicely indeed, even in plastic. It should also be noted that unlike most porn stars whose cocks are reproduced in the form of dildos, Ridgeston is not particularly well hung, nor are his strategic measurements emphasized. The appeal thus lies elsewhere: in the naturalizing mixture of the curious and the wholesome.)

It makes sense, then, that the Bel Ami boys are generally represented as untouched by certain aspects of Western civilization, including the stern identity compartments of "gay" and "straight."[34] In other words, their sexuality is imagined intact, just like their cocks, much in the tradition of straight trade— albeit representing a particularly clean boy-next-door version thereof, one for which the foreskin yet adds a particularly organic, spicy flavor of queer wholesomeness. As is well known, many men indoctrinated into modern gay identity sexually prefer naturally "straight" men (particularly those prone to horsing around with other guys). It is as though another gay-identified person were "corrupted" by culture—and, when circumcised, corrupted twice over. The fantasy of polymorphous sexuality—innocence as horniness, an undiscriminating horniness—seems to acquire visual confirmation in the premodern nature of the frisky foreskins.

............................

There is much more to the foreskin than meets the innocent eye. Trivial as it may seem to many of us, the foreskin is a surprisingly prominent cultural presence, not least in the United States, precisely where it is supposed to be marginal. A highly ambivalent body part, the foreskin lends itself in a paradigmatic, versatile way to the theorizing of desire. It has been seen as dirty and dubious in various historical contexts—from the "foreskin is disgusting" dictum of the Talmud to twentieth-century American hygienicist circumcision policy—all the way to recent speculation on HIV and foreskins. On the other hand, circumcision and the uncovered glans of the penis have been deemed ungainly and obscene, both in Christian traditions and in ancient Greece, where foreskins represented the aesthetic norm (indeed, some American foreskin aficionados draw quite explicitly from this ancient tradition of Greek foreskin appreciation).[35] Recently, due to anticircumcision activity in the United States, many circumcised men have come to consider foreskinned penises more natural and genuine, even in a sense cleaner (because they are unsoiled by the tampering of medical science). These men emphasize the natural "good" bacteria that dwell under the foreskin—a kind of ambiguous filth that becomes clean because it may actually defend the body from intruding "bad" bacteria or viruses.

Thus, depending on the historical situation and ideological concerns, the presence as well as absence of the foreskin could be deemed unseemly or indecent. The scenarios of desire and disavowal looming about the foreskin render it a culturally expressive—as well as endlessly perplexing—issue. They indicate a persistent fetishistic fascination, which becomes a case in point when seeking to understand desire's perverse relation to its seeming opposites, repression and disgust. One thing, at least, seems indisputable in light of the evidence: the attempt to control—to censor, cut off, cleanse, or aestheticize—will result in sexualization and end up producing intricate cultures of desire around the dubious object. The modern practice of circumcision can itself be understood (quite literally) as a perversion—an ideology that rejects bodily nature by invoking functional rationality and hygiene, and, gradually, normalcy: the naturalness of modern tradition. The repressed, however, will return, now in the form of a seedy curiosity, electrified by its outlaw status. And finally, that charge of curious marginality will end up tending to a culture of sociality.

I would like to end with a little anecdote concerning a colleague of mine who heard a version of this chapter in Finland a few years ago. (He is a European man who was circumcised as a youth due to a particular medical problem.) Fascinated, he admitted that he had actually never come to think of foreskins as objects of desire. So here was a circumcised gay man who didn't really care for foreskin—an exception to the rule? Alas, a year or so later he enthusiastically reported that he was now totally "into foreskin" and that people's cut-uncut status had acquired major relevance since my talk. "Oh dear," I thought to myself, "I've created a monster!" To be sure, fetishism is infectious—a social phenomenon, just like fandom. I hope this chapter hasn't created more monsters. On the other hand, what if it has? After all, foreskins are fun.

## Notes

1. See, for example, J. Butler, "The Force of Fantasy," 490, 498, 500–503; Meyer, *Outlaw Representation*, 212–19; L. Williams, "Second Thoughts on *Hard Core*," 3, 165, 174 n15.

2. For an aesthetic-sensitive reading of Mapplethorpe's photographs that yet remains insensitive to the foreskin, see Danto, *Playing with the Edge*, 106–17, 130–34. Arthur C. Danto is hardly one to skirt an issue for reasons of propriety, and he does make ample notice of the awesome spectacularity of the Mapplethorpean dick, especially in the circumcised case of the 1976 photograph *Mark Stevens* (Mr. 10 1/2).

3. Paige, "The Ritual of Circumcision," 2–4.

4. Paige, "The Ritual of Circumcision," 6. After the Second World War, the number of circumcised men rose to 80 percent, reaching its apex in the mid-1960s. See Gilman, *Making the Body Beautiful*, 288; and Lauman, Masi, and Zuckerman, "Circumcision in the United States."

5. Quoted in Hodges, "The Ideal Prepuce in Ancient Greece and Rome," 389.

6. Frisky Boy, "Thick 'n Creamy French Dish," FriskyFans.org, September 25, 2007.

7. For a post-Freudian account of desire, dirt, and class topography (in Finnish), see: Kalha, "Halu alennuksessa."

8. See the *Club Mandom* 1 page on BijouGayMovies.com, accessed April 23, 2011, http://www.bijougaymovies.com/Club_Mandom_1_Blue_Collar_Cheese_Factory.

9. Laumann, Masi, and Zuckerman, "Circumcision in the United States." The democratization of circumcision didn't take place until after the Second World War. Karen Ericksen Paige estimates the frequency of circumcision in the late 1930s to have been 75 percent in middle-class families and 25 percent in lower social strata. Paige, "The Ritual of Circumcision," 4.

10. Freud's theory of fetishism is a very specific attempt at understanding the dynamic of desire and disavowal. Here fetishism establishes itself as queerly essential to the male heteronormative psychosocial makeup, as it is imagined as substitute for the mother's phallus, which the boy child discovers to be missing. Due to this "trauma" and eventual disavowal (*Verleugnung*), the restless gaze is averted and focuses instead on substitutes — feet, shoes, stockings, and so on — which become sexually charged. Freud goes as far as to suggest that this fetishistic disavowal is what saves men from homosexuality, a perversion that might otherwise ensue from the trauma. As is well known, Freud's "boyish" scenario tends to disregard women's various fetishisms as well as those of the men who are not saved from homosexual perversion.

11. Wortis, *My Analysis with Freud*, 150.

12. Krafft-Ebing, *Psychopathia Sexualis*, 21.

13. Statements compiled by John A. Erickson and Jeffrey R. Wood from Tornwings .com, September 25, 2007.

14. I stress here the Greek *algos*, meaning pain, for it is a particularly physical sense of longing or homesickness that is here evoked.

15. Freud, "Analysis of a Phobia of a Five Year Old Boy."

16. Statements compiled by John A. Erickson and Jeffrey R. Wood from Tornwings .com, September 25, 2007. See, on the other hand, Jason's comment (p. 6) on his "circumfetish." The term *docking* refers to an increasingly popular form of sexual intimacy wherein one's partner's foreskin is pulled over one's own penis. This is an intriguing form of all-male "penetrative" union, suggestive of a "familial" narrative that is both generative and nostalgically looking backward.

17. "JackinQ&A," JackinWorld, September 25, 2007, accessed March 24, 2014, http://www.jackinworld.com/questions-answered/jackinqa-and-qa-archive.

18. Mercer, *Welcome to the Jungle*, 171–209. As a black gay man, Mercer unpacks the racist imagination invoked by Mapplethorpe with acute sensitivity; however, as an uncut Englishman, Mercer takes for granted — hence fails to pay attention to — the other tautological difference of the man in the polyester suit.

19. Mercer, *Welcome to the Jungle*, 185.

20. As Freud notes, sublimation is attainable only for the privileged few — those who, as it were, tend to wear three-piece suits. While all suits might be understood to be "synthetic," this particular suit makes clear that the project of civilization is always already doomed for failure. See Freud, *Civilization and Its Discontents*, 30.

21. See also Mercer, *Welcome to the Jungle*, 187. This ambivalence is echoed by the dissonance between blackness and the suit: blackness may represent the sublime symbolically, but its status in terms of the practice of sublimation has traditionally been dubi-

ous (consider here Freud, but also, say, blackness in the Burkean sublime, or Kobena Mercer's first take on Mapplethorpe). The line between *sublime* and *slime*, however, seems to remain forever ambiguous.

22. Barthes, "Wilhelm von Gloeden," 196. He writes, "These little Greek gods . . . have rather dirty peasant hands with big rough fingernails, worn feet that are none too clean, and very visibly swollen foreskins."

23. See Barthes, *Incidents*, 38. He writes, "Gérard, whose father is French and whose mother is a native woman, wants to show me the way to the Gazelle d'Or; he sprawls in the car in order to reveal his charms; then, as a rare delicacy, a final, irresistible argument: 'You know, my thing, it's not cut!'"

24. Here we might juxtapose a Gloeden photograph of three youths with the cover of the Latin Fan Club film *Fantastic Foreskin!* to see how Gloeden's Latinate naturalism anticipates the modern taste for Latin dick, while both disclose the nature of their sleazy arcadia to be, as it were, a copy without an original.

25. Edelman, *No Future*.

26. The book was published in Germany by Bruno Gmünder (2009) and the photographs are by one "Giovanni," an Italian fashion photographer.

27. Eigo, foreword to *Un\*/Cut*, 6. Eigo's text also recalls Danto's reading of *Man in a Polyester Suit*, which stresses the cock's uncanny confrontation and likens it to the image of an age-old deity. As was the case with Mercer, Danto does not seem to pay attention to the foreskin. See Danto, *Playing with the Edge*, 106–17, 130–34.

28. Edelman, *No Future*, 89.

29. The Barthesian *punctum* is a "sting, speck, cut, little hole—that accident which pricks me (but also bruises me, is poignant to me)." See Barthes, *Camera Lucida*, 27.

30. *Bel Ami Postcard Book*, no. 31 (Germany: Bruno Gmünder, 2001).

31. Indeed, Bel Ami films are a case in point when analyzing postcommunist states' urgent will to pornographic capitalism—or our will to appropriate the natural wealth of Eastern Europe. The "transnationalist" phenomenon has been analyzed with insight by Rich Cante and Angelo Restivo, focusing on the case of Kristen Bjorn: "When the communist regimes of Central and Eastern Europe fell, what emerged in their place was the nation-state ready to take its place in the frenzy of transnational capitalism. And what these nations had to market was men." See Cante and Restivo, "The 'World' of All-Male Pornography," 121. I would only add that what these states had to offer was *uncut* men. In any case, the postcommunist world quickly became a fantastic locus for disseminating utopian—premodern, precapitalist—notions of sexuality. East European men also continue to embody, as it were, an "Orientalist" fantasy, which has lengthy traditions in queer economies of desire. In Finland, for example, Russian and Slavic men tend to be considered more rugged and down-to-earth, hence more desirable, than Scandinavians; in Sweden, Finnish men are considered more rough and "primitive" (i.e., desirable), et cetera. Here it seems that desire finds perpetual archaism in moving eastward—not because "light comes from the east" (*ex oriente lux*), but because primal darkness seems to dwell there.

32. F. Johnson, "The Next Best Thing," 9.

33. A slightly different ad was published in the July 2001 issue, which also features an article on the empowering effects of foreskin restoration (focusing on a procedure called "tugging"), right next to an ad for Bel Ami's "limited edition collector's magazine" (fea-

turing a typically outdoorsy image of four uncut Bel Ami stars frolicking in what looks like an endless ocean).

34. Kalha, "Sen pituinen se," 401–3.

35. See Kalha, "Sen pituinen se," 404–8, for a discussion (in Finnish) of the classical preputial paradigm and its echoes in contemporary uncut connoisseurship.

# 20

# Stadler's Boys; or, The Fictions
# of Child Pornography

Steven Ruszczycky

> Though my account will lapse into coarseness, flippancy, lies, and pure pornography, you must never forget that I truly and impossibly did love him.
> —Matthew Stadler, Allan Stein

The things that we find both treacherous and repugnant nevertheless contain important insights about how we engage the world around us: this is the problem expressed in the epigraph, taken from Matthew Stadler's 1999 novel Allan Stein. I expand on the narrator's plea to argue that it is through an investigation of not simply offensive things themselves but also the various strategies we deploy to deal with them that we stand to gain important insights into human sexuality. Yet what is it, exactly, about the narrator's account that would be so off-putting? Allan Stein tells the story of a young teacher from the Pacific Northwest who, disgraced by allegations of having slept with one of his adolescent male students, impersonates a curator friend and travels to Paris in order to procure a set of Picasso sketches on his friend's behalf. The curator friend, Herbert Widener, believes that the sketches may prove that Picasso modeled the young boy of his painting Boy Leading a Horse (1905–1906) on Gertrude Stein's young nephew, Allan Stein. Yet during his research the imposter Herbert seduces—and is seduced by—Stéphane, the fifteen-year-old son of his Parisian hosts. The two run away together to the south of France, where their relationship quickly deteriorates as the narrator's identity is exposed.

The narrator's plea cautions readers that his narrative, as one about a love between a man and a barely pubescent boy, lapses at times into pure child pornography. A cursory survey of newspaper databases, daytime talk shows, and nightly news programs would confirm child pornography's status as a topic sure to generate as much debate as declarations of disgust, and thus affirm the narrator's cause for concern. Such a survey, however, would also reveal child pornography as a source of persistent cultural fascination. This is the ambivalent relation to child pornography that the narrator's plea and Stadler's novel capture so well: despite the reluctance we may feel upon reading the narrator's warning, the titillation it provides keeps us reading.

Following the work of scholars such as Richard D. Mohr and Jacqueline Rose, I claim that one of the ways that we have managed to deal with this ambivalent relation to child pornography is to project the desire to see it onto others; we do so because these representations—and the responses they engender—trouble our seemingly secure sense of who we are. These strategies of denial and projection are in fact central to the prevailing notion of what child pornography is as it has emerged from a thorny history of court rulings, legislation, and psychological studies. Within the United States, child-pornography law is primarily thought of as a means for protecting children from exploitation. However, the law erects a powerful edifice that has two principal functions. First, it insists that child pornography is not a representation, subject to the deceptions of the signifier, but is evidence of a real crime committed against a real child. Second, it imagines a discrete population of pedophiles as the primary producers, distributors, and consumers of sexually explicit materials involving children. These two functions permit the censure of child pornography at the same time as they provide indirect access to the kinds of representations they condemn.

Moreover, in permitting both circuitous access and a sanitized excitement, child-pornography law bears important similarities to pornography itself. An analysis of the way that the law operates as a fiction—with very real effects—about what child pornography is and who uses it will be useful in challenging the particular notions of sexuality, subjectivity, and sociality subtending legal discourse. Despite the ease with which one might critique the strategies of child-pornography law, child pornography's perilous legal status places a formidable barrier in the way of any attempt to understand the more basic question of why sexually explicit representations of children have the capacity to both entice and disgust us in the first place. The mere expressed intention to view visual child pornography is enough to incur both the full force of child-pornography law and intense moral rebuke. Since written forms of child pornography remain (for the moment) largely free of legal prohibition and enjoy a much murkier moral status, these texts offer one possible solution to the problem of the legal barrier. Novels such as Stadler's *Allan Stein* provide a tentatively secure site in which to pursue these basic questions.

Like child-pornography law, which finds shelter in its status as law, *Allan Stein* is shifting, inconsistent, and at times sexually explicit in ways that readers would likely find objectionable were it expressed in a form other than the literary. Unlike child-pornography law, however, the novel's deceptions are its virtues. Its status as fiction and, according to the narrator, as child pornography affords us a chance to inquire into the fantasies at stake in such texts. In the final section of this chapter, I offer a reading of Stadler's novel in the context of his own interest in intergenerational sex and youth sexuality. This reading illustrates what literary pornography may have to tell us about the fantasies at stake in sexually explicit representations of children. I conclude by suggesting that careful attention to literary examples of child pornography may provide one way out of the contemporary political and moral mess that such representations produce. They may do so by indicating new modes of ethical relation between adults and youths that begin with rethinking one's own relation to what is most troubling about the self.

## Child Pornography, Pedophiles, and Realness

While erotic representations of children have existed for some time, our current understanding of child pornography did not emerge until the law identified it as a social and legal problem at the end of the 1970s. Until this moment, child pornography enjoyed a relatively quiet commercial existence. A number of scholars suggest that magazines and films containing sexually explicit images of children were relatively easy to find, if not widely available. These texts were both imported from Europe and manufactured domestically on a small scale. The modest heyday of child pornography ended as child abuse emerged as a social and political problem within the larger feminist project of identifying forms of domestic violence that previously had been shielded from legal scrutiny by the privatized space of the home. These intervention efforts had complicated consequences: at the same time that these campaigns identified children's well-being as a problem for state intervention, they also provided leverage for antiporn feminists and conservative critics to censor child pornography in particular, and hard-core pornography in general.[1]

Yet such developments depended on a prior historical shift within the broader legal discourse of obscenity. As Loren Glass argues, "Unlike obscenity, the term *pornography* has no official legal status, but it was frequently used over the course of the century precisely in response to the muddle that arose when literary texts were deemed obscene."[2] With first *Roth v. United States* (1957) and then *Miller v. California* (1973), the Supreme Court established a relative definition of obscenity that evaluated a text according to "contemporary community standards," rather than the intrinsic value a work might have as determined by literary experts. As Glass and others note, if publishers and booksellers clearly market and restrict works to communities deemed capable of handling those works in a responsible manner, then they will likely remain immune from obscenity charges.[3] This development in obscenity law produced a flexible mechanism for determining when a work lost legal immunity, and the text's relative value for a specific community served as this mechanism's most significant feature. The "end of obscenity," in other words, made it so that moral and legal objections to a text depend less on the intrinsic qualities of that text than its relation to those who encountered it.

The history of obscenity law provides an important backdrop for the emergence by the end of the century of child pornography as a distinct legal category. As Chuck Kleinhans notes, key to this emergence was the law's specific concern with visual images rather than written text.[4] The Protection of Children Against Sexual Exploitation Act of 1977, for example, prohibited the use of children in the production of obscene materials, which largely directs the law toward photographic and filmic forms of representation. Between 1978 and 2000, a series of national laws and court decisions at the federal and district levels, too many to survey in this chapter, continued to develop a legal definition of child pornography in other ways. In 1982 the Supreme Court's decision in New York v. Ferber ruled that child pornography constituted its own constitutional category exempt from First Amendment protection; thus, child pornography became the exception to what Glass claims to be the categorical distinction between "pornography" and "obscenity."[5]

During the 1990s, the law continued to define, debate, and redefine the definition of child pornography with two significant outcomes. First, these debates broadened the scope of what visual contents could meet the definition of child pornography. In 1994 the lower court decision in United States v. Knox determined that an image could meet the standard of "lascivious exhibition of the genitals" even if the child were fully clothed.[6] As a result, a wide range of images, including family photographs of children, often depicted nude, bathing, or dressed in costumes, could potentially constitute child pornography.[7] Second, the legal wrangling over child pornography, in ways parallel to developments in contemporary sociological discourses, furnished the images with a documentary quality: child pornography constituted evidence of a crime.[8] The Child Pornography Protection Act (1996), for example, defined virtual child pornography, computer-generated or "recombinant photorealistic images" that transplant an image of a child's head on to the body of a nude adult, as legally suspect.[9] As Kleinhans reports, the 2002 Supreme Court decision in Ashcroft v. Free Speech Coalition overturned this decision, arguing that "visual child pornography remains centrally defined by the fact that it is the recording of a crime and that its production creates victims. With virtual images, the 6–3 majority reasoned, these two elements are not present."[10] Yet in doing so, the Court further affirmed the documentary quality of the image as an important condition for defining child pornography.

This emphasis on the realness of child pornography surfaced again roughly five years later, when the Supreme Court affirmed the 2003 Prosecutorial

Remedies and Other Tools to End the Exploitation of Children Today Act, otherwise known as the PROTECT Act. The Court's 2008 decision in *United States v. Williams* upheld the act's definition of child pornography that emphasized not only an image's contents but also the viewer's intent. Critics argued that the decision potentially exposed to prosecution any individual who requested or offered to share child pornography, even if those images only contained adults masquerading as children or virtual child pornography. Justice Antonin Scalia swiftly dismissed these concerns in his majority opinion: "An offer to provide or request to receive virtual child pornography is not prohibited by the statute. A crime is committed only when the speaker believes or intends the listener to believe that the subject of the proposed transaction depicts *real* children."[11] The Court's ruling in *United States v. Williams* constitutes a subtle but important shift in the law, as the question of the viewer's intent increasingly supplemented the evidentiary or documentary quality of the image for the law's definition of child pornography. In a way that seems to pervert the previous decades' development of a community standards–based definition of obscenity, child-pornography law thus does not extend but *revokes* legal immunity because of a text's value for a particular community of viewers.

This brief history of child-pornography law demonstrates its development as a specific hermeneutic not only of texts but of persons. Child pornography, as defined by the law, is less a genre composed of specific tropes and conventions than a pathological response to an often documentary representation. Yet, as Amy Adler shows, the ability for anyone to adopt this pathological response remains at the heart of child-pornography law. In her analysis of the 1989 California district court case *United States v. Dost*, Adler reveals how the law requires one to adopt the subjective position of a pedophile in order to determine whether or not an image constitutes child pornography. The Dost test, established by the court's ruling, provides a set of six guidelines for assessing a particular image. While some guidelines direct the examiner to consider the child's pose, state of undress, or perceived "willingness to engage in sexual activity," the most telling factor is the sixth, which asks the examiner to consider "whether the visual depiction is intended or designed to elicit a sexual response in the viewer."[12] For Adler, the Dost test exemplifies the tendency of child-pornography law to produce what she terms a *pedophilic gaze*: "The law requires us to study pictures of children to uncover their potential sexual meanings, and in doing so it explicitly exhorts us to take on the perspective of the pedophile."[13] Following Michel Foucault's critique of the deployment of sexuality, she persuasively argues that child-pornography law remains a key force for a continued incitement to discourse around the sexuality of children.[14]

Adler's careful history of child-pornography law, however, falls short in its critique of the law. "It still seems better to have proliferating discourses about the danger of child exploitation," she argues, "than to have the exploitation itself."[15] Yet the problem of the subject's pathological desire and pleasure has surpassed the problem of children's exploitation when it comes to child-pornography law. Moreover, the current implementation of child-pornography laws ensures a great deal of collateral damage, as parents, artists, and business owners can unwittingly fill the role of pedophile trading in child pornography. In addition, as Ralph Underwager and Hollida Wakefield suggest, investigations into allegations of child pornography and child abuse can often be just as or even more traumatic than whatever violence the child in question may have suffered.[16] Adler's primary concern is that child-pornography law contributes to a vaguely elaborated process she terms the *sexualization of children*, by which she means that the pedophilic gaze causes a change in how we perceive children as sexual beings.[17] If this is true, then the change it causes seems to produce an insufficient notion of children's sexuality by insisting that whatever the previous notion was, it was de facto better. At the heart of Adler's critique, the question of children's sexual innocence remains unanswered.

Adler correctly points out that Foucault identifies children's sexuality as one of the key areas of knowledge through which power attaches itself to the body. However, what Adler forgets is that the endless interrogation of our desires is in part an experience of pleasure, derived from the evasions, seductions, and revelations—what Foucault described as the "*perpetual spirals of power and pleasure*"—that characterize the confessional mode.[18] According to Adler's formulation, child-pornography law exemplifies the discursive production of sexuality and the extension of biopower into everyday life, but in order to have any chance of success in the endless scrutiny of images for a sexual truth, we must adopt the position of a pedophile. The implication seems to be that the pedophilic gaze thus requires that we have either some familiarity with or some capacity for recognizing what is sexually exciting about children. To paraphrase Justice Potter Stewart: we know it when we see it; but we only know it because we have already some capacity to experience pedophilic desire. In other words, the pedophilic gaze ensures that child-pornography law can only function if we find the potential pedophile within ourselves.

Child-pornography law enjoins the viewer to place images under intense scrutiny, but in doing so, it directs the viewer in a similar pursuit of truth that Linda Williams has attributed to pornography itself. According to Williams, hard-core pornography constitutes one of the many "medical, psychological, juridical, and pornographic discourses [that] have functioned as transfer points of knowledge, power, and pleasure."[19] In particular, hard-core moving-image pornography uses its various conventions to render the otherwise ever-elusive truth of female pleasure visible on screen. The genre thus bears a significant resemblance to what Jon Davis identifies as a recent trend in both mainstream and independent films with thematic interests in pedophilia.[20] For Davis, these films deploy a series of structural techniques to compensate for the unrepresentability of illicit intergenerational sex acts on screen, what Davis calls "the black hole of representation that is arguably at the center of every pedophile movie."[21] However, Davis's pedophile movies and Williams's hard-core pornography achieve very different things from child pornography, as it is subject to the intense scrutiny of child-pornography law. If Davis's and Williams's respective accounts describe filmic conventions that attempt to make visible on screen the truth of the Other's desire, then child pornography makes visible the perverse desire of the viewing subject, who finds in the provocation of his or her desire the grounds for prohibiting the image being viewed. The trouble with child-pornography law occurs when it asserts that this pathological desire is the exclusive property of a pathological subject: the pedophile.

As Richard Mohr suggests, the series of moves by which one participates in and then disavows a desire for the child appears to structure not just the law but also the wider public sphere. Mohr coins the phrase the pedophilia of everyday life to explain how, in spite of the legal ban on child pornography, viewers find enjoyment in the sexiness of children through the texts and images that constitute our everyday experience. This catalog of mundane, pedophilic delights includes Hollywood family films, clothing advertisements, public-service announcements, and news coverage of child sexual abuse scandals. These texts provide just enough exposure to the sexual appeal of children while effacing any conscious knowledge one might have of what makes these images so exciting in the first place. What prevents one from becoming fully conscious of one's attraction to these images is the creation of a pathological subjectivity that can carry the burden of one's disavowed desires as well as become the object of one's condemnation. Mohr writes, "Society needs the pedophile: his existence allows everyone else to view sexy children innocently. But his conceptualization by society must not be allowed to be rich enough to be interesting, to constitute a life."[22] The unconscious fantasies that dictate how child-pornography law functions seem to extend far beyond the courtroom walls.

A telling example of the phenomenon Mohr describes comes from Philip Jenkins's study of the moral panics that occurred around the issue of child pornography during the early 1990s. At the same time as expanding case law intensified the prohibitions on child pornography, the United States experienced an efflorescence of popular crime literature by authors such as Jonathan Kellerman, Robert Campbell, James N. Frey, and Andrew Vachss, whose novels featured pedophile villains. Describing this body of popular literature,

Jenkins writes: "Kellerman's *When the Bough Breaks* featured the Gentlemen's Brigade, a voluntary social work group that concealed a network of elite child molesters and 'closet sickos.' Ron Handberg's *Savage Justice* had as its villain a judge who used pornographic videos to seduce pubescent boys and whose extensive connections enabled him to escape detection and to silence critics, by murder if necessary."[23] The sudden popularity of crime novels with themes of child abuse and pedophile villains is suggestive. Jenkins's brief account lends credence to Mohr's otherwise polemical claim that prohibitions incite circuitous routes to oblique pleasures, and that the pathological subject provides one means for disavowing these enjoyments. According to this logic, one finds pleasure not only in seeing the villainous pedophile punished by the law but also in acting as the pedophile's fellow traveler as he or she commits violent deeds.

More significant, however, is Mohr's claim that "society seems to need these images. And the images are allowed to the extent that they are buffered, not read in the first instance as sexual representations."[24] Mohr insists that the social depends on these images and on the process of provocation and disavowal that characterizes one's relation to them. A number of scholars have already broached the question of why something akin to the pedophilia of everyday life might be so necessary, yet two of the most influential accounts belong to James Kincaid and Lee Edelman. According to Kincaid's cultural-historical analysis, the modern child's innocence and purity served as a counter to the rational man of the Enlightenment: "The child was figured as *free of* adult corruptions; *not yet burdened with* the weight of responsibility, mortality, and sexuality."[25] The result, however, is that the child becomes a blank screen that displays whatever fantasies the adult wishes to project there. According to Edelman's queer psychoanalytic account, the figure of the child serves as the linchpin in the collective libidinal fantasy of a redemptive future that structures U.S. politics.[26] As this future's primary inheritor and as the means by which the citizen inhabits it via his or her identification with the child, the child ensures a conservative political order that prizes sexual reproduction and heteronormativity to the point of violently opposing all other forms of social and political organization. The particulars of Edelman's and Kincaid's respective insights aside, their accounts demonstrate various ways in which the desirability of children is not simply the product of pathology but central to the constitution of the modern subject.

The work of Mohr, Edelman, and Kincaid gestures toward more than a problem in the relation between children and the modern adult subject, who may or may not adequately recognize the child as a sexual being. While these relations are definitely at stake, the more central question concerns how notions of children and pedophiles manage one's relation to the Otherness that divides the subject from within. In making this claim, I echo Jacqueline Rose's 1984 psychoanalytic investigation of children's fiction, *The Case of Peter Pan; or, The Impossibility of Children's Fiction*, and second her insistence on the value of Freud's work for thinking about the connections between representations of children and subjectivity. Rose claims with respect to her own study: "The most crucial aspect of psychoanalysis for discussing children's fiction is its insistence that childhood is something in which we continue to be implicated and which is never simply left behind."[27] Just as Freud's analysis of his own childhood memories' fictional quality revealed those memories as attempts to reconcile present conflicts through the endless reworking of personal history, children's fiction concerns the relation between children and adults insofar as the children in question are the adults who tell the story.

According to Rose, children's fiction tends to imagine childhood in terms of a strict biological development through a series of discrete stages. This is a problem because the sequential model of psychosexual development fails to take on childhood's persistent revision within the psychic life of the subject. While acknowledging Freud's own equivocal stance on psychosexual development in his *Three Essays on the Theory of Sexuality*, Rose nevertheless sees as key his reframing of childhood sexuality in terms of fantasy: "[Freud] described how infantile sexuality starts to turn on a number of questions which the child sets itself, questions about its own origin (the birth of the child) and its sexual identity (the difference between the sexes) which the child will eventually have to resolve. By describing the child's development in terms of a *query*, Freud moves it out of the realm of an almost biological sequence, and into that of fantasy and representation where things are not so clear."[28] As Rose observes, these questions are central to the subject's self-constitution, but at the same time they are never completely answerable because they address the child's status regarding his or her own Otherness: "Behind the question about origins is the idea of a moment when the child did not exist, and behind the question about difference is the recognition that the child's sexual identity rests solely in its differentiation from something (or someone) it is not."[29] The fact that these incomplete answers can come only through language, itself constituted by its own semantic short-circuits and deceptions, further highlights childhood's status as a never-ending inquiry into the subject's own meaning.

For Rose, the problem with most children's fiction is "the most emphatic refusals and demands" it makes by insisting on the child's linguistic and erotic innocence: "There should be no disturbance at the level of language, no challenge to our own sexuality, no threat to our status as critics, and no question of our relation to the child."[30] Another way to phrase Rose's claim is that the child of children's fiction affirms a particular form of subjectivity, whose truth lies hidden in an origin of linguistic and sexual innocence, while repressing the disturbing effects of the unconscious that render such sub-jectivity untenable. There is no such thing as a subject of linguistic or sexual innocence. Yet children's fiction manages its partial repression of this fact through a representational scheme that reorganizes these forces into a more palatable—if highly overdetermined—form.

The relevance of Rose's argument about children's fiction for my own claims rests not in the assertion that the children who appear in pornographic videos and images do not exist, or that their exploitation is negligible. Rather, Rose's insights help to expose law's notion of child pornography as a legal fiction that, like dominant trends in children's fiction, avoids some of the more pressing questions of modern subjectivity. Child-pornography law con-stitutes the normal subject by insisting that the image in question is both innocent and documentary. As a document of desire, the image can then con-stitute a population of pathological consumers. The pedophile, whose sup-posedly tumultuous childhood explains his or her deviant desires, and the sense of realness, which absolves the text from the difficulties of representa-tion, together constitute the law's fictions of child pornography: child por-nography exhibits real children suffering real acts of violence, which only real pedophiles could possibly enjoy. Following Rose as much as Mohr, I argue that these conventions help normal subjects evade questions about their libidinal investment in both children and child pornography that they sequester within the pedophile.

These legal fictions have less to do with the texts themselves than with common anxieties about who uses child pornography and why. If Mohr is even half correct about the pedophilia of everyday life, then these anxious questions miss the wider problematic of children's sexuality. It seems that any attempt to interrogate the cultural and political work that representation of children's sexuality may perform will fall short without first attending to how child-pornography law directs one's attention away from such efforts in first place. Doing so would require that scholars approach child pornography in terms other than those provided to us by the law. One of the ways to do this would be to follow Laura Kipnis when she describes pornography, in terms resonant with Rose's own claims, as "a place where problematic social issues get expressed and negotiated."[31] Thus, texts deemed child pornography may have a great deal to tell us about the fantasies and contradictions that orga-nize not only Mohr's pedophilia of everyday life or the conservative political structure that Edelman dubs "reproductive futurism" but also how we under-stand the psychic strategies that we develop against our desires, pleasures, and the world we inhabit.[32]

The central problem remains, however, that child pornography is still a genre defined by its legal prohibition. My intention is neither to endorse nor to censor child pornography as we currently understand it. Rather, I argue that leaving a body of representations completely in the hands of the law is dangerous precisely for the way it inhibits rational discussion of what these images may mean. Child abuse will happen regardless of whether or not academics discuss child pornography, and this violence is likely to continue not simply as physical injury or sexual exploitation but also as the larger systemic violence that prevents children from having supportive social environments, schools to attend, and food to eat. As Pat Califia writes: "Neglect, violence, and the sexual abuse of children are shocking offenses, yet they are terribly ordinary acts."[33] Moreover, Ian Hacking has shown in "The Making and Molding of Child Abuse" that the history of child abuse as a concept "has been in the direction of dividing more and more types of behavior into normal and deviant."[34] These divisions become problematic when we forget that the apparently objective scientific knowledge of the normal is at the same time a moral prescription that ought to be questioned. The problem of child abuse is not simply a matter of adults oppressing children, but one of the central axes along which complex relations of power emerge among a variety of subjects. A better analysis of child-pornography law and child pornography may show us how such representations maintain and extend these relations in ways irreducible to the facile categories of pathological viewers and innocent victims.

No longer simply a means for preventing the exploitation of children, child-pornography law distributes normal and pathological subjectivities through the evidentiary status it assigns to the image. The law thus prohibits the careful analysis of child pornography as a visual genre on both legal and ethical grounds. However, the law has largely ignored sexually explicit *written* representations of children. I suggest that this is a result of the historical shift away from written texts toward visual images as the primary target of legal censure. In addition to differential attitudes regarding the cultural function of text over images, written texts generally sidestep the immediate and pressing question of exploitation because one does not need a real child to produce such a text in the first place. Of course, to say that the law has ignored written texts is not the same thing as saying that such texts are immune from it; however, the law's current lack of interest in written representations of children's sexuality, or sexuality writ large, affords scholars an opportunity to explore some of the problems simultaneously raised and foreclosed by visual forms. As I noted with respect to Jenkins's discussion of the sex-crime novels that grew to great popularity during the early 1990s, fiction has served as a surrogate source of the pleasures that readers could not find elsewhere. If the pornographic image of the child remains off-limits, then pornographic novels and other written texts provide literary scholars with an alternative route to some of these questions.[35]

Stadler's Boys

Matthew Stadler's small but incredibly rich oeuvre is a prime candidate for thinking through the problems that child pornography raises. This is the case in part because most of his novels take up the theme of sex between an adult and a barely pubescent boy, whose indeterminate pubertal status highlights the difficulty in evaluating or diagnosing a desire for minors based on standardized models of sexual development. Stadler's particular focus on man–boy relations also helps to specify gender's significance for accounts of such sexual relations, which the law often occludes through its use of the gender-neutralized category of "the child." The history of statutory rape laws provides a brief but useful example. As various scholars have noted, statutory rape laws were conceived during much of the twentieth century as a means to protect women's chastity and, as a consequence, were applied only to women under the age of consent. During the 1970s, following new conceptualizations of child abuse, reformers sought to protect all children, boys and girls, by neutralizing the gendered language of the law. However, this formal gender equality subsequently became a means to disproportionately prosecute gay men. In addition, many men report that intergenerational relationships with older men during their teenage years were often benign if not also deeply formative experiences.[36] The history of such laws thus reveals the dangers of losing sight of the child's gender, and it is through the specific figure of the boy that Stadler explores the ethical possibilities between men and men to be. However, Stadler's take on these relations also forms the basis for thinking more generally about intimacies, explicitly sexual and otherwise, forged along differentials of age.

Stadler's interest in the specificities of man–boy relations characterizes some of his other work as well, including an oft-cited feature story for the independent Seattle newspaper the *Stranger* on the North American Man-Boy Love Association (NAMBLA) held in Stadler's hometown in 1995. On account of his novel *The Sex Offender* (1994), NAMBLA's members invited Stadler to the conference as a guest speaker, and the account he produced of the clandestine event remains one of the best pieces written on the organization. Stadler's report traces the history of NAMBLA as it emerged out of the gay and lesbian rights movement of the early 1970s, when its members found themselves marginalized by the growing public debate about child abuse and pornography that intensified over the following years. Mainstream gay and lesbian politics abandoned NAMBLA early on, because the organization seemed incompatible with the movement's exchange of sex radicalism for respectability.[37] Stadler remains critical of the conference participants' politically naive "embrace of all the perversities of sex and affection," but he is nonetheless sympathetic with their attempts to challenge prevailing sexual and social norms: "Only in a distant future—if we ever step back from our deep, deep feelings about children and begin to rationally assess their sexuality, particularly that of teenagers—will the age-of-consent laws be changed. This will be possible only if we care enough about kids to stop condemning them to the role of angels from some realm apart, and to begin to grant them power over their real experience as human beings."[38]

Stadler also found that conference participants, in addition to discussing political strategy, spent much of their time discussing sexual fantasies, retelling experiences with live boys, and trading images of children. Yet, as if anticipating Mohr's argument about the pedophilia of everyday life, the vast majority of these images consisted of mainstream commercial films and advertisements. Stadler writes, "I had found NAMBLA's 'porn,' and it was Hollywood. It was network television, Sunday ad supplements, Nickelodeon, and the Disney channel. NAMBLA doesn't need to manufacture porn, because America manufactures it for them."[39] Another one of the virtues of Stadler's article is the degree of candor with which the men he interviews explain why they find these images appealing. One participant, whom Stadler identifies only as John, does so by contrasting these texts with "real porn": "Real porn has nothing to do with boys—that's what so strange about, you know, 'boy porn.' I mean, what boy would ever make boy porn? It's just sexy to gay men. It's gay porn, and the boys just happen to be in it. Sometimes I like the boys, but in a porn movie they're not doing anything sexy, you know, like just being boys. Now, if some boys actually got together with a video camera and made their own porn, that could be sexy."[40] What gives these images their erotic allure is, in fact, the absence of sex. This absence coincides with an absence of adulthood, since the only way to return sex to the image is to remove the adult who would be responsible for framing the shot and arranging the scene. John's interpretation of these images seems to jibe with Kincaid's assertion about the erotic innocence of children. Yet John's understanding differs to the extent that his boys retain some creative potential that could be put to use in making "their own porn." While the boy may be an absence of something, he is defined by some other, elusive positive content.

John's account suggests that the men of the NAMBLA conference do not have an indiscriminate interest in children but rather a distinct set of fantasies involving boys, wherein the boy—and not the child—serves as a particularly dense nexus of meanings. Stadler's article makes clear the centrality of the boy, and I suggest that it is the peculiar fantasy of the boy as an erotic yet elusive potential that Stadler addresses in much greater detail in his novel *Allan Stein*. Published in 1999 by Grove Press, the novel follows close on the heels of his feature on NAMBLA for the *Stranger*. Yet what makes *Allan Stein* particularly relevant for a discussion of child pornography, beyond the narrator's opening insistence on portions of his narrative as "pure pornography," is that the plot depends on the narrator's relation to an image of a nude child.

The image in question is Picasso's painting *Boy Leading a Horse*, and the narrator impersonates his friend Herbert Widener, a curator, in order to travel to Paris to secure the sketches that might identify the boy in the image as Gertrude Stein's nephew, the eponymous Allan. In a discussion of the painting that Herbert has with his host family, Miriam Dupaignes, the mother of Stéphane, provides a description of the depicted boy that resonates with John's own take on the eroticism of boys. She explains: "This is one of the features of the Picasso Herbert speaks of, the most erotic and moving aspect of it—that it is a boy. He has tremendous power because he is nothing yet, no one, and so he has the power in him to be a god, like all children do, you see? If Picasso had painted a man leading the horse, just imagine it. This man would be someone, some man who will never be a god at all, just a man, without the limitless power this boy has."[41] Miriam's description makes explicit John's implication of an elusive potential as the source of a boy's eroticism. Yet Miriam's description is far more complex and interesting. While it may be easy to recognize the eroticism in the anonymous nude boy, it's much more difficult to understand in what way a boy can be said to be powerful. Children are usually construed as vulnerable and in need of protection, but according to Miriam, a boy retains a degree of power unparalleled by any man. To further complicate matters, while a man is "someone," a boy is "no one" in addition to being a "nothing," a depersonalized entity that draws its power from an unexercised potential. It seems important to stress the indefinite article as well; Miriam speaks of "a boy" versus "the boy," thus emphasizing the boy's indefinite nature while reserving this nature for the boy alone. The eroticism of a boy appears linked to the power he keeps in reserve, the potential power he retains but loses in the moment he exercises it to become a man.

The narrator privately gushes over Miriam's description: "Oh, God bless her. A mother knows so much most men will never know."[42] While it is important that he singles out the mother as having privileged access to this knowledge, I want to defer discussing the mother for a moment in order to point out that what structures the narrator's relation to the image also structures his relation to Stéphane. The boy frequently acts as an informal guide to the narrator as he halfheartedly conducts his curatorial errands, and in this way Stéphane serves as a source for much of the narrator's meditations on the boy's eroticism. The following passage is especially telling:

> Language was the least of our barriers. Stéphane hovered behind a scrim, trapped inside a body whose proportions and angularity perfectly ex-

pressed something to me . . . "becoming," I'd like to say, but it might have been nostalgia. His posture as he led me, the narrowing shoulders, the lilt of his arms and bounce of his blue knapsack that kept disappearing into the crowd, enthralled me by pointing elsewhere—away from him. The hollow of his back and then the turn at the hips, his long thighs, became abstractions, pure equations, so that he engaged that part of my mind that also loves geometry or angels.⁴³

Stéphane's lack of familiarity with English contributes to his dropping away from the narrator's space of attention, which is now fully occupied with the formal elements of the boy's body. The narrator is not simply interested in the boy's body as it is composed of flesh, but, as the language of his description suggests, he is taken with the form that the body expresses. The telling slip that substitutes *angels* for the perhaps more appropriately geometric term *angles* at once signals to the reader the subjectivized nature of the narrative and suggests that the boy's form is not something immediately present to the narrator's experience. The boy as a kind of form is potentially transcendent of Stéphane's body, which nevertheless serves as the substance that replicates it. Finally, the narrator hints that the Picasso painting provides inspiration for this form: just as the boy leads the horse, Stéphane leads the narrator through the streets of Paris.

The narrator provides two terms for the relationship between Stéphane's body and its form, *becoming* and *nostalgia*, and each describes a very different phenomenon. On the one hand, nostalgia as a sentimental longing for a past time or state seems to conflict with the rupture of the self from itself that characterizes becoming. However, the narrator may have nostalgia for the potential he embodied in his own youth but has lost in his adulthood. The tension the narrator sees between Stéphane as a boy of lived experience and the form of the boy glimpsed in the contours of Stéphane's body would be this nostalgia's trigger. Another way to understand this scene would be to read it in terms of Miriam's description of the Picasso painting. The aestheticized vocabulary that the narrator deploys in describing this scene, as well as its status as a fully subjectivized account being retold to us from the narrator's present moment, helps to legitimize this move. The narrator, as the one who is "just a man," must deal with the loss of his own power to be nothing yet become anything. Although his deceptions and identity theft serve as an attempt to reactivate this lost potential, these efforts pale before what is invested in the form of the boy. As he recalls watching Stéphane move ahead of him, the narrator recognizes the boy's power, and thus his erotic appeal, as emanating from his form as pure potential. Yet the real boy, Stéphane, keeps blocking this view with the body that locates him as an embodied subject.

The final lines of the novel help to clarify this point. After a successful seduction (it is unclear whether it is the narrator's or Stéphane's victory), the narrator lies to Miriam about taking her son on a short trip to southern France in order to abduct the boy. Stéphane, who requires a special diet, becomes ill at the same time that Miriam discovers that the narrator is an imposter. She demands, via letter, that he return Stéphane. The narrator reveals his first name as Matthew, and he and Stéphane part ways. Alone and having wandered off into the woods at night, the narrator concludes the novel with the following sentences: "I have imagined that whole worlds dwell in the body of a boy and have pried with words to relax these meanings from their hiding place, to coax the boy into the open. He stood still for a moment, caught in the warmth of my regard, and when I reached for him he was gone."[44]

These lines raise a series of questions for the reader. Just as Matthew brought Stéphane to an obscure town in the south of France, the temporal and spatial coordinates of the narrative become unclear. The novel opens with Matthew's account of his and Stéphane's arrival at their destination before leaping back in time to narrate the series of events that brought Matthew to France. As the novel comes to a close, Matthew and Stéphane have already parted ways, and the final scene seemingly exceeds the boundaries of the opening frame. There is also the question of the narrator's effort to extract worlds of meaning from the body of a boy. Does the narrator's attempt to pry with words refer to his verbal seductions of Stéphane, or does it index the larger narrative as an attempt to give form to Matthew's own lost potential? The latter question troubles any attempt to claim that the events that exceed the boundaries of the narrative frame should be understood as actually happening or, at the very least, as somehow less subjectivized than the rest of the narrative. Finally, there is the matter of the boy. By the time Matthew and Stéphane arrive at their destination, the narrator has ceased to refer to Stéphane by his first name and instead uses the term *boy*. From this, two possible explanations follow: either the narrator has ceased to recognize Stéphane in his specificity as an embodied subject or the narrative is purely fantasy.

At this point it is important to keep in mind that what has served as the ostensible motivation for the narrator throughout much of the novel is his pursuit of the sketches that will prove that a real boy, Allan Stein, lies behind the erotic image of the boy in Picasso's painting. This theme repeats in the living tableau the narrator imagines as he watches Stéphane move ahead of him, and it appears once more in the novel's final scene. At stake in these scenes is a set of questions similar to those raised in discussions of child pornography, particularly as they address the realness of the image. Yet Stadler's novel marshals realism, with its particular emphases on the psychic life of the subject, against the documentary, evidentiary quality such images obtain from the law. While such images invite indisputable claims about the world, the novel challenges the possibility of such claims in the first place. The novel's conclusion presents an interpretive dilemma wherein it becomes impossible to draw a clear line between the novel's world and the narrator's subjective experience of it. Yet rather than asserting the impossibility of knowing anything about the world, Stadler presents fantasy as the subject's sole means for interfacing with that world. There is no text or image, the novel suggests, that makes claims on the realness of things that is not already shot through with the fantasies of the interpreting subject.

Stéphane does not fare well by the novel's end. He becomes ill on account of the narrator's carelessness over his diet, which, the reader is repeatedly informed, must be strictly maintained. The individual who delivers these constant reminders is the boy's mother, Miriam. Yet this fact is not meant to assert the mother's unequivocal superiority over the pedophile. We should keep in mind that Miriam is the first to describe the boy in Picasso's painting as a highly erotic form of potential. It is safe to infer that Miriam has experienced this erotic draw and therefore engages the world through a similar set of fantasies. Miriam is a loving mother, but she is stern with Stéphane, especially over the regulation of his diet. Pat Califia, writing about his own experience of being a parent, explains this dynamic well: "Raising a child involves making all kinds of decisions that the child resents and opposes. Most children do not want to sleep in their own beds, take medicine, nap, get a shot, give up the baby bottle, get a bath, eat vegetables, learn their multiplication tables, etc. In order to avoid having every interaction turn into a pitched battle, adults condition their offspring to obey and please them. While this meets with varying degrees of success, there's never a time when the playing field is level."[45] The interaction between caretaker and child takes on a Foucauldian character, as the two engage in a play of seduction, resistance, tension, and repression, in a conflict between the child's desires and what the adult perceives as best for the child's well-being.

For Califia, the relationship between child and caretaker is never equal because of the adult's superior position. However, as *Allan Stein* suggests, it would be incorrect to assume that children are vulnerable because they are completely powerless. In conjunction with the figure of the caretaker, the novel demonstrates that the child, here conceived as a boy, may be vulnerable, but he is not without power. Matthew is seduced, hurt, and humiliated by Stéphane as much as he is the seducer and abductor. In contrast to the narrator, the novel offers the caretaker in the form of the boy's mother, Miriam, who is in an ethical position with respect to the tangle of seductions, tensions, and resistances that compose the child-caretaker relation. Miriam fully acknowledges the eroticism of the boy in Picasso's painting, yet her role as caretaker, which is not dependent on sex, prescribes a particular means of engaging that eroticism as it expresses itself in the body of her son. The narrator caves to each of Stéphane's whims. While the boy seems to thoroughly enjoy his relation with Matthew, the narrator's permissiveness still leads the boy to fall ill. What Matthew forgets—which the caretaker remembers—is that the boy is only glimpsed, caught in the warmth of one's regard, for an instant in the young body of a child of lived experience. One of the important implications of the caretaker as an ethical position, as a way of relating to the child, is that even if fantasy functions as one's means for interfacing with the world, an interface that depends on one's self-relation, it remains possible to act in a way that is not necessarily hostile or indifferent to the forms of life that one encounters there. Fantasy is the necessary condition for all forms of action, from the most violent to the most generative.[46]

There is much more to be said about *Allan Stein* and Matthew Stadler's oeuvre, just as there is much more to be said about child pornography and the fantasies that it expresses. The fictions of realness and de facto abuse that characterize contemporary discussions of child pornography are in urgent need of revision, because their insistence on the image as a record of something real effaces the complex fantasies that produce that realness as an effect of reading. This is not to deny the fact that children have been and still are exploited for the production of child pornography; this is rather to argue that our established frameworks efface this exploitation better than they expose it. The legal discourses that prevail in current discussions of child pornography serve only to disavow the subject's psychic investments in the desirability of children and to avoid the larger question of just what, exactly, a child is. Thus it becomes easier to ignore the systematic forms of violence perpetuated against both children and adults. One of the necessary tasks for scholars is to challenge the legal definition of child pornography through an elaboration of the genre as a genre—that is, a normative set of conventions that does social and political work. Literary pornography may be one of the best places to begin, in order to circumvent the law's prohibitions and safeguard against its overzealous advocates.

In his discussion of the pedophilia of everyday life, Mohr argues that one of its problematic effects is that we are prevented from conceptualizing the pedophile in such a way as "to be rich enough to be interesting, to constitute a life."[47] I find this phrase provocative because, like this chapter's epigraph, it suggests that there is something of value in thinking through the pedophilic relation. Especially provocative is Mohr's claim that the pedophile can and should be interesting—attractive to us as a way of living in the world. Opponents of this argument will claim that this is precisely the danger of child pornography—that it makes pedophilia attractive. Perhaps. But as I have argued, child-pornography law already does this. The questions remain as to what exactly this means and whether, as Mohr suggests, pedophilia may constitute a politically and ethically viable form of life. In the process of considering these questions, we might find ourselves delightfully scandalized to learn that child pornography has something valuable to show us about youth, desire, and life itself.

## Notes

For their thoughts on this difficult subject, I would like to thank Tim Dean, David Squires, and my fellow colleagues enrolled in the History and Theory of Pornography seminar held at the University at Buffalo, SUNY, in the spring of 2010.

1. A number of scholars have written more-extended accounts of the relations among antiporn feminism, conservative U.S. politics, and the emergence of child abuse as a social problem. See Califia, "No Minor Issues"; P. Jenkins, *Beyond Tolerance*, 32; Levine, *Harmful to Minors*; and O'Toole, *Pornocopia*, 217–45. For a detailed account of the complex connections between antiporn feminism and conservative U.S. politics, see Strub, *Perversion for Profit*, 213–55.

2. Glass, "Redeeming Value," 360.

3. The 1968 U.S. Supreme Court ruling in *Ginsberg v. State of New York* established the assessment of obscenity according to the "ethical and moral development" of a particular social group likely to encounter the work in question. Normative categories, such as "adult" and "youth," reflected assumptions about an individual's acquired capacity to integrate sexually explicit material into a regime of sexual self-management. While adults could perform this task successfully, youth had not yet learned successful self-management and would risk self-corruption. See Hunter, Saunders, and Williamson, *On Pornography*, 214.

4. Kleinhans, "Virtual Child Porn," 73.

5. Glass, "Redeeming Value," 360.

6. Adler, "The Perverse Law of Child Pornography," 239–40.

7. The experience of photographers and academics such as Marian Rubin, Jacqueline Livingston, Marilyn Zimmerman, Betsy Schneider, and David Sonenschein reveal instances where law enforcement officials considered family photographs of children, often depicted as nude, bathing, or dressed in costumes, as potential child pornography. See Rubin et al., " 'Not a Pretty Picture' "; and Sonenschein, "Sources of Reaction to 'Child Pornography.' " For an extended overview of the various scandals surrounding perceived instances of child pornography, see Califia, "No Minor Issues."

8. For examples, see O'Donnell and Milner, *Child Pornography*, 70; and Taylor and Quayle, *Child Pornography*, 4.

9. Kleinhans, "Virtual Child Porn," 75.

10. Kleinhans, "Virtual Child Porn."

11. United States v. Williams, 553 U.S. 285 (2008).

12. Quoted in Adler, "The Perverse Law of Child Pornography," 262.

13. Adler, "The Perverse Law of Child Pornography," 262.

14. Adler, "The Perverse Law of Child Pornography," 272.

15. Adler, "The Perverse Law of Child Pornography," 272.

16. See Underwager and Wakefield, "Sexual Abuse, Anti-sexuality, and the Pornography of Power." The authors argue that, like Adler's pedophilic gaze, criminal investigations produce their own body of pornographic representation through the interrogation of perceived child victims.

17. Adler, "The Perverse Law of Child Pornography," 265.

18. Foucault, *The History of Sexuality*, 45.

19. L. Williams, *Hard Core* (1999), 35.

20. These films include Pedro Almodóvar's *Bad Education* (2004), Asia Argento's *The Heart Is Deceitful above All Things* (2004), Miranda July's *Me You and Everyone We Know* (2005), Gregg Araki's *Mysterious Skin* (2004), Todd Solondz's *Palindromes* (2004), and Nicole Kassell's *The Woodsman* (2004).

21. Davis, "Imagining Intergenerationality," 377.

22. Mohr, "The Pedophilia of Everyday Life," 20.

23. P. Jenkins, *Moral Panic*, 155.

24. Mohr, "The Pedophilia of Everyday Life," 20.

25. Kincaid, *Erotic Innocence*, 15.

26. Edelman, *No Future*, 11–13.

27. Rose, *The Case of Peter Pan*, 12.

28. Rose, *The Case of Peter Pan*, 16.

29. Rose, *The Case of Peter Pan*, 16.

30. Rose, *The Case of Peter Pan*, 20.

31. Kipnis, *Bound and Gagged*, 62.

32. Edelman, *No Future*, 2.

33. Califia, "No Minor Issues," 60.

34. Hacking, "The Making and Molding of Child Abuse," 287–88.

35. In making this move from the fictions of child-pornography law to literature, I am indebted to Kathryn Bond Stockton's excellent *The Queer Child*. Stockton argues that literary fiction and film "imagine and present what sociology, Law, and History cannot pierce, given established taboos surrounding children. Novels and films, in their inventive forms, are rich stimulators of questions public cultures seem to have no language for encountering" (10).

36. See Cocca, *Jailbait*, 18–19; and Fischel, "Per Se or Power?," 287–90, which draws much from Cocca's study. While Joseph Fischel is aware that many gay men often report favorably on relationships with older men during their teenage years, he argues convincingly for retaining the gender neutrality of youth as a protected legal class. Fischel's argument for revising statutory rape laws around a notion of sexual autonomy, rather than consent and force, may offer a more nuanced approach to adjudicating power differentials within sexual relationships.

37. Stadler, "Keeping Secrets," 17.

38. Stadler, "Keeping Secrets," 17.

39. Stadler, "Keeping Secrets," 15.

40. John quoted in Stadler, "Keeping Secrets," 15.

41. Stadler, *Allan Stein*, 82.

42. Stadler, *Allan Stein*, 82.

43. Stadler, *Allan Stein*, 117.

44. Stadler, *Allan Stein*, 263.

45. Califia, "No Minor Issues," 63.

46. In her reading of Henry James's novella *The Pupil*, Stockton provides another example of how fantasy, conceived in terms of the "fetishistic delay and stasis" of Deleuzian masochism, might offer a basis for an ethical pedophilic relation between a man and a boy. If Stéphane's occlusion within Matthew's sexual fantasy results in his rapidly declining health, then, in James's story, the masochistic verbal play that holds pupil and tutor together provides a means to pleasure while forestalling the boy's eventual death. Stockton, *The Queer Child*, 84, 78–88.

47. Mohr, "The Pedophilia of Everyday Life," 20.

# 21

## Stumped

*Tim Dean*

The French writer Annie Ernaux, noting what she observed in Paris on March 18, 1994, recounts the following scene: "At the top of the escalator, at Les Halles, a man was begging. Protruding slightly from his pants, cut off at the knees, were the stumps of his amputated legs. They looked like the tips of two huge penises."[1] Although *Things Seen*, the book in which this observation appears, concerns neither disability nor pornography, I want to designate this encounter at Les Halles as a "disability porn" moment, since it represents an exemplary instance where physiological impairment is rendered as pornographic. What makes the scene pornographic is Ernaux's analogy for the stumps ("like the tips of two huge penises"), which imagines gargantuan genitals where others might see merely evidence of misfortune. Why offer such a provocative comparison? Doubtless Ernaux, a socially conscious writer and meticulous prose stylist, wishes to convey the obscenity of poverty at the site of France's most famous shopping center. It is likely that the man she encounters is impoverished and homeless *because* his legs have been amputated. Indeed, the long-standing link between disability and destitution has been explained by tracing the term *handicapped* to the economic situation of the disabled: "We were beggars, caps in hand," writes one disability theorist.[2]

Drawing attention to the beggar's stumps, Ernaux makes visible what is supposed to remain outside public view—the obscenity of disability as well as of poverty. Her image of the anonymous amputee means to evoke not only pity but also outrage at a biopolitical system that exacerbates conditions of bodily impairment and vulnerability by failing to provide adequate care for all bodies, irrespective of their heterogeneity or their widely varying capacities (including the capacity to pay). Yet her description of the stumps as resembling "the tips of two huge penises" evokes something else, too. Her candor as a writer compels Ernaux to acknowledge that unexpectedly exposed portions of human anatomy—especially when somehow anomalous—are liable to evoke also desire. It is the disquieting combination of sensations aroused—sympathy, curiosity, outrage, desire—that makes disability sex and its representation so difficult to talk about coherently. This chapter is about that difficulty and about the complex pleasure of staring at anatomical forms that significantly diverge from normative embodiment. Since pornography thrives on corporeal anomaly, it should not surprise us to discover that twenty-first-century porn scenes perpetuate viewing conventions established by nineteenth-century freak shows or, indeed, that disabled people are making their own pornography and embracing the erotic connotations of freakery.

"All Freaks are perceived to one degree or another as erotic," argues Leslie Fiedler in one of the earliest critical studies of freakery.[3] Claiming more emphatically than Ernaux that corporeal anomaly tends to provoke desire in those who witness it, Fiedler maintains that this desire "is itself felt as freaky, however, since it implies not only a longing for degradation but a dream of breaching the last taboo against miscegenation."[4] In Fiedler's terms, it is both the desire and its object that are regarded as "freaky," such that anomalous embodiment is wont to trigger eros automatically, as it were. His reference to miscegenation reminds us that just as interracial porn emphasizes contact between phenotypically distinct anatomies (in order to highlight the contrast and hence the frisson of transgressing a boundary), so disability porn conventionally features extraordinary bodies in sexual contact with the more normatively bodied.[5] In such configurations, the desire at stake involves a culturally overdetermined fascination with bodily difference, where "difference" is construed relative to the putatively normal or unmarked subject. However, my concern lies less with the sociocultural construction of the nonnormative subject as different (or freakish) than with that subject's own desires. I'm interested, that is, in how people with disabilities are fabricating sexual subjectivities out of a history of libidinized objectification.

Contemporary pornography is useful for this enterprise because it so notably preoccupies itself with anatomies that can be presented as freakish, whether by emphasizing larger-than-average genitals, breasts, and "booties"; by highlighting unusual body modifications; or by contrasting normative embodiment with corporeal excess, as in fat porn, midget porn, tranny porn ("chicks with dicks"), and amputee porn.[6] Through its relentless focus on spectacles of the extraordinary body—and particularly the extraordinary feats that bodies may be induced to perform—pornography today constantly invokes the freak show. More explicitly than freak shows, however, porn eroticizes the nonnormative body and its capacities. In so doing, porn is not simply exploiting anomalous embodiment via techniques of spectacularization; it is also making disability sexy. The pornography that interests me reveals how bodily anomaly—indeed, nonnormativity in its many guises—can be erotically attractive; this porn's significance lies in its commitment to making the nonnormative hot. If the specter of disability hovers around the margins of contemporary porn thanks to its use of freak-show conventions, this is not a version of disability that viewers necessarily are encouraged to identify themselves against.[7] On the contrary, in the realm of sexuality enfreakment appears as desirable. Both straight and queer pornographies have initiated a process of destigmatizing the term *freak*, transfiguring what was once an insult into an accolade.[8]

The porn archive that I examine here—that of amputee sex between men—contributes to this project of eroticizing bodily variance. Much has been written about heterosexual instances of this kind of sex, with the overwhelming majority of attention focused on able-bodied men who desire female amputees—the so-called devotees, whose desire tends to be treated as pathological.[9] We feel so sure that being disabled is undesirable that we harbor suspicions about anyone who finds disabled bodies attractive. Critiques of amputee sex generally ignore its incidence among gay men; psychiatric and feminist discussions of this phenomenon are strikingly heteronormative. It is as if its critics refuse to acknowledge those instances of amputee sex that are most unequivocally enjoyable for its participants, since to acknowledge them would entail shifting the terms of debate from pathology and exploitation to pleasure. Far safer to decry the sexual abuse of the disabled than to think about either disabled persons' erotic desires or what consensual disability sex really entails.[10]

This is where bringing disability studies into conjunction with queer critique may be especially useful. What disability theory shares in common with queer theory is a commitment to finding anomalous bodies and nonnormative corporeal practices not merely defensible but positively desirable. Together these approaches may illuminate not just the archive of gay amputee porn but all pornographies that manifest a concern with extraordinary embodiment. Although I focus here on a specific archive, the issues I discuss go well beyond that archive, since disability represents a universal predicament rather than a purely minority question. All human bodies are vulnerable to accident, injury, and illness; all are subject to infirmity and the contingencies of time. We need disability theory to help us grasp the full range of corporeal variation and shared human vulnerability, on the one hand, while we need queer theory to help us appreciate erotic variation and the tyranny of the normal, on the other.[11] If, from this conjoined perspective, much ostensibly straight porn ends up looking rather queer, then it becomes all the more apparent that the meaning of pornographic images lies primarily in how they are viewed or read. No matter how explicit pornographic images may be, their meaning is neither essential nor self-evident. A disability perspective can transform how we look at pornography. Disability changes the meanings of pornography; the reverse may be true as well.

## "What the Hell Is Going On?"

One way that anomalously embodied persons exercise agency in a disabling world is by "getting their freak on." Freaks are not only talking back, in Joshua Gamson's terms, but also fucking back.[12] If the medicalization of corporeal anomaly historically led to its desexualization, then what I'm calling disability porn should be acknowledged as part of the resistance to the medical model that characterizes the modern disability rights movement. Disability porn tacitly recognizes how an older tradition of exoticizing anomalous embodiment—a tradition that includes the freak show—may be appropriable for very different political ends. While the circumstance of being culturally immobilized as an exotic object is doubtless unwelcome, it nevertheless confers a peculiar kind of power that can be mobilized through sexual activity. Recent social and technological conditions have enabled some crips to seize that power.

When people with disabilities publicize their sexual activity in the form of pornography, they activate an unstable circuit of gazes, attitudes, and emotions. Making themselves visible as sexual subjects rather than merely as exotic objects, people with disabilities are announcing that they have not only rights but also desires—desires that many folks still view as unacceptably perverse. These desires may be harder to acknowledge as legitimate than disability rights have been to grant. We tend to withhold compassion from those regarded as excessively desirous; it is easier to countenance minority identities than minority sexual practices. In some cases, *any* manifestation of erotic desire is regarded as excessive—as if people with disabilities, in their dependence on able-bodied good will, should behave like children whose imperative is to safeguard our fantasy of their sexual innocence. To discover that disabled folks are more interested in getting laid than in being pitied can seem to be an affront to established notions of victimhood and able-bodied privilege.[13]

The unstable circuit of gazes, attitudes, and emotions that disability porn mobilizes is evident in a viral video known as "2 Guys 1 Stump." Captioned "Military Gay Amputee Foot Fisting," this clip features two white men—one with close-cropped graying hair and a missing leg, the other sporting a buzz cut and goatee—engaged in stump fucking. The amputee's leg stump, just below knee-level, is behaving exactly like the tip of a huge penis, lunging vigorously in and out of the other man's gaping rectum. The camera is positioned so that penetration is clearly visible, as is the delight on the face of the man being penetrated.[14] Aficionados of this practice refer to it as stump fucking or, occasionally, stumping; *foot fisting* is not merely an oxymoronic term but also blatantly inaccurate, since the man *has no foot* on the limb engaged in sexual activity.

The inaccuracy of the video's caption testifies to some difficulty in seeing what's going on, a difficulty that results not from inadequate lighting or amateurish camerawork but from the normative structuring of vision. Seeing what one is not accustomed to seeing, even when one is accustomed to seeing lots of pornography, tends to generate a symptomatic response. There is no evidence that either of the men having sex in the video has any connection with the armed forces, yet much of the furor surrounding "2 Guys 1 Stump" stems from the caption's misidentification as "*Military* Gay Amputee Foot Fisting." What makes it plausible that either of these men could be veterans of the conflict in Iraq or Afghanistan is the fact that those wars have been sending home amputees in record numbers. In contrast to twentieth-century wars, "for the first time in American history, 90% of the wounded [now] survive their injuries"; indeed, the percentage of amputee veterans is the highest since the Civil War.[15] Given how the U.S. military has become a veritable disability production line, we should not be surprised when barrack buddies invent ways of having sex and creating porn with their new anatomies. I was thoroughly convinced, when a student showed me "2 Guys 1 Stump" in the context of my graduate seminar on pornography, that what we were seeing was two military vets obtaining their jouissance at the expense of those who not only consign them to being cannon fodder but, in the process, nullify their sexuality. The response posted immediately beneath the clip seemed to sum up the predominantly negative reaction to it: "This is why they don't let gays in the military." I understood "2 Guys 1 Stump" as not just a fuck video but a fuck-you video.

My initial delight over this example of queers and crips employing homemade porn as a medium of political protest dissipated once it became clear that there was little evidence to support the "military" designation. On News filter.org, a website closely associated with military personnel, the same clip circulates with a different title: "Handicapped Stump Man Legfucks Another Guy's Butt."[16] This description, while less patently inaccurate, betrays as readily as "2 Guys 1 Stump" that the video has been appropriated from its original maker. As with so much online pornography, this video has been alienated from its original context and edited for a different audience. It has been retrofitted for maximum shock value by abbreviation, recaptioning, overlaying a comedic soundtrack, and splicing in a rapid reaction clip at the very end.

Instantly recognizable to a certain generation as the Super Mario Bros. Starman theme ringtone derived from Nintendo video games, the soundtrack of "2 Guys 1 Stump" comprises a rapid-fire electronic melody with a cartoon-like quality that tends to make listeners smile. Whoever added this soundtrack to the video clip has managed to synchronize its hectic tempo with the fast-paced rhythm of the men's stump fucking, thereby casting their erotic activity in a comic light. Setting gay amputee sex to a Pac-Man tune makes it look as if one man's butt is eating the other man's leg. After laughing at this video's incongruity, which the overlaid soundtrack serves to enhance, we might consider what's at stake in representing someone else's sexuality in absurdist terms. It's not that porn—or, indeed, sex—should never be funny; quite the contrary. But mocking the ways in which minority groups such as queers and the disabled have sex suggests a distinctly hostile attitude toward them.

This attitude is compounded by the reaction shot that has been spliced in at the end of the clip. The final few seconds cut to a scene from the cult horror film *Tremors*, in which Kevin Bacon and his sidekick gaze in shock at something monstrous outside the frame. "What the hell is going on? I mean, what the hell is going on?" exclaims the outraged Bacon, in a line that became a catchphrase for a while during the nineties.[17] Here Kevin Bacon is the one who is stumped. The Hollywood star has been enlisted as a surrogate for the normative viewer who thus is tutored in how to react: heteronormativity entails not understanding this clip. You are supposed to feel like you have no idea "what the hell is going on"; any other response to the scene would be suspect. You are not supposed to feel aroused by the image or curious about the erotic practice it depicts. Normative spectatorship relies upon the maintenance of a certain ignorance—what Eve Kosofsky Sedgwick called "the privilege of un-knowing."[18] Hence most of the comments responding to this video ostentatiously perform confusion or horror: "What the hell IS going on?"; "WTF???" By echoing Bacon, these viewers protest their resolutely normal sexuality in the face of queer crip practices.

There is no small irony in needing to watch queer disability sex to qualify as sexually normal. "2 Guys 1 Stump" exploits the psychic mechanism of dis-avowal by prompting viewers to watch minority sexual practices about which they're encouraged to express disgust or outrage. The video presents two versions of being stumped, a queer and a normative version, with the implication that viewers should choose between them. The queer version offers the plea-sure of seeing a disability-sex encounter, while the normative version offers the pleasure of identifying with a movie star in recoil from that encounter. Both Bacon and the man on his back in the video, despite their manifold differences, are performing being stumped. I refer to the mechanism of dis-avowal here in the sense that it is necessary to conjure the spectacle of queer crip sex in order to access the pleasure of recoiling from it. Disgust represents not simply a reaction against pleasure but an unacknowledged form of pleasure in itself: the ego-enhancing pleasure of feeling superior to the objects of one's regard.

Whoever made "2 Guys 1 Stump" got the idea to splice in the reaction shot—as well as the video's title—from "2 Girls 1 Cup," an infamous viral video that some years ago provided ample opportunity for public performances of sexual disgust. According to the thoroughly researched Wikipedia page devoted to it, "2 Girls 1 Cup" was the nickname given to a one-minute preview for a Brazilian scat porno that "features two women conducting themselves in fetishistic intimate relations, including defecating into a cup, taking turns ostensibly consuming the excrement, and vomiting it into each other's mouths."[19] The title "2 Girls 1 Cup" was borrowed from a U.S. public-health video made to discourage the sharing of drinking vessels in the interests of hygiene. Its genius as an appropriated title lies in the degree to which disgust at the prospect of someone sipping from your water bottle pales in comparison with the spectacle of young women avidly eating shit. This viral video precipitated the emergence of a new Internet genre: the reaction clip: "Around mid-October 2007, video sites such as YouTube were flooded with videos depicting others' reactions to watching the video for the first time."[20] It was the thousands of filmed reactions to it, quite as much as the video itself, that made "2 Girls 1 Cup" iconic.

Although reaction clips performing disgust at "2 Guys 1 Stump" also are available online, they are less numerous because this video comes with its own built-in reaction shot. The genre of the reaction clip, as with the phenomenon of viewers posting comments in response to online porn scenes, offers scholars of pornography a hitherto unavailable source of data. For decades research on the effects of porn consumption has struggled to find ways of measuring its impact; now viewers are volunteering their responses in droves. To be sure, these reactions likely are as staged as the erotic acts to which they're responding. Yet although viewers' posted comments and filmed reactions hardly constitute objective data, they remain a significant source of material for analysis and interpretation. For example, online responses to pornography—whether in the form of posted comments, reaction clips, or clickable thumbs-up and thumbs-down icons—enable us to gauge what the majority of viewers will admit to finding arousing and what they will not. Public performances of disgust represent a way of policing pleasure by dividing its sources into viable and nonviable. Disgust marks the boundary, for cultures as for individuals, between what may be included and what must be expelled. Since that boundary is variable rather than immutable, the performance of disgust is always culturally conditioned and, in that sense, political. Here I'm suggesting not that disgust is necessarily invalid, only that it too readily gets mobilized to delegitimate the erotic practices of minority populations. And yet the signal advantage of public performances of disgust lies in how they recognize—albeit in violently negative mode—the presence of desire. Disgust constitutes a significant form of testimony. This practice that compels me to proclaim my disgust to the world is thereby acknowledged as desirable, indeed pleasurable, for *someone*.

## The Pleasures of Stump Grinding

Having endeavored to diagnose the fantasmatic logic of a porn clip that lasts for fewer than thirty seconds, I'd like now to consider the video that was appropriated to make "2 Guys 1 Stump." The original video, titled "Stump Grinder," runs for more than five minutes; without the Super Mario Bros. soundtrack and the *Tremors* reaction shot, it conveys a quite different meaning. What in "2 Guys 1 Stump" was pictured as absurd, even horrifying, in "Stump Grinder" is clearly erotic, not only for the men in the video but also for their audience on Xtube.com, judging by the profusion of laudatory comments that have been posted in response to it. The creator of "Stump Grinder," who is also the one being penetrated in the scene, is a gay man from Walhalla, South Carolina, who goes by the screen name of "scversasspig" (South Carolina versatile ass pig) and whose profile boasts: "15+ million views for my videos." This is a man with an audience. An amateur pornographer with a devoted following, he describes himself thus: "Very fit, lean, muscled, hung, sexy 54 year old man living in Upstate, SC, USA, looking for play buddies into FF/assplay [FF refers to fist fucking]. Extremely talented punchfist bottom, experienced top with large but patient hands. 5'9", 140, 7+cut THICK, smooth, buzz cut, s&p goatee, adventurous, passionate and playful! For those who are curious, I enjoy my FF without chemical enhancement."[21] This individual, remarkably in shape for a middle-aged man, is not a "devotee" advertising for amputee partners but a broad-minded person who appears to welcome the possibility of a disability-sex encounter. It is as if the openness of his ass, capable of accommodating a fist or a limb stump, correlates with the openness of his mind. Although nothing on his web page mentions disability or amputees, several of his many videos show him getting stumped by various amputee fuck buddies.

On the section of his profile describing what he seeks in a partner, the South Carolinian has specified "be poz friendly," thereby suggesting his own serostatus. Just as sex involving HIV-positive men could be construed as disability sex, so the popular subgenre of bareback porn may be understood under the rubric of disability pornography. In *Unlimited Intimacy* I argue that deliberately "unsafe" sex allegorizes an ethic of openness toward the other;

here that ethic is manifest in a disposition of sexual hospitality toward the disabled other.[22] Putting the matter in this way captures only part of the story, however, since it is not just the erotic activity pictured in "Stump Grinder" but *both men's bodies* that are interpretable as nonnormative, albeit with differing degrees of legibility. Erotic openness toward disability encourages the recognition that it is less a question of distinct corporeal identities than of a fundamental kinship between bodies that are but artificially segregated into disabled and nondisabled. When these bodies come together, we see not that they're the same but that their conjunction dissolves the invidious disabled/able-bodied binary.

This point becomes more evident in *Stump*, a commercially produced feature-length film about amputee sex from the bareback pornographer Dick Wadd.[23] *Stump* stars Eyton, a young Dutchman whose legs have both been amputated (one above the knee, the other below) and who, though conventionally handsome, has never appeared in porn before. As the film begins Eyton is wheeling his way down a Los Angeles street, only to be intercepted by Bud, a fearsomely tattooed and heavily pierced regular in many Dick Wadd features. Bud invites Eyton to "a dungeon party" and, after winning his reluctant consent, carefully wheels him into a space that is barely wheelchair accessible. Presenting matter-of-factly on film the maneuvers necessary to get a wheelchair into a sex space (rather than simply editing them out) communicates to viewers that this pornotopia can accommodate routine disability equipment in addition to its more obviously erotic prostheses.

After a long sequence in which his stumps are kissed, massaged, and tongued in a highly sensual manner, Eyton is fucked first by one man and then by another. The pièce de résistance comes when Eyton uses his shorter thigh to stump-fuck Bud—an experience that the latter describes as "probably the most fucking erotic thing I've ever done in my life!"[24] Although Eyton's verbal commentary during the scene indicates that he too finds it erotic ("You feel that stump? I've got my whole leg up your butt!"), his cock is not erect while stump fucking, unlike some of the amputees in the South Carolinian's amateur videos. Because the point at which his limb has been amputated makes what Eyton wields much heftier than the below-the-knee stumps in those amateur videos, the proceedings in *Stump* are more physiologically impressive yet less visually spectacular. The anatomical configuration makes it hard to see the stump entering or exiting Bud's hole.

What rivals Eyton's leg stumps for visual impact in this film is the sudden appearance of condoms. As in all this pornographer's films, the fucking and fisting in *Stump* are performed bareback, with plenty of fluid exchange—except when Eyton is fucked or when he fists the other performers. It is actually quite shocking when men who have been penetrating each other without protection abruptly don rubbers to fuck the amputee. At those moments we realize that, unlike the other men, Eyton must be HIV-negative and wants to stay that way. He has achieved something remarkable in starring in a bareback porno while insisting that those who penetrate him wear protection on film. As the appearance of condoms provokes reflection on his serostatus, so it also draws attention to the likelihood that his partners in Stump are HIV-positive. The audience is encouraged to see something that is not initially obvious on screen—namely, that all the participants are disabled in one guise or another. They may be performing impressive feats, but none of them is normatively bodied.

Insofar as they all give the lie to the pornographic myth of the perfect body, Stump's anatomies demonstrate that pleasure comes from elsewhere than perfection or intactness. The film offers an allegory for how sites of injury may be transformed into sites of pleasure. It is this transformation, rather than the feat of inserting a thigh stump into an anus, that makes the central encounter between Eyton and Bud appear genuinely erotic. The pornographer acknowledges this when he notes, in his website description of Stump, that "the true climax of this video is Eyton's sexual awakening to the possibilities available to a man without feet." [25] Gauged not by the visibility of money shots or the volume of piss that punctuates the proceedings, this film's climax lies in its star's transition from one state to another. The process of "sexual awakening" represents a kind of movement that does not require legs and that may be accomplished when its subject is physically immobilized, as Eyton is for much of the film. By means of this paradoxical mobilization through immobility, he gains access not just to the sex dungeon and potential porn stardom but also to a broadening of erotic possibility. If the purpose of disability activism is to increase access and mobility for those with physiological impairments in order to expand the possibilities available to them, then Stump pictures one way in which that might happen. This may be as impressive a feat for pornography to accomplish as that of capturing the act of taking a stump up one's butt.

## Sexual Mobility

The hypothesis that sex lends itself to a certain psychical mobility bears particular significance in the context of disability. To transform a site of injury or impairment into a site of pleasure—and then to consent to having that transformation witnessed in the form of pornography—constitutes an exemplary kind of labor. The amputee in "Stump Grinder," by transforming his stump into a giant penis, shows himself to be more mobile rather than less. When Annie Ernaux compares the Parisian beggar's stumps to "the tips of two huge penises," she performs an imaginative act of metaphoric transformation. But when a gay amputee transmutes his missing limb into a sexual organ, he's performing the more radical act of remapping his body's erogenous zones — an act that testifies to the lability of pleasure and desire. Far from a matter of "overcoming" disability, this process entails embracing it in order to intensify one's pleasure.

Here we might recall Freud's point that "any other part of the body can acquire the same susceptibility to stimulation as is possessed by the genitals and can become an erotogenic zone."[26] Redescribing sexuality in terms of fantasy rather than anatomy, Freud shows how what we call our erogenous zones are not biologically fixed but potentially itinerant. The burden of the psychoanalytic theory of sexuality is less that anatomy is destiny than that *fantasy unsettles anatomy*. This discovery, far from leaving Freud stumped, steers him toward one of his queerest conclusions — that the psychically transformed anatomical regions "then behave exactly like genitals."[27] At the level of fantasy, limb stumps really can become huge penises. Whereas amputation has reduced the physical mobility of the men in these porn scenes, it nonetheless has increased their psychical mobility, rendering them sexually more adventurous, capable of going places in fantasy that others barely have conceived.

The psychical work involved in transforming an amputated limb into an erogenous zone has extensive implications. Since the amputees in these films are not missing a functional penis, we would be mistaken in regarding their psychical transformation as merely compensatory. They have, in a sense, grown an extra penis; or, to put it somewhat differently, they have converted a source of pain into a source of pleasure. Although the official literature on amputation is replete with descriptions of phantom pain, I have yet to find any acknowledgment of what might be called *phantom pleasure* as a consequence of limb loss. Rather than a case of phantom limb syndrome, whereby the mind compensates for loss by experiencing sensation in regions that are no longer part of the body, we have here a case of limbs that are generating and experiencing genital sensations. This is, to say the least, a better deal for everyone involved.

"Being an amputee is fundamentally a plus, rather than a minus, when it comes to sexual attraction," confirms Derek Douglas, a gay man who lost his lower right arm in a construction accident. Given that, as far as I have been able to ascertain, the videos I'm discussing were not made by amputees, it's worth hearing at length what this disabled man has to say about the erotic dimensions of his stump:

> An amputated arm can be a major turn on to certain people. It doesn't take
> a lot of imagination to leap to a phallic context. My friends kid me about

having a super dick. It's not unusual for a partner to want to lick or suck my stump. Actually, the end of my stump is quite sensitive and erotic in certain situations. And yes when lubed-up—well, you get the picture. The concept is fisting without a fist. In answer to your [implied] question: Yes I have on numerous occasions. And yes it puts them on the ceiling. Not to get into too much level of detail, but the end of my stump is naturally extremely sensitive, logically because of the severed nerve endings. The only other natural extremity with [a] similar amount of nerve endings is the head of the penis—quite literally. Is it erotic in the same sense as the penis? No, not exactly, but stroking it directly along the line of the scar (where the skin and muscle tissue was stitched over the bone) does produce a very unique sensation. When we sit and watch TV or relax, my boyfriend frequently massages my stump and it is very pleasurable.[28]

Using his stump to fuck other men is, according to Douglas, enormously pleasurable for both them and him. As became evident in Stump, this kind of disability sex involves not only wielding the stump as a giant phallus ("super dick") but also tonguing, kissing, sucking, and caressing it. Although Douglas describes his pleasure in purely physiological terms, based on the preponderance of nerve endings at the point of amputation, elsewhere in the interview he makes clear that incorporating the stump into his body image and hence into his sexuality entailed a complex psychological process. Developing an erogenous zone is never a purely physiological or cognitive act. There is a kind of psychical labor involved in constructing new sexual practices and the erogenous zones that accompany them—a labor that pornography serves to facilitate.

The creation of new possibilities of pleasure ought to be understood not just as an individual response to injury or impairment but also as part of a collective enterprise that stems from the history of sexual politics. Gay men, especially those who practice SM, are well versed in "inventing new possibilities of pleasure with strange parts of their body," suggests Michel Foucault.[29] In conversations late in life about sexuality and ethics, Foucault frequently turned to the subject of SM, which he characterized as "a creative enterprise," one that shows how "we can produce pleasure with very odd things, very strange parts of our bodies, in very unusual situations."[30] Here Foucault—like Freud before him—sounds as though he could be describing the practice of stump fucking. Surprisingly consistent with a psychoanalytic account of the mobility of erotogenicity beyond genitalia, Foucault refers in the same interview to "the desexualization of pleasure," a phrase more accurately translated as the *degenitalization* of pleasure.[31] Foucault's point is that we are mistaken in treating genital stimulation or orgasm as the source and model of all bodily pleasure. The difference between Freud and Foucault on this score, however, is that whereas Freud focuses on fantasy, Foucault focuses on practices. (My own sense is that, in thinking about sexuality, methodologically one should focus on both.) The practices to which Foucault refers have a history—and have given rise to a specific subculture—that helps to contextualize stump fucking.

We catch glimpses of that subculture in the South Carolinian's online profile, as well as in the leather iconography evident in both his amateur videos and Dick Wadd's commercial productions. Here *fist fucking* (abbreviated to FF in the online profile) serves as a metonym for a whole range of practices associated with SM and leather sex. What's striking about these practices in gay pornography is how they decenter the visual and narrative focus from penises and orgasm to other parts of the body. In fisting scenes, as the camera focuses on hands and anal sphincters, the men engaged in this activity often are shown as either semierect or detumescent.[32] One might say that their pleasure has shifted from the genital region or that erotogenicity is being purposely extended in order to maximize pleasure. Anal stimulation, in this porn subgenre, often represents not a prelude to penile penetration but an end in itself. It is not just the lips, the mouth, and the throat (as well as the ass cheeks, the anus, the rectum, and the prostate) that become available to stimulation in SM; it is also the hands, the feet, and any limb stumps, along with the nipples, the chest, and the torso. The entirety of the body's surface may be slapped, spanked, or flogged with varying degrees of intensity; the scalp may be shaved; the head may be hooded; any part of the body may be sheathed or restrained (including one's breath). And this is just the beginning. Such varied techniques for producing pleasure "with very odd things, very strange parts of our bodies, in very unusual situations" are developed and transmitted within a subculture whose pornography is vital to its existence.

*Disability and Porn Pedagogy*

When it comes to nonnormative sex, porn always has a pedagogical function. The pornography that interests me shows how to elicit pleasure from regions of the body that one might have been unaware could yield pleasure; it demonstrates practices that one may not have previously imagined; it suggests how to cultivate nongenital parts of the body (the hand, the sphincter, the stump) for sexual encounters; and it reveals a greater range of anatomies that may be considered desirable. In other words, this pornography pictures something for me that I didn't necessarily already know or feel. Pornography and disability thus go together less in terms of exploitation than in terms of demonstrating different bodies' astonishingly varied capacities, including their capacities for pleasure. The pedagogy of pornography entails not so much imitation of what one sees others doing on screen but rather the process of making visible a range of options—options that remain irreducible to mere consumer choices. This kind of porn pedagogy serves democratic culture insofar as it conspicuously broadens the opportunities for what one might do with one's body and how one might generate pleasure. It extends the horizon of possibility by furnishing conditions for sexual mobility.

In suggesting how a pornography of disability may be enabling, I mean to question the persistent assumption that sexual pleasure tends to be generated at the expense of less powerful individuals or groups—in this case, people with disabilities. There is nothing inherently sinister about taking pleasure in staring at anomalous bodies or marveling at what naked bodies can do; as Rosemarie Garland-Thomson argues, we don't necessarily disenfranchise the objects of our regard when we stare at them.[33] Yet the legacy of the hermeneutics of suspicion, and particularly of certain versions of psychoanalysis, has bequeathed us a daunting lexicon that functions above all to pathologize the pleasures of looking. *Objectification, fetishism, voyeurism, exhibitionism, incorporative identification, violent disidentification*—all these terms render the pleasures of looking as deeply suspect and in need of demystification. If we cannot talk about looking without recourse to these terms (or their cognates), we'll forever stop short of grasping what's most fully at stake in a whole range of experiences of visual pleasure. I'm not proposing that the pleasures of looking are innocent or uncomplicated, but we might see something different if we regarded those pleasures from a critical perspective less tinged with paranoia.

Yet to claim, as I have thus far, that the pleasure manifested by its amputee participants exculpates disability porn from any charge of exploitation does not go far enough. Even when all the on-screen participants appear to be freely and consensually enjoying themselves, we worry that the able-bodied viewer's pleasure may be derived at the expense of the nonnormatively embodied persons whose actions compose the film. It is hard to shake the notion that if viewers regard themselves as normatively embodied, then their getting off on watching disabled bodies must be ethically dubious. According to this perspective, the viewer's gaze exacerbates the disabled body's vulnerability by taking pleasure in fetishizing or otherwise dominating it as a specular object. Indeed, pornography's focus on extraordinary anatomies lends itself to the all-too-familiar disciplinary project of regulating bodies by stabilizing their identities, thus rendering them more susceptible to classification and control. We participate in that normalizing project when we take pleasure in consolidating our own identities at the expense of others'—as in the invidious depiction of crip sex in "2 Guys 1 Stump." Doubtless much pornography, by investing heavily in identity categories, works toward this normalizing effect.[34]

Conversely, however, porn's emphasis on action—its relentless displays of what different bodies are capable of doing—works against this normalizing effect by downplaying the significance of identity in favor of what, borrowing from Frances Ferguson, we may designate as relative value. Insofar as it privileges acts over identities, pornography disperses rather than consolidates normalizing power. I extrapolate this point from Ferguson's distinctive account, which connects the late eighteenth-century pornographic revival with the historically coincident emergence of utilitarianism, in order to demonstrate homologies between the Marquis de Sade's writing and Jeremy Bentham's educational philosophy, both of which exemplify what she calls utilitarian social structures. "Pornography, like Bentham's Panopticon, was central in moving politics from a way of representing property rights to a way of capturing the importance of actions, and of using the social group as a way of establishing a relative value for individual actions," she argues.[35] What utilitarianism did to action, in the terms of her study's subtitle, was to elevate its significance as a measure of social value—and, in so doing, to counter the claims of inherited status as the basis for enfranchisement and social power.

Comparing Sadian pornography to Bentham's panopticon writings, Ferguson is not rehearsing the critical commonplace that modern society subjects its members to an essentially anonymous gaze that disciplines bodies and desires, thereby curtailing our freedom. Instead, she's locating in utilitarian social structures a set of techniques for making hypervisible the value of any individual relative to his or her standing in a group. Here visibility is advantageous rather than otherwise because it allows everyone to see what others are capable of doing, not just who they are. Ferguson's description of panopticism revises the standard reading of Bentham derived from Foucault's *Discipline and Punish* by shifting the emphasis from penality to education. Insofar as utilitarian educational philosophy, organized around competition and ranking, focused on rewards more than on punishments, the classroom was, in fact, distinguishable from the prison.

The appeal of the utilitarian system lies in its commitment to social mobility: "No longer would merit be judged on the basis of what family one came from or even whom one knew. Instead, Panoptic examinations made it possible for the merit of even the poor and unwashed to become apparent."[36] Utilitarian social structures remain central to democratic modernity because "they opened opportunities and access that would have been unimaginable in a strictly class-based or wealth-based society."[37] We have become so accustomed to Foucault's reading of Bentham that Ferguson's emphasis on access and equality of opportunity doubtless comes as a surprise; her account enables us to see not only Bentham but also Foucault (and, indeed, pornography) in a startling new light. Further, her emphasis on access—and on the institutionalization of mechanisms for safeguarding opportunities for mobility—resonates with a disability-politics agenda.

What connects Ferguson's account with disability issues is what connects utilitarianism with pornography—the question of mobility. Utilitarian pedagogy shares in common with the porn pedagogy I've been describing a focus on constant movement: bodies are perpetually in motion and changing places following a logic of testing and evaluation. (Can you spell this word? What about this one? Can you take this dildo up your ass? How about this stump?)[38] Utilitarian social organization, like pornography, provides a structure of representation within which value becomes both hypervisible and subject almost immediately to revision, as actions (rather than identities) determine an individual's placement in the configuration. Ferguson construes the structured movement of children among places in the Benthamite classroom (like the rule-bound movement of participants in a spelling bee) in terms of both social mobility and the harder-to-perceive mobility of power relations. Three kinds of mobility are involved here—physical, social, and political. The radically egalitarian presupposition underlying utilitarianism is that it's not who you are or where you come from but what you can do that decides your position in these social arrangements.

How exactly does this work in pornography? The rigorous antiessentialism of Ferguson's argument leaves her uninterested in the specifics of pornographic content; by contrast, I've focused on very specific, even marginal, pornographic contents, which I've claimed have significance beyond their particularity as a disability-porn archive. On the one hand, pornography may be explicable through reference to the abstract choreography of dance, whereby the identities of individual bodies remain subordinate to temporary positions within a structure that excites bodily movement in order to promote its visibility. And, indeed, one disabled porn actor has distinguished sex in private from sex on camera in just these terms: "Sex on film is about lighting and choreography; I don't consider it sex."[39] On the other hand, pornography as a utilitarian social structure is comparable to the rather different spectacle of competitive sporting events. As Ferguson puts it: "Pornography, . . . like lists of the ten or twenty or one hundred 'best of . . . ,' like scores of athletic games, intensively uses comparison and displays relative value to create extreme perceptibility."[40] Translating Ferguson's account into a disability context, we might say that watching pornography resembles watching the Paralympics, insofar as one takes pleasure in the spectacle of bodies in action—bodies whose prowess and relative value depend not on their intactness but on what they can do (and *do* do) in a highly structured situation. The point, in utilitarian terms, would be to increase the number of highly structured situations; what we need is more pornography, not less. (This could explain, as much as justify, the proliferation of porn online.)

Pornography—like sports, like dance—works to make acutely visible what bodies can do; like the Paralympics, it is particularly interested in what different kinds of bodies can do. As we observed when comparing "2 Guys 1 Stump" with "Stump Grinder" (the video from which it was appropriated), the viewing context invariably raises ethical issues about how pornographic images are mobilized. Since the meaning and, indeed, the politics of any image lie less in its content than in what is done with the image, we cannot tell for certain just by looking what uses any particular pornographic image may be enlisted to serve. It is extraordinarily reductive to assume that pornography will be used always and only for masturbation or for the propping up of my own identity at someone else's expense. Just as the archive of gay amputee porn reveals comparatively unexpected ways of generating pleasure, not to mention startling uses of human anatomy, so likewise we may imagine less predictable, more inventive uses for pornography itself. The point is not to prescribe (or proscribe) particular uses but to significantly expand the range of possibilities. By making explicit what's not immediately evident in stump porn, I've tried to contribute to that project. Specifically, I've argued that making disability sex into pornography works to render perceptible subtle forms of mobility— psychic or erotogenic mobility—that are as hard to capture as the social and political kinds of mobility analyzed so incisively by Ferguson (and, in different contexts, by scholars working in disability studies).

Whereas in the popular imagination to be stumped is to be stymied (the opposite of mobility), in the films I've discussed, being stumped grants access to extraordinary mobility. The difficulty of registering that mobility is connected to what Linda Williams two decades ago identified as the difficulty of capturing adequate visual evidence of pleasure.[41] Williams showed how the late nineteenth-century emergence of cinematic technology could be understood as part of a broader endeavor to make the truths of sex available to sight. An "incitement to see" developed as the correlative of what Foucault famously called the "incitement to speak" about sex; and both served disciplinary power by creating sexual identities that function as mechanisms of control over otherwise unruly bodies.[42] What Ferguson emphasizes, in contrast, is how making actions especially visible can work against, rather than in the service of, disciplinary power by rendering identities increasingly irrelevant. Insofar as pornography, whether written or filmed, excels at making actions visible, it thereby generates possibilities for movement that loosen the bonds of identity.

If disability porn publicizes disabled bodies exercising their sexual agency, it also shows how ability and disability are inextricably intertwined rather than opposed. The transformation of stumps into erogenous zones represents just one example of pleasure's capacity to destabilize corporeal identities. Pornography is particularly adept at making us see how identities—including that of able-bodiedness—dissolve under the pressure of pleasure. When we start to see our bodies as the basis for something other than self-recognition, we can take pleasure in (rather than simply feeling anxious about) the corporeal kinship that connects all human anatomies. In the perspective opened up by certain pornographies, disability represents the ground not for identity but for transformation. Insofar as disability porn mobilizes its viewers to discover their bodies' hitherto unknown capacities, this archive enables us to see much more than it contains.

## Notes

For inspiration and feedback, I wish to thank Maria Almanza, Janet Lyon, Amanda Morrison, Steven Ruszczycky, Ramón Soto-Crespo, David Squires, Joseph Valente, and Cynthia Wu.

1. Ernaux, Things Seen, 24–25.

2. Clare, Exile and Pride, 67. Eli Clare concedes that the link between handicapped and cap in hand is not strictly etymological (140); however, it helps to remind us of the systemic connections between physiological impairment and economic disadvantage. The figure of the "unsightly beggar"—and the history of U.S. laws regulating the appearance of disabled bodies in public—is the subject of a major recent study on indigence, disability, and urban space; see Schweik, The Ugly Laws.

3. Fiedler, Freaks, 137.

4. Fiedler, Freaks, 137.

5. On interracial porn and boundary transgression, see L. Williams, "Skin Flicks on the Racial Border." In the subgenre of so-called midget porn, the impulse is to see somebody with dwarfism fucking a normatively bodied partner. Unlike Tom Thumb weddings a century ago, contemporary midget porn never features two people with dwarfism coupled with each other; the contrast in scale is rigorously maintained. Perhaps for this reason, I have never come across any examples of gay midget porn; the subgenre is both resolutely heterosexual and, at the same time, unremittingly queer. See, for example, The Adventures of Diablo, the Crippled Midget (directed by Diablo, 2006) and Midget Gang-Bang (directed by Apocalypse Joe, 2000). On the phenomenon of Tom Thumb weddings, see Stewart, On Longing, 117–25.

6. In her groundbreaking study Bound and Gagged, Laura Kipnis reads fat porn and tranny porn, among other pornographic subgenres, as allegories of U.S. culture's fantasies about gender, consumption, and excess. Although her principal analytic category is gender rather than disability, her discussions are illuminating in a disability studies context. On heterosexual fat porn, see Kulick, "Porn"; on gay fat porn, see Bunzl, "Chasers."

7. My understanding of the freak show derives from a number of scholarly sources.

Rachel Adams, in *Sideshow U.S.A.*, argues persuasively that rather than disappearing in the latter half of the twentieth century, freak-show conventions persisted in American culture through to the present (though she mentions pornography only in passing [210]). My description of disability as extraordinary embodiment draws on Garland-Thomson, *Extraordinary Bodies*; and Garland-Thomson, *Freakery*, although I demur from her blanket assertion that "a freak show's cultural work is to make the physical particularity of the freak into a hypervisible text against which the viewer's indistinguishable body fades into a seemingly neutral, tractable, and invulnerable instrument of the autonomous will, suitable to the uniform abstract citizenry democracy institutes." Garland-Thomson, "From Wonder to Error: A Genealogy of Freak Discourse in Modernity," 10. The pornography that interests me solicits the viewer to identify with, rather than against, the freaks. In *Freak Show*, Robert Bogdan employs the phrase *the pornography of disability* as a term of censure in his account of how entertainment institutions transformed human bodily anomalies into the spectacle of freaks.

8. *Superfreaks* is the title of a video series featuring predominantly African American performers that ran to seventeen videos and was produced by mainstream straight-porn company Elegant Angel during the early 2000s. Brian Pumper, a performer-cum-rapper associated with Elegant Angel, departed in 2009 to form his own porn studio, which he named Freaky Empire. Two noteworthy gay feature-length films that adapt freak-show conventions for their carnival sideshow and circus themes are *Carny* (directed by Brian Mills and Harold Creg, 2003) and *Cirque Noir* (directed by Brian Mills, 2005). In addition to heavily tattooed and pierced performers, *Cirque Noir* features two semiprofessional clowns (one of whom has a cleft tongue), an acrobatic trapeze artist, a strong man, and a rubber man named Stretch who performs remarkable anatomical feats. In the film's most original scene, the penis of the FTM transgender performer Buck Angel becomes detached while inside Tober Brandt's ass, and the two gay muscle guys who've been having sex with Buck discover to their consternation that, despite his hypermasculine appearance and demeanor, "he's got a pussy!"

9. See, for example, Elman, "Disability Pornography"; and Money and Simcoe, "Acrotomophilia, Sex and Disability."

10. Focusing here on sex involving physically disabled men, I leave aside more complex issues surrounding sex with cognitively impaired persons, where questions of consent are especially vexed. Doubtless the disabling social arrangements that impede and constrain people with physical impairments also make them more vulnerable to coercion or sexual exploitation. However, my working assumption throughout this chapter is that the pornography I discuss has been produced with the full consent of all its participants.

11. I take the phrase *the tyranny of the normal* from Fiedler's *The Tyranny of the Normal*, in recognition of how Fiedler's work tackled queer and disability issues avant la lettre.

12. Gamson, *Freaks Talk Back*.

13. For example, studies of people with spinal cord injuries find that some of them rank the capacity to have sex as more desirable than the ability to walk again. See Tepper, "Lived Experiences That Impede or Facilitate Sexual Pleasure and Orgasm in People with Spinal Cord Injury."

14. The video clip is available at http://www.2guys1stump.com, accessed June 4, 2010.

15. These statistics are provided in the astonishing documentary film *Alive Day Memories: Home from Iraq* (directed by Jon Alpert and Ellen Goosenberg Kent, 2007). To the military statistics should be added the numbers of those who end up as amputees by

other means, whether through injury, medical intervention in disease processes such as diabetes, or congenital accident. A recent study concludes that "one in 190 Americans is currently living with the loss of a limb. Unchecked, this number may double by the year 2050." Ziegler-Graham et al., "Estimating the Prevalence of Limb Loss in the United States," 423. Significantly, this study excludes amputations resulting from armed conflict and those performed at Veterans Administration hospitals; the authors note that "estimates of amputations during Operation Iraqi Freedom and Operation Enduring Freedom alone exceed 600" (427). These figures suggest that the United States is now producing more amputees than it can keep track of, let alone care for or accommodate.

16. "Handicapped stump man legfucks another guy's butt," uploaded by bungduck, Newsfilter.org, 2009, accessed June 10, 2010, http://www.newsfilter.org/video/52535 /Handicapped_stump_man_legfucks_another_guy's_butt/.

17. See *Tremors* (directed by Ron Underwood, 1990).

18. Sedgwick, *Tendencies*, 23–51.

19. See the Wikipedia page for "2 Girls 1 Cup," accessed June 10, 2010, http://www .en.wikipedia.org/wiki/2_Girls_1_Cup.

20. See the Wikipedia page for "2 Girls 1 Cup."

21. The Xtube.com profile for scversasspig is available at http://www.xtube.com/com munity/profile.php?user=scversasspig, accessed June 10, 2010.

22. See Dean, *Unlimited Intimacy*, chapter 4.

23. See *Stump* (directed by Dick Wadd, 2003).

24. "Bud," "Getting a Leg Up," 40. (This article was published under the name "Bud," though he also publishes under the name "Bud Hole.") Contextualizing Eyton's appearance in this film, the author adds: "I think it's really important to point out that this guy did it because he was curious about trying something that would open up new sexual avenues for him (i.e., using his stump as a huge cock); he also said that he 'wanted to see what it would be like to be an amputee sex symbol.' . . . He left the video shoot with me and on the drive home, told me that this experience had changed his life and was probably the most positive thing that had happened to him since the accident that caused him to lose his legs."

25. See http://www.dickwadd.com/osc/product_info.php?products_id=44, accessed June 25, 2007.

26. Freud, *Three Essays on the Theory of Sexuality*, 184.

27. Freud, *Three Essays on the Theory of Sexuality*, 183–84. I discuss further the implications of this aspect of psychoanalytic theory in Dean, *Beyond Sexuality*, 251–57.

28. See Mark Allen, "Mark Allen's Disability Interviews," accessed June 15, 2010, http://www.markallencam.com/disabilityderek.html.

29. Foucault, "Sex, Power, and the Politics of Identity," 165.

30. Foucault, "Sex, Power, and the Politics of Identity," 165.

31. Foucault, "Sex, Power, and the Politics of Identity," 165.

32. See, for example, *Devil in the Rain* (directed by Harold Creg and Mike Cole, 1998).

33. See Garland-Thomson, *Staring*. She draws on the object relations psychoanalysis of D. W. Winnicott, among other sources, to argue that staring can function as a life-sustaining form of acknowledgment. Staring would constitute something like recognition in Hegel's terms. Several of the amputees interviewed in *Alive Day Memories* describe how looking directly at their amputations works as a crucial act of acknowledgment that helps to make real their new bodily forms. Learning to live with an amputated limb or

limbs requires renegotiating what Lacanians call the mirror stage; it requires, in other words, social recognition through an exchange of looks.

34. Similarly, most of the chapters collected in Garland-Thomson's *Freakery* focus on the consolidation of normative identities at the expense of the nonnormative.

35. Ferguson, *Pornography, the Theory*, xv.

36. Ferguson, *Pornography, the Theory*, 20.

37. Ferguson, *Pornography, the Theory*, 20.

38. I should acknowledge that even as I'm drawing on Ferguson's analysis for the final stage of my argument, I may be distorting it beyond recognition. Certainly the way in which Ferguson connects pornography to pedagogy differs from how I'm linking them. It is not simply that she considers pornography and pedagogy in the historically specific terms of utilitarianism. Ferguson also rehearses an argument against what could be construed as the position I'm advancing on the value of minority porn pedagogy—a position that she identifies primarily with the work of Gayle Rubin. She observes that for Rubin pornography "not only doesn't cause harms to women but . . . serves a positive educational purpose. Pornography, in [Rubin's] treatment, has developed to the point of dividing into a variety of genres with a variety of target audiences; it performs a major service by educating a self-selecting audience into the possibility of sexual self-realization. The meaning of the pornographic object, in other words, is its audience's self-image. From this perspective, pornography teaches by giving one anticipations of certain actions that are merely an incidental expression of the sexual identity one has already (if only proleptically) achieved." Ferguson, *Pornography, the Theory*, 42–43.

I share Ferguson's dissatisfaction with the self-recognition model of pornography and am trying to make apparent how pornography can work pedagogically *without* having to appeal to anyone's self-image or sexual identity. Through various vectors of mobility, disability porn works by defusing identity into a world of possibility; its appeal may lie precisely in its promise of the dissolution or deferral of social and sexual identities.

39. Aidan Shaw, a British gay porn actor and writer, quoted in the documentary *Thinking XXX* (directed by Timothy Greenfield-Saunders, 2006).

40. Ferguson, *Pornography, the Theory*, xiv.

41. See Linda Williams, *Hard Core* (1989).

42. See Foucault, *The History of Sexuality*, 18.

# APPENDIX

## Clandestine Catalogs: A Bibliography
## of Porn Research Collections

*Caitlin Shanley*

This list of clandestine catalogs gives credence to the archivist Hilary Jenkinson's famous claim that archivists exist "in order to make other people's work possible." Librarians, archivists, and other information enthusiasts did much of the detective work I relied on in compiling this bibliography, offering a tremendous number of suggestions for materials to feature. Librarianly anxieties about creating a fully complete record plagued me as I tried to incorporate as much of the information as possible. I hope that this tool will offer some sense of the diversity of materials relevant to the field of pornography research, but it does not, truly cannot, attempt to be a comprehensive document. Instead I have tailored this list to accentuate the material profile of the various "porn archives" that the preceding chapters of this volume explore. Because many of those archives are digital, theoretical, or simply inaccessible to most researchers, the list intends to facilitate access to relevant sex materials conserved in institutional settings. The hope is that future archival studies of pornography will continue the important transnational and interdisciplinary conversation taken up in this volume. That conversation and the diversity of collections listed provide strong evidence that porn is multitudinous. If the keepers of necessarily, but unintentionally, excluded collections revolt and insist on public recognition for their sex materials, perhaps this list will play the role of instigator as well as facilitator. That would be the surest sign of its worth.

AMERICAN GENRE FILM ARCHIVE

PO Box 28741
Austin, TX 78755
United States
http://www.americangenrefilm.com/

The American Genre Film Archive (AGFA) is a not-for-profit archive that houses and lends 35 mm prints of genre films. The collection centers on independent genre films from the exploitation era of the 1960s through the 1980s, including sexploitation films. Though pornography is not explicitly part of any collection's policy, a number of pornographic films fall into the genres on which they focus.

## BIBLIOTHÈQUE NATIONALE DE FRANCE

11 Quai François Mauriac
75706 Paris
France
http://www.bnf.fr

The L'Enfer collection, famously described in a 1913 bibliography by Guillaume Apollinaire, Fernand Fleuret, and Louis Perceau, holds one of the world's most prolific and long-standing collections of pornographic and erotic materials. The bibliography describes nearly one thousand titles of erotic French poetry.

## BRITISH LIBRARY

St Pancras
96 Euston Road
London
NW1 2DB
England
http://www.bl.uk/

A key collection of historical pornographic materials, the British Library's Private Case has been the subject of speculation, folklore, and history. Written before its catalog escaped staff-only circulation, Peter Fryer's *Private Case—Public Scandal* was the first historical study of the collection. During the same period the library began transferring Private Case materials to the General Catalog. In 1981 Patrick J. Kearney published an updated catalog titled *The Private Case*. Although the library has continued to integrate its contents into the main collection, the Private Case holds a wide-ranging collection of sexology, erotic classics, and pornographic texts from the seventeenth and eighteenth centuries; more-recent hard-core pornography; and gay erotica.

## BROWNE POPULAR CULTURE LIBRARY

William T. Jerome Library
Bowling Green State University
Bowling Green, OH 43403
United States
http://www.bgsu.edu/colleges/library/pcl/

In addition to manuscripts, rare books, and other archival resources, the Browne Popular Culture Library collects nontraditional library materials, including dime novels, story papers, and nickel weeklies; pulp magazines, fanzines, and other amateur publications; comic books and graphic novels; and posters, postcards, greeting cards, and mail-order catalogs. Of particular interest are collections of erotic pulp fiction, vintage paperbacks, adult comics, explicit romance novels, and sex manuals.

## CANADIAN LESBIAN AND GAY ARCHIVES

PO Box 699, Station F
50 Charles Street East
Toronto, ON M4Y 2N6
Canada
http://clga.ca/

In addition to archival collections, The Canadian Lesbian and Gay Archives (CLGA) maintains the James Fraser Library, a research library that holds a significant collection of periodical titles along with fiction and nonfiction monographs, including erotica.

## CENTER FOR SEX AND CULTURE

2261 Market Street Box 455-A
San Francisco, CA 94114
United States
http://www.sexandculture.org

The Center for Sex and Culture maintains a comprehensive collection of both cataloged and uncataloged print and archival materials; only underage material is excluded. Research materials include personal collections, organization records (notably the lesbian-feminist BDSM organizations Samois and early Society of Janus), VHS porn by the cubic yard, 1970s-era porn movie posters, pulp erotica, and antique vibrators.

## CINEMATECA BRASILEIRA

Largo Senador Raul Cardoso, 207
Vila Clementino
04021-070, São Paulo
Brazil
http://www.cinemateca.gov.br/
http://www.bcc.org.br/

Incorporated in 1984 as a branch of the Ministry of Education and Culture, Cinemateca Brasileira hosts an extensive filmography of Brazilian films from 1897 to the present. Its database includes annotated entries for more than forty thousand titles, many of which are recognized as pornochanchadas (erotic slapsticks popular during the 1970s and 1980s). The associated Banco de Conteúdos Culturais features an online archive of movie posters, film stills, and promotional photographs for well-known pornochanchadas, including *Mulher objeto, A árvore dos sexos, Histórias que nossas babás não contavam, Como é boa nossa empregada, O bem dotado: O homem de Itu*, and its sequel, *A virgem o dem dotado*.

DAVID M. RUBENSTEIN RARE BOOK AND MANUSCRIPT LIBRARY

Duke University
Box 90185
Durham, NC 27708
United States
http://library.duke.edu/rubenstein/index.html

Composed of collecting areas in the documentary arts, advertising history, and women's history and culture, among others, the David M. Rubenstein Library houses diverse items and groupings of materials with pornographic content. Discrete collections of interest include extensive collections of gay American pulps, gay male mysteries, and police stories; one of the largest collections of lesbian pulp fiction in North America; the Reevy Collection of Books on the History of Sexuality, which consists of several hundred Cold War–era paperbacks depicting sensationalized versions of scientific works on American sexual behaviors; and periodical collections that include runs of titles generally considered pornographic, including *On Our Backs, Screw*, and *Drummer*.

DEUTSCHE KINEMATHEK

Potsdamer Straße 2
10785 Berlin
Germany
http://www.deutsche-kinemathek.de/

The Deutsche Kinemathek collects films and cinema ephemera, focusing on German filmmakers and avant-garde and experimental film. Collections include early stag films, notably including erotic silent films produced by the Viennese Saturn company. The museum regularly accepts donations of erotic and pornographic films; while these items become part of the museum collections, regrettably they are largely uncataloged at present.

EROTIC HERITAGE MUSEUM

3275 Industrial Road
Las Vegas, NV 89109
United States
http://www.eroticheritagemuseumlasvegas.com/

The Erotic Heritage Museum describes its origin as "a partnership of a Preacher and a Pornographer." The museum houses more than seventeen thousand square feet of permanent and featured exhibits of materials that depict sex and love acts, focusing on erotic artifacts, fine art, and film.

EYE FILM INSTITUTE NETHERLANDS

Vondelpark 3
PO Box 74782
1070 BT Amsterdam
Netherlands
http://eyefilm.nl/

An amalgamation of four separate Dutch film organizations, the EYE Film Institute Netherlands was founded in 2010 to provide educational and research opportunities and to advance film culture in the Netherlands. Along with curating and providing access to an extensive film collection, EYE staff are working on a project to document Dutch opinions of erotica from the 1960s to the 1980s, including conducting original interviews with porn directors and theater managers from that era.

FALES LIBRARY AND SPECIAL COLLECTIONS

The Downtown Collection
New York University
70 Washington Square South, Third Floor
New York, NY 10012
United States
http://www.nyu.edu/library/bobst/research/fales/

The Fales Library has sexually explicit materials scattered throughout its collections, especially those dealing with downtown New York City art and sexuality. Some highlights include the Gay and Lesbian Pulp Novel collection, the MIX Archive of Experimental LGBT Film and Video, the Gay Cable Network Archives, the Peter Allen Lewis Collection of Safe Sex Pamphlets, Serpent's Tail/High Risk Books Archives, and the personal papers of such people as Dennis Cooper, David

Wojnarowicz, Robert Blanchon, Erich Maria Remarque, Jay Blotcher, Jimmy De-Sana, Tim Dlugos, Richard Hell, Gary Indiana, and Terence Sellers. The downtown New York City collection documents the literary and art scenes of the 1970s through the present and contains notable titles such as *Screw, Bomb, Cover,* and *Punk,* as well as an extensive queer zine collection.

### FILM AND TELEVISION ARCHIVE

Outfest Legacy Project for LGBT Film Preservation
University of California, Los Angeles
Los Angeles, CA 90095
United States
http://www.cinema.ucla.edu/collections

The Outfest Legacy Project for LGBT Film Preservation formed in 2005 as a partnership between the UCLA Film and Television Archive and the Outfest organization. This unique project focuses on the preservation of independent LGBT films and contains historically significant pornographic titles. Additionally, the UCLA Library and Special Collections have numerous collections of interest to pornography scholars, from Henry Miller erotica manuscripts to pulp-fiction collections to Spanish-language *novelas pasionales.*

### GEORGE KELLY PAPERBACK AND PULP FICTION COLLECTION

Lockwood Library Special Collections
University at Buffalo
420 Capen Hall
Buffalo, NY 14260
United States
http://library.buffalo.edu/specialcollections/

The University at Buffalo Special Collections houses nearly eight hundred erotic novels in the George Paperback and Pulp Fiction Collection, which comprises more than 25,000 pulp-fiction books and magazines. Erotic titles include novels by authors such as Arthur Adlon, J. G. Ballard, Lolah Burford, Robert Colby, Harlan Ellison, Carlton Gibbs, Matt Harding, William Moore, Jack Pine, and Steve Yardley, as well as several anonymous titles, including *Bizarre Sexual Fantasies,* volume 13. The entire Kelly collection is cataloged and searchable online. Also of note at the same institution is the Poetry Collection. It holds more than nine thousand entrepreneurial little literary magazine titles from across the world of poetry, many of which are associated with various sexual liberation movements.

Elihu Burritt Library
Central Connecticut State University
1615 Stanley Street
New Britain, CT 06050
United States
http://library.ccsu.edu/help/spcoll/equity/index.php

The Gender Equity Collection at Elihu Burritt Library has a few collections of particular relevance to LGBTQ researchers, including collections of gay and lesbian pulp fiction from the mid-twentieth century, explicit graphic novels from the late 1960s through early 1970s, and materials related to Connecticut gay and lesbian film festivals.

### THE GROVE PRESS FILM COLLECTION

Harvard Film Archive
Carpenter Center for the Visual Arts
24 Quincy Street
Cambridge, MA 02138
United States
http://hcl.harvard.edu/hfa/collections/grove_press.html

The Harvard Film Archive was a recipient of materials from the Grove Press's film division after it disbanded in 1985. The Grove Press Film Collection at the Harvard Film Archive consists of international nonmainstream films dating from the 1910s to the 1970s. Among these include Grove Press Erotic Classic cartoons, live-action sexology films, and other films that challenge traditional sexual mores.

### GULF COAST ARCHIVE AND MUSEUM OF GAY, LESBIAN, BISEXUAL AND TRANSGENDER HISTORY

PO Box 130192
Houston, TX 77219
United States
http://gcam.org/

The Gulf Coast Archive and Museum collects pornographic magazines, images, videos, and books, along with unique archival collections that include pornographic materials. Significant book collections include a complete run of Naiad Press books, along with collections from St. Martin's, Plume, and Alyson. Periodical runs include collections of *Male Art, In Heat, Mandate, Masturbation and Fantasy, Masturbation and Youth, Playguy, Phallic Development in the Young Adult as Well as Mature*

Adult, Galerie 1 and 2, Alternate, Muscles 'a Go-Go, Muscleboy, The Young Physique, Acme Physique Illustrated, Gay Mexico I & II, JR-First Annual, Mannlich, QQ Magazine, Beefcake, In Touch, and After Dark.

## HOWARD GOTLIEB ARCHIVAL RESEARCH CENTER

Boston University
771 Commonwealth Avenue
Boston, MA 02215
United States
http://www.bu.edu/dbin/archives/

The Howard Gotlieb Archival Research Center holds three resources of particular relevance for porn researchers. The Robert Rimmer collection contains numerous publications that Rimmer used as research for his work, including catalogs and promotional brochures from various video and film distributors and mail-order companies and magazines focusing on adult videos from the 1980s. Rimmer was known for his novels featuring open marriages and sexual experimentation in the 1960s and 1970s, and later his creation of the X-Rated Videotape Guide in 1984 (the first such guide). The Myles Eric Ludwig Collection includes runs of Penthouse, Viva, and other pornographic magazines that the novelist and editor contributed to and worked on. The last collection of note is the papers of Samuel Steward, who was a prolific American writer and novelist in many genres, including male homosexual erotica under the pseudonym "Phil Andros." His papers include his extensive personal collection of gay pornographic magazines, dating from the 1960s and 1970s.

## HUMAN SEXUALITY COLLECTION

Division of Rare and Manuscript Collections
2B Carl A. Kroch Library
Cornell University
Ithaca, NY 14853
United States
http://rmc.library.cornell.edu/HSC/

The Human Sexuality Collection of the Cornell Division of Rare and Manuscript Collections contains materials that record diverse perspectives on sexuality. The collection has grown from an original donation from the Mariposa Education and Research Foundation, which included films, artwork, and erotica. Other materials of note document the politics of pornography, including books censored on grounds of sexually controversial subject matter; the papers of the Guild Press publisher H. Lynn Womack, detailing operations of the press as part of the pornography industry; and collections of antiporn materials from feminist and other perspectives.

## INSTITUTE FOR THE ADVANCED STUDY OF HUMAN SEXUALITY

1523 Franklin Street
San Francisco, CA 94109
United States
http://www.iashs.edu/library.html

The Institute for the Advanced Study of Human Sexuality (IASHS) maintains a library system of eighteen specialty libraries. Along with collecting videotapes of previous IASHS lectures and seminars, these libraries contain books, magazines, pamphlets, journals, videotapes, films, photographs, slides, and illustrations. Collection strengths include erotica and sex-pattern films.

## INTERNATIONAL INSTITUTE OF SOCIAL HISTORY

PO Box 2169
1000 CD Amsterdam
Netherlands
http://www.iisg.nl/archives/en/index.php

The International Institute of Social History seeks to collect documentation and facilitate research on international social and economic histories, with a focus on the history of social and emancipatory movements. The institute maintains archival, audiovisual, library-research, and documentation collections. Within the archives, one collection of note is the Erotica Collection, which includes sex leaflets, erotic manuscripts and handmade publications, books, comics, journals, photographs, and other documents from mainly the Netherlands and other Western European countries, spanning from 1900 to 1989.

## ISRAELI POPULAR LITERATURE COLLECTION

Charles Trumbull Hayden Library
Arizona State University Libraries
PO Box 871006
Tempe, AZ 85287
United States
http://lib.asu.edu/

The Charles Trumbull Hayden Library at Arizona State University houses a unique collection of Israeli popular literature materials. This collection, known as Isra-

Pulp, consists of materials including westerns, comic books, science fiction, espionage, war novels, mysteries, and erotic pulp fiction from the 1930s through the present. Of particular note is the subgenre known as "stalag," which consists of pornographic Nazi-exploitation pulp.

THE KINSEY INSTITUTE FOR RESEARCH IN SEX,
GENDER, AND REPRODUCTION

Indiana University
Morrison Hall 302
1165 E. Third Street
Bloomington, IN 47405
United States
http://www.kinseyinstitute.org/index.html

Perhaps the most significant collection of sex materials in the United States, the Kinsey Institute purposefully collects erotic materials in order to preserve cultural notions of what is erotic as it changes over time. Materials range from noted works of scholarship to pop-culture publications.

LEATHER ARCHIVES AND MUSEUM

6418 North Greenview Avenue
Chicago, IL 60626
United States
http://www.leatherarchives.org

The Leather Archives and Museum displays and collects materials pertaining to leather and related lifestyles, including fetishism, sadomasochism, and other queer sexual practices. The institution is composed of library collections of published materials, films, and electronic resources; museum collections of original art and artifacts; and archival collections of unpublished papers and records. Collecting areas of note include both published and unpublished video and film, erotic art, leather sexuality periodicals, and photography.

THE LOUIS ROUND WILSON SPECIAL COLLECTIONS LIBRARY

University of North Carolina, Chapel Hill
Campus Box #3948
Chapel Hill, NC 27514
United States
http://www.lib.unc.edu/wilson/

The Louis Round Wilson Special Collections Library at the University of North Carolina, Chapel Hill, does not seek to collect pornographic materials intentionally, but it houses significant collections due to publisher or press collections that also address other collecting areas. In particular, the Grove Press Imprint Collection represents a comprehensive record of the press from 1949 through the mid-1980s, due to the library's collecting focus on the poets of the Beat generation.

## THE MASS OBSERVATION ARCHIVE

Special Collections
The Library
University of Sussex
Brighton
BN1 9QL
England
http://www.massobs.org.uk

Maintained by the University of Sussex, the Mass Observation Archive collects materials documenting everyday life in the United Kingdom. One unique collection is the Sexual Behaviour 1939–1950 collection, which contains results of a 1949 sex survey, and the archive holds other printed materials on sexual attitudes, birth control, and "lonely hearts" organizations in Britain during the midcentury.

## MUSÉE DE L'EROTISME

72 Boulevard de Clichy
75018 Paris
France
http://www.musee-erotisme.com/

The Musée de l'Erotisme houses and showcases erotic art in various media. Permanent holdings include collections of contemporary, sacred, and popular art.

## MUSEO ARCHEOLOGICO NAZIONALE DI NAPOLI

Piazza Museo Nazionale, 19
80135 Naples
Italy
http://museoarcheologiconazionale.campaniabeniculturali.it/

The National Archaeological Museum in Naples houses the Secret Cabinet (Gabinetto Segreto), a collection of sexually explicit artworks excavated from Pompeii and Herculaneum. Items include frescos, pottery, and statues—one of which is the collection's most famous item, a marble statue of Pan copulating with a goat. Although access has been restricted variously since its foundation in 1821, the Secret Cabinet is now open to the public.

## MUSEUM OF SEX

233 Fifth Avenue
New York, NY 10016
United States
http://www.museumofsex.com/

Established in 2002, the Museum of Sex is dedicated to preserving the history of human sexuality and promoting open discussions about sex. The museum maintains a permanent collection of artifacts, a research library, and a multimedia library that houses films in various formats. Of particular interest is the Ralph Whittington Collection, a significant collection of pornography amassed beginning in the 1970s by the porn enthusiast and former Library of Congress curator Ralph Whittington.

## NATIONAL FILM CENTER

National Museum of Modern Art, Tokyo
3-7-6 Kyobashi, Chuo-ku, Tokyo
104-0031
Japan
http://www.momat.go.jp

The National Film Center of the National Museum of Modern Art, Tokyo, preserves and provides access to films and research materials related to Japanese cinema. Of interest may be holdings of soft-core erotic titles known as "pink films," including the "Roman porno" films produced by major production studios during the 1970s and 1980s.

## ONE NATIONAL GAY AND LESBIAN ARCHIVES

909 W. Adams Boulevard
Los Angeles, CA 90007
United States
http://www.onearchives.org/

The ONE National Gay and Lesbian Archives, in collaboration with the Online Archive of California, has made available substantial collections of early muscle magazines, tapes, and a large pulp-fiction collection. Additionally, the books collection consists of 23,000 volumes, including rare and unusual titles featuring sexually explicit content.


ORGONE ARCHIVE

3312 Ward Street
Pittsburgh, PA 15213
United States
http://www.orgonearchive.com/

The Orgone Archive maintains and screens extensive collections of fringe films. The curator, Greg Pierce, has described the specializations of the archive as "inscrutable epiphanies, toilet trims, unknown what-have-yous, perfect industrial rolls, home movie printing tests, corporate comedies, Warholian strikebreaking screeds, the all-around beautiful and everything else." Pierce also maintains a stand-alone inventory of pornographic films.


THE PRIDE LIBRARY

D. B. Weldon Library
The University of Western Ontario
London, Ontario, N6A 3K7
Canada
http://www.uwo.ca/pridelib/

The Pride Library seeks to obtain and provide access to various materials related to LGBTQ communities, and to advocate for intellectual freedom as an integral part of Canadian society. Unique collections include the Queer Graphica Collection of zines, comic books, graphic novels, and other illustrated volumes focused on LGBTQ themes; the Canadian Lesbian Fiction Addicts Collection of titles authored by members of the online "lesfic" community; and collections of queer pulp titles.


SAN FRANCISCO MEDIA ARCHIVE/ODDBALL FILM AND VIDEO

275 Capp Street
San Francisco, CA 94110
United States
http://www.sfm.org/sfma1.html
http://www.oddballfilm.com/

Though they are two different institutions in name and nonprofit status (Oddball provides stock footage while the San Francisco Media Archive is a publicly accessible archive and library), the San Francisco Media Archive and Oddball Film and Video share a common space, curator, and mission. Among other independent and avant-garde films, noteworthy materials in their collections include Reg 8 mm and Super 8 mm "Smokers" (silent adult films), adult feature films, peep-show loops, and a large collection of pulp erotica, magazines, and books.

## SCHLESINGER LIBRARY ON THE HISTORY OF WOMEN IN AMERICA

Radcliffe Institute for Advanced Study
Harvard University
10 Garden Street
Cambridge, MA 02138
United States
http://www.radcliffe.edu/schlesinger_library.aspx

The Schlesinger Library holds a number of collections of antipornography materials, most notably collections of papers of the renowned antiporn feminists Andrea Dworkin and Catharine MacKinnon, along with the records of the Women Against Pornography activist group.

## SPECIAL COLLECTIONS RESEARCH CENTER

Syracuse University Library
E.S. Bird Library, Room 600
Syracuse University
Syracuse, NY 13244
United States
http://scrc.syr.edu

One major collection of note is the Pulp Literature and Science Fiction collection of archival, monograph, and audiovisual materials documenting the mass production of dime novels and the rise of science fiction. Another significant collection is the Grove Press Records collection, which contains the papers of the publishing house, along with manuscript production and film files. A detailed inventory of the Grove Press Records is now available online. The Special Collections Research Center also houses a considerable number of Grove Press titles within the rare books holdings.

TARLTON LAW LIBRARY

University of Texas, Austin
727 East Dean Keeton Street
Austin, Texas 78705
United States
http://tarlton.law.utexas.edu/

The University of Texas's Tarlton Law Library houses a collection of "litigated literature," which represents the efforts of library staff and faculty members to collect pornography during the late 1960s in light of threats to the porn industry's legality. The library also collects men's and nudist magazines from the late 1950s and early 1960s, some of which served as evidence in local obscenity trials. Additionally, the library houses a collection of a number of paperback titles that were subject to litigation by the Warren Supreme Court.

VERN AND BONNIE BULLOUGH COLLECTION ON SEX AND GENDER

Oviatt Library
California State University, Northridge
18111 Nordhoff Street
Northridge, CA 91330
United States
http://library.csun.edu/Collections/SCA/SC/Bullough

The Vern and Bonnie Bullough Collection on Sex and Gender documents the history of sexual attitudes and studies of human sexuality. Composed of books, periodicals, manuscripts, and archival documents, the collection provides access to a number of important titles relating to homosexuality, sexual behavior, and sex education. The collection is cataloged and searchable online, while another collection of note at the university's Special Collections and Archives remains uncataloged: Len's Fabulous Physique Photo Collection consists of photographs of gay life from the 1950s through the 1980s.

# FILMOGRAPHY

Alpert, Jon, and Ellen Goosenberg Kent, directors. *Alive Day Memories: Home from Iraq*. 2007.

Amenábar, Alejandro, director. *Tesis*. 1996.

Apocalypse Joe, director. *Midget Gang-Bang*. 2000.

Barry, Evy, director. "Does Snuff Exist?" *The Dark Side of Porn*. April 18, 2006.

Bell, Barbara, and Anna Lorentzon, directors. *Graphic Sexual Horror*. 2009.

Blanchon, Robert, director. *let's just kiss + say goodbye*. 1995.

Borden, Lizzy, director. *Forced Entry*. 2002.

Brennan, Brian, director. *Fantastic Foreskin!* 2006.

Brownfield, Anna, director. *The Band*. 2009.

Caserta, Tom, director. *Club Mandom 1: Blue Collar Cheese Factory*. 1990.

Costello, Shaun, director. *Forced Entry*. 1972.

Creg, Harold, and Mike Cole, directors. *Devil in the Rain*. 1998.

Damiano, Gerard, director. *Deep Throat*. 1972.

———, director. *The Devil in Miss Jones*. 1973.

Denis, Claire, director. *Beau Travail*. 1999.

Diablo, director. *The Adventures of Diablo, the Crippled Midget*. 2006.

Dougherty, Cecilia, director. *Gone*. 2001.

———, director. *Grapefruit*. 1989.

Dougherty, Cecilia, and Leslie Singer, directors. *Joe-Joe*. 1993.

Findlay, Michael, Roberta Findlay, and Horacio Fredriksson, directors. *Snuff*. 1976.

Fleischer, Richard, director. *Mandingo*. 1975.

Frears, Stephen, director. *Prick Up Your Ears*. 1987.

Greenfield-Saunders, Timothy, director. *Thinking XXX*. 2006.

Hottentot, Venus, director. *Aphrodite Superstar*. 2006.

Houston, Shine Louise, director. *Champion*. 2008.

———, director. *The Crash Pad*. 2005.

———, director. *In Search of the Wild Kingdom*. 2007.

———, director. *Superfreak*. 2006.

Huston, John, director. *Reflections in a Golden Eye*. 1967.

Lamonte, director. *The Last of the Boricuas*. 1994.

Marchand, Raúl, director. *12 Horas*. 2001.

Marsh, James, director. *Man on Wire*. 2008.

Metzger, Radley, director. *Score*. 1974.

Mills, Brian, director. *Cirque Noir*. 2005.

Mills, Brian, and Harold Creg, directors. *Carny*. 2003.

Moya, Alvaro de, director. *A b . . . profunda*. 1984.

Nguyen, Tan Hoang, director. *7 Steps to Sticky Heaven*. 1995.

———, director. *Forever Bottom!* 1999.

———, director. *K.I.P.* 2002.

———, director. *Maybe Never (but I'm counting the days)*. 1996.

Peirce, Kimberly, director. *Boys Don't Cry*. 1999.

Poole, Wakefield, director. *Boys in the Sand*. 1971.

Powell, Michael, director. *Peeping Tom*. 1960.

Richhe, William, director. *International Skin*. 1985.

Rico, Ron. *Papi and Chulo*. 2003.

———. *Chico con leche*. 2002.

Roberts, Mel, Jr., and Marty Stevens, directors. *101 Men*. 1998.

Roth, Eli, director. *Hostel*. 2005.

Schrader, Paul, director. *Hardcore*. 1979.

Spinelli, Anthony, director. *SexWorld*. 1978.

Tarantino, Quentin, director. *Inglourious Basterds*. 2009.

Tate, Tim, director. *Secret Histories: Kinsey's Paedophiles*. 1998.

Underwood, Ron, director. *Tremors*. 1990.

Uncredited, director. *Rican Gang Bang*. 1997.

Uncredited, director. *Rican Sizzle Gang Bang 2*. 1997.

Wadd, Dick, director. *Niggas' Revenge*. 2001.

———, director. *Stump*. 2003.

Waller, Anthony, director. *Mute Witness*. 1994.

West, Wash, director. *The Hole*. 2003.

# BIBLIOGRAPHY

Abbeele, Georges Van Den. "Sade, Foucault, and the Scene of Enlightenment Lucidity." *Stanford French Review* 11, no. 1 (1987): 7–16.

Abbott, Steve. Letter. *Gay Sunshine* 44–45 (1980): 4.

Abreu, Nuno Cesar. *Boca do Lixo: Cinema e classes populares.* Campinas, Brazil: Editora Unicamp, 2006.

Adams, Rachel. *Sideshow U.S.A.: Freaks and the American Cultural Imagination.* Chicago: University of Chicago Press, 2001.

Adler, Amy. "The Perverse Law of Child Pornography." *Columbia Law Review* 101, no. 2 (March 2001): 209–73.

Agamben, Giorgio. "The Face." In *Means without End*, translated by Vincenzo Binetti and Cesare Casarino, 91–100. Minneapolis: University of Minnesota Press, 2000.

———. "Notes on Gesture." In *Means without End*, translated by Vincenzo Binetti and Cesare Casarino, 49–60. Minneapolis: University of Minnesota Press, 2000.

Algarín, Miguel. *Mongo Affair.* New York: A Nuyorican Press, 1978.

Alonso, María Mercedes. *Muñoz Marín vs. the Bishops: An Approach to Church and State.* Hato Rey, Puerto Rico: Publicaciones Puertorriqueñas, 1998.

Andrade, Oswald de. "Manifesto antropófago." In *A utopia antropofágica*, 47–52. São Paulo: Editora Globo, 1928.

Andrews, David. *Soft in the Middle: The Contemporary Softcore Feature in Its Contexts.* Columbus: Ohio State University Press, 2006.

Anonymous. *My Secret Life.* New York: Grove Press, 1966.

Anson, Margaret [pseudo]. *The Merry Order of St. Bridget, Personal Recollections of the Use of the Rod.* York: Printed by author, 1857.

Antin, David. "Modernism and Postmodernism: Approaching the Present in Modern American Poetry." In *Radical Coherency: Selected Essays on Art and Literature, 1966 to 2005*, 161–96. Chicago: University of Chicago Press, 2011.

———. "Some Questions about Modernism." In *Radical Coherency: Selected Essays on Art and Literature 1966 to 2005*, 197–226. Chicago: University of Chicago Press, 2011.

Anzaldúa, Gloria. *Borderlands/La Frontera: The New Mestiza.* San Francisco: Aunt Lute Books, 1987.

Arendt, Hannah. *Eichmann in Jerusalem: A Report on the Banality of Evil.* New York: Viking Press, 1963.

Arondekar, Anjali. *For the Record: On Sexuality and the Colonial Archive in India*. Durham, NC: Duke University Press, 2009.

Ashworth, Lucian. "Clashing Utopias: H. G. Wells and Catholic Ireland." In *The Reception of H. G. Wells in Europe*, edited by Patrick Parrinder and John S. Partington, 267–79. London: Continuum, 2005.

Assunção, Teodoro Rennó. "Relações oblíquas com a pornochanchada em 'P III: Duas vezes Ela' de Paulo Emílio Sales Gomes." *Revista de Estudos Portugueses* 28, no. 3 (2008): 196–212.

Attwood, Feona, ed. *Porn.com: Making Sense of Online Pornography*. New York: Peter Lang, 2010.

———. "Reading Porn: The Paradigm Shift in Pornography Research." *Sexualities* 5, no. 1 (2002): 91–105.

Attwood, Feona, and I. Q. Hunter. "Not Safe for Work? Teaching and Researching the Sexually Explicit." *Sexualities* 12, no. 5 (2009): 547–57.

Avellar, José Carlos. "A teoria da relatividade." In *Anos 70: Cinema*, edited by J. C. Bernadet and R. Monteiro, 62–96. Rio de Janeiro: Europa Empresa Gráfica Editora, 1979.

Aydemir, Murat. *Images of Bliss: Ejaculation, Masculinity, Meaning*. Minneapolis: University of Minnesota Press, 2007.

Backlash. "Women's views on the proposal." Backlash-uk.org. Accessed July 31, 2010, http://www.backlash-uk.org.uk/womensviews.html.

Baier, Annette. "Trust and Antitrust." *Ethics* 96, no. 2 (1986): 231–60.

Barnes, David. "Raheem." In *Meatmen: An Anthology of Gay Male Comics*, vol. 22, edited by Winston Leyland, 103–12. San Francisco: Leyland Publications, 1998.

Barthes, Roland. *Camera Lucida: Reflections on Photography*. New York: Hill and Wang, 1981.

———. *Incidents*. Translated by Richard Howard. Berkeley: University of California Press, 1992.

———. "Wilhelm von Gloeden." In *The Responsibility of Forms*, translated by Richard Howard, 195–97. Berkeley: University of California Press, 1985.

Bartlett, Neil. *Who Was That Man? A Present for Mr. Oscar Wilde*. London: Serpent's Tail, 1988.

Bataille, Georges. *Erotism: Death and Sensuality*. San Francisco: City Lights, 1986.

———. "Formless." In *Visions of Excess: Selected Writings, 1927–1939*, edited and translated by Allan Stoekl, 31. Minneapolis: University of Minnesota Press, 1985.

Baudrillard, Jean. "War Porn." Translated by Paul A. Taylor. *International Journal of Baudrillard Studies* 2, no. 1 (January 2005). http://www.ubishops.ca/baudrillardstudies/.

Beauvoir, Simone de. *The Marquis de Sade: An Essay by Simone de Beauvoir with Selections from His Writings Chosen by Paul Dinnage*. Translated by Paul Dinnage and Annette Michelson. New York: Grove Press, 1953.

———. "Must We Burn Sade?" Translated by Annette Michelson. In *The Marquis de Sade: 120 Days of Sodom and Other Writings*, translated by Richard Seaver and Austryn Wainhouse, 3–64. New York: Grove Press, 1966.

Beckson, Karl, ed. *Oscar Wilde: The Critical Heritage*. London: Routledge and Kegan Paul, 1970.

Belasco. *The Brothers of New Essex: Afro Erotic Adventures*. San Francisco: Cleis Press, 2000.

Bell, Barbara. *Stacking in Rivertown*. New York: Simon and Schuster, 2002.

Benton, Nick. "Who Needs It?" *Gay Sunshine* 1 (1970): 2.

Benveniste, Émile. *Problems in General Linguistics*. Coral Gables, FL: University of Miami Press, 1971.

Bernard, Bruce, and Derek Birdsall. *Lucian Freud*. New York: Random House, 1996.

Bernardi, Daniel. "Interracial Joysticks: Pornography's Web of Racist Attractions." In *Pornography: Film and Culture*, edited by Peter Lehman, 220–43. New Brunswick, NJ: Rutgers University Press, 2006.

Bersani, Leo. *The Freudian Body: Psychoanalysis and Art*. New York: Columbia University Press, 1986.

———. "Is the Rectum a Grave?" "AIDS: Cultural Analysis/Cultural Activism," *October* 43 (Winter 1987): 197–222.

Blanchot, Maurice. "Sade." In *The Marquis de Sade: The Complete Justine, Philosophy in the Bedroom, and Other Writings*, translated by Richard Seaver and Austryn Wainhouse, 37–72. New York: Grove Press, 1965.

Bogdan, Robert. *Freak Show: Presenting Human Oddities for Amusement and Profit*. Chicago: University of Chicago Press, 1988.

Bois, Yve-Alain, and Rosalind Krauss. *Formless: A User's Guide*. Cambridge, MA: MIT Press, 1997.

Bourdieu, Pierre. *Distinction: A Social Critique of the Judgement of Taste*. Translated by Richard Nice. Cambridge, MA: Harvard University Press, 1984.

Boyle, Karen, ed. *Everyday Pornography*. New York: Routledge, 2010.

Bredbeck, Gregory W. "Anal/yzing the Classroom: On the Impossibility of a Queer Pedagogy." In *Professions of Desire: Lesbian and Gay Studies in Literature*, edited by George E. Haggerty and Bonnie Zimmerman, 169–82. New York: Modern Language Association of America, 1995.

Briggs, Laura. *Reproducing Empire: Race, Sex, Science, and U.S. Imperialism in Puerto Rico*. Berkeley: University of California Press, 2002.

Bronson, A. A., and Philip Aarons. "AA Bronson Interviews Philip Aarons." In *Queer Zines*, edited by A. A. Bronson and Philip Aarons, 10–13. New York: Printed Matter, 2008.

Brown, Jeffrey A. *Black Superheroes, Milestone Comics, and Their Fans*. Jackson: University Press of Mississippi, 2001.

Bud. "Getting a Leg Up." *Instigator Magazine* 1, no. 4 (2004): 40.

Bunzl, Matti. "Chasers." *Fat: The Anthropology of an Obsession*, edited by Don Kulick and Anne Meneley, 199–210. New York: Penguin, 2005.

Burroughs, William. Interview with Laurence Collinson and Roger Baker. *Gay Sunshine* 21 (1974): 1–2.

Burton, Antoinette, ed. *Archive Stories: Facts, Fictions, and the Writing of History*. Durham, NC: Duke University Press, 2005.

Burton, Richard. "Terminal Essay." In *Sexual Heretics: Male Homosexuality in English Literature from 1850 to 1900*, edited by Brian Reade, 58–192. London: Routledge and Kegan Paul, 1970. 1

Buscombe, Edward. "Generic Overspill: A Dirty Western." In *More Dirty Looks: Gender, Pornography and Power*, edited by Pamela Church Gibson, 27–30. London: British Film Institute, 2004.

Butler, Heather. "What Do You Call a Lesbian with Long Fingers? The Development of Lesbian and Dyke Pornography." *Porn Studies*, edited by Linda Williams, 167–97. Durham, NC: Duke University Press, 2004.

Butler, Judith. "The Force of Fantasy: Feminism, Mapplethorpe, and Discursive Excess." In *Feminism and Pornography*, edited by Drucilla Cornell, 487–508. Oxford: Oxford University Press, 2000.

———. *Frames of War: When Is Life Grievable?* New York: Verso, 2009.

Caleb, Amanda, ed. *Teleny*. Kansas City: Valancourt Press, 2010.

Califia, Pat. "No Minor Issues: Age of Consent, Child Pornography, and Cross-Generational Relationships." In *Public Sex: The Culture of Radical Sex*, 2nd ed., 54–96. San Francisco: Cleis Press, 2000.

Camille, Michael, and Adrian Rifkin, eds. *Other Objects of Desire: Collectors and Collecting Queerly*. Oxford: Wiley-Blackwell, 2002.

Campbell, James. *Exiled in Paris: Richard Wright, James Baldwin, Samuel Beckett, and Others on the Left Bank*. Berkeley: University of California Press, 2003.

Campos, Haroldo de. "The Rule of Anthropophagy: Europe under the Sign of Devoration." Translated by M. T. Wolff. *Latin American Literary Review* 14 (1996): 42–60.

Cante, Rich C., and Angelo Restivo. "The 'World' of All-Male Pornography: On the Public Place of Moving-Image Sex in the Era of Pornographic Transnationalism." In *More Dirty Looks: Gender, Pornography and Power*, edited by Pamela Church Gibson, 110–26. London: British Film Institute, 2004.

Cappock, Margarita. "The Motif of Meat and Flesh." In *Francis Bacon and the Tradition of Art*, edited by Wilfried Seipel, Barbara Steffen, and Christoph Valli, 311–27. Milan: Skira, 2003.

Caputi, Jane. *The Age of Sex Crime*. London: The Women's Press, 1987.

Carol, Avedon. "Snuff: Believing the Worst." In *Bad Girls and Dirty Pictures: The Challenge to Reclaim Feminism*, edited by Alison Assiter and Carol Avedon, 126–30. London: Pluto Press, 1993.

Carrillo, Héctor. *The Night Is Young: Sexuality in Mexico in the Time of AIDS*. Chicago: University of Chicago Press, 2002.

Carter, Angela. *The Sadeian Woman and the Ideology of Pornography*. New York: Pantheon, 1978.

Cartmell, Deborah, with I. Q. Hunter, Heidi Kaye, and Imelda Whelehan. *Trash Aesthetics: Popular Culture and Its Audience*. London: Pluto Press, 1997.

Casavini, Pieralessanddro. "Translator's Foreword." In *Justine: or, Good Conducted Well Chastised*. Translated by Pieralessanddro Casavini, xi–xvi. Paris, France: Olympia Press, 1954.

Certeau, Michel de. *The Practice of Everyday Life*. Translated by Steven Rendall. Berkeley: University of California Press, 1984.

Champagne, John. *The Ethics of Marginality: A New Approach to Gay Studies*. Minneapolis: University of Minnesota Press, 1995.

———. "Stop Reading Films! Film Studies, Close Analysis, and Gay Pornography." *Cinema Journal* 36, no. 4 (1997): 76–97.

Charcot, Jean-Martin, and Valentin Magnan, "Inversion du sense génital et autres perversions génitale." *Archives de neurologie* 7 (1882): 55–60.

Chun, Wendy Hui Kyong. *Control and Freedom: Power and Paranoia in the Age of Fiber Optics*. Cambridge, MA: MIT Press, 2006.

Clare, Eli. *Exile and Pride: Disability, Queerness, and Liberation*. Cambridge, MA: South End Press, 1996.

Clay, Steve, and Rodney Phillips, eds. *A Secret Location on the Lower East Side: Adventures in Publishing, 1960–1980*. New York: Granary Books, 1998.

Clover, Carol. *Men, Women, and Chainsaws: Gender in the Modern Horror Film*. Princeton, NJ: Princeton University Press, 1993.

Cocca, Carolyn E. Jailbait: The Politics of Statutory Rape Laws in the United States. Albany: State University of New York Press, 2004.

Cohen, Ed. "Writing Gone Wilde: Homoerotic Desire in the Closet of Representation." PMLA 102, no. 5 (1988): 801–13.

Colligan, Colette. A Publisher's Paradise: Expatriate Literary Culture in Paris, 1890–1960. Amherst: University of Massachusetts Press, 2014.

Cook, Matt. London and the Culture of Homosexuality, 1885–1914. Cambridge, UK: Cambridge University Press, 2003.

Cornell, Drucilla, ed. Feminism and Pornography. Oxford: Oxford University Press, 2000.

Cornog, Martha, ed. Libraries, Erotica, Pornography. Phoenix, AZ: Oryx, 1991.

———. "Providing Access to Materials on Sexuality." In Libraries, Erotica, Pornography, 166–87. Phoenix, AZ: Oryx, 1991.

———. "What Happens When Libraries Subscribe to Playboy?" In Libraries, Erotica, Pornography, 144–65. Phoenix, AZ: Oryx, 1991.

Cornog, Martha, and Timothy Perper. "For Sex, See Librarian: An Introduction." In Libraries, Erotica, Pornography, edited by Martha Cornog, 1–35. Phoenix, AZ: Oryx, 1991.

Coutt, Henry T. "Perverted Proverbs." In Library Jokes and Jottings: A Collection of Stories Partly Wise but Mostly Otherwise, 125–26. London: Grafton & Co, 1914.

Crimp, Douglas. "Mario Montez, for Shame." In Regarding Sedgwick: Essays on Queer Culture and Critical Theory, edited by Stephen Barber and David L. Clark, 57–70. New York: Routledge, 2002.

Cross, Paul J. "The Private Case: A History." In The Library of the British Museum: Retrospective Essays on the Department of Printed Books, edited by P. R. Harris, 201–40. London: The British Library, 1991.

Crowley, Ronan. "Dressing Up Bloom for 'Circe.'" James Joyce Broadsheet 87 (October 2010): 3.

Cvetkovich, Ann. An Archive of Feelings: Trauma, Sexuality, and Lesbian Public Cultures. Durham, NC: Duke University Press, 2003.

Danner, Mark. "Donald Rumsfeld Revealed." New York Review of Books. January 9, 2014, 65–69.

———. "Frozen Scandal." New York Review of Books. December 4, 2008, 26–28.

———. "Rumsfeld: War and the Consequences Now." New York Review of Books. December 19, 2013, 87–91.

———. "Rumsfeld: Why We Live in His Ruins." New York Review of Books. February 6, 2014, 36–40.

Danto, Arthur C. "Lucian Freud." The Nation, January 24, 1994, 100–104.

———. Playing with the Edge: The Photographic Achievement of Robert Mapplethorpe. Berkeley: University of California Press, 1996.

Darwin, Charles. The Descent of Man and Selection in Relation to Sex. Vol. 2. London: John Murray, 1871.

Davidson, Michael. Guys Like Us: Citing Masculinity in Cold War Poetics. Chicago: University of Chicago Press, 2003.

Davis, Jon. "Imagining Intergenerationality: Representation and Rhetoric in the Pedophile Movie." GLQ 13, no. 2–3 (2007): 377.

Dean, Tim. Beyond Sexuality. Chicago: University of Chicago Press, 2000.

———. "The Biopolitics of Pleasure." South Atlantic Quarterly 111, no. 3 (2012): 477–96.

———. "Sam Steward's Pornography: Archive, Index, Trace." In Passionate Professions:

Samuel Steward and the Politics of the Erotic, edited by Debra Moddelmog and Martin Joseph Ponce. Columbus: Ohio State University Press, forthcoming.

———. Unlimited Intimacy: Reflections on the Subculture of Barebacking. Chicago: University of Chicago Press, 2009.

Debord, Guy. Comments on the Society of the Spectacle. Translated by Malcolm Imrie. London: Verso, 1998.

———. The Society of the Spectacle. Translated by Donald Nicholson-Smith. New York: Zone Books, 1995.

Decena, Carlos Ulises. Tacit Subjects: Belonging, Same-Sex Desire, and Daily Life among Dominican Immigrant Men. Durham, NC: Duke University Press, 2011.

Deitcher, David. "Looking at a Photograph, Looking for a History." In The Passionate Camera: Photography and Bodies of Desire, edited by Deborah Bright, 22–36. New York: Routledge, 1998.

Delany, Samuel R. Times Square Red, Times Square Blue. New York: New York University Press, 1999.

Deleuze, Gilles. Cinema 1: The Action-Image. Translated by Hugh Tomlinson and Robert Galeta. Minneapolis: University of Minnesota Press, 1989.

———. "Louis Wolfson; or, The Procedure." In Essays Critical and Clinical, 7–20. Minneapolis: University of Minnesota Press, 1997.

———. Masochism: Coldness and Cruelty. New York: Zone Books, 1991.

———. "Mysticism and Masochism." In Desert Islands and Other Texts, 1953–1974, edited by David Lapoujade, 131–34. Los Angeles: Semiotext(e), 2004.

———. "To Have Done with Judgment." In Essays Critical and Clinical, 126–35. Minneapolis: University of Minnesota Press, 1997.

D'Emilio, John. Sexual Politics, Sexual Communities: The Making of a Homosexual Minority in the United States, 1940–1970. Chicago: University of Chicago Press, 1983.

Dennis, Kelly. Art/Porn: A History of Seeing and Touching. Oxford: Berg, 2009.

Derrida, Jacques. Archive Fever: A Freudian Impression. Translated by Eric Prenowitz. Chicago: University of Chicago Press, 1996.

———. "Autoimmunity: Real and Symbolic Suicides." In Philosophy in a Time of Terror: Dialogues with Jürgen Habermas and Jacques Derrida, edited by Giovanna Borradori, 85–136. Chicago: University of Chicago Press, 2003.

———. "Faith and Knowledge: The Two Sources of 'Religion' at the Limits of Reason Alone." In Acts of Religion, edited by Gil Anidjar, 40–101. London: Routledge, 1998.

De Simone, Antonio. "The History of the Museum and the Collection." In Eros in Pompeii: The Erotic Art Collection of the Museum of Naples, edited by Michael Grant and Antonia Mulas, 168–69. New York: Stewart, Tabori and Chang, 1997.

Dines, Gail. Pornland: How Porn Has Hijacked Our Sexuality. Boston: Beacon Press, 2010.

Dines, Gail, Robert Jensen, and Ann Russo. Pornography: The Production and Consumption of Inequality. New York: Routledge, 1998.

Donato, Eugenio. "The Museum's Furnace: Notes toward a Contextual Reading of Bouvard and Pecuchet." In The Script of Decadence: Essays on the Fictions of Flaubert and the Poetics of Romanticism, 56–79. New York: Oxford University Press, 1993.

Downing, Lisa. "Pornography and the Ethics of Censorship." In Film and Ethics: Foreclosed Encounters, by Lisa Downing and Libby Saxton, 76–89. London: Routledge, 2009.

Doyle, Jennifer. "Between Friends." In A Companion to Lesbian, Gay, Bisexual, Transgender, and

*Queer Studies*, edited by George E. Haggerty and Molly McGarry, 325–40. Malden, MA; Oxford: Blackwell, 2007.

Duany, Jorge. *The Puerto Rican Nation on the Move: Identities on the Island and in the United States.* Chapel Hill: University of North Carolina Press, 2002.

Duncan, Michael, and Christopher Wagstaff, eds. *An Opening of the Field: Jess, Robert Duncan, and Their Circle.* Portland, OR: Pomegranate Communications Inc., 2013.

Duncan, Robert. *The H.D. Book.* Berkeley: University of California Press, 2010.

———. "Preface." In *Bending the Bow*, i–x. New York: New Directions, 1968.

Dworkin, Andrea. *Pornography: Men Possessing Women.* New York: Perigree Books, 1979.

Echard, Siân. "House Arrest: Modern Archives, Medieval Manuscripts." *Journal of Medieval and Early Modern Studies* 30, no. 2 (2000): 185–210.

Eco, Umberto. *The Infinity of Lists.* Translated by Alastair McEwen. New York: Rizzoli, 2009.

Edelman, Lee. *No Future: Queer Theory and the Death Drive.* Durham, NC: Duke University Press, 2004.

Eigo, Jim. Foreword to *Un\*/Cut*, by Giovanni. Berlin: Bruno Gmünder Verlag, 2009.

Elias, James E., Veronica Diehl Elias, Vern Bullough, and Gwen Brewer, eds. *Porn 101: Eroticism, Pornography, and the First Amendment.* Amherst, NY: Prometheus Books, 1999.

Ellis, Havelock. *Studies in the Psychology of Sex.* New York: Random House, 1936.

Elman, R. Amy. "Disability Pornography: The Fetishization of Women's Vulnerabilities." *Violence against Women* 3, no. 3 (1997): 257–70.

Emerson, Ralph Waldo. "Books." In *The Collected Works of Ralph Waldo Emerson*, vol. 7, *Society and Solitude*, edited by Ronald Angelo Bosco and Douglas Emory Wilson, 95–112. Cambridge, MA: Belknap Press of Harvard University Press, 2007.

Ernaux, Annie. *Things Seen.* Translated by Jonathan Kaplansky. Lincoln: University of Nebraska Press, 2010.

Escoffier, Jeffrey. *Bigger Than Life: The History of Gay Porn Cinema from Beefcake to Hardcore.* Philadelphia: Running Press, 2009.

Fairholt, Frederick William. *A Dictionary of Terms in Art.* London: Hall & Virtue, 1854.

Falkon, Felix Lance, with Thomas Waugh. *Gay Art: A Historic Collection of Gay Art.* Vancouver: Arsenal Pulp Press, 2006.

Fanon, Frantz. *Black Skin, White Masks.* Translated by Richard Philcox. New York: Grove Press, 2008.

Farrer, Peter, ed. *Confidential Correspondence on Cross Dressing: 1911–1915.* Liverpool, UK: Karn Publications Garston, 1997.

Feipel, Louis N. "Questionable Books in Public Libraries — I." *The Library Journal* 47 (October 15, 1922): 857–61.

Ferguson, Frances. *Pornography, the Theory: What Utilitarianism Did to Action.* Chicago: University of Chicago Press, 2004.

Fiedler, Leslie. *Freaks: Myths and Images of the Secret Self.* New York: Simon and Schuster, 1978.

———. *The Tyranny of the Normal: Essays on Bioethics, Theology and Myth.* Boston: David R. Godine, 1996.

Fillion, Patrick. *Hot Chocolate.* Berlin: Bruno Gmünder Verlag, 2006.

———. *Rapture # 3.* Art by Patrick Fillion. Vancouver, Canada: Class Comics, January 2009.

———. *Space Cadet #1.* Art by Bob Grey. Vancouver, Canada: Class Comics, April 2010.

Findlay, Eileen J. Suárez. *Imposing Decency: The Politics of Sexuality and Race in Puerto Rico, 1870–1920*. Durham, NC: Duke University Press, 1999.

Fischel, Joseph J. "Per Se or Power? Age and Sexual Consent." *Yale Journal of Law and Feminism* 22 no. 2 (2010): 279–341.

Foster, Hal. "An Archival Impulse." *October* no. 110 (2004): 3–22.

Foucault, Michel. *Abnormal: Lectures at the Collège de France, 1974–1975*. Edited by Valerio Marchetti and Antonella Salomoni, translated by Graham Burchell. New York: Picador, 2003.

———. *The Archaeology of Knowledge*. Translated by A. M. Sheridan Smith. New York: Pantheon, 1972.

———. *Birth of Biopolitics: Lectures at the Collège de France, 1978–1979*. Edited by Arnold I. Davidson, translated by Graham Burchell. New York: Palgrave Macmillan, 2008.

———. *Discipline and Punish: The Birth of the Prison*. Translated by Alan Sheridan. New York: Vintage Books, 1995.

———. "Friendship as a Way of Life." In *Essential Works of Foucault, 1954–1984*, vol. 1, *Ethics: Subjectivity and Truth*, edited by Paul Rabinow, translated by Robert Hurley and others, 135–40. New York: New Press, 1997.

———. *Histoire de la sexualité 1: La volonté de savoir*. Paris: Gallimard, 1976.

———. *History of Madness*. Edited by Jean Khalfa, translated by Jonathan Murphy and Jean Khalfa. London: Routledge, 2006.

———. *The History of Sexuality*. Vol. 1, *An Introduction*. Translated by Robert Hurley. New York: Random House, 1978.

———. *Madness and Civilization: A History of Insanity in the Age of Reason*. Translated by Richard Howard. New York: Vintage, 1965.

———. "A Preface to Transgression." In *Language, Counter-memory, Practice*, edited by Donald F. Bouchard, 29–52. Ithaca, NY: Cornell University Press, 1977.

———. "Sex, Power, and the Politics of Identity." In *The Essential Works of Foucault, 1954–1984*, vol. 1, *Ethics: Subjectivity and Truth*, edited by Paul Rabinow, translated by Robert Hurley, 163–73. New York: New Press, 1997.

Fox, Claire F. "Pornography and 'the Popular' in Post-revolutionary Mexico: The Club Tívoli from Spota to Isaac." In *Visible Nations: Latin American Cinema and Video*, edited by Chon A. Noriega, 143–73. Minneapolis: University of Minnesota Press, 2000.

Freeman, Elizabeth. "Turn the Beat Around: Sadomasochism, Temporality, History." *differences* 19, no. 1 (2008): 32–70.

———. *The Wedding Complex: Forms of Belonging in Modern American Culture*. Durham, NC: Duke University Press, 2002.

Freitas, Marcel de Almeida. "Pornochanchada: Capítulo estilizado e estigmatizado da história do cinema nacional." *Comunicação e política* 11, no. 1 (2004): 57–105.

Freud, Sigmund. "Analysis of a Phobia of a Five Year Old Boy." In *Case Histories I: "Dora" and "Little Hans,"* vol. 8, 169–306. Harmondsworth, UK: Pelican, 1977.

———. *Beyond the Pleasure Principle*. Translated by James Strachey. New York: Norton, 1961.

———. *Civilization and Its Discontents*. New York: W. W. Norton, 1989.

———. *Delusion and Dream: An Interpretation in the Light of Psychoanalysis of Gradiva, a Novel, by Wilhelm Jensen, Which Is Here Translated*. Translated by Helen M. Downey. New York: Moffat, Yard, and Co., 1922.

———. "The Disillusionment of the War." In *The Standard Edition of the Complete Psychological Works of Sigmund Freud*, vol. 14, 1914–1916, translated by James Strachey, 273–300. London: The Hogarth Press, 1957.

———. *Three Essays on the Theory of Sexuality*. Vol. 7, *The Standard Edition of the Complete Psychological Works of Sigmund Freud*, edited and translated by James Strachey, 125–243. London: Hogarth Press, 1953.

Fryer, Peter. *Private Case—Public Scandal*. London: Secker & Warburg, 1966.

Gallop, Jane. "The Student Body." In *Thinking through the Body*, 41–54. New York: Columbia University Press, 1998.

———. "The Teacher's Breasts." In *Anecdotal Theory*, 23–35. Durham, NC: Duke University Press, 2002.

Gamson, Joshua. *Freaks Talk Back: Tabloid Talk Shows and Sexual Nonconformity*. Chicago: University of Chicago Press, 1998.

Garland-Thomson, Rosemarie. *Extraordinary Bodies: Figuring Physical Disability in American Culture and Literature*. New York: Columbia University Press, 1997.

———, ed. *Freakery: Cultural Spectacles of the Extraordinary Body*. New York: New York University Press, 1996.

———. "From Wonder to Error: A Genealogy of Freak Discourse in Modernity." In *Freakery: Cultural Spectacles of the Extraordinary Body*, edited by Rosemarie Garland-Thomson, 1–19. New York: New York University Press, 1996.

———. *Staring: How We Look*. Oxford: Oxford University Press, 2009.

Genet, Jean. "The Tightrope Walker." In *Genet, Fragments of the Artwork*. Translated by Charlotte Mandell, 69–83. Stanford: Stanford University Press, 2003.

Gerard, E. *The Land beyond the Forest: Facts, Figures, and Fancies from Transylvania*. Vol. 2. Edinburgh: William Blackwood, 1888.

Gertzman, Jay A. *Bookleggers and Smuthounds: The Trade in Erotica, 1920–1940*. Philadelphia: University of Pennsylvania Press, 1999.

Gibson, Ian. *The English Vice: Beating, Sex and Shame in Victorian England and After*. London: Duckworth, 1978.

———. *The Erotomaniac: The Secret Life of Henry Spencer Ashbee*. London: Faber, 2001.

Gibson, Pamela Church, ed. *More Dirty Looks: Gender, Pornography and Power*. 2nd ed. London: British Film Institute, 2004.

Gibson, Pamela Church, and Roma Gibson, eds. *Dirty Looks: Women, Pornography, Power*. London: BFI Publications, 1993.

Gilman, Sander. *Making the Body Beautiful: A Cultural History of Aesthetic Surgery*. Princeton, NJ: Princeton University Press, 1999.

Ginsberg, Allen. Interview with Allen Young. *Gay Sunshine* 16 (1973): 1, 4–10.

Glass, Loren. *Counterculture Colophon: Grove Press, the Evergreen Review, and the Incorporation of the Avant-Garde*. Stanford, CA: Stanford University Press, 2013.

———. "Redeeming Value: Obscenity and Anglo-American Modernism." *Critical Inquiry* 32, no. 2 (Winter 2006): 341–61.

Goldman, Albert. "The Old Smut Peddler." *Life* 67, no. 9 (August 29, 1969): 49–53.

Gontarski, Stanley. "Introduction: The Life and Times of Grove Press." In *The Grove Press Reader: 1951–2000*, edited by Stanley Gontarski, xi–xxxvii. New York: Grove, 2001.

Gorfinkel, Elena. "Dated Sexuality: Anna Biller's VIVA and the Retrospective Life of Sexploitation Cinema." *Camera Obscura* 26 (2011): 95–135.

————. "The Tales of Times Square: Sexploitation's Secret History of Place." In *Taking Place: Location and the Moving Image*, edited by John David Rhodes and Elena Gorfinkel, 55–76. Minneapolis: University of Minnesota Press, 2011.

Gornick, Vivian, and Barbara Moran, eds. *Woman in Sexist Society*. New York: Basic Books, 1971.

Gray, Kevin. "What, Censor Us?" *Details*, December 2003, 132–37.

Green, Jonathon, and Nicholas J. Karolides. *The Encyclopedia of Censorship*. New York: Facts on File, 2005.

Guillory, John. *Cultural Capital: The Problem of Literary Canon Formation*. Chicago: University of Chicago Press, 1993.

Gurney, Edmund. *The Power of Sound*. London: Smith, Elder, 1880.

Gurney, Edmund, Frederic W. H. Myers, and Frank Podmore. *Phantasms of the Living*. Abridged ed. London: Kegan Paul, Trench, Trubner, 1918.

Hacking, Ian. "The Making and Molding of Child Abuse." *Critical Inquiry* 17, no. 2 (Winter 1991): 253–88.

Halberstam, Judith. *In a Queer Time and Place: Transgender Bodies, Subcultural Lives*. New York: New York University Press, 2005.

————. "The Joe-Joe Effect." *GLQ* 1, no. 3 (1994): 359–63.

————. *The Queer Art of Failure*. Durham, NC: Duke University Press, 2011.

Hall, Lesley A. "Sex in the Archives." *Archives: the Journal of the British Records Association* 25, no. 93 (April 1995): 1–12.

Hall, Richard. Letter. *Gay Sunshine* 44/45 (1980): 5.

Halperin, David. "Deviant Teaching." In *A Companion to Lesbian, Gay, Bisexual, Transgender, and Queer Studies*, edited by George E. Haggerty and Molly McGarry, 146–67. Malden, MA; Oxford: Blackwell, 2007.

————. *Saint Foucault: Towards a Gay Hagiography*. Oxford: Oxford University Press, 1995.

Hanson, Ellis. "Teaching Shame." In *Gay Shame*, edited by David M. Halperin and Valerie Traub, 132–64. Chicago: University of Chicago Press, 2009.

Harris, Frank. *My Life and Loves*. New York: Grove Press, 1963.

Harrison, Martin. *In Camera, Francis Bacon; Photography, Film and the Practice of Painting*. New York: Thames & Hudson, 2005.

Hart, Lynda. *Between the Body and the Flesh: Reforming Sadomasochism*. New York: Columbia University Press, 1998.

Haver, William. "Really Bad Infinities: Queer's Honour and the Pornographic Life." *Parallax* 5, no. 4 (1999): 9–21.

Haynes, E. S. P. "The Taboos of the British Museum Library." *The English Review* 16 (December 1913): 123–34.

Heins, Marjorie. *Not in Front of the Children: "Indecency," Censorship, and the Innocence of Youth*. New York: Hill and Wang, 2001.

Herring, Scott. *Another Country: Queer Anti-urbanism*. New York: New York University Press, 2010.

————. "Material Deviance: Theorizing Queer Objecthood." *Postmodern Culture* 21, no. 2 (January 2011).

Hersh, Seymour M. *Chain of Command: The Road from 9/11 to Abu Ghraib*. New York: Harper Collins, 2004.

Hoare, Peter. "The Libraries of the Ancient University to the 1960s." In *The Cambridge His-*

tory of Libraries in Britain and Ireland, vol. 3, 1850–2000, edited by Alistair Black and Peter Hoare, 321–44. Cambridge, UK: Cambridge University Press, 2006.

Hodges, Frederick M. "The Ideal Prepuce in Ancient Greece and Rome: Male Genital Aesthetics and Their Relation to Lipodermos, Circumcision, Foreskin Restoration, and the Kynodesme." The Bulletin of the History of Medicine 75, no. 3 (Fall 2001): 375–405.

Hoff, Joan. "Why Is There No History of Pornography?" In For Adult Users Only: The Dilemma of Violent Pornography, edited by Susan Gubar and Joan Hoff, 17–46. Bloomington: Indiana University Press, 1989.

Holland, Merlin, and Rupert Hart-Davis, eds. The Complete Letters of Oscar Wilde. London: Fourth Estate, 2000.

Hopkins, Patrick. "Rethinking Sadomasochism: Feminism, Interpretation, and Simulation." Hypatia 9, no. 1 (1994): 116–41.

Hunt, Lynn. "Introduction: Obscenity and the Origins of Modernity, 1500–1800." In The Invention of Pornography: Obscenity and the Origins of Modernity, 1500–1800, ed. Lynn Hunt, 9–45. New York: Zone, 1993.

———, ed. The Invention of Pornography: Obscenity and the Origins of Modernity, 1500–1800. New York: Zone, 1993.

Hunt, Michael H. Ideology and U.S. Foreign Policy. New Haven, CT: Yale University Press, 1987.

Hunter, Ian, David Saunders, and Dugald Williamson. On Pornography: Literature, Sexuality, and Obscenity Law. New York: Macmillan, 1992.

Indiana, Cindy. "In the Stacks and in the Sack: An Undercover Look at Librarians in Erotica." In Revolting Librarians Redux: Radical Librarians Speak Out, edited by Katia Roberto and Jessamyn West, 100–104. Jefferson, NC: McFarland, 2003.

Jackson, Earl, Jr. "Explicit Instruction: Teaching Gay Male Sexuality in Literature Classes." In Professions of Desire: Lesbian and Gay Studies in Literature, edited by George E. Haggerty and Bonnie Zimmerman, 136–55. New York: Modern Language Association of America, 1995.

———. Strategies of Deviance: Studies in Gay Male Representation. Bloomington: Indiana University Press, 1995.

Jackson, Neil. "The Cultural Construction of Snuff: Alejandro Amenábar's Tesis (Thesis, 1996)." Kinoeye 3, no. 5 (2003).

Jameson, Fredric. "The Vanishing Mediator; or, Max Weber as Storyteller." In The Ideologies of Theory, Essays 1971–1986. Vol. 2, The Syntax of History, 3–34. Minneapolis: University of Minnesota Press, 1988.

Jenkins, Henry. "Foreword: So You Want to Teach Pornography?" In More Dirty Looks: Gender, Pornography and Power, edited by Pamela Church Gibson, 1–7. 2nd ed. London: British Film Institute, 2004.

Jenkins, Philip. Beyond Tolerance: Child Pornography and the Internet. New York: New York University Press, 2003.

———. Moral Panic: Changing Concepts of the Child Molester in Modern America. New Haven, CT: Yale University Press, 1998.

Johnson, Eithne, and Eric Schaefer. "Soft Core/Hard Gore: Snuff as a Crisis in Meaning." Journal of Film and Video 45, nos. 2–3 (1993): 40–59.

Johnson, Floyd. "The Next Best Thing." Unzipped, May 2000, 9.

Johnson, Randal. The Film Industry in Brazil: Culture and the State. Pittsburgh, PA: University of Pittsburgh Press, 1987.

Johnson, Randal, and Robert Stam. *Brazilian Cinema*. New York: Columbia University Press, 1995.

Jones, E. Michael. *Degenerate Moderns: Modernity as Rationalized Sexual Misbehavior*. San Francisco: Ignatius, 1993.

Jones, James H. *Alfred C. Kinsey: A Public/Private Life*. New York: W. W. Norton, 1997.

Juffer, Jane. *At Home with Pornography: Women, Sex, and Everyday Life*. New York: New York University Press, 1998.

Juhasz, Joseph B. "Minoru Yamasaki." In *Contemporary Architects*, edited by Muriel Emanuel. New York: St. James Press, 1994.

Julien, Isaac. "Confessions of a Snow Queen: Notes on the Making of *The Attendant*." In *The Film Art of Isaac Julien*, edited by Amanda Cruz, David Deitcher, David Frankel, and Isaac Julien, 79–82. Annandale-on-Hudson, NY: The Center for Curatorial Studies, Bard College, 2000.

Kalha, Harri. "Halu alennuksessa: Sigmund Freud ja matalan vetovoima." In *Pornoakatemia!*, edited by Harri Kalha, 78–113. Turku: Eetos, 2007.

———. "Sen pituinen se: Esinahka halu ja toiseus." In *Pornoakatemia!*, edited by Harri Kalha, 376–415. Turku: Eetos, 2007.

Kane, Daniel. *All Poets Welcome: The Lower East Side Poetry Scene in the 1960s*. Berkeley: University of California Press, 2003.

Kant, Immanuel. *Religion within the Bounds of Bare Reason*. Translated by Werner S. Pluhar. Indianapolis, IN: Hackett, 2009.

Katz, Bill. "The Pornography Collection." *Library Journal* 96 (December 1971): 4060–66.

Kearney, Patrick J. *The Private Case: An Annotated Bibliography of the Private Case Erotica Collection in the British (Museum) Library*. London: Landesman, 1981.

Keehnen, Owen. *Rising Starz: Interviews with the Hottest New Stars of Gay Adult Video*. Herndon: Star Books, 2010.

Kendrick, Walter. *The Secret Museum: Pornography in Modern Culture*. New York: Viking, 1987.

Kerekes, David, and David Slater. *Killing for Culture: An Illustrated History of the Death Film from Mondo to Snuff*. London: Creation Books, 1995.

Kertess, Klaus. "Crucifictions." Foreword to *Assemblies of Magic*, by John O'Reilly, 11–17. Santa Fe, NM: Twin Palm Publishers, 2002.

Kierkegaard, Søren. *Works of Love*. Translated by Howard and Edna Hong. New York: Harper Perennial, 2009.

Kincaid, James. *Erotic Innocence: The Culture of Child Molesting*. Durham, NC: Duke University Press, 1998.

Kipnis, Laura. *Bound and Gagged: Pornography and the Politics of Fantasy in America*. Durham, NC: Duke University Press, 1998.

Kleinhans, Chuck. "In Focus: Visual Culture, Scholarship, and Sexual Images." *Cinema Journal* 46, no. 4 (summer 2007): 96–132.

———. "Virtual Child Porn: The Law and the Semiotics of the Image." In *More Dirty Looks: Gender, Pornography, and Power*, edited by Pamela Church Gibson, 71–84. London: British Film Institute, 2004.

Klossowski, Pierre. "Nature as Destructive Principle." Translated by Joseph McMahon. In *The Marquis de Sade: 120 Days of Sodom and Other Writings*, translated by Richard Seaver and Austryn Wainhouse, 65–86. New York: Grove Press, 1966.

———. *Sade mon prochain*. Paris, France: Editions du Seuil, 1947.

Krafft-Ebing, Richard von. *Psychopathia Sexualis*. Edited by Domino Falls. London: Velvet Publications, 1997.

Kulick, Don. "Porn." In *Fat: The Anthropology of an Obsession*, edited by Don Kulick and Anne Meneley, 77–92. New York: Penguin, 2005.

LaBelle, Beverly. "Snuff—The Ultimate in Woman-Hating." In *Take Back the Night: Women on Pornography*, edited by Laura Lederer, 272–78. New York: William Morrow and Company, 1980.

Lacy, Dan. "Censorship and Obscenity." ALA *Bulletin* 59 (June 1965): 471–76.

Ladenson, Elisabeth. *Dirt for Art's Sake: Books on Trial from Madame Bovary to Lolita*. Ithaca, NY: Cornell University Press, 2007.

Laplanche, Jean, and Jean-Bertrand Pontalis. "Fantasy and the Origins of Sexuality." *Formations of Fantasy*, edited by Victor Burgin, James Donald, and Cora Kaplan, 5–34. London: Methuen, 1986.

———. "Phantasy (or Fantasy)." In *The Language of Psycho-Analysis*. Translated by Donald Nicholson-Smith, 314–419. New York: Norton, 1973.

Lauman, Edward, with Christopher Masi and Ezra Zuckerman. "Circumcision in the United States: Prevalence, Prophylactic Effects, and Sexual Practice." *Journal of the American Medical Association* 277, no. 13 (1997): 1052–57.

Lazo, Rodrigo. "Migrant Archives: New Routes in and out of American Studies." *States of Emergency: The Object of American Studies*, edited by Russ Castronovo and Susan Gillman, 36–54. Chapel Hill: University of North Carolina Press, 2009.

Legman, Gershon. *The Horn Book: Studies in Erotic Folklore and Bibliography*. New Hyde Park, NY: University Books, 1964.

———. Introduction to *The Private Case: An Annotated Bibliography of the Private Case Erotica Collection in the British (Museum) Library*, by Patrick J. Kearney, 3–34. London: Landesman, 1981.

———. "The Lure of the Forbidden." In *Libraries, Erotica, Pornography*, edited by Martha Cornog, 36–68. Phoenix, AZ: The Oryx Press, 1991.

Lehman, Peter. "Introduction: 'A Dirty Little Secret'—Why Teach and Study Pornography?" In *Pornography: Film and Culture*, edited by Peter Lehman, 1–21. New Brunswick, NJ: Rutgers University Press, 2006.

———, ed. *Pornography: Film and Culture*. New Brunswick, NJ: Rutgers University Press, 2006.

Lély, Gilbert. *The Marquis de Sade: A Definitive Biography*. Translated by Alec Brown. New York: Grove Press, 1961.

Lester, Julius. "Woman—The Male Fantasy." *Evergreen Review* 14, no. 82 (September 1970): 31–34.

Levin, Jennifer Burns. "How Joyce Acquired 'The Stale Smut of Clubmen': Photo Bits in the Early-Twentieth Century." *James Joyce Quarterly* 46 (Winter 2009): 255–68.

Levine, Judith. *Harmful to Minors: The Perils of Protecting Children from Sex*. Minneapolis: University of Minnesota Press, 2002.

Leyland, Winston. "Gay Radical Press: 1972." *Gay Sunshine* 15 (1972): 5.

———, ed. *Gay Roots: An Anthology of Gay History, Sex, Politics, and Culture*. Vol. 2. San Francisco: Gay Sunshine Press, 1993.

———, ed. *Gay Sunshine Interviews: Volume 1*. San Francisco: Gay Sunshine Press, 1978.

———, ed. *Gay Sunshine Interviews: Volume 2*. San Francisco: Gay Sunshine Press, 1978.

————. Introduction to *Gay Roots: Twenty Years of Gay Sunshine*. Edited by Winston Leyland, 13–30. San Francisco: Gay Sunshine Press, 1991.

————, ed. *Teleny: A Novel Attributed to Oscar Wilde*. San Francisco: Gay Sunshine Press, 1984.

Liszt, Franz. *The Gipsy in Music*. 2 vols. Translated by Edwin Evans. London: William Reeves, 1926.

Litvak, Joseph. "Discipline, Spectacle, and Melancholia in and around the Gay Studies Classroom." In *Pedagogy: The Question of Impersonation*, edited by Jane Gallop, 19–27. Bloomington: Indiana University Press, 1995.

Lockhart, William, and Robert McClure. "Censorship of Obscenity: The Developing Constitutional Standards." *Minnesota Law Review* 45, no. 1 (November 1960): 5–121.

————. "Literature, the Law of Obscenity, and the Constitution." *Minnesota Law Review* 38, no. 4 (March 1954): 295–395.

Loftus, David. *Watching Sex: How Men Really Respond to Pornography*. New York: Thundermouth Press, 2002.

Love, Heather. *Feeling Backward: Loss and the Politics of Queer History*. Cambridge, MA: Harvard University Press, 2007.

MacKinnon, Catharine. *Feminism Unmodified: Discourses on Life and Law*. Cambridge, MA: Harvard University Press, 1987.

————. *Only Words*. Cambridge, MA: Harvard University Press, 1993.

Madison, Steven. "Online Obscenity and Myths of Freedom: Dangerous Images, Child Porn, and Neoliberalism." In *Porn.com: Making Sense of Online Pornography*, edited by Feona Attwood, 17–33. New York: Peter Lang, 2010.

Manoff, Marlene. "Theories of the Archive from across the Disciplines." *Libraries and the Academy* 4, no. 1 (2004): 9–25.

Mapplethorpe, Robert. *Black Book*. New York: St. Martin's Press, 1986.

Marcus, Sharon. "At Home with the Other Victorians." *South Atlantic Quarterly* 108, no. 1 (2009): 119–45.

Marcus, Steven. *The Other Victorians: A Study of Sexuality and Pornography in Mid-Nineteenth-Century England*. New York: Basic Books, 1964.

Marder, Elissa. "On 'Psycho-Photography': The 'Case' of Abu Ghraib." *English Language Notes* 44, no. 2 (2006): 231–42.

Marquet, Antonio. *El crepúsculo de heterolandia: mester de jotería*. Mexico City: Universidad Autónoma Metropolitana, 2006.

————. *Sexy Thrills: Undressing the Erotic Thriller*. Urbana: University of Illinois Press, 2007.

Massumi, Brian. "The Archive of Experience." In *Information Is Alive: Art and Theory on Archiving and Retrieving Data*, edited by Joke Brouwer and Arjen Mulder, 142–51. Rotterdam: V2 Publishing, 2003.

McCracken, Scott. *Pulp: Reading Popular Fiction*. Manchester, UK: Manchester University Press, 1998.

McElroy, Wendy. *XXX: A Woman's Right to Pornography*. New York: St. Martin's Press, 1995.

McGann, Jerome. *Black Riders: The Visible Language of Modernism*. Princeton, NJ: Princeton University Press, 1993.

Meeker, Martin. *Contacts Desired: Gay and Lesbian Communications and Community, 1940s–1970s*. Chicago: University of Chicago Press, 2006.

Mendes, Peter. *Clandestine Erotic Fiction in English, 1800–1930*. Aldershot, UK: Scolar Press, 1993.

Mercer, Kobena. "Imagining the Black Man's Sex." In *Photography/Politics: Two*, edited by Pat Holland, Jo Spence, and Simon Watney, 61–69. London: Comedia/Metheun, 1987.

———. "Skin Head Sex Thing: Racial Difference and the Homoerotic Imaginary." In *How Do I Look? Queer Film and Video*, edited by Bad Object-Choices, 169–222. Seattle: Bay Press, 1991.

———. *Welcome to the Jungle: New Positions in Black Cultural Studies*. New York: Routledge, 1994.

Merewether, Charles, ed. *The Archive: Documents of Contemporary Art*. Cambridge, MA: MIT Press, 2006.

Meyer, Richard. *Outlaw Representation: Censorship and Homosexuality in Twentieth-Century American Art*. New York: Oxford University Press, 2002.

Miller, Francine Koslow. "John O'Reilly's Assemblies of Magic." Afterword to *Assemblies of Magic*, by John O'Reilly, 176–85. Santa Fe, NM: Twin Palm Publishers, 2002.

Miller, Monica L. *Slaves to Fashion: Black Dandyism and the Styling of Black Diasporic Identity*. Durham, NC: Duke University Press, 2009.

Millett, Kate. *Sexual Politics*. New York: Touchstone, 1970.

Mitchell, W. J. T. *Cloning Terror: The War of Images, 9/11 to the Present*. Chicago: University of Chicago Press, 2011.

Mohr, Richard D. "The Pedophilia of Everyday Life." In *Curiouser: On the Queerness of Children*, edited by Steven Bruhm and Natasha Hurley, 17–30. Minneapolis: University of Minnesota Press, 2004.

Molz, Kathleen. "The Public Custody of the High Pornography." *American Scholar* 36 (1966–67): 93–103.

Money, John, and Kent W. Simcoe. "Acrotomophilia, Sex and Disability: New Concepts and Case Report." *Sexuality and Disability* 7, nos. 1–2 (1985): 43–50.

Moon, Eric. "'Problem' Fiction." *Library Journal* 87 (1962): 484–85.

Moore, Everett T. "Broadening Concerns for Intellectual Freedom." *Library Quarterly* 38, no. 4 (October 1968): 309–14.

Moore, Patrick. *Beyond Shame: Reclaiming the Abandoned History of Radical Gay Sexuality*. Boston: Beacon Press, 2004.

Myles, Eileen. "Gay Sunshine, 1971." *Animal Shelter* 2 (2012): 187–95.

Nancy, Jean-Luc. "The Confronted Community." In *The Obsessions of Georges Bataille: Community and Communication*, edited by Andrew J. Mitchell and Jason Kemp Winfree, 19–30. Albany: State University of New York Press, 2009.

———. *The Creation of the World; Or, Globalization*. Translated by François Raffoul and David Pettigrew. Albany: SUNY Press, 2007.

———. *The Discourse of the Syncope: Logodaedalus*. Translated by Saul Anton. Stanford, CA: Stanford University Press, 2008.

———. *Dis-enclosure: The Deconstruction of Christianity*. Edited by John D. Caputo. Translated by Bettina Bergo, Gabriel Malenfant, and Michael B. Smith. New York: Fordham University Press, 2008.

———. *L'Équivalence des Catastrophes (Après Fukushima)*. Paris, France: Editions Galilée, 2012.

———. *A Finite Thinking*, edited by Simon Sparks. Stanford, CA: Stanford University Press, 2003.

———. "The Intruder." In *Corpus*, translated by Richard A. Rand, 161–70. New York: Fordham University Press, 2008.

———. *Noli Me Tangere: On the Raising of the Body*. Translated by Sarah Clift, Pascale-Anne Brault, and Michael Naas, edited by John D. Caputo. New York: Fordham University Press, 2008.

———. "On a Divine Wink." In *Dis-enclosure: The Deconstruction of Christianity*, translated by Bettina Bergo, Gabriel Malenfant, and Michael B. Smith, edited by John D. Caputo, 104–20. New York: Fordham University Press, 2008.

———. "The Vestige of Art." In *The Muses*, translated by Peggy Kamuf, 81–100. Stanford, CA: Stanford University Press, 1996.

Nelson, James G. *Publisher to the Decadents: Leonard Smithers in the Careers of Beardsley, Wilde, Dowson*. University Park: Pennsylvania State University Press, 2000.

Newmahr, Staci. *Playing on the Edge: Sadomasochism, Risk, and Intimacy*. Bloomington: Indiana University Press, 2011.

Newman, M. W. "The Smut Hunters." In *The Smut Hunters*, n.p. Los Angeles: All America Distributors, 1964.

Nguyen Tan Hoang. *A View from the Bottom: Asian American Masculinity and Sexual Representation*. Durham, NC: Duke University Press, 2014.

———. "The Resurrection of Brandon Lee." In *Porn Studies*, edited by Linda Williams, 223–70. Durham, NC: Duke University Press, 2004.

Nicholson, Geoff. *Sex Collectors: The Secret World of Consumers, Connoisseurs, Curators, Creators, Dealers, Bibliographers, and Accumulators of "Erotica."* New York: Simon & Schuster, 2006.

Nye, Robert A. *Masculinity and Male Codes of Honor in Modern France*. New York: Oxford University Press, 1993.

O'Donnell, Ian, and Claire Milner. *Child Pornography: Crime, Computers, and Society*. Portland, OR: Willan Publishing, 2007.

Olson, Charles. "Projective Verse." In *Collected Prose*, edited by Donald Allen and Benjamin Friedlander, 239–49. Berkeley: University of California Press, 1997.

Olster, Stacey. *The Trash Phenomenon: Contemporary Literature, Popular Culture, and the Making of the American Century*. Athens: University of Georgia Press, 2003.

O'Reilly, John. *Assemblies of Magic*. Santa Fe, NM: Twin Palm Publishers, 2002.

Osborne, Thomas. "The Ordinariness of the Archive." *History of the Human Sciences* 12, no. 2 (1999): 51–64.

Osterweil, Ara. "Andy Warhol's *Blow Job*: Toward the Recognition of a Pornographic Avant-Garde." In *Porn Studies*, edited by Linda Williams, 431–60. Durham, NC: Duke University Press, 2004.

O'Toole, Laurence. *Pornocopia: Porn, Sex, Technology and Desire*. London: Serpent's Tail, 1998.

Paige, Karen Ericksen. "The Ritual of Circumcision." *Human Nature* (May 1978): 40–48.

Patai, Raphael. *The Arab Mind*. New York: Scribner, 1973.

Patterson, Zabet. "Going On-line: Consuming Pornography in the Digital Era." In *Porn Studies*, edited by Linda Williams, 104–24. Durham, NC: Duke University Press, 2004.

Paul, Pamela. *Pornified: How Pornography Is Transforming Our Lives, Our Relationships, and Our Families*. New York: Times Books, 2005.

Paulhan, Jean. "The Marquis de Sade and His Accomplice." In *The Marquis de Sade: The Complete Justine, Philosophy in the Bedroom, and Other Writings*. Translated by Richard Seaver and Austryn Wainhouse, 3–36. New York: Grove Press, 1965.

Peniston, William A. *Pederasts and Others: Urban Culture and Sexual Identity in Nineteenth-Century Paris*. Binghamton, NY: Harrington Park Press, 2004.

Penley, Constance. "Crackers and Whackers: The White Trashing of Porn." In *Porn Studies*, edited by Linda Williams, 309–31. Durham, NC: Duke University Press, 2004.

Pershing, Gwendolyn L. "Erotica Research Collections." *Libraries, Erotica, Pornography*, edited by Martha Cornog, 188–98. Phoenix, AZ: Oryx, 1991.

Peters, John Durham. *Courting the Abyss: Free Speech and the Liberal Tradition*. Chicago: University of Chicago Press, 2005.

Petley, Julian. "Pornography, Panopticism and the Criminal Justice and Immigration Act 2008." *Sociology Compass* 3, no. 3 (2009): 417–32.

———. "'Snuffed Out': Nightmares in a Trading Standards Officer's Brain." In *Unruly Pleasures: The Cult Film and Its Critics*, edited by Graham Harper and Xavier Mendik, 203–19. Guildford: FAB Press, 2000.

Pietri, Pedro. *Puerto Rican Obituary/Obituario Puertorriqueño*. 1973. San Juan, Puerto Rico: Isla Negra Editores, 2000.

Pomeroy, Wardell B. *Dr. Kinsey and the Institute for Sex Research*. New York: Harper & Row, 1972.

Quignard, Marie-Françoise, and Raymond-Josué Seckel. *L'Enfer de la bibliothèque: Éros au secret*. Paris: Bibliothèque nationale de France, 2007.

Quinn, Sandra. "The Last of the Boricuas." In *Chicano/Latino Homoerotic Identities*, edited by David William Foster, 217–30. New York: Garland Publishing, 1999.

Ramírez de Arellano, Annette B. *Colonialism, Catholicism, and Contraception*. Chapel Hill: University of North Carolina Press, 1983.

Rancière, Jacques. *The Emancipated Spectator*. Translated by Gregory Elliott. London: Verso, 2009.

Ranganathan, S. R. *The Five Laws of Library Science*. Madras, India: The Madras Library Association; London: Edward Golston, 1931.

Réage, Pauline. *Story of O*. Translated by Sabine d'Estrée. New York: Grove Press, 1965.

Rembar, Charles. *The End of Obscenity: The Trials of Lady Chatterley, Tropic of Cancer, and Fanny Hill*. New York: Bantam Books, 1968.

Retort. *Afflicted Powers: Capital and Spectacle in a New Age of War*. London: Verso, 2005.

Ricco, John Paul. *The Decision between Us: Art and Ethics in the Time of Scenes*. Chicago: University of Chicago Press, 2014.

Roberts, Lewis. "Trafficking in Literary Authority: Mudie's Select Library and the Commodification of the Victorian Novel." *Victorian Literature and Culture* 34, no. 1 (2006): 1–25.

Rocha, Glauber. "An Aesthetic of Hunger." In *New Latin American Cinema*, edited by Michael T. Martin, 59–61. Detroit, MI: Wayne State University Press, 1997.

Rodriguez, Juana María. "Gesture and Utterance: Fragments from a Butch-Femme Archive." In *A Companion to Lesbian, Gay, Bisexual, Transgender, and Queer Studies*, edited by George E. Haggerty and Molly McGarry, 282–91. Malden, MA: Blackwell, 2007.

Roque Ramírez, Horacio N. "A Living Archive of Desire." In *Archive Stories: Facts, Fictions, and the Writing of History*, edited by Antoinette Burton, 111–35. Durham, NC: Duke University Press, 2005.

Rose, Jacqueline. *The Case of Peter Pan; or, The Impossibility of Children's Fiction*. Philadelphia: University of Pennsylvania Press, 1993.

Rubin, Marian, Jackie Livingston, Marilyn Zimmerman, and Betsy Schneider. "'Not a Pretty Picture': Four Photographers Tell Their Personal Stories about Child 'Pornography' and Censorship." In *Censoring Culture: Contemporary Threats to Free Expression*, edited by Robert Atkins and Svetlana Mintcheva, 213–27. New York: The New Press, 2006.

Russo, Linda. "Poetics of Adjacency: 0–9 and the Conceptual Writing of Bernadette Mayer and Hannah Weiner." In *Don't Ever Get Famous: Essays on New York Writing after the New School*, 122–50. Champaign, FL: Dalkey Archive Press, 2006.

Sacco, Dena T., Rebecca Argudin, James Maguire, Kelly Tallong, and Cyberlaw Clinic. *Sexting: Youth Practices and Legal Implications*. Research publication no. 2010–8, Berkman Center for Internet and Society, Harvard University, June 22, 2010.

Sade, D. A. F. de. *Justine: or, Good Conduct Well Chastised*. Translated by Pieralessanddro Casavini. Paris: Olympia Press, 1954.

Sanders, Ed. *The Family: The Story of Charles Manson's Dune Buggy Attack Battalion*. New York: Dutton, 1971.

Santiago, Esmeralda. *When I Was Puerto Rican*. New York: Vintage, 1993.

Sartre, Jean-Paul. *Saint Genet: Actor and Martyr*. Translated by Bernard Frechtman. New York: Pantheon, 1963.

Saussure, Ferdinand de. *Course in General Linguistics*. Translated by Wade Baskin. New York: McGraw-Hill, 1966.

Scarry, Elaine. *The Body in Pain: The Making and Unmaking of the World*. New York: Oxford University Press, 1987.

Schaefer, Eric. *Bold, Daring, Shocking, True! A History of Exploitation Films, 1919–1959*. Durham, NC: Duke University Press, 1999.

———. "Dirty Little Secrets: Scholars, Archivists, and Dirty Movies." *The Moving Image* 5, no. 2 (2005): 79–105.

———, ed. *Sex Scene: Media and the Sexual Revolution*. Durham, NC: Duke University Press, 2014.

Schell, Jonathan. "Torture and Truth." *The Nation*, May 27, 2009, 15–18.

Schmied, Wieland. *Francis Bacon: Commitment and Conflict*. Munich: Prestel, 2006.

Schweik, Susan M. *The Ugly Laws: Disability in Public*. New York: New York University Press, 2009.

Scott, Darieck. *Extravagant Abjection: Blackness, Power, and Sexuality in the African American Literary Imagination*. New York: New York University Press, 2010.

———. "Love, Rockets and Sex." *The Americas Review* 22, nos. 3–4 (1994): 73–106.

Seaver, Richard. "An Anniversary Unnoticed." *Evergreen Review* 9, no. 36 (June 1965): 53–60, 89–92.

———. "Publisher's Preface." In *The Marquis de Sade: The Complete Justine, Philosophy in the Bedroom, and Other Writings*, translated by Richard Seaver and Austryn Wainhouse, xvii–xxii. New York: Grove Press, 1965.

Sedgwick, Eve Kosofsky. "Shame, Theatricality, and Queer Performativity: Henry James's *The Art of the Novel*." In *Gay Shame*, edited by David M. Halperin and Valerie Traub, 49–82. Chicago: University of Chicago Press, 2009.

———. *Tendencies*. Durham, NC: Duke University Press, 1993.

Shaw, Lisa, and Stephanie Dennison. *Brazilian National Cinema*. New York: Routledge, 2007.

Shelley, Percy Bysshe. "The Coliseum: A Fragment." In *Essays, Letters from Abroad, Transla-*

tions and Fragments, vol. 1, edited by Mary Shelley, 168–81. London: Edward Moxon, 1840.

Shively, Charles. Letter. *Gay Sunshine* 44, no. 5 (1980): 3.

Sigel, Lisa Z. *Governing Pleasures: Pornography and Social Change in England, 1815–1914.* Piscataway, NJ: Rutgers University Press, 2002.

Singer, P. W. *Wired for War: The Robotics Revolution and Conflict in the 21st Century.* New York: The Penguin Press, 2009.

Slade, Joseph. *Pornography and Sexual Representation: A Reference Guide.* 2 vols. Westport, CT: Greenwood Press, 2001.

———. "Violence in the Hard-Core Pornographic Film: A Historical Survey." *Journal of Communication* 34, no. 3 (September 1984): 148–63.

Smith, Clarissa. "Pleasure and Distance: Exploring Sexual Cultures in the Classroom." *Sexualities* 12, no. 5 (2009): 568–85.

Smith, F. B. "Labouchere's Amendment to the Criminal Law Amendment Bill." *Historical Studies* 17 (1976): 165–75.

Smith, Terry. *The Architecture of Aftermath.* Chicago: University of Chicago Press, 2006.

Sonenschein, David. "Sources of Reaction to 'Child Pornography.'" In *Porn 101: Eroticism, Pornography, and the First Amendment*, edited by James E. Elias, Veronica Diehl Elias, Vern Bullough, and Gwen Brewer, 527–33. Amherst, NY: Prometheus Books, 1999.

Sontag, Susan. "Regarding the Torture of Others." *New York Times Magazine*, May 23, 2004, accessed April 16, 2011, http://www.nytimes.com/2004/05/23/magazine/regarding-the-torture-of-others.html.

Soto-Crespo, Ramón E. *Mainland Passage: The Cultural Anomaly of Puerto Rico.* Minneapolis: University of Minnesota Press, 2009.

Souza Nunes Martins, William. "As múltiplas formas de censura no cinema brasileiro: 1970–1980." *Iberoamerica Global* 1, no. 1 (February 2008): 29–42.

Spencer, Herbert. "The Origin of Music." *Mind* 15 (1890): 449–68.

Spicer, Jack. "Poetry and Politics." In *The House That Jack Built*, edited by Peter Gizzi, 152–72. Middletown, CT: Wesleyan University Press, 1998.

Spivak, Gayatri Chakravorty. "The Rani of Sirmur: An Essay in Reading the Archives." *History and Theory* 24, no. 3 (1985): 247–72.

———. "Terror: A Speech after 9–11." *boundary 2* 31, no. 2 (Summer 2004): 81–111.

Spring, Justin. *Secret Historian: The Life and Times of Samuel Steward, Professor, Tattoo Artist, and Sexual Renegade.* New York: Farrar, Straus and Giroux, 2010.

Spring, Justin, and Sam Steward. *An Obscene Diary: The Visual World of Sam Steward.* New York: Elysium Press, 2010.

Stadler, Matthew. *Allan Stein.* New York: Grove Press, 1999.

———. "Keeping Secrets: NAMBLA, the Idealization of Children, and the Contradictions of Gay Politics." *Stranger*, March 20, 1997, 8–15.

Stavans, Ilán. "The Latin Phallus." In *The Latino Studies Reader: Culture, Economy and Society*, edited by Antonia Darder and Rodolfo D. Torres, 228–40. Malden, MA: Blackwell, 1998.

Steedman, Carolyn. *Dust: The Archive and Cultural History.* New Brunswick, NJ: Rutgers University Press, 2002.

Steffen, Barbara. "The Representation of the Body: Velasquez-Bacon." In *Francis Bacon and the Tradition of Art*, edited by Wilfried Seipel, Barbara Steffen, Christoph Valli, 205–7. Milan: Skira, 2003.

Stevens, Kenneth R. "United States v. 31 Photographs: Dr. Alfred C. Kinsey and Obscenity Law." Indiana Magazine of History 71, no. 4 (December 1975): 299–300.

Steward, Sam. "Dr. Kinsey Takes a Peek at S/M: A Reminiscence." In Leatherfolk: Radical Sex, People, Politics and Practice, edited by Mark Thompson, 81–90. Boston: Alyson Publications, 1991.

Stewart, Susan. On Longing: Narratives of the Miniature, the Gigantic, the Souvenir, the Collection. Durham, NC: Duke University Press, 1993.

Stine, Scott Aaron. "The Snuff Film: The Making of an Urban Legend." Skeptical Inquirer 23, no. 3 (1999).

St. Jorre, John de. Venus Bound: The Erotic Voyage of the Olympia Press and Its Writers. New York: Random House, 1994.

Stockton, Kathryn Bond. The Queer Child; or, Growing Sideways in the Twentieth Century. Durham, NC: Duke University Press, 2009.

Stoler, Ann Laura. Along the Archival Grain: Epistemic Anxieties and Colonial Common Sense. Princeton, NJ: Princeton University Press, 2009.

Strebeigh, Fred. "Defining Law on the Feminist Frontier." Equal: Women Reshape American Law, October 6, 1991, accessed July 31, 2010, http://www.equalwomen.com/nyt magazine.1991.html.

Strout, Ruth French. "The Development of the Catalog and Cataloging Codes." The Library Quarterly 26, no. 4 (October 1956): 254–75.

Strub, Whitney. Perversion for Profit: The Politics of Pornography and the Rise of the New Right. New York: Columbia University Press, 2011.

Symonds, John Addington. Many Moods: A Volume of Verse. London: John Murray, 1878.

———. A Problem in Modern Ethics: Being an Inquiry into the Phenomenon of Sexual Inversion. London, 1896.

———. "To Havelock Ellis, July 1891." In The Letters of John Addington Symonds, vol. 3, edited by Herbert M. Schueller and Robert L. Peters, 587–88. Detroit, MI: Wayne State University Press, 1969.

———. "Vulgar Errors." In A Problem in Modern Ethics: Being an Inquiry into the Phenomenon of Sexual Inversion, 9–15. London: n.p., 1896.

Szogyi, Alex. "A Full Measure of Madness." New York Times Book Review, July 25, 1965, 4, 22.

Taylor, Diana. The Archive and the Repertoire: Performing Cultural Memory in the Americas. Durham, NC: Duke University Press, 2003.

Taylor, Max, and Ethel Quayle. Child Pornography: An Internet Crime. New York: Brunner-Routledge, 2003.

Taylor, Paul A. "The Pornographic Barbarism of the Self-Reflecting Sign." International Journal of Baudrillard Studies 4, no. 1 (January 2007).

Tepper, Mitchell S. "Lived Experiences That Impede or Facilitate Sexual Pleasure and Orgasm in People with Spinal Cord Injury." PhD dissertation, University of Pennsylvania, 2001.

Thurschwell, Pamela. Literature, Technology, and Magical Thinking, 1880–1920. Cambridge, UK: Cambridge University Press, 2001.

Turner, James Grantham. "The Whores Rhetorick: Narrative, Pornography, and the Origins of the Novel." Studies in Eighteenth-Century Culture 24, no. 1 (1995): 297–306.

Underwager, Ralph, and Hollida Wakefield. "Sexual Abuse, Anti-sexuality, and the Pornography of Power." In Porn 101: Eroticism, Pornography, and the First Amendment, edited by James E. Elias, Veronica Diehl Elias, Vern Bullough, and Gwen Brewer, 520–26. Amherst, NY: Prometheus Books, 1999.

Upchurch, Charles. *Before Wilde: Sex between Men in Britain's Age of Reform.* Berkeley: University of California Press, 2009.

Vismann, Cornelia. *Files: Law and Media Technology.* Translated by Geoffrey Winthrop-Young. Stanford, CA: Stanford University Press, 2000.

Wainhouse, Austryn. "On Translating Sade." *Evergreen Review* 10, no. 42 (August 1966): 50–56.

Warner, Michael. *Publics and Counterpublics.* New York: Zone Books, 2002.

———. *The Trouble with Normal: Sex, Politics and the Ethics of Queer Life.* New York: Free Press, 1999.

Waugh, Thomas. *Hard to Imagine: Gay Male Eroticism in Photography and Film from Their Beginnings to Stonewall.* New York: Columbia University Press, 1996.

———. *Lust Unearthed: Vintage Gay Graphics from the DuBek Collection.* Vancouver: Arsenal Pulp Press, 2004.

———. *Out/Lines: Underground Gay Graphics before Stonewall.* Vancouver: Arsenal Pulp Press, 2002.

Weber, Max. *On Charisma and Institution Building*, edited by S. N. Eisenstadt. Chicago: University of Chicago Press, 1968.

Weiss, Margot. *Techniques of Pleasure: BDSM and the Circuits of Sexuality.* Durham, NC: Duke University Press, 2011.

White, Chris. "The Metaphors of Homosexual Colonialism and Tourism." *Victorian Literature and Culture* 23 (1999): 1–22.

Wilde, Oscar. *The Picture of Dorian Gray: The 1890 and 1891 Texts.* Vol. 3, *The Complete Works of Oscar Wilde*, edited by Joseph Bristow. Oxford: Oxford University Press, 2005.

Wilde, Oscar, and others. *Teleny.* Edited by John McRae. London: Gay Men's Press, 1986.

Williams, Linda. *Hard Core: Power, Pleasure, and the "Frenzy of the Visible."* Berkeley: University of California Press, 1989.

———. *Hard Core: Power, Pleasure, and the "Frenzy of the Visible."* 2nd ed. Berkeley: University of California Press, 1999.

———, ed. *Porn Studies.* Durham, NC: Duke University Press, 2004.

———. "Porn Studies: Proliferating Pornographies On/Scene; An Introduction." In *Porn Studies*, edited by Linda Williams, 1–23. Durham, NC: Duke University Press, 2004.

———. *Screening Sex.* Durham, NC: Duke University Press, 2008.

———. "Second Thoughts on *Hard Core*: American Obscenity Law and the Scapegoating of Deviance." In *More Dirty Looks: Gender, Pornography and Power*, edited by Pamela Church Gibson, 165–75. London: British Film Institute, 2004.

———. "Skin Flicks on the Racial Border: Pornography, Exploitation, and Interracial Lust." In *Porn Studies*, edited by Linda Williams, 271–308. Durham, NC: Duke University Press, 2004.

———. "Studying 'Soft' Sex." *Film Quarterly* 62, no. 1 (2008): 86–88.

———. "'White Slavery' versus the Ethnography of 'Sexworkers': Women in Stag Films at the Kinsey Archive." *The Moving Image* 5, no. 2 (Fall 2005): 107–34.

Williams, Linda Ruth. *The Erotic Thriller in Contemporary Cinema.* Bloomington: Indiana University Press, 2005.

Wilson, Edmund. "The Vogue of the Marquis de Sade." In *The Bit between My Teeth: A Library Chronicle 1950–1965*, 158–73. New York: Macmillan, 1965.

Wiseman, Jay. *S/M 101: A Realistic Introduction*. San Francisco: Greenery Press, 1989.
Wizisla, Erdmut. "Preface." In Walter Benjamin, *Walter Benjamin's Archive: Images, Texts, Signs*, translated by Esther Leslie, edited by Ursula Marx, Gudrun Schwarz, Michael Schwarz, and Erdmut Wizisla, 1–6. London: Verso, 2007.
Wolk, Douglas. *Reading Comics: How Graphic Novels Work and What They Mean*. Cambridge, MA: Da Capo, 2007.
Wollheim, Richard. *Painting as an Art*. Princeton, NJ: Princeton University Press, 1987.
Wortis, Joseph. *My Analysis with Freud*. London: Jason Aronson, 1994.
Wypijewski, JoAnn. "The Love We Lost." *The Nation*, February 8, 2010, 6–7.
Yamashiro, Jennifer. "In the Realm of the Sciences: The Kinsey Institute's 31 Photographs." In *Porn 101: Eroticism, Pornography, and the First Amendment*, edited by James E. Elias, Veronica Diehl Elias, Vern Bullough, and Gwen Brewer, 32–52. Amherst, NY: Prometheus Books, 1999.
Yudell, Michael. "Kinsey's Other Report." *Natural History* 108, no. 6 (1999): 80–81.
Zhou, Liana. "Characteristics of Material Organization and Classification in the Kinsey Institute Library." *Cataloguing and Classification Quarterly* 35, nos. 3–4 (2003): 335–53.
Ziegler-Graham, Kathryn, Ellen J. MacKenzie, Patti L. Ephraim, Thomas G. Travison, and Ron Brookmeyer. "Estimating the Prevalence of Limb Loss in the United States: 2005 to 2050." *Archives of Physical Medicine and Rehabilitation* 89 (2008): 422–29.
Ziolkowski, Jan M. "Introduction." *Obscenity: Social Control and Artistic Creation in the European Middle Ages*, edited by Jan M. Ziolkowski, 3–18. Leiden: Brill, 1998.
Žižek, Slavoj. *The Plague of Fantasies*. London: Verso, 1997.
Zornick, George. "The Porn of War." *The Nation*, September 22, 2005, accessed April 16, 2011, http://www.thenation.com/article/porn-war.

# NOTES ON CONTRIBUTORS

JENNIFER BURNS BRIGHT teaches literature, sexuality studies, and food studies at the University of Oregon. She holds a PhD in English from the University of California, Irvine, and has published recently on James Joyce's pornography sources, early Joyce studies, and restaurant culture in America and Europe. She is completing a manuscript on representations of masochism in early twentieth-century pornography, medical studies, and modernist texts.

EUGENIE BRINKEMA is an assistant professor of contemporary literature and media at the Massachusetts Institute of Technology. She is the author of *The Forms of the Affects* (2014), and her articles on film, violence, sexuality, and psychoanalysis have appeared in *Camera Obscura, Criticism, differences,* and *Discourse.* She is currently working on a project on finitude and the horror film.

JOSEPH BRISTOW is a professor of English at the University of California, Los Angeles. His recent books include an edited collection, *Wilde Discoveries: Traditions, Histories, Archives* (2013), and a monograph (coauthored with Rebecca N. Mitchell), *Oscar Wilde's Chatterton: Literary History, Romanticism, and the Art of Forgery* (2014).

ROBERT L. CASERIO, professor of English at The Pennsylvania State University, University Park, is the editor of *The Cambridge Companion to the Twentieth-Century English Novel* (2009), and is a coeditor, with Clement Hawes, of *The Cambridge History of the English Novel* (2012).

RONAN CROWLEY is an Alexander von Humboldt postdoctoral research fellow at the University of Passau, Germany. He received a PhD in English from the University at Buffalo (SUNY) in 2014.

TIM DEAN is a professor of English and comparative literature at the University at Buffalo (SUNY), where he is also the director of the Center for the Study of Psychoanalysis and Culture. He is the author of *Beyond Sexuality* (2000) and *Un-*

limited Intimacy: Reflections on the Subculture of Barebacking (2009), as well as a coeditor of Homosexuality and Psychoanalysis (2001). His new book is What Is Psychoanalytic Thinking? (forthcoming).

ROBERT DEWHURST is a PhD candidate in the Department of English at the University at Buffalo (SUNY) and a participant in its Poetics Program. He lives in Los Angeles, where he is completing a dissertation on the American poet John Wieners.

LISA DOWNING is a professor of French discourses of sexuality at the University of Birmingham, UK. She is the author of five books, the coeditor of five others, and the author of numerous journal articles and book chapters in the fields of sexuality and gender studies, literature, film, and Continental thought. Her particular research interests lie in the history and politics of sexual perversion, in queer theory and ethical theory, and in Foucauldian and feminist responses to psychoanalysis. Her most recent monograph is The Subject of Murder: Gender, Exceptionality, and the Modern Killer (2013).

FRANCES FERGUSON teaches in the English department at the University of Chicago and is the author of Pornography, the Theory: What Utilitarianism Did to Action (2004). She is currently working on the rise of mass education in the eighteenth and early nineteenth centuries and on a brief history of reading and practical criticism.

LOREN GLASS is a professor of English at the University of Iowa. His publications include Authors Inc.: Literary Celebrity in the Modern United States (2004), Obscenity and the Limits of Liberalism (2011), and Counterculture Colophon (2013).

HARRI KALHA is adjunct professor of Art History and Gender Studies at the University of Helsinki. He is the author of many award-winning books in Finnish. His most recent books include Taidetta seksin vuoksi (on Tom of Finland, 2012), Ihme ja kumma (on proto-surrealist postcards, 2012), and Kokottien kultakausi ("The Golden Age of the Cocotte," 2013). For the last book, Kalha was nominated for the prestigious Finlandia award for best non-fiction book published in his country.

MARCIA KLOTZ teaches at the University of Arizona. Having previously worked in the field of German studies, she is now a member of the English department, focusing on critical theory, literature, film, and sexuality studies.

PRABHA MANURATNE is a lecturer in the English department at the University of Kelaniya, Sri Lanka, and a PhD candidate in the Department of English at the

University at Buffalo (SUNY). Her present research focuses on representations of violence in contemporary culture.

MIREILLE MILLER-YOUNG is an associate professor of feminist studies at the University of California, Santa Barbara. Her book, *A Taste for Brown Sugar: Black Women, Sex Work, and Pornography* (2014), examines black women's representations, performances, and labors in the adult entertainment industry. Along with Constance Penley, Celine Parreñas Shimizu, and Tristan Taormino, she is an editor of *The Feminist Porn Book: The Politics of Producing Pleasure* (2013).

NGUYEN TAN HOANG is an associate professor of English and film studies at Bryn Mawr College. He is the author of *A View from the Bottom: Asian American Masculinity and Sexual Representation* (2014). His critical writings have appeared in *Porn Studies* (2004), *Vectors: Journal of Culture and Technology in a Dynamic Vernacular* (2006), and *Resolutions 3: Video Praxis in Global Spaces* (2012). His experimental videos— including *Forever Bottom!* (1999), *PIRATED!* (2000), and *K.I.P.* (2002)—have screened at the Museum of Modern Art in New York, the National Museum of Modern Art at the Pompidou Center, the Getty Center, and numerous film and media festivals.

JOHN PAUL RICCO is the author of *The Logic of the Lure* (2002) and *The Decision between Us: Art and Ethics in the Time of Scenes* (2014). His chapter in this collection is part of his current book project, "The Outside not Beyond: Pornographic Faith and the Economy of the Eve." He is the coeditor of a special issue of the *Journal of Visual Culture* on Jean-Luc Nancy (2010) and the editor of an issue of the journal *Parallax* on the conceptual theme of "unbecoming." He is currently an associate professor of contemporary art, media theory, and criticism at the University of Toronto.

STEVEN RUSZCZYCKY received his PhD from the Department of English at the University at Buffalo (SUNY) in 2014. In addition to *Porn Archives*, his work has appeared in *Genre: Forms of Discourse and Culture*. He is currently completing a manuscript, "Vulgar Genres: On Pornography, Sexuality, and the Privatization of Fantasy," about the history of gay pornographic writing and processes of social differentiation in the U.S. during the late twentieth and early twenty-first centuries.

MELISSA SCHINDLER is a PhD candidate in the Department of English at the University at Buffalo (SUNY). Her dissertation focuses on the function of ethic names in colonial and postcolonial narratives from Brazil, Ghana, and India.

DARIECK SCOTT is an associate professor of African American studies at the University of California, Berkeley. Scott is the author of *Extravagant Abjection: Black-*

ness, Power, and Sexuality in the African American Literary Imagination (2010), winner of the 2011 Alan Bray Memorial Prize of the Modern Language Association GL/Q Caucus. Scott is also the author of the novels Hex (2007) and Traitor to the Race (1995), and the editor of Best Black Gay Erotica (2004).

CAITLIN SHANLEY is an instruction librarian and subject specialist for American studies, Asian studies, and women's studies at Temple University. She holds an MS in library science from the University of North Carolina, Chapel Hill, and has published on games and information literacy, sex materials in archival collections, and learning technologies. Her latest project explores connections among librarianship, critical pedagogy, and feminist/social justice praxis, with particular attention to the Girls Rock movement.

RAMÓN E. SOTO-CRESPO is an associate professor of transnational studies, American studies, and comparative literature at the University at Buffalo (SUNY). His articles have appeared in American Literary History, Modern Language Notes, Modern Fiction Studies, Contemporary Literature, and Textual Practice. He is the author of Mainland Passage: The Cultural Anomaly of Puerto Rico (2009). His chapter "Porno Rícans" is part of the book-length manuscript "Hemispheric Trash: Despised Forms in the Cultural History of the Americas."

DAVID SQUIRES is a PhD candidate in the Department of English at the University at Buffalo (SUNY). His dissertation provides a critical investigation of modern literature and the rise of library science between 1870 and 1950. His work on pornography also appears in The Librarian Stereotype (2014).

LINDA WILLIAMS teaches film and media at the University of California, Berkeley. Her books on pornography include Hard Core: Power, Pleasure and the "Frenzy of the Visible" (1989/1999) and the misnamed anthology Porn Studies (Duke University Press, 2004).

# INDEX

Campos, Haroldo de, 319–20
Cante, Richard, 30, 397n31
Caputi, Jane, 252, 254
*Carny* (Mills and Greg), 438n8
Carol, Avedon, 251
Carpenter, Edward, 109
Carrillo, Héctor, 303
Carter, Angela, 141
Caserio, Robert L., 18
Caspar, J. L., 153
Catholicism, 128–29, 223, 309
censorship, 17–18, 127–28; of child por-
   nography, 401–3; as complicit with
   heteronormativity, 75, 243, 258–59;
   institutional, 109, 115–17; and law, 79,
   104, 131, 252–54; self-, 72–73; state,
   140–41, 319, 324–26, 333, 336n24,
   358; of violent pornography, 285–86;
   of war porn, 358, 360
Champagne, John, 31, 304
*Champion* (Houston), 19, 234–39, 241,
   245–46
Charcot, Jean-Martin, 153–54, 158,
   160n33
Chicago Public Library, 104
*Chico con leche* (Rico), 310
child pornography, 6–7, 23–24, 285,
   399–401; and law, 401–4, 408–9, 414–
   17; and mainstream media, 405–6,
   411
Child Pornography Protection Act (1996),
   402
Children's Internet Protection Act (2000),
   103, 121–22n2
Chun, Wendy Hui Kyong, 34
Cinema Novo, 320–21, 325, 334, 335n7
circumcision, 23, 376–78, 381, 384–87,
   389, 394–95. *See also* foreskin
*Cirque Noir* (Mills), 438n8
Clare, Eli, 437n2
Class Comics, 201
class, social, 13–14, 32–33, 44–47, 107,
   434–35; and access to pornography,
   54–55, 83, 107; and desire, 379–82;
   and shame, 321–22; and taste, 22, 92,
   317–19, 321, 327–28, 332, 337n29

Cleland, John, 135
Cleveland Street affair, 149, 159–60n16
Clips4Sale (website), 242
Clover, Carol, 286; *Men, Women, and Chain-
   saws*, 52
*Club Mandom* (Caserta), 379–81, 391
*Cocktails* (Borden), 263
Cohen, Ed, 144
Colan, Gene, 186
Collins, Jess, 220, 232n13
Comfort, Alex, 48
comics, 18–19, 30, 184–92, 194–211
Communications Decency Act (1996),
   306
Comstock, Anthony, 122n9
Comstock, Tony, 241
Condom World, 306–9
confessions: bodily, 8, 266; and power,
   404; of sexual pleasure, 118, 164, 264,
   369; of sexual truth, 32, 258; and sub-
   jectivity, 150
consent, 9, 20–21, 52, 369; age of, 145,
   411; in BDSM, 287–88, 294–98; con-
   tractual forms of, 40–41, 297, 363; in
   moving-image porn, 253–58, 263–65,
   273
Cook, Matt, 150
Cooper, Dennis, 217, 231
copyright, 11, 90, 107
Cornog, Martha, 92–95
Corot, Jean-Baptiste-Camille, 170
counterarchive, 10–11
counterpornography, 16, 63, 69
Crash Pad Series (Houston), 236, 239,
   240, 241, 243, 244, 245
Creeley, Robert, 214, 220
Criminal Justice and Immigration Act
   2008, 255–59
Criminal Law Amendment Act (1885),
   145
Crimp, Douglas, 77n35
Critchley, Simon, 343
Cross, Paul, 113–14
Crowley, Ronan, 3, 17
cruising, 144, 150
Cvetkovich, Ann, 226–27, 230

Damiano, Gerard, 250, 317; *Devil in Miss Jones*, 69. See also *Deep Throat*
Danner, Mark, 343
Danto, Arthur, 178, 395n2, 397n27
Darwin, Charles, 156
Davidson, Michael, 232n17
Davis, Jon, 405
Dawes, Charles Reginald, 114
Dean, Tim, 35, 41; *Beyond Sexuality*, 97n12; *Unlimited Intimacy*, 25n18, 31, 266, 277, 283n14, 427–28
Debord, Guy, 216, 340
Decena, Carlos Ulises, 303
*Deep Throat* (Damiano), 21–22, 69, 250; compared to *A b . . . profunda*, 317–19, 320, 327–31, 333–34
Deitcher, David, 226, 229
Delaine, Remy, 378–79
Delany, Samuel R., 12–13; *Times Square Red, Times Square Blue*, 31
Deleuze, Gilles, 297, 338, 342–43, 350–51, 353–54n7
Del Rio, Vanessa (Ana Maria Sanchez), 235
D'Emilio, John, 224, 230
Dennis, Kelly, 34
Dennison, Stephanie, 323
DePew, Daniel, 258–59
DeRosa, Tony, 223
Derrida, Jacques, 71, 97n14, 338–40, 347–49; *Archive Fever*, 4–5, 280
*Devil in Miss Jones, The* (Damiano), 69
DeVoe, Diana, 240
Dewey Decimal Classification, 93, 117
Dewhurst, Robert, 19
Dickens, Charles, 138
difference, 12, 16, 318; bodily, 375, 421–22; class, 13–14; ethnopolitical, 361, 364–66, 370; gender, 163, 181; and pedagogy, 67, 73–74; as Otherness, 187, 400, 406–7; racial, 70–71, 183, 185–86, 205–10, 388–89; religious, 50
Dines, Gail, 260n9, 261n31
Dingwall, Eric, 114
Dinnage, Paul, 129–30

disability, 420–23; representations of, 423–29; and sexual mobility, 429–37
disability porn, 16, 24, 420–23, 427–29, 432–37; compared to freak shows, 421–22, 437–38n7. See also stumping
disability studies, 24, 422–23
*Discipline and Punish* (Foucault), 47, 87, 434–35
disgust, 425–27; and desire, 378, 387, 394–95; moral, 399–400; and obscenity, 255–56; in response to art, 156, 178
Ditko, Steve, 196
domination, 174–75; erotics of, 173, 364–66, 433; in pornography, 12, 20–21, 181, 238–39, 285; racial, 190–91
Dominó, Gerardo (Álvaro de Moya), 317–18, 327
Donato, Eugenio, 85–86
Dorff, Stephen, 189
Dostoevsky, Fyodor, 131
*Double Portrait of Lucian Freud and Frank Auerbach* (Bacon), 177
Dougherty, Cecilia, 65–67
Douglas, Derek, 430–31
Douglas, Lord Alfred, 120
Downing, Lisa, 20, 21, 285
Dowson, Ernest, 147–48
Doyle, Jennifer, 74
Duany, Jorge, 313
Dumas, Alexandre (fils), 149, 151
Duncan, Robert, 220, 222, 232n13
Dworkin, Andrea, 141, 253–54, 261n31
Dyer, Richard, 31

Eakins, Thomas, 177
*Early Morning, An* (O'Reilly), 179–81
Echard, Siân, 111
Eco, Umberto, 114
Edelman, Lee, 214, 389–90, 406, 408
education. See pedagogy
Edwards, Brent Hayes, 26n23
Eigner, Larry, 217
Eigo, Jim, 390
Elias, James E., 41n1; *Porn 101*, 30, 35, 37
El Kholti, Hedi, 231

Ellis, Havelock, 113; *Studies in the Psychology of Sex*, 109–10
embodiment: extraordinary, 421–22, 423, 425, 432–33; and subjectivity, 413–14; textual, 215
Embrafilme (Empresa Brasileira do Filme Nacional), 325
Emerson, Ralph Waldo, 105
England, Lynndie, 367
erection, 155, 167–68; and castration, 185–86, 190, 195; and detumescence, 432; and ethnicity, 196, 312–13; and foreskin, 386, 391
Ernaux, Annie, 420, 429–30
erogenous zones, 286–87, 430–32, 436–37
*Eros Denied* (Young), 136
erotica, 33–34, 116–17; black, 235; as distinct from pornography, 53
Erotika Biblion Society, 147, 152, 159n1
Escoffier, Jeffrey, 31
ethics, 22, 73, 338, 352; of archiving, 13; of caretaking, 415–17; of openness, 427–28; of pornographic representation, 21, 318, 436; and strangeness, 281
Evergreen Club, 135–37, 139
*Evergreen Review* (periodical), 130, 133–37, 140
evidence: archival, 5; documentary, 192, 402; empirical, 251–52; historical, 3, 138, 226; legal, 24, 400, 402–3, 409; medical, 153; photographic, 359; social, 9
Extreme Associates, 20, 263–64, 277

*Fag Rag* (newspaper), 214, 222, 225
Fairholt, Frederick William, 106
faith, pornographic, 338–42, 347, 350–53
Falcon Studios, 310
Falkon, Felix Lance, 192
*Falling Man, The* (Drew), 350–51
Fanon, Frantz, 183, 193, 388
*Fantastic Foreskin!* (Brennan), 381–83, 391
fantasy, 23–24, 36, 37–38, 62; of archives, 86, 280; criminalization of,

20, 255–59, 401; cultural, 309, 423; and pornographic conventions, 31, 41, 82; and psychoanalysis, 208–9, 268, 380–88, 392–94, 405–9, 414–16, 419n46, 430–32; and race, 184–86, 190–95, 201, 205–11, 235, 310; and reality, 252–54, 310–11, 357, 362–63, 369; representations of, 169, 244; and spectatorship, 69–70, 240; and violence, 249–51, 286, 297–98, 299n15, 364–66, 370
Farrer, Peter, 113
Federal Depository Library Program, 105
feminism, 163, 244–45, 401, 422; and critiques of porn, 12, 17–18, 20, 140–41, 260n9, 285–86, 369; as methodology, 10–11, 29, 31–33, 36, 61, 63, 72–75, 265; and sadomasochism, 285, 363; sex-positive, 19–20, 66, 257; and snuff films, 249–54, 257–59
Feminist Porn Awards (Toronto), 19, 234
Ferguson, Frances, 1; on action, 24; on context of pornography, 357–58; on Marquis de Sade, 141; and pedagogy, 15–17; on pornographic content, 21, 87–89, 98n20; on social mobility, 14, 434–36, 440n38. See also *Pornography, the Theory*
fetish and fetishism, 23–24, 65, 154, 396n10; devotees of, 387, 422, 427; of foreskin, 375, 383–87, 392, 395; of print materials, 111, 114, 132–33; as social phenomenon, 395
FetLife (website), 291
Fiedler, Leslie, 421, 438n11
Fillion, Patrick, 19, 194, 201–6, 208, 211
film studies: as discipline, 14–15, 29–31, 35, 38; methodology of, 52, 90, 268
Findlay, Eileen J. Suárez, 308–9
Findlay, Michael, 249, 363
Findlay, Roberta, 249, 363
Fischel, Joseph, 418n36
Fish, Stanley, 50
First Amendment, 252, 367; defense of, 37–38, 254; material unprotected by, 117, 305, 402

fisting, 217–19, 424, 427, 431–32
Flaubert, Gustave, 44, 55, 85, 130
*Flaying of Marsyas, The* (Titian), 170–75
*Forced Entry* (Borden), 20, 263–79,
    282nn3–4, 283n22
foreskin, 23, 375–78, 394–95; in pornog-
    raphy, 378–82; as fetish object, 383–
    87; and race, 389–94
Fortescue, G. K., 108
*Fossil Fuckers* (Borden), 263
Foucault, Michel, 8–9, 24, 71, 89; on
    archive, 4, 10, 25n8, 303–4; *ars erotica*
    versus *scientia sexualis*, 14; on discipline,
    47–48, 52, 58, 87, 141, 436; on fisting,
    217 19; on friendship, 73, 77nn22–23;
    on madness, 3, 25n5; on pleasure,
    431–32; on power, 60; on subjugated
    knowledge, 11. *See also specific works*
Fowlie, Wallace, 132
Fox, Claire F., 315n6
Fraga, Ody, 334
Franco, James, 284
*'Frank' and I*, 139
Freeman, Elizabeth, 73–74, 297
free speech: and inequality, 49–50; legally
    protected, 306; and liberalism, 133–34;
    and pornography, 44–45, 252–54; and
    scholarship, 38, 113
Freitas, Marcel de Almeida, 324
Fremont-Smith, Eliot, 78–79
Freud, Lucian, 18, 167–70, 172, 175, 177–
    78, 181. *See also specific works*
Freud, Sigmund, 5, 287, 388; *Beyond the
    Pleasure Principle*, 110, 270; on fetishism,
    383–87, 396n10; *Interpretation of Dreams*,
    110; "Rat Man" case, 169; on sublima-
    tion, 396n20; theory of sexuality, 24,
    290, 407, 430, 432; on trauma, 270; on
    war, 370
Fryer, Peter, 112
*Fuck You: A Magazine of the Arts*, 220–22
Fung, Richard, 32
*Furies* (newspaper), 214
futurity: affirmative, 313; archival, 92,
    226, 229–30; and belief, 342–43; cata-
    strophic, 348–49; and children, 406;

erotic, 310, 314; and memory, 97n14;
    political, 347; in sadomasochistic play,
    297–98; sexual, 68, 70

Gallop, Jane, 72–73
*Games People Play* (Berne), 136
Gamson, Joshua, 423
Garland-Thomson, Rosemarie, 433,
    438n7, 439–40nn33–34
Garner, Richard, 26n27
Garnett, Richard, 109, 114
Gay Liberation Front, 223
*Gay Liberator* (newspaper), 214
Gay Men's Press, 149
gay pornography, 18–20, 23–24, 246,
    360; as archive, 16, 67–69, 119–20, 164;
    and art, 167, 170, 175; and disability,
    427–39; foreskin in, 378–82, 390–94;
    history of, 139, 144; race in, 183–84,
    202, 211; studies of, 30–31, 62–63
gay rights movement, 214, 217, 219, 229,
    410
*Gay Roots* (Leyland), 231n1
*Gay Sunshine* (periodical), 19, 213–14; and
    community, 228–31, 232n10; as queer
    archive, 222–28; and pornopoetic col-
    lage, 214–22, 232n13
*Gay Sunshine Interviews*, 224
Gay Sunshine Press, 149, 228, 231n1
gaze: averted, 392, 396n10; openness to,
    293; panoptic, 75, 434; pedophilic,
    403–4; unstable, 423; as violent, 364,
    433
Genet, Jean, 130, 134, 139, 224, 352
genres, 20, 37–39, 174; BDSM as, 285–
    87, 290, 363; cinematic, 21–22, 240,
    272, 275, 317, 319–27, 335n7; of comic
    books, 184–92, 194, 195; digital, 360,
    362, 368, 370, 426; hybrid, 33–34,
    110; and law, 403, 408–9, 416; novel
    as, 53–56; porn as, 2–3, 29, 32, 264,
    268–69, 277; portraiture as, 225–26;
    of sex acts, 116–17, 219, 369; snuff as,
    249–52, 260n11; sub-, 24, 31, 310–11,
    427, 432, 437nn6–7
Gerard, Emily, 156

Gerli, Jake, 30
Getty, Ann, 140
Gibson, Ian, 26n32, 122n21, 123n23, 124n46
Gibson, Pamela Church, 94
Ginsberg v. New York, 142n22, 417n3
Ginsberg, Allen, 217, 222, 224–25, 229
Ginzburg, Ralph, 135
Ginzburg v. United States, 135
Giorno, John, 217
Girodias, Maurice, 130
Glass, Loren, 17–18, 401
GLBT Historical Society (San Francisco), 226, 229–30
globalization, 21, 338–40, 344
Gloeden, Wilhelm von, 389–90, 397n24
Glück, Robert, 217
Goldin, Nan, 256
Goldman, Albert, 139–40
Good Gay Poets (imprint), 222. See also Fag Rag
Good Vibrations (sex shop), 243
Goodwin, Willard, 377
Gorfinkel, Elena, 34
Gornick, Vivian, 140
GotWarPorn (website), 357, 368–69, 370
Graphic Sexual Horror (Bell and Lorentzon), 21, 284, 289–90; criticism of, 294; making of, 292–93
Great Speckled Bird, The (newspaper), 228
Greene, David, 225–26
Green Girls, 138
Grove Press, 17–18, 87, 127–41, 411; and censorship, 78–79, 128; and democratization, 128–29; and liberalism, 132–34; and Olympia Press, 130, 139; and paratext, 130–34, 137–39
Guantánamo Bay, 369
Gurney, Edmund, 156–57
Gynecocracy, 138

Hacking, Ian, 409
Halberstam, Judith, 67, 76n12, 214, 227, 230
Hall, Lesley A., 110
Hall, Richard, 231

Halperin, David, 73, 77n25, 219
Hanson, Ellis, 73, 75, 76n12
harassment, sexual, 16, 48–50, 62, 82, 88, 97n6, 295–96
Hardcore (Schrader), 260n1
Hard Core (Williams), 29–30, 36–37, 90, 163–64, 404–5; on genre, 174; on pornographic form, 267–69; on violence in pornography, 250–51, 285, 363; on visibility in pornography, 20, 264–65, 282n6–7
Hardy, James Earl, 195
Hardy, Thomas, 138
harm, 9, 48–50, 53, 57, 59, 88, 253. See also violence
Harriet Marwood, Governess, 138
Harris, Kaplan, 233n32
Harrison, Martin, 173
Hart, Lynda, 297
Haver, William, 338, 354n16
Haynes, E. S. P., 109–10
health: physical, 69, 153–55, 419n46; public, 61, 426; sexual, 146, 158
Heine, Maurice, 127, 129, 132
Herring, Scott, 26n23, 26n31, 231n2
heteronormativity, 12–14, 72–74, 406, 422, 424–25; and misogyny, 157–58; and psychoanalysis, 396n10
Hidell, Alek James (Brandon Iron), 263
Hillyer, Minette, 30
Hirsch, Charles, 148–49, 152, 159n1
History of Sexuality, The (Foucault), 18, 127–29, 137, 258, 361, 404, 436
Hitchcock, Alfred, 246
Hitler, Adolf, 133–34, 211n6
HIV/AIDS, 19, 67–70, 214, 394, 427–29
Hoffman, Chloe, 246
Hole, The (West), 246
Holmes, John, 235
homoeroticism: in art, 18, 64; in comics, 191–92; in literature, 18, 144–46, 149, 155, 158; and subculture, 150, 222, 226
homosexuality, 157–58; criminalization of, 120, 144–46; and cultural difference, 225; defense of, 58, 144, 152; and desire, 146, 152, 210–11; and friend-

ship, 73–74; geographies of, 149–50, 229–30; history of, 68, 226–27; pathologization of, 18, 153–55, 384, 396n10; traditions of, 146, 224–25, 228–29; visibility of, 313–14. *See also* identity: sexual

*Honcho* (magazine), 69

*Hostel* (Roth), 250, 259

*Hot Chocolate* (Fillion), 202

Hotmovies (website), 242

Hottentot, Venus, 240

Houston, Shine Louise, 19–20; *Champion*, 234–39, 241, 245–46; Crash Pad Series, 236, 239, 240, 241, 243, 244, 245; *In Search of the Wild Kingdom*, 236, 239, 245; *Snapshot*, 240; *Superfreak*, 236

human rights, 358

Hume, David, 342

Hunter, Ian, 417n3

Hun, The, 195

Hunt, Lynn, 1, 6, 22; *The Invention of Pornography*, 2, 35

Hurley, Robert, 127

*Hustler* (magazine), 310

*I Am Curious (Yellow)* (Sjöman), 139

I Blame the Patriarchy (website), 260n9

identity, 423, 433–37; corporeal, 24, 427–29; ethnic, 303, 311–13; gender, 49, 52, 72; intersectional, 62–65; racial, 70, 183, 210–11; sexual, 12–14, 20, 23, 74–75, 256–57, 394, 407; social, 33, 228; and subjectivity, 165–67

identity politics, 72, 214, 313, 378, 434

images: of children, 6–7, 256, 401–9, 411–12, 414, 416; digital, 7–10, 15, 22–23, 346, 357; drawn, 184, 192, 211n4; queer, 66, 216, 244–45; reality of, 251–52, 255, 285–86, 363; solicitation of, 164–65, 167, 168, 175, 438n7; of war, 22–23, 339, 358–64, 367–70. *See also* representation; spectacle

*Incest Lovers, The*, 139

industry, porn, 8, 38, 175, 211, 263; Black women's experience of, 240–41; and conditions of production, 255; and dis-

tribution, 241–42, 255; and labor practices, 208, 243–44, 295

*In Search of the Wild Kingdom* (Houston), 236, 239, 245

Insex (website), 21, 284, 286; and community, 290–93, 298; and consent, 293–97; history of, 287–90, 299n13

intergenerational relationships, 63, 74, 401, 405, 410–11

*International Skin* (Richhe), 61

Internet, 6–9, 19, 140, 175; access to, 49, 97n6, 105, 118, 122n2; as archive, 35, 378–79; as condition of possibility, 285; and interactivity, 21, 34, 164–67, 287, 288–90, 365–70; and porn distribution, 30, 239, 241–42; reaction clip, 424, 426–27; regulation of, 306; and social networks, 181, 215, 356–58, 362

interpassivity, 165–67, 172, 173, 174, 181

interracial porn, 67, 70–71, 194, 210, 235, 421

intimacy, 174, 278; and archives, 9; and fantasy, 380; intergenerational, 410; mediated, 21, 293, 298; between men, 144, 146; narrative, 150; in pornography, 236–37

inversion, sexual, 153–54

Isherwood, Christopher, 224

Jackson, Earl, Jr., 74–75; *Strategies of Deviance*, 31

Jakobson, Roman, 85

Jameson, Fredric, 128

Jarmusch, Jim, 246

Jeffreys, Sheila, 260n9

Jenkins, Henry, 62

Jenkins, Philip, 405–6

Joe-Joe (Dougherty and Singer), 66, 76n8

Johnson, Eithne, 250–51

Johnson, Randal, 323, 331, 335n20

Jordan, Fred, 136

Josephson, Larry, 253–54

Joyce, James, 130–31; *Ulysses*, 110–11

*Joy of Sex, The* (Comfort), 48–49, 56

Juffer, Jane, 35

Julien, Isaac, 193, 207, 209

Liman, Carl, 153
Limbaugh, Rush, 361–62
Liszt, Franz, 156
Little Caesar (magazine), 231
Litvak, Joseph, 72
LiveLeak (website), 22, 357–58, 362, 364–67, 370
Loftus, David, 34
Longhurst, Liz, 286
Lorca, Frederico García, 224–25
Lorentzon, Anna, 292–93. See also Graphic Sexual Horror
Los borrachos (Velázquez), 167
Loud, Lance, 66
Love, Heather, 74, 77n29
Lucky Lukas (Duroy), 391–92
Luhmann, Niklas, 46
Lustful Turk, The, 138

Macey, David, 217–19
MacKinnon, Catharine, 16, 57, 140–41; Only Words, 252–53; on snuff, 252–54, 260–61n14
Madison, Steven, 42n24
Madness and Civilization (Foucault), 141
Magnan, Valentin, 153–54, 158
Malanga, Gerard, 224
Mandingo (Fleischer), 70–71, 210
Manhattans (band), 68
Man in a Polyester Suit (Mapplethorpe), 23, 375–76, 379, 381, 387–89
Man in Blue (Bacon), 174
Manoff, Marlene, 26n22
Manon Lescaut (Prévost), 149, 151
Man on Wire (Marsh), 349–50
Man Posing (Freud), 167–68
Manroot (magazine), 217
Manuratne, Prabha, 22–23
Man with a Maid, A, 138–39
Mapplethorpe, Robert, 23, 256, 375–76; and race, 32, 64–65, 381, 387–88. See also Man in a Polyester Suit
Marchand, Raúl, 307
Marcus, Sharon, 150
Marcus, Steven, 35; Other Victorians, 38, 137–38

Marder, Elissa, 360
Mariah, Paul, 215–20, 223, 227
marketplace: aesthetic demands of, 238–39; and explicit representation, 38, 55; international, 115; literary, 128, 134–35; niche, 46, 135–36; online, 243; for print, 109–10, 146–48; state-regulated, 324–25
Marquet, Antonio, 303
Martin, Nina, 33–34
Marvel Comics, 186, 190–91, 196–97, 202, 206
Marx, Karl, 57
masculinity, 18–19, 21, 64–65, 245; and education, 73; hyper-, 76n6, 185, 195; Latino, 303, 311–13, 330, 332, 381
masochism. See sadomasochism
Massenet, Jules, 151
masturbation, 8, 154, 165, 169, 377, 436
Mattachine Review (magazine), 220, 224
Mayer, Bernadette, 232n17
McCracken, Scott, 315n18
McDowell, Curt, 34
McElroy, Wendy, 94
McGann, Jerome, 215
McRae, John, 144, 159n1
medicine: authority of, 158, 330; and circumcision, 377–78, 384, 394; and medical discipline, 109–10, 147, 153, 404; and medicalization of body, 423; and normativity, 388–89; and patholo-gization, 18, 146, 153–54; fictional practitioners of, 329–30
Meese Report, 360
Memoirs of Count Alexis, 139
Memoirs of a Woman of Pleasure (Cleland), 135
Memoirs v. Massachusetts, 305
memory, 7, 120; cultural, 3–4, 10, 103, 227–28, 251; sexual, 70
Mendes, Peter, 146, 152
Mercer, Kobena, 32, 42n7, 64–65, 388, 396–97n21
Meredith, George, 138
Merlin (journal), 130
Merlin collective, 130, 132

obscenity, 3, 4, 37–41, 106, 118, 420; and Comstockery, 79, 104, 122n9; as distinct from art, 111; as distinct from pornography, 44, 59–60, 402; end of, 17–18, 78–79, 92, 128–29, 140–41; and Extreme Associates, 263; history of, 125n70, 304–6, 314; law, 20–21, 54–55, 108, 112, 115–16, 135, 255; variable, 135, 401–3, 417n3

*Occupied Territory* (O'Reilly), 170

*Occupied Territory #12 — Eigner* (O'Reilly), 170

Office for Contemporary Anarchy, 367

*Off Our Backs* (magazine) 41n1

Ogrish (website), 357–58, 365

Olson, Charles, 231–32n6

Olympia Press, 114, 130; and Traveler's Companion series, 139

one (magazine), 220

*120 Days of Sodom* (Sade), 127, 131

*On Our Backs* (magazine), 41n2

Ono, Yoko, 66

on/scenity, 37–39, 61, 69, 93, 316n26, 376. See also Williams, Linda

ontology, 254, 271, 339, 347, 353n3, 363

*Opening of Misty Beethoven, The* (Paris), 16

oral sex, 67; analingus, 277–78; blow job, 39, 196; cunnilingus, 72, 317, 331, 332; deep throating and throat-fucking, 263, 266; face-fucking, 271; fellatio, 39, 196–97, 332, 358; irrumation, 41; lick, 196, 430–31; suck, 198, 273, 379–80

O'Reilly, John, 18, 167, 170, 175–81. See also specific works

orientalism, 147, 155, 157–58, 397n31

Orlovsky, Peter, 225

Orton, Joe, 66

Osterweil, Ara, 34, 369

O'Toole, Laurence, 34

Paige, Karen Ericksen, 396n9

*Painter and Model* (Freud), 168

*Painter Working, Reflection* (Freud), 177–78

Palmieri, Edmund L., 116

*Pan and the Goat*, 8

Panizzi, Anthony, 108

*Papi and Chulo* (Rico), 310

Paris, Henry, 16

passivity, 18, 73, 163–64, 168–81, 278, 320; and interpassivity, 165–67

Patterson, Zabet, 30, 165–67, 172, 174, 181, 311

Paulhan, Jean, 131

Peacock, Jere, 112

*Pearl, The*, 138–39

pedagogy, 15–17, 45–46, 66, 68, 73–75, 80–82; as function of pornography, 432–33, 435; and teaching pornography, 61–63, 76–77n19

pedophilia, 23–24, 258–59, 400, 403, 416–17; in literature, 405–6, 415; and subjectivity, 408–9

*Peeping Tom* (Powell), 260n1

penetration, 169–73, 312; anal, 177–79, 294, 424; and masculinity, 195, 199–201; and mastery, 73, 370; in pornography, 41, 253, 271–72, 275–79, 428–29, 432

Penguin Books, 54

Peniston, William A., 153

Penley, Constance, 32

*Penthouse* (magazine), 21, 305

performance: art, 288; in pornography, 235, 239, 243–44, 363; sexual, 67, 71–72; solo, 310–11; as teacher, 62, 75

Perper, Timothy, 92–94

Peters, John Durham, 133–34

Petit, Philippe, 349–50

Petley, Julian, 255

Petronius, 147

Pettus, Christophe, 241

Peyre, Henri, 132

phallus, 2, 18–19, 73, 163; democratization of, 313–14; gay, 145–46, 152–58; and gender ideology, 377, 389, 396n10; as signifier, 179, 183–85, 195, 197; stump as, 420, 423, 429–31

*Phantasms of the Living* (Society of Psychical Research), 157

phantom pain, 430

*Philosophy in the Bedroom* (Sade), 131

Picasso, Pablo, 215, 399, 412–13
Pietri, Pedro, 312
Pink and White Productions, 234, 237, 241, 244
Pinney, Morgan, 223
Plato, 73, 146, 152
*Playboy* (magazine), 11, 21, 94, 136, 305
pleasure, 9–10, 22–23, 298, 333, 421–22; of collecting, 13–15; as constitutive of pornography, 40–41, 257–58; degenitalized, 219, 290, 429–32, 435–37; and disgust, 387, 425–27; forced, 264–66, 272–73, 282n6; homoerotic, 18, 145–46, 152, 155–58; and knowledge, 86, 90, 350; men's, 31, 79; and power, 29, 163–66, 175, 318, 361–62, 404–6, 433–34; and race, 184, 196–201, 210; of reading, 114, 409; trans, 238–39; transgressive, 313; and violence, 285–86, 356–58, 363–70; women's, 19, 66, 288, 322, 328–30
Plumb, J. H., 138
Polaroid (camera), 14, 26n34; and montage, 167, 170, 175–77
Pompeii, 5, 8; discovery of, 2–3, 53–56; in literature, 146, 154, 341; and sexually explicit representations, 83, 106
Pontalis, Jean-Bertrand, 209
Poole, Wakefield, 34
pornochanchadas, 21–22, 317–19, 321–28, 332–34, 336nn27–28
pornography, 1–3, 6–9, 15–24; as archive, 9–12, 222–28; and art, 167–81; and boredom, 55, 268, 369; circulation of, 138–41, 146–50, 213–14, 228–31, 241–42, 310–14; classification of, 82–86, 109–14; collection of, 12–15, 87–91, 103–9, 119–21; connotations of, 36–40; consumption of, 163–65, 240, 358, 362, 366–70, 426–27; etymology, 106; and form, 264–79; heterogeneity of, 30, 46, 279–81; history of, 53, 234–35; music in, 68, 155–56, 290, 323, 368–69, 424–25; online (*see* Internet); production of, 62–72, 234–40, 244, 287–90, 292–96, 324–26, 334; regula-

tion of, 78–82, 91–96, 115–18, 251–59, 304–9, 336n24; relation to sexual explicitness, 33–34, 48, 317–19, 341; semantic use of, 340, 343; as social danger, 133, 285. *See also specific types*
*Pornography, the Theory* (Ferguson), 15–16, 44–45; compared to *Hard Core*, 89–90, 436; on context of pornography, 357–58; on Marquis de Sade, 141; on pornographic content, 87–88; on social mobility, 14, 434–36, 440n38; on tort law, 56–57
pornotopia, 313, 428
*Porn Studies* (Williams), 30–34, 37–38
PorYes Feminist Porn Awards, 245
power, 20–21, 145, 185, 240, 249, 329–31; administrative, 80–81, 96; archival, 4–5, 85; distribution of, 22, 52–54, 71–72, 323; economic, 242–43, 293–96; and gender, 141, 186, 253, 312, 318; mobility of, 423, 434–46; and pedagogy, 73–75, 77n30; and pleasure, 29, 163–65, 174–75, 365–66, 370, 404, 433–37; relations, 60, 244, 258–59, 409, 412–15; self-exhausting, 339, 344; and shame, 63–64, 75, 358–62; subversive, 132, 315–16n23, 328; transformative, 66–67, 190–91, 194–95, 198–99; visibility of, 47–51, 436–37. *See also* biopolitics; superheroes
*Priapeia*, 147, 150, 154
Priapus, 2, 5, 9, 154; as Mysian god, 146
*Prick Up Your Ears* (Frears), 76n8
print culture, 2; institutions of, 17, 92–93, 108–9, 121, 128, 146–47; and publics, 112, 213–14, 222, 230; regulation of, 79
Printed Matter, Inc., 220–22
privacy, 18; in archives, 103, 107–8; and the body, 266; domestic, 140, 150; personal, 224–25, 291
Private Case, 13, 103, 116–17, 137; access to, 93, 99n42, 111–14, 125n84; history of, 108–10, 123n27
privilege, 259; able-bodied, 423; economic, 13; educational, 46–47, 74;

erotic, 210; identity-based, 87; white, 209

Protection of Children Against Sexual Exploitation Act (1977), 402

psychoanalysis, 51, 433; and death drive, 5; and fantasy, 24, 208–9, 406–8, 430–32; and fetish, 23, 383–87, 396n10

public sphere, 5, 50, 105, 356, 405; and counterpublics, 17, 47, 118, 230–31; and social change, 111–12

Puccini, Giacomo, 151

Puerto Rico, 21, 303–9

Puig, Manuel, 314

Pumper, Brian, 438n8

Putnam (G. P. Putnam's Sons), 135

queer studies: and antisocial thesis, 389–90, 406; and archives, 10–11, 19, 222, 226–31; and disability studies, 24, 422–23; as discipline, 29, 30–31; and feminism, 245; methodology of, 12, 16; and pedagogy, 63, 66–67, 72–75; and temporality, 214

Quinn, Sandra, 315–16n23

racism: and fantasy, 210; imperial, 320, 364, 366; in pornography, 32–33, 235; and sexuality, 64, 183, 194; and white supremacy, 193

Rage Against the Man-chine (website), 260n9

Ram, Markus, 183–84, 191, 203, 208, 211

Ramirez, Richard, 264, 271, 275, 283n19

Ramírez de Arellano, Annette B., 308, 315nn8–9

Ramparts (magazine), 136

Ramsay, Peggy, 66

Rancière, Jacques, 351

Ranganathan, S. R., 91

rape, 62, 253, 257, 346–47, 358–59; in film, 264–65, 267, 270–72, 276, 278–79, 282–83nn7–8; in literature, 154, 158; statutory, 410, 418n36

Rawls, John, 50

Réage, Pauline, 16, 78

realism, 5, 9–10, 19, 178, 184, 290–91;

literary, 414–15; and regulation of pornography, 254–55; and sexiness, 191–92; and violence in pornography, 273, 285–86, 363

Reflections in a Golden Eye (Huston), 71

Reichenbach, Carlos, 334

Rembar, Charles, 142n2

Reno v. ACLU, 306

representation: of children (see under images); of disability sex, 421, 425; inadequate, 85–91; of orifices, 178–81, 266; pornographic, 2, 5–6, 23, 235, 288–90, 298; pornopoetic, 222–28; possibility of, 303–4, 311–14; pro-filmic, 267–68, 274–75; queer, 12–14, 16, 18–20, 236; racial, 19, 23, 32–33, 76n6, 183–211, 244–45, 388; realistic, 9, 254–57, 291–92, 363–64, 400; of rough sex, 262–63, 265; sexual, 33, 38, 50, 62, 75, 83, 394; and social systems, 44–45, 53–55; of violence, 249, 270–72, 285–87, 357–62, 369

repression: cultural, 313–14, 319; institutional, 45–47, 96; sexual, 169, 191, 395, 407–8, 415

repressive hypothesis, 18, 127–28, 258

Réstif de la Bretonne, Nicolas-Edme, 53

Restivo, Angelo, 30, 397n31

revolution, sexual, 111–12, 127, 129, 235

Rican Gang Bang, 310

Rican Sizzle Gang Bang 2, 310

Ricco, John Paul, 20, 22–23

Richhe, William, 61

Ricketts, Charles, 147

Ridgeston, Lukas, 391–94

Rifkin, Adrian, 26n31

riot grrrl, 227

Rocha, Glauber, 320–23, 335n7

Rodriguez, Juana María, 71–72

Roque Ramírez, Horacio N., 313

Rose, Jacqueline, 407–8

Rosset, Barney, 128–29, 135–36, 139–40

Rossetti, Dante Gabriel, 151

Roth, Eli, 250

Roth v. United States, 116, 125n70, 305, 401

Rousseau, Jean-Jacques, 58–59

snuff films, 20, 249–54, 258–59, 260n1, 260–61n14
Society for Psychical Research, 152, 155–57
soft core porn, 33–34, 42n9, 240
Sontag, Susan, 359–60
Soto-Crespo, Ramón E., 21
Soup (magazine), 228, 231
Souza Nunes Martins, William de, 336n24
space and spatiality, 2, 16–17, 47–50, 79–96; community-based, 230; democratic, 313–14; disciplinary, 105–6, 118, 120–21; domestic, 140, 150, 401; negative, 328; organization of, 108–9, 117–18; safe, 62–63; shared, 342, 347, 350, 352; wheelchair accessible, 428
spectacle, 51, 186, 191, 314, 323, 349–50; abolition of, 165; of extraordinary embodiment, 421, 425–26, 435; of foreskin, 23, 375–77, 381, 387–88, 392; of humiliation, 22, 338–39; society of, 216, 339–40, 342–45, 348; of violence, 265, 289, 296, 362–63
Spencer, Herbert, 156
Spicer, Jack, 228, 230
Spivak, Gayatri Chakravorty, 25n6, 354n32
Spock, Benjamin, 377
Spring, Justin, 14, 116, 119–20
Sprinkle, Annie (Ellen Steinberg), 94
Squires, David, 16–17
Sri Lanka, 356–57
Stadler, Matthew, 23, 399–401, 410–16; Sex Offender, 410. See also Allan Stein
stag film, 11, 30, 90, 444
Stark, Scott, 34
Starr Report, 30
Stavans, Ilán, 313–14
Stein, Gertrude, 215, 399, 412
stereotype: of Asian male, 32, 64–65; of black men, 32, 183, 194, 388; of black women, 245; and hypersexuality, 96, 184–85, 245, 330; of Latin American leaders, 332–33; racist, 210, 370
Sterling Memorial Library (Yale), 116

Sterne, Laurence, 151
Steward, Samuel, 14, 110, 116, 119–21
Stewart, Potter, 40, 57, 404
St. John, Maria, 30
Stockton, Kathryn Bond, 418n35, 419n46
Stoler, Ann Laura, 25n6, 25n20
Stonewall, 19, 31, 213–14, 226
Story of O, The (Réage), 16, 78–82, 86, 88, 92, 140
Straayer, Chris, 94
Strebeigh, Fred, 260n14
Strout, Ruth F., 83
Study from the Human Body (Bacon), 175
Study of a Nude (Bacon), 177
Stump (Wadd), 428–29
"Stump Grinder," 427–28, 429, 436
stumping, 423–32, 436
subjectivity: and abjection, 339, 343–44; borderland, 304, 311–14; coherence of, 268, 290, 297–98; and desire, 11–12, 13, 81–82, 209, 403–6, 413–16; deviant, 259, 407–9; homosexual, 150, 384; and language, 56–57, 72; and passivity, 166–67, 169, 174–75, 278; and race, 64–66, 70–71, 185, 187–89; 364; sexual, 63, 69, 74, 230, 347, 400, 421, 423
Summers, Montague, 109, 123n32
Superfreak (Houston), 236
superheroes, 19, 184–87, 191–92, 194–205, 209–11
Supreme Court (U.S.), 24, 135, 306, 401–3, 417n3. See also specific cases
surveillance, 46, 51–52, 55–58, 255, 339; military, 362–63, 368–69; and technology, 9, 22, 357
Swan's Dirty Rag, The (magazine), 231
Swimming Hole, The (Eakin), 177
Swinburne, Algernon Charles, 131, 151
Symonds, John Addington, 145, 152–53, 155
Szogyi, Alex, 134

Taormino, Tristan, 246
Tardieu, Auguste Ambroise, 153–55, 158
Tariff Act (1930), 115

taste: erotic, 11, 13, 258; popular, 22, 317–19, 323, 337n29; regulations of, 256; rhetoric of, 92, 97n4; sexual, 329

Taylor, Paul, 340

Tea, Michelle, 229–30

technology, 1–9, 14–15, 18–19, 21–22, 34; cataloging, 83, 86, 117–18; digital, 164–65, 175, 241–43, 288–90; film, 33, 90, 173, 140, 173, 363, 436; media, 39, 61; networking, 25n12, 215, 357–58, 367, 370; pornography as, 87–89; print, 83, 117, 213; video, 69–70, 235, 240, 274, 276. *See also specific types*

*Teleny*, 18, 144, 158; literary ambition of, 146–47; medicine in, 153–54; music in, 146, 155–57; publication history of, 145, 148–50, 159n1; romance in, 150–52

temporality: and anachronism, 340; borderland, 304; of consent, 297–98; dissonance of, 389; interruptions in, 271, 273; narrative, 274–75; of print circulation, 105, 230; queer, 214; of war, 348

terrorism, 299n13, 345, 347–49

*Tesis* (Amenábar), 260n1

Thomas, Paul, 246

*Three Studies for a Crucifixion* (Bacon), 172

*Three Studies of Figures on Beds* (Bacon), 172–73

Thurschwell, Pamela, 155

Times Square, 12–13

Titan Media, 310

Titian (Tiziano Vecellio), 170–73, 175, 178–79. *See also Flaying of Marsyas*

TLA Entertainment Group, 303

*Tomb of Dracula* (comic), 186–87

Tom of Finland, 195, 203

*To Patrick (1975–97)* (O'Reilly), 175–77

tort law, 56–59

torture, 347–48, 369; at Abu Ghraib, 344–45, 358–62; in Marquis de Sade, 51; opposed to sadomasochistic play, 297; of women, 252

torture porn, 259, 286, 339, 340

trafficking, sexual, 145

transgression, 41, 94, 295; and desire, 379–82; of taboos, 313, 421

trash: as aesthetic, 22, 318–19, 324–29, 331–32; as archive, 21, 313, 315n18; and pornography, 84, 88

Treasure Island Media, 40–41

*Tremors* (Underwood), 425

Trinity College Library Dublin, 104, 107, 111

Trocchi, Alexander, 130

tropicália, 320–21, 325, 335n7

*Tropic of Cancer* (Miller), 17, 78, 128, 140

*12 horas* (Marchand), 307

*Two Figures* (Bacon), 173

"2 Girls 1 Cup," 426

"2 Guys 1 Stump," 423–27, 436

typography, 213–14, 220, 225, 231, 381

*Un\*/Cut* (Giovanni), 390, 391

*Undershirt* (O'Reilly), 167

Underwager, Ralph, 404

*United States v. Dost*, 403

*United States v. Knox*, 402

*United States v. 31 Photographs*, 115–16

*United States v. Williams*, 403

UnseenWar (website), 367

Upchurch, Charles, 159n7

utilitarianism, 15–16, 45–49, 58–59, 87, 434–36

utopia and utopianism: and minorities, 19, 20, 192, 210; pornographic, 273–74, 282n7; sexual, 397n31. *See also* pornotopia

*Valhalla* (Peacock), 112

Velázquez, Diego Rodríguez de Silva y, 167

Vermeer, Johannes, 17

Vidal, Gore, 224

*Village Voice*, 136

Vismann, Cornelia, 4

violence, 20–23, 49–51, 365–70, 416; aesthetics of, 262–63, 269–71, 277–81, 310, 320–21; affective, 63–64; bodily, 265–67, 272–74; against children, 401, 404, 406, 408–9; as constitutive of

CPSIA information can be obtained
at www.ICGtesting.com
Printed in the USA
FSHW021127030520
69807FS

9 780822 356806